Nutrient Requirements of Cats

Revised Edition, 1986

Subcommittee on Cat Nutrition
Committee on Animal Nutrition
Board on Agriculture
National Research Council

National Academy Press   2101 Constitution Avenue, NW   Washington, DC 20418

NOTICE: The project that is the subject of this report was approved by the Governing Board of the National Research Council, whose members are drawn from the councils of the National Academy of Sciences, the National Academy of Engineering, and the Institute of Medicine. The members of the committee responsible for the report were chosen for their special competences and with regard for appropriate balance.

This report has been reviewed by a group other than the authors according to procedures approved by a Report Review Committee consisting of members of the National Academy of Sciences, the National Academy of Engineering, and the Institute of Medicine.

The National Research Council was established by the National Academy of Sciences in 1916 to associate the broad community of science and technology with the Academy's purposes of furthering knowledge and of advising the federal government. The Council operates in accordance with general policies determined by the Academy under the authority of its congressional charter of 1863, which establishes the Academy as a private, nonprofit, self-governing membership corporation. The Council has become the principal operating agency of both the National Academy of Sciences and the National Academy of Engineering in the conduct of their services to the government, the public, and the scientific and engineering communities. It is administered jointly by both Academies and the Institute of Medicine. The National Academy of Engineering and the Institute of Medicine were established in 1964 and 1970, respectively, under the charter of the National Academy of Sciences.

This study was supported by the U.S. Department of Agriculture, Agricultural Research Service, under Agreement No. 59-32U4-5-6, and by the Center for Veterinary Medicine, Food and Drug Administration of the U.S. Department of Health and Human Services, under Cooperative Agreement No. FD-U-000006-05-1. Additional support was provided by the American Feed Industry Association, Inc. Any opinions, findings, conclusions, or recommendations expressed in this publication are those of the authoring subcommittee and do not necessarily reflect the views of the sponsors.

Library of Congress Cataloging-in-Publication Data
Nutrient requirements of cats.

   (Nutrient requirements of domestic animals)
   Bibliography: p.
   Includes index.
   1. Cats—Food.   I. National Research Council (U.S.). Subcommittee on Cat Nutrition.   II. Series: Nutrient requirements of domestic animals (Unnumbered)
SF447.6.N88   1986   636.8'08'52   86-8685

ISBN 0-309-03682-8

Printed in the United States of America

Preface

This report is one of a series issued under the direction of the Committee on Animal Nutrition, Board on Agriculture, National Research Council. It was prepared by the Subcommittee on Cat Nutrition, and is a revision and expansion of the 1978 edition of *Nutrient Requirements of Cats*. A substantial quantity of new information on cat nutrition has been published since the last edition. Estimates of all the amino acid requirements, including taurine, have been included. New information on diet and acid-base balance has been included with an emphasis on how diet composition affects the risk of feline urological syndrome (FUS). The essential fatty acid requirements have been included in this edition. There has been an expansion of the section on other feed ingredients, including dietary effects of such items as sodium benzoate and propylene glycol. Finally, an increased number of feed ingredients used for cat diets has been included in the feed composition tables and nutritional values for many other ingredients have been updated.

This new edition describes the minimal requirements of the growing kitten based on nutrient availability similar to that found when purified diets are used as the sole food source. For nutrients where information on minimal requirements was not available, minimal quantities known to give satisfactory performance were used or estimates were made based on other species. Guidelines are given for applying these minimal requirements to diets containing natural feedstuffs. General recommendations are also given for maintenance and reproduction for the adult cat. The reader interested in the management of the cat as a laboratory animal is referred to a report entitled *Laboratory Animal Management—Cats*, 1978, which is available from the Institute of Laboratory Animal Resources, National Research Council.

The subcommittee is indebted to Selma P. Baron and Philip Ross of the Board on Agriculture for their assistance in the production of this report; to the members of the Committee on Animal Nutrition for their suggestions; and to Ronald S. Anderson, Norlin J. Benevenga, Richard D. Kealy, and Duane E. Ullrey for their comprehensive reviews and constructive comments on the report. We are especially grateful to John A. Pino who reviewed the report for the Board on Agriculture.

Subcommittee on Cat Nutrition

QUINTON R. ROGERS, *Chairman*
University of California, Davis

DAVID H. BAKER
University of Illinois

KENNETH C. HAYES
Brandeis University

PETER T. KENDALL
Pedigree Petfoods

JAMES G. MORRIS
University of California, Davis

iii

Contents

Tables

Nutrient Requirements of Cats

Revised Edition, 1986

1 **Introduction**

An examination of the nutritional requirements of the cat, as compared to other domesticated and laboratory animals, shows some striking differences and supports the view that several aspects of metabolism in the cat have evolved in response to the cat's adherence to a strict carnivorous diet (MacDonald et al., 1984c). These metabolic differences have resulted in several nutritional requirements that are unique (Morris and Rogers, 1982). Some of these special nutrients that are required by the cat are found normally in animal products but not in plants. These include arachidonate, taurine, and preformed vitamin A (i.e., carotene cannot be utilized). Differences in enzyme activities result in absolute requirements for niacin and arginine, and in a higher requirement for protein. These and other lesser differences are considered in detail under sections for each nutrient.

Behaviorally, the cat is also different from most domestic animals. Many biological variables that exhibit rhythmicity in most mammals have little rhythmicity in the cat. Thus, the cat, when fed ad libitum, eats and drinks randomly throughout the day and night rather than being nocturnal or diurnal (Mugford, 1977; Kane et al., 1981b). Meals are rather small, so the cat normally eats about 8 to 16 meals during a 24-hour period. Even though this appears to be their natural feeding behavior (feral cats eat a wide variety of small prey that include such animals as mice, birds, lizards, insects, etc.), adult cats at maintenance can adapt to being fed only once a day. Growing kittens and pregnant and lactating queens, however, require feeding at more frequent intervals.

The relatively short gastrointestinal tract of the cat results in a rapid rate of passage and therefore somewhat lower digestibility for many natural feedstuffs than that of the dog or rat (Kendall et al., 1983). Therefore, high-quality foods best serve this species.

As might be expected, the cat also has different taste preferences than omnivores and herbivores. The cat is not responsive to a sweet flavor but does respond to the taste of certain amino acids and peptides (Beauchamp et al., 1977; White and Boudreau, 1975). Thus, meat extracts and peptides (commonly from tissue digests) have positive acceptance properties for the cat. Animal fats also generally improve the palatability of cat diets with little preferential difference exhibited among rendered fats (Kane et al., 1981a) as long as fats are not rancid. Finally, the texture of the food is important. The cat generally prefers solid, moist foods to dry, powdery foods. Nevertheless, when started at a young age, kittens can be trained to eat a wide variety of textures and flavors. Thus, adequate acceptable diets can be prepared from natural foodstuffs (using both animal and plant products) as is common for commercial cat foods. Also, diets that are both nutritionally adequate and acceptable can be prepared from purified carbohydrates, fats, proteins, amino acids, vitamins, and minerals (purified diets). More details in this area may be found in the chapter on "Formulated Diets for Cats."

Details about the nutritional requirements of the cat are presented throughout the text, and a complete summary of the requirements of growing kittens is given in Table 2. Few nutritional requirements are known for the adult cat for maintenance or for pregnancy and lactation. Where requirements are known for individual nutrients for stages of life other than for growth, they are listed in footnotes to Table 2. The brevity of the footnotes denotes the paucity of available data.

While the nutrient requirements in this report are based on published research and practical experience, some of the values, although known to be adequate, are probably not minimal requirements. A margin of safety was not intentionally incorporated into these recommendations. It is important to note that the require-

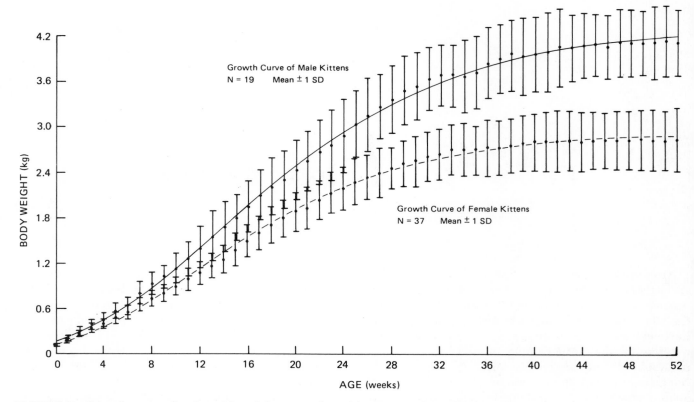

FIGURE 1   Growth curves of male and female kittens. Adapted from Loveridge (1986a).

ments for many of the nutrients listed in Table 2 have been established using purified diets (e.g., amino acid diets were used in determining the amino acid requirements), and therefore an allowance for a product of lower digestibility (and/or availability) should be used when the nutrients are supplied by foodstuffs. The availability of minerals would be expected to vary considerably, depending on the feed source. Compounds occurring in foods such as phytic acid or chitin may markedly reduce the availability of minerals from feed sources and were not considered in the expression of the minimal requirements determined using purified diets.

Thus, minimal requirements as shown in the tables assume that nutrient availability is equal to that of purified diets.

Growth curves for male and female short-haired, domestic cats are shown in Figure 1 to present a normal growth response (Loveridge, 1986a). Breeds vary considerably in size such that a normal, lean, full-grown cat may weigh anywhere from 2 to 6 kg.

Finally, these nutrient requirements are based on the best information available; modifications should be made as environmental and other circumstances may warrant.

2 Nutrient Requirements

ENERGY

Energy is not itself a nutrient but is rather a property contributed to diets by the three nutrients: fats (lipids), carbohydrates, and proteins. Energy is expressed in either kilocalories (kcal) or kilojoules (kJ). One kcal is equivalent to 4.184 kJ.

Cats require energy for support of metabolism during maintenance, growth, reproduction, and lactation. In the absence of adequate energy, animal performance will be suboptimal, and there will be depletion of energy and other nutrient stores.

Energy Content of Diets and Ingredients

Energy content of animal diets and energy requirements have been stated in at least three different ways: (1) gross energy (E), which is the total chemical energy arising from complete combustion of a food as is determined in a bomb calorimeter; average E values for carbohydrate, fat, and protein are 4.15, 9.40, and 5.65 kcal/g, respectively; (2) digestible energy (DE), which is the food E minus E of the feces; and (3) metabolizable energy (ME), which is the food E minus E of the feces and urine. Although these concepts apply to the cat, the DE and ME concentrations of many cat food ingredients have not been experimentally determined. For this reason, estimated ME values of 4 kcal/g for dietary carbohydrate and protein and 9 kcal/g for dietary fat have been employed in most of the published studies concerned with energy requirements of the cat. Based on data derived from metabolism studies with commercial cat diets (see Table 3, page 43), calculated ME values overestimate in vivo ME values by as much as 30 percent (M. A. Norvell, Quaker Oats Co., personal communication, 1976; Kendall et al., 1982a, 1985). Alternative methods for calculating the ME concentrations of cat

diets are compared in the chapter on formulated diets for cats. At present no single equation or series of calorie factors can be recommended for calculating ME concentration of all types of cat diets. In vivo dietary ME values can be estimated from determined DE values and for some canned diets, from proximate analysis or E alone (Kendall et al., 1985). The determined E and neutral detergent fiber values appear to offer some promise for more accurate prediction of ME concentration of dry cat diets, but further studies are needed.

Because few data are available on in vivo DE or ME concentration of cat food ingredients, values determined for swine have been used in tables, when cat values are absent, rather than those calculated from Atwater factors as in the previous report (NRC, 1978a). Swine ME values have been well verified as compared to most other simple-stomached mammals and show reasonable agreement with those determined in cats when direct comparisons are available (P. T. Kendall, Pedigree Petfoods, Melton Mowbray, UK, personal communication, 1985). Calculated ME values for feed ingredients for cats are precluded by the lack of data on apparent digestibility for most feed ingredients. It is hoped that future studies will be carried out to define in vivo energy content of the common foods used in cat diets, so that predictive relationships can be developed.

Basis for Establishing Energy Requirements

The mature body weights of domestic cats *Felis domesticus* range from about 2 to 6 kg compared with more than 200 kg for lions (*Panthera leo*) and tigers (*Panthera tigris*). Whether the mass exponent of $W^{0.73}$ proposed by Brody et al. (1934) for interspecific extrapolation of energy requirements is appropriate throughout the cat family or whether $W^{0.67}$ should be used as the intraspecies mass exponent as suggested by Heusner

3

(1985) remains unclear. However, since the various breeds of domestic cats differ so little in mature size, energy requirements listed in this publication will continue to be expressed per unit of body weight. Indeed Kendall et al. (1983) found no extra precision when energy requirements of adult domestic cats were scaled to mass exponents of body weight (kg) of either 0.75 or 0.67, compared with unity.

Data from which estimates of energy requirements can be made are available from two sources: short-term measurements of gaseous exchange or heat production, and longer-term measurements of food intake and body weight or body energy changes. Theoretically, both approaches should give similar values. However, activity is limited in a respiration chamber or metabolism cage, and most studies in chambers have measured fasting heat production rather than maintenance energy requirements. Several previous estimates of energy requirements from feeding trials with cats must be interpreted with caution, because dietary energy intakes were based on Atwater factor calculations rather than direct measurement (Miller and Allison, 1958; Scott, 1968). Unless diets of very high digestibility are used, these values are likely to be serious overestimates.

Requirements for Adult Maintenance

Energy requirements for maintenance of adults have been estimated by several investigators. MacDonald et al. (1984c), using the calorimetric data of Benedict (1938) and Carpenter (1944), calculated the daily requirement (1.5 times basal heat production) for the cat as 87 kcal ME/kg body weight (BW).

Various estimations of energy requirements of cats reported in the literature have been based on measurements of food intake. Krehl et al. (1955) reported daily ME intakes of 65 kcal/kg BW for maintenance of young adult cats. Daily maintenance energy estimates for mature adults in confined conditions range from 60 to 70 (Miller and Allison, 1958; Gisler and Ewing, 1964; Skultety, 1969; Burger et al., 1984) to 80 kcal ME/kg BW (Greaves and Scott, 1960). The latter value may be biased upwards because Atwater factors of 4 kcal/g for protein and carbohydrate and 9 kcal/g for fat were applied to high-fiber canned diets containing 4 percent sugar beet pulp and 20 percent potato flake as fed.

Kendall et al. (1983) reported a mean daily DE requirement for maintenance of six adult cats in metabolism cages of 76 kcal/kg BW, based on 6 months' continuous measurement of DE intake and body weight change. This value is equivalent to a daily ME requirement of 68 kcal/kg BW, assuming a urinary energy loss of 1.25 kcal/g digestible crude protein intake. While no

definitive value for maintenance energy requirement can be derived from the above data, it would appear that a value of about 70 kcal ME/kg BW is reasonable for inactive cats. Higher energy intakes are probably appropriate for maintenance of active cats. Miller and Allison (1958) reported that adult cats allowed to exercise in runs increased their calculated daily energy intakes to 80 to 90 kcal/kg BW compared with 60 kcal/kg BW in metabolism cages. When the above estimate is adjusted downwards to account for the probable bias in ME intakes from the use of Atwater factors, a daily ME requirement of about 80 kcal/kg BW is recommended.

Requirements for Growth

Miller and Allison (1958) observed that the daily ME requirements of growing kittens rapidly declined with advancing age from about 250 kcal/kg BW at 5 weeks to about 100 kcal/kg BW at 30 weeks of age. By 50 weeks of age daily ME intakes stabilized at about 60 kcal/kg BW for cats kept in metabolism cages and at about 85 kcal/ kg BW for cats allowed to exercise in runs. Miller and Allison (1958) used a purified diet in their studies. Comparable ME intakes for growing kittens have been subsequently reported by a number of investigators. Waterhouse and Carver (1962) found mean daily ME intakes of 128, 95, and 76 kcal/kg BW for kittens 18, 30, and 56 weeks of age, respectively. Loveridge (1986a) measured mean daily Atwater ME intakes of 220 and 145 kcal/kg BW at 10 and 20 weeks of age, respectively, for 52 kittens fed commercial canned foods. In contrast, Greaves (1965) observed lower daily ME intakes of 152, 114, and 102 kcal/kg BW for kittens 11, 17, and 21 weeks of age. The lower ME intakes reported by Greaves (1965) are probably explained by a lower food intake required to support somewhat smaller mean daily body weight gains of 16 and 10 g per cat for male and female kittens, respectively, from 12 to 20 weeks compared with 18 and 16 g per cat reported by Loveridge (1986a). Allison et al. (1956) suggested that daily ME intakes of 160 kcal/kg BW may represent a lower limit for satisfactory growth in young kittens.

Figure 1 outlines the growth response for 19 male and 37 female kittens from birth to 52 weeks of age (Loveridge, 1986a). These kittens were raised in a specific pathogen-free derived cat colony and were given commercial canned diets.

Requirements for Gestation and Lactation

Queens appear to require about 25 percent more energy for gestation than for maintenance. Smith (1974) observed mean daily ME intakes of approximately 90

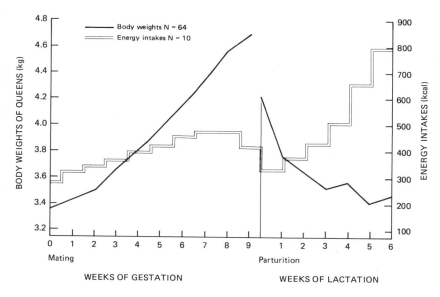

FIGURE 2 Weekly body weights and mean metabolizable energy intakes of queens during gestation and lactation. Adapted from Loveridge (1986b).

kcal/kg BW during gestation for queens fed a commercial diet. Scott (1966) has suggested that average daily ME requirements based on dietary Atwater ME concentrations are about 100 kcal/kg BW. This may be slightly high when ME is based on direct in vivo ME determination. More recently, voluntary energy intakes of cats have been measured throughout gestation and lactation by Loveridge (1986b). The pattern of body weight change during gestation and lactation is outlined in Figure 2 based on data for 64 individual cats, together with weekly averages of calculated (Atwater) ME intake for 10 of these cats. During gestation the mean body weight of the queens increased from 3.4 to 4.7 kg, while calculated daily voluntary ME intakes showed a steady but consistent increase from about 270 to 470 kcal ME per cat. This level of calculated ME intake is equivalent to 93 to 109 kcal/kg BW and is in quite close agreement with the earlier observations (Scott, 1966; Smith, 1974). It would appear from the postparturient weight loss of the queens as seen in Figure 2 that for satisfactory reproductive performance the body weight gain in pregnancy should include net tissue accretion in preparation for lactation, rather than gain in fetal and placental and associated membrane weight alone.

Energy intakes for lactation increase substantially and may exceed 250 kcal ME/kg BW at the peak of lactation (Smith, 1974), since food energy needs represent that for the queen plus her kittens. Scott (1968) has pointed out that female cats tend to lose body weight during lactation even when allowed to eat palatable formulated diets ad libitum. This is supported by the data of Loveridge (1986b) outlined in Figure 2, which show a drop in mean body weight of queens from about 4.2 kg

postpartum to about 3.4 kg after 6 weeks of lactation. Mean daily ME intakes for 10 queens showed an increase from about 330 in the first week postpartum to 800 kcal per cat plus kittens in week 6 of lactation. These values approximate to 90 to 270 kcal ME/kg maternal BW/day, respectively.

More detailed data on mean daily calculated ME intakes of queens in lactation are outlined in Table 1 by litter size and week of lactation. These values are based on the work of Loveridge (1986b) using a specific pathogen-free derived cat colony given canned foods that are known to support satisfactory queen and kitten performance.

Energy Allowances

Recommended daily ME allowances for cats in various physiological states are outlined in Table 1. These allowances represent estimates of probable energy needs of cats and are intended to serve as practical feeding guides. They do not necessarily represent the precise energy requirement of a specific animal for optimum performance. It should be recognized that the energy requirements of cats vary with age, activity, body condition, insulative characteristics of hair coat, environmental circumstances, and temperature acclimatization. In the case of lactating queens, allowances have been detailed by litter size and week of lactation. The values are based on total voluntary ME intake for queen and kittens during the period shown, and thus ME intakes for the queen only will be lower than stated from about weeks 4 to 6 of lactation.

CARBOHYDRATES

Although no known dietary carbohydrate requirement exists for the cat, dry commercial diets usually contain 40 percent or more carbohydrate and are well utilized. Based on research with chickens (Renner, 1964; Renner and Elcombe, 1964; Brambila and Hill, 1966; Edwards and Hart, 1971), rats (Goldberg, 1971; Akrabawi et al., 1974), and dogs (Belo et al., 1976; Romsos et al., 1976), it is probable that cats can be maintained without dietary carbohydrate if the diet furnishes sufficient fat (and thus glycerol) and protein (containing glucogenic amino acids) from which the metabolic requirement for glucose can be derived.

Greaves and Scott (1963) noted that substitution of dextrin for sucrose in a purified diet resulted in greater food intakes by adult cats. Hardy et al. (1977) and Teeter et al. (1978b) have obtained excellent growth rates in young kittens fed purified amino acid diets containing carbohydrate as a 1:1 ratio of cornstarch to sucrose. Trudell and Morris (1975) measured intestinal lactase and sucrase activities up to 109 days of age in kittens maintained from weaning (8 weeks) on either a basal ground beef and mutton diet or the basal diet plus lactose or sucrose (at 20 percent of diet dry matter). There was considerable individual variation in disaccharidase activity, but it did not appear related to the presence of carbohydrate in the diet.

The liver of most omnivorous animals has two enzymes, glucokinase and hexokinase, which catalyze the phosphorylation of glucose to glucose-6-phosphate. Hexokinase has a low K_m for glucose, whereas glucokinase has a high K_m and operates mainly when the liver receives a high load of glucose from the portal vein. The activity of glucokinase in the liver of the cat is extremely low, whereas the activity of hexokinase is in the normal range (Ballard, 1965). Carnivores with omnivorous dietary habits, e.g., domestic dog, possess both enzymes. Therefore, one would predict that they might have a greater capacity to metabolize a high-glucose meal than the cat, but this does not appear to have been tested.

Fiber is not generally considered essential for simple-stomached mammals including cats, although including some fiber in the diet is not uncommon in commercial practice. Energy density of the diet is reduced by fiber, and therefore including some fiber in the diet may contribute to maintenance of ideal body weight in adult sedentary cats fed ad libitum.

With the advent of semimoist cat foods there has been renewed interest in the taste response of cats and their tolerance for mono- and disaccharides, since these sugars are important in the formulation of these diets. Sucrose does not enhance diet palatability for cats (Pfaffmann, 1955; Carpenter, 1956; Zotterman, 1956), perhaps because there are few sucrose-sensitive nerve endings in feline taste buds. Nevertheless, interactions between sucrose and other dietary components can affect taste preference (Bartoshuk et al., 1971, 1975; Frings, 1951).

Digestibility

Trudell and Morris (1975) estimated the apparent digestibility of individual carbohydrates using the feed-to-fecal ratios of chromic oxide to carbohydrate. The basal ground beef and mutton diet was fed to near-mature domestic short-haired cats with the test carbohydrates constituting about 20 percent of diet dry matter. The apparent digestibilities (percent) were: glucose, 99.8; sucrose, 99.8; lactose, 99.1; dextrin, 97.6; starch, 96.1; cellulose, −0.73.

Using the same technique and a ground meat basal diet, Pencovic and Morris (1975) studied the apparent digestibility of starch (added at 35 percent of diet dry matter) found in corn or wheat grain. Apparent starch digestibilities (percent) for coarsely ground, finely ground, or coarsely ground and cooked grains were, respectively: corn, 79, 94, and 88; wheat, 92, 97, and 96. It was concluded that starch from corn and wheat, especially when finely ground, is well utilized by the cat.

Morris et al. (1977) studied the effects of age and the addition of sucrose and lactose on the β-fructofuranidase (sucrase) and β-galactosidase (lactase) activities of the small intestine. Intestinal β-galactosidase activity decreased with age (71–106 days) in kittens. However, the activities of neither enzyme were affected by addition of sucrose or lactose to the all-meat diet.

The apparent digestibilities of nitrogen-free extract in commercial cat foods (canned and dry type) ranged from 82 to 87 percent (L. G. Miller, The Carnation Co., personal communication, 1985). Apparent digestibilities of "total carbohydrate" (assayed by the method of Dubois et al., 1956) in dry-type commercial cat food ranged from 90 to 95 percent (R. D. Kealy, Ralston Purina Co., personal communication, 1985).

The fiber contents of ingredients used in cat diets are listed in Table 7 as crude fiber. It should be noted that the crude fiber can be a very misleading parameter of "indigestible" fiber content, particularly with ingredients high in poorly soluble indigestible materials such as cellulose, hemicellulose, lignin, and chitin. A more appropriate criterion of insoluble fiber might be neutral-detergent fiber (NDF). Unfortunately, NDF values for common ingredients used in feline diets are not available at present.

FAT

Dietary fat functions as a concentrated energy source, serves as a carrier for fat-soluble vitamins, provides essential fatty acids, and influences diet acceptance by the cat.

Analytical Procedures

Materials extracted from cat food with anhydrous diethyl ether are termed crude fat and include primarily glycerides of fatty acids, although small amounts of other substances such as cholesterol, chlorophyll, or xanthophylls, which have no known nutritional significance for the cat, may also be included. In expanded or baked cat foods, complete release of glycerides will not result unless ether extraction is preceded by acid hydrolysis. Thus, using crude fat, levels for low fat diets may underestimate total fat by more than 50 percent (Budde, 1952; Hoffman, 1953). The fat (including phospholipids) in certain animal products is extracted more completely by a chloroform-methanol mixture. Thus, use of fat content derived from ether extraction may lead to underestimates of the calculated energy potential in these diet ingredients so that acid hydrolysis followed by chloroform-methanol extraction is the preferred approach (Cox and Pearson, 1962).

Digestibility

Morris et al. (1977) reported apparent digestibility of crude fat in a diet of beef and mutton to be 99 percent, and M. A. Norvell (personal communication, 1976) found that apparent digestibilities of crude fat in several commercial cat foods ranged from 85 to 94 percent (see Table 3, page 43). Kane et al. (1981a) found that the apparent digestibility of fat was 90 percent when fed at 10 percent of the dry matter but was 97 to 99 percent when fed at 25 or 50 percent of the dry matter. Humphreys and Scott (1962) have shown that dietary fat concentration could be raised to 64 percent (dry matter basis) without an increase in the proportion of fecal fat, indications of ketonuria, or significant pathological changes in the cardiovascular system. These observations suggest that cats have the capacity to tolerate and utilize high levels of dietary fat.

Dietary Fat Concentration

Relatively high dietary fat concentrations, from both animal and plant sources, have been routinely used in feeding experiments with cats. Purified diets composed of 25 to 30 percent fat and 30 to 40 percent protein are commonly fed, whereas dry, commercial cat foods usually contain 8 to 12 percent fat. Generally, high-fat diets appear to be more palatable than low-fat diets (Greaves, 1965; Kendall, 1984).

Both the amount and source of dietary fat influence food acceptance and growth in kittens (Kane et al., 1981a; MacDonald et al., 1983). Diets containing 25 percent hydrogenated coconut oil were found to be unpalatable and failed to support growth. Even when acceptance was improved by adding small amounts of essential fatty acids as safflower oil or chicken fat, normal growth was not restored. By contrast, hydrogenated beef tallow did support growth in kittens, although tested for only 7 weeks. This difference between fats was attributed to palatability, since the hydrogenated beef tallow diet was consumed at almost five times the level of the hydrogenated coconut oil diet. Further studies by the Davis group (MacDonald et al., 1985) indicate that diets containing medium-chain triglycerides are poorly accepted by cats and that caprylic acid as low as 1 g/kg diet caused the diet to be unpalatable. Similarly, kittens chose beef tallow (nonhydrogenated) over chicken fat (3:1), although no significant difference in choice was noted between diets containing 35 percent fat as hydrogenated tallow and those containing regular beef tallow (MacDonald et al., 1983). Other results (Kane et al., 1981a) indicate that diets containing 25 percent fat are selected over those containing 10 percent or 50 percent fat. Beef tallow was selected over butter and chicken fat, but no preference was apparent among beef tallow, lard, or partially hydrogenated vegetable oil. Scott (1966) found satisfactory performance in kittens fed diets containing 22 percent fat.

Schneck and Cumberland (1968) observed that growing kittens responded to a 10 percent dietary fat addition with a reduction in dry matter intake relative to the unsupplemented control group. Total energy consumption for the experimental period was about the same for both groups, and weight gain as a percentage of the original body weight was not significantly different. This suggests that energy intake of the cat is maintained with diets of varying dietary energy densities.

Because the metabolizable energy concentration of fat is approximately 2.25 times that of protein and carbohydrate, changes in fat level alter the caloric density of the diet. This may necessitate adjustment of other nutrient concentrations, particularly proteins, vitamins, and minerals, in order to maintain appropriate intakes of these nutrients. For example, if proportions of other nutrients are not increased as the dietary caloric density increases, energy intake may be adequate but intake of proteins, vitamins, and minerals may be inadequate (Elvehjem and Krehl, 1947; Crampton, 1964).

Fat is a good energy source, provides a vehicle for carrying fat soluble vitamins and essential fatty acids into the diet, and may improve palatability. A need for fat above and beyond that required as essential fatty acids has not been demonstrated.

Essential Fatty Acids (EFA)

Investigations of the essential fatty acid needs of two Felidae species have been reported. Most studies of the metabolism of polyunsaturated fatty acids (PUFA) have been conducted on rats, which have relatively high $\Delta 6$- and $\Delta 5$-desaturase activities associated with the ability to convert linoleic acid (18:2n6) to the prostaglandin precursors dihomo-γ-linolenic acid (20:3n6) and arachidonic acid (20:4n6), respectively. It had been assumed that other species can desaturate polyunsaturated fatty acids equally well. However, Rivers et al. (1975, 1976a,b,c) and Hassam et al. (1977) originally presented evidence that cats fail to convert linoleic ($\Delta 6$-desaturase) to γ-linolenic acid (18:3n6) or dihomo-γ-linolenic acid ($\Delta 5$-desaturase) to arachidonic acid, implicating the need for dietary 20:4n6, which is available only from animal sources. Subsequent studies by MacDonald et al. (1983, 1984a,b,c,d) demonstrated the essentiality of dietary linoleate (5 g/kg diet), in its own right, as a factor affecting skin water permeability, as well as the failure of the cat to convert 18:2n6 to 18:3n6, 20:3n6, or 20:4n6 due to a presumed lack of both $\Delta 6$- and $\Delta 5$-desaturase activities. In addition their data suggested a selective ability of the hepatic $\Delta 5$-desaturase to convert 20:2n6-11,14 to 20:3n6-5,11,14, but not 20:3n6-8,11,14 to 20:4n6-5,8,11,14. However, feeding cats evening primrose oil, rich in 18:3n6 (Frankel and Rivers, 1978), improved the physical status of cats fed safflower oil, but failed to enhance conversion of 18:3n6 to 20:4n6 as evidenced by plasma phospholipid fatty acids. It was concluded that $\Delta 5$-desaturase was absent but that 18:3n6 and/or 20:3n6 were biologically important fatty acids since they improved physical condition. In contrast, Sinclair et al. (1979) fed the methyl ester of 18:3n6 to kittens consuming no PUFA or injected radiolabeled 18:2n6 or 20:3n6 into kittens fed safflower oil and found evidence for conversion of 18:3n6 and 20:3n6 (but not 18:2n6) to 20:4n6, concluding that $\Delta 5$-desaturase was active, whereas the $\Delta 6$-desaturase was not.

A requirement for dietary 18:2n6 and 20:4n6 in cats was established with studies of reproductive function in both sexes by MacDonald et al. (1984d). By feeding linoleate with or without arachidonate it was possible to demonstrate that 20:4n6 was required by female cats to deliver viable kittens, whereas 18:2n6 alone was sufficient to maintain seminiferous tubule architecture and spermatogenesis in males. Furthermore, conversion of linoleate to arachidonate by the testes was evident from phospholipid fatty acid profiles, indicating at least some $\Delta 5$- and $\Delta 6$-desaturase activity in the testes, in contrast to the questionable $\Delta 5$ and lack of $\Delta 6$ activity in liver.

These reproduction studies demonstrated that 0.04 percent of the energy (200 mg/kg diet) supplied as 20:4n6 was adequate for assuring pregnancy and lactation except when additional fish oil (tuna oil) was fed (MacDonald et al., 1984d). The latter contains n3 fatty acids (20:5n3, 22:6n3), which both compete with 20:4n6 for incorporation into glyceryl lipids and may depress the $\Delta 5$-desaturase activity, as well.

It seems prudent to recommend including both 18:2n6 and 20:4n6 in any diet intended for cats. Five and 0.2 g of lineolate and arachidonate/kg diets, respectively, are recommended as the minimum requirements.

Signs of Deficiency

Rivers (1982) listed several changes attributed to EFA deficiency in cats (listlessness, dry hair coat with dandruff, poor growth, and increased susceptibility to infection), and MacDonald et al. (1984a) have detailed the pathology involved after 1.5 to 2.5 years of EFA-deficient diets. EFA-deficient cats develop reduced feed efficiency without changing body weight gain. Scaly skin and markedly increased water loss through the skin were accompanied by alopecia and focal exudative dermatitis on the flanks and ventral surfaces of selective females. Livers were enlarged and fatty, and kidneys also revealed histologic evidence of fatty infiltration. These changes were corrected by feeding 18:2n6 alone, but prevention of mild mineralization of kidneys (MacDonald et al., 1984a) and changes in platelet aggregation (MacDonald et al., 1984b) depended on 20:4n6 supplementation. They concluded that dietary linoleate probably provides for functions dependent on physical properties of membranes, whereas arachidonate was needed in processes requiring eicosanoid formation, such as reproduction and platelet aggregation.

The variation in diet composition, age and sex of cats, tissues examined, and method of assessment have all served to complicate interpretation of the several studies cited. Kittens have been raised and maintained for up to 2 years on purified diets containing vegetable oil (Hayes et al., 1975a; Schmidt et al., 1976) without observed differences in growth or overt signs of EFA deficiency (reproduction not studied), which suggests that cats can be maintained without dietary 20:4n6. Furthermore, undiscovered nutrient interactions presumably vary the demand or in vivo synthetic capacity of the various EFA.

PROTEIN

Cats require protein in the diet to supply amino acids that cannot be synthesized at a rate commensurate with optimal performance (essential amino acids) and to supply nitrogen required for synthesis of dispensable amino acids and other nitrogenous compounds such as purines, pyrimidines, heme, and creatine. The following 10 alpha-amino acids were shown by Rogers and Morris (1979) to be essential for the growing kitten.

Arginine	Leucine	Threonine
Histidine	Lysine	Tryptophan
Isoleucine	Methionine	Valine
	Phenylalanine	

When any one of the above 10 amino acids was deleted from an otherwise complete purified amino acid-based diet, food intake decreased and body weight loss occurred. Returning the amino acid to the diet restored food intake and body weight gain. The minimal requirements for these 10 essential amino acids have been determined only for growing kittens (generally between 10 and 20 weeks of age). Younger and older kittens may have different requirements. With the exception of methionine, no values are available for minimal essential amino acid requirements of adult cats for maintenance or for pregnancy and lactation.

The minimal requirements were determined using purified diets. These diets had an ME value about 4.7 to 5 kcal/g and nitrogen was supplied as crystalline amino acids.

When diets are formulated from natural ingredients the quantities of amino acids in the diet should be greater than those listed in Table 2. These greater quantities are necessary because digestibility (availability) of amino acids in natural ingredients is less than that from free amino acids.

Nitrogen Requirements of Cats

Published studies prior to the 1980s on the protein requirements of the growing kitten and adult cat were done without knowledge of the quantitative requirements for essential amino acids. Therefore, no differentiation could be made between a response to an essential amino acid and to protein (nitrogen) per se. In the last edition of *Nutrient Requirements of Cats* (NRC, 1978a), the protein requirement was set at 280 g/kg diet. The sum of the nitrogen of the current minimal essential amino acid requirements of the growing kitten (Table 2) times 6.25 is equivalent to about one-fourth to one-fifth of this quantity of protein. It would, therefore, appear that a high proportion of the protein requirement of the growing kitten and adult cat must be for amino nitrogen for synthesis of dispensable amino acids and other compounds containing nitrogen.

Several estimates have been made of the nitrogen requirements of the growing kitten. Anderson et al. (1980b) gave kittens diets varying from 21.5 to 29.4 g of nitrogen/kg diet (134 to 184 g crude protein/kg diet). In one experiment they found a linear growth response to level of nitrogen in the diet and in the other essentially no response.

Smalley et al. (1985) gave growing kittens either amino acid-based diets or casein-based diets supplemented with essential amino acids. All diets exceeded the essential amino acid requirements. They suggested that 180 to 200 g of protein equivalent (N × 6.25)/kg diet was required to maximize both body weight gain and nitrogen retention. When all the data are pooled for the growing kitten, the relationships between growth (gain in body weight and nitrogen retention) and protein content of the diet gradually approach a plateau without a definite "breakpoint." Recently, Rogers and Morris (personal communication, 1985), in studies in which all the essential amino acids were added at their minimum requirements (MacDonald et al., 1984c) plus tryptophan at 1.5 g/kg diet, and total dispensable amino acids added to bring the protein content (N × 6.25) to 200 g/kg diet, a substantial growth response was obtained by the addition of dispensable amino acids equivalent to 40 g crude protein/kg diet. These results indicate that a higher concentration of nitrogen is required for maximal growth if the essential amino acids are not present in excess of their requirements as in the diets used by Smalley et al. (1985). A minimum requirement of protein (N × 6.25) of 240 g/kg diet is recommended.

Burger et al. (1984) reported that most adult cats could maintain good health and condition when given a diet containing about 120 g crude protein/kg diet that included all essential amino acids at the minimal requirements for growth suggested by Anderson et al. (1980b). There are no proteins known that supply the essential amino acids at the concentration used by Burger et al. (1984) when the diets contain 120 g protein (N × 6.25)/kg. Adult cats (like kittens) might also respond to a higher concentration of dietary nitrogen if the essential amino acid concentration were not in excess of minimal requirements. This may account in part for the higher requirement suggested by NRC (1978a) for the adult cat when protein per se was used. If an additional quantity of nitrogen is added to the diet containing 120 g protein equivalent/kg diet in proportion to that suggested for kittens (see above), the minimum protein (N × 6.25) requirement would be 144 g/kg diet. Rounding this value, a minimum protein (N × 6.25) of 140 g/kg diet is recommended for the adult cat.

Both the growing kitten and adult cat have higher nitrogen requirements than most other domestic mammals (Rogers and Morris, 1982a, 1983). Cats (and presumably other strict carnivores) have a reduced capacity to regulate the activity of the transaminases and urea-cycle enzymes (Rogers et al., 1977) with change of dietary protein intake. Thus, cats require a relatively high intake of nitrogen to accommodate this high obligatory nitrogen loss.

Arginine

Morris and Rogers (1978a,b), using a purified diet, demonstrated that arginine was an essential amino acid. When near-adult cats were given a diet containing 16.6 g L-arginine/kg they grew normally. However, when arginine was omitted from the diet, clinical signs of hyperammonemia appeared within 3 h of ingestion of a single meal. These signs included vocalization (moaning), emesis, ptyalism, hyperactivity, hyperesthesia, ataxia, tetanic spasms, emprosthotonus, extended limbs with exposed claws, apnea, and cyanosis, which in some cases led to death. When arginine was substituted with isomolar quantities of ornithine, near-adults cats did not develop hyperammonemia. However, Morris et al. (1979) demonstrated that while kittens given an arginine-free diet containing ornithine were protected from hyperammonemia, even high concentrations of ornithine did not support growth. Normal growth occurred when citrulline replaced arginine, but the efficiency of utilization of citrulline was less than that of arginine (C. Johanssen, J. G. Morris, and Q. R. Rogers, University of California, Davis, personal communication, 1985).

Dietary arginine is required for optimal growth in rats (Borman et al., 1946), and in its absence, growth rate is reduced to about half maximal (Milner and Visek, 1974). This indicates that rats are capable of synthesizing some arginine de novo, but the rate of synthesis is suboptimal. In contrast, cats given an arginine-free diet not only do not grow, but they also lose body mass at a rate greater than when given diets devoid of any other essential amino acid. This observation indicates that the capacity of cats to synthesize arginine is much less than that of rats. The metabolic basis for this difference between species appears to be primarily due to the low activity of the enzyme pyrroline-5-carboxylate synthase in the intestinal mucosa. Rogers and Phang (1985) showed that the specific activity of this enzyme in the cat is only about 18 percent of that in the rat and only about 5 percent as active per kilogram body weight. A second factor limiting ornithine synthesis in the small intestine is the low activity of the enzyme ornithine amino transferase (Morris, 1985), which is also about 20 percent that of the rat.

The requirement of the kitten for arginine for maximal growth does not appear to exceed 8.3 g/kg diet (Anderson et al., 1979a; Costello et al., 1979, 1980). However, Costello et al. (1979) showed that at this level of dietary arginine, urinary orotic acid excretion was elevated, and they suggested that 10.5 g arginine/kg diet was necessary to normalize both growth and orotic acid excretion. A value of 10 g of arginine/kg diet is recommended for the minimum requirement.

Histidine

The histidine requirement of the kitten was shown by Rogers and Morris (1979) to be no greater than 6 g/kg diet. Anderson et al. (1980a) gave kittens diets containing 0, 3.0, 6.0, and 9.0 g histidine/kg and on the basis of growth rate, suggested a requirement of 3 g histidine/kg diet. Quam et al. (1986) reported that food intake, rates of body weight gain, and nitrogen retention attained plateau values at 2.1 g histidine/kg diet. However, weanling kittens given diets containing either 2.0 or 2.5 g histidine/kg diet later developed bilateral cataracts, a histidine concentration of 3 g/kg diet was required to support normal hematological values in young kittens. A requirement of 3 g histidine/kg diet is therefore recommended for the minimum requirement of growing kittens.

Isoleucine

Rogers and Morris (1979) reported that isoleucine was an essential amino acid for the growing kitten and that a diet containing 9.0 g isoleucine/kg would support growth rates similar to those occurring in kittens receiving a diet containing 18 g isoleucine/kg. Anderson et al. (1980c) did not observe a significant growth response in kittens fed levels of isoleucine above 3 g/kg diet.

Hargrove et al. (1984a) measured growth rate, nitrogen retention, and plasma amino acid concentrations of kittens given diets containing various levels of isoleucine. Using an asymptotic curve-fitting method, maximal growth and nitrogen retention occurred at 6.2 and 8.4 g isoleucine/kg diet, respectively. However, kittens given the diet containing 4.6 g isoleucine/kg diet gained 30 g/day, and the authors suggested the requirement may not exceed this level. Kittens given diets containing suboptimal levels of isoleucine (less than 3.8 g/kg diet) had crusts of dried exudate around the eyes. Cultures from the conjunctiva of these kittens indicated the presence of staphylococcal organisms, and the authors suggested that a deficiency of isoleucine may have induced a lack of membrane integrity or impaired immunity. Clinical signs disappeared when the dietary concentration of isoleucine was increased.

Hargrove et al. (1984a) also observed that isoleucine concentration in plasma was not a useful indicator of the dietary requirement. Moreover, dietary concentrations of isoleucine did not affect the concentrations of the other branched-chain amino acids (valine and leucine) in plasma.

A minimum requirement of 5.0 g isoleucine/kg diet is recommended for the growing kitten.

Leucine

Rogers and Morris (1979) reported similar growth rates in kittens receiving purified diets containing either 12 or 24 g leucine/kg diet. Anderson et al. (1980c), on the basis of feed intake and rate of weight gain, suggested a minimal leucine requirement for growth of 12 g leucine/kg diet. Hargrove et al. (1984a) reported requirements of 7.8 g and 10.6 g for maximal weight gain and nitrogen retention respectively, of growing kittens. However, levels as low as 5 g leucine/kg diet gave gains and nitrogen retentions two-thirds of maximal. Increasing the dietary concentration of leucine from 5 g to 20 g/kg diet resulted in a decrease to about one-third in the concentrations of the other branched-chain amino acids in plasma. The rate of catabolism of isoleucine and valine may be a function of the leucine concentration in the diet.

A dietary concentration of 12.0 g leucine/kg diet is recommended as the minimum requirement for the growing kitten.

Lysine

Jansen et al. (1975) demonstrated that the rate of body weight gain of cats given a diet based on wheat gluten could be increased by a lysine supplement. Rogers and Morris (1979), using crystalline amino acid diets, showed that lysine was an essential amino acid for the growing kitten, and the requirement (as lysine·HCl) did not exceed 14 g/kg diet. Anderson et al. (1979a) also using crystalline amino acid diets indicated that the requirement did not exceed 8 g/kg diet. This dietary concentration is in agreement with that found by J. O'Donnell, Q. R. Rogers, and J. G. Morris (University of California, Davis, personal communication, 1985), who used both gain and nitrogen retention as criteria of adequacy. A minimum requirement of 8 g lysine/kg diet is recommended.

Methionine

Early studies on the methionine requirement of the kitten by Dymsza and Miller (1964) and Rambaut and Miller (1965, 1967) led these authors to suggest that the

young and adult cat had a very low requirement for methionine. In 1974, Ritter and Owens reported that the addition of methionine to a diet based on casein and gelatin increased the growth rate of cats. They inferred from these observations that methionine was essential for the cat and suggested a requirement of 9 g methionine in the presence of 0.6 g cystine/kg diet (F. N. Owens, Oklahoma State University, personal communication, 1985).

Teeter et al. (1978a), using a purified amino acid diet containing high concentrations of cystine, taurine, and sulfate, demonstrated that methionine was an essential amino acid for the growing kitten and adult cat. In another study, also with amino acid diets, Teeter et al. (1978b) showed that the methionine requirement of the kitten in the presence of excess cystine was 4.5 g/kg diet. When cystine was added to a diet containing 4.5 g methionine/kg, growth rate plateaued at 4.5 g cystine/kg diet. These results indicated that cystine may supply about half the sulfur amino acid requirement of the growing kitten and that the total sulfur amino acid requirment was 9 g/kg diet, half of which must be methionine.

The methionine requirement of the growing kitten given purified amino acid diets was also studied by Schaeffer et al. (1982a). They reported that in the absence of cystine, growth rate and nitrogen retention attained maximal values at 7 g and 7.5 g methionine/kg diet, respectively. In a diet containing adequate cystine (6.0 g/kg), growth and nitrogen retention plateaued at 3.3 and 3.9 g/kg, added methionine, respectively (Smalley et al., 1983).

The slightly different estimates of requirements in the above studies arise from the different increments of methionine tested by both groups of researchers. Because Schaeffer et al. (1982a) and Smalley et al. (1983) used smaller increments than Teeter et al. (1978a,b), these values are suggested as the minimum requirements for growth, i.e., a total methionine plus cystine requirement of 7.5 g/kg diet of which 4.0 g/kg must be supplied as methionine. These requirements for methionine are based on a diet containing adequate levels of choline (3 g/kg diet). If the diet contains suboptimal levels of choline (or other methyl donors), the requirement for methionine will be greater. The D isomer of methionine is utilized by the cat (Teeter et al., 1978a; K. A. Smalley, Q. R. Rogers, and J. G. Morris, University of California, Davis, personal communication, 1985). The latter authors fed growing kittens diets containing 5.5, 7.0, or 15 g/kg of either the D or the L isomer of methionine. Nitrogen retention values indicated that when methionine was growth-limiting the efficiency of utilization of D-methionine varied from 73 to 89 percent of that for L-methionine.

The calcium salt of DL-OH-methionine appears to be poorly utilized by the growing kitten given an amino acid-based diet. When added as a supplement to a soy-based diet its efficiency of utilization was greater than with an amino acid diet, but still not equal to L-methionine (Teeter et al., 1978a).

The reason for the high-sulfur amino acid requirement of the cat, compared to other mammals, e.g., the dog (Burns and Milner, 1981; Blaza et al., 1982; Hirakawa and Baker, 1984), is not readily apparent. The urine of the cat contains the branched-chain sulfur amino acid felinine (Datta and Harris, 1951; Westall, 1953), which may be a territorial marker. However, its synthesis in the male cat should not require more than 0.5 g of methionine or cystine/kg diet (MacDonald et al., 1984c). Methionine and cystine may act to a limited extent as precursors for synthesis of the beta sulfonic amino acid taurine, which is discussed in a later section. However, the quantity of sulfur amino acids equivalent to the taurine requirement of the cat does not exceed 0.5 g/kg diet.

Limited data are available on the sulfur amino acid requirements of the adult cat for maintenance. Studies of Burger (I. H. Burger, Pedigree Petfoods, personal communication, 1985) suggest that the total sulfur amino acid requirement for maintenance was greater than 2.4 g, but less than 4.0 g/kg diet. Subsequent work indicates the requirement to be 3 g total sulfur amino acids/kg diet.

Phenylalanine

Rogers and Morris (1979) using crystalline amino acid diets demonstrated that phenylalanine was an essential amino acid for the growing kitten and suggested that the requirement for phenylalanine was not greater than 7.5 g/kg diet when the diet contained 10 g tyrosine/kg diet. These authors also showed that tyrosine was a dispensable amino acid.

Anderson et al. (1980a) gave kittens crystalline amino acid-based diets with varying phenylalanine and tyrosine concentrations. On the basis of body weight gain, they showed that the total aromatic amino acid requirement (phenylalanine plus tyrosine) of the kitten did not exceed 10 g/kg diet, of which half could be supplied by tyrosine. Morris and Rogers (1983) determined the requirement for these amino acids in growing kittens. In the absence of tyrosine, growth rate and nitrogen retention were maximized at 8.5 g/phenylalanine/kg diet, whereas when tyrosine was present in the diet in excess (10 g/kg diet) growth rate and nitrogen retention were maximized at 3.5 g phenylalanine/kg diet.

A minimum requirement of phenylalanine plus tyrosine of 8.5 g/kg diet is recommended for the growing kitten. Half of this requirement should be provided by phenylalanine.

Threonine

Rogers and Morris (1979) demonstrated that threonine was an essential amino acid for the growing kitten and that the requirement did not exceed 7 g/kg diet. Anderson et al. (1980c) in two experiments gave kittens amino acid diets with varying levels of threonine. In the first experiment, 8.0, 11.0, and 14.0 g/kg diet were used, and, in the second experiment, 6.0, 7.0, and 8.0 g/kg were tested. However, significant differences were not observed in rates of body weight gain in either experiment.

Titchenal et al. (1980) gave kittens threonine-imbalanced and -deficient diets. They suggested that the requirement was between 7 and 10 g threonine/kg diet. Near maximal weight gains were observed at 6 g threonine/kg diet. Kittens fed threonine-deficient diets grew suboptimally and developed neurological dysfunctions. Clinical signs included ataxia, incoordination, dysequilibrium, and a defective righting reflex. Carpal joints were affected, resulting in abnormal conformation of the forelimbs. Also, reduced flexion and extension of the hip, stifle, and hock resulted in stilted pelvic limb movements. Evidence of neurologic dysfunction appeared as early as the fifth day of ingestion of the imbalanced diet. The clinical signs and absence of histopathological changes in the carpal joints, peripheral nerves, spinal cord, or brain suggested that the deficiency of threonine induced cerebellar dysfunction.

A minimum dietary requirement of 7 g threonine/kg diet is recommended for the growing kitten.

Tryptophan

Rogers and Morris (1979) demonstrated the essentiality of tryptophan for the growing kitten and they indicated that the requirement was no greater than 2 g/kg diet. Anderson et al. (1980a) suggested a requirement of 1.5 g/kg diet, although kittens in their study grew rather poorly. Hargrove et al. (1983), on the basis of rate of body weight gain and nitrogen retention, reported a minimum requirement of 1.1 g tryptophan/kg diet. However, Q. R. Rogers and J. G. Morris (University of California, Davis, personal communication, 1985) have found that when all the essential amino acids are present in the diet at their minimum requirements (tryptophan 1.1 g/kg diet) total amino acids provided a protein equivalent (N × 6.25) of 200 g/kg diet, tryptophan severely limits growth. Therefore, a minimum requirement of 1.5 g tryptophan/kg diet is recommended.

Valine

Hardy et al. (1977) demonstrated that valine was an essential amino acid for the growing kitten. Growth rate and nitrogen retention of kittens given a diet containing 6 g valine/kg was the same as when the diet contained 18 g valine/kg. Anderson et al. (1980c), using a similar amino acid mixture to that used by Hardy et al. (1977), also reported a minimum requirement of 6 g valine/kg diet. P. Wright, J. G. Morris, and Q. R. Rogers (University of California, Davis, personal communication, 1985) found that 4 g valine/kg diet was suboptimal for kittens given an amino acid diet. However, 6 g valine/kg diet gave maximal weight gain and nitrogen retention.

A minimum dietary requirement of 6 g valine/kg diet is recommended for the growth of kittens.

Amino Acid Availability from the Diet

While the amino acid composition of dietary protein is a useful index of nutritive value, not all the amino acids in the ingested food are absorbed. A variable proportion of dietary protein is indigestible, and processing methods may result in changes in digestibility and structure of individual amino acids. Processing may enhance or reduce the nutritive value of proteins. Some raw plant products contain inhibitors of proteolytic digestion, e.g., soybeans contain trypsin inhibitors, which are inactivated by cooking, which also enhances digestibility. In contrast, the nutritional value of protein in the diet may be lowered as a result of heat damage either to the dietary ingredients in the course of their manufacture as in drying meat meals or during preparation of the complete diet in the process of extrusion or retorting. Some of the major types of processing damage that may occur to proteins are:

1. Excessive heat, especially in the presence of sugars or oxidized lipids, can induce cross linkage of amino acids and render proteins resistant to digestion. The availability of all amino acids in these proteins is decreased. This type of heat damage is encountered in the manufacture of dried animal tissue meals.

2. Mild heat treatment of proteins or free amino acids in the presence of reducing sugars can reduce the availability of amino acids. The epsilon amino group of lysine reacts with the reducing sugar to form compounds that are resistant to digestion, thereby rendering lysine unavailable.

3. Exposure of proteins to strong alkali solutions can result in racemization of L-amino acids and formation of compounds such as lanthionine and lysinoalanine. The latter is absorbed from the gut and in high concentration can result in damage to the kidney.

4. Oxidative damage of proteins may occur when proteins are stored with polyunsaturated lipids. Oxidation products of lipids react with methionine, tryptophan, and histidine reducing their bioavailability.

In the formulation of diets, allowances should be made for the amino acid composition of the proteins in the dietary ingredients and the digestibility and availability of the amino acids in the proteins. For high-quality natural ingredients a value of 80 to 90 percent availability is suggested, whereas for low-quality proteins a value of 60 to 70 percent should be used.

Amino Acid Interactions

Little work has been done on the effect of disproportionalities among dietary amino acids in the cat. The rat and cat appear to have similar sensitivities to a dietary excess of methionine. A methionine concentration of 25 g/kg diet was reported by Fau et al. (1983) to cause depression in food intake and growth in kittens. Kittens were capable of exhibiting some adaptation to diets containing up to 35 g methionine/kg diet. However, Fau et al. (1984) showed that the cystathionase activity in the liver of the cat was less than that in the liver of the rat and was probably the limiting step for transsulfuration in the cat.

Intolerance of growing kittens to glutamic acid in the diet at 90 g/kg diet or higher has been reported by Deady et al. (1981a). High concentrations of glutamic acid appeared to increase the requirement of the kitten for thiamin. Titchenal et al. (1980) reported that growing kittens given threonine-imbalanced diets had depressed food intakes and body weight gains compared to kittens given balanced diets. Threonine-imbalanced or -deficient diets both resulted in the development of neurological lesions that were resolved when dietary threonine was increased.

The growing kitten appears relatively less sensitive to antagonisms among the branched-chain amino acids than the rat. Hargrove et al. (1984b) was unable to demonstrate a depression of feed intake or body weight gain resulting from the addition of 100 g branched chain amino acids/kg diet. From the limited data available, it appears that the cat may be less sensitive to imbalances and antagonisms than the rat.

Taurine (Feline Central Retinal Degeneration)

In 1964 Scott et al. reported corneal and retinal lesions in cats given a vitamin A-deficient purified diet based on 350 g casein/kg diet. Supplemental vitamin A gave remission of the corneal, but not the retinal lesions. A similar vitamin-A deficient diet based on meat protein produced corneal but not retinal lesions. In the following year, Morris (1965) reported cats given a relatively low-protein, vitamin A-supplemented diet based on casein became totally blind after 9 months. These cats developed lesions confined to and associated with degeneration of the retina. Earlier, Rubin (1963) described atrophy of the rods and cones of three aged cats of unknown nutritional history. This was followed by reports of other naturally occurring cases (Bellhorn et al., 1974) and laboratory-induced cases (Rabin et al., 1973) of the disease. The link with taurine deficiency was made soon thereafter (Hayes et al., 1975b).

Typical feline central retinal degeneration (FCRD) occurs in adult cats or older kittens and is associated with mydriasis and reduced visual acuity with only partial loss of vision except in advanced cases. Ophthalmoscopic examination of affected cats reveals lesions of the area centralis of the retina. In a developing lesion the normal bright yellow tapetum initially appears dark and granular, then later develops into a hyperreflective focal lesion. By the time the lesion develops to this stage, extensive destruction of the visual elements has occurred. Electrophysiologic recordings indicate that cone timing delays are among the first detectable changes, closely followed by a decrease in amplitude of the visual response. The cone timing delays are correlated with disorientation of the cone outer segments and the degeneration of the rods and cones (Schmidt et al., 1977). The hyperreflective focus represents an irreparable loss of photoreceptor cells and disordered structure of the underlying tapetum. The detailed progression of the degenerative changes has been followed in a series of nutritional studies (Rabin et al. 1973, 1976; Hayes et al., 1975a,b; Sturman et al., 1981). These workers found that, while this condition did not develop in cats given a commercial diet or a semipurified diet containing lactalbumin, it was regularly seen in cats receiving semipurified diets containing casein as the only protein source. The condition appeared to be partially reversed when the semipurified diet contained egg albumen. The earliest changes in the electroretinogram occurred within 3 months with extensive degeneration within 6 months, but total blindness took up to 2 years to develop.

Since casein is relatively low in sulfur amino acids (in particular cystine) and because the mammalian retina contains high levels of taurine (one product of methionine via cystine metabolism in most mammals), Hayes et al. (1975b) measured the concentration of free amino acids in the retina and plasma. After 3 to 12 months, all cats fed the casein diets showed evidence of retinal degeneration. None of the cats given the commercial diet exhibited eye lesions, and retinal taurine concentrations of these cats were two to six times higher than in cats receiving casein. Further studies with kittens (Berson et al., 1976; Schmidt et al., 1976, 1977) showed that development of the retinal lesion could be prevented by supplemental taurine but not methionine and cystine. This suggested that the synthesis of taurine from methionine via cystine in the cat may be suboptimal for the maintenance of effective concentrations of taurine in the eye.

Subsequently, Knopf et al. (1978) demonstrated that while limited amounts of ^{35}S cystine could be converted to taurine, this conversion was not sufficient to maintain the body taurine pool. These workers were unable to demonstrate incorporation of ^{35}S sulfate into taurine in the cat. Hardison et al. (1977), working with perfused cat liver, concluded that some synthesis of taurine via the cysteine sulfinic acid decarboxylase pathway occurred, but its quantitative significance was not determined.

A taurine-free diet fed to newborn kittens causes a depression in growth (K. C. Hayes, Brandeis University, personal communication, 1985) and when fed to queens during gestation and lactation produced kittens with low birth weight, poor survival, reduced growth, cerebellar dystrophy, and abnormalities in skeletal growth and motor ability (Sturman et al., 1985a), all of which were prevented by taurine supplementation (500 mg taurine/kg diet) (Sturman et al., 1985b).

For most mammals the bile salts contain a mixture of taurine and glycine conjugates. When confronted with a tissue deficiency of taurine, glycine conjugates are readily synthesized. Rabin et al. (1976) showed that the cat is unable to alternate between glycine and taurine conjugation, and the bile salts are conjugated exclusively with taurine. Bile salt production represents an obligatory loss of taurine for the cat (Sturman et al., 1978) even though some of this taurine is recovered in the enterohepatic circulation. This loss, coupled with the low efficiency of hepatic synthesis of taurine from methionine and cystine, would appear to explain the sensitivity of the cat to a dietary deficiency of taurine.

REQUIREMENTS

Although FCRD has been induced in a number of studies involving cats given taurine-free diets (Hayes et al., 1975a; Anderson et al., 1979b; Burger and Barnett, 1980) few long-term studies have been undertaken to determine a dietary requirement. Also, any estimated requirement will be a function of the concentration of sulfur amino acids in the diet and presumably the physiological state of the cat (O'Donnell et al., 1981).

Burger and Barnett (1982) gave cats diets containing

200 or 500 mg taurine/kg diet for periods up to 45 weeks. They found one case of FCRD out of five cats given the 200 mg/kg diet, and none for cats given the 500 mg/kg diet. They suggested a requirement of 500 mg taurine/kg diet. The diet they used contained 8.9 g methionine and 6.4 g cystine/kg.

Rogers and Morris (1982b) gave eight groups of cats diets containing either 0, 250, 375, or 500 mg taurine/kg with either 9 or 16 g sulfur amino acids/kg. Plasma concentration of taurine after 17 months was a function of both dietary taurine and sulfur amino acids (SAA). Four of the five cats receiving the zero taurine plus 9 g/kg sulfur amino acid diet had clinical FCRD, and all five cats exhibited decreased electroretinogram (ERG) amplitudes of the rods and cones. No clinical cases of FCRD occurred in the cats given the 250 mg taurine/kg diet, but two out of the six cats receiving the 250 mg taurine plus 16 g sulfur amino acid diet had reduced ERG amplitudes, but no abnormalities were apparent in the group fed 375 or 500 mg taurine/kg diet.

A requirement of 400 mg taurine/kg diet is suggested for the growing kitten and for maintenance of the adult. A minimal requirement for reproduction would be 500 mg taurine/kg diet.

MINERALS

That cats require minerals is indisputable. However, there is a scarcity of data on both the qualitative and quantitative requirements for this class of nutrients. Some minerals (calcium, phosphorus, sodium, potassium, magnesium, iron, copper, zinc, and iodine) have been shown to be indispensable for the cat, while others (chlorine, manganese, sulfur, cobalt, selenium, molybdenum, fluorine, chromium, silicon, and perhaps tin, nickel, and vanadium) have been assumed essential by analogy with other species.

The major obstacles in gathering such information have been the failure to develop (until recently) a readily acceptable chemically defined diet suitable for the study of mineral requirements. Nevertheless, many researchers have successfully raised cats fed purified diets from which guidelines for mineral requirements may be extrapolated.

Minerals are fundamental in maintaining acid-base balance, tissue structure, and osmotic pressure, as well as being essential components of many enzyme systems. Minerals exhibit numerous interrelationships, and thus proper balance is important in assessing the adequacy of minerals within a diet. In addition, some minerals, while essential to health, may be detrimental if consumed in excess.

Calcium and Phosphorus

REQUIREMENTS

Calcium (Ca) and phosphorus (P) are so closely interrelated, both nutritionally and metabolically, that they will be discussed together. Calcium and phosphorus in the form of hydroxyapatite crystals [$3Ca_3(PO_4)_2 \cdot Ca(OH)_2$] are the major minerals involved in the structural rigidity of bones and teeth. Calcium is also intimately involved in blood clotting and in impulse transmission at the neuromuscular junction. Since the cat is born with small stores of calcium—about 0.75 g (Jackson, 1968a)—and requires 200 to 400 mg calcium per day (approximately 6 to 8 g/kg diet) for good bone development, a dietary deficiency of this mineral can quickly result in a variety of complications. A healthy adult cat has between 18 and 40 g of calcium in its skeleton, depending upon size. The cat will maintain almost normal plasma calcium levels (9.5 to 10.5 mg/dl) at the expense of depleting bone stores; however, as these stores are exhausted, the cat may suffer bone fractures, extended blood-clotting time, and develop nervous disorders.

Phosphorus is likewise involved in many metabolic processes in addition to bone formation, including energy transfer. The ratio of calcium to phosphorus is important in both absorption and utilization of these minerals when one or both are near their requirement. Scott and Scott (1967) have shown optimal utilization by the cat when dietary calcium:phosphorus ratios ranged between 0.9:1 to 1.1:1. Gershoff et al. (1957b) induced rickets in kittens with a vitamin D-deficient diet when the calcium:phosphorus ratio was either 1:1 or increased to 3:1. The pathology caused by the deficiency was most severe at 1:1, presumably because food intake and growth were depressed by the 3:1 ratio. A ratio of 0.04:1 (Anonymous, 1962) has also produced bone pathology. Thus, calcium or phosphorus should not be indiscriminately added to the diet of cats that exhibit signs of calcium or phosphorus deficiency; but, rather, the dietary concentrations of these minerals should be determined, and any supplement should provide both the desired concentrations and the desired ratio.

Most feed ingredients used in feline diets are richer in phosphorus than calcium. However, phosphorus provided from plant materials such as cereal grains and oilseed products is present largely as phytate phosphorus. From studies with other species it seems reasonable to conclude that the bioavailability of phytate phosphorus is approximately 30 percent. A ratio of calcium to bioavailable phosphorus of between 1:1 and 2:1 has proven acceptable for diets of other simple-stomached animals.

The metabolism of calcium and phosphorus is closely related to that of vitamin D. When calcium and phosphorus are available in limited amounts, inadequate vitamin D may result in ineffective utilization of these minerals. The requirement for vitamin D is discussed more completely in the section on vitamins. Iodine has also been shown to influence calcium utilization. Roberts and Scott (1961), feeding a diet of raw minced sheep's heart, showed that iodine supplementation of this low-calcium diet not only lowered calcium losses in urine and feces compared to the unsupplemented diet, but also initiated positive calcium balance.

Scott (1965) has reported that growing kittens as well as 9-month-old adult cats require about 200 to 400 mg calcium per day, depending on the proportions of other dietary constituents. Kittens fed a purified diet thrived on daily phosphorus intakes of 150 to 200 mg per kitten when the calcium:phosphorus ratio was maintained between 0.9:1 and 1.1:1. However, when fed raw meat, the phosphorus intake from the meat was about 400 mg per day. Thus, it was necessary to raise the calcium intake in order to bring the calcium:phosphorus ratio to 1:1. When all these data are considered, dietary concentrations of 8 g/kg of calcium and 6 g/kg phosphorus is recommended for the growing kitten.

SIGNS OF DEFICIENCY AND IMBALANCE

The most commonly encountered nutritional bone disease in cats results from nutritional secondary hyperparathyroidism (Bennett, 1976). It is seen most often in kittens and young adult cats and is commonly associated with the feeding of incorrectly supplemented, meat-rich diets. Cardiac and skeletal muscle have a calcium:phosphorus ratio of approximately 1:20, and the calcium concentration is approximately 0.025 percent (dry basis). As a consequence, there is a marked deficiency of calcium in relation to the need of this element in bone formation. The result of consuming such a diet is osteitis fibrosa (Krook et al., 1963), also called osteodystrophia fibrosa (Palmer, 1968; Jackson, 1968b), osteogenesis imperfecta (Coop, 1958), and osteoporosis (Jowsey and Gershon-Cohen, 1964). Locomotor disturbance is seen, with limping and ultimately reluctance to move. Radiographic examination provides evidence of generalized decrease in bone density, loss of fine trabeculation, and thinning of cortices (Rowland et al., 1968). Morphological changes in the parathyroid include hypertrophy, hyperplasia, and disappearance of dark chief cells (Krook, 1965). The underlying cause is a dietary calcium deficiency and inadequate absorption of available calcium due to excess phosphorus, resulting in hypocalcemia and release of parathormone. This hormone acts on bone, kidney, and intestine to help restore serum calcium levels to normal. The resorption of bone to release calcium exceeds bone formation and results in a loss of bone mass. Jowsey and Gershon-Cohen (1964) were able to reverse some of the bone changes when adult cats, previously fed a low-calcium diet, were offered supplements containing calcium. Wing (1967) found, with young cats, that reversal of nutritional osteitis fibrosa was accomplished most effectively with a dietary calcium: phosphorus ratio of 2:1 (10 g Ca to 5 g P/kg diet) rather than 1:1 or 3:1.

Magnesium

REQUIREMENTS

Scott (1960, 1964) has observed good performance in cats fed diets containing approximately 160 to 200 mg of magnesium (Mg) per kilogram of dry diet. More recently, magnesium deficiency was produced in 16-week-old kittens by feeding a purified diet containing 50 or 100 mg magnesium/kg dry diet as magnesium sulfate (Chausow et al., 1985). At 50 mg/kg, kittens grew poorly and exhibited muscular weakness, hyperirritability, convulsions, anorexia, reduced bone and serum magnesium concentration, and calcification of the aorta. In a follow-up study 100, 400, or 700 mg magnesium/kg dry diet were fed to kittens for 8 weeks. At 100 mg/kg intake the serum magnesium level was depressed after only 1 week and persisted throughout the 8-week experiment. Both the 400 and 700 mg/kg levels of magnesium maintained serum magnesium near 2.5 mg/100 ml serum throughout the trial. Based upon this work and studies conducted in other species, a dietary magnesium level of 400 mg/kg dry diet is suggested as a minimum requirement.

Consumption of excessive magnesium by cats (>3.5 g/kg diet) has been linked to urinary calculi in the form of struvite crystals (magnesium ammonium phosphate), which contribute to urinary obstruction of the male urethra (Kallfelz et al., 1980), otherwise known as the feline urological syndrome (FUS). The absolute level of magnesium per se is probably not critical, providing its interrelationship with other minerals and dietary factors is adequate to maintain an acidic urinary pH (see discussion of FUS). Nevertheless, it seems prudent to not intentionally add an excess of magnesium to cat diets.

Potassium

REQUIREMENTS

Potassium (K) is found in high concentration within cells and in much smaller concentrations in extracellular fluids. It is especially critical to muscle function and is involved with fluid and ionic balance. When a deficiency does occur, depressed reflexes or cardiac failure may be observed. Potassium is also instrumental in the maintenance of the mechanisms to fight infection.

Dietary levels of potassium that have been fed successfully at 1.6 to 4.0 g/kg dry diet (Scott, 1964). However, the requirement for growing kittens is dependent on the level of dietary protein (Hills et al., 1982). In a 33 percent soy protein diet, 3 g potassium/kg was adequate, but this requirement increased to 5 g/kg with a 68 percent soy protein diet. Deficiency signs included anorexia, retarded growth, emaciation, lethargy, locomotive problems, unkempt fur, and hypokalemia. Based on these observations and usual dietary protein content of cat diets a minimum level of 4 g/kg dry weight is recommended.

Natural foodstuffs may not always contain adequate amounts of potassium, but uncomplicated deficiencies are rare.

Sodium and Chloride

REQUIREMENTS

Sodium (Na) and chloride (Cl) are essential for normal metabolism and are easily supplied by common salt. Scott and Scott (1967) reported that the water intake of a cat may be increased 50 to 100 percent by adding salt at the rate of 1 percent to the diet. However, the healthfulness of such a procedure for any length of time is questionable since high sodium intake has been implicated in causing hypertension.

Although levels of sodium in the range from 400 to 600 mg/kg diet have been fed successfully (Scott, 1964), little evidence exists for determination of a minimum requirement. Similarly, chloride has been fed at 1900 mg/kg diet without apparent harm (Scott, 1960), but a minimum requirement was not established. Based on requirements of other small mammals, a minimum requirement of 500 mg and 1900 mg per kg dry diet for sodium and chloride, respectively, is recommended.

SIGNS OF DEFICIENCY

Signs of deficiency include weight loss, severe alopecia, and dryness of skin. A chloride deficiency may cause a severe alkalosis.

Iron and Copper

REQUIREMENTS

Iron (Fe) and copper (Cu) are both essential for prevention of anemia in the cat. Iron is present in hemoglobin, myoglobin, certain enzymes, and as ferritin and hemosiderin. The amount of iron in the body of the cat at different stages of development has been determined by Spray and Widdowson (1950).

Copper is required for normal iron metabolism, but also has many other diverse functions. Among these is production of myelin, melanin, and connective tissue. The latter involves the synthesis of desmosine and isodesmosine and the formation of cross-linkages, which lend strength to blood vessel walls and the organic matrix of bone. Clinical signs of copper deficiency vary with the individual and severity of the deficiency; however, bone abnormalities may occur. Doong et al. (1983) have produced copper deficiency in weaned kittens fed a purified diet containing 0.58 mg Cu/kg diet or in offspring of queens fed the same level of copper for the last 30 days of gestation and during the lactation period. Although anemia was not consistently observed in kittens fed the low copper diet, both liver copper concentration and hepatic Cu-Zn-superoxide dismutase activity were depressed. Moreover, signs of connective tissue lesions were seen in kittens born to and weaned from queens fed diets containing less than 1 mg Cu/kg diet. Since no conclusive results are available on the minimal requirement of Cu in the kitten, 5 mg Cu/kg diet is recommended, based on the requirement of the rat (NRC, 1978b).

Chausow and Czarnecki (1985) studied 6-week-old kittens fed an iron-deficient casein-dextrose diet (5 mg Fe/kg diet) over a 30-day period. Dietary treatments consisted of the basal diet (5 mg Fe/kg), 30, 55, 80, 105, and 130 mg Fe/kg, the supplemental iron being provided as $FeSO_4 \cdot 7H_2O$. Both hemoglobin and hematocrit at day 30 increased linearly from 6.4 g/100 ml and 16.5 percent, respectively, in kittens fed 5 mg Fe/kg to 11.6 g/100 ml and 28.0 percent in those fed 80 mg Fe/kg. There was no further response in either of these iron-sensitive parameters at Fe increments above 80 mg Fe/kg diet. From these results an iron requirement of about 80 mg Fe/kg diet (3.8 mg/day) is recommended for young kittens fed a phytate-free purified diet.

It is important to keep in mind that an iron requirement established with a phytate-free purified diet represents a "minimum" requirement. Thus, it is clear from the scientific literature that not only phytate but other nutrient excesses (e.g., zinc) as well can materially decrease the efficiency of gut absorption of iron and copper (Erdman, 1979; Southern and Baker, 1983a,b; Bafundo et al., 1984a). Although 80 mg Fe/kg diet is adequate for kittens fed purified diets, this level may be inadequate under conditions where bioavailability is low. Still to be determined, moreover, are the relative bioavailabilities of iron from heme and nonheme sources for cats, and within nonheme sources, the relative utilization of inorganic iron salts deserves attention.

Based upon results with other species, however, it seems likely that (a) heme (i.e., from meat sources) iron is well utilized; (b) iron sulfate may be assimilated twice as efficiently as iron carbonate; and (c) iron oxides have very little if any iron bioavailability for animals.

Requirements of 80 mg Fe/kg diet and 5 mg Cu/kg diet are recommended for growing kittens.

Iodine

REQUIREMENTS

Iodine (I) serves as a component of the thyroid hormones thyroxine and triiodothyronine, which are involved in the control of the rate of cellular metabolism. An interaction with calcium metabolism has been described by Scott (1959), Scott and Greaves (1961), and Roberts and Scott (1961).

Recommended iodine levels in published literature range from 1.4 to 4.0 mg/kg dry diet (Scott, 1964). Data from other species suggest that the minimum requirement would not exceed 350 μg/kg diet for the kitten.

SIGNS OF DEFICIENCY OR TOXICITY

Although the reported incidence is rare, iodine deficiency has been observed in zoo felids (Ratcliff, 1956; Fiennes and Graham-Jones, 1960) as well as in domestic cats (Greaves et al., 1959). Clinical signs include thyroid hypertrophy, alopecia, abnormal calcium metabolism, and death. Further, Scott (1960) reported that iodine deficiency caused fetal resorption, while estrus and libido were unaffected.

Scott (1964) stated that relatively high doses of iodine (up to 5 mg I/day) are tolerated by euthyroid cats, but hypothyroid individuals subjected to these amounts show toxic signs, which include anorexia, fever, and weight loss.

It is worth noting that in recent years (first reported in 1980) a substantial number of adult cats, typically between 6 and 20 years old, have been diagnosed with hyperthyroidism and elevated circulating thyroxine and triiodothyronine levels (see Peterson et al., 1983). Whether this is related to a dietary factor(s), including an increase in iodine intake or its metabolism, is presently unknown and awaits further investigation.

Zinc

REQUIREMENTS

Zinc (Zn) is found in trace amounts, but is widely distributed throughout the body. Certain tissues (e.g.,

male reproductive tissue, pancreas, choroid tissue of the eye) contain relatively high concentrations of zinc, but tissues such as bones, teeth, and skin account for a far larger total quantity of zinc in an animal's body. As a component or activator of numerous body enzymes, it is important in the metabolism of nucleic acids, carbohydrate, protein, and fat. The zinc requirement of weanling kittens fed a soy-based purified diet was found by Kane et al. (1981c) not to exceed 15 mg Zn/kg diet based upon growth and lack of gross deficiency signs. Male kittens, however, showed evidence of impaired testicular function when fed 15 mg Zn/kg over an 8-month period. This suggests that during growth, male kittens have a higher requirement for zinc than females. Male kittens fed 67 mg Zn/kg diet showed no evidence of testicular degeneration.

Kane et al. (1981c) also fed kittens a diet based upon EDTA-washed soy protein isolate in an attempt to produce severe zinc deficiency signs. The basal diet in this study contained only 0.7 mg Zn/kg diet. Although classic zinc deficiency signs were produced in kittens fed this diet for 8 weeks, the parakeratosis and other dermal lesions were less severe than that which has been observed previously in zinc-deficient pigs and dogs. Good weight gains and no zinc deficiency signs were observed in kittens fed the EDTA-treated soy diet containing 52 mg zinc/kg diet.

Excess dietary calcium when provided in phytate-containing diets is known to antagonize zinc via formation of an insoluble Zn-Ca-phytate complex in the gut. Kane et al. (1981c) added excess calcium (2 percent added $CaHPO_4$) to their soy protein isolate-based diets containing 15 mg Zn/kg and still failed to observe either reduced weight gains or skin lesions. In a preliminary report, however, Aiken et al. (1978) reported skin lesions and reduced growth when a vegetable protein-based diet containing 40 mg Zn/kg was fed to young kittens. Whether breed differences or some other factor accounts for the disparity between the Kane et al. (1981c) and Aiken et al. (1978) results cannot be determined.

The minimal requirement of zinc for gestation and lactation has not been determined. A high dietary zinc requirement (50-100 mg/kg diet) is known for several species for fetal development. A deficiency causes several congenital abnormalities (e.g., cleft palate, hairlessness).

Coccidiosis has been shown to increase the zinc requirement of chickens (Southern and Baker, 1983a,b). Whether a similar effect would occur in coccidial-infected cats remains problematic. Excess dietary cadmium has also been shown to exacerbate a zinc deficiency in chicks (Bafundo et al., 1984b), while excess inorganic lead, iron, or copper ingestion seemed to have little or no effect on zinc status (Bafundo et al., 1984a,c; Southern and Baker, 1983b).

A minimum requirement of 15 mg zinc/kg diet is recommended for kittens fed diets containing a low quantity of compounds known to decrease zinc bioavailability, e.g., phytate and fiber, under which conditions 50 mg/kg diet should suffice.

SIGNS OF DEFICIENCY OR TOXICITY

Signs of zinc deficiency include emaciation, parakeratosis, achromotrichia, testicular dysfunction, general debility, and retarded growth. Although zinc toxicity has not been reported in the cat, levels of 2000 mg/kg or more have been observed to produce iron- or copper-deficiency anemia in other species (Bafundo et al., 1984a).

Manganese

REQUIREMENTS

Manganese (Mn) is an essential factor for several enzymes and is necessary for proper bone formation and reproduction. Satisfactory performance of kittens has been obtained by feeding levels of 4 mg/kg dry diet (Scott, 1960, 1964). This level is recommended with an appropriate increase for a diet of higher caloric density than that fed by Scott (1960, 1964); that is, 5 mg manganese/kg diet.

Cobalt

Cobalt (Co) is an integral component of vitamin B_{12}. Other functions of cobalt in the tissues have not been identified. A deficiency of vitamin B_{12} is characterized by anemia, poor growth, and lack of resistance to infections. Based on research with other species, there is no evidence that cobalt is needed when adequate vitamin B_{12} is present in the diet, and therefore no requirement is recommended.

Selenium

Selenium (Se) deficiency in cats has not been observed, although it would appear likely from work with other species that a specific dietary requirement does exist. Much of the selenium present in common feed ingredients used in cat foods exists as selenomethionine. This compound provides a readily bioavailable source of selenium, except under conditions of dietary methionine deficiency. Inorganic salts of selenite or selenate are good sources of selenium. Some fish products are very rich in selenium. Levels of selenium in excess of 5 mg/kg diet

are toxic for many animal species, but have not been reported to be toxic to the cat. Based on the requirement of selenium in other species, a minimal requirement of 100 μg Se/kg diet is recommended.

Sulfur, Fluorine, Molybdenum, Tin, Silicon, Nickel, Vanadium, and Chromium

There are no published data on the requirements of cats for sulfur, fluorine, molybdenum, tin, silicon, nickel, vanadium, and chromium, although a physiological need for these elements has been demonstrated in other species.

EFFECT OF ACID-BASE BALANCE ON NUTRIENT REQUIREMENTS

The mineral composition of the diet dictates the acid-base status of the animal. The effects of diet composition on acid-base balance have generally not been considered when diets are formulated for cats, and this inattention may be a major factor contributing to the current high incidence of feline struvite urolithiasis, which represents the majority of cases reported under the general term FUS (feline urological syndrome) (Fishler, 1955; Carbone, 1965; Rich and Kirk, 1969; Lewis and Morris, 1983, 1984; Taton et al., 1984a,b; Buffington et al., 1985).

Large quantities of acid are normally formed from carbon dioxide generated during metabolic processes (Alberti and Cuthbert, 1982). Pulmonary excretion, the primary mode of excretion of the carbon dioxide, maintains pH homeostasis related to this source of acid. Unless metabolic disturbances such as keto- or lactic-acidosis occur, no net acid is produced or consumed during the complete catabolism of neutral lipids and carbohydrate. The catabolism of phospholipids may affect acid-base balance, depending on the quantity of phosphate hydrolyzed and extent of protonation of free phosphate groups (i.e., pH of the ingested phospholipid). Catabolism of amino acids from proteins to urea, carbon dioxide, sulphate, and water generates net acid (acid forming) due to production of sulfates during oxidation of the sulfur amino acids (Hunt, 1956). Carnivores eating high-protein diets thus produce net amounts of acid (from sulfur amino acid catabolism), which results in an acid urine. Excretion of excess acid in the urine restores proper tissue hydrogen ion and electrolyte concentrations.

In contrast, herbivores ingest largely vegetable materials, which contain large amounts of potassium and organic anions. The organic anions are protonated during catabolism and then oxidized to carbon dioxide and water (base forming), leaving an excess of potassium and base (bicarbonate ion) to be excreted. An alkaline urine results, and homeostasis is likewise restored.

The influence of dietary mineral composition (ash) on overall acid-base balance was recognized in the nineteenth century by documenting the "acid-forming" effects of dietary chloride, phosphorus, and sulfur and the "base-forming" effects of dietary sodium, potassium, calcium, and magnesium (see Hills, 1973). Lack of complete absorption of magnesium, calcium, and phosphate, however, precludes prediction of urinary pH from dietary mineral composition. Thus, to fully assess the net acid-base effect of a given foodstuff, it must be fed under a standard set of conditions and the net acid (base) excretion measured (see Camien et al., 1966, 1969; Gonick et al., 1968).

Homeostatic mechanisms (primarily renal) that enable the animal to excrete either acid or base (resulting in either acidic or alkaline urine) allow regulation of blood pH over a wide range of net acid or base intake (or production). If, however, the capability of the animal to excrete acid or base is exceeded, acidemia or alkalemia develops. The medical treatment of acid-base abnormalities commonly present in certain diseases is dealt with in detail in the physiology and medical literature (Porter and Lawrenson, 1982). Minimal research has addressed the question of diet-induced acidemia and alkalemia and their impact on nutrient requirements of the cat. For example, these conditions influence calcium and potassium balance.

Acidemic kittens avoid high-protein diets in favor of low-protein diets (Cook et al., 1985); avoidance of the high-protein diet lessens the acid load. Indeed, it has been shown that when offered a choice, the cat (N. Cook, Q. R. Rogers, and J. G. Morris, University of California, Davis, personal communication, 1985) and the rabbit (Hermus et al., 1983) will correct an acid-base deficit (or excess) by selecting the proper diet.

A major nutritional factor contributing to feline urolithiasis appears to be ingestion of abnormally large quantities of base-forming elements in the diet, which result in an alkaline urine. In the normal situation, a feral cat eats a carnivorous diet and produces a urine with a pH of 6.0 to 7.0. Since the cat evolved as a desert animal, it has the capacity to produce high urinary concentrations of many waste products in order to conserve water (Schmidt-Nielsen, 1964). These waste products include magnesium, ammonium, and phosphate ions that may crystallize in neutral and alkaline urine to form struvite uroliths (Fishler, 1955; Carbone, 1965; Rich and Kirk, 1969; Lewis and Morris, 1983). Below 6.6, struvite remains largely in solution, while if the urinary pH rises above 7.1, the formation product is exceeded and crystallization may occur spontaneously.

FUS includes various clinical signs, but is often characterized by dysuria, hematuria, cystitis, and urinary tract obstruction (Osbaldiston and Taussig, 1970; Osborne and Lees, 1978; Lewis and Morris, 1984). This term has been used and applied to the domestic cat as a broad descriptor for urethral obstruction arising not only from the formation of calculi, but also from the presence of sabulous and matrix plugs. The common lesion in the female is vesicular calculi, while in the male urethral obstruction by either microcalculi, sabulous plugs, or matrix plugs is more common (Carbone, 1965; Rich and Kirk, 1968; Sutor et al., 1970; Jackson and Colles, 1974).

The reported incidence of FUS in domestic cats appears to have increased from a low incidence in the 1950s to around 0.6 percent of the population in the mid-1970s (Willeberg, 1984) and 0.85 percent in the mid-1980s (Lawler et al., 1985). About 3 to 7 percent (Willeberg, 1984) or even a higher percent (Reif, 1977) of cats presented at veterinary clinics are diagnosed as having FUS.

For several decades the etiology of FUS has been elusive (Willeberg, 1984). Numerous potential causative factors have been suggested, including infection, both bacterial and viral; alkaline urine; castration; endocrine imbalance; high ash level of the diet; high dietary magnesium, phosphate, and nitrogen; low water intake; obesity; dry cat foods; stricter confinement of cats; less frequent urination, e.g., during rainy weather) (see extensive reviews by Finco et al., 1975; Greene and Scott, 1983; Lewis and Morris, 1984; Obsorne et al., 1984). There has been great difficulty in attempting to determine the primary cause and in reproducing experimental results from one laboratory to another.

Environmental changes affecting the cat population during the last 30 years include more strict confinement and a greater dependence on commercial foods. Commercial cat foods, especially dry cat foods, contain significant amounts of vegetable-based ingredients. Unless special precautions are taken, vegetable ingredients in cat foods can result in the production of neutral or slightly alkaline urine.

Although it has been known for decades that urinary pH is one factor involved (Vermeulen et al., 1951), differences found in urinary pH of affected cats were often ascribed to urinary stasis or infection rather than to the mineral composition of the diet. This has resulted in most experimenters not reporting the urinary pH caused by the specific diet fed. Most of the dietary effects studied were in association with diets that produced a urinary pH around neutrality, and with the alkaline tide the pH of the urine would often reach 7.3 to 8.0 (Lewis and Morris, 1984; Taton et al., 1984a,b). Under dietary conditions that produce a urinary pH around neutrality, high dietary magnesium is one factor that contributes to high incidence of FUS (Jackson, 1972; Rich et al., 1974; Lewis et al., 1978; Kallfelz et al., 1980; Lewis and Morris, 1984). Lack of recognition of the base-forming properties of magnesium oxide appears to have resulted in an inordinate emphasis being focused on magnesium as an etiologic agent. Recent experiments using magnesium chloride as the form of added magnesium have shown that high dietary magnesium does not result in any signs of FUS if an acid urine is produced (Buffington et al., 1985). Under conditions in which the urinary pH is around neutrality, water intake, water and high salt intake (therefore urinary volume), frequency of urination, and calcium and phosphate levels may also be important in decreasing or enhancing crystallization of struvite in the urinary tract. (See Osborne and Kruger [1984] for a discussion of initiation and growth of uroliths.) Some of these variables, plus others such as infection and level of ash (depending upon composition), could also affect urinary pH.

It has been demonstrated that dropping the urinary pH not only prevents FUS, but also causes formed stones to dissolve (Taton et al., 1984a,b), and since struvite plugs will form at low dietary magnesium concentrations if the urinary pH is 7.5 or higher (Cook, 1985), the most important dietary factors in the etiology of FUS appear to be those that affect urinary pH. The recent work of Taton et al. (1984a,b) and Buffington et al. (1985) has therefore re-emphasized the role of urinary pH on the development of FUS in an animal that has been evolutionarily adapted to produce acidic urine. This evidence suggests that special attention should be given to the mineral composition of cat foods in order to assure the consistent production of cat urine at a pH below 6.6.

A word of caution is appropriate on the possible consequences of chronic acidemia to such a degree that the urinary pH is kept consistently near 5.5. Chronic acidosis mobilizes bone to provide phosphate for hydrogen ion buffering (Brosnan and Brosnan, 1982). Steenbock et al. (1914) described this type of bone dissolution in pigs and calves, and Jaffe et al. (1932) found in all age groups of dogs studied that the acidifying effect of ammonium chloride administration on bone calcium concentrations was strongly associated with calcium intake. That is, dogs receiving adequate calcium showed less decalcification than those receiving a low-calcium diet. As might be expected, since calcification of bone is acid forming, the acidifying effect of ammonium chloride was more pronounced in younger dogs. More recently, in rats (Beck and Webster, 1976) and humans (Wachman and Bernstein, 1970) metabolic acidosis increased calcium and phosphate mobilization mediated by an increase in parathyroid hormone activity. Since there is no

experimentally published work on the cat concerning the effect of chronic acidemia on bone density or on calcium requirement, the acid-forming constituents in the diet should be limited to the production of urine at a pH above the minimal urinary pH obtainable (the average minimal urinary pH obtainable in cats is about 5.5 [Taton et al., 1984a,b; Buffington et al., 1985]). Long-term experiments are essential to determine the minimal calcium requirement for maintaining optimal calcium homeostasis in various age groups when feeding diets that produce urine at a pH between 5.5 and 6.6. While long-term studies have not been published, it appears that for minimum FUS risk, the urinary pH should be less than 6.6.

VITAMINS

Very limited research has been conducted on vitamin requirements of the cat. Recommendations of quantitative needs are based on both published and unpublished research with cats and extrapolation from data on other species. Since several vitamins are rather unstable, and their destruction may be promoted by light, heat, oxidation, moisture, rancidity, or certain mineral elements, sufficient amounts should be provided to ensure that the recommended concentrations will be present when the diet is consumed. Just as important is recognition that excessive intake of vitamins A and D may be harmful.

Vitamin A

REQUIREMENTS

Cats require preformed vitamin A in their diet since they lack the ability to effectively convert β-carotene to vitamin A (Ahmad, 1931; Rea and Drummond, 1932; Gershoff et al., 1957a). This is true whether β-carotene is presented in the diet or intravenously. Carotenoid pigments are not normally found in plasma or other tissues.

Lowe et al. (1957) found, and Moore et al. (1963) confirmed, that the kidney of the cat contains much higher concentrations of vitamin A than do the kidneys of other species (cats, >100 IU/g; hens, >3; dogs, >12; pigs, 5; rabbits and sheep, 4; cattle and goats, >1. One retinol equivalent equals 3.3 IU of vitamin A). Nevertheless, liver vitamin A appears to constitute the primary vitamin A reserve, and liver concentrations tend to be related more closely to dietary intake than do kidney concentrations. Vitamin A depletion may result in exhaustion of both liver and kidney levels, but not infrequently, some kidney vitamin A is detectable when liver vitamin A can no longer be measured. When liberal amounts of vitamin A were included in the diet, liver vitamin A concentrations (mean of 3,500 IU/g) were many times those in the kidney (mean of 77 IU/g) (Moore et al., 1963).

Scott and Thompson (1969) found that the vitamin A concentration in the diet of the queen influenced the concentration of vitamin A in the liver and kidneys of the unsuckled newborn kitten. However, when the mother's diet contained adequate vitamin A, suckling produced a marked increase in liver vitamin A levels as compared to the effect on kidney levels.

Liver, cod liver oil, and retinyl acetate or palmitate are satisfactory sources of vitamin A for the cat. Within limits (1–26 percent fat in the diet), vitamin A absorption, as estimated by serum vitamin A levels, appears positively related to dietary fat concentration (Gershoff et al., 1957a).

Although Scott and Scott (1964) concluded that cats required 1,600 to 2,000 IU/day, studies designed to define the vitamin A requirement have not been published. Unpublished data (K. Knox, University of Connecticut, 1982) suggest that 64 μg of retinol/kg of body weight daily maintains adequate plasma vitamin A concentrations (greater than 40 μg/dl) in weaned kittens. The next level studied (256 μg retinol/kg body weight) appeared more than necessary.

In long-term studies (Rogers and Morris, personal communication, 1985) 4,000 IU (1.2 mg) retinol/kg diet was not adequate for pregnancy in that several kittens were born hairless or afflicted with cleft palate. An intake of 6,000 IU (1.8 mg) retinol/kg diet prevented deformities and provided for normal kitten development during lactation. From these data one would predict that 1 mg retinol/kg diet should satisfy the minimum requirement for growth in kittens, whereas 1.8 mg/kg should meet the minimum needs for pregnancy and lactation.

SIGNS OF DEFICIENCY

While Scott et al. (1964) reported conjunctivitis, xerosis with keratitis and vascularization of the cornea, photophobia, delay in the pupillary response to light, retinal degeneration, and the formation of cataracts in cats fed semipurified diets for 6 to 20 months, oral supplements of vitamin A did not prevent all of these lesions. These workers concluded that the continuous feeding of casein interfered with proper utilization of dietary vitamin A. Morris (1962), feeding a similar diet, noted that the histological lesions of the retina were "somewhat similar to, but not quite identical with, the lesion shown in vitamin A deficiency by other species." Since neither diet contained taurine, the retinal lesions presumably were complicated by taurine deficiency (Rabin et al., 1973; Hayes et al., 1975a,b).

Gershoff et al. (1957a) observed squamous metaplasia in the respiratory tract, conjunctiva, salivary glands, and endometrium. Subpleural cysts without apparent bronchial communication and lined by keratinizing squamous epithelium were also seen. Extensive infectious sequelae were common in the lung and occasionally in the conjunctiva and salivary glands. Local dysplasia of pancreatic acinar tissue and marked hypoplasia of the seminiferous tubules, depletion of adrenal cortical lipid, and focal atrophy of the skin were also observed. Skeletal and neurological lesions were not demonstrated, due apparently to the failure to induce the deficiency early enough to retard bone growth.

Bartsch et al. (1975) described ataxia, "star gazing," blindness, and intermittent convulsions in African lion cubs presumed to be vitamin A-deficient. There was severe thickening of the cranium, compression of the brain, and partial herniation of the cerebellum.

SIGNS OF TOXICITY

Deforming cervical spondylosis in cats has been attributed by Seawright et al. (1967) to prolonged, excessive intake of vitamin A. The naturally occurring disease is associated with the near-exclusive feeding of raw liver and milk, and it can be duplicated by large supplements of vitamin A in a lean beef and milk diet. The levels of dietary vitamin A supplied by liver, which induced skeletal lesions, ranged from 17 to 35 μg retinol/g body weight, while 15 μg retinol/g body weight added to the meat diet over 41 weeks produced no effect. The next higher level of supplemental vitamin A (30 μg retinol/g body weight) produced lethargy after 10 weeks and spondylosis after 24 weeks. The primary lesions consisted of an extensive osseocartilagenous hyperplasia about the first three diarthroidal joints of the cervical vertebrae. There was also a marked lipid infiltration of the reticulohistiocytic cells of the liver, lungs, spleen, and hepatic lymph node and of the tubular epithelium of the renal cortex. Plasma vitamin A levels ranged from 452 to 1,281 μg retinol/dl in affected cats. Liver and kidney vitamin A concentrations were 15,442 to 39,750 and 100 to 4,083 μg/g, respectively.

In subsequent work, Clark et al. (1970a) verified that these lesions could be produced by excessive vitamin A, even when dietary concentrations and the ratio of calcium and phosphorus were optimum. These workers (Clark, 1970, 1973; Clark et al., 1970b) also found that abnormalities in long bone morphology could be produced when kittens were dosed with high levels of vitamin A at the time of most active bone growth. The long bones were shorter than normal, osteoporotic, and the cartilagenous epiphyseal plates suffered extensive damage, resulting in reduced endochondral bone growth. Seawright and Hrdlicka (1974) described a proliferative gingivitis, retarded development of the osseous alveolar processes, and tooth loss due to excess vitamin A.

Vitamin D

REQUIREMENTS

Vitamin D is involved in the metabolism of calcium and phosphorous, and probably magnesium. In the rat and chick it has been shown that cholecalciferol (vitamin D_3) is absorbed in the small intestine, hydroxylated in the liver to 25-hydroxycholecalciferol and in the kidney to 1,25-dihydroxycholecalciferol. The latter compound appears to play a significant role in promoting calcium absorption. Both ergocalciferol (vitamin D_2) and cholecalciferol have been used successfully in the diet for growth and reproduction of confined cats (R. D. Kealy, personal communication, 1985).

Gershoff et al. (1957b) found that 250 IU of cholecalciferol given orally, twice a week, prevented the development of rickets in kittens fed a semipurified diet from 3 to 6 months of age to 21 months of age. The exacerbations and remissions of rickets in unsupplemented cats, which survived longer than 12 months, suggest that the vitamin D requirement of older cats is low. The latter conclusion is supported by the observation that no signs of deficiency occurred in adult cats fed a vitamin D-free diet for a year in the absence of sunlight (Rivers et al., 1979). For kittens, the minimal requirement should be provided by 500 IU (12.5 μg) of vitamin D per kg of diet.

SIGNS OF DEFICIENCY

Severe rickets in kittens was produced using vitamin D-deficient diets containing either 1 percent calcium and 1 percent phosphorus or 2 percent calcium and 0.65 percent phosphorus (Gershoff et al., 1957b). Weight gain was less with the latter diet, and rickets was less severe. Serum alkaline phosphatase activity increased markedly in the third month, peaked during the fifth to seventh months, and decreased through the twenty-first month. Serum calcium and inorganic phosphorus concentrations decreased markedly during the acute phase of rickets in cats fed 1 percent calcium and 1 percent phosphorus. The cats that died during acute rickets had a lower percent femur ash than cats supplemented with vitamin D. The deficient cats had enlarged costochondral junctions ("rachitic rosary") with disorganization in the region of new bone formation and excessive osteoid.

SIGNS OF TOXICITY

Effects of overdosage of vitamin D were observed at necropsy in a cat that had been given 5 million IU of vitamin D_3 and 2.5 million IU of vitamin A by mouth over a 6-month period. The cat received these vitamins as treatment for a skin ailment, but gradually lost weight and died suddenly. The great vessels, including aorta and the carotid arteries, and the adrenals were heavily calcified, and calcium was deposited in the stomach wall and parathyroids. No increased fragility of bones was noted (Suter, 1957).

Vitamin E

REQUIREMENTS

The need for vitamin E in the diet of cats is markedly influenced by dietary composition. Cordy (1954), Coffin and Holzworth (1954), Munson et al. (1958), and Griffiths et al. (1960) have noted an association of steatitis (yellow fat disease—presumed vitamin E deficiency) with consumption of fish-based diets, particularly red tuna.

Cordy (1954) fed a commercial cat food containing mostly fish, but including about 10 percent cereal products, to weaned kittens from 6 to 8 weeks of age for 16 weeks. In addition, each cat was given, orally 6 days a week, 1 ml of fish-liver oil containing 1,500 IU vitamin A and 200 IU vitamin D. One of the kittens receiving no supplemental vitamin E died at 30 days. The remaining animals appeared healthy and were sacrificed after 16 weeks. At necropsy all four unsupplemented kittens and one of two receiving 10 mg DL-α-tocopherol per day showed signs of vitamin E deficiency. The kittens receiving 20 or 40 mg/day were normal (see below).

Gershoff and Norkin (1962) fed a semipurified diet, with or without 5 percent tuna oil, to 3- to 6-month-old kittens for periods up to 13.5 months. Basal diet composition (in percent) was: casein, 32; vitamin E-free lard, 20; sucrose, 42.7; Hegsted salts IV, 4; cod liver oil, 1; and a vitamin mix. Steatitis was not observed in any of the cats receiving the basal diet without tuna oil, even in the absence of vitamin E supplementation. However, four out of six of these cats exhibited focal interstitial myocarditis, focal myositis of the skeletal muscle, and periportal mononuclear infiltration in the liver. When 17 IU of vitamin E (as D-α-tocopheryl acetate) per kilogram of diet was provided, one out of four cats exhibited myositis. Supplemental vitamin E at 34 or 68 IU/kg of diet prevented all lesions. When 5 percent tuna oil was substituted for 5 percent of the lard, steatitis was severe in cats unsupplemented with vitamin E. The severity of steatitis was diminished by supplemental vitamin E, but was not entirely prevented by 34 IU/kg of diet. When 136 IU/kg of diet were provided, no lesions were seen. Despite the awareness of the relationship between vitamin E intake and steatitis, cases in cats still occur occasionally (Gaskell et al., 1975).

Tocopherol is found in eight isomeric forms (four tocols, four tocotrienols) in nature, but it is agreed that α-tocopherol is the biologically important isomer. Gamma-tocopherol, found in considerable quantity in soybean oil, has considerably less (only 10 percent) of the biological activity attributed to α-tocopherol and is not typically included in the dietary allowance. HPLC is currently the preferred method of analysis, and, unlike the original colorimetric assay, it readily distinguished among isomers (Bieri et al., 1979). The minimum requirement for cats is set at 30 mg α-tocopherol/kg diet, but it is presumed that a relatively low-fat diet (< 10 percent dry weight) containing antioxidants and adequate selenium would greatly reduce this requirement. High-PUFA diets, especially those containing fish oil, may increase the suggested minimum three- to four-fold.

SIGNS OF DEFICIENCY

Steatitis has been noted when sources of highly unsaturated fatty acids have been fed in the absence of adequate supplemental vitamin E. The adipose tissue is yellow to orange-brown and very firm. Microscopically, the fat shows focal neutrophilic infiltration with some mononuclear cells. Acid-fast ceroid pigment is present as globules and as peripheral rings in the fat cell vacuoles.

While gross fat pigmentation was not seen by Gershoff and Norkin (1962) in cats not fed tuna oil, some cats unsupplemented with vitamin E exhibited microscopic changes in the subcutaneous adipose tissue. These consisted of focal cuffing of capillaries and arterioles with mononuclear cells. Some of the fat cells had fine yellowish granules in thickened rims of cytoplasm, and similar granules were seen in some interstitial cells, probably macrophages or fibroblasts. Also seen were focal interstitial myocarditis and rarely muscle fiber degeneration, focal myositis of the skeletal muscle, and periportal mononuclear infiltration in the liver.

In a preliminary report, Stephan and Hayes (1978) induced severe vitamin E deficiency with hemolytic anemia and steatitis by feeding a diet containing 15 percent stripped safflower oil without α-tocopherol. Clinical signs of deficiency were prevented by supplementing with α-tocopheryl acetate at 100 IU/kg diet.

Vitamin K

REQUIREMENTS

Presumably the cat, like other higher vertebrates that have been studied, has a metabolic vitamin K requirement for the carboxylation of certain glutamyl residues of specific proteins such as prothrombin. Neither vitamin K absorption nor function has been studied in cats. Reber and Malhotra (1961) found that an irradiated beef diet, which caused hemorrhages in weanling rats, did not cause death, loss of weight, or prolonged prothrombin times when fed to cats for 40 weeks. The concentration of vitamin K in the diet was calculated to be 60 μg/kg of solids. Although a minimum requirement has never been demonstrated for cats, a level of 100 μg/kg is suggested. In other species, on a weight basis, menadione is about as effective as phylloquinone in preventing prolongation of clotting time, whereas it may take several times as much menadione as phylloquinone to cure an existing deficiency (John W. Suttie, University of Wisconsin, personal communication, 1986).

SIGNS OF DEFICIENCY

Vitamin K deficiency has not been reported in the cat, but hypoprothrombinemia and hemorrhage might be expected.

Thiamin

REQUIREMENTS

Odom and McEachern (1942) produced thiamin deficiency in cats by giving them the same diet that Cowgill (1921) used to induce thiamin deficiency in dogs. Everett (1944) provided a detailed account of thiamin deficiency in the cat. He showed that daily injections of 0.5 mg thiamin would prevent neurological disorders and maintain weight (or produce gains) in adult cats given an autoclaved dog food diet. This diet was supplemented with riboflavin, pyridoxine, and calcium pantothenate. Loew et al. (1970) calculated that the thiamin requirement for maintenance of a cat weighing about 3 kg was about 0.36 mg/day or 0.1 mg/50 kcal ME. Deady et al. (1981a) gave kittens purified amino acid diets containing 4.4 mg thiamin/kg diet. When the diet contained high levels of glutamic acid (90 followed by 120 g/kg diet or vice versa), kittens developed severe neurological signs of thiamin deficiency, which responded to parenteral thiamin.

A functional inadequacy of thiamin may be induced either by consumption of a thiamin-deficient diet or by ingestion of uncooked food containing the enzyme thiaminase. Some species of fish contain thiaminase (Smith and Proutt, 1944; Jubb et al., 1956; Loew et al., 1970). Carp and saltwater herring, but not perch, catfish, butterfish, or spots, may produce thiamin deficiency. Thiamin is readily destroyed by heat, especially under neutral or alkaline conditions, and extensive losses may occur in canned cat foods during processing and storage (Baggs et al., 1978). Sufficient thiamin has to be present in the food before processing to ensure that adequate amounts are present after processing and reasonable storage.

A requirement of 5 mg thiamin/kg diet is suggested as the minimal requirement for growth. This concentration appears adequate for gestation and lactation (J. G. Morris and Q. R. Rogers, University of California, Davis, personal communication, 1985).

SIGNS OF DEFICIENCY

Everett (1944) described three stages of thiamin deficiency in cats: (1) induction, characterized by anorexia; (2) critical, characterized by sudden appearance of neurological disorders, particularly of the postural mechanisms, and by short tonic convulsive seizures; (3) terminal, characterized by progressive weakness, prostration, and death. The anorexia of stage (1) frequently appears within 1 to 2 weeks of ingestion of a deficient diet and may be accompanied by emesis (Jubb et al., 1956; Deady et al., 1981a,b). Neurological disorders in the critical stage (2) include impairment of labyrinthine righting reactions, as shown by ventroflexion of the head, loss of righting in the air, and defective conscious proprioception. Affected cats, when suspended by their hind limbs, keep their heads ventroflexed on the sternum instead of the normal dorsoflexion. In addition, ventroflexion of the head causes cats to somersault as they jump from a table (Jubb et al., 1956). The impaired vestibulolocular reflexes observed include decreased nystagmus time and an impaired or slow pupillary light reflex. Affected kittens also have dilated pupils.

Electrocardiographic changes due to thiamin deficiency have been described by Toman et al. (1945). These included sinus bradycardia, which developed as early as the second week. Tachycardia was less frequent and seen later. Disorders in rate regularity and impulse formation responded promptly to thiamin treatment. Changes in the ventricular complex (QRS prolongation and other changes and T wave) were slower to respond.

Cats affected with thiamin deficiency may exhibit spontaneous seizures, which may be accompanied by brief periods of tachycardia followed by severe bradycardia.

A number of pathological changes of the central nervous system have been described. In acute cases, bilateral symmetrical hemorrhages of the brain in the periventricular gray matter have been recorded. Considerable variation occurred in the number of nuclear masses of the brain involved. The main nuclei involved in order of frequency were: inferior colliculi, medial vestibular, lateral geniculate, habenular and occulomo-

tor nuclei in the accessory vestibular, cuneate and red nuclei (Jubb et al., 1956; Deady et al., 1981a,b).

The measurement of erythrocyte transketolase stimulation by thiamin pyrophosphate (Brin and Vincent, 1965) has been used in the diagnosis of thiamin deficiency in the cat (Baggs et al., 1978; Deady et al., 1981a,b). However, a decrease in the concentration of thiamin pyrophosphate in the blood of rats has been shown to precede changes in transketolase activity (Warnock et al., 1978) and may be a superior test for the cat. Thiamin and its phosphate esters in tissues may be conveniently measured by high-performance liquid chromatography (Ishii et al., 1979).

Riboflavin

REQUIREMENTS

Microbial synthesis of riboflavin occurs in the gastrointestinal tract of a number of animal species. However, the extent of synthesis appears to depend on the animal and the type of carbohydrate in the diet. In the cat, the contribution of symbiotically synthesized riboflavin is not known. This vitamin loses biological activity when exposed to light.

Leahy et al. (1967), using 6- to 8-week-old kittens (about 700 g body weight) and a semipurified diet (containing 35 percent vitamin-free casein, 50 percent sucrose, 5 percent cellulose, 4 percent peanut oil, and 6 percent minerals (which did not include a source of copper or zinc) and vitamins, concluded that riboflavin requirements for growth did not exceed 100 μg/day, or approximately 1 mg/kg of diet. The authors reported similar concentrations of riboflavin in the liver and muscle of kittens given the high fecal residue diet with and without supplemental riboflavin. Intestinal synthesis of riboflavin by microorganisms may have contributed to the daily intake of the vitamin and resulted in an artificially low estimate of the requirement.

Gershoff et al. (1959a) studied the effects of a low-carbohydrate, high-fat diet (46 percent of the ME from fat) or a high-carbohydrate, low-fat diet (11 percent of the ME from fat) on the riboflavin requirements of 3- to 6-month-old kittens. Casein provided 25 percent of the ME in both diets. The authors concluded that a high-carbohydrate, low-fat diet favored synthesis of riboflavin by intestinal microorganisms as indicated by greater urinary and fecal excretion. The high-carbohydrate diet may also have favored utilization or retention of riboflavin. Although these authors reported that two cats were maintained in excellent health for more than 34 months on the high-carbohydrate diet plus 3 mg riboflavin/kg diet. Cats were routinely reared in their laboratory on the low-carbohydrate, high-fat diet plus 4 mg riboflavin/kg diet for up to 2 years. A minimal requirement of 4 mg riboflavin/kg diet is suggested for growth.

SIGNS OF DEFICIENCY

Gershoff et al. (1959a) reported that in acute riboflavin deficiency, cats exhibited anorexia, loss of weight, and periauricular alopecia with epidermal atrophy. In chronic riboflavin deficiency, cats developed cataracts, fatty livers, and testicular hypoplasia. Erythrocyte glutathione reductase activity is currently the preferred test for diagnosis of riboflavin deficiency in man. Factors affecting the assay are described by Thurnham and Rathakette (1982).

Vitamin B₆

REQUIREMENTS

Carvalho da Silva et al. (1959b), using 3- to 4-month-old kittens fed a semipurified diet, reported that 1 mg of pyridoxine given orally, three times per week, would prevent signs of deficiency and would support satisfactory growth and a normal hemogram. Vitamin B₆-deficient cats resumed growth and attained normal weights for age when given oral doses of 1 to 10 mg pyridoxine per day. One animal given 0.5 mg per day recovered, but another given 0.25 mg per day did not. Gershoff et al. (1959b) using 3- to 6-month-old kittens fed a semipurified diet, reported that 1 mg of pyridoxine HCl/kg diet was not adequate for all cats, but a 2 mg pyridoxine HCl/kg permitted normal growth and hematology. However, urinary excretion of oxalate was greater in cats given a diet containing 2 mg pyridoxine/kg than those receiving a diet containing 4 mg pyridoxine/kg diet. A minimal requirement of 4 mg pyridoxine/kg diet is recommended for growing kitten.

SIGNS OF DEFICIENCY

Carvalho da Silva et al. (1959b) reported growth depression, a mild microcytic, hypochromic anemia with elevated serum iron; convulsive seizures; and irreversible kidney lesions consisting of areas of tubular atrophy and dilatation, fibrosis, and intratubular deposits of birefringent crystals in cats receiving a vitamin B₆-deficient diet. Tissue pyridoxine levels were 50 percent of supplemented controls. Gershoff et al. (1959b) reported similar signs and identified the birefringent crystals as calcium oxalate monohydrate. He also showed that the urine of vitamin B₆-deficient cats contained large amounts of oxalate.

Niacin

REQUIREMENTS

The niacin requirement of many animal species can be satisfied by synthesis of the vitamin from tryptophan. The cat liver has all the enzymes for niacin synthesis. However, the rate of removal of an intermediate in the pathway (alpha-amino-beta-carboxymuconic epsilon semialdehyde) is so rapid that virtually no niacin is produced (Suhadolnick et al., 1957; Ikeda et al., 1965). In whole animal studies, Carvalho da Silva et al. (1952) showed that administration of a tryptophan load to cats did not result in increased urinary nicotinamide excretion. Heath et al. (1940) described lesions of feline pellagra that responded to daily oral doses of 80 to 100 mg of nicotinic acid. After a few days of treatment with this level, the daily oral dose was lowered to 30 mg. Carvalho da Silva (1950) reported that supplementation of a purified diet (containing all vitamins except vitamin B₁ and niacin) with 2.5 mg of nicotinic acid three times a week produced satisfactory growth, a normal hemogram, and good health for at least 12 months. However, in a later publication Carvalho da Silva et al. (1952) when referring to their earlier paper, stated 4 mg of nicotinic acid three times a week maintained good health. In cats made niacin deficient, Carvalho da Silva et al. (1952) found that periodic subcutaneous injections of 2 to 3 mg of nicotinic acid or nicotinamide produced a favorable response. They concluded, however, that the optimum parenteral dose was about 10 mg. In short-term studies with growing cats weighing 800 to 900 g, Braham et al. (1962) found that an oral intake of 5 mg of nicotinic acid per day was adequate as measured by N-methyl nicotinamide excretion. They also reported that the cat is able to utilize the niacin from raw and lime-treated corn to an equal extent. In the absence of further information, the minimal requirement of 40 mg niacin/kg diet is suggested.

SIGNS OF DEFICIENCY

Heath et al. (1940) observed weight loss, anorexia, weakness, and apathy in deficient cats. Thick saliva with a foul odor drooled from the mouth. The oral cavity was characterized by ulceration of the upper palate; the tongue was fiery red in color and had an area about cm wide of ulceration and congestion along the anterior border. Carvalho da Silva et al. (1952) noted unkempt fur and diarrhea but no buccal lesions. An association with respiratory diseases was common and contributed to early death.

Supplemental niacin activity can be provided as

ther niacin or niacinamide. Either source of niacin activity is acceptable. Work with the chick has indicated that niacinamide contains somewhat more niacin activity per unit weight than niacin (Baker et al., 1976). No comparable studies have been done on the cat.

Pantothenic Acid

REQUIREMENTS

Gershoff and Gottlieb (1964) fed 3-month-old kittens a purified diet (32.1 percent casein, 37.6 percent sucrose, 12.5 percent corn oil, 12.5 percent hydrogenated fat, 1.0 percent cod liver oil, and mineral and vitamins). Based on weight gain, freedom from deficiency signs, and the efficiency with which p-amino-benzoic acid was acetylated, these workers concluded that 3 mg of calcium pantothenate/kg diet was inadequate, but 5 mg of calcium pantothenate/kg diet was sufficient for the period of the test (nearly 2 years). A minimum requirement of 5 mg of pantothenate/kg diet is suggested. Only the dextrorotatory form of the vitamin (D-pantothenic acid) has vitamin activity.

SIGNS OF DEFICIENCY

The terminal stages of acute pantothenic acid deficiency were observed after 2.0 to 4.5 months in kittens fed an unsupplemented semipurified diet (Gershoff and Gottlieb, 1964). The deficiency state was characterized chiefly by emaciation. Moderate to marked fatty metamorphosis of the liver was noted, with both fine and coarse vacuolar formation. Giant, blunted villi were seen in some areas of the jejunum and upper ileum with the tops of the villi in some animals showing infarct necrosis. No losses or graying of hair and blood dyscrasias were observed.

Folacin

REQUIREMENTS

Carvalho da Silva et al. (1955) were not able to induce folacin deficiency in 2- to 3-month-old-kittens with a purified diet containing no added folic acid or vitamin B_{12} unless 0.6 to 2.0 percent of sulfaguanidine or sulfathalidine was included. A growth response was obtained in sulfa-treated, deficient kittens with either two oral doses of 0.8 mg of folic acid administered 24 hours apart or with one oral dose of 1.0 mg of folic acid. The latter treatment produced a response that persisted for about a month.

Amyes et al. (1975) determined the folic acid concen-

trations of cat erythrocytes, plasma, and liver and found that these values declined from birth to 32 days. However, no information was presented on the diet of queens that gave birth to and nursed the kittens.

Thenen and Rasmussen (1978) demonstrated that weanling kittens fed a purified diet based on casein and lard without added folacin (diet provided only 2 μg/kg BW/day) for 10 weeks developed megaloblastic erythropoiesis and marked depletion of plasma and liver folic acid. Control kittens receiving 1.36 mg total folacin per kilogram of diet were normal.

In the absence of an experimentally determined value for the cat, a minimal requirement of 800 μg/kg diet as suggested for swine (NRC, 1979) as adjusted for dietary energy density.

SIGNS OF DEFICIENCY

When a deficiency was induced by adding sulfa drugs to a purified diet, affected cats exhibited weight loss, anemia (with macrocytic tendencies), and leucopenia. Blood clotting time was increased, and plasma iron concentrations were elevated (Carvalho da Silva et al., 1955). Schalm (1974) has described a megaloblastic anemia in an adult cat that responded to vitamin B_{12} and folic acid administration.

Biotin

REQUIREMENTS

Carey and Morris (1975, 1977), using 3-month-old kittens, fed a purified diet containing 32 percent of a protein source, 38 percent sucrose, 25 percent animal and vegetable fat, and minerals and vitamins (except biotin). When the protein source was vitamin-free casein, signs of biotin deficiency were not seen, even when the diet contained 2 percent succinyl sulfathiazole to limit microbial synthesis in the intestine. Replacement of 58 to 100 percent of the vitamin-free casein with dried egg white and including 2 percent succinyl sulfathiazole resulted in deficiency signs that disappeared when 0.25 mg of D-biotin was administered subcutaneously every other day. Presumably, avidin in the egg white rendered biotin unavailable. Cats probably do not require a dietary source of biotin except under abnormal conditions (diets containing raw egg white or antimicrobials or if animals are germ-free). A purified diet containing 60 μg biotin/kg supported pregnancy and lactation in queens and normal growth in kittens (Kang, Morris, and Rogers, personal communication, 1985). Therefore, with adjustment for dietary caloric density, a requirement of 70 μg/kg diet is recommended.

Carey and Morris (1975, 1977) produced biotin deficiency by including 18.5 to 32.0 percent egg white in a purified diet for kittens. Growth was normal to about 150 days, but by this time dried secretions were evident around the eyes, nose, and at the angle of the mouth. Also seen were scaly dermatitis of the nasolabial-mandibular region, general alopecia, and hypersalivation. These signs increased in severity and were later accompanied by bloody diarrhea and marked anorexia and emaciation. There was also a decrease in the activity of hepatic propionyl CoA carboxylase.

Vitamin B_{12}

REQUIREMENTS

A need for vitamin B_{12} in a purified diet fed to weaned kittens has been established (Keesling and Morris, 1975; Morris, 1977). However, the quantitative requirement has not been determined.

A purified diet containing 20 μg vitamin B_{12}/kg supported pregnancy and lactation in queens and growth in kittens. This diet also maintained a normal concentration of hemoglobin in blood (Kang, Morris, and Rogers, personal communication, 1985). A minimal requirement of 20 μg vitamin B_{12}/kg diet is suggested.

SIGNS OF DEFICIENCY

Morris (1977) reported that kittens given a vitamin B_{12}-deficient diet at first grew normally for 3 to 4 months, after which growth ceased. Subsequently, body weight was lost at an accelerating rate until supplementation was initiated with parenteral vitamin B_{12} which restored weight gain. Hemoglobin, hematocrit, and bone cytology remained normal, probably because of high concentrations of folic acid in the diet (10 mg/kg), which overcame the consequences of folate "trapped" as methyl folate (Shane and Stokstad, 1985).

Choline

REQUIREMENTS

Carvalho da Silva et al. (1959a) reported that a diet containing 420 g casein and 240 g hydrogenated coconut fat/kg diet and a supplement of 1 g choline/kg diet produced some growth in young cats but did not prevent fatty infiltration of the liver. When the choline was increased to 5 g/kg diet, rate of growth was increased and fat content of the liver decreased.

Anderson et al. (1979c) used an amino acid-based diet containing 4.5 g methionine, 4.5 g cystine, 1.0 g taurine, and 250 g of turkey fat/kg diet. They found that rate of growth was maximized at 1 g choline/kg diet, but liver lipid concentration was still elevated. Increasing the choline to 3 g/kg reduced liver lipids. They also demonstrated that methionine was an effective methyl donor for the cat. Methionine provided in excess of its dietary requirement as an amino acid can totally replace the dietary need for choline on an iso-methyl basis.

Schaeffer et al. (1982b) investigated the effect of five dietary concentrations of choline between 0 and 3 g/kg diet on rate of body weight gain and liver lipids. The diet used was based on soy protein and contained 4 g methionine/kg diet (which approximates the kittens' minimal requirement), and additional cystine. They suggested the requirement for maximal growth and minimal liver lipid was 2.4 g choline/kg diet. This value has been used as the minimal requirement.

SIGNS OF DEFICIENCY

Decreased food intake and growth rate and increased lipid content of the liver have been reported (Carvalho da Silva et al., 1959a; Anderson et al., 1979c; Schaeffer et al., 1982b). Perilobular infiltration of the liver has been described by Carvalho da Silva et al. (1959a). Hypoalbuminemia was reported by Mansur Guerios and Hoxter (1962), but was not found by Schaeffer et al. (1982b).

Ascorbic Acid

Repeated trials have failed to demonstrate a need for dietary ascorbic acid in cats (Carvalho da Silva, 1950). Successful growth and reproduction are routinely obtained with commercial and purified (Kang, Morris, and Rogers, personal communication, 1985) diets containing no supplemental ascorbic acid.

3 Water

Water is the single most important nutrient necessary to sustain normal function of all living cells. The nonfat component of mammals contains about 73 percent water. Most mammals can lose nearly all their reserves of glycogen and fat, half the body protein stores, and 40 percent of their body weight and survive. However, mammals are much less tolerant to losses of body water.

Cats can withstand acute dehydration slightly better than dogs with water losses reaching up to 20 percent of body weight (Adolph, 1947). Although cats can tolerate some depletion of their body water for a short period, they must in the long run remain in water balance. The losses of water from the body must be offset by an equal intake of water. At normal temperatures, water is lost from the body via the lungs, skin, urine, milk, and feces. At high temperatures, an additional loss may occur via saliva, which is used to wet the fur and provide evaporative cooling (Robinson and Lee, 1941). The body gains water from "free water" present in liquids and solid foods and "oxidation water" arising from the catabolism of carbohydrates, fats, and protein. Oxidation of 1 g of starch, fat, and protein results in the production of 0.556, 1.071, and 0.396 g of oxidation water, respectively (Schmidt-Nielsen, 1964).

A number of studies have been conducted in which the ratio of free water to dry matter intake of cats has been measured (Carver and Waterhouse, 1962; Thrall and Miller, 1976; Holme, 1977; Jackson and Tovey, 1977; Seefeldt and Chapman, 1979). Anderson (1983) summarized these data and showed that for commercial dry foods the ratio of water to dry matter intake varied from 2.0 to 2.8:1 and for canned foods from 3.0 to 5.7:1. Kane et al. (1981b), in a study of eating and drinking patterns of the cat, reported lower ratios of water to dry matter intake for two purified diets (1.1:1 and 1.4:1) than those reported by Anderson (1983) for commercial diets. However, they found similar ratios to those reported by Anderson (1983) for commercial dry and canned foods (1.9:1 and 3.5:1, respectively). In these studies cats given dry commercial food ad libitum drank water about the same number of times as they ate (16.0 versus 15.7 times/day, respectively). All studies on water and dry matter intakes of cats indicate higher total free water to dry matter ratios for cats given commercial canned food diets than for cats given commercial dry foods. That is, cats given dry food do not voluntarily consume water to equal the ratio of water to dry matter of cats given canned diets containing about 75 percent moisture. In satisfying the requirement for energy, cats consume more water from a canned diet than they would take in if they were eating an entire small mammal.

The cat is able to achieve a maximal urinary osmolar concentration much greater than that in man (Schmidt-Nielsen, 1964), and so is more efficient in conserving water. Adult cats can maintain normal health in the absence of drinking, when given high-moisture diets, e.g., fresh fish (Prentiss et al., 1959) and can utilize sea water to facilitate excretion of the urea load from high-protein diets (Wolf et al., 1959).

It is recommended that fresh clean water be available at all times to cats regardless of their age or diet.

4 Formulated Diets for Cats

Cats require specific nutrients, not specific feedstuffs. Nevertheless, cats are quite individualistic in their feeding behavior and frequently exhibit food preferences that have been conditioned by previous dietary experience. Conditioned diet preference should not be confused with nutrient requirements. While cats are carnivorous in the wild, satisfactory diets containing significant amounts of vegetable matter have been developed. However, in commercial cat diets a proportion of animal tissue is retained to satisfy specific nutrient requirements, e.g., arachidonic acid and taurine, and to improve the acceptability of the diet. Thus, strict vegetarian diets fed alone are not nutritionally adequate for cats, even if such diets are sufficiently palatable to be readily eaten.

The nutritional needs of domestic cats are increasingly being met by commercial cat foods. While there are a large number of products available, these fall into the three basic types described below.

DRY-TYPE CAT FOODS

Low in moisture content (usually about 7 to 12 percent), these foods commonly contain ground, whole or dehulled cereal grains (e.g., wheat, corn, oats, barley), cereal by-products (e.g., corn gluten meal, mill run, wheat germ meal), soybean products (e.g., soybean meal, soy flour, soy protein concentrate), animal products (e.g., poultry by-product meal, meat meal, and meat and bone meal, meat by-products), marine products (e.g., fish meal, condensed fish solubles), milk products (e.g., dried whey, dried skimmed milk, sodium caseinate), fats and oils (e.g., cod liver oil, animal fat), and mineral and vitamin supplements. Crude fat content usually ranges from 8 to 12 percent on a dry basis. These fat levels are achieved by spraying a liqui-

fied fat on an extruded product or incorporating fat in the core material. Crude protein content varies from ? to 36 percent on a dry basis. Processing methods (fr quently expansion, extrusion, or baking) serve to pa tially gelatinize starch for improved digestibility. Th extruded product is often sprayed with various prote digests to increase product acceptability.

SEMIMOIST CAT FOODS

Intermediate in moisture content (usually 25 to ? percent), these foods incorporate a level of water-sol ble solids such as sugar, sodium chloride, sorbates, ar low-molecular-weight alcohols (e.g., propylene glycc sufficient to stabilize the product through available w ter control and to prevent spoilage without refriger tion. Semimoist cat foods commonly contain fresh frozen meats (e.g., liver, kidney, tripe), animal b product meals (e.g., meat, poultry, liver), whole or d hulled cereal grains (e.g., corn, wheat, barley, oats cereal by-products (e.g., corn gluten meal, whe flour), marine products (e.g., fish meal, condensed fi solubles), soybean products (e.g., soybean meal, s flour, soy protein concentrate), fats and oils (e.g., ar mal fat), and mineral and vitamin supplements. Cru protein content usually ranges from 28 to 40 percent al crude fat from 10 to 15 percent on a dry basis. The foods are commonly marketed in a sealed pouch of a si convenient for feeding single meals.

CANNED CAT FOODS

Relatively high in moisture content (usually 72 to ? percent in the United States), these foods are usually fc mulated to be nutritionally complete. They may al serve as a highly palatable, specialty food that adds variety to the cat's diet but which may not be nutritionally complete. The label should be examined for guarantees of nutritional adequacy. Complete foods usually have crude protein levels ranging from 28 to 50 percent and crude fat levels from 10 to 40 percent on dry basis. They are commonly formulated from fresh or frozen meats (e.g., lung, liver, kidney, spleens, tripe, udders, bone, blood, poultry by-products), animal by-product meals (meat, poultry), marine products (e.g., fish, fish meals), and mineral and vitamin supplements. Some formulations also contain whole or dehulled cereal grains (e.g., corn, wheat, barley), soybean products (e.g., textured soy protein derived from soy flour or soy protein concentrate), fats and oils (e.g., vegetable oil), and cereal by-products (e.g., wheat bran). Specialty canned formulations are generally high-protein (40 to 65 percent) meat- or fish-based products with mineral or vitamin supplements added. In all canned cat foods particular attention is needed to ensure that adequate thiamin levels are present post-processing, because thiamin is especially heat labile and up to 80 percent may be lost during canning. Canned cat foods should be supplemented to several times the thiamin requirement to ensure adequacy after processing.

NUTRIENT CONTENT OF COMMERCIAL DIETS

Metabolism trials have been conducted on commercial cat diets (M. A. Norvell, Quaker Oats Company, personal communications, 1976; Kendall et al., 1982a,b, 1985). The proximate composition, apparent digestibility, and metabolizability of the various types of commercial cat diets are shown in Table 3. The average apparent digestibilities of crude protein, crude fat, and nitrogen-free extract were appreciably less (78, 75, and 72 percent, respectively) than the digestibility figures (91, 96, and 96 percent, respectively) used in developing Atwater's (Harris, 1966) estimated ME values of 4, 9, and 4 kcal/g. Table 3 also outlines calculated metabolizable energy (CME) values by diet type according to four different methods (CME_1 to CME_4). Method 1 (CME_1) calculates ME on the basis of Atwater factors; method 2 (CME_2) uses measured apparent digestibility coefficients to adjust E values to an estimated ME; method 3 (CME_3) uses the regression equations derived by Kendall et al. (1982a,b) to calculate ME of dry and canned diets; method 4 (CME_4) adjusts measured in vivo DE values to ME by subtracting 0.9 kcal/g digestible crude protein in the diet, which is the E value of urinary urea. The latter value does not include the energy from components in urine that are not associated

with the complete catabolism of protein. However, the 0.9 kcal/g digestible crude protein has been verified experimentally in cat metabolism trials (P. T. Kendall, Pedigree Petfoods, personal communication, 1986). The footnotes to Table 3 explain the derivation of CME_1 to CME_4 values in detail.

Kendall et al. (1985) compared these four methods of estimating ME content of cat diets with in vivo determined ME values. The exception was that an adjustment factor of 1.25 kcal/g digestible crude protein was used for CME_4 rather than 0.9 kcal/g digestible crude protein reported in Table 3:

Prediction of ME from	Linear Regression Equation	Coefficient of Determination (R^2)	Residual Standard Deviation (RSD)
Atwater factors (CME_1)[a]	$ME = 0.09 + 0.76\,CME_1$[b]	0.96	0.214
Measured apparent digestibility coefficients and E values (CME_2)	$ME = 0.09 + 0.93\,CME_2$	0.96	0.228
Regression equations (CME_3)			
(a) dry diets	$ME = 0.47 + 0.84\,CME_3$	0.78	0.149
(b) canned	$ME = 0.02 + 0.96\,CME_3$	0.95	0.049
DE by subtracting 1.25 kcal digestible crude protein (CME_4)	$ME = 0.01 + 1.02\,CME_4$	1.00	0.04

[a]Subscripts refer to the various methods.
[b]In vivo determined ME (kcal/g, as fed).

All methods, except CME_3 for dry diets, reliably estimated relative ME values of cat diets, but absolute ME was overestimated by methods 1 and 3 (dry diets only) and to a lesser extent by method 2. Method 3 gives close agreement with in vivo ME of canned diets, while method 4 closely agrees with in vivo ME for all diets and would be further improved by the use of 0.9 kcal/g digestible crude protein rather than 1.25 kcal/g. Thus, an accurate estimate of in vivo ME content of commercial cat diets can be obtained by adjustment of DE values by subtracting an assumed energy value for urinary urea (CME_4), or by applying apparent digestibility coefficients and E values for major organic nutrients (CME_2). In addition, the ME of certain canned diets can be predicted from proximate composition according to the multiple regression equation of Kendall et al. (1982). However, no single method appears to be applicable for cat diets of all types unless preceded by in vivo digestibility studies. The use of Atwater factors is not recommended unless apparent digestibility values above 90 percent are measured for crude protein, fat, and nitrogen-free extract.

Estimates of daily food requirements for cats are presented in Table 4. These estimates take into consideration the recommended daily ME allowances per kilogram body weight in Table 1 for the range of body weights in Figure 1. The E concentrations used for the dry matter in dry-type, semimoist, and canned cat foods were 3.2, 4.1, and 4.0 kcal/g, respectively. As fed these values would be 2.9, 3.0, and 1.1 kcal/g, respectively. Specific calculations should be made for cat foods with different composition. It should be emphasized, however, that these estimates are just guides, and a healthy cat will normally regulate energy intake in relation to its needs provided palatable food is available.

GUIDELINES FOR FORMULATING DIETS FROM NATURAL INGREDIENTS

Diets based upon natural ingredients often have nutrient bioavailabilities less than that found in purified diets. Intact proteins require enzymic digestion in the gut, B vitamins must be released from their bound forms, and both of these groups of nutrients may not be completely hydrolyzed from all natural feedstuffs. Trace elements may be rendered poorly available because of binding to phytate or fiber. While nutrient requirements listed in Table 2 are appropriate for purified feline diets, formulated diets from natural ingredients require adjustment factors to assure nutrient adequacy. Guidelines discussed below are intended to bridge the gap between minimum nutrient concentrations in purified diets and those thought necessary for typical commercial diets. The factors suggested have generally been derived from studies on species other than the cat. Adjustment of some of these factors may be necessary at a later date when bioavailability data become available for the cat.

Protein Amino Acids

Protein digestibility and hence amino acid bioavailabilities generally will not exceed 90 percent for natural ingredients commonly used in cat foods. Some proteineacous ingredients, however, may be no more than 50 percent digestible, particularly those rich in collagen protein (Baker and Parsons, 1985). Moreover, excessive heat processing procedures sometimes used in preparing commercial products may enhance or lower amino acid bioavailability. Considering the array of ingredients used in typical feline diets, some of which are high and some low in digestibility, an average correction factor of 1.3 is suggested. Thus, the total minimum concentrations of each essential amino acid necessary in a practical-type diet can be estimated by multiplying the purified diet requirement in Table 2 by 1.3.

Vitamins

Little information is available on the bioavailability of fat-soluble vitamins. Requirements listed in Table 2 are expressed on the basis of a specific form of each fat-soluble vitamin, i.e., retinol, cholecalciferol, α-tocopherol, and phylloquinone. Other forms or isomers may be present in natural ingredients and may, in turn, contribute vitamin bioactivity to the cat. Information concerning this can be found in the text, but if more specific and detailed information is desired, other references should be consulted.

Vitamin E deserves special mention when dealing with diets based upon natural ingredients. Diets containing a high level of polyunsaturated fatty acids (PUFA, e.g., in fish oil) may lead to a three- to four-fold increase in the vitamin E requirement. Diets low in PUFA and containing supplemental selenium and/or antioxidant, on the other hand, may not necessitate the 30 mg/kg α-tocopherol activity listed in Table 2. Based upon the available information at this time and the high digestibility of triglycerides, it would appear that, with the exception of vitamin E for diets high in PUFA, the levels of fat-soluble vitamin activity listed in Table 2 are suitable for both purified and practical-type diets.

B vitamins exist both in bound and free forms. Thus, they are not always completely available when consumed by animals. Niacin and folacin are examples of two B vitamins that are poorly available.

Intestinal B-vitamin biosynthesis likely furnishes some bioavailable B-vitamin activity to cats, although information does not exist in cats to quantify the extent of this contribution. Unlike dogs, rabbits, and rodents, however, cats engage in minimal coprophagy, and therefore they would be expected to derive less B-vitamin activity from intestinal synthesis than would occur for the other species mentioned.

Work done with other species suggests that a general bioavailability correction factor of 1.6 should be applied to the B-vitamin requirements listed in Table 2 when extrapolating them to animals consuming practical-type diets (e.g., Molitoris and Baker, 1976; Yen et al., 1976; Anderson et al., 1978; Southern and Baker, 1981). Thiamin is a special case, however, because it is extremely heat labile. Thus, while multiplying requirement values in Table 2 by 1.6 will likely suffice for practical-diet B vitamins in general, the reader is referred to pages 24 and 31 for special precautions concerning thiamin.

Minerals

Other than phosphorus, little definitive information exists on the bioavailability of essential macro-elements

Feline diets are generally high in phosphorus, and a majority of that present exists as meat- or bone-derived phosphorus, which, relative to $CaHPO_4$ (an accepted standard), is close to 100 percent bioavailable. Plant-derived phosphorus, on the other hand, is largely bound to phytate and as such should be considered no more than 30 percent bioavailable. Because of this, dry cat foods for kittens during the first 4 weeks postweaning may require up to 8 g total phosphorus per kilogram of dry diet. Other than this adjustment, requirements for the other macro-elements (Ca, Mg, K, Na, Cl) listed in Table 2 may be applied to both purified and practical-type diets.

Essential trace elements contained in natural ingredients are not fully bioavailable to the animals consuming them. Unfortunately, few data exist to quantify their bioavailability in cats. Evidence with other species, however, suggests that both phytate and fiber can bind trace elements and thereby render them less available. Phytate binding of trace elements is, moreover, enhanced by excess dietary calcium. The binding constant for zinc is particularly high such that the minimal requirement for zinc may be up to 4 times higher when determined with a soy-based diet than with a casein-based diet. The zinc requirement listed in Table 2 was set on the assumption that a soy-protein purified diet was fed.

Factors other than phytate and fiber can affect trace-element bioavailability. Thus, recent evidence with chicks has shown that a feed ingredient like menhaden fish meal possesses mineral unavailability factors (Halpin and Baker, 1986). Fish meals are assumed to contain neither phytate nor fiber, but contain measurable levels of neutral detergent fiber, probably mostly chitin and chitin-like materials (D. H. Baker, University of Illinois, personal communication, 1986). Whether animal products other than fish contain factors reducing trace-element availability is unknown.

The difficulty in assigning guidelines for extrapolating trace-element requirements from purified diets to practical diets is multifaceted. Not only may trace elements be less available in diets based upon natural ingredients than in those based upon purified ingredients, but factors present in the natural ingredients may further lower the bioavailability of *inorganic* sources of the trace elements. Moreover, mineral-mineral interactions can come into play. Classic examples of these are excess dietary phosphorus lowering iron bioavailability and excess dietary zinc lowering the bioavailability of both iron and copper. A low ratio of dietary inorganic cations relative to anions may result in excessive spillage of cations (e.g., K) in the urine. For example, high-protein diets, perhaps by virtue of sulfate production and excretion in the urine, increase the potassium requirement of cats (Hills et al., 1982). This phenomenon was taken into consideration, however, in setting the minimal potassium requirement for growth of the kitten. It seems clear that mineral additions to a diet cannot be made indiscriminately. The kind of dietary (organic) ingredients, the source of each inorganic mineral supplement, and mineral-mineral interactions must all be considered carefully before fortifying practical-type diets with sources of mineral elements. To provide a margin of safety to protect against unavailability factors present in diets based upon natural ingredients, an adjustment factor of 1.3 is suggested for iron, copper, and iodine.* A correction factor of 1.5 is suggested for zinc and manganese. Selenium probably requires no correction, because food-borne selenium exists primarily as seleno-methionine whose selenium moiety is essentially totally available relative to sodium selenate or sodium selenite.

---

*Some colorants, e.g., erythrosin, contain considerable quantities of iodine which is wholly unavailable and yet analytically shows abundant iodine.

5 Other Food Constituents

FOOD ADDITIVES

Information on the effects of food additives in cats is scarce because routine toxicity testing is rarely conducted on this species. Where a nonrodent mammal is required for testing, usually the dog or pig (or possibly ferret) is chosen rather than the cat. Avoidance of the cat as a test animal is probably partly due to its reputation as a finicky eater. More important, however, is the cat's unusual sensitivity to some chemicals because of differences in the pathways of metabolism of these compounds in the cat compared with other animals. Consequently, results obtained from screening tests might not be readily applicable to other mammals (including man) and could give an unrealistically severe assessment of the toxicity of an additive.

BENZOIC ACID AND RELATED COMPOUNDS

Benzoic acid and its salts are used in human foods as preservatives, particularly as antifungal agents. Cats are much more susceptible than other mammals to these compounds because of their reduced ability to detoxify them. In most species benzoic acid derivatives are metabolized by dual pathways of conjugation with glycine and glucuronic acid to produce hippuric acid and benzoyl glucuronate, respectively (Bridges et al., 1970). The glucuronide pathway, which has the greater capacity, is defective in the cat and only the glycine pathway is operative (Williams, 1967). This defect is responsible for cats' hypersensitivity to other phenolic compounds, including aspirin. Bedford and Clarke (1972) found that the highest continuous daily intake of benzoic acid that could be tolerated for 15 days was 200 mg/kg body

weight (BW). An intake of 300 mg/kg BW/day caused mild hyperesthesia from which the cat recovered, but higher doses caused aggression, hyperesthesia, and death. Although it is theoretically possible to stipulate a safe concentration of benzoic acid on the basis of these results, in practice the use of this additive in cat foods is not advisable because of the low margin of safety, the possibility of overdispensing or inadequate mixing resulting in high concentrations in certain batches, and its relatively poor preservative action at the concentrations permitted by the observed no-adverse-effect level. Benzyl alcohol poisoning has also been reported in cats (Cullison et al., 1983) that had received lactated Ringer's solution containing benzyl alcohol as a preservative. In the body the alcohol is rapidly oxidized to benzoic acid and hence is toxic to the cat. Because of the problems associated with benzoic acid in the cat, safer and more effective alternatives to this chemical are recommended for use in pet foods. Sorbic acid produced no adverse effects in cats when fed at concentrations up to 2 percent of a canned meat-based diet (Bedford and Clarke, 1973). The effective antifungal concentration is only about 0.2 percent. Phillips et al. (1978) found that radioactively labelled p-hydroxybenzoic acid, when fed to cats at doses up to 130 mg/kg, was rapidly excreted in the urine. Only one major metabolite was identified, p-hydroxyhippuric acid. The same results were obtained in animals pretreated with the compound in the diet for 28 days. Studies with the ethyl and n-propyl esters showed a similar route of metabolism except that in this case two major metabolites were identified, p-hydroxyhippuric acid and free p-hydroxybenzoic acid. As with sorbic acid, the tested intakes of these compounds are sufficient to allow their use in foods. The concentrations used are typically up to 0.2 percent on dry matter or about 50 mg/kg BW/day for an adult cat.

34

COLOR

Cats appear to possess limited color perception (De Reuck and Knight, 1965); however, a variety of artificial and natural colorants are added to cat foods to enhance human appeal for such products. Many colorants (e.g., caramel) are used on the basis of work carried out in other species (CRC, 1972). Therefore, this section only considers colorants where direct data on the cat are available.

One of the few long-term toxicity tests conducted in the cat is a teratogenicity study of the food color amaranth (F, D, and C Red No. 2) reported by Khera et al. (1976). Cats were given doses of amaranth up to 265 mg/kg BW/day for a time period extending from 0 to 22 days before conception to days 61 to 62 of gestation. Kittens were then delivered by Caesarean section. There was no evidence of embryotoxicity at any dose level. Maternal indices (including incidences of pregnancy, nonpregnancy, and abortion) also showed no adverse effects related to amaranth. For this color the cat study gave results similar to those obtained in other species, including the dog.

Amaranth is one of the azo group of colors that, on reduction in the body, yield aniline compounds. These are well-known inducers of Heinz body formation in animals. Heinz bodies are small inclusion particles in erythrocytes that result from the oxidative degradation of hemoglobin, and the cat erythrocyte is reported to be particularly sensitive to the induction of these inclusions. Cats have therefore been used to test the effects of several azo colors on Heinz body induction, namely amaranth (JECFA, 1975), tartrazine (JECFA, 1964), azorubine, also known as carmoisine (JECFA, 1974b), and sunset yellow (Khera and Munro, 1979). Doses up to 1 g/day were given for periods up to 35 days. Negative results for Heinz body formation were obtained for all colors tested.

Another color that has been tested in cats is titanium dioxide. This is a white pigment possessing considerable "coloring power," which is used widely throughout the food industry. Two cats were fed 3 g/day of technical grade titanium dioxide for 390 days. Two other cats received the same intake for 175 and 300 days. No adverse effects were seen during the trial or on histopathological examination (JECFA, 1970).

SODIUM NITRITE

Sodium nitrite is a widely employed human food additive used particularly as an antimicrobial agent and also as a color stabilizer or fixative, especially in meat products, where it reacts with the heme pigments myoglobin and hemoglobin to form stable nitrosyl derivatives. A considerable amount of research has been conducted on this additive, and there is a report of a feeding trial in one cat that received an average of 39 mg of sodium nitrite daily over 105 days without ill effects (JECFA, 1974a). This is equivalent to an intake of approximately 105 mg/kg body weight/day for an adult (4 kg) animal.

PROPYLENE GLYCOL (1,2 PROPANEDIOL)

Propylene glycol is a low-molecular-weight alcohol used in the control of water activity in human and pet foods. The biological effects of propylene glycol have been the subject of general reviews (Morris et al., 1942; Ruddick, 1972), but no direct studies have been published for cats. However, it is known that the lipids in cat erythrocyte are sensitive to oxidants and increased numbers of Heinz bodies have been observed in cats given diets containing propylene glycol (K. C. Hayes, Brandeis University, personal communication, 1985). Thus, the use of high levels of propylene glycol might be expected to decrease the life of the erythrocyte resulting in hemolytic anemia in cats.

OTHER FOOD ITEMS

There are few incidences in which food itself has been reported to cause adverse effects in cats. An obvious exception to this is liver, but this has already been discussed in the section on vitamin A. Allergic reactions to food have been reported in the cat, but even here the scale of the problem is difficult to assess and incidences between 1 and 30 percent have been suggested. The sites usually affected are the skin and alimentary tract. Although a detailed discussion of the problem is outside the scope of this publication, the subject has been reviewed recently by Stogdale et al. (1982).

Onion poisoning has been described in the cat by Kobayashi (1981), who reported a hemolytic anemia and an increase in Heinz bodies in cats that had consumed onion soup. Hemoglobinuria also occurred when large quantitites of soup were ingested. Clinical signs disappeared with the cessation of onion feeding and the poisoning was not considered to pose a clinical problem unless consumption was excessive or prolonged.

One further item worth mentioning under this heading is the possible risk of poisoning from cocoa and related products. Although this has not been reported in cats, it is well documented in dogs and presents a risk of intoxication from what would normally be considered a harmless material. The toxic principle is the methylxanthine derivative theobromine and the signs of poisoning are vomiting, diarrhea, sudden collapse, and death. The oral LD_{50} for cats is 200 mg/kg BW and, as cocoa contains 1.5 to 2.0 percent theobromine (Sutton, 1981), it would theoretically need only 40 to 50 g to provide a potentially lethal dose. Chocolate has a much lower theobromine content of around 0.2 percent (Glauberg and Blumenthal, 1983) and is therefore less of a hazard.

6 Composition of Feeds

Tables 5–10 present the composition of some cat food ingredients. Nutrient concentrations are organized as follows:

Table 5:   Fats, fatty acids, and ME composition
Table 6:   Taurine content
Table 7:   Composition of ingredients, excluding minerals and amino acids
Table 8:   Mineral composition
Table 9:   Mineral sources
Table 10:   Amino acid composition

METABOLIZABLE ENERGY (ME)

Since ME values for cat food ingredients have not been published, the figures in Table 8 are largely those derived for swine (NRC, 1982). For some ingredients DE values directly determined in cats have been converted to ME using the equation: ME (kcal/kg) = DE − (digestible crude protein × 1.25 kcal/g).

NOMENCLATURE

In Tables 5, 7, 8, 9, and 10, names of the feeds are based on a scheme proposed by Harris et al. (1981). The names are designed to give a qualitative description of each product, where such information is available and pertinent. A complete name consists of as many as eight components separated by commas and written in linear form. The components are as follows:

Origin (or parent material)
Species, variety, or kind
Part eaten
Process(es) and treatment(s) to which product has been subjected
Stage of maturity
Cutting or crop
Grade or quality designations
Classification

Feeds of the same origin (and the same species, variety, or kind, if one of these is stated) are grouped into eight classes.

The numbers and the classes they designate are as follows:

1. Dry forages or dry roughages
2. Pasture, range plants, and forages fed green
3. Silages
4. Energy feeds
5. Protein supplements
6. Minerals
7. Vitamins
8. Additives

Feeds that in the dry state contain, on the average, more than 18 percent of crude fiber are classified as forages and roughages. Feeds that contain 20 percent or more of protein are classified as protein supplements. Feeds that contain less than 20 percent of protein and less than 18 percent of crude fiber are classified as energy feeds. (These guidelines are approximate, and there is some overlapping.)

Abbreviations have been devised for some of the terms in the feed names (Table 10).

The following list shows how three feeds are described:

Components of Name	Feed No. 1	Feed No. 2	Feed No. 3
Origin (or parent material)	fish	soybean	wheat
Species, variety, or kind	herring		soft white winter
Part eaten	whole	seeds	
Process(es) and treatment(s) to which product has been subjected	fresh	meal solv extd	grain
Grade or quality designations		44% protein	
Classification: first digit in International Feed Number (IFN)	(5) protein supplements 5-01-999	(5) protein supplements 5-04-604	(4) energy feeds 4-05-337

Thus, the names of the three feeds are written as follows:

No. 1: Fish, herring, whole, fresh
No. 2: Soybean, seeds, meal solv. extd., 44 percent protein
No. 3: Wheat, soft white winter, grain

The analytical data are expressed in the metric system and are shown on a dry basis. See Table 12 for weight-unit conversion factors.

Analytical data may differ in the various NRC reports because the data are updated for each report. The names may also differ as feeds are more precisely characterized or as official definitions change. However, if the feed is the same, the International Feed Number will remain the same.

LOCATING NAMES IN THE TABLES

To locate in Tables 5, 7, 8, and 10 the name of a feed, one must first know the name of the parent material (i.e., the origin of the feed) and usually the variety or kind of parent material. The first word of each name is the name of the parent material. Parent materials are of four types: plant, animal, poultry, and fish. For a feed derived from a plant, the origin term is the name of the plant (e.g., BARLEY, OATS). For a feed derived from animals or poultry, the origin term is the name of the animal or bird (e.g., CATTLE, CHICKEN, WHALE). For a feed of fish origin, the origin term is FISH followed by the species or variety (e.g., FISH, COD; FISH, MENHADEN).

When the specific origin of a feed derived from poultry or fish is not known, the origin term is POULTRY or FISH. When a specific origin of a feed derived from animals is not known the origin term is the name of the animal product (e.g., BLOOD, meal). Fats or oils are listed under the term FATS AND OILS, and the various kinds of molasses or syrups are listed under MOLASSES.

A six-digit International Feed Number is listed after the feed name. The first digit is the class of the feed, the remaining five digits identify the specific feed within the class. The numbers may be used as the "numerical name" of a feed when performing linear programming with electronic computers.

The common name of the parent material is followed by the specific name (example: BARLEY, *Hordeum vulgare*).

Tables

TABLE 1   Daily Metabolizable Energy Intakes Observed for Cats

Kitten[a] (age, weeks)	Body Weight (kg)		(kcal/kg BW)	Expected Bodyweight (gain g/day)		Adult[b]	(kcal/kg BW)
	Male	Female		Male	Female		
10	1.1	0.9	250	20	14	inactive[b]	70
20	2.5	1.9	130	14	11	active[b]	80
30	3.5	2.7	100	7	4	gestation[c]	100
40	4.0	3.0	80	—	—		

Lactation[d] (kcal/kg BW)

Litter size	1	2	3	4	5	6
Lactation week						
1	60	76	92	108	124	124
2	66	83	100	117	134	134
3	72	94	116	138	160	160
4	78	106	134	162	190	190
5	84	117	150	183	217	250
6	90	136	182	228	274	320

[a] The kitten allowances are adapted from Miller and Allison (1958).

[b] The allowances for adult cats refer to in vivo ME data and apply to cats of 50 weeks of age or greater. The value for inactive cats is adapted from Kendall et al. (1983); that for active cats is based on several studies (see text).

[c] The allowances for gestation are based on work by Scott (1968) and Loveridge (1986b).

[d] The allowances for lactation are adapted from Loveridge (1986b) based on voluntary intakes for queens of mean BW 3.8 kg after parturition. Values from about week 4 onward include energy intake by kittens.

NOTE: The intakes other than for normal adult cats were based on studies where ME intakes were calculated using Atwater factors of 4 kcal/g for dietary protein and carbohydrate and 9 kcal/g for dietary fat. Such ME allowances are likely to be some 20 percent higher compared with those based on determined in vivo ME (Kendall et al., 1985) depending on food type.

TABLE 2   Minimum Requirements for Growing Kittens (units per kg of diet, dry basis)[a]

Nutrient	Unit	Amount	Nutrient	Unit	Amount
Fat[b]			Sodium	mg	500
Linoleic acid	g	5	Chloride	g	1.9
Arachidonic acid	mg	200	Iron	mg	80
Protein[c] (N × 6.25)	g	240	Copper	mg	5
Arginine	g	10	Iodine	μg	350
Histidine	g	3	Zinc	mg	50
Isoleucine	g	5	Manganese	mg	5
Leucine	g	12	Selenium	μg	100
Lysine	g	8	Vitamins		
Methionine plus cystine	g	7.5	Vitamin A (retinol)	mg	1 (3333 IU)
(total sulfur amino acids)			Vitamin D (cholecalciferol)	μg	12.5 (500 IU)
Methionine	g	4	Vitamin E[e] (α-tocopherol)	mg	30 (30 IU)
Phenylalanine plus tyrosine	g	8.5	Vitamin K[f] (phylloquinone)	μg	100
Phenylalanine	g	4	Thiamin	mg	5
Taurine	mg	400	Riboflavin	mg	4
Threonine	g	7	Vitamin B₆ (pyridoxine)	mg	4
Tryptophan	g	1.5	Niacin	mg	40
Valine	g	6	Pantothenic acid	mg	5
Minerals			Folacin (folic acid[f])	μg	800
Calcium	g	8	Biotin[f]	μg	70
Phosphorus	g	6	Vitamin B₁₂ (cyanocobalamin)	μg	20
Magnesium	mg	400	Choline[g]	g	2.4
Potassium[d]	g	4	Myo-inositol[h]	—	—

[a]Based on a diet with an ME concentration of 5.0 kcal/g dry matter fed to 10- to 20-week-old kittens. If dietary energy density is greater or lesser, it is assumed that these requirements should be increased or decreased proportionally. Nutrient requirement levels have been selected based on the most appropriate optimal response (i.e., growth, nitrogen retention, metabolite concentration or excretion, lack of abnormal clinical signs, etc.) of kittens fed a purified diet. Some of these requirements are known adequate amounts rather than minimum requirements. Since diet processing (such as extruding or retorting) may destroy or impair the availability of some nutrients, and since some nutrients, especially the trace minerals, are less available from some natural feedstuffs than from purified diets, increased amounts of these nutrients should be included to ensure that the minimum requirements are met. The minimum requirements presented in this table assume availabilities similar to those present in purified diets.

[b]No requirement for fat is known apart from the need for essential fatty acids and as a carrier of fat-soluble vitamins. Some fat normally enhances the palatability of the diet.

[c]Assuming that all the minimum essential amino acid requirements are met.

[d]The minimum potassium requirement increases with protein intake (see text, page 17).

[e]This minimum should be adequate for a moderate to low-fat diet. It may be expected to increase three- to four-fold with a high PUFA diet, especially when fish oil is present.

[f]These vitamins may not be required in the diet unless antimicrobial agents or antivitamin compounds are present in the diet.

[g]Choline is not essential in the diet but if this quantity of choline is not present the methionine requirement should be increased to provide the same quantity of methyl groups.

[h]A dietary requirement for myo-inositol has not been demonstrated for the cat. However, almost all published studies in which purified diets have been used have included myo-inositol at 150 to 200 mg/kg diet and no studies have tested a myo-inositol-free diet.

NOTE: The minimum requirements of all the nutrients are not known for the adult cat at maintenance. It is known that these levels of nutrients are adequate and that protein and methionine can be reduced to 140 and 3 g/kg diet, respectively. It is likely that the minimum requirements of all the other nutrients are also lower for maintenance than for the growing kitten.

The minimum requirements of all the nutrients are not known for reproduction for the adult male or female cat. It is known that with the following modifications the Nutrient Allowances as recommended in the 1978 NRC report are adequate for gestation and lactation (in units/kg purified diet, note these recommendations are based on 4.0 kcal/g dry diet): arachidonate, 200 mg; zinc, 40 mg; vitamin A, 5500 IU; and taurine, 500. It is probable that the minimum requirements for growing kittens in this table would satisfy all requirements for reproduction if the following were modified as shown: vitamin A, 6000 IU/kg diet, and taurine, 500 mg/kg diet.

TABLE 3 Proximate Composition, Apparent Digestibility, and Digestible and Metabolizable Energy of Some Commercial Cat Diets

Number of Determinations	Dry Type		Semimoist	Canned	
	1[a]	29[b]	2[a]	2[a]	28[b]
Composition (percent)					
Dry matter	93.3	91.7	71.3	28.0	20.8
Crude protein	35.3	33.0	25.1	10.8	9.6
Crude fat	9.7	9.3	9.8	4.0	4.6
Crude fiber	2.7	—	0.7	0.6	—
Nitrogen-free extract	38.2	41.1	22.3	10.1	4.2
Ash	7.4	10.5	6.5	2.6	2.3
Propylene glycol	—	—	7.0	—	—
Gross energy (kcal/g)	4.55	4.22	3.65	1.44	1.10
Apparent digestibility (percent)					
Crude protein	78.3	76.0	83.2	80.1	80.5
Crude fat	85.3	72.3	93.9	88.6	76.1
Nitrogen-free extract	78.8	75.4	80.6	75.1	70.2
Gross energy	80.6	75.4	86.3	80.5	78.9
Digestible energy (kcal/g)	3.67	3.18	3.15	1.16	0.87
Metabolizable energy (kcal/g)	3.54	2.94	2.95	1.11	0.79
CME_1 (kcal/g)[c]	3.81	3.80	3.11	1.19	0.97
CME_2 (kcal/g)[d]	3.25	3.02	2.70	1.09	1.79
CME_3 (kcal/g)[e]	3.24	2.92	—	1.00	0.81
CME_4 (kcal/g)[f]	3.42	2.95	2.96	1.08	0.80

[a]Data from Norvell (1976). Each diet was fed to 16 adult cats housed in individual metabolism cages. All products were fed for a 7-day adjustment period and a 6-day collection period.

[b]Data from Kendall et al. (1985). Each diet was fed to 6 adult cats in individual metabolism cages. Experimental protocol was as for Norvell (1976), except collection periods were 7 days and fat was measured in food and feces by the acid ether extraction method.

[c]Calculated ME_1 values were calculated as follows (dry-type diet):

	Nutrient/Diet	ME (kcal/g)	ME (kcal)
Crude protein	0.353	× 4	= 1.41
Crude fat	0.097	× 9	= 0.87
Nitrogen-free extract	0.382	× 4	= 1.53
			3.81

Propylene glycol in the semimoist diets was assigned an ME value of 4.7 kcal/g (Weil et al., 1971). The use of CME_1 overestimated in vivo ME by 7 to 29 percent on average, depending on food type.

[d]Calculated ME_2 values were calculated as follows (dry-type diet):

	Nutrient/Diet	Apparent Digestibility Coefficient	E (kcal/g)	ME (kcal)
Crude protein	0.353	× 0.783	× 4.4	= 1.22
Crude fat	0.097	× 0.853	× 9.4	= 0.78
Nitrogen-free extract	0.382	× 0.788	× 4.15	= 1.25
				3.25

The E value for crude protein was derived by subtraction of energy loss in urine (1.25 kcal/g) from the average gross energy of crude protein (5.65 kcal/g). The CME_2 values for the other diets were estimated in the same way, except that propylene glycol in the semimoist foods was assigned an ME value of 4.7 kcal/g. The CME_2 values ranged from 92 to 103 percent on average of those measured in vivo.

[e]Calculated ME_3 values were calculated using regression equations (Kendall et al., 1985).

Dry-type diets:

$CME_3 = 0.99$ gross energy $- 1.26$ (kcal/g), $R^2 = 0.53$; RSD $= 0.15$ (kcal/g)

Canned-type diets:

$CME_3 =$ crude protein $\times 3.9 +$ ether extract $\times 7.7 +$ nitrogen-free extract $\times 3.0 - 0.05$. $R^2 = 0.94$, RSD $= 0.06$ (kcal/g)

[f]Calculated ME_4 values were calculated as follows:

$CME_4 =$ food DE $- 0.9$ kcal/g protein digested, e.g., for 29 dry-type diets,

$CME_4 = 3.18 - 0.251 \times 0.9 = 2.95$ kcal/g.

The E value of urinary urea is based on 151.6 kcal/mole urea equivalent to 5.4 kcal/g N or 0.86 kcal/g crude protein. The CME_4 values ranged on average from 97 to 101 percent of in vivo determined ME values.

TABLE 4   Estimated Daily Food Allowances for Cats

Cat	Weight[a] of Cat (kg)	Dry Type[b] (g/kg body wt.)	(g/cat)	Semimoist[c] (g/kg body wt.)	(g/cat)	Canned[d] (g/kg body wt.)	(g/cat)
Kitten							
10 weeks	0.9–1.1	78	70–86	83	75–91	227	204–250
20 weeks	1.9–2.5	41	78–103	43	82–108	118	224–295
30 weeks	2.5–3.8	31	78–118	33	83–125	91	228–346
40 weeks	2.9–3.8	25	73–95	27	78–103	73	212–277
Adult[e]							
Inactive	2.2–4.5	22	48–90	23	51–99	64	141–288
Active	2.2–4.5	25	55–113	27	59–122	73	160–329
Gestation	2.5–4.0	31	78–124	33	83–132	91	228–364
Lactation[f]	2.2–4.0	78	172–312	83	182–332	227	499–908

[a]Derived from Figure 1 by setting lower limit at mean weight of females minus one standard deviation and the upper limit at mean weight of males plus one standard deviation.

[b]Dry matter, 90 percent; ME, 3.2 kcal/g.

[c]Dry matter, 70 percent; ME, 3.0 kcal/g.

[d]Dry matter, 25 percent; ME, 1.1 kcal/g.

[e]Fifty weeks of age or older.

[f]Queens nursing 4-5 kittens in week 6 of lactation.

TABLE 5 Fat, Fatty Acid (FA), and Metabolizable Energy Composition of Feed Ingredients[a]

COMMON NAME Genus species / Short name	International Feed Number	Dry Matter (%)	Ether Extract[b] (%)	Saturated[c] Fat (%)	Unsaturated[c] Fat (%)	Linoleic[c] Acid (%)	Linoleic[b] Acid (%)	Arachidonic[b] Acid (%)	ME (kcal/kg)
ANIMAL									
tallow, see FATS and OILS									
BARLEY Hordeum vulgare, grain	4-00-549	89.0	2.1	0.6	1.4	0.27	—	—	2870
CORN Zea mays									
dent yellow grain	4-02-935	89.0	4.5	0.9	3.7	2.05	—	—	3724
distillers solubles dehy	5-02-844	93.0	9.5	2.0	7.5	4.80	—	—	2900
gluten meal	5-02-900	91.0	2.0	1.5	6.8	4.21	—	—	3907
dent yellow, hominy feed	4-03-011	90.0	7.2	1.2	6.1	3.71	—	—	3382
CRAB Callinectes sapidus									
cannery residue meal (crab meal)	5-01-663	92.0	1.9	0.5	1.3	0.35	—	—	1328
FATS AND OILS									
bran oil	4-14-504	100.0	100.0	18.5	81.1	36.50	—	0	8047
fat (lard), swine	4-04-790	100.0	100.0	35.9	64.1	18.30	—	0.3–1.0[d]	7850
fat, bacon	4-15-582	100.0	100.0	42.3	56.7	6.8	0.6	—	—
fat, beef	4-25-306	100.0	100.0	44.9	55.1	1.9	1.2	1.0	—
fat, lamb	4-24-921	100.0	100.0	52.1	47.9	2.4	2.4	—	—
fat, rabbit	4-24-923	100.0	100.0	43.3	56.7	19.9	9.4	1.8	—
fat, turkey	4-24-924	100.0	100.0	36.5	63.5	19.0	1.0	4.8	—
fat, brain, lamb	4-15-583	100.0	100.0	41.4	58.6	0.2	0.8	2.4	—
fat, kidney, lamb	4-15-584	100.0	100.0	45.4	54.6	6.1	3.0	5.3	—
fat, kidney, beef	4-15-585	100.0	100.0	56.3	42.7	3.6	0.4	1.9	—
fat, kidney, swine	4-15-586	100.0	100.0	43.5	56.5	8.7	0.4	5.0	—
fat, liver, beef	4-15-587	100.0	100.0	49.6	50.4	5.5	1.9	4.8	—
fat, liver, swine	4-15-588	100.0	100.0	41.6	58.4	11.0	0.4	10.7	—
margarine, hard animal and vegetable oils	4-15-589	84.0	96.4	37.5	62.5	4.2	0.1	6.6	—
margarine, hard vegetable oily only	4-15-590	84.0	96.4	38.2	61.8	9.1	0.5	0	—
margarine, soft animal and vegetable oils	4-15-591	84.0	96.4	30.7	69.3	8.1	0.4	6.1	—
margarine, soft vegetable oils only	4-15-592	84.0	96.4	33.1	66.9	19.3	1.8	0	—
margarine soft, polyunsaturated vegetable oils only	4-15-593	84.0	96.4	24.7	75.3	49.3	0.6	0	—
offal fat, poultry	4-09-319	100.0	100.0	39.1	60.9	22.30	—	0.5–1.0[d]	8044
oil, coconut	4-09-320	100.0	100.0	90.3	9.7	1.10	—	0	8047
oil, corn	4-07-882	100.0	100.0	12.3	87.7	55.40	1.6	0	8047
oil, fish, menhaden	7-08-049	100.0	100.0	40.0	60.0	2.70	—	20.0–25.0[d]	—
oil, flax, common (linseed oil)	4-14-502	100.0	100.0	8.2	91.8	13.90	—	0	8047
oil, safflower	4-20-526	100.0	100.0	10.5	89.5	72.70	0.5	0	8047
oil, evening primrose[e]	4-15-591	100.0	100.0	8.5–13.5	86.5–91.5	73.0[e]	10.4[e]	0	8047
oil, soybean	4-07-983	100.0	100.0	14.7	85.3	51.9	7.4	0	7283
oil, cotton seed	4-20-836	100.0	100.0	26.8	73.2	53.0	1.4	0	8047
oil, rapeseed low erucic acid	4-20-834	100.0	100.0	6.9	93.1	23.0	10.0	0	8047
oil, sunflower	4-20-833	100.0	100.0	10.4	89.6	65.7	—	0	8047
tallow, animal	4-08-127	100.0	100.0	47.6	52.4	4.3	—	0.0–0.2[d]	8343
white grease	4-20-959	100.0	100.0	—	—	1.1	—	0	—
FISH									
solubles, condensed	5-01-969	51.0	12.8	5.7	7.1	0.39	—	—	3217
menhaden, meal mech extd	5-02-009	92.0	10.5	4.8	3.6	0.12	—	—	3200

TABLE 5—Continued

COMMON NAME *Genus species* Short name	International Feed Number	Dry Matter (%)	Ether Extract[b] (%)	Saturated[c] Fat (%)	Unsaturated[c] Fat (%)	Linoleic[b] Acid (%)	Linoleic[b] Acid (%)	Arachidonic[b] Acid (%)	ME (kcal/kg)
FISH, COD *Gadus morrhua-Gadus macrocephalus*									
liver oil	7-01-993	100.0	99.9	—	—	—	—	—	—
FLAX *Linum usitatissimum*									
common, meal solv extd (linseed meal)	5-02-048	91.0	1.9	0.4	1.5	0.41	—	0	2797
MEAT Animal									
meal, rendered	5-00-385	94.0	10.6	5.0	5.7	0.36	—	—	2371
with blood, meal tankage rendered (tankage)	5-00-386	92.0	8.8	4.4	4.5	0.30	—	—	2275
MILK Cattle									
fresh	5-01-168	13.4	30.6	61.1	38.9	0.4	0.4	—	—
skimmed dehy	5-01-175	94.0	1.0	0.40	0.60	0.01	—	—	3777
OATS *Avena sativa*									
grain	4-03-309	89.0	5.1	1.20	3.90	1.67	—	0	2668
PEANUT *Arachis hypogaea*									
kernels, meal mech extd (peanut meal)	5-03-649	92.0	7.3	1.70	5.50	1.36	—	0	3741
POULTRY									
by-product, meal rendered	5-03-798	93.0	12.5	4.50	8.00	1.98	—	—	3058
CHICKEN *Gallus domesticus*									
eggs, without shells, fresh	5-08-114	25.2	43.3	37.9	62.1	4.0	—	0.3	—
SORGHUM *Sorghum vulgare*									
milo grain	4-04-444	92.0	3.2	0.70	2.50	1.20	—	0	3585
SOYBEAN *Glycine max*									
seeds	5-04-610	92.0	20.0	3.30	16.7	8.66	—	0	3905
flour by-product (soya-bean mill feed)	4-04-594	90.0	6.8	1.3	5.4	3.29	—	0	1032
soybean, seeds meal solv extd 44% protein	5-20-637	90.0	1.1	0.03	0.08	0.61	—	0	3090
soybean, seeds 100 hulls, meal solv extd 49% protein	5-20-638	90.0	0.6	0.3	0.6	0.39	—	0	3485
WHEAT *Triticum* spp									
bran	4-05-190	89.0	3.4	0.9	3.7	2.53	—	0	2320
grain	4-05-211	89.0	1.9	0.4	1.5	0.65	—	0	3200
middlings, lt 9.5% fiber	4-05-205	89.0	5.2	1.0	4.1	2.79	—	0	
WHEY *Bos* spp									
dehy (cattle)	4-01-182	93.0	0.9	0.6	0.3	0.01	—	—	3190
YEAST *Saccharomyces cerevisiae*									
brewers dehy	7-05-527	93.0	1.1	0.2	0.8	0.05	—	—	2707

[a] Data adapted from Edwards (1964) and Paul and Southgate (1978) except when indicated.

[b] Expressed as percent (by weight) of the ingredient on a dry basis (100 percent matter).

[c] Expressed as percent (by weight) of the total fatty acids in the ingredient as fed. Fatty acids comprise about 95 percent of the weight of triglycerides, assuming the average triglyceride contains one glycerol, one 16 carbon fatty acid, and two 18 carbon fatty acids. Conversion factors for fat in brain, kidney, liver, and eggs were as recommended by Anderson (1976).

[d] Data adapted from Hilditch and Williams (1964).

[e] Median values from Hudson (1984).

TABLE 6   Taurine Content of Selected Foods (mg/kg, wet weight)[a]

Item	Uncooked		Baked[b]		Boiled[c]	
	Mean	Range/ ± SE	Mean	Range	Mean	Range
Beef muscle	362	150–472	133	96–125	60	58–63
Beef liver	192	144–270	141	68–184	73	36–95
Beef kidney	225	180–247	138	130–144	76	68–88
Lamb muscle	473	446–510	257	220–284	126	91–184
Lamb kidney	239	128–440	154	81–290	51	47–55
Pork muscle	496	394–690	219	126–390	118	91–184
Pork liver	169	110–228	85	70–100	43	30–54
Chicken muscle	337	300–380	229	140–310	82	71–180
Cod	314	233–396	294	260–328	161	125–198
Oysters	698	390–1238	264	217–308	89	59–122
Clams	2400	1450–3700	1017	587–1700	446	264–794
Milk, cows, colostrum[d]	38	± 7				
Milk, cows[d]	1.3	± 0.3				
Milk, cats[d]	359	± 42				

[a]Potential significance of free taurine in the diet. Adapted from Roe and Weston (1965).
[b]Homogenate baked 30 min at 177°C.
[c]Homogenate boiled 15 min in deionized water. Very high proportions of tissue taurine may be recovered in the cooking fluid.
[d]Taurine concentration in mg/liter. Adapted from Rassin et al. (1978).

TABLE 7 Composition of Some Common Cat Feeds, Excluding Minerals and Amino Acids on a Dry Basis (moisture-free)

Entry Number	COMMON NAME *Genus species* Short name	International Feed Number[a]	Dry Matter (%)	ME (kcal/kg)	Protein (%)	Ether Extract (%)	Crude Fiber (%)	Cellulose (%)	Ash (%)
	BARLEY *Hordeum vulgare*								
001	grain	4-00-549	89	3299.0	13.0	2.0	5.7	—	2.7
002	grain, Pacific Coast	4-07-939	89	3293.0	10.1	2.3	7.1	—	2.8
	BLOOD, ANIMAL								
003	fresh	5-26-007	15	—	—	—	—	—	—
004	meal spray dehy	5-00-381	93	4192.0[b]	95.6	1.1	0.6	—	7.1
	BONE, ANIMAL								
005	meal steamed	6-00-400	96	—	11.4	2.7	2.1	—	73.4
006	phosphate	6-00-406	98	—	—	—	—	—	—
	BREAD								
007	dehy	4-07-944	95	—	13.0	2.4	—	—	2.4
	BUTTERMILK *Bos taurus*								
008	dehy	5-01-160	92	3300.0	34.4	5.6	0.4	—	9.9
	CANOLA *Brassica napus-Brassica campestris*								
009	seeds, meal prepressed, solv extd, low erucic acid, low glucosinolates	5-06-145	93	—	40.9	3.3	12.9	—	6.8
	CASEIN								
010	dehy	5-01-162	93	2991.0	93.8	0.9	0.2	—	2.6
	CATTLE, *see* HAMBURGER								
011	chucks, fresh	5-17-896	39	—	47.7	50.0	—	—	—
012	lips, fresh	5-07-940	30	—	60.0	23.3	—	—	—
013	livers, fresh	5-01-166	28	3173.0[b]	69.6	18.3	0.6	—	4.9
014	lungs, fresh	5-07-941	24	—	65.0	38.9	2.9	—	—
015	spleens, fresh	5-07-942	24	3940.0[b]	68.7	16.1	4.0	—	6.0
016	tripe	5-09-806	33	5504.0[b]	46.1	43.6	0.5	—	3.4
017	udders, fresh	5-07-943	20	5587.0[b]	58.6	30.0	1.2	—	7.4
	CHICKEN, *see* POULTRY								
	CORN, DENT YELLOW *Zea mays indentata*								
018	distillers grains w solubles dehy	5-28-236	93	3070.0	29.3	10.2	10.0	42.0	4.9
019	distillers solubles, dehy	5-28-237	92	3369.0	31.0	9.2	4.8	—	7.7
020	germ, meal wet milled solv extd	5-28-240	92	3295.0	22.6	1.6	13.3	—	4.2
021	gluten, meal, 60%	5-28-242	90	3907.0	67.9	2.0	2.8	9.7	2.4
022	grain, flaked	4-28-244	90	—	11.2	2.2	0.7	—	1.0
023	hominy feed	4-03-011	90	3748.0	11.8	6.3	5.5	22.9	3.1
024	grain	4-02-935	89	3724.0	9.9	4.2	2.9	—	1.5
	COTTON, *Gossypium* spp								
025	seeds, meal prepressed solv extd, 41% protein	5-07-872	90	2745.0	45.7	1.2	14.1	—	7.0
026	seeds, meal solv extd, 41% protein	5-01-621	91	2592.0	45.4	1.6	13.4	26.9	7.1
027	seeds wo hulls, meal prepressed solv extd, 50% protein	5-07-874	93	—	54.0	1.4	8.8	—	7.1
	CRAB *Callinectes sapidus-Cancer* spp-*Paralithodes camschatica*								
028	cannery residue, meal	5-01-663	92	1328.0	35.0	2.4	11.6	—	44.6
	DEXTROSE								
	FISH, ALEWIFE *Pomolobus pseudoharengus*								
029	meal mech extd	5-09-830	90	3711.0	69.4	13.6	1.1	—	15.4
030	whole, fresh	5-07-964	26	—	75.8	19.1	—	—	—
	FISH, ANCHOVY *Engraulis ringen*								
031	meal mech extd	5-01-985	92	2695.0	69.8	4.5	1.1	—	16.0
	FISH, CARP *Cyprinus carpio*								
032	meal mech extd	5-01-987	90	—	58.6	—	—	—	—
033	whole, fresh	5-01-986	31	—	61.9	29.4	—	—	9.4
	FISH, CATFISH *Ictalurus* spp								
034	meal mech extd	5-09-835	94	—	55.3	—	—	—	—
035	whole, fresh	5-07-965	22	—	—	—	—	—	—
	FISH, COD *Gadus morrhua-Gadus macrocephalus*								
036	meal mech extd	5-01-998	—	—	—	—	—	—	—
	FISH, FLOUNDER Bothidae (family), Pleuronectidae (family)								
037	whole, fresh	5-01-996	17	—	88.2	2.9	—	—	—
	FISH, HADDOCK *Melanogrammus aeglefinus*								
038	whole, fresh	5-07-966	20	—	93.8	0.5	—	—	—
	FISH, HAKE *Merluccius* spp-*Urophycis* spp								
039	whole, boiled	5-07-967	26	—	57.8	20.4	0.2	—	—
040	whole, boiled acidified	5-07-968	25	—	—	21.2	1.1	—	11.2
041	whole, fresh	5-07-969	20	—	59.6	14.6	0.2	—	12.0
	FISH, HERRING *Clupea harengus*								
042	meal mech extd	5-02-000	92	3026.0	78.3	9.2	0.8	—	11.5
043	whole, fresh	5-01-999	29	—	63.1	30.5	—	—	6.8

Entry Number	Nitrogen-Free Extract (%)	Biotin (mg/kg)	Choline (mg/kg)	Folic Acid (mg/kg)	Niacin (mg/kg)	Pantothenic Acid (mg/kg)	Pyridoxine (mg/kg)	Riboflavin (mg/kg)	Thiamin (mg/kg)	Vitamin A (mg/kg)	Vitamin D (IU/kg)	Vitamin E (mg/kg)
	76.1	0.17	1162	8.8	61.3	9.1	7.3	1.8	5.0	—	—	25.0
	77.0	0.17	1162	0.6	52.7	8.0	3.3	1.7	4.7	—	—	30.0
	—	—	—	—	—	—	—	—	—	—	—	—
	0.2	0.22	306.0	0.4	18.0	5.4	4.7	1.4	0.5	—	—	—
	10.2	—	—	—	4.4	2.5	—	2.9	—	—	—	—
	—	—	—	—	—	—	—	—	—	—	—	—
	51.9	—	—	—	30.0	—	—	2.1	—	—	—	—
	49.7	0.31	1891.0	0.4	9.3	40.1	2.6	33.1	3.7	2.4	—	7.0
	25.9	0.90	6700.0	2.3	201.6	13.6	3.3	—	—	—	—	—
	4.2	0.05	230.0	0.5	1.1	3.2	0.4	1.6	0.5	—	—	—
	—	—	—	0.3	114.8	—	—	—	—	—	—	—
	—	—	—	—	—	—	—	—	—	—	—	—
	6.6	3.51	5093.0	8.3	269.0	164.0	18.0	92.2	6.3	131.7	—	25.0
	—	0.12	7933.0	0.9	49.0	2.6	1.8	8.4	2.8	1.0	—	13.0
	5.3	0.16	2036.0	4.8	25.0	8.2	1.3	15.3	3.1	0.9	—	56.5
	6.4	0.09	509.6	0.3	33.2	3.9	0.6	—	—	0.5	—	1.5
	2.8	0.30	4320.0	0.3	102.0	46.7	6.8	14.6	32.7	2.7	—	49.0
	45.7	0.85	2803.0	1.0	79.0	15.3	6.4	10.0	3.1	—	600.0	43.0
	47.3	1.79	5151.0	1.4	134.0	25.2	12.0	22.7	7.3	—	—	55.5
	58.3	0.24	1785.0	0.2	42.0	4.6	6.8	4.2	4.9	—	—	94.0
	25.8	0.21	390.0	0.3	66.0	3.9	7.4	2.2	0.3	—	—	15.0
	84.9	—	—	—	—	—	—	—	—	—	—	—
	73.4	0.15	1154.8	0.4	51.0	9.1	12.2	2.0	8.9	—	—	—
	80.6	0.07	697	0.4	27.0	4.5	7.0	1.1	3.9	—	—	10.0
	31.9	0.61	3166.3	2.8	44.3	8.1	5.0	4.9	3.7	—	—	—
	32.5	0.61	3058.0	2.8	45.0	15.0	5.8	5.0	7.3	—	—	17.0
	28.8	0.48	3184.0	1.0	48.0	15.4	6.8	5.0	8.8	—	—	12.0
	6.4	0.07	2179.0	0.1	49.0	7.0	7.2	6.7	0.5	—	—	—
	0.6	—	4465.0	—	35.9	10.6	—	3.9	0.1	4.3	—	6.2
	—	—	—	—	—	—	—	—	—	—	—	—
	9.6	0.21	4023.4	0.2	87.6	10.9	5.1	8.2	0.5	—	—	4.0
	—	—	—	—	—	—	—	—	—	—	—	—
	—	—	—	—	67.6	—	—	—	—	—	—	—
	—	—	—	—	—	—	—	—	—	—	—	—
	—	—	—	—	—	—	—	—	—	—	—	—
	—	—	—	—	—	—	—	—	—	—	—	—
	—	—	—	—	—	—	—	—	—	—	—	—
	—	—	—	—	—	—	—	—	—	—	—	—
	10.4	—	—	—	—	—	—	—	—	—	—	—
	—	—	—	—	—	—	—	—	—	—	—	—
	13.6	—	—	—	—	—	—	—	—	—	—	—
	0.2	0.53	3750.0	0.4	93.0	18.8	5.1	10.0	0.4	—	—	—
	—	—	—	—	130.8	—	5.0	—	—	—	—	—

TABLE 7—*Continued*

Entry Number	COMMON NAME *Genus species* / Short name	International Feed Number[a]	Dry Matter (%)	ME (kcal/kg)	Protein (%)	Ether Extract (%)	Crude Fiber (%)	Cellulose (%)	Ash (%)
	FISH, MACKEREL ATLANTIC *Scomber scombrus*								
044	whole, fresh	5-07-971	28	—	48.7	32.7	—	—	11.3
	FISH, MACKEREL *Scomber japonicus*								
045	Pacific, whole, fresh	5-07-972	30	—	72.5	24.2	—	—	—
	FISH, MENHADEN *Brevoorti tyrannus*								
046	meal mech extd	5-02-009	92	3200.0	66.7	10.5	1.0	—	20.9
	FISH, REDFISH *Sciaenops ocellata*								
047	meal mech extd	5-07-973	93	2772.0	61.0	9.8	1.0	—	27.1
	FISH, ROCKFISH *Sebastodes* spp								
048	whole, fresh	5-07-974	21	—	89.6	8.5	—	—	—
	FISH, SALMON *Oncorhynchus* spp-*Salmo* spp								
049	meal mech extd	5-02-012	94	—	65.8	12.6	0.3	—	19.1
050	whole, fresh	5-02-011	32	—	66.2	31.9	—	—	—
	FISH, SARDINE *Clupea* spp-*Sardinops* spp								
051	meal mech extd	5-02-015	93	2717.0	70.0	5.4	1.1	—	17.0
	FISH, SMELT *Osmerus* spp								
052	whole, fresh	5-07-975	21	—	88.6	10.0	—	—	—
	FISH, SOLE Soleidae (family)								
053	whole, fresh	5-07-976	20	—	65.5	21.0	0.2	—	12.3
	FISH, TUNA *Thunnus thynnus-Thunnus albacares*								
054	cannery residue	5-07-977	61	—	55.5	21.8	—	—	—
055	meal mech extd	5-02-023	93	2554.0	63.6	7.4	0.9	—	23.6
	FISH, TURBOT *Psetta maxima*								
056	whole, fresh	5-07-978	25	—	57.3	24.3	0.2	—	12.8
	FISH, WHITE Gadidae (family)-Lophidae (family)-Rajidae (family)								
057	meal mech extd	5-02-025	91	2912.0	68.4	5.1	0.6	—	25.4
	FISH, WHITING *Gadus merlangus*								
058	whole, fresh	5-07-979	23	—	69.9	8.7	—	—	—
	FISH								
059	livers, meal mech extd	5-01-968	93	—	67.7	18.6	1.3	—	6.6
060	racks, dehy grnd (bone with heads)	5-17-891	78	3542.0[b]	65.5	5.0	—	—	18.4
061	solubles, condensed	5-01-969	51	3217.0	61.8	12.2	1.0	—	20.0
062	solubles, dehy	5-01-971	92	3036.0	69.1	9.4	2.5	—	13.7
	FLAX *Linum usitatissimum*								
063	seeds, meal solv extd (linseed meal)	5-02-048	90	2797.0	38.4	1.6	10.1	—	6.5
064	glucose monohydrate	4-02-891	90	—	—	—	—	—	—
	HAMBURGER *Bos taurus*								
065	fresh 10% fat (cattle)	5-17-899	32	—	65.3	31.5	—	—	3.2
066	fresh 20% fat (cattle)	5-17-897	40	—	45.0	53.3	—	—	—
	HOMINY FEED, *see* CORN, hominy								
	HORSE *Equus caballus*								
067	meat, fresh	5-07-980	31	—	63.6	32.5	0.9	—	—
	KELP, *see* SEAWEED								
	LINSEED, *see* FLAX								
	LIVER, ANIMAL								
068	meat dehy	5-00-389	92	—	71.3	17.0	1.5	—	6.8
	MEAT, ANIMAL								
069	meal rendered	5-00-385	92	2258.0[b]	59.1	7.7	2.9	—	30.0
070	w blood w bone meal tankage rendered	5-00-387	93	2846.0	50.2	13.7	2.4	—	30.4
071	w bone, meal rendered	5-00-388	93	2000.0[b]	53.9	10.7	2.6	—	35.0
	MILK								
072	dehy (cattle)	5-01-167	96	—	26.6	27.7	0.2	—	5.7
073	cottage cheese	5-08-001	21	—	81.0	1.4	—	—	4.8
074	whey albumin (cattle)	5-01-177	92	—	52.5	1.1	0.9	—	31.6
075	fresh (cattle)	5-01-168	12	—	26.7	29.5	—	—	6.2
076	skimmed fresh (cattle)	5-01-170	10	—	—	1.0	—	—	6.9
077	skimmed dehy (cattle)	5-01-175	94	3745.0	35.4	1.2	0.2	—	8.4
	MILLET, FOXTAIL *Setaria italica*								
078	grain	4-03-102	89	3241.0	12.8	4.6	8.3	—	3.8
	MOLASSES *Beta vulgaris altissima*								
079	beet sugar, molasses mt 48%	4-00-668	78	3002.0	8.5	0.2	—	—	11.4
080	invert sugar mt 79.5 degrees brix, sugar cane, molasses dehy	4-04-695	94	2632.0	10.3	0.9	6.7	—	13.3
081	sugar cane, molasses, mt 46% invert, sugar mt 79.5 degrees brix	4-04-696	74	2951.0	5.8	0.1	0.5	—	13.2
	OATS *Avena sativa*								
082	cereal by-product, lt 4% fiber (feeding oat meal) (oat middlings)	4-03-303	91	3779.0	16.3	7.0	4.0	—	2.5
083	grain	4-03-309	89	3012.0	13.2	5.2	11.9	29.6	3.4

Dietary Number	Nitrogen-Free Extract (%)	Biotin (mg/kg)	Choline (mg/kg)	Folic Acid (mg/kg)	Niacin (mg/kg)	Pantothenic Acid (mg/kg)	Pryridoxine (mg/kg)	Riboflavin (mg/kg)	Thiamin (mg/kg)	Vitamin A (mg/kg)	Vitamin D (IU/kg)	Vitamin E (mg/kg)
	—	0.12	3422.0	8.5	24.0	17.9	1.2	9.6	2.9	25.6	—	—
	—	—	—	—	—	—	—	—	—	—	—	—
	0.8	0.20	3398.0	0.2	60.0	9.4	4.2	5.0	0.6	—	—	5.0
	1.1	0.18	3681.0	—	44.0	9.0	—	7.0	0.2	—	—	—
	—	—	—	—	—	—	—	—	—	—	—	—
	2.7	—	2990.0	—	27.0	7.4	—	6.2	0.9	—	—	—
	—	—	—	—	—	—	—	—	—	—	—	—
	6.5	0.11	3518.0	—	81.0	11.8	—	5.8	0.3	—	—	—
	1.0	—	—	—	—	—	—	—	—	—	—	—
	4.5	0.22	3227.0	—	155.0	8.4	—	7.3	1.6	—	—	—
	5.5	—	—	—	—	—	—	—	—	—	—	—
	0.1	0.09	4718.6	0.4	65.0	10.9	5.8	10.0	1.8	—	—	—
	—	—	—	—	—	—	—	—	—	—	—	—
	5.8	—	—	—	—	—	—	—	—	—	—	—
	4.4	0.28	6679.7	0.4	347.9	70.7	24.2	25.5	—	—	—	—
	11.7	0.45	5741.5	0.7	269.2	54.0	21.2	15.0	—	—	—	—
	43.5	—	1544.0	1.4	37.0	16.3	9.5	3.2	8.4	—	—	—
	—	—	—	—	—	—	—	—	—	—	—	—
	—	—	—	—	157.7	—	—	5.7	—	—	—	—
	—	—	—	—	105.3	—	—	—	—	0.3	—	—
	—	0.08	1043.0	0.8	16.0	4.8	0.7	—	1.4	2.6	—	—
	3.6	0.02	12281.0	6.0	221.0	31.5	—	39.1	0.2	—	—	—
	—	0.13	2110.0	0.4	60.0	6.4	4.5	5.0	0.6	—	—	1.0
	3.3	0.08	2224.6	0.6	62.9	5.2	—	5.0	—	—	—	—
	2.7	0.11	2196.0	0.4	55.0	5.9	6.3	5.0	0.2	—	—	1.0
	39.9	0.40	—	—	9.0	23.8	4.9	19.0	3.9	3.6	353.0	—
	12.9	—	—	—	5.0	—	—	13.0	—	0.2	—	—
	13.9	—	—	—	2.2	7.9	—	9.0	—	—	—	—
	37.6	—	7310.9	—	10.1	68.0	—	10.0	—	—	—	—
	60.6	—	—	—	11.5	36.9	—	20.0	—	3.4	—	—
	54.8	0.35	1479.8	0.7	12.2	38.6	4.4	20.0	—	—	446.2	9.6
	70.6	—	—	—	37.0	—	—	1.0	—	—	—	—
	80.0	—	1063.0	—	53.0	5.8	—	2.0	—	—	—	5.0
	68.8	—	—	—	—	—	—	—	—	—	—	5.5
	80.2	0.92	1027.1	0.1	49.0	50.3	5.7	3.0	1.2	—	—	7.3
	70.2	0.24	1276.7	0.5	26.3	19.4	—	1.0	7.7	—	—	26.0
	66.1	0.30	1084.4	0.4	15.6	11.1	1.1	1.0	7.1	—	—	16.8

TABLE 7—*Continued*

Entry Number	COMMON NAME *Genus species* Short name	International Feed Number[a]	Dry Matter (%)	ME (kcal/kg)	Protein (%)	Ether Extract (%)	Crude Fiber (%)	Cellulose (%)	Ash (%)
084	groats	4-03-331	90	3269.6	17.6	6.8	2.8	—	2.4
085	hulls	1-03-281	92	940.0	4.1	1.5	33.0	74.3	6.6
	PEA *Pisum* spp								
086	seeds	5-03-600	90	3416.0	26.4	1.2	6.1	—	3.2
	PEANUT *Arachis hypogaea*								
087	kernels, meal solv extd (peanut meal)	5-03-650	92	3295.0	54.5	2.4	10.3	—	6.3
	POTATO *Solanum tuberosum*								
088	tubers, dehy	4-07-850	91	3581.0	8.9	0.5	2.3	—	7.9
	POULTRY, CHICKEN *Gallus domesticus*								
089	broilers, whole fresh	5-07-945	24	—	76.5	20.2	—	—	—
090	eggs, fresh whole	5-01-213	30	—	42.6	31.1	—	—	31.4
091	eggs, fresh white	5-01-210	13	—	87.1	4.3	—	—	4.7
092	feet fresh	5-07-947	33	—	54.5	23.1	—	—	16.6
093	gizzards fresh	5-07-948	25	—	80.4	10.8	—	—	6.0
094	heads, fresh	5-07-949	33	—	57.6	18.2	—	—	—
095	by-product (viscera with feet and heads)	5-07-951	—	4515.0[b]	—	—	—	—	—
096	by-product, meal rendered (viscera with feet and heads)	5-03-798	93	4062.9[b]	62.4	14.1	2.4	—	15.1
097	hens, whole fresh	5-07-950	33	2829.0	60.3	24.1	1.5	—	3.1
098	viscera, fresh	5-07-985	26	—	54.4	32.3	0.9	—	7.7
	POULTRY FEATHERS								
099	hydrolyzed meal	5-03-795	93	3456.5[b]	92.9	5.5	1.5	—	3.4
100	PROPYLENE GLYCOL	8-03-809	100	4700.0	—	—	—	—	—
	RICE *Oryza sativa*								
101	bran w germ (rice bran)	4-03-928	91	3387.0	14.2	14.9	13.1	30.9	11.9
102	grain	4-03-939	89	3063.0	8.6	2.0	10.2	—	4.9
103	groats polished	4-03-942	89	4020.0	8.2	0.5	0.4	—	0.6
104	polishings	4-03-943	90	3814.0	13.2	13.9	3.5	—	8.4
105	grain, boiled	4-27-273	—	—	—	—	—	—	—
	RYE								
106	secale cereal grain	4-04-047	88	3327.0	13.7	1.7	2.5	18.6	1.9
	SEAWEED, KELP *Laminariales* (Order)- *Fucales* (Order)								
107	whole, dehy	4-08-073	91	—	7.1	0.5	7.4	—	38.6
	SESAME *Sesamum indicum*								
	SHRIMP *Pandalus* spp-*Penaeus* spp								
108	cannery residue meal (shrimp meal)	5-04-226	90	2339.0	50.0	4.3	15.6	—	29.7
	SORGHUM *Sorghum bicolor*								
109	grain	4-04-383	90	3585.0	12.8	2.9	2.8	23.0	2.0
	SOYBEAN *Glycine max*								
110	seeds, meal solv extd	5-04-604	90	—	50.5	1.3	6.4	—	6.9
111	seeds wo hulls, meal solv extd	5-04-612	90	3500.0	52.9	0.6	3.8	7.0	6.5
112	flour, concentrate (70% protein)	5-08-038	92	4164.0	91.8	0.6	0.1	—	3.8
113	isolate (80% protein)	5-24-811	96	—	94.0	—	—	—	—
114	seeds heat processed	5-04-597	90	—	41.1	20.3	5.6	—	5.1
115	flour, solvent extd	5-04-593	93	—	55.3	0.8	2.7	—	6.5
	SUCROSE								
116	sucrose	4-06-176	100	3673.0	—	—	—	—	—
	SUNFLOWER *Helianthus* spp								
117	seeds wo hulls, meal mech extd	5-04-738	93	2951.0	43.7	9.2	13.7	—	7.2
118	seeds wo hulls, meal solv extd	5-04-739	93	2851.0	48.8	3.1	12.7	—	8.1
	SWINE *Sus scrofa*								
119	livers, fresh	5-04-792	30	—	68.8	16.5	0.3	—	5.3
120	lungs, fresh	5-26-140	16	3913.0[b]	88.6	—	—	—	—
	TOMATO *Lycopersicon esculentum*								
121	pomace	5-05-041	92	—	22.9	10.7	27.2	54.8	7.4
	TURKEY *Meleagris gallopavo*								
122	mature birds, offal, fresh	5-07-984	—	—	—	—	—	—	—
123	young birds, offal, fresh	5-07-985	—	—	—	—	—	—	—
124	viscera, fresh	5-08-616	31	—	43.4	43.1	—	—	—
	WHALE *Balaena glacialis-Balaenoptera* spp- *Physeter catadon*								
125	meat, fresh	5-07-986	29	—	70.8	25.8	—	—	3.4
	WHEAT *Triticum aestivum*								
126	bran	4-05-190	89	2491.0	16.5	3.4	11.2	47.1	7.5
127	flour, bard red spring	4-08-113	89	3591.0	14.4	1.4	2.0	—	0.5
128	flour, lt 2% fiber	4-05-199	88	3873.0	15.5	1.9	1.0	—	1.7
129	germ meal	5-05-218	88	3798.0	27.6	9.6	3.5	—	4.9
130	grain	4-05-211	89	3660.0	14.7	2.0	2.9	12.2	2.0
131	grain, hard red spring	4-05-258	88	3339.0	14.4	2.1	2.9	—	1.9
132	grain, hard red winter	4-05-268	87	3627.0	14.4	2.2	2.8	—	2.0
133	grain, screenings	4-05-216	89	2638.0	14.9	3.2	6.0	—	3.5
134	grain, soft red winter	4-05-294	88	3533.0	12.9	1.8	2.6	—	2.1

ry nber	Nitrogen-Free Extract (%)	Biotin (mg/kg)	Choline (mg/kg)	Folic Acid (mg/kg)	Niacin (mg/kg)	Pantothenic Acid (mg/kg)	Pryridoxine (mg/kg)	Riboflavin (mg/kg)	Thiamin (mg/kg)	Vitamin A (mg/kg)	Vitamin D (IU/kg)	Vitamin E (mg/kg)
	70.4	—	1264.0	0.6	11.0	15.4	1.1	1.0	7.2	—	—	16.5
	54.9	—	281.0	1.0	10.0	3.4	2.4	1.0	0.7	—	—	—
	63.0	0.20	612.4	0.2	34.3	31.1	2.2	2.0	5.2	—	—	3.3
	28.5	0.36	2048.9	0.7	192.0	39.8	6.4	5.0	6.2	—	—	3.2
	80.5	0.11	2879.0	0.7	37.0	22.0	15.5	1.0	—	—	—	—
	—	—	—	—	—	—	—	—	—	—	—	—
	—	—	—	—	—	—	—	—	—	—	—	—
	3.9	—	—	1.3	7.5	20.2	0.3	23.3	—	—	—	—
	—	0.08	523.1	2.4	117.2	12.6	1.9	2.0	—	0.5	—	13.1
	2.8	—	—	—	180.0	—	—	—	—	—	—	—
	—	—	—	—	—	—	—	—	—	—	—	—
	—	—	—	—	—	—	—	—	—	—	—	—
	4.3	0.09	645.1	0.5	50.0	11.8	4.7	11.2	0.2	—	—	2.0
	11.0	—	—	—	—	—	—	—	—	—	—	—
	4.8	—	—	—	—	—	—	—	—	—	—	—
	—	0.05	962.0	0.2	23.0	9.7	4.7	2.0	0.1	—	—	—
	—	—	—	—	—	—	—	—	—	—	—	—
	45.9	0.47	1357.0	2.4	330.0	25.2	14.6	2.0	24.7	—	—	66.7
	74.3	0.09	1111.3	0.5	35.0	9.9	5.0	1.0	3.2	—	—	9.6
	90.3	—	1018.0	0.2	17.0	3.9	0.4	0.6	0.7	—	—	4.0
	61.0	0.68	1383.0	—	560.0	51.4	30.9	2.0	22.1	—	—	100.0
	—	—	—	—	—	—	—	—	—	—	—	—
	80.2	0.06	479.0	0.7	16.2	8.5	2.9	1.0	4.2	—	—	17.0
	46.4	—	301.2	—	25.2	7.7	—	2.0	—	—	—	—
	7.4	—	6110.5	—	—	—	—	4.0	—	—	—	—
	79.5	0.29	762.0	0.2	51.8	11.3	6.0	1.0	4.7	—	—	—
	34.8	0.36	2915.0	0.7	31.0	18.2	6.7	3.2	6.7	—	—	—
	34.8	0.36	3054.0	0.8	24.0	16.4	5.5	3.3	3.4	—	—	2.0
	3.7	—	2.0	—	5.5	3.8	—	0.8	0.4	—	—	—
	—	—	—	—	—	—	—	—	—	—	—	—
	28.1	0.32	2688.9	3.9	24.4	17.4	—	2.9	—	—	—	—
	34.7	0.78	2420.2	—	46.1	15.2	—	3.0	—	—	—	—
	99.9	—	—	—	—	—	—	—	—	—	—	—
	26.2	—	808.9	—	148.7	—	—	2.6	—	—	—	—
	27.3	—	3923.3	—	261.9	43.9	14.8	2.6	—	—	—	12.0
	9.1	2.49	—	6.9	544.0	77.9	10.0	90.3	7.7	—	—	—
	—	0.32	14373.0	0.9	80.0	4.1	2.2	13.4	2.2	—	—	—
	31.9	—	—	—	—	—	—	6.7	12.3	—	—	—
	—	—	—	—	—	—	—	—	—	—	—	—
	—	—	—	—	—	—	—	—	—	—	—	—
	—	—	—	—	—	—	—	—	—	—	—	—
	—	—	—	—	—	—	—	2.7	3.1	19.2	—	—
	60.2	0.42	1382.6	2.0	221.0	31.4	11.6	4.0	9.4	—	—	20.0
	81.7	—	1076.0	0.1	14.0	7.7	1.2	0.6	2.6	—	—	2.6
	79.9	—	1102.3	0.1	29.4	7.0	1.0	0.6	2.1	—	—	—
	54.4	0.24	3465.3	2.4	77.0	21.0	11.3	6.0	25.8	—	—	159.7
	78.4	0.11	1032.0	0.5	65.8	12.7	4.2	1.0	4.8	—	—	17.4
	76.9	0.13	1152.6	0.5	65.0	11.0	5.8	1.0	4.8	—	—	14.4
	76.7	0.12	1133.2	0.4	59.7	11.4	3.4	1.0	4.8	—	—	12.5
	72.4	—	979.7	0.5	65.4	12.7	—	1.0	—	—	—	—
	80.5	—	1008.9	0.5	60.4	11.4	3.6	1.0	5.1	—	—	17.5

TABLE 7—*Continued*

Entry Number	COMMON NAME *Genus species* Short name	International Feed Number[a]	Dry Matter (%)	ME (kcal/kg)	Protein (%)	Ether Extract (%)	Crude Fiber (%)	Cellulose (%)	Ash (%)
135	grain, soft white winter	4-05-337	89	3756.0	11.5	1.7	2.6	—	1.8
136	grits	4-07-852	90	3616.0	12.7	1.0	0.4	—	0.5
137	mill run, lt 9.5% fiber	4-05-206	90	2900.0	16.7	4.6	9.1	—	5.7
138	red dog, lt 4.5% fiber	4-05-203	88	3261.0	17.8	3.8	3.3	26.4	2.8
139	shorts, lt 7.0% fiber	4-05-201	88	3246.0	18.7	5.2	7.2	—	5.0
140	middlings, lt 9.5% fiber	4-05-205	88	3200.0	17.6	4.5	8.5	—	5.5
	WHEAT DURUM *Triticum durum*								
141	grain	4-05-224	88	3492.0	15.6	2.0	2.6	—	1.9
	WHEY *Bos taurus*								
142	dehy	4-01-182	93	3337.0	12.9	0.8	0.2	0.3	10.4
143	low lactose, dehy (dried whey product)	4-01-186	91	2915.0	17.0	1.1	0.2	—	16.5
	YEAST *Saccharomyces cerevisiae*								
144	brewers, dehy	7-05-527	93	3078.0	47.7	1.0	3.2	—	7.0
145	primary, dehy	7-05-533	93	—	51.8	1.1	3.3	—	8.6
	YEAST *Candida utilis*								
146	petroleum, solv extd, dehy	7-09-836	92	—	51.1	—	—	—	—
	YEAST *Torulopsis utilis*								
147	torula, dehy	7-05-534	93	2597.0	50.8	1.7	2.7	—	8.6

[a]First digit is class of feed: 1. dry forages and roughages; 2. pasture, range plants, and forages fed green; 3. silages; 4. energy feeds; 5. protein supplements; 6. mineral vitamins; 8. additives.

[b]Kendall (1985).

ry nber	Nitrogen-Free Extract (%)	Biotin (mg/kg)	Choline (mg/kg)	Folic Acid (mg/kg)	Niacin (mg/kg)	Panto-thenic Acid (mg/kg)	Pryri-doxine (mg/kg)	Ribo-flavin (mg/kg)	Thiamin (mg/kg)	Vitamin A (mg/kg)	Vitamin D (IU/kg)	Vitamin E (mg/kg)
	82.3	0.12	1097.0	0.4	68.3	12.3	5.3	1.3	5.3	—	—	34.2
	85.4	—	—	—	—	—	7.8	1.0	—	—	—	—
	63.9	0.34	1118.0	1.2	129.0	15.2	12.3	2.0	17.0	—	—	33.8
	72.3	0.12	1647.6	0.9	52.1	15.0	6.3	2.0	25.9	—	—	42.4
	63.9	—	1119.8	1.7	119.0	24.8	8.2	4.0	21.7	—	—	40.7
	65.9	—	—	—	—	—	—	—	—	—	—	20.0
	77.9	—	—	0.4	50.6	10.1	3.4	1.1	7.3	—	—	—
	76.6	0.38	1921.0	0.9	11.4	49.6	3.4	29.4	4.3	0.2	—	0.2
	65.2	0.54	4387.3	1.0	19.0	79.8	4.8	50.0	5.4	—	—	—
	41.1	1.12	4133.9	10.4	476.4	87.6	39.4	36.0	99.2	—	—	2.3
	35.1	1.74	—	33.6	324.7	336.9	—	41.0	—	—	—	—
	—	—	—	—	—	—	—	—	—	—	—	—
	36.2	1.26	3184.2	27.6	547.2	112.2	37.1	53.0	6.6	—	—	—

TABLE 8 Mineral Composition of Some Common Cat Feeds on a Dry Basis (moisture-free)

Entry Number	COMMON NAME *Genus species* Short name	International Feed Number[a] (%)	Dry Matter (%)	Calcium (%)	Phosphorus (%)	Magnesium (%)	Sodium (%)	Potassium (%)	Chlorine (%)	Copper (mg/kg)	Iodine (mg/kg)	Iron (mg/kg)	Manganese (mg/kg)	Selenium (mg/kg)	Sulfur (%)	Zinc (mg/kg)
	BARLEY, *Hordeum vulgare*															
001	grain	4-00-549	89	0.03	0.40	0.16	0.04	0.54	0.17	11.2	0.05	56.2	18.1	0.18	0.17	44.4
002	grain, Pacific Coast	4-07-939	89	0.06	0.36	0.14	0.02	0.60	0.17	9.0	—	123.6	18.0	0.11	0.16	17.1
	BLOOD, ANIMAL															
003	fresh	5-26-007	—	—	—	—	—	—	—	—	—	—	—	—	—	—
004	meal, spray dehy	5-00-381	93	0.31	0.24	0.22	0.33	0.11	0.27	8.8	—	4000.0	6.9	—	0.37	350.0
	BONE, ANIMAL															
005	meal, steamed	6-00-400	96	28.9	13.4	0.57	0.42	0.19	0.01	16.1	—	1072.6	38.8	—	0.36	380.7
006	phosphate	6-00-406	98	24.3	18.8	0.01	0.02	0.02	—	5.4	—	411.0	20.5	—	0.05	165.3
	BREAD *Triticum aestivum*															
007	dehy (wheat)	4-07-944	95	0.16	0.16	0.04	0.89	0.16	1.46	2.5	—	27.9	—	—	1.30	13.1
	BUTTERMILK *Bos taurus*															
008	dehy	5-01-160	92	1.44	1.01	0.52	0.90	0.16	0.48	1.1	—	9.1	3.8	0.13	0.09	44.0
	CANOLA *Brassica napus-Brassica campestris*															
009	seeds, meal prepressed solv extd, low erucic acid, low glucosinolates	5-06-145	93	0.74	1.30	0.61	0.01	1.19	—	85.0	—	93.6	54.2	1.00	1.35	80.8
	CASEIN															
010	dehy, *see*	5-01-162	93	0.67	0.93	0.01	0.01	0.01	—	4.5	—	19.0	4.1	—	—	35.1
	CATTLE, *see* HAMBURGER															
011	chucks, fresh	5-17-896	39	0.03	0.48	—	1.66	0.91	—	—	—	71.4	—	—	—	—
012	lips, fresh	5-07-940	30	—	—	—	—	—	—	—	—	—	—	—	—	—
013	livers, fresh	5-01-166	28	0.04	0.82	0.04	0.35	0.72	—	22.0	0.31	165.0	10.0	—	—	95.0
014	lungs, fresh	5-07-941	24	0.06	0.69	0.03	0.69	0.33	—	5.0	—	322.0	0.0	0.35	—	55.0
015	spleens, fresh	5-07-942	24	0.02	1.13	0.05	0.58	0.91	—	1.0	0.76	1691.0	—	—	—	81.0
016	tripe	5-09-806	33	0.44	0.40	0.02	0.15	0.11	—	3.4	—	3.2	15.3	—	—	33.8
017	udders, fresh	5-07-943	20	2.62	1.37	0.08	0.58	0.79	—	3.0	—	102.0	3.0	0.54	—	104.0
	CHICKEN, *see* POULTRY															
	CORN, DENT YELLOW *Zea mays indentata*															
018	distillers grains, w soluble dehy	5-28-236	93	0.15	0.73	0.18	0.57	0.44	0.18	58.0	—	259.0	25.0	0.42	0.33	91.0
019	distillers solubles, dehy	5-28-237	92	0.33	1.58	0.65	0.25	1.80	0.28	89.0	0.12	610.0	80.0	0.36	0.40	92.0
020	germ, meal wet milled solv extd	5-28-240	92	0.04	0.55	0.17	0.04	0.38	0.04	5.0	—	370.0	4.0	0.37	0.33	114.0
021	gluten, meal, 60%	5-28-242	90	0.03	0.49	0.17	0.05	0.22	0.08	5.0	0.02	254.0	7.0	0.92	0.64	40.0
022	grain, flaked	4-28-244	90	0.02	—	0.04	—	—	—	—	—	39.2	4.1	—	—	12.8
023	hominy feed	4-03-011	90	0.03	0.57	0.20	0.11	0.65	0.07	14.8	—	111.2	16.6	0.17	0.14	36.8
024	grain	4-02-935	89	0.02	0.31	0.14	0.01	0.36	0.04	3.0	—	25.0	5.1	0.04	0.13	13.0
	COTTON *Gossypium* spp															
025	seeds, meal prepressed solv extd, 41% protein	5-07-872	90	0.17	1.18	0.53	0.04	1.38	0.07	20.0	—	189.7	22.5	1.00	0.34	69.4
026	seeds, meal solv extd, 41% protein	5-01-621	91	0.18	1.21	0.59	0.05	1.52	0.05	21.4	—	206.3	23.0	1.00	0.29	68.0
027	seeds wo hulls, meal prepressed solv extd, 50% protein	5-07-874	93	0.19	1.24	0.50	0.06	1.56	0.05	16.0	—	120.0	25.0	—	0.56	79.4

Entry	Description	Ref. No.														
	Paralithodes camschatica															
028	cannery residue, meal	5-01-663	92	15.7	1.72	1.02	0.95	0.49	1.63	35.5	0.06	4719.0	144.0	4.00	0.27	107.4
	FISH, ALEWIFE *Pomolobus pseudoharengus*															
029	meal mech extd	5-09-830	90	5.49	3.06	0.16	0.25	0.63	—	19.0	—	654.0	21.1	1.9	—	111.1
030	whole, fresh	5-07-964	25.8	—	0.85	—	—	—	—	—	—	—	—	—	—	—
	FISH, ANCHOVY *Engraulis ringen*															
031	meal mech extd	5-01-985	92	4.08	2.70	0.27	0.95	0.78	1.08	10.0	3.41	233.5	12.0	1.47	0.84	114.0
	FISH, CARP *Cyprinus carpio*															
032	meal mech extd	5-01-987	90	—	—	—	—	—	—	—	—	—	—	—	—	—
033	whole, fresh	5-01-986	31	0.23	1.14	1.14	0.23	1.29	—	40.0	—	—	—	—	—	—
	FISH, CATFISH *Ictalurus* spp															
034	meal mech extd	5-09-835	94	7.77	—	—	—	—	—	28.0	—	—	—	—	—	—
035	whole, fresh	5-07-965	22	—	—	—	—	—	—	—	—	—	—	—	—	—
	FISH, COD *Gadus morrhua-Gadus macrocephalus*															
036	meal mech extd	5-01-992	86	—	—	—	—	—	—	—	—	—	—	—	—	—
	FISH, FLOUNDER Bothidae (family)-Pleuronectidae (family)															
037	whole, fresh	5-01-996	17	—	—	—	—	—	—	—	—	—	—	—	—	—
	FISH, HADDOCK *Melanogrammus aeglefinus*															
038	whole, fresh	5-07-966	20	0.10	0.91	0.12	0.64	1.60	0.86	10.2	—	32.1	—	—	1.18	16.0
	FISH, HAKE *Merluccius* spp-*Urophycis* spp															
039	whole, boiled	5-07-967	26	—	—	—	—	—	—	—	—	—	—	—	—	—
040	whole, boiled acidified	5-07-968	25	—	—	—	—	—	—	—	—	—	—	—	—	—
041	whole, fresh	5-07-969	20	3.06	1.93	—	—	—	—	—	—	—	—	—	—	—
	FISH, HERRING *Clupea harengus*															
042	meal mech extd	5-02-000	93	2.40	1.82	0.16	0.65	1.18	1.08	6.1	0.57	124.5	5.2	2.13	0.50	135.8
043	whole, fresh	5-01-999	29	0.09	0.89	0.36	0.36	2.04	0.21	3.3	—	42.7	—	—	0.53	13.9
	FISH, MACKEREL ATLANTIC *Scomber scombrus*															
044	whole, fresh	5-07-971	28	3.64	1.83	0.10	0.56	0.55	—	2.9	0.76	149.8	—	—	—	78.0
	FISH, MACKEREL *Scomber japonicus*															
045	Pacific, whole, fresh	5-07-972	30	0.07	0.67	0.08	0.36	1.00	0.27	5.3	—	27.8	—	—	0.50	13.9
	FISH, MENHADEN *Brevoortia tyrannus*															
046	meal mech extd	5-02-009	92	5.67	3.14	0.17	0.75	0.77	0.60	11.3	1.19	500.0	40.4	2.34	0.61	157.5
	FISH, REDFISH *Sciaenops ocellata*															
047	meal mech extd	5-07-973	93	6.96	3.64	—	0.11	0.32	—	—	—	—	8.3	1.90	—	—
	FISH, ROCKFISH *Sebastodes* spp															
048	whole, fresh	5-07-974	21	—	—	—	—	—	—	—	—	—	—	—	—	—
	FISH, SALMON *Oncorhynchus* spp-*Salmo* spp															
049	meal mech extd	5-02-012	94	5.88	3.72	—	—	—	—	12.8	—	193.0	8.5	1.91	—	—
050	whole, fresh	5-02-011	32	0.22	0.68	0.07	0.11	1.12	0.16	27.0	—	19.4	—	—	0.47	22.2
	FISH, SARDINE *Clupea* spp-*Sardinops* spp															
051	meal mech extd	5-02-015	93	4.95	2.88	0.11	0.19	0.35	0.44	22.0	—	321.0	25.0	1.90	0.33	—
	FISH, SMELT *Osmerus* spp															
052	whole, fresh	5-07-975	21	—	1.29	—	—	—	—	—	—	—	—	—	—	—
	FISH, SOLE Soleidae (family)															
053	whole, fresh	5-07-976	20	3.19	2.00	—	—	—	—	—	—	—	—	—	—	—

TABLE 8—Continued

Entry Number	International Feed Number[a] (%)	COMMON NAME, *Genus species* / Short name	Dry Matter (%)	Calcium (%)	Phosphorus (%)	Magnesium (%)	Sodium (%)	Potassium (%)	Chlorine (%)	Copper (mg/kg)	Iodine (mg/kg)	Iron (mg/kg)	Manganese (mg/kg)	Selenium (mg/kg)	Sulfur (%)	Zinc (mg/kg)
		FISH, TUNA *Thunnus thynnus-Thunnus albacares*														
054	5-07-977	cannery residue	61	—	—	—	—	—	—	—	—	—	—	—	—	—
055	5-02-023	meal mech extd	93	8.48	4.54	0.25	0.80	0.77	1.09	11.0	—	383.0	9.0	4.64	0.73	227.0
		FISH, TURBOT *Psetta maxima*														
056	5-07-978	whole, fresh	25	1.25	0.88	—	—	—	—	—	—	—	—	—	—	—
		FISH, WHITE Gadidae (family)-Lophidae (family)-Rajidae (family)														
057	5-02-025	meal mech extd	91	7.25	4.37	0.20	0.51	0.49	0.55	4.5	—	280.5	10.5	1.77	0.53	75.9
		FISH, WHITING *Gadus merlangus*														
058	5-07-979	whole, fresh	24	—	—	—	—	—	—	—	—	—	—	—	—	—
		FISH														
059	5-01-968	livers, meal mech extd	93	—	—	—	—	—	—	—	—	—	—	—	—	—
060	5-17-891	racks, dehy grnd (bone with heads)	—	—	—	—	—	—	—	—	—	—	—	—	—	—
061	5-01-969	solubles, condensed	51	0.32	1.14	0.06	4.86	3.24	5.81	92.4	—	547.5	26.2	3.9	0.25	85.6
062	5-01-971	solubles, dehy	92	1.09	1.36	0.81	1.12	1.55	—	21.5	—	1019.4	32.5	2.9	0.48	310.1
		FLAX *Linum usitatissimum*														
063	5-02-048	seeds, meal solv extd (linseed meal)	90	0.43	0.89	0.66	0.15	1.53	0.04	29.0	—	354.0	42.0	0.91	0.43	—
064	4-02-891	glucose	90	—	—	—	—	—	—	—	—	—	—	—	—	—
		HAMBURGER *Bos taurus*														
065	5-17-899	fresh 10% fat (cattle)	32	0.04	0.61	0.04	1.30	0.59	1.74	5.4	—	97.8	—	—	0.35	69.6
066	5-17-897	fresh 20% fat (cattle)	40	0.03	0.39	—	1.68	0.72	—	—	—	67.8	—	—	—	—
		HOMINY FEED, *see* CORN, hominy														
		HORSE *Equus caballus*														
067	5-07-980	meat, fresh	31	0.07	1.06	0.04	0.18	0.38	—	0.20	0.29	167.0	0.5	—	—	60.0
068	5-07-981	meat w bone, fresh	36	—	—	—	—	—	—	—	—	—	—	—	—	—
		KELP, *see* SEAWEED, KELP														
		LINSEED, *see* FLAX														
		LIVER, ANIMAL														
069	5-00-389	meal dehy	92	0.61	1.36	0.11	—	—	—	96.5	—	681.0	9.5	—	—	66.8
		MEAT, ANIMAL														
070	5-00-385	meal rendered	92	8.0	4.1	0.32	1.60	0.58	1.18	10.2	—	522.8	12.6	0.54	0.55	79.2
071	5-00-387	w blood, w bone meal (tankage) rendered	93	12.01	5.82	—	—	—	—	—	—	—	—	0.28	0.28	—
072	5-00-388	w bone, meal rendered	93	8.7	4.4	1.09	0.77	1.43	0.80	1.6	1.41	699.9	14.3	0.28	0.50	101.1
		MILK *Bos taurus*														
073	5-01-167	dehy, cattle	96	0.93	0.74	0.09	0.39	1.12	1.55	1.0	—	8300.0	0.5	0.32	0.32	22.8
074	5-08-001	cottage cheese	21	0.43	0.85	—	1.38	0.34	—	—	—	18.9	—	—	—	—
075	5-01-168	fresh (cattle)	12	0.93	0.75	0.10	0.38	0.13	0.92	0.8	—	—	—	—	—	23.0
076	5-01-170	skimmed fresh (cattle)	10	1.31	1.04	0.12	0.47	1.29	0.54	11.6	—	—	2.3	—	0.32	51.0
077	5-01-175	skimmed dehy (cattle)	94	1.36	1.09	0.13	0.54	1.70	0.96	12.4	—	40.0	2.3	0.13	0.34	40.9
078	5-01-177	whey albumin (cattle)	92	11.8	4.37	—	—	—	—	—	—	—	—	—	—	—
		MILLET, FOXTAIL *Setaria italica*														
079	4-03-102	grain	89	—	0.46	—	—	0.35	—	—	—	107.5	—	—	—	—

No.	Feed Name	Ref. No.	%													
080	beet sugar, molasses mt 48%	4-00-668	78	0.16	0.03	0.29	1.48	6.07	1.64	21.6	—	87.4	5.8	—	0.60	18.0
081	invert sugar mt 79.5 degrees brix,	4-04-695	94	1.10	0.45	0.47	0.20	3.60	—	79.4	2.10	250.0	57.3	—	0.46	33.0
082	sugar cane, molasses, mt 46% invert, sugar mt 79.5 degrees brix, blackstrap	4-04-696	75	1.00	0.11	0.43	0.22	4.01	3.04	65.7	2.10	263.5	58.8	—	0.47	20.9
	OATS *Avena sativa*															
083	cereal by-product, IH 4% fiber (feeding oat meal) (oat middlings)	4-03-303	91	0.08	0.48	0.16	0.10	0.55	0.06	5.7	—	421.0	48.0	—	0.24	154.0
084	grain	4-03-309	89	0.09	0.38	0.16	0.06	0.45	0.10	6.7	0.11	71.6	40.1	0.24	0.23	39.2
085	groats	4-03-331	90	0.08	0.48	0.13	0.06	0.39	0.09	6.7	0.12	82.0	31.0	—	0.22	0.1
086	hulls	1-03-281	92	0.15	0.15	0.09	0.04	0.62	0.08	4.5	—	110.6	20.4	—	0.15	—
	PEA *Pisum* spp															
087	seeds	5-03-600	90	0.14	0.46	0.14	0.05	1.06	0.06	—	—	72.4	3.2	—	—	25.7
	PEANUT *Arachis hypogaea*															
088	kernals, meal solv extd (peanut meal)	5-03-650	93	0.39	0.66	0.30	0.03	1.25	0.03	17.0	0.07	154.0	29.0	—	0.33	22.0
	POTATO *Solanum tuberosum*															
089	tubers, dehy	4-07-850	91	0.08	0.22	0.12	0.01	2.16	0.40	—	—	—	2.5	—	0.09	2.2
	POULTRY, CHICKEN *Gallus domesticus*															
090	heads, fresh	5-07-949	33	—	—	—	—	—	—	—	—	—	—	—	—	—
091	broilers, whole fresh	5-07-945	24	0.04	0.82	—	—	—	—	—	—	81.0	—	—	—	—
092	eggs, fresh whole	5-01-213	30	22.20	0.33	—	—	—	—	—	—	—	—	—	—	—
093	eggs, fresh white	5-01-210	13	0.08	0.08	0.08	1.27	1.15	—	—	—	2.5	—	—	—	1.7
094	feet fresh	5-07-947	33	6.45	2.33	0.10	0.38	0.26	—	2.1	0.37	96.0	1.7	—	—	48.6
095	gizzards fresh	5-07-948	25	0.04	0.42	0.26	0.96	0.66	—	—	—	116.0	—	—	—	—
096	by-product fresh (viscera with feet and heads)	5-07-951	—	—	—	—	—	—	—	—	—	—	—	—	—	—
097	by-product meal rendered (viscera with feet and heads)	5-03-798	93	3.76	1.96	0.19	0.35	0.7	0.4	15.0	3.31	473.0	12.0	0.83	0.56	129.0
098	hens, whole fresh	5-07-950	33	0.03	0.59	0.22	0.83	0.31	—	—	—	—	—	—	—	—
099	viscera	5-07-985	26	—	—	—	—	—	—	—	—	—	—	—	—	—
	POULTRY FEATHERS															
100	hydrolyzed meal	5-03-795	93	0.33	0.67	0.19	0.68	0.29	0.30	7.9	0.05	242.0	12.9	0.98	1.61	77.3
101	**PROPYLENE GLYCOL**	8-03-809	100	—	—	—	—	—	—	—	—	—	—	—	—	—
	RICE *Oryza sativa*															
102	bran w germ (rice bran)	4-03-928	91	0.08	1.59	0.94	0.04	1.87	0.08	12.1	—	206.6	372.4	0.44	0.20	41.3
103	grain	4-03-939	89	0.06	0.27	0.15	0.02	0.62	0.09	5.8	—	141.5	70.1	—	0.05	24.4
104	groats polished	4-03-942	89	0.03	0.13	0.02	0.02	0.12	0.04	3.0	—	16.0	12.0	—	0.09	2.0
105	polishings	4-03-943	90	0.05	1.49	0.66	0.05	1.41	0.12	8.8	—	89.8	140.5	—	0.19	70.0
	RYE *Secale cereale*															
106	grain	4-04-047	88	0.07	0.36	0.12	0.03	0.51	0.03	8.6	—	71.8	82.3	0.44	0.17	32.2
	SEAWEED, KELP Laminariales (Order)-Fucales (Order)															
107	whole, dehy	1-08-073	91	2.72	0.27	0.93	4.60	1.42	—	6.9	—	980.3	1352.7	0.44	—	38.3
	SESAME *Sesamum indicum*															
108	seeds, meal mech extd	5-04-220	93	2.17	1.46	0.50	0.04	1.35	0.07	—	—	100.0	52.0	—	0.35	107.5
	SHRIMP *Pandalus* spp-*Penaeus* spp															
109	canary residue meal (shrimp meal)	5-04-226	90	9.0	2.06	0.60	1.74	0.92	1.15	—	—	116.0	33.0	—	—	31.5
	SORGHUM *Sorghum bicolor*															
110	grain	4-04-383	90	0.06	0.35	0.15	0.03	0.39	0.08	10.8	0.04	66.6	10.9	0.50	0.15	47.1

TABLE 8—Continued

Entry Number	COMMON NAME, *Genus species* Short name	International Feed Number[a] (%)	Dry Matter (%)	Calcium (%)	Phosphorus (%)	Magnesium (%)	Sodium (%)	Potassium (%)	Chlorine (%)	Copper (mg/kg)	Iodine (mg/kg)	Iron (mg/kg)	Manganese (mg/kg)	Selenium (mg/kg)	Sulfur (%)	Zinc (mg/kg)
	SOYBEAN *Glycine max*															
111	seeds, meal solv extd	5-04-604	89	0.27	0.72	0.32	0.04	2.30	0.04	20.0	0.15	156.9	34.2	0.48	0.47	57.9
112	seeds hulls, meal solv extd	5-04-612	90	0.22	0.71	0.33	0.02	2.36	0.05	22.5	0.12	145.0	41.3	0.11	0.48	63.5
113	protein flour concentrate, more than 70% protein	5-08-038	93	0.06	0.74	0.02	0.13	0.01	0.02	15.4	0.35	84.7	6.0	0.15	0.76	32.3
114	flour oil residue, solvent extd	5-04-593	93	0.30	0.70	0.27	0.001	2.04	0.22	15.8	—	154.4	32.4	0.30	0.44	33.1
115	isolate (90% protein)	5-24-811	96	—	—	—	—	—	—	—	—	—	—	—	—	—
116	seeds, heat processed	5-04-597	90	0.21	0.66	0.23	0.03	1.89	—	—	—	—	—	—	—	—
117	SUCROSE	4-06-176	99	—	—	—	—	—	—	—	—	—	—	—	—	—
	SUNFLOWER *Helianthus* spp															
118	seeds wo hulls, meal mech extd	5-04-738	93	0.43	1.15	0.72	0.04	1.29	0.18	19.5	—	96.2	21.7	1.91	0.22	100.9
119	seeds wo hulls, meal solv extd	5-04-739	93	0.45	1.01	0.74	0.04	1.29	0.17	22.3	—	117.1	20.4	2.3	0.23	105.5
	SWINE *Sus scrofa*															
120	livers, fresh	5-04-792	30	0.04	0.85	1.22	0.24	0.85	—	187.0	1.12	480.0	6.0	1.12	—	146.0
121	lungs, fresh	5-26-140	16	0.05	0.39	1.05	—	0.96	0.04	0.0	0.82	475.0	—	—	—	68.0
	TOMATO *Lycopersicon esculentum*															
122	pomace dehy	5-05-041	92	0.43	0.60	0.20	—	3.63	—	32.6	—	4600.0	51.0	—	—	—
	TURKEY *Meleagris gallopavo*															
123	mature birds, offal, fresh	5-07-984	—	—	—	—	—	—	—	—	—	—	—	—	—	—
124	young birds, offal, fresh	5-07-985	—	—	—	—	—	—	—	—	—	—	—	—	—	—
125	viscera, fresh	5-08-616	31	—	—	—	—	—	—	—	—	—	—	—	—	—
	WHALE *Balaena glacialis-Balaenoptera* spp-*Physeter caladon*															
126	meat fresh	5-07-986	29	0.03	0.48	—	0.28	0.07	0.06	—	0.07	—	—	—	—	—
	WHEAT *Triticum aestivum*															
127	bran	4-05-190	90	0.14	1.31	0.64	0.03	1.37	0.06	15.0	0.07	180.0	129.0	0.72	0.24	106.2
128	flour, hard red spring	4-08-113	89	0.04	0.28	0.11	0.01	0.23	0.11	0.7	0.10	4.2	4.1	0.34	0.25	6.7

#	Feed	IFN														
129	flour, lt 2% fiber	4-05-199	88	0.04	0.33	0.06	0.01	0.06	0.10	1.0	0.10	6.0	4.0	0.17	0.24	7.0
130	germ meal	5-05-218	88	0.06	1.07	0.28	0.03	1.06	0.07	10.4	—	66.2	149.9	0.52	0.30	135.1
131	grain	4-05-211	89	0.06	0.39	0.15	0.03	0.55	0.08	6.5	0.10	57.6	60.0	0.2	0.20	20.0
132	grain, hard red spring	4-05-258	88	0.05	0.42	0.16	0.02	0.41	0.09	6.8	—	64.3	42.2	0.30	0.17	43.3
133	grain, hard red winter	4-05-268	87	0.05	0.42	0.13	0.02	0.49	0.06	5.7	—	39.2	34.3	0.33	0.15	39.8
134	grain, screenings	4-05-216	89	0.14	0.38	0.24	0.05	0.91	—	2.6	—	131.0	32.5	0.68	0.22	43.9
135	grain, soft red winter	4-05-294	88	0.06	0.40	0.11	0.01	0.46	0.08	8.0	—	32.8	37.8	0.05	0.12	47.7
136	grain, soft white winter	4-05-337	89	0.07	0.44	0.13	0.02	0.46	0.09	7.8	—	40.0	40.0	0.05	0.13	30.0
137	grits	4-07-852	90	0.03	0.12	—	0.00	0.09	—	—	—	16.7	—	—	—	—
138	mill run, lt 9.5% fiber	4-05-206	90	0.07	1.13	0.53	0.24	1.34	—	20.6	—	105.4	115.8	—	0.34	—
139	red dog, lt 4.5% fiber	4-05-203	88	0.06	0.60	0.21	0.02	0.59	0.14	7.1	—	52.2	59.1	0.37	0.25	73.7
140	shorts, lt 7.0% fiber	4-05-201	88	0.10	0.91	0.31	0.03	1.09	0.06	13.0	—	83.1	129.1	0.54	0.23	115.9
141	middlings, lt 9.5% fiber	4-05-205	89	0.07	1.0	0.40	0.03	1.3	0.03	20.0	—	65.0	45.0	0.7	0.20	60.0
142	WHEAT DURUM *Triticum durum* grain	4-05-224	88	0.11	0.41	0.18	—	0.50	—	7.8	—	47.6	35.0	1.02	—	22.0
143	WHEY *Bos taurus* dehy (cattle)	4-01-182	93	1.00	0.82	0.14	0.66	1.19	0.08	49.9	—	181.1	6.3	0.06	1.11	3.4
144	low lactose, dehy (dried whey product) (cattle)	4-01-186	93	1.60	1.18	0.23	1.54	3.16	1.10	7.5	10.55	262.0	8.6	0.06	1.15	8.4
145	YEAST *Saccharomyces cerevisiae* brewers dehy	7-05-527	93	0.15	1.47	0.26	0.08	1.82	0.08	41.3	0.36	89.7	7.2	0.98	0.46	41.9
146	primary dehy	7-05-533	93	0.39	1.86	0.39	—	—	0.02	—	—	324.0	4.0	—	0.62	—
147	YEAST *Candida utilis* petroleum solv extd dehy	7-09-836	92	0.02	5.87	—	—	4.02	—	—	—	—	—	—	—	—
148	YEAST *Torulopsis utilis* torula dehy	7-05-534	93	0.59	1.73	0.15	0.12	2.06	0.09	35.0	2.69	15.0	6.0	0.05	0.59	45.0

[a]First digit is class of feed: 1. dry forages and roughages; 2. pasture, range plants, and forages fed green; 3. silages; 4. energy feeds; 5. protein supplements; 6. minerals; 7. vitamins; 8. additives.

TABLE 9   Common Mineral Sources for Cats

Mineral	Source	Chemical Formula	Mineral Content[a]			
Calcium	Calcium carbonate		40 % Ca	0.02 % Na		
	Limestone		38 % Ca	0.05 % Na	0.01 % F	
Calcium and phosphorus	Bone meal		24 % Ca	12.6 % P	0.37 % Na	0.05 % F
	Phosphate, curacao		36 % Ca	14 % P	0.3 % Na	0.54 % F
	defluorinated		30–34 % Ca	18 % P	5.7 % Na	0.16 % F
	dicalcium		18–24 % Ca	18.5 % P	0.6 % Na	0.14 % F
	mono and dicalcium		16–19 % Ca	21 % P	0.6 % Na	0.20 % F
	soft rock		17 % Ca	9 % P	0.1 % Na	1.2 % F
	sodium tripoly		0	25 % P	31.2 % Na	0.03 % F
Sodium and chlorine	Sodium chloride		39.3 % Na	60.7 % Cl		
Iron	Ferrous sulfate	$FeSO_4\ H_2O$	32.9 % Fe			
	Ferrous sulfate	$FeSO_4\ 7H_2O$	20.1 % Fe			
	Ferric ammonium citrate		16.5–18.5 % Fe			
	Ferrous fumarate	$FeC_4\ H_2O_4$	32.9 % Fe			
	Ferric chloride	$FeCl_3\ 6H_2O$	20.7 % Fe			
	Ferrous carbonate	$FeCO_3$	48.2 % Fe			
	Ferric oxide	Fe_2O_3	69.9 % Fe			
	Ferrous oxide	FeO	77.8 % Fe			
Copper	Cupric carbonate	$CuCO_3\ Cu(OH)_2$	57.5 % Cu			
	Cupric chloride	$CuCl_2\ 2H_2O$	37.3 % Cu			
	Cupric hydroxide	$Cu(OH)_2$	65.1 % Cu			
	Cupric oxide	CuO	79.9 % Cu			
	Cupric sulfate	$CuSO_4\ 5H_2O$	25.4 % Cu			
Manganese	Manganese carbonate	$MnCO_3$	47.8 % Mn			
	Manganous chloride	$MnCl_2\ 4H_2O$	27.8 % Mn			
	Manganous oxide	MnO	77.4 % Mn			
	Manganese sulfate	$MnSO_4\ 5H_2O$	22.7 % Mn			
	Manganous sulfate	$MnSO_4\ H_2O$	32.5 % Mn			
Zinc	Zinc carbonate	$5ZnO\ 2CO_3\ 4H_2O$	56.0 % Zn			
	Zinc chloride	$ZnCl_2$	48.0 % Zn			
	Zinc oxide	ZnO	80.3 % Zn			
	Zinc sulfate	$ZnSO_4\ 7H_2O$	22.7 % Zn			
	Zinc sulfate	$ZnSO_4\ H_2O$	36.4 % Zn			
Iodine	Calcium iodate	$Ca(IO_3)_2$	65.1 % I			
	Potassium iodide	KI	76.4 % I			
	Cuprous iodide	CuI	66.6 % I			
	Penta calcium orthoperiodate	$Ca_3(IO_6)_2$	39.3 % I			
Selenium	Sodium selenite	Na_2SeO_3	45.6 % Se	26.6 % Na		
	Sodium selenate	Na_2SeO_4	41.8 % Se	24.3 % Na		

[a]Actual mineral levels in technical grade sources may vary.

TABLE 10 Amino Acid Composition of Some Common Cat Feeds on a Dry Basis (moisture-free)

Entry Number	COMMON NAME *Genus species* / Short name	International Feed Number	Dry Matter (%)	Crude Protein (%)	Arginine (%)	Glycine (%)	Histidine (%)	Iso-leucine (%)	Leucine (%)	Valine (%)	Lysine (%)	Methionine (%)	Cystine (%)	Phenylalanine (%)	Tyrosine (%)	Threonine (%)	Tryptophan (%)
	BARLEY *Hordeum vulgare*[a]																
001	grain	4-00-549[a]	89[b]	13.0	0.66	0.45	0.33	0.55	0.90	0.70	0.45	0.20	0.27	0.72	0.37	0.47	0.16
002	grain, Pacific Coast	4-07-939	89	10.1	0.54	0.40	0.24	0.45	0.67	0.52	0.33	0.15	0.20	0.54	0.34	0.34	0.14
	BLOOD, ANIMAL																
003	fresh	5-26-007	—	—	—	—	—	—	—	—	—	—	—	—	—	—	—
004	meal spray dehy	5-00-381	93[b]	95.6	4.10	4.20	5.66	0.95	12.71	9.25	7.50	1.08	1.18	7.04	2.68	4.24	1.44
	BONE, ANIMAL																
005	meal steamed	6-00-400	96	11.4	1.79	—	—	—	—	—	0.95	0.21	0.11	—	—	—	0.05
006	phosphate	6-00-406	98	—	—	—	—	—	—	—	—	—	—	—	—	—	—
	BREAD *Triticum aestivum*																
007	dehy (wheat)	4-07-944	95	13.0	—	—	—	—	—	—	0.22	0.19	0.19	—	—	—	—
	BUTTERMILK *Bos taurus*																
008	dehy	5-01-160	92	34.4	1.17	0.51	0.92	2.62	3.48	2.80	2.47	0.76	0.42	1.58	1.08	1.64	0.53
	CANOLA *Brassica napus-Brassica campestris*																
009	seeds, meal prepressed, solv extd, low erucic acid, low glucosinolates	5-06-146	93	40.9	2.49	2.02	1.15	1.62	2.85	2.09	2.63	0.73	0.51	1.63	1.00	1.84	0.47
	CASEIN																
010	dehy	5-01-162	93	93.8	3.88	1.93	2.99	5.18	9.68	6.95	8.59	2.85	0.23	5.33	5.77	4.61	1.13
	CATTLE *Bos taurus*																
011	chucks	5-17-896	39	47.7	—	—	—	—	—	—	—	—	—	—	—	—	—
012	lips, fresh	5-07-940	30	60.0	—	—	—	—	—	—	—	—	—	—	—	—	—
013	livers, fresh	5-01-166	28[c]	69.6	3.56	3.35	2.48	2.90	5.29	3.89	5.72	1.62	0.97	3.35	2.05	2.92	0.86
014	lungs, fresh	5-07-941	24	65.0	3.10	5.57	1.13	1.37	2.74	1.09	2.59	0.61	0.66	1.46	1.04	1.42	0.28
015	spleens, fresh	5-07-942	24	68.7	—	—	—	—	—	—	—	—	—	—	—	—	—
016	tripe, dressed (lime treated)	5-09-806	33[c]	46.1	5.50	8.13	2.25	3.12	5.25	3.88	6.25	1.88	1.00	3.00	2.25	3.38	1.00
017	udders, fresh	5-07-943	20	58.6	—	—	—	—	—	—	—	—	—	—	—	—	—
	CHICKEN, see POULTRY																
	CORN, DENT YELLOW *Zea mays indentata*																
018	distillers grains w solubles dehy	5-28-236	93	29.3	1.05	0.61	0.70	1.08	2.37	1.40	0.81	0.65	0.47	1.29	0.80	0.99	0.20
019	distillers solubles, dehy	5-28-237	92	31.0	1.14	1.20	0.76	1.36	2.29	1.51	0.98	0.54	0.44	1.41	1.03	1.09	0.32
020	germ, meal wet milled solv extd	5-28-240	92	22.6	1.43	1.20	0.76	0.76	1.97	1.31	0.98	0.64	0.44	0.98	0.76	1.19	0.21
021	gluten, meal, 60%	5-28-242	90	68.9	2.14	1.82	1.36	2.54	11.23	3.04	1.0	2.12	1.23	4.19	3.27	2.19	0.30
022	grain, flaked	4-28-244	90	11.2	0.49	0.40	0.31	0.31	1.40	0.53	0.28	0.17	0.28	0.50	0.44	0.39	0.11
023	hominy feed	4-03-011	90	11.1	0.52	0.44	0.22	0.44	0.93	0.54	0.44	0.14	0.14	0.39	0.54	0.44	0.10
024	grain	4-02-935	89	9.9	0.50	0.45	0.22	0.42	1.24	0.58	0.27	0.22	0.20	0.53	0.57	0.44	—
	COTTON, *Gossypium spp*																
025	seeds, meal prepressed solv extd, 41% protein	5-07-872	90	46.0	5.10	1.89	1.22	1.48	2.67	2.10	1.90	0.58	0.71	2.47	1.13	1.47	0.32
026	seeds, meal solv extd, 41% protein	5-01-621	91	45.4	4.66	2.14	1.22	1.65	2.70	2.17	1.86	0.64	0.84	2.46	1.15	1.51	0.60
027	seeds wo hulls, meal prepressed solv extd, 50% protein	5-07-874	93	54.0	5.20	3.03	1.30	2.00	3.03	2.32	2.08	0.81	1.13	2.81	0.87	1.78	0.67
	CRAB *Callinectes sapidus-Cancer spp-Paralithodes camschatica*																
028	cannery residue, meal	5-01-663	92	35.0	1.80	1.89	0.53	1.26	1.67	1.59	1.50	0.57	0.26	1.26	1.26	1.09	0.32
	FISH, ALEWIFE *Pomotobus pseudoharengus*																
029	meal mech extd	5-09-830	90	69.4	4.96	3.91	2.02	3.59	5.07	3.79	5.08	2.02	0.51	3.07	2.40	3.45	0.65
030	whole, fresh	5-07-964	26	75.8	—	—	—	—	—	—	—	—	—	—	—	—	—
	FISH, ANCHOVY *Engraulis ringen*																
031	meal mech extd	5-01-985	92	69.8	3.98	3.90	1.66	3.27	5.25	3.67	5.33	2.10	0.64	2.93	2.37	2.91	0.80
	FISH, CARP *Cyprinus carpio*																
032	meal mech extd	5-01-987	90	58.6	—	—	—	—	—	—	1.56	—	—	—	—	—	—
033	whole, fresh	5-01-986	31	61.9	—	—	—	—	—	—	—	—	—	—	—	—	—

64

TABLE 10—Continued

Entry Number	COMMON NAME Genus species Short name	International Feed Number	Dry Matter (%)	Crude Protein (%)	Arginine (%)	Glycine (%)	Histidine (%)	Isoleucine (%)	Leucine (%)	Valine (%)	Lysine (%)	Methionine (%)	Cystine (%)	Phenylalanine (%)	Tyrosine (%)	Threonine (%)	Tryptophan (%)
	FISH, CATFISH Ictalurus spp																
034	meal, mech extd	5-09-835	94	55.3	—	—	—	—	—	—	—	—	—	—	—	—	—
035	whole, fresh	5-07-965	22	—	—	—	—	—	—	—	—	—	—	—	—	—	—
	FISH, COD Gadus morrhua-Gadus macrocephalus																
036	meal mech extd	5-01-992	84	73.1	—	—	—	—	—	—	—	—	—	—	—	—	—
037	whole, fresh	5-01-988	—	—	—	—	—	—	—	—	—	—	—	—	—	—	—
	FISH, FLOUNDER Bothidae (family)-Pleuronectidae (family)																
038	whole, fresh	5-01-996	17	88.2	—	—	—	—	—	—	—	—	—	—	—	—	—
	FISH, HADDOCK Melanogrammus aeglefinus																
039	whole, fresh	5-07-966	20	93.8	—	—	—	—	—	—	—	—	—	—	—	—	—
	FISH, HAKE Merluccius spp-Urophycis spp																
040	whole, boiled	5-07-967	26	57.8	—	—	—	—	—	—	—	—	—	—	—	—	—
041	whole, boiled acidified	5-07-968	25	—	—	—	—	—	—	—	—	—	—	—	—	—	—
042	whole, fresh	5-07-969	20	59.6	—	—	—	—	—	—	—	—	—	—	—	—	—
	FISH, HERRING Clupea harengus																
043	meal mech extd	5-02-000	93	77.7	5.20	4.96	1.83	3.46	5.74	4.71	6.13	2.26	0.77	3.00	2.44	3.23	0.87
044	whole, fresh	5-01-999	29	63.1	—	—	—	—	—	—	—	—	—	—	—	—	—
	FISH, MACKEREL Scomber scombrus																
045	Atlantic, whole, fresh	5-07-971	28	48.7	—	—	—	—	—	—	—	—	—	—	—	—	—
	FISH, MACKEREL Scomber japonicus																
046	Pacific, whole, fresh	5-07-972	30	72.5	—	—	—	—	—	—	—	—	—	—	—	—	—
	FISH, MENHADEN Brevoortia tyrannus																
047	meal mech extd	5-02-009	92[b]	65.8	4.12	4.55	1.59	3.10	4.89	3.51	5.25	1.92	0.70	2.70	2.15	2.72	0.74
	FISH, REDFISH Sciaenops ocellata																
048	meal mech extd	5-07-973	93	61.0	4.36	4.35	1.39	3.72	5.22	3.55	7.04	1.94	0.44	2.68	1.81	2.79	0.65
	FISH, ROCKFISH Sebastodes spp																
049	whole, fresh	5-07-974	21	89.6	—	—	—	—	—	—	—	—	—	—	—	—	—
	FISH, SALMON Oncorhynchus spp-Salmo spp																
050	meal mech extd	5-02-012	94	65.3	5.59	5.59	—	—	—	—	8.17	1.72	0.75	—	—	—	0.54
051	whole, fresh	5-02-011	32	66.2	—	—	—	—	—	—	—	—	—	—	—	—	—
	FISH, SARDINE Clupea spp-Sardinops spp																
052	meal mech extd	5-02-015	93[c]	70.0	2.93	4.89	1.96	3.59	6.30	4.40	6.41	2.17	0.86	2.15	3.00	2.79	0.54
	FISH, SMELT Osmerus spp																
053	whole, fresh	5-07-975	21	89.6	—	—	—	—	—	—	—	—	—	—	—	—	—
	FISH, SOLE Soleidae (family)																
054	whole, fresh	5-07-976	20	65.5	—	—	—	—	—	—	—	—	—	—	—	—	—
	FISH, TUNA Thunnus thynnus-Thunnus albacares																
055	cannery residue	5-07-977	61	55.5	3.65	4.30	1.94	2.50	4.09	3.01	4.14	1.56	0.45	2.30	1.86	2.46	0.60
056	meal mech extd	5-02-023	93	63.6	3.44	4.40	1.89	2.64	4.09	2.98	4.37	1.58	0.50	2.32	1.82	2.49	0.62
	FISH, TURBOT Psetta maxima																
057	whole, fresh	5-07-978	25	57.3	—	—	—	—	—	—	—	—	—	—	0.44	0.41	—
	FISH, WHITE Gadidae (family)-Lophidae (family)-Rajidae (family)																
058	meal mech extd	5-02-025	91	68.4	4.42	4.89	1.47	2.99	4.79	3.32	4.98	1.85	0.82	2.51	2.01	2.82	0.73
	FISH, WHITING Gadus merlangus																
059	whole, fresh	5-07-979	23	69.9	—	—	—	—	—	—	—	—	—	—	—	—	—

No.	Feed	Ref. No.	DM %														
060	FISH — livers, meal mech extd	5-01-968	93	67.7	—	—	—	—	—	—	—	—	—	—	—	—	—
061	racks, dehy grnd (bone w heads)	5-17-891	—	—	—	—	—	—	—	—	—	—	—	—	—	—	—
062	solubles, condensed	5-01-969	51	61.8	3.16	6.69	2.28	2.08	3.65	2.50	3.39	0.98	0.59	1.82	0.78	1.69	0.61
063	solubles, dehy	5-01-971	92	69.1	3.02	6.40	2.37	2.12	3.43	2.41	3.57	1.09	0.72	1.61	0.85	1.47	0.55
064	FLAX *Linum usitatissimum* — seeds, meal solv extd (linseed meal)	5-02-048	90	38.4	3.25	1.93	0.77	1.87	2.24	1.93	1.28	0.60	0.67	1.62	1.21	1.35	0.56
065	HAMBURGER *Bos taurus* — fresh 10% fat	5-17-899	36[c]	65.3	2.21	2.32	1.11	1.55	2.49	1.71	2.71	0.88	0.39	1.49	1.10	1.38	0.39
066	fresh 20% fat	5-17-897	39	45.0	—	—	—	—	—	—	—	—	—	—	—	—	—
	HOMINY FEED, see CORN, hominy																
067	HORSE *Equus caballus* — meat, fresh	5-07-980	31	63.6	—	—	—	—	—	—	—	—	—	—	—	—	—
068	meat w bone, fresh	5-07-981	36	51.4	—	—	—	—	—	—	—	—	—	—	—	—	—
	LINSEED, see FLAX																
069	LIVER, ANIMAL — meal dehy	5-00-389	92	71.3	4.50	6.05	1.60	3.36	5.74	4.49	5.22	1.32	0.97	3.15	1.84	2.70	0.64
070	MEAT, ANIMAL — meal rendered	5-00-385	92	59.1	4.05	6.85	1.41	1.74	3.61	2.50	3.26	0.82	0.72	1.85	0.91	1.89	0.39
071	w blood, w bone meal tankage rendered	5-00-387	93	50.2	3.03	7.08	1.90	2.01	5.67	3.68	3.57	0.74	0.29	2.46	—	2.35	0.67
072	w bone, meal rendered	5-00-386	93	53.9	3.80	6.96	1.08	1.80	3.33	2.61	3.14	0.71	0.70	1.84	0.96	1.78	0.33
073	MILK — dehy (cattle)	5-01-167	96	26.6	0.96	—	0.75	1.39	2.67	1.81	2.35	0.64	0.42	1.39	1.39	1.07	0.43
074	fresh (cattle)	5-01-168	12[c]	26.7	—	0.31	—	2.58	2.03	2.03	2.27	0.69	—	1.33	—	1.33	0.39
075	skimmed dehy (cattle)	5-01-175	94	35.4	1.40	—	0.92	2.30	3.50	2.43	3.00	0.96	0.40	1.60	0.12	1.66	0.46
076	skimmed fresh (cattle)	5-01-170	10	31.2	—	—	—	—	—	—	2.90	—	—	—	—	—	—
077	cottage cheese	5-08-001	21	81.0	—	—	—	—	—	—	—	—	—	—	—	—	—
078	whey albumin (cattle)	5-01-177	92	52.5	—	—	—	—	—	—	2.92	—	—	—	—	—	—
079	MILLET, FOXTAIL *Setaria italica* — grain	4-03-102	89	12.8	0.72	0.40	0.35	0.63	1.49	0.62	0.19	0.30	0.22	0.57	0.39	0.37	0.99
080	MOLASSES — beet sugar, molasses mt 48%	4-00-668	78	8.5	—	—	—	—	—	—	—	—	—	—	—	—	—
081	invert sugar mt 79.5 degrees brix, sugar cane, molasses dehy	4-04-695	94	10.3	—	—	—	—	—	—	—	—	—	—	—	—	—
082	sugar cane, molasses, mt 46% invert, sugar mt 79.5 degrees brix	4-04-696	74	5.8	—	—	—	—	—	—	—	—	—	—	—	—	—
083	OATS *Avena sativa* — cereal by-product, lt 4% fiber (feeding oat meal) (oat middlings)	4-03-303	91	16.3	0.89	0.69	0.33	0.61	1.16	0.81	0.58	0.23	0.28	0.76	0.79	0.53	0.22
084	grain	4-03-309	89	12.8	0.90	0.56	0.27	0.58	1.0	0.76	0.56	0.20	0.25	0.66	0.60	0.48	0.18
085	groats	4-03-331	90	17.6	0.99	0.67	0.30	0.57	1.02	0.79	0.60	0.24	0.22	0.76	0.55	0.49	0.21
086	hulls	1-03-281	92	5.2	0.16	0.16	0.09	0.08	0.16	0.22	0.18	0.08	0.07	0.15	0.16	0.15	0.08
087	PEA *Pisum* spp — seeds	5-03-600	90	26.4	1.56	1.22	0.80	1.22	2.00	1.44	1.78	0.34	0.19	1.44	—	1.04	0.27
088	PEANUT *Arachis hypogaea* — kernels, meal solv extd (peanut meal)	5-03-650	93	54.5	5.91	2.90	1.28	2.26	3.22	1.96	1.89	0.47	0.82	2.96	2.15	1.56	0.70
089	POTATO *Solanum tuberosum* — tubers, dehy	4-07-850	91	8.9	0.28	—	0.17	0.28	0.66	0.40	0.45	0.11	0.08	0.44	—	0.52	0.15
090	POULTRY, CHICKEN *Gallus domesticus* — heads, fresh	5-07-949	33	57.6	—	—	—	—	—	—	—	—	—	—	—	—	—
091	broilers, whole fresh	5-07-945	—	—	—	—	—	—	—	—	—	—	—	—	—	—	—
092	eggs, fresh whole	5-01-213	30	42.6	2.90	1.58	1.16	2.99	4.20	3.26	3.32	1.60	1.16	2.73	1.98	2.44	0.86
093	eggs, fresh white	5-01-210	13	87.1	4.96	3.19	1.93	5.18	7.40	6.36	5.24	3.30	2.10	3.35	3.41	3.78	1.31
094	feet fresh	5-07-947	33	54.5	—	—	—	—	—	—	—	—	—	—	—	—	—
095	gizzards fresh	5-07-948	25	80.4	—	—	—	—	—	—	—	—	—	—	—	—	—
096	by-product, fresh (viscera with feet and heads)	5-07-951	—	—	—	—	—	—	—	—	—	—	—	—	—	—	—
097	by-product, meal rendered (viscera with feet and heads)	5-03-798	93[b]	62.4	4.30	6.34	1.61	2.16	3.98	2.80	3.10	1.06	1.12	2.25	0.58	2.15	0.57
098	hens, whole fresh	5-07-950	—	—	—	—	—	—	—	—	—	—	—	—	—	—	—
099	chicken viscera	5-07-985	26	54.4	—	—	—	—	—	—	—	—	—	—	—	—	—
100	POULTRY FEATHERS — hydrolyzed meal	5-03-795	93	92.9	5.83	6.78	0.37	3.51	7.23	5.99	1.80	0.58	3.76	3.51	6.78	3.69	0.54

66

TABLE 10—Continued

Entry Number	COMMON NAME Genus species / Short name	International Feed Number	Dry Matter (%)	Crude Protein (%)	Arginine (%)	Glycine (%)	Histidine (%)	Isoleucine (%)	Leucine (%)	Valine (%)	Lysine (%)	Methionine (%)	Cystine (%)	Phenylalanine (%)	Tyrosine (%)	Threonine (%)	Tryptophan (%)
	RICE *Oryza sativa*																
101	bran w germ (rice bran)	4-03-928	91	14.2	0.98	0.88	0.36	0.57	0.99	0.82	0.65	0.22	0.11	0.64	0.75	0.33	0.17
102	grain	4-03-939	89	8.6	0.65	0.57	0.15	0.36	0.65	0.52	0.31	0.18	0.13	0.38	0.64	0.28	0.13
103	groats polished	4-03-942	89	8.2	0.50	0.83	0.20	0.50	0.80	0.60	0.32	0.28	0.11	0.60	0.70	0.40	0.11
104	polishings	4-03-943	90	13.6	0.87	0.79	0.27	0.46	0.89	0.84	0.63	0.24	0.11	0.51	0.70	0.44	0.14
	RYE *Secale cereale*																
105	grain	4-04-047	88	13.7	0.60	0.56	0.30	0.53	0.79	0.64	0.47	0.19	0.21	0.64	0.30	0.41	0.13
	SEAWEED, KELP Laminariales (order)-Fucales (order)																
106		1-08-073	91	7.1	—	—	—	—	—	—	—	—	—	—	—	—	—
	SESAME *Sesamum indicum*																
107	seeds, meal mech extd	5-04-220	93	47.1	5.30	4.54	1.17	2.28	3.58	2.59	1.40	1.29	0.64	2.38	2.15	1.77	0.86
	SHRIMP *Pandalus* spp-*Panaeus* spp																
108	cannery residual meal (shrimp meal)	5-04-226	90	43.0	2.58	1.45	0.97	1.67	2.63	1.89	2.28	0.93	0.52	1.72	1.22	1.40	0.40
	SORGHUM *Sorghum vulgare*																
109	grain	4-04-383	90[b]	10.0	0.40	0.36	0.26	0.40	1.32	0.59	0.26	0.21	0.21	0.52	0.40	0.37	0.08
	SOYBEAN *Glycine max*																
110	seeds, meal solv extd	5-04-604	89[b]	49.4	3.69	2.57	1.29	2.69	3.96	2.63	3.29	0.74	0.77	2.55	1.44	2.03	0.70
111	seeds wo hulls, meal solv extd	5-04-612	90[b]	53.9	3.80	2.54	1.47	2.86	4.24	3.02	3.53	0.83	0.86	2.34	2.23	2.12	0.74
112	flour, concentrate (70% protein)	5-08-038	93	90.4	7.20	3.55	2.26	4.95	7.10	4.73	5.91	0.87	1.00	4.62	3.33	3.55	0.87
113	flour, oil residue solvent extd	5-04-593	93	55.3	4.58	1.77	1.35	2.04	3.57	1.99	4.81	0.61	0.69	2.14	1.54	1.69	0.85
114	isolate (90% protein)	5-24-811	96	94.0	3.80	3.80	—	4.50	7.90	4.60	5.60	—	—	5.20	3.70	3.30	—
115	seeds, heat processed	5-04-597	90	41.1	3.11	2.22	0.99	2.22	3.11	2.00	2.67	0.57	0.71	2.00	1.33	1.67	0.61
	SUCROSE																
116	sucrose	4-06-176	99	—	—	—	—	—	—	—	—	—	—	—	—	—	—
	SUNFLOWER *Helianthus* spp																
117	seeds wo hulls, meal mech extd	5-04-738	93	43.7	3.66	—	0.97	1.90	2.66	2.17	1.71	1.01	—	1.94	1.08	1.47	0.52
118	seeds wo hulls, meal solv extd	5-04-739	93	48.8	3.76	2.89	1.50	2.99	4.17	3.48	1.83	0.77	0.76	3.15	1.28	2.29	0.76
	SWINE *Sus scrofa*																
119	livers, fresh	5-04-792	30.5[c]	69.8	3.69	3.47	2.57	3.02	5.48	4.02	5.93	1.68	1.01	3.47	2.12	3.02	0.89
120	lungs, fresh	5-26-140	—	—	—	—	—	—	—	—	—	—	—	—	—	—	—
	TOMATO *Lycopersicon esculentum*																
121	pomace dehy	5-05-041	92	23.0	1.30	—	0.43	0.76	1.85	1.09	1.74	0.11	—	0.98	0.98	0.78	0.22
	TURKEY *Meleagris gallopavo*																
122	mature birds, offal fresh	5-07-984	—	—	—	—	—	—	—	—	—	—	—	—	—	—	—
123	young heads, offal fresh	5-07-985	—	—	—	—	—	—	—	—	—	—	—	—	—	—	—
124	viscera fresh	5-08-616	31	43.4	—	—	—	—	—	—	—	—	—	—	—	—	—

No.	Feed name	Feed No.	—	—	—	—	—	—	—	—	—	—	—	—	—	—	—
125	WHALE *Balaena glacialis-Balaenoptera* spp-*Physeter catadon* meat fresh	5-07-986	29	70.8	—	—	—	—	—	—	—	—	—	—	—	—	—
126	WHEAT *Triticum aestivum* bran	4-05-190	90	17.4	1.09	1.00	0.38	0.66	1.01	0.81	0.66	0.25	0.35	0.54	0.43	0.46	0.33
127	flour, hard red spring	4-08-113	89	14.4	0.54	0.55	0.29	0.60	1.03	0.64	0.32	0.27	0.39	0.78	0.46	0.42	0.19
128	flour, lt 2% fiber	4-05-199	88	15.5	0.47	0.52	0.32	0.63	1.01	0.58	0.30	0.15	0.28	0.70	0.28	0.34	0.11
129	germ meal	5-05-218	88	27.6	2.07	1.65	0.70	1.07	1.67	1.31	1.73	0.47	0.53	1.05	0.84	1.07	0.34
130	grain	4-05-211	89	14.7	0.69	0.66	0.34	0.55	1.01	0.68	0.44	0.23[b]	0.32[b]	0.69	0.41	0.45	0.17
131	grain, hard red spring	4-05-258	88	16.2	0.73	0.68	0.31	0.60	1.04	0.69	0.44	0.23	0.25	0.75	0.51	0.44	0.17
132	grain, hard red winter	4-05-268	87	16.2	0.67	0.83	0.25	0.67	1.08	0.72	0.46	0.22	0.30	0.82	0.49	0.43	0.21
133	grain, screenings	4-05-216	89	14.9	0.77	0.60	0.34	0.50	0.83	0.62	0.48	0.29	0.14	0.55	0.26	0.38	0.14
134	grain, soft red winter	4-05-294	88	12.9	0.73	0.62	0.36	0.51	1.02	0.65	0.46	0.24	0.41	0.72	0.43	0.44	0.30
135	grain, soft white winter	4-05-337	89	11.5	0.45	0.55	0.23	0.47	0.66	0.49	0.35	0.17	0.25	0.51	0.44	0.36	0.14
136	grits	4-07-852	90	12.7	—	—	—	—	—	—	—	—	—	—	—	—	—
137	mill run, lt 9.5% fiber	4-05-206	90	16.7	1.04	0.59	0.44	0.78	1.33	0.89	0.64	0.37	0.26	—	0.56	0.56	0.23
138	red dog, lt 4.5% fiber	4-05-203	88	17.4	1.09	0.84	0.47	0.63	1.21	0.82	0.67	0.26	0.42	0.74	0.52	0.56	0.22
139	shorts, lt 7.0% fiber	4-05-201	88	18.7	1.35	1.08	0.50	0.66	1.24	0.94	0.90	0.31	0.41	0.76	0.53	0.68	0.24
140	middlings, lt 9.5% fiber	4-05-205	88	17.6	1.20	—	—	—	—	—	0.80	0.30	0.40	—	—	—	0.24
141	WHEAT DURUM *Triticum durum* grain	4-05-224	88	15.6	0.67	0.52	0.31	0.55	1.60	0.62	1.19	0.16	0.15	0.61	0.33	0.42	0.30
142	WHEY *Bos taurus* dehy	4-01-182	93	12.9	0.37	0.32	0.19	0.88	1.28	0.73	1.04	0.20	0.32	0.35	0.27	0.96	0.20
143	low lactose, dehy (dried whey product)	4-01-186	91	17.0	0.74	1.14	0.11	0.99	1.26	0.33	1.62	0.63	0.63	0.55	0.22	0.55	0.20
144	YEAST *Saccharomyces cerevisiae* brewers dehy	7-05-527	93	47.7	2.35	2.24	1.15	2.30	3.43	2.49	3.47	0.75	0.54	1.95	1.60	2.22	0.53
145	primary dehy	7-05-533	93	51.8	2.81	—	6.05	3.89	4.00	3.46	4.10	1.08	0.54	2.70	—	2.70	0.43
146	YEAST *Candida utilis* petroleum solv extd dehy	7-09-836	92	51.1	—	—	—	—	—	—	—	—	—	—	—	—	—
147	YEAST *Torulopsis utilis* torula dehy	7-05-534	93	50.8	2.80	2.80	1.51	3.11	3.76	3.11	4.09	0.86	0.65	3.23	2.26	2.80	0.54

[a]First digit is class of feeds: 1. dry forages and roughages; 2. pasture, range plants, and forages fed green; 3. silages; 4. energy feeds; 5. protein supplements; 6. minerals; 7. vitamins; 8. additives.
[b]Methionine and Cystine data from Wicker (personal communication, Degussa Corporation, 1984).
[c]Amino Acid data from Paul and Southgate (1978).

TABLE 11   Abbreviations for Terms Used in Tables 5, 7, 8, and 10

dehy	dehydrated
extd	extracted
g	gram
gr	grade
grnd	ground
IU	International Units
kcal	kilocalories
kg	kilogram(s)
lt	less than
mech extd	mechanically extracted, expeller extracted, hydraulic extracted, or old process
μg	microgram(s)
mg	milligram(s)
mt	more than
s-c	suncured
solv extd	solvent extracted
spp	species
w	with
wo	without

TABLE 12   Weight-Unit Conversion Factors

Units Given	Units Wanted	For Conversion Multiply by
lb	g	453.6
lb	kg	0.4536
oz	g	28.35
kg	lb	2.2046
kg	mg	1,000,000.
kg	g	1,000.
g	mg	1,000.
g	μg	1,000,000.
mg	μg	1,000.
mg/g	mg/lb	453.6
mg/kg	mg/lb	0.4536
μg/kg	μg/lb	0.4536
kcal	Mcal	1,000.
kcal	kJ	4.184
kJ	kcal	0.239
kcal/kg	kcal/lb	0.4536
kcal/lb	kcal/kg	2.2046
ppm	μg/g	1.
ppm	mg/kg	1.
ppm	mg/lb	0.4536
mg/kg	%	0.0001
ppm	%	0.0001
mg/g	%	0.1
g/kg	%	0.1

TABLE 13   Fat-Soluble Vitamin Equivalents

Vitamin A

1 retinol equivalent (RE)	= 1 μg retinol
	= 1.147 μg retinyl acetate
	= 3.3 IU vitamin A
1 IU vitamin A	= 0.3 μg retinol

Vitamin D

1 μg vitamin D	= 40 IU
Ergocalciferol (D$_2$)[a]	
Cholecalciferol (D$_3$)[b]	
1 IU vitamin D	= 0.025 μg D$_3$

Vitamin E

1 mg DL-α-tocopheryl acetate	= 1 IU
1 mg DL-α-tocopherol	= 1.1 IU
1 mg D-α-tocopheryl acetate	= 1.36 IU
1 mg D-α-tocopherol[c]	= 1.49 IU

Vitamin K

Expressed as "phylloquinone equivalents." No IU developed for this vitamin.

[a]plant source
[b]animal source
[c]natural form in foodstuffs

References

Adolph, E. F. 1947. Signs and symptoms of desert dehydration. Pp. 226–240, Chapter 14, *in* Physiology of Man in the Desert, E. F. Adolph and Associates, eds. New York: Interscience.

Ahmad, B. 1931. The fate of carotene after absorption in the animal organism. Biochem. J. 25:1195.

Aiken, T. D., L. E. Schnepper, R. M. Forbes, and J. E. Corbin. 1978. The effect of a low-zinc diet on the growth and skin condition in cats. P. 27 *in* Proc. 112th Annu. Meet., Am. Soc. Anim. Sci. Midwest Sect., Jan. 5–6, 1978. (Abstr. 71)

Akrabawi, S. S., M. M. Saegert, and J. P. Salji. 1974. Studies on the growth and changes in metabolism of rats fed on carbohydrate-deficient fatty acid-based diets supplemented with graded levels of maize starch. Br. J. Nutr. 32:209.

Alberti, K. G. M. M., and C. Cuthbert. 1982. The hydrogen ion in normal metabolism: a review. P. 1019 *in* Metabolic Acidosis, R. Porter and G. Lawrenson, eds. CIBA Foundation Symp. 87. London: Pitman.

Allen, R. D. 1982. Feedstuffs ingredient analysis table. Feedstuffs 54(30):25.

Allison, J. B., S. A. Miller, J. R. McCoy, and M. K. Brush. 1956. Studies on the nutrition of the cat. N. Am. Vet. 37:38.

Amyes, S. J. G., P. M. M. Roberts, and P. P. Scott. 1975. The effect of age on the blood and liver folate concentrations of laboratory animals. Proc. Nutr. Soc. 34:25A.

Anderson, B. A. 1976. Comprehensive evaluation of fatty acids in foods. VII. Pork products. J. Am. Diet. Assoc. 69:44.

Anderson, P. A., D. H. Baker, and S. P. Mistry. 1978. Bioassay determination of the biotin content of corn, barley, sorghum, and wheat. J. Anim. Sci. 47:645.

Anderson, P. A., D. H. Baker, and J. E. Corbin. 1979a. Lysine and arginine requirements of the domestic cat. J. Nutr. 109:1368.

Anderson, P. A., D. H. Baker, J. E. Corbin, and L. C. Helper. 1979b. Biochemical lesions associated with taurine deficiency in the cat. J. Anim. Sci. 49:1227.

Anderson, P. A., D. H. Baker, P. A. Sherry, and J. E. Corbin. 1979c. Choline-methionine interrelationship in feline nutrition. J. Anim. Sci. 49:522.

Anderson, P. A., D. H. Baker, P. A. Sherry, and J. E. Corbin. 1980a. Histidine, phenylalanine-tyrosine and tryptophan requirements for growth of the young kitten. J. Anim. Sci. 50:479.

Anderson, P. A., D. H. Baker, P. A. Sherry, and J. E. Corbin. 1980b. Nitrogen requirement of the kitten. Am. J. Vet. Res. 41:1646.

Anderson, P. A., D. H. Baker, P. A. Sherry, R. G. Teeter, and J. E. Corbin. 1980c. Threonine, isoleucine, valine and leucine requirements of the young kitten. J. Anim. Sci. 50:266.

Anderson, R. S. 1983. Fluid balance and diet. Pp. 19–25 *in* Proc. 7th Kal Kan Symp. Ohio State University. Sept. 24–25, 1983. Columbus.

Anonymous. 1962. Annotations: The feeding and nutrition of cats. J. Small Anim. Pract. 3:19.

Bafundo, K. W., D. H. Baker, and P. R. Fitzgerald. 1984a. The iron-zinc interrelationship in the chick as influenced by *Eimeria acervulina* infection. J. Nutr. 114:1306.

Bafundo, K. W., D. H. Baker, and P. R. Fitzgerald. 1984b. *Eimeria acervulina* infection and the zinc-cadmium interrelationship in the chick. Poult. Sci. 63:1828.

Bafundo, K. W., D. H. Baker, and P. R. Fitzgerald. 1984c. Lead toxicity in the chick as affected by excess copper and zinc and by *Eimeria acervulina* infection. Poult. Sci. 63:1594.

Baggs, R. B., A. deLaHunta, and D. R. Averill. 1978. Thiamine deficiency encephalopathy in a specific-pathogen-free cat colony. Lab. Anim. Sci. 28:323.

Baker, D. H., and C. M. Parsons. 1985. Recent Advances in Amino Acid Nutrition. Tokyo, Japan: Ajinomoto Publ. Co. 48 pp.

Baker, D. H., J. T. Yen, A. H. Jensen, R. G. Teeter, E. N. Michel, and J. H. Burns. 1976. Niacin activity in niacinamide and coffee. Nutr. Rep. Int. 14:115.

Ballard, F. J. 1965. Glucose utilization in mammalian liver. Comp. Biochem. Physiol. 14:437.

Bartoshuk, L. M., M. A. Harned, and L. H. Parks. 1971. Taste of water in the cat: effects on sucrose preference. Science 171:699.

Bartoshuk, L. M., H. L. Jacobs, T. L. Nichols, L. A. Hoff, and J. J. Ryckman. 1975. Taste rejection of nonnutritive sweetners in cats. J. Comp. Physiol. Psychol. 89:971.

Bartsch, R. C., G. D. Imes, Jr., and J. P. J. Smit. 1975. Vitamin A deficiency in the captive African lion cub, *Panthero leo* (Linnaeus, 1758). Onderstepoort J. Vet. Res. 42:43.

Beauchamp, G. K., O. Maller, and J. G. Rogers, Jr. 1977. Flavor preferences in cats (*Felis catus* and *Panthera* sp.). J. Comp. Physiol. Psychol. 91:1118.

Beck, N., and S. K. Webster. 1976. Effects of acute metabolic acidosis on parathyroid hormone action and calcium mobilization. Am. J. Physiol. 230:127.

Bedford, P. G. C., and E. G. C. Clarke. 1972. Experimental benzoic acid poisoning in the cat. Vet. Rec. 90:53.

Bedford, P. G. C., and E. G. C. Clarke. 1973. A preliminary study of the suitability of sorbic acid for use as a preservative in cat food preparations. Vet. Rec. 92:55.

Bellhorn, R. W., G. D. Aguirre, and M. B. Bellhorn. 1974. Feline central retinal degeneration. Invest. Ophthalmol. 13:608.

Belo, P. S., D. R. Romsos, and G. A. Leveille. 1976. Influence of diet on glucose tolerance, on the rate of glucose utilization and on gluconeogenic enzyme activities in the dog. J. Nutr. 106:1465.

Benedict, F. G. 1938. Vital Energetics. Carnegie Institution of Washington Publ. No. 513. Washington, D.C.

Bennett, D. 1976. Nutrition and bone disease in the dog and cat. Vet. Rec. 98:313.

Berson, E. L., K. C. Hayes, A. R. Rabin, S. Y. Schmidt, and G. Watson. 1976. Retinal degeneration in cats fed casein. II. Supplementation with methionine, cysteine or taurine. Invest. Ophthalmol. 15:52.

Bieri, J. G., T. J. Tolliver, and G. L. Catignani. 1979. Simultaneous determination of a-tocopherol and retinol in plasma or red cells by HPLC. Am. J. Clin. Nutr. 32:2143.

Blaza, S. E., I. H. Burger, D. W. Holme, and P. T. Kendall. 1982. Sulfur-containing amino acid requirements of growing dogs. J. Nutr. 112:2033.

Borman, A., T. R. Wood, H. C. Black, E. G. Anderson, M. J. Oesterling, M. Womack, and W. C. Rose. 1946. The role of arginine in growth with some observations on the effects of arginic acid. J. Biol. Chem. 166:585.

Braham, J. E., A. Villareal, and R. Bressani. 1962. Effect of lime treatment of corn on the availability of niacin for cats. J. Nutr. 76:183.

Brambila, S., and F. W. Hill. 1966. Comparison of neutral fat and free fatty acids in high lipid-low carbohydrate diets for the growing chicken. J. Nutr. 88:84.

Bridges, J. W., M. R. French, R. L. Smith, and R. T. Williams. 1970. The fate of benzoic acid in various species. Biochem. J. 118:47.

Brin, M., and W. A. Vincent. 1965. The diagnosis of thiamine adequacy in the dog by use of the erythrocyte enzyme, transketolase. J. Am. Vet. Med. Assoc. 147:1649.

Brody, S., R. C. Proctor, and U. S. Ashworth. 1934. Growth and development with special reference to domestic animals. XXXIV. Basal metabolism, endogenous nitrogen, creatinine and neutral sulfur excretions as functions of bodyweight. Univ. Mo. Agric. Exp. Stn. Res. Bull. No. 221. University of Missouri, Columbia.

Brosnan, J. T., and M. E. Brosnan. 1982. Dietary protein, metabolic acidosis, and calcium balance. Adv. Nutr. Res. 4:77.

Budde, E. F. 1952. The determination of fat in baked biscuit type of dog foods. J. Assoc. Off. Agric. Chem. 35:799.

Buffington, C. A., Q. R. Rogers, J. G. Morris, and N. E. Cook. 1985. Feline struvite urolithiasis: Magnesium effect depends on urinary pH. Feline Pract. 15:29.

Burger, I. H., and K. C. Barnett. 1980. Essentiality of taurine for the cat. Pp. 13–33 in Proc. Kal Kan Symp. Columbus, Ohio, 1979.

Burger, I. H., and K. C. Barnett. 1982. The taurine requirement of the adult cat. J. Small Anim. Pract. 23:533.

Burger, I. H., S. E. Blaza, P. T. Kendall, and P. M. Smith. 1984. The protein requirement of adult cats for maintenance. Feline Pract. 14:91.

Burns, R. A., and J. A. Milner. 1981. Sulfur amino acid requirements of the immature Beagle dog. J. Nutr. 111:2117.

Camien, M. N., L. M. Smith, T. J. Reilly, and D. H. Simmons. 1966. Determinations of total cation-forming mineral elements in feces and urine and its relation to renal "net acid" excretion. Proc. Soc. Exp. Biol. Med. 123:686.

Camien, M. N., D. H. Simmons, and H. C. Gonick. 1969. A critical reappraisal of "acid-base" balance. Am. J. Clin. Nutr. 22:786.

Carbone, M. G. 1965. Phosphocrystalluria and urethral obstruction in the cat. J. Am. Vet. Med. Assoc. 147:1195.

Carey, C. J., and J. G. Morris. 1975. Biotin deficiency in the cat. J. Anim. Sci. 41:309. (Abstr. 259)

Carey, C. J., and J. G. Morris. 1977. Biotin deficiency in the cat and the effect on hepatic propionyl CoA carboxylase. J. Nutr. 107:330.

Carpenter, J. A. 1956. Species differences in taste preferences. J. Comp. Physiol. Psychol. 49:139.

Carpenter, T. M. 1944. The effects of sugars on the respiratory exchange of cats. J. Nutr. 28:315.

Carvalho da Silva, A. 1950. The domestic cat as a laboratory animal for experimental nutritional studies. II. Comparative growth and hematology on stock and purified rations. Acta Physiol. Lat. Am. 1:26.

Carvalho da Silva, A., R. Fried, and R. C. de Angelis. 1952. The domestic cat as a laboratory animal for experimental nutrition studies. III. Niacin requirements and tryptophan metabolism. J. Nutr. 46:399.

Carvalho da Silva, A., R. C. de Angelis, M. A. Pontes, and M. F. Mansur Guerios. 1955. The domestic cat as a laboratory animal for experimental nutrition studies. IV. Folic acid deficiency. J. Nutr. 56:199.

Carvalho da Silva, A., M. F. Mansur Guerios, and S. R. Monsao. 1959a. The domestic cat as a laboratory animal for experimental nutrition studies. VI. Choline deficiency. J. Nutr. 67:537.

Carvalho da Silva, A., A. B. Fajer, R. C. De Angelis, M. A. Pontes, A. M. Giesbrecht, and R. Fried. 1959b. The domestic cat as a laboratory animal for experimental nutrition studies. VII. Pyridoxine deficiency. J. Nutr. 68:213.

Carver, D. S., and H. N. Waterhouse. 1962. The variation in water consumption of cats. Proc. Anim. Care Panel 12:267.

Chausow, D. G., and G. L. Czarnecki. 1985. Estimation of the dietary iron requirement for the weanling kitten. P. 294 in Proc. Am. Soc. Anim. Sci. (Abstr.)

Chausow, D. G., R. M. Forbes, G. L. Czarnecki, and J. E. Corbin. 1985. Experimentally induced magnesium deficiency in growing kittens. P. 295 in Proc. Am. Soc. Anim. Sci. (Abstr.)

Chemical Rubber Company (CRC). 1972. Handbook of Food Additives, 2nd ed, Vol II. Cleveland, Ohio.

Clark, L. 1970. The effect of excess vitamin A on longbone growth in kittens. J. Comp. Pathol. 80:625.

Clark, L. 1973. Growth rates of epiphyseal plates in normal kittens and in kittens fed excess vitamin A. J. Comp. Pathol. 83:447.

Clark, L., A. A. Seawright, and J. Hrdlicka. 1970a. Exostoses in hypervitaminotic cats with optimal calcium-phosphorus intakes. J. Small Anim. Pract. 11:553.

Clark, L., A. A. Seawright, and R. J. W. Gartner. 1970b. Longbone abnormalities in kittens following vitamin A administration. J. Comp. Pathol. 80:113.

Coffin, D. L., and J. Holzworth. 1954. "Yellow fat" in two laboratory cats: acid-fast pigmentation associated with a fish-base ration. Cornell Vet. 44:63.

Cook, N. E. 1985. The importance of urinary pH in the prevention of Feline Urologic Syndrome. Pet Food Industry, March/April, pp. 24–31.

Cook, N. E., E. Kane, Q. R. Rogers, and J. G. Morris. 1985. Self selection of dietray casein and soy-protein by the cat. Physiol. Behav. 34:583.

Coop, M. C. 1958. A treatment for osteogenesis imperfecta in kittens. J. Am. Vet. Med. Assoc. 132:299.

Cordy, D. R. 1954. Experimental production of steatitis (yellow fat disease) in kittens fed a commercial canned cat food and prevention of the condition by vitamin E. Cornell Vet. 44:310.

Costello, M. J., J. G. Morris, and Q. R. Rogers. 1979. The arginine requirement of the growing cat. Western Section, American Society of Animal Science 30:133.

Costello, M. J., J. G. Morris, and Q. R. Rogers. 1980. Effect of dietary arginine level on urinary orotate and citrate excretion in growing kittens. J. Nutr. 110:1204.

Cowgill, G. R. 1921. A contribution to the study of the relation between vitamin-B and the nutrition of the dog. Am. J. Physiol. 57:420.

Cox, H. E., and D. Pearson. 1962. General methods-fat. Pp. 26–28 in Chemical Analysis of Foods. London: Churchill.

Crampton, E. W. 1964. Nutrient-to-calorie ratios in applied nutrition. J. Nutr. 82:353.

Cullison, R. F., P. D. Menard, and W. B. Buck. 1983. Toxicosis in cats from use of benzyl alcohol in lactated Ringer's solution. J. Am. Vet. Med. Assoc. 181:61.

Datta, S. P., and H. Harris. 1951. A convenient apparatus for paper chromatography. Results of a survey of urinary amino-acid patterns of some animals. J. Physiol. 114:39P.

Deady, J. E., B. Anderson, J. A. O'Donnell, J. G. Morris, and Q. R. Rogers. 1981a. Effects of level of dietary glutamic acid and thiamin on food intake, weight gain, plasma amino acids, and thiamin status of growing kittens. J. Nutr. 111:1568.

Deady, J. E., Q. R. Rogers, and J. G. Morris. 1981b. Effect of high dietary glutamic acid on the excretion of 35-S-thiamin in kittens. J. Nutr. 111:1580.

De Reuck, A. V. S., and J. Knight. 1965. Colors vision physiology and experimental psychology. CIBA Foundation Symposium:325.

Doong, G., C. L. Keen, Q. R. Rogers, J. G. Morris, and R. B. Rucker. 1983. Selected features of copper metabolism in the cat. J. Nutr. 113:1963.

Dubois, M., K. A. Gilles, J. K. Hamilton, P. A. Rebers, and F. Smith. 1956. Colorimetric method for determination of sugars and related substances. Anal. Chem. 28:350.

Dymsza, H. A., and S. A. Miller. 1964. Dietary methionine requirement of the cat. Fed. Proc. 23:186. (Abstr. 512)

Edwards, H. M., Jr. 1964. Fatty acid composition of feeding stuffs. Ga. Agric. Exp. Stn. Tech. Bull. N.S. 36. University of Georgia, Athens.

Edwards, H. M., Jr., and P. Hart. 1971. Carcass composition of chickens fed carbohydrate-free diets containing various lipid energy sources. J. Nutr. 101:989.

Elvehjem, C. A., and W. A. Krehl. 1947. Imbalances and dietary interrelationships in nutrition. J. Am. Vet. Med. Assoc. 135:279.

Erdman, J. W. 1979. Oilseed phytates: Nutritional implications. J. Am. Oil Chem. Soc. 56:736.

Everett, G. M. 1944. Observations on the behavior and neurophysiology of acute thiamin deficient cats. Am. J. Physiol. 141:439.

Fau, D., K. A. Smalley, Q. R. Rogers, and J. G. Morris. 1983. Effects of excess dietary methionine in the kitten. Fed. Proc. 42:542. (Abstr. 1469)

Fau, D., J. G. Morris, Q. R. Rogers, and R. A. Freedland. 1984. Excess dietary methionine in the kitten: effect on liver metabolism. Fed. Proc. 43:466. (Abstr. 1058)

Fiennes, R. N. T. W., and O. Graham-Jones. 1960. Studies of a nutritional disease (osteodystrophia fibrosa) of young lions associated with changes in the skeleton and symptoms of muscular weakness. Proc. Zool. Soc. Lond. 133:573.

Finco, D. R., S. K. Kneller, and W. A. Crowell. 1975. Diseases of the urinary system in Feline Medicine and Surgery, 2nd ed., E. J. Catcott, ed. Santa Barbara, Calif.: Am. Vet. Publ., Inc.

Fishler, J. 1955. Urolithiasis or urethral impaction in the cat. J. Am. Vet. Med. Assoc. 127:121.

Frankel, T. L., and J. P. W. Rivers. 1978. The nutritional and metabolic impact of γ-linolenic acid (18:3n6) on cats deprived of minimal lipid. Br. J. Nutr. 39:227.

Frings, H. 1951. Sweet taste in the cat and the taste-spectrum. Experientia 7:424.

Gaskell, C. J., A. H. Leedale, and S. W. Douglas. 1975. Pansteatitis in the cat: A report of four cases. J. Small Anim. Pract. 16:117.

Gershoff, S. N., and L. S. Gottlieb. 1964. Pantothenic acid deficiency in cats. J. Nutr. 82:135.

Gershoff, S. N., and S. A. Norkin. 1962. Vitamin E deficiency in cats. J. Nutr. 77:303.

Gershoff, S. N., S. B. Andrus, D. M. Hegsted, and E. A. Lentini. 1957a. Vitamin A deficiency in cats. Lab. Invest. 6:227.

Gershoff, S. N., M. A. Legg, F. J. O'Connor, and D. M. Hegsted. 1957b. The effect of vitamin D-deficient diets containing various Ca:P ratios on cats. J. Nutr. 63:79.

Gershoff, S. N., S. B. Andrus, and D. M. Hegsted. 1959a. The effect of the carbohydrate and fat content of the diet upon the riboflavin requirement of the cat. J. Nutr. 68:75.

Gershoff, S. M., F. F. Faragalla, D. A. Nelson, and S. B. Andrus. 1959b. Vitamin B6 deficiency and oxalate nephrocalcinosis in the cat. Am. J. Med. 27:72.

Gisler, D. B., and D. E. Ewing. 1964. A free access dry ration for cats. Lab. Anim. Care 14:91.

Glauberg, A., and H. P. Blumenthal. 1983. Chocolate poisoning in the dog. J. Am. Anim. Hosp. Assoc. 19:246.

Goldberg, A. 1971. Carbohydrate metabolism in rats fed carbohydrate-free diets. J. Nutr. 101:693.

Gonick, H. C., G. Goldberg, and D. Mulcare. 1968. Reexamination of the acid-ash content of several diets. Am. J. Clin. Nutr. 21:898.

Greaves, J. P. 1965. Protein and calorie requirements of the feline. Pp. 33-45 in Canine and Feline Nutritional Requirements, O. Graham-Jones, ed. London: Pergamon Press.

Greaves, J. P., and P. P. Scott. 1960. Nutrition of the cat. 3. Protein requirements for nitrogen equilibrium in adult cats maintained on a mixed diet. Br. J. Nutr. 14:361.

Greaves, J. P., and P. P. Scott. 1963. The influence of dietary carbohydrate on food intake of adult cats. Proc. Nutr. Soc. 22:iv. (Abstr.)

Greaves, J. P., M. G. Scott, and P. P. Scott. 1959. Thyroid changes in cats on a high protein diet, raw heart. J. Physiol. 148:73P.

Greene, R. W., and R. C. Scott. 1983. Diseases of the bladder and urethra. In Textbook of Veterinary Internal Medicine, 2nd ed. E. J. Ettinger, ed. Philadelphia: W. B. Saunders Co.

Griffiths, R. C., G. W. Thornton, and J. E. Willson. 1960. Pansteatitis ("yellow fat") in cats. J. Am. Vet. Med. Assoc. 137:126.

Halpin, K. M., and D. H. Baker. 1986. Long-term effects of corn, soybean meal, wheat bran and fish meal on manganese utilization in the chick. Poult. Sci. In press.

Hardison, W. G. M., C. A. Wood, and J. H. Proffitt. 1977. Quantification of taurine synthesis in the intact rat and cat liver. Proc. Soc. Exp. Biol. Med. 155:55.

Hardy, A. J., J. G. Morris, and Q. R. Rogers. 1977. Valine requirements of the growing kitten. J. Nutr. 107:1308.

Hargrove, D. M., Q. R. Rogers, and J. G. Morris. 1983. The tryptophan requirement of the kitten. Br. J. Nutr. 50:487.

Hargrove, D. M., Q. R. Rogers, and J. G. Morris. 1984a. Leucine and isoleucine requirements of the kitten. Br. J. Nutr. 52:595.

Hargrove, D. M., Q. R. Rogers, and J. G. Morris. 1984b. Lack of branched chain amino acid antagonism in the cat. Fed. Proc. 43:300. (Abstr. 92)

Harris, L. E. 1966. Biological Energy Interrelationships and Glossary of Energy Terms. Washington, D.C.: National Academy of Sciences.

Harris, L. E., L. C. Kearl, and P. V. Fonnesbeck. 1981. A Rationale for Hominy Feeds. International Feedstuffs Institute, Utah Agric. Exp. Stn. Bull. 501, Utah State University, Logan.

Hassam, A. G., J. P. W. Rivers, and M. A. Crawford. 1977. The failure of the cat to desaturate linoleic acid; Its nutritional implications. Nutr. Metab. 21:321.

Hayes, K. C., A. R. Rabin, and E. L. Berson. 1975a. An ultrastructural study of nutritionally induced and reversed retinal degeneration in cats. Am. J. Pathol. 78:505.

Hayes, K. C., R. E. Carey, and S. Y. Schmidt. 1975b. Retinal degeneration associated with taurine deficiency in the cat. Science 188:949.

Heath, M. K., J. W. MacQueen, and T. D. Spies. 1940. Feline pellagra. Science 92:514.

Hermus, R. J. J., C. E. West, and E. J. van Weerden. 1983. Failure of dietary-casein-induced acidosis to explain the hypercholesterolemia of casein-fed rabbits. J. Nutr. 113:618.

Heusner, A. A. 1985. Body size and energy metabolism. Annu. Rev. Nutr. 5:267.

Hilditch, T. P, and P. N. Williams. 1964. The Chemical Constitution of Natural Fats. New York: John Wiley & Sons.

Hills, A. G. 1973. Acid-base Balance—Chemistry, Physiology, Pathophysiology. Baltimore: Williams and Wilkins Co.

Hills, D. L., J. G. Morris, and Q. R. Rogers. 1982. Potassium requirement of kittens as affected by dietary protein. J. Nutr. 112:216.

Hirakawa, D. A., and D. H. Baker. 1984. Sulfur amino acid nutrition of the growing puppy. P. 3 in Proc. Am. Soc. Anim. Sci., 17th Annual Meeting, Midwestern Sect., Chicago, Illinois. (Abstr.)

Hoffman, H. H. 1953. Report on crude fat in baked dog food. J. Assoc. Off. Agric. Chem. 36:208.

Holme, D. W. 1977. Research into the feline urological syndrome. Pp. 40–45 in Proc. 1st Kal Kan Symp. Ohio State University, Sept. 19–20, 1977, Columbus.

Hudson, B. J. F. 1984. Evening primrose (*Oenothera* spp) oil and seed. J. Assoc. Off. Chem. Soc. 61:540.

Humphreys, E. R., and P. P. Scott. 1962. The addition of herring and vegetable oils to the diet of cats. Proc. Nutr. Soc. 21:xviii.

Hunt, J. N. 1956. The influence of dietary sulphur on the urinary output of acid in man. Clin. Sci. 15:119.

Ikeda, M., H. Tsuji, S. Nakamura, A. Ichiyama, Y. Nishizuka, and O. Hayaishi. 1965. Studies on the biosynthesis of nicotinamide adenine dinucleotide. II. A role of picolinic carboxylase in the biosynthesis of nicotinamide adenine dinucleotide from tryptophan in mammals. J. Biol. Chem. 240:1395.

Ishii, K., K. Sarai, H. Sanemori, and T. Kawasaki. 1979. Concentrations of thiamine and its phosphate esters in rat tissues determined by high-performance liquid chromatography. J. Nutr. Sci. Vitaminol. 25:517.

Jackson, O. F. 1968a. Nutritional requirements of cats with special reference to the skeleton. J. S. Afr. Vet. Med. Assoc. 39:18.

Jackson, O. F. 1968b. Feline osteodystrophy, its treatment and prevention. J. S. Afr. Vet. Med. Assoc. 39:27.

Jackson, O. F. 1972. Urolithiasis in laboratory and domestic cats. Vet. Rec. 91:292.

Jackson, O. F., and C. M. Colles. 1974. Experimental matrix plug production in male cat urine following a natural case of urolithiasis due to matrix plug. J. Small Anim. Pract. 15:701.

Jackson, O. F., and J. D. Tovey. 1977. Water balance studies in domestic cats. Feline Pract. 7:30.

Jaffe, H. L., A. Bodansky, and J. P. Chandler. 1932. Ammonium chloride decalcification, as modified by calcium intake: The relation between generalized osteoporosis and ostitis fibrosa. J. Exp. Med. 56:823.

Jansen, G. R., M. A. Deuth, G. M. Ward, and D. E. Johnson. 1975. Protein quality studies in growing kittens. Nutr. Rep. Int. 11:525.

JECFA. 1964. 8th report of Joint FAO/WHO Expert Committee on Food Additives. WHO/Food Additives/66.25. p. 88.

JECFA. 1970. 13th report of Joint FAO/WHO Expert Committee on Food Additives. WHO/Food Additives/70.36. p. 55.

JECFA. 1974a. 17th report of Joint FAO/WHO Expert Committee on Food Additives. WHO Food Additives Series No. 5. p. 97.

JECFA. 1974b. 18th report of Joint FAO/WHO Expert Committee on Food Additives. WHO Food Additives Series No. 16. p. 47.

JECFA. 1975. 19th report of Joint FAO/WHO Expert Committee on Food Additives. WHO Food Additives Series No. 8. p. 10.

Jowsey, J., and J. Gershon-Cohen. 1964. Effect of dietary calcium levels on production and reversal of experimental osteoporosis in cats. Proc. Soc. Exp. Biol. Med. 116–437.

Jubb, K. V., L. Z. Saunders, and H. V. Coates. 1956. Thiamine deficiency encephalopathy in cats. J. Comp. Pathol. 66:217.

Kallfelz, F. A., J. D. Bressett, and R. J. Wallace. 1980. Urethral obstruction in random source SPF male cats induced by dietary magnesium. Feline Pract. 10:25.

Kane, E., J. G. Morris, and Q. R. Rogers. 1981a. Acceptability and digestibility by adult cats of diets made with various sources and levels of fat. J. Anim. Sci. 53:1516.

Kane, E., Q. R. Rogers, J. G. Morris, and P. M. B. Leung. 1981b. Feeding behavior of the cat fed laboratory and commercial diets. Nutr. Res. 1:499.

Kane, E., J. G. Morris, Q. R. Rogers, P. J. Ihrke, and P. T. Cupps. 1981c. Zinc deficiency in the cat. J. Nutr. 111:14.

Keesling, P. T., and J. G. Morris. 1975. Vitamin B$_{12}$ deficiency in the cat. J. Anim. Sci. 41:317. (Abstr. 289)

Kendall, P. T. 1984. The use of fat in dog and cat diets. Pp. 383 in Fats in Animal Nutrition, J. Wiseman, ed. Butterworths: Boston.

Kendall, P. T., P. M. Smith, and D. W. Holme. 1982a. Factors affecting digestibility and *in vivo* energy content of cat foods. J. Small Anim. Pract. 25:538.

Kendall, P. T., D. W. Holme, and P. M. Smith. 1982b. Comparative evaluation of net digestive and absorptive efficiency in dogs and cats fed a variety of contrasting diets. J. Small Anim. Pract. 23:577.

Kendall, P. T., S. E. Blaza, and P. M. Smith. 1983. Comparative digestible energy requirements of adult Beagles and domestic cats for bodyweight maintenance. J. Nutr. 113:1946.

Kendall, P. T., I. H. Burger, and P. M. Smith. 1985. Methods of metabolisable energy estimation in cat foods. Feline Pract. 15:38.

Khera, K. S., and I. C. Munro. 1979. A review of the specifications and toxicity of synthetic food colours permitted in Canada. CRC Crit. Rev. Toxicol. 6:81.

Khera, K. S., G. Roberts, G. Trivett, G. Terry, and C. Whalen. 1976. A teratogenicity study with amaranth in cats. Toxicol. Appl. Pharmacol. 38:389.

Knopf, K., J. A. Sturman, M. Armstrong, and K. C. Hayes. 1978. Taurine: an essential nutrient for the cat. J. Nutr. 108:773.

Kobayashi, K. 1981. Onion poisoning in the cat. Feline Pract. 11:22.

Krehl, W. A., G. R. Cowgill, and A. D. Whedon. 1955. Non deleterious effects of polyoxyethylene esters in the nutrition of rats and cats. J. Nutr. 55:35.

Krook, L. 1965. On the etiology of primary parathyroid hyperplasia. Rev. Can. Biol. 24:63.

Krook, L., R. B. Barrett, K. Usui, and R. E. Wolke. 1963. Nutritional secondary hyperparathyroidism in the cat. Cornell Vet. 53:224.

Lawler, D. F., D. W. Sjolin, and J. E. Collins. 1985. Incidence rates of feline lower urinary tract disease in the United States. Feline Pract. 15:13.

Leahy, J. S., K. W. G. Shillam, C. E. Waterhouse, and H. Partington.

1967. Studies of the riboflavin requirements of the kitten. J. Small Anim. Pract. 8:351.

Lewis, L. D., and M. L. Morris, Jr. 1983. Feline urolithiasis. Pp. 1-40 in Small Animal Clinical Nutrition, 1st ed. Topeka: Mark Morris Associates.

Lewis, L. D., and M. L. Morris, Jr. 1984. Feline urologic syndrome: Causes and clinical management. Vet. Med. 79:323.

Lewis, L. D., F. H. C. Chow, G. F. Taton, and D. W. Hamar. 1978. Effect of various dietary mineral concentrations on the occurrence of feline urolithiasis. J. Am. Vet. Med. Assoc. 172:559.

Loew, F. M., C. L. Martin, R. H. Dunlop, R. J. Mapletoft, and S. I. Smith. 1970. Naturally-occurring and experimental thiamin deficiency in cats receiving commercial cat food. Can. Vet. J. 11:109.

Lowe, J. S., R. A. Morton, and J. Vernon. 1957. Unsaponifiable constituents of kidney in various species. Biochem. J. 67:228.

Loveridge, G. G. 1986a. Factors affecting growth performance in male and female kittens. Anim. Tech. In press.

Loveridge, G. J. 1986b. Body weight changes and energy intakes of cats during gestation and lactation. Anim. Tech. 37:15.

MacDonald, M. L., Q. R. Rogers, and J. G. Morris. 1983. Role of linoleate as an essential fatty acid for the cat independent of arachidonate synthesis. J. Nutr. 113:1422.

MacDonald, M. L., B. C. Anderson, Q. R. Rogers, C. A. Buffington, and J. G. Morris. 1984a. Essential fatty acid requirements of cats: Pathology of essential fatty acid deficiency. Am. J. Vet. Res. 45:1310.

MacDonald, M. L., Q. R. Rogers, and J. G. Morris. 1984b. Effects of dietary arachidonate deficiency on the aggregation of cat platelets. Comp. Biochem. Physiol. 78C:123.

MacDonald, M. L., Q. R. Rogers, and J. G. Morris. 1984c. Nutrition of the domestic cat, a mammalian carnivore. Annu. Rev. Nutr. 4:521.

MacDonald, M. L., Q. R. Rogers, J. G. Morris, and P. T. Cupps. 1984d. Effects of linoleate and arachidonate deficiencies on reproduction and spermatogenesis in the cat. J. Nutr. 114:719.

MacDonald, M. L., Q. R. Rogers, and J. G. Morris. 1985. Aversion of the cat to dietary medium-chain triglycerides and caprylic acid. Physiol. Behav. 35:371.

Mansur Guerios, M. F., and G. Hoxter. 1962. Hypoalbuminemia in choline deficient cats. Protides Biol. Fluids Proc. Colloq. 10:199.

Miller, S. A., and J. B. Allison. 1958. The dietary nitrogen requirements of the cat. J. Nutr. 64:493.

Milner, J. A., and W. J. Visek. 1974. Orotate, citrate, and urea excretion in rats fed various levels of arginine. Proc. Soc. Exp. Biol. Med. 147:754.

Molitoris, B. A., and D. H. Baker. 1976. Choline availability in soybean meal. J. Anim. Sci. 42:481.

Moore, T., I. M. Sharman, and P. P. Scott. 1963. Vitamin A in the kidney of the cat. Res. Vet. Sci. 4:397.

Morris, H. J., A. A. Nelson and H. O. Calvery. 1942. Observations on the chronic toxicities of propylene glycol, diethylene glycol, ethylene glycol mono-ethyl-ether and diethylene glycol mono-ethyl-ether. J. Pharmacol. Exp. Ther. 74:266.

Morris, J. G. 1977. The essentiality of biotin and vitamin B_{12} for the cat. Pp. 15–18 in Kal Kan Symposium for Treatment of Dog and Cat Diseases, Ohio State University, Sept. 19–20, 1977.

Morris, J. G. 1985. Nutritional and metabolic responses to arginine in carnivores. J. Nutr. 115:524.

Morris, J. G., and Q. R. Rogers. 1978a. Ammonia intoxication in the near-adult cat as a result of a dietary deficiency of arginine. Science 199:431.

Morris, J. G., and Q. R. Rogers. 1978b. Arginine: An essential amino acid for the cat. J. Nutr. 108:1944.

Morris, J. G., and Q. R. Rogers. 1982. Metabolic basis for some of the nutritional peculiarities of the cat. In Recent Advances in Feline Nutrition, A. T. B. Edney, ed. Waltham Symposium No. 4. J. Small Anim. Pract. 23:599.

Morris, J. G., and Q. R. Rogers. 1983. Amino Acid Requirements of Growing Kittens. Fourth Annu. Pet Food Inst. Tech. Symp. Sept. 23, 1983. Washington, D.C.: Pet Food Institute.

Morris, J. G., J. Trudell, and T. Pencovic. 1977. Carbohydrate digestion by the domestic cat (Felis catus). Br. J. Nutr. 37:365.

Morris, J. G., Q. R. Rogers, D. L. Winterrowd, and E. M. Kamikawa. 1979. The utilization of ornithine and citrulline by the growing kitten. J. Nutr. 109:724.

Morris, M., Jr. 1962. Feline degeneration retinopathy. M.S. thesis. University of Wisconsin, Madison.

Morris, M. L. 1965. Feline degenerative retinopathy. Cornell Vet. 55:296.

Mugford, R. A. 1977. External influences on the feeding of carnivores. Pp. 25–50 in The Chemical Senses and Nutrition, M. R. Kare and O. Maller, eds. New York: Academic Press.

Munson, T. O., J. Holzworth, E. Small, S. Witzel, T. C. Jones, and H. Luginbuhl. 1958. Steatitis ("yellow fat") in cats fed canned red tuna. J. Am. Vet. Med. Assoc. 133:563.

National Research Council (NRC). 1978a. Nutrient Requirements of Cats. Washington, D.C.: National Academy of Sciences.

National Research Council (NRC). 1978b. Nutrient Requirements of Laboratory Animals, 3d ed. Washington, D.C.: National Academy of Sciences.

National Research Council (NRC). 1979. Nutrient Requirements of Swine. Washington, D.C.: National Academy of Sciences.

National Research Council. 1982. United States-Canadian Tables of Feed Composition. Washington, D.C.: National Academy Press.

National Research Council (NRC). 1984. Nutrient Requirements of Poultry. Washington, D.C.: National Academy Press.

Odom, G., and D. McEachern. 1942. Subarachnoid injection of thiamine in cats: unmasking of brain lesions by induced thiamine deficiency. Proc. Soc. Exp. Biol. Med. 50:28.

O'Donnell, J. A., III, Q. R. Rogers, and J. G. Morris. 1981. Effect of diet on plasma taurine in the cat. J. Nutr. 111:1111.

Osbaldiston, G. W., and R. A. Taussig. 1970. Clinical report on 46 cases of feline urological syndrome. Vet. Med. Small Anim. Clin., May 1970.

Osborne, C. A., and J. M. Kruger. 1984. Initiation and growth of uroliths. Vet. Clin. North Am. 14:439.

Osborne, C. A., and G. E. Lees. 1978. Feline cystitis, urethritis, urethral obstruction syndrome. Part 1. Etiopathogenesis and clinical manifestations. Mod. Vet. Pract. 59:173.

Osborne, C. A., G. R. Johnston, D. J. Polzin, J. M. Kruger, E. M. Poffenbarger, F. W. Bell, D. A. Feeney, S. Goyal, T. F. Fletcher, J. A. Newman, J. B. Stevens, and M. F. McMenomy. 1984. Redefinition of the Feline Urologic Syndrome: Feline lower urinary tract disease with heterogenous causes. Vet. Clin. North Am. 14:409.

Palmer, N. C. 1968. Osteodystrophia fibrosa in cats. Austr. Vet. J. 44:151.

Paul, A. A., and D. A. T. Southgate. 1978. In McCance and Widdowson's The Chemical Composition of Foods. New York: Elsevier/North-Holland Biomedical Press.

Pencovic, T. A., and J. G. Morris. 1975. Corn and wheat starch utilization by the cat. J. Anim. Sci. 41:325. (Abstr. 318)

Peterson, M. E., P. P. Kintzer, P. G. Cavanagh, P. R. Fox, D. C. Ferguson, G. F. Johnson, and D. V. Becker. 1983. Feline hyperthyroidism: Pretreatment clinical and laboratory evaluation of 131 cases. J. Am. Vet. Med. Assoc. 183:103.

Pfaffmann, C. 1955. Gustatory nerve impulses in rat, cat, and rabbit. J. Neurophysiol. 18:429.

Phillips, J. C., C. S. Topp, and S. D. Gangolli. 1978. The metabolism of ethyl and n-propyl-p-hydroxybenzoate ("parabens") in male cats. Toxicol. Lett. 2:237.

Porter, R., and G. Lawrenson, eds. 1982. Metabolic Acidosis. CIBA Foundation Symp. 87. London: Pitman.

Prentiss, P. G., A. V. Wolf, and H. A. Eddy. 1959. Hydropenia in cat and dog. Ability of the cat to meet its water requirements solely from a diet of fish or meat. Am. J. Physiol. 196:625.

Quam, D. D., J. G. Morris, and Q. R. Rogers. 1986. Histidine requirement of kittens for growth, haematopoiesis and prevention of cataracts. Br. J. Nutr. In press.

Rabin, A. R., K. C. Hayes, and E. L. Berson. 1973. Cone and rod responses in nutritionally induced retinal degeneration in the cat. Invest. Ophthalmol. 12:694.

Rabin, B., R. J. Nicolosi, and K. C. Hayes. 1976. Dietary influence on bile acid conjugation in the cat. J. Nutr. 106:1241.

Rambaut, P. C., and S. A. Miller. 1965. Studies of sulfur amino acid nutrition in the adult cat. Fed. Proc. 24:373. (Abstr. 1348)

Rambaut, P. C., and S. Miller. 1967. Studies in feline sulfur amino acid metabolism. Proc. VII Int. Congress of Nutrition (1966) Hamburg 164. New York: Pergamon Press. (Abstr.)

Rassin, D. K., J. A. Sturman, and G. E. Gaull. 1978. Taurine and other free amino acids in milk of man and other mammals. Early Hum. Dev. 2:1.

Ratcliff, H. L. 1956. Adequate diets for captive wild animals and notes on tuberculin tests for apes and monkeys. Bull. Penrose Res. Lab., Philadelphia, Pa.

Rea, J. L., and J. C. Drummond. 1932. Formation of vitamin A from carotene in the animal organism. Z. Vitam. Horm. Fermentforsch. 1:177.

Reber, E. F., and O. P. Malhotra. 1961. Effect of feeding a vitamin K-deficient ration containing irradiated beef to rats, dogs and cats. J. Nutr. 74:191.

Reif, J. S. 1977. Feline urethral obstruction: A case control study. J. Am. Vet. Med. Assoc. 170:1320.

Renner, R. 1964. Factors affecting the utilization of "carbohydrate-free" diets by the chick. I. Level of protein. J. Nutr. 84:322.

Renner, R., and A. M. Elcombe. 1964. Factors affecting the utilization of "carbohydrate-free" diets by the chick. II. Level of glycerol. J. Nutr. 84:327.

Rich, L. J., and R. W. Kirk. 1968. Feline urethral obstruction: Mineral aspects. Am. J. Vet. Res. 29:2149.

Rich, L. J., and R. W. Kirk. 1969. The relationship of struvite crystals to urethral obstruction in cats. J. Am. Vet. Med. Assoc. 154:153.

Rich, L. J., M. I. Dysart, F. H. C. Chow, and D. Hamar. 1974. Urethral obstruction in male cats: Experimental production by addition of magnesium and phosphate to diet. Feline Pract. 4:44.

Ritter, S. M., and F. N. Owens. 1974. Methionine requirements of the growing cat. J. Anim. Sci. 39:981. (Abstr.)

Rivers, J. P. W. 1982. Essential fatty acids in cats. J. Small Anim. Pract. 23:563.

Rivers, J. P. W., A. J. Sinclair, and M. A. Crawford. 1975. Inability of the cat to desaturate essential fatty acids. Nature 258:171.

Rivers, J. P. W., A. J. Sinclair, D. P. Moore, and M. A. Crawford. 1976a. The abnormal metabolism of essential fatty acids in the cat. Proc. Nutr. Soc. 35:66A.

Rivers, J. P. W., A. G. Hassam, and C. Alderson. 1976b. The absence of ω-desaturase activity in the cat. Proc. Nutr. Soc. 35:67A.

Rivers, J. P. W., A. G. Hassam, M. A. Crawford, and M. R. Brambell. 1976c. The inability of the lion, *Panthera leo* L., to desaturate linoleic acid. FEBS Lett. 67:269.

Rivers, J. P. W., T. C. Frankel, S. Juttla, and A. W. M. Hay. 1979. Vitamin D in the nutrition of the cat. Proc. Nutr. Soc. 38:364.

Roberts, A. H., and P. P. Scott. 1961. Nutrition of the cat. 5. The influence of calcium and iodine supplements to a meat diet on the retention of nitrogen, calcium and phosphorus. Br. J. Nutr. 15:73.

Robinson, K. and D. H. K. Lee. 1941. Reactions of the cat to hot atmospheres. Proc. R. Soc. Queensl. 53:159.

Roe, D. A., and M. O. Weston. 1965. Potential significance of free taurine in the diet. Nature 205:287.

Rogers, Q. R., and J. G. Morris. 1979. Essentiality of amino acids for the growing kitten. J. Nutr. 109:718.

Rogers, Q. R., and J. G. Morris. 1982a. Do cats really need more protein? J. Small Anim. Pract. 23:521.

Rogers, Q. R., and J. G. Morris. 1982b. Report to the Pet Food Institute, Feline Task Force. 3rd Annu. Pet Food Inst. Tech. Symp. Sept. 24, 1982. Kansas City, Mo.

Rogers, Q. R., and J. G. Morris. 1983. Protein and amino acid nutrition of the cat. Pp. 333–336 in AAHA's 50th Annu. Meet. Proc.

Rogers, Q. R., and J. M. Phang. 1985. Deficiency of pyrroline-5-carboxylate synthase in the intestinal mucosa of the cat. J. Nutr. 115:146.

Rogers, Q. R., J. G. Morris, and R. A. Freedland. 1977. Lack of hepatic enzymatic adaptation to low and high levels of dietary protein in the adult cat. Enzyme 22:348.

Romsos, D. R., P. S. Belo, M. R. Bennink, W. G. Bergen, and G. A. Leveille. 1976. Effects of dietary carbohydrate, fat and protein on growth, body composition and blood metabolite levels in the dog. J. Nutr. 106:1452.

Rowland, G. N., C. C. Capen, and L. A. Nagode. 1968. Experimental hyperparathyroidism in young cats. Path. Vet. 5:504.

Rubin, L. F. 1963. Atrophy of rods and cones in the cat retina. J. Am. Vet. Med. Assoc. 142:1415.

Ruddick, J. A. 1972. Toxicology, metabolism and biochemistry of 1, 2 propanediol. Toxicol. Appl. Pharmacol. 21:102.

Schaeffer, M. C., Q. R. Rogers, and J. G. Morris. 1982a. Methionine requirement of the growing kitten, in the absence of dietary cystine. J. Nutr. 112:962.

Schaeffer, M. C., Q. R. Rogers, and J. G. Morris. 1982b. The choline requirements of the growing kitten in the presence of just adequate dietary methionine. Nutr. Res. 2:289.

Schalm, O. W. 1974. Megaloblastic marrow cytology in the cat: vitamin B12 and folic acid deficiencies (and) erythroleukemia. Feline Pract. 4:16.

Schmidt, S. Y., E. L. Berson and K. C. Hayes. 1976. Retinal degeneration in cats fed casein. I. Taurine deficiency. Invest. Ophthalmol. 15:47.

Schmidt, S. Y., E. L. Berson, G. Watson, and C. Huang. 1977. Retinal degeneration in cats fed casein. III. Taurine deficiency and ERG amplitudes. Invest. Ophthalmol. 16:673.

Schmidt-Nielsen, K. 1964. Desert Animals. Physiological Problems of Heat and Water. New York: Oxford University Press.

Schneck, G. W., and V. Cumberland. 1968. The effect of 10 percent dietary fat addition on the growth rate of cats. Vet. Rec. 83:486.

Scott, P. P. 1959. Calcium and iodine deficiency in meat-fed cats with reference to osteogenesis imperfecta. Proc. Br. Small Anim. Vet. Assoc., p. 84.

Scott, P. P. 1960. Some aspects of the nutrition of the dog and cat. II. The cat. Vet. Rec. 72:5.

Scott, P. P. 1964. Nutritional requirements and deficiencies. In Feline Medicine and Surgery, E. J. Catcott, ed. Santa Barbara, Calif: Am. Vet. Publ. Inc.

Scott, P. P. 1965. Minerals and vitamins in feline nutrition. Pp. 75 in Canine and Feline Nutrition Requirements, O. Graham-Jones, ed. London: Pergamon Press.

Scott, P. P. 1966. Nutrition. Pp. 1–31 in Diseases of the Cat, G. T. Wilkinson, ed. London: Pergamon Press.

Scott, P. P. 1968. The special features of nutrition of cats, with observations on wild felidae nutrition in the London Zoo. Pp. 21–39 *in* Comparative Nutrition of Wild Animals, M. A. Crawford, ed. New York: Academic Press.

Scott, P. P., and J. P. Greaves. 1961. Nutrition of the cat. 4. Calcium and iodine deficiency on a meat diet. Br. J. Nutr. 15:35.

Scott, P. P., and M. G. Scott. 1964. Vitamin A and reproduction in the cat. J. Reprod. Fertil. 8:270.

Scott, P. P., and M. G. Scott. 1967. Nutritive requirements for carnivora. Pp. 163-186 *in* Husbandry of Laboratory Animals. London: Academic Press.

Scott, P. P., and S. Y. Thompson. 1969. The influence of maternal intake of vitamin A on liver and kidney stones in kittens. J. Physiol. 201:79P.

Scott, P. P., J. P. Greaves, and M. G. Scott. 1964. Nutritional blindness in the cat. Exp. Eye Res. 3:357.

Seawright, A. A., and J. Hrdlicka. 1974. Pathogenetic factors in tooth loss in young cats on a high daily oral intake of vitamin A. Austr. Vet. J. 50:133.

Seawright, A. A., P. B. English, and R. J. W. Gartner. 1967. Hypervitaminosis A and deforming cervical spondylosis of the cat. J. Comp. Pathol. 77:29.

Seefeldt, S. L., and T. E. Chapman. 1979. Body water content and turnover in cats fed dry and canned rations. Am. J. Vet. Res. 40:183.

Shane, B., and E. L. R. Stokstad. 1985. Vitamin B_{12}-folate interrelationships. Annu. Rev. Nutr. 5:115.

Sinclair, A. J., J. G. McLean, and E. A. Monger. 1979. Metabolism of linoleic acid in the cat. Lipids 14:932.

Skultety, F. M. 1969. Alterations of caloric intake in cats following lesions of the hypothalamus and mid brain. Ann. N.Y. Acad. Sci. 157:861.

Smalley, K. A., Q. R. Rogers, and J. G. Morris. 1983. Methionine requirement of kittens given amino acid diets containing adequate cystine. Br. J. Nutr. 49:411.

Smalley, K. A., Q. R. Rogers, J. G. Morris, and L. L. Eslinger. 1985. The nitrogen requirement of the weanling kitten. Br. J. Nutr. 53:501.

Smith, B. A. 1974. Effects of early under-nutrition in the kitten: behavior, electroencephalography and brain composition. Ph.D. thesis, Colorado State University, Fort Collins.

Smith, D. C., and L. M. Proutt. 1944. Development of thiamine deficiency in the cat on a diet of raw fish. Proc. Soc. Exp. Biol. Med. 56:1.

Southern, L. L., and D. H. Baker. 1981. Bioavailable pantothenic acid in cereal grains and soybean meal. J. Anim. Sci. 53:403.

Southern, L. L., and D. H. Baker. 1983a. *Eimeria acervulina* infection and the zinc-copper interrelationship in the chick. Poult. Sci. 62:401.

Southern, L. L., and D. H. Baker. 1983b. Zinc toxicity, zinc deficiency and zinc-copper interrelationship in *Eimeria acervulina*-infected chicks. J. Nutr. 113:688.

Spray, C. M., and E. M. Widdowson. 1950. The effect of growth and development on the composition of mammals. Br. J. Nutr. 4:332.

Steenbock, H., V. E. Nelson, and E. B. Hart. 1914. Acidosis in omnivora and herbivora and its relation to protein storage. J. Biol. Chem. 19:399.

Stephan, Z. F., and K. C. Hayes. 1978. Vitamin E deficiency and essential fatty acid status of cats. Fed. Proc. 73:706. (Abstr.)

Stogdale, L., L. Bomzon, and P. B. van den Berg. 1982. Food allergy in cats. J. Am. Anim. Hosp. Assoc. 18:188.

Sturman, J. A., D. K. Rassin, K. C. Hayes, and G. E. Gaull. 1978. Taurine deficiency in the kitten: Exchange and turnover of (35S) taurine in brain, retina and other tissues. J. Nutr. 108:1462.

Sturman, J. A., G. Y. Wen, H. M. Wisniewski, and K. C. Hayes.

1981. Histochemical localization of zinc in the feline tapetum. Effect of taurine depletion. Histochemistry 72:341.

Sturman, J. A., R. C. Moretz, J. H. French, and H. M. Wisniewski. 1985a. Taurine deficiency in the developing cat: Persistence of the cerebellar external granule cell layer. J. Neurosci. Res. 13:405.

Sturman, J. A., R. C. Moretz, J. H. French, and H. M. Wisniewski. 1985b. Postnatal taurine deficiency in the kitten results in persistence of the cerebellar external granule cell layer: Correction by taurine feeding. J. Neurosci. Res. 13:521.

Suhadolnik, R. J., C. O. Stevens, R. H. Decker, L. M. Henderson, and L. V. Hankes. 1957. Species variation in metabolism of 3-hydroxyanthranilate to pyridinecarboxy acids. J. Biol. Chem. 228:973.

Suter, P. 1957. Zur Gefahr der Uberdosierung von vitamin-D praparaten. Schweiz. Arch. Tierheilkd. 99:421.

Sutor, D. J., S. E. Wooley, and O. F. Jackson. 1970. Crystalline material from the feline bladder. Res. Vet. Sci. 11:298.

Sutton, R. H. 1981. Cocoa poisoning in a dog. Vet. Rec. 109:563.

Taton, G. F., D. W. Hamar, and L. D. Lewis. 1984a. Evaluation of ammonium chloride as a urinary acidifier in the cat. J. Am. Vet. Med. Assoc. 184:433.

Taton, G. F., D. W. Hamar, and L. D. Lewis. 1984b. Urinary acidification in the prevention and treatment of feline struvite urolithiasis. J. Am. Vet. Med. Assoc. 184:437.

Teeter, R. G., D. H. Baker, and J. E. Corbin. 1978a. Methionine essentiality for the cat. J. Anim. Sci. 46:1287.

Teeter, R. G., D. H. Baker, and J. E. Corbin. 1978b. Methionine and cystine requirements of the cat. J. Nutr. 108:291.

Thenen, S. W., and K. M. Rasmussen. 1978. Megaloblastic erythropoiesis and tissue depletion of folic acid in the cat. Am. J. Vet. Res. 39:1205.

Thrall, B. E., and L. G. Miller. 1976. Water turnover in cats fed dry rations. Feline Pract. 6:10.

Thurnham, D. I., and P. Rathakette. 1982. Incubation of NAD(P)H$_2$: glutathione oxidoreductase (EC 1.6.4.2) with flavin adenine dinucleotide for maximal stimulation in the measurement of riboflavin status. Br. J. Nutr. 48:459.

Titchenal, C. A., Q. R. Rogers, R. J. Indrieri, and J. G. Morris. 1980. Threonine imbalance, deficiency and neurologic dysfunction in the kitten. J. Nutr. 110:2444.

Toman, J. E. P., G. M. Everett, R. H. Oster, and D. C. Smith. 1945. Origin of cardiac disorders in thiamine-deficient cats. Proc. Soc. Exp. Biol. Med. 58:65.

Trudell, J. I., and J. G. Morris. 1975. Carbohydrate digestion in the cat. J. Anim. Sci. 41:329. (Abstr. 332)

Vermeulen, C. W., H. D. Ragins, W. J. Grove, and R. Goetz. 1951. Experimental urolithiasis. III. Prevention and dissolution of calculi by alteration of urinary pH. J. Urol. 66:1.

Wachman, A., and D. S. Bernstein. 1970. Parathyroid hormone in metabolic acidosis. Its role in pH homeostatis. Clin. Orthop. 69:252.

Warnock, L. G., C. R. Prudhomme, and C. Wagner. 1978. The determination of thiamin pyrophosphate in blood and other tissues, and its correlation with erythrocyte transketolase activity. J. Nutr. 108:421.

Waterhouse, N. H., and D. S. Carver. 1962. Growth rate, food and calorie consumption of laboratory cats. Proc. Anim. Care Panel 12:271.

Westall, R. G. 1953. The amino acids and other ampholytes of urine. 2. The isolation of a new sulphur-containing amino acid from cat urine. Biochem. J. 55:244.

White, T. D., and J. C. Boudreau. 1975. Taste preferences of the cat for neurophysiologically active compounds. Physiol. Psychol. 3:405.

Willeberg, P. 1984. Epidemiology of naturally occurring Feline Urologic Syndrome. Vet. Clin. North Am. 14:455.

Williams, R. T. 1967. Comparative patterns of drug metabolism. Fed. Proc. 26:1029.

Wing, P. C. 1967. The reversibility of nutritional osteitis fibrosa. Diss. Abstr. (B) 27:3735B.

Wolf, A. V., P. G. Prentiss, L. G. Douglas, and R. J. Swett. 1959. Potability of sea water with special reference to the cat. Am. J. Physiol. 196:633.

Yen, J. T., A. H. Jensen, and D. H. Baker. 1976. Assessment of the concentration of biologically available vitamin B-6 in corn and soybean meal. J. Anim. Sci. 42:866.

Zotterman, Y. 1956. Species differences in water taste. Acta Physiol. Scand. 37:60.

Index

115014

Learning Languages through Technology

Edited by Elizabeth Hanson-Smith and Sarah Rilling

TESOL **Teachers of English to Speakers of Other Languages, Inc.**

Typeset in Minion and Eurostile
by Capitol Communication Systems, Inc., Crofton, Maryland USA
Printed by United Graphics, Inc., Mattoon, Illinois USA
Indexed by Coughlin Indexing, Annapolis, Maryland USA

Teachers of English to Speakers of Other Languages, Inc.
700 South Washington Street, Suite 200
Alexandria, Virginia 22314 USA
Tel 703-836-0774 • Fax 703-836-6447 • E-mail tesol@tesol.org • http://www.tesol.org/

Publishing Manager: Carol Edwards
Copy Editor: Sarah J. Duffy
Additional Reader: Ellen Garshick
Cover Design: Tomiko Chapman

ISBN 9781931185363
Library of Congress Control No. 2006909048

Table of Contents

Chapter 1

Introduction: *Using Technology in Teaching Languages*

Elizabeth Hanson-Smith
Command Performance/Computers for Education
Sacramento, California USA

Sarah Rilling
Kent State University
Kent, Ohio USA

Computers and other electronic technologies have come to permeate many daily activities, whether checking bank statements and booking vacations online or sending e-mail and recording voice messages on a cell phone. It should come as no surprise, then, to find that to a great extent, these technologies have been co-opted by the field of education in general, and TESOL in particular. In 1999, Carla Meskill posed a scenario hypothetically taking place twenty minutes into the future (that is, in 2005) in which a high school student on his way home from class opens his laptop on a train and interacts with his private electronic tutor. He reviews the day's lesson (a courtroom simulation); examines the video recording and text discourse; makes notes about vocabulary; and prepares for the next day's lesson using keyboard, voice, and video tools (Meskill 1999). What is amazing is the degree to which that scenario has come true, especially as various technologies—cell phones, laptops, iPods, personal digital assistants (PDAs)—converge. Most teachers have probably been to conferences where the hotels, convention centers, and Internet cafes are totally "wired" (that is, wireless) for Internet use. Open your laptop and you are online; open your cell phone and you are online. Access to the Web can take place anytime, anywhere.

Permeation of technology is seen everywhere. Whole countries, such as Turkey, are building the electronic infrastructure to connect all students, and eventually all citizens, to the Web for educational purposes. The University of Western Cape, in South Africa, recently welcomed its first e-learning students from the Universities of Dar es Salaam and Zambia to a transnational, multi-institutional online degree program in information technology (IT) and telecommunications policy. In the United States, Maine's laptop initiative put portable computers in the hands of all schoolchildren, who took them on virtual and actual field trips, collecting data and writing reports for such varied projects as community oral history and the investigation of local water quality (Curtis 2003). The University of Texas at Austin, College of Education (n.d.) laptop initiative seeks "to immerse future teachers in technology-rich environments so that they become competent in using technology learning tools in their instruction" (¶1). Other laptop programs in the schools have proven highly successful in engaging students in academic literacy skills (Warschauer et al. 2004), and there is talk of a solar- or hand-powered "$100 laptop" (OLPC 2006, ¶2). Meanwhile, universities are delivering lectures online via audio files and podcasting. Collaborations between and among classrooms and teachers are taking place daily, around the clock and around the world (e.g., the GLOBE project described by Kennedy in chapter 7 of this volume).

Integrating technologies into language pedagogy has become a reality for TESOL practitioners even as students around the world increasingly need both English and technology skills for their future careers in the workforce (Shetzer and Warschauer 2000; Thatcher 2005). Personal computers, cell phones, and PDAs are but a few of the electronic devices that teachers increasingly are using to meet the digital needs of diverse learners in the twenty-first century. Interestingly, English is not the only beneficiary, as technology is also allowing less commonly spoken languages, such as Welsh, to spread and strengthen.

Learning Languages through Technology offers a broad survey of how language learning takes place with and through computer technologies. Each chapter situates practices within specific contexts and supports those practices through research. The authors, from educational institutions in many regions of the world, offer examples of a wide variety of technologies, from the lowest levels, such as word processing and scanning, to high-end multimedia and interactive communications through voice and video on the Internet. Where appropriate, an appendix to each chapter lists the tools, software, and Web sites that its authors have found helpful in using technology with learners. This volume demonstrates how teachers captivate the imagination of learners, from schoolchildren to postgraduates, by providing real-world purposes for language while also posing important questions about how learning proceeds with new technologies. Text, video, and voice tools have become relatively inexpensive and increasingly easy for educators to use, and they play an important role in creating lessons and communicating with students and fellow teachers. Describing authentic, collaborative tasks that involve learners in using and expanding their language and technology skills together, each author contributes to the description of tools and technologies that can provide learners with multiple avenues for language development.

Technology for Learning Languages

With technological tools increasingly available in educational contexts around the world, ESOL professionals are incorporating a variety of applications into their administrative and teaching duties. Three types of practices typify current technology uses for teachers:

1. *Administrative*—The teacher uses the computer for administrative or organizational functions, such as record keeping; word processing to produce texts (i.e., creating lesson plans and student materials); e-mailing parents; or participating in professional development (see Dahlman and Tahtinen, chapter 16; Stevens, chapter 19).

2. *Blended*—The teacher uses computers with students in an environment that combines face-to-face (f2f) classrooms with computerized tasks (see Kennedy, chapter 7; Almeida d'Eça, chapter 12; Jewell, chapter 13). Blended practices include

   - using single, stand-alone computers in the corner of a classroom for group information gathering or writing projects,
   - taking classes into a computer lab or classroom on scheduled days,
   - teaching in a fully computerized classroom (one workstation per student) with a combination of f2f and computer collaborations,
   - using home or public computers as the site for information retrieval and discussion outside of class. (Egbert 2005)

3. *Distance*—The teacher uses computers to support distance learning, where learners meet only virtually (see Kim, chapter 5; Schramm and Mabbott, chapter 18). Distance courses maximize the use of the computer as a communications tool and a nexus of information through the various multimedia functions that are increasingly accessible on and through the Internet. Distance courses usually employ a course management system (see Trites, chapter 15; Gommlich and Minick, chapter 17).

ESOL teachers and administrators are turning to computer technologies to make many of their tasks more efficient. Many studies, including Sokolik's (see chapter 11), indicate student approval of new technologies. To understand why using technology can make language learning faster, easier, less painful, and more engaging, we refer to the conditions that make language learning possible, which we as educators try to incorporate each time we prepare our lessons. The following eight conditions for optimal language learning environments were outlined in Egbert and Hanson-Smith's (1999) now classic *CALL Environments: Research, Practice, and Critical Issues*:

1. Learners have opportunities to interact with each other and negotiate meaning.
2. Learners interact in the target language with an authentic audience.
3. Learners are involved in authentic tasks.
4. Learners are exposed to and encouraged to produce varied and creative language.
5. Learners have enough time and feedback.
6. Learners are guided to attend mindfully to the learning process.
7. Learners work in an atmosphere with an ideal stress/anxiety level.
8. Learner autonomy is supported. (Egbert, Chao, and Hanson-Smith 1999, 6)

A technology-rich environment can support all these conditions and thus become an optimal setting for language acquisition, a setting that breaks out of the constricted environment of the typical paper-and-chalkboard classroom. However, these eight conditions refer to learner activity, and it is often unclear to teachers how they can best provide a technology-rich environment that supports these types of activities. This volume meets the need for examples of instructional activities that pre- and in-service teachers can use to prepare computer-supported curricula.

Technology provides two paths to optimal language learning conditions: software (which increasingly is delivered over the Internet) and Internet communications. If one thinks for a moment of multimedia CDs or DVDs, it is evident that learners are exposed through such materials to a wide variety of language (Condition 4); they get instant feedback (Condition 5); they are able to repeat words and phrases as often as they wish during practice (Conditions 5, 6, 7, and 8); they are given rewards and incentives to practice, such as games and entertaining challenges, as well as opportunities to explore and manipulate language (Conditions 6 and 7); and they are able to access the disks where, when, and as often as they want (Condition 8). Adding the Internet to this mix, especially live text and voice chat, curricular collaborations, and Web-based media projects, provides abundant opportunities for interaction with native speakers and peers, the negotiation of meaning, authentic audience, and authentic tasks (Conditions 1, 2, 3, and 4).

Short of adoption by a target-language-speaking family before the age of seven, technology is perhaps the best environment that language teachers can devise for learning, as even the earliest studies suggest. (For meta-analyses of a broad range of quantitative studies on the effectiveness of teaching and learning with technology, see Glennan and Melmed 1996; Waxman, Lin, and Michko 2003.) As technology spreads through the kinds of infrastructure currently projected—wireless anytime, anywhere; free access at libraries and community centers; access to the Internet through a home's electrical current—technology is only going to get better.

Research on Technology in Language Learning

A sign of the maturity of computer-assisted language learning (CALL) is that a respectable body of research, including quantitative as well as structured qualitative and action research studies, has come into existence over the past five years or so. More than five thousand research and pedagogy articles on CALL, published since 1988, have been compiled into a database documented by Jung (2005). While early writings about CALL often focused on the how-to-do-it aspect, there is now a considerable body of quantitative investigation in CALL, often using the unique features of technology as part of the research. The following are just a few examples: a study of the appropriateness and acceptability of synthesized speech in various CALL software programs (Handley and Hamel 2005; Petrushin 2001); recordings of keystroke and eye gaze to investigate usability (B. Smith and Gorsuch 2004); computer-based pre- and posttests and chronological profiles to measure learning gains and assist performance (Belz 2004); an examination of developing conversational skill in recordings of synchronous voice chat (Payne and Whitney 2002); patterns of repair or negotiated interaction recorded in text and voice chat (Jepson 2005); and an analysis of students' reflections using the computer's ability to record visual and aural interaction in a voice conference (Levy and Kennedy 2004).

Further indications that CALL research has come of age are the appearance and increased recognition of highly respected, refereed online journals in the field, such as *Lan-*

guage *Learning & Technology*, *Reading Online*, and *TESL-EJ*. According to a study published in *Nature*, articles appearing online are over 300 percent more likely to be cited than those appearing in paper text alone (Lawrence 2002), so the presence of both appropriate research and a technologically appropriate distribution of its results has been a major advance in the field of CALL. Beatty, as long ago as 2003, listed eight journals and newsletters devoted to computer technology in language learning, seven international annual CALL conferences, and nine professional organizations focusing on CALL issues. Those numbers continue to grow every year. Recent issues of two major journals, *System* (2004, volume 32) and *Computers and Composition* (2005, volume 22), have focused on concerns specific to language learners in technology-enhanced environments, demonstrating the importance given to learners in online environments and the interdisciplinary nature of and interest in such research. Each of the chapters in this volume has found support in the now solid body of research about CALL, which has gone well beyond anecdotal evidence and how-to articles.

Another significant indicator of CALL's respectability in and importance to the field of language pedagogy is the changed focus of research. Early studies in the field made a concerted effort to compare so-called traditional courses to computer-assisted courses. The effort has proven futile. There is no single or unified traditional method, nor is there a single or unified approach to CALL. And there is no way to readily compare paper-and-chalkboard classes to computer-mediated classes; the introduction of computer mediation changes far too many variables in types of tasks and individual motivation. In addition, such comparisons imply that computers could perform the functions of teachers, which, in most respects, they do not (Egbert, Chao, and Hanson-Smith 1999). In case after case, teachers report that integrating technology into instruction goes beyond merely changing the media for completing course tasks and delivering assignments. Instead, students are engaging in authentic learning projects (e.g., WebQuests, slide shows, photo Weblogs [Web + log, or blog], and video productions) that are facilitated by the use of technology, and they are involved in quite different processes than more traditional forms of paper-based research and writing. Researching language learning or language development tasks in computer-enhanced environments must focus on context-sensitive, unique loci—each with its own cultural and rhetorical reality—from which other teacher-researchers can gain insights (De Pew and Miller 2005; Warschauer 2000b).

Research on language learning with and through technology also crosses disciplinary lines, resulting in new research methodologies (Chapelle 2004) with concomitant instructional implications. Simply scanning the tables of contents of online journals indicates that recent studies in CALL draw on research in second language acquisition, foreign and second language learning, composition studies, applied linguistics (including corpus linguistics), and the cognitive and social sciences. Studies also cross international boundaries (e.g., studies of European Union teacher attitudes toward computers in education; Kollias et al. 2005; Veermans and Cesareni 2005). In addition, universities are gradually learning new ways to value research and service that integrate twenty-first-century technologies into instruction (Gruber 2000). Of greatest importance, research informs classroom practice, as demonstrated by the chapters in this volume.

Learning Languages through Technology reflects the fact that there are now as many ways to use computers and the Internet as there are traditional, land-based methods of teaching, and it is becoming increasingly difficult to find classrooms that do not somehow make use of electronic technologies, even if it is simply a student e-mailing a teacher about next week's test. While many students around the world are just being introduced to technology in education, their responses universally reflect those of the students involved in the Maine laptop experiment mentioned earlier; as diSessa (2000) puts it, computers offer children the opportunity to learn "with a pleasure and commitment that only a privileged few now feel toward school learning" (p. ix). In turn, instructors are "reinvigorated by a new way of teaching that encourages real-world problem-solving and individual student initiative" (Curtis 2003, ¶1). Many of the chapters in this volume demonstrate this new attitude and the high motivation that characterizes much of the experimentation with CALL. Rather than contrasting CALL to the traditional classroom, many carefully planned research projects are comparing how different types of computer and Internet use can affect learning (see Chen, Belkada, and Okamoto 2004, who look at different types of group work in a Web-based course; Trites, chapter 15 in this volume). The Questions and Activities at the end of each section in the volume are intended to lead the reader further into this discussion of the role technology plays in learning—both currently and in the future.

The Organization of This Volume

This text is divided into four sections. The first, Language Development Online: Skill Building through Technology, deals with what might be thought of as current best practices in using technology within the four skill areas of reading, writing, speaking, and listening. The authors embed considerations of grammar, vocabulary, rhetoric, and culture in various ways throughout these chapters because teaching with and through technology seems to lend itself particularly well to holistic language approaches.

The second section, Content-Based and Task-Based Learning: Collaborative CALL, proves how well the Internet supports content-rich curricula, both in the exploration of content Web sites and in the ability to ensure that students work collaboratively, locally as well as globally. In contrast to instructor-based learning, in which much of the input comes from the teacher and interaction often takes place primarily between the teacher and the class as a whole (e.g., lecture mode), computer-mediated communication tools dominate how this section's authors plan and conduct courses and activities. The locus of power in the classroom shifts from the sage on the stage to students and student teams. Many of the activities involve local group work as well as collaborations with peers throughout cyberspace. Instead of depending upon imagined scenarios and hypothetical situations, students apply their technology skills in tasks with large doses of authenticity.

The third section, Authentic Audience in a Web-Based World, describes several different educational settings—elementary school, high school, an intensive English program, and graduate teacher education courses—all delivered either through blended (on- and off-campus) or wholly online courses. As learning increasingly takes place outside the walls of a school, teachers must be alert to reducing isolation, promoting interconnections among students and between students and themselves, and fostering social interactivity that is both emotionally rewarding and educationally inspiring.

The last section of this volume, Constructivism in Professional Development, offers practical advice for structuring meaningful educational scenarios that can be applied in subject-matter courses and language courses, as well as in teacher education. Constructivism (and its related variant, *connectivism*; Siemens 2004), as theme and approach, runs throughout the entire volume. It implies the creation of meaning, beyond simply putting two and two together or getting the correct answers on a test, and the social interactivity that supports, enhances, and reinforces learning. Constructivism is perhaps the simple answer to the question, "How do people know as much as they do with as little information as they get?" (Landauer and Dumais 1997, ¶1). While behavioral approaches break down learning into its smallest parts, each to be mastered bit by bit, a constructivist approach provides large quantities of input—usually in a hands-on fashion. This approach allows students to interact with the materials and each other, to explore and create, all the while relying and expanding on what they already know, both individually and collectively, to construct and use new meanings. The sum is always greater than the parts, and individualization in learning takes place as students, consciously or unconsciously, absorb new concepts and vocabulary, making them their own. Important aspects of such learning opportunities, particularly as enhanced by technology, include reflecting on one's own educational processes, collaborating with others to complete projects, and interacting socially to create and sustain communities of practice.

Each chapter in this volume opens with a preview of ideas to ponder before reading. Each of the four sections begins with a preview of the chapters it contains and concludes with a thought-provoking chapter focused on a particular issue in technology and pedagogy. Follow-up questions for class discussion, further research, and activities appear at the end of each section. We hope that these elements will be helpful to in-service teachers who are using or thinking about using technology, or for further classroom explorations of CALL with a teacher educator.

Language Development Online: Skill Building through Technology

This section considers some of the more interesting technology-enhanced approaches in the four skill areas of speaking (González, chapter 2), reading (Sevier, chapter 3), writing (Reppen and Vásquez, chapter 4), and listening (Kim, chapter 5). These approaches include synchronous voice chat for oral skills; concordancing for reading and vocabulary; interactive, guided modules for elements of academic composing; and micro- and macrolistening strategies online. While exercises, quizzes, and games for grammar and vocabulary have become commonplace on the Web, these authors include rhetoric, culture, content genre, research, and communication in global approaches to language teaching that also support structured and individualized learning. The concluding issue-focused chapter in this section deals with the problem of autonomy in learning a highly social skill—language. Robb (chapter 6) asks if teachers are abandoning learners in their eagerness to let learners be independent. How much teaching is too little?

Chapter 2

Using Synchronous Communication Collaboratively in ESP

Dafne González
Universidad Simón Bolívar
Caracas, Venezuela

Preview

As the Internet becomes increasingly speedy, voice chat, Web telephony, podcasts, and radio webcasting are evincing rapid growth in popularity. In this chapter González offers a number of activities that make use of voice chat rooms—virtual environments for learning that are highly motivating, in sometimes surprising ways—for the students in her English for architecture class. To properly prepare voice chat activities, she relies on the principles of communicative language learning: content- and task-based activities; student collaboration in pairs, triads, and groups; and interactive, constructivist notions of how learning proceeds when students create their own language exercises, generate their own glossary, and construct online oral presentations and complex real-time events with authentic audiences.

Before you read:

- What kinds of Internet applications (e.g., e-mail, chat) do you already use? How extensively? What else do you use the Internet to achieve in your daily personal or professional life?

- Have you used voice chat technologies on the Internet? Have you used other voice technologies (e.g., podcasts, online video)? How? How do these applications provide appropriate learning environments for developing language skills?

Language and Content on the Web

Teaching EFL to English for specific purposes (ESP) students in an academic setting presents several challenges to teachers: finding authentic materials for the specific field; engaging students' motivation in the subject when they and their content teachers usually do not consider English to be an important course; getting students to speak the target language to reach the aspired communicative competence when they do not see the need to communicate with English in their daily lives; and, most of all, dealing with content for which most language teachers do not have the necessary preparation or knowledge. Facing such challenges, in turn, means learning by doing through self-instruction (Orr 1995).

The arrival of computers and the Internet in the language classroom has permitted teachers to face some of these challenges with a new vision. ESP practitioners have found the Web to be an infinite source of materials. Moreover, the Internet and the World Wide Web, its multimedia documents and protocols, provide access to a great variety of formats that cater to students' different cognitive and learning styles, for example, plain text, hypertext, images, graphics, sound, video, and virtual kinesthetic activity in simulations. However, having an abundance of materials and modes of communication does not solve the problem of how teachers use computers to keep students motivated and engaged. Coghlan (2005) calls technology's impact on students the WOW! factor, and it has to be exploited because it will wear off if students and teachers use the computer simply as a book.

Making use of authentic materials found on the Web is, of course, very important, but teachers have to consider other aspects that are paramount if learning is to take place in a language course: enabling interaction with real audiences to promote negotiation of meaning, and providing enough and appropriate feedback (Egbert, Chao, and Hanson-Smith 1999). The method for putting all these ingredients together is the key to any successful lesson, and working with technologies is no exception. Using Web tools, teachers can create the necessary conditions for communicative teaching and learning. If teachers stick to the premises that (1) the reason for learning a language is communicating with a purpose—one that is meaningful to both speaker/writer and listener/reader—and (2) learning is a social phenomenon, then interaction and collaboration emerge as the factors to promote students' learning. In this context, Web tools can play an important role.

Computer-mediated communication (CMC) can be carried out synchronously, in real time, or asynchronously, in delayed mode, allowing teachers to deal with all four language skills. Asynchronous tools, which include e-mail, message forums, Weblogs (blogs, which allow visitor comments), and wikis (Web pages that can be edited collaboratively online), are helpful in reading and writing, while synchronous tools, especially voice tools, can be used to practice speaking and listening. Text-based e-conversations have been found to promote the negotiation of meaning (Pelletieri 2000), and computerized voice chat further enhances interaction and collaboration.

In this chapter, I describe in detail some activities I have used in undergraduate English for architecture courses at Universidad Simón Bolívar, in Caracas, Venezuela. These can be adapted to any ESP or even general English (GE) course. Since the ability to speak English and communicate with English speakers from other countries is a key goal in the architecture undergraduate program, voice chat is the leading medium, but other tools have been incorporated as ubiquitously as possible. Although I had been using similar collaborative activities in my face-to-face (f2f) classes for many years, when I found suitable electronic media, my classes became even more interesting, and my students used the target language more intensively. Part of the interest and excitement is generated by talking live to international guests, something that really brings home the WOW! factor. My students use English to talk about architecture while learning to use the computer and the Internet. To quote from student responses to an anonymous course evaluation, "This is great for our daily life, and our future jobs," and "We are learning and having fun."

Communication, Collaboration, and Content-Based Learning

The activities described in this chapter are based on the premise that language learning is a social and cognitive phenomenon (see Dewey 1916/1966; Piaget 1965; Vygotsky 1978) and that it integrates awareness of structural elements, the internal cognitive processes of individuals, and their interaction with the context. Fairclough (1999) argues that texts or discourses are social spaces where two fundamental social processes take place: cognition and social interaction, both of paramount importance for communicative language learning. If students are to be communicatively competent in the target language, interaction and negotiation of meaning should be carried out with authentic audiences. Sociolinguistic and strategic competencies also need interaction—the use of language with others to negotiate meaning. CMC, especially chat, is a significant means to achieve these competencies and takes students well beyond other electronic media. To help my students become communicatively competent in the broadest sense, I have tried to intertwine three main strands in my course activities: *communicative approaches*, *cooperative learning*, and *content-based instruction*.

Communicative language teaching has given birth to various pedagogical techniques and approaches, but those best reflecting this approach in the classroom are content-based (Brinton, Snow, and Wesche 2003), task-based (Nunan 2001; Willis 1996), and cooperative learning techniques (Kagan 1994; LeLoup and Ponterio 2000). As the name implies, in the task-based approach, tasks are the fundamental unit of the lesson. They should promote real communication through activities in which the language is used to carry out meaningful real-life tasks, not just to practice a set of structures. Teachers have three main roles within this approach: selecting, adapting, or designing the tasks; facilitating their implementation; and creating techniques to help students notice the forms of the language (Schmidt 1994b), thus converting them into intake (Gass 1997), without having to plan the whole lesson around grammar or vocabulary. Tasks provide not only the input and output (Swain 1985) but also the opportunities for negotiation of meaning since students learn the language through communicative interactions (Pica 1994) while carrying out the activities. Following the tenets of communicative language teaching, I have designed the online activities for my architecture course as a set of successive tasks that are part of a larger project, the final product of each course.

Cooperative learning (CL), a second major strand in planning communicative lessons, focuses on group learning, with its roots in ancient tribal customs. CL has traditionally been part of educational practices, and its effectiveness has been reported in many studies (e.g., D. González 2004b, 2004c; D. W. Johnson, Johnson, and Holubec 1988; Slavin 1995). Maximum use of activities involving pairs, triads, and small groups puts students at the center of the educational process. Interaction, collaboration, common and individual goals, rules for team work—these are some of the strategies of CL, with a focus on the role of social interaction in learning. One of the many advantages of CL is the possibility of working with heterogeneous groups consisting of mixed-ability students, which is the case in many ESP and GE courses.

Content-based instruction (CBI) integrates language with content instruction. CBI and ESP emphasize the need to use authentic materials, work in cooperative groups, and promote the use of higher-order thinking and study skills that might be transferable to other areas of study or work. The conscious use of metacognitive strategies for students to plan, monitor, and reflect on their own learning is another element of CBI that promotes learner autonomy and represents the kinds of demands faced in higher-level schooling and occupations.

These three teaching-learning principles—the communicative approach, CL, and CBI—can be harmoniously integrated into a blended (f2f and online) course, and I use the graphic in Figure 2.1 as a reminder to integrate them into my planning.

I have not mentioned the motivational aspect of language learning, but not because it

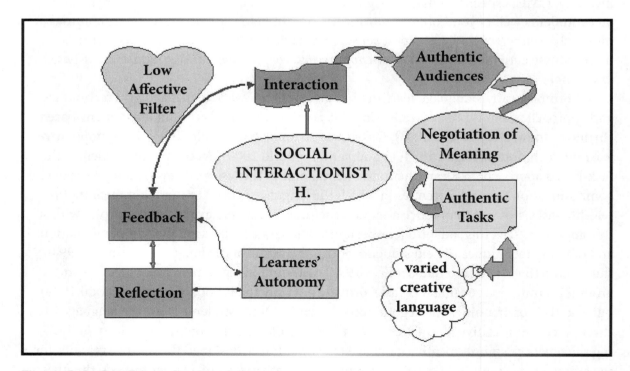

Figure 2.1. Conditions for Acquisition
Source: D. González 2004b.

is unimportant. On the contrary, it is the umbrella under which the other aspects should be developed. The use of tasks and CL techniques in a content-based methodology integrated with the use of CMC tools should be, and has been in my classes, a trigger to increase motivation. Technology provides the WOW! factor, and it is hoped that the collaborative tasks—learning with and from each other—make that effect enduring. In the following section, I describe some computer-assisted language learning and CMC activities that have been successful with my architecture students.

Applying Communicative Principles Online

As can be inferred from the previous section, what I want to achieve in my computer and f2f blended courses is interaction and collaboration with real audiences using authentic materials, and I have found that voice chat is the application that best suits my purpose. Depending on the sophistication of the chat application, in a typical voice chat environment, speakers take turns by "raising a hand" to indicate their intention to take the floor. Only one person may speak at a time, and the moderator may control turn taking. Meanwhile, participants may text chat in another scrolling frame. Users share Web pages by typing in URLs, which become active links, or the moderator "pushes" a Web page to the whiteboard window for all to see or transmits a presentation slide show from a computer. Users may also upload photos to the whiteboard and draw or type text into it (see Figure 2.2 for an example of a whiteboard used in a voice chat at LearningTimes.org [n.d.]). In the most elegant chat spaces (which may include using a webcam to enhance the live, f2f feeling), all the displayed Web pages, the voice recording, and the text log or transcript are saved as one large file that recreates the entire experience. In applications without a whiteboard, such as Yahoo! Messenger (2005), the audio and text log are saved as separate files.

Through my experiences with chat while presenting at and attending online conferences, I have identified several characteristics of the medium that support communicative approaches and enhance language learning:

- interaction with real audiences (those who listen in order to get the message and not its form)
- reception of input and production of output
- immediate feedback from interlocutors
- no restrictions regarding location
- opportunity for negotiation of meaning
- collaborative learning for the purpose of knowledge construction
- opportunity for intake
- chatlogs (written transcription of chat) that allow further analysis of conversation and add coherence to the different threads
- promotion of learner autonomy (See also D. González 2003b.)

After discussing how I plan online or blended courses for interactivity, I provide some examples of activities with voice chat that I have used with my students.

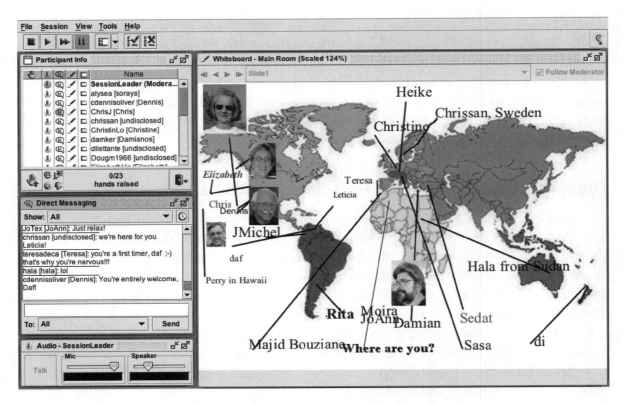

Figure 2.2. Voice Chat Whiteboard with Photos and Drawings

Source: Webheads in Action virtual office in LearningTimes.org, sponsored by a Global Collaboration Grant and Elluminate (http://home.learningtimes.net/learningtimes?go=1042112; login required).

Planning of Online Learning

I design an entire blended course before it starts—syllabus, timetable, activities, exercises, resources, and all. I start a Moodle (2005; a course management system [CMS]) or a Yahoo! Group (2006), both of which are free. These *communication centers* are our virtual learning environments, online platforms where students find all the information pertaining to the courses and where we interact asynchronously. (Although both platforms have a text chat feature, we prefer to use Yahoo! Messenger [2005], which offers more advantages.) Whereas all assignments in Moodle are posted in the forums created for each activity, in Yahoo! Groups I create my own folders for this purpose, and then I post each lesson plan with step-by-step instructions and links to resources, such as online dictionaries. In this way, students can go back to them whenever necessary. Students need only an e-mail account and Web access to use either platform.

I also create a separate Web page for each of my courses to show to other teachers who are not enrolled in my password-protected courses. These Web pages contain all the lesson plans, activities, and links, but without any specific student information. In this way, I protect my students' privacy should they not want their work to be seen by other teachers. For teachers who do not know how to create a Web page, there are other alternatives to presenting content online, such as blogs; wikis (Web pages that can be edited collaboratively online);

and even free templates to generate lessons quickly with, for example, Filamentality (2006), WebWizard (n.d.), DiscoverySchool.com: Teaching Tools (Discovery Education 2005), LessonPro (Strategic Studies 1999–2002), or Module Maker (McKenzie 2000), to name a few.

By incorporating Web pages into my courses, I do not require students to be physically present in the computer room, which mainly serves as a resource for those who do not have easy access to computers or the Internet from other locations. Students can attend the class from a remote location, or if the group agrees, they can meet on other days to complete their assignments because they have a week for each one. The following are some examples of course activities.

Image Descriptions and Drawings

By using pictures and voice chat on the Web, I give a new twist to a familiar picture-pair activity to practice descriptive terms and listening-speaking skills in a content area (see boxed text below). The voice chat can be recorded to give the instructor a window onto every student's performance.

Another way to carry out this activity is to give a pair of students prerecorded descriptions, and then both students have to find the picture being described. Both are encouraged to discuss why they do or do not consider a picture to be the one described. Because architecture students love drawing, I use another variant of this activity to allow them to draw the images being described. For this task, I use Groupboard (n.d.), an application that allows students to draw on a whiteboard collaboratively in groups of up to five. (Any other whiteboard, such as NetMeeting [2000], could also be used.) Students can use the text chat provided on the site or the voice chat in Yahoo! Messenger (2005) to communicate while drawing.

Image Description Activity

1. Students are assigned a classmate to work with, or they can select whom they want to work with.
2. Students open a voice chat.
3. One student opens a Web page, blog, or any other Web document that has four to five pictures (I use architectural pictures: buildings, houses, bridges, door knobs, doors, windows, balconies, etc.), and the other student opens a Web document with the descriptions of these elements.
4. The student with the descriptions selects one of them and reads or summarizes it to his or her classmate.
5. The student with the pictures tries to select the one that the other student describes verbally. The student trying to guess the answer can ask questions when something is not clear. Both students can use text chat to clarify doubts.
6. Students take turns describing or selecting images.
7. Students can use online dictionaries to look up unknown words. These words will be added to a class glossary.

Jigsaw Reading

The jigsaw reading activity (see boxed text below) is a more complex information-gap group activity that emulates professional research teams on a modest scale. Students obtain information from a reading that is too long to be read by each student in a single class, or the activity can be used simply to make the reading process less tedious and more meaningful. I select readings to complement the topics we cover in the f2f class. Online note taking is encouraged.

Expert Jigsaw Groups

This information-gap activity has wider dimensions than the jigsaw reading activity. The task works well when the class has many resources for a broad topic with subtopics. The idea is that each group of students becomes expert on a subtopic. One member of each group then joins another group to share expertise on the topic.

Jigsaw Reading Activity

1. Students are divided into groups of three to five, depending on the length of the reading, and are assigned the Web page and section to be read individually.
2. While reading, students take notes using a word processor or electronic notebook.
3. They summarize the content, meanwhile looking up words in an online dictionary and writing down the vocabulary that is not familiar to them.
4. Once students have finished reading and taking notes, they join the members of their group for a voice chat conference. One of the members opens the conference and invites the others.
5. The student who has the first part of the text explains his or her reading part to the rest of the group. The others can ask questions when they do not understand something.
6. Once all parts of the reading have been explained, the group discusses questions previously assigned by the teacher.
7. One of the students in the group saves the chat and posts it to the CMS (part of the group's assessment).
8. Students write individual summaries of the reading on their blog or post them to a specified forum or folder. Sometimes they are asked to make an audio recording of the summary, using a desktop tool such as Handybits (2005), for individual assessment.
9. Each student copies new vocabulary found in the reading, with corresponding meanings, to the glossary section of Moodle (2005) or to a folder if using Yahoo! Groups (2006).
10. Students are encouraged to read some of their classmates' summaries and to write comments.
11. Students perform follow-up activities, such as answering questions, creating tables, writing or recording a summary, creating timelines, or making drawings, depending on the content and structure of the reading.

Expert Jigsaw Groups Activity

First Group Creation

1. Students are divided into groups of three to five.
2. Each group is assigned a different topic.
3. Each member of the group gets one to three links to Web pages corresponding to a subtopic.
4. Each member goes over the Web pages and takes notes to report back to the group.
5. Each group calls a voice chat conference.
6. Each member gives a report, and the group discusses the main points of the subtopic.
7. The recording and chat log are saved and posted for others to listen to and read.

Second Group Creation

1. The second groups are made up of one member from each of the previous groups. In that way, each group has an expert in each subtopic.
2. The new groups hold a chat conference.
3. Members present and discuss their specialized information.
4. Group members come to agreement regarding the whole topic.
5. Students complete follow-up activities as in the Jigsaw Reading Activity.

I offer two examples of these activities (see boxed text above) taken from my architecture classes. In the first, the aim of the unit is for students to learn the characteristics of Modernism in Valencia, Spain. I have twenty-five descriptions of Modernist buildings and their corresponding pictures, and twenty-five students in the class. Each student in the first group of five selects a building and its pictures, studies them, and writes a summary for their group mates. During the voice chat, they look for the characteristics of their five buildings and jot them down. In this way, five groups of students describe the characteristics of five buildings per group. Then one member from each group joins another group and, in a voice chat, discusses the five characteristics brought from the original team. At the end of this second chat, the class has covered the twenty-five buildings and is able to discuss the general characteristics of Modernism in Valencia. Since I listen in on each chat, and the prompt materials are written in English, the students must use the target language for the discussion.

In the second example, the aim is to learn about different elements needed to plan a house. For this activity, each group member becomes expert in one of the following areas: flooring, siding, plumbing, roofing, kitchen, energy efficiency, windows, or doors. The whole group must decide which house they will work with. Individuals select their favorite house plan from a set of Web pages and describe it according to what they have learned in their professional program about rhythm, acoustics, space, scale, and circulation. They try to persuade others to vote for their choice. The group votes using an online poll in which they can see all the house plans and cast their votes. Once the whole group has selected a house, the students must choose various external elements, such as location and type of inhabitants. They are then given Web page links where they read the information for each specialist role and select the most suitable materials and appliances. Then, as a group, they evaluate and defend their selections during a voice chat. Finally, they present the product to the rest of the class. All the discussions are carried out in voice chat, and the students save the text chat logs and recordings so that everyone in the class can read and hear them.

The idea behind these activities is that each student has a piece of information that is essential for the others to complete the task assigned to the group. Collaboration, interaction, and negotiation of meaning are some of the means to perform these activities. A particularly helpful aspect of these activities is the dictionary that students create with the words they do not know, not the ones I think they do not know. They do it in a collaborative process for the benefit of the whole group. To allow the students to practice the vocabulary they have chosen, I use their lists to create interactive online exercises that students can do on their own at anytime. I also ask them to contribute their own vocabulary exercises, such as crossword puzzles, Hangman, or practice in matching words to definitions or pictures. I provide links to online exercise creators, such as Quia Web (Quia 1998–2006) or Makers Pages (n.d.). The exercises that the students create are also posted to the CMS for easy access.

Video Chat

For a whole-class video and chat activity, I use Real English videos (The Marzio School and Real English 2006), which are recorded in the street with authentic native and nonnative speakers of English (rather than actors) and complemented with Hot Potatoes (Arneil and Holmes 2005) interactive exercises. After watching the videos and completing the exercises, students are invited to chat with their classmates and me about the videos, and finally they write entries in their blogs. These entries can reflect their opinions about the videos, or they can be a story based on the people in the videos. The first time we used this activity, I invited several international teachers to voice chat with the students, and Mike Marzio, the creator of the videos, was one of them, to students' surprise and pleasure.

I frequently use videos with architectural content taken from the Web. I prepare interactive exercises for previewing, to help activate students' previous knowledge on the subject and, at the same time, to introduce vocabulary and structures heard in the video. After watching the video, and discussing the content via text and voice chat, students create postviewing activities in pairs or triads. These activities are completed by the other groups, and in this way, students receive feedback on both content and form.

Online Presentations

My students have always presented their projects f2f to their classmates, but because many new voice tools have become available online, I decided that it was time for them to start presenting live online to an international audience. In one unit, students had to evaluate a structure in Caracas and present their findings to an international audience in a voice chat using a presentation slide show. Students were involved in collaborative planning from the beginning. The first step was to create an evaluative checklist. They formed groups to discuss the elements that should be considered when evaluating a building, according to the literature and their own knowledge of the subject. Each group presented a checklist, and through an electronic poll the class voted on which checklist everyone should use. Once the checklist was chosen, in pairs or triads the students selected a building and created Microsoft Power-Point (2006) presentations with photos, taking into consideration all the aspects contained in the checklist. I invited my international colleagues to be our guests for these presentations. We met online at the Alado (n.d.) voice chat room, and the students presented their work, speaking as they showed the PowerPoint slides (see Figure 2.3). Our guests asked questions both orally and in text, and these were answered orally by the presenters and, at times, in the text chat by classmates.

The voice conference was a fabulous experience for the students because they had an ideal authentic audience who listened to them for the information they wanted to transmit and not for the mistakes they might make. Most of our guests had never been to Caracas, so they were genuinely interested, and the students were motivated to convey their admiration for and pride in the buildings they described. As unbelievable as it might sound, the students unanimously said they had felt more at ease in this online presentation, which was the first time for all of them, than when they presented f2f to their classmates, who already knew most of the things they had to say. Our guests wrote authentic congratulatory messages to the students after the presentation, and these were posted on the course Web page with the slide shows and the students' pictures.

Figure 2.3. Students Participate in Voice Chat with International Scholars

Consulting Hours

Since I have been teaching online, I have held two-thirds of my consulting hours online. Students meet me through Yahoo! Messenger (2005) or at some other online venue we agree on in advance. We use text chat, voice chat, or a combination. In this way, I have more time to devote to students than when I see them in my office on a restricted schedule. If more than two students want to consult me at the same time, I open a conference and chat with them both. In these sessions, sometimes students have answers to each other's questions, therefore making it a collaborative learning experience. I have gotten to know my students better because we also chat about topics we cannot cover when there is a line of students waiting outside the door to talk to me. Some prefer to send e-mails until they get used to chatting—usually thought of as merely social—with the teacher.

Challenges and Future Directions

Getting started with blended and online teaching was not an easy task. In the first stages, I did not find support from the university because nobody else had dared to get involved in this kind of online activity. The extent of other language teachers' work on the Web did not go beyond asking students to do some reading online to get the main idea of the text; thus, the university had not been faced with the need to create an infrastructure to satisfy teachers' requests. It is still difficult to find a computer lab for my classes since these are generally reserved for computer students. The only way I can solve this problem is by booking the lab well in advance—two or three months before a trimester begins. Convincing the lab administrators to let me download the text and voice applications needed for my classes is another obstacle that I have to overcome every time I am assigned to a new lab. However, once the technicians see what I do in my courses, especially having speakers from all over the world join in, they change their attitude. These days, I am allowed to install all the applications needed for each course, and I have even been invited to give workshops about the use of Web tools for all the professors at the university and to teach graduate courses on the use of technology in education.

Planning the courses, creating Web pages, looking for resources, designing materials, moderating, and tutoring are time-consuming activities that represent an extra workload, especially when e-teaching is not recognized or even understood by the administration. Although I spend many more hours than my other colleagues getting my courses ready, all the extra effort is worth the satisfaction I get when I look at my students' smiling faces, when I share in their enthusiasm in class, and when I see how they use the language to communicate.

Most of my students are motivated from the beginning; they have never experienced this kind of learning before. However, the first weeks are difficult for those who have never worked with computers. It takes patience, scaffolding, and reassurance to let them find out for themselves that it is not difficult but fun. Their feedback at the end of each course has been a motivation to carry on (see this chapter's appendix for comments).

I hope that the activities described in this chapter will be helpful for ESP teachers as well as for teachers of GE. The idea I would like to convey is that having a great many materials is indeed helpful, but what makes an online teaching-learning experience a success are the activities and tasks that teachers design to use those materials, tasks that must be planned with the objectives and students in mind (D. González and St. Louis 2002). Ways to provide opportunities for input and output, and the principles of promoting interaction, collaboration, negotiation of meaning, and student autonomy, are on my mind when planning activities for f2f, online, or blended courses. The student comments in the appendix, from the latest version of a course on architecture and urban planning, are an indication of how enthusiastic students become about this type of motivating experience.

Some of the activities mentioned in this chapter had international guest speakers or visitors, which was possible because my colleagues and I belong to online communities of language teachers. Communities of practice (see Stevens, chapter 19 in this volume) are the best places to start learning and practicing to be an online or blended teacher. I am fortunate to belong to Webheads in Action, a virtual community of language teachers worldwide, who explore Web communication tools, share best teaching practices, and collaborate in online projects and conferences (for more information, see D. González 2004a, 2005). Thanks to all of them (and especially to those who have taken part in my projects and helped me learn how to use CMC tools for my students' benefit), my courses are successful in helping students practice language while building confidence, communication, and content skills and knowledge.

Appendix A—Chapter 2
E-Journal Student Comments on an
Architecture and Urban Planning Course, 2005

Hi teacher! Well, first of all, I would like to give you some feedback about the whole learning system. I think it is awesome to have a space to interact more personally with the teachers, and to have a platform so we can work outside the college. I think that it is known that we usually don't have so much time left for works, other than the "entregas" (architects and urban planners alike) , and working this way is a nice advantage to people that has internet at home. The use of technology for learning is something that should be used, not only in this course, but also in other courses.

About the f2f class, well, as with all the english courses before this one, my first impression was that all english teachers are fun and happy, it is nice to have a teacher that motivates us and brings us some happiness to our lives, those people that never stop smiling are the ones that we always tend to remember. I expect to have a nice experience with the course, as I am interested in all of these computer stuff.

WE don't ned F2F classes . . . On-line classes are the best way. . This is the first class ever, and I'm loving every minute. .!!!!! Thanks for this new way to learn . . . and the best thing is that IS FOR FREE!!!! LOL

Even though I could not be in the first class, I have a lot of expectations about this course "English for Architects and Urban Planners." I think It's an important course that will help us several things such as learning new archtectonic and urban planning vocabulary, develping our writting skills, speaking more fluid.

Besides, One of my biggest expectations about this course is developing new skills that we are not used to develop in other courses like using webtools for learning and interacting online with guest speakers. I use computers (Word, Excel, Power Point) a lot for writing compositions and essays, but I don't usually use a lot of internet as a learning methods; that's why I have big expectations on this part (webtools) of this course.

Dafne i hope in the future i will find people like you, becuase you try very hard to do your job in the best way.

Appendix B—Chapter 2
Web Sites, Internet Tools, and Software for
Online Interaction

Alado	http://www.alado.net
Discovery School.com:Teaching Tools	http://school.discovery.com/teachingtools/teachingtools.com
Filamentality	http://www.filamentality.org/wired/fil/
Groupboard	http://www.groupboard.com/
Handybits	http://www.handybits.com/voicemail.htm
Hot Potatoes	http://hotpot.uvic.ca
Lesson Pro.net	http://www.lessonpro.net/
Makers Pages	http://lang.swarthmore.edu/makers/
Microsoft PowerPoint	http://office.microsoft.com/powerpoint
Module Maker	http://questioning.org/module/module.html
Moodle	http://moodle.org/
NetMeeting	http://www.microsoft.com/windows/netmeeting
Quia Web	http://www.quia.com/web/
Real English	http://www.real-english.com/
The WebWizard	http://www.the-webwizard.co.uk/
Yahoo!Groups	http://groups.yahoo.com/
Yahoo!Messenger	http://messenger.yahoo.com/

Chapter 3

Problems of Time and Exposure in Vocabulary Acquisition: An Electronic Solution

Marti Sevier
Simon Fraser University
Vancouver, British Columbia, Canada

Preview

The "beginner's paradox" (Coady 1997, 230) accounts for the frustration experienced by language learners attempting to enter a university with only a basic level of vocabulary and a minimal reading speed. Sevier summarizes what is known about reading, noting that random access to new vocabulary through extensive reading may be a slow process for learners who hope to enter a university within a year. She offers concordancing as a means to make vocabulary learning faster and easier, particularly in English for academic purposes (EAP) intensive programs. Once students (and teachers) become familiar with an online concordancer, such as The Compleat Lexical Tutor (Cobb 2006), they may explore and process language in depth. Sevier offers a number of activities that can be accomplished with this online tool.

Before you read:

- What kinds of vocabulary learning activities are you already familiar with? Do any make use of computer technologies? If so, which ones?

- Have you ever used a concordancer? To what purpose?

- A corpus is a collection of texts, either spoken or written. What kinds of texts have you gathered for learners' materials or for language or classroom research? Were these e-texts?

The Challenge of Reading

One of the greatest challenges facing international students in North American universities is the immense reading load required in many mainstream courses. Students leaving Simon Fraser University's pre-entry English Bridge Program are usually advised to take at least one mathematics course, to reduce that load and allow more time to acclimatize to the demands of reading. These students, like their counterparts elsewhere, consistently list poor vocabulary as one of their greatest concerns in reading (and writing) academic texts. A lack of vocabulary renders reading a difficult, sometimes impossible task; unable to grasp individual lexical items, learners may not be ready to read in chunks and thus may be forced to read in a halting, word-by-word manner that leaves them incapable of grasping main ideas or distinguishing them from supporting details. Coady (1997) describes the "beginners' paradox" (p. 230), which is a dilemma also faced by large numbers of EAP learners (even though they are technically not beginners at all): "How [do they] learn enough words to read with even modest comprehension at the threshold level of 3,000 word families, and, beyond that, an independent level of 5,000 families?" (p. 230). These numbers do not even account for specialty vocabulary required in the disciplines.

Despite recommendations that the best way to increase vocabulary is incidentally, through the multiple exposures provided by extensive reading (Coady 1997; Krashen 1994), the fact remains that this is a time-consuming process. Informal testing of EAP students in my classes shows that when reading academic texts, few manage more than two hundred words per minute. At this rate, a relatively short academic paper of four thousand words would take twenty minutes to read once, and could easily take twice that long should the reader pause to make notes, highlight key phrases, or check words in the dictionary. Thus learners understandably may feel that EAP reading is an endurance race in which the goal of completion supersedes that of comprehension.

In this chapter I summarize recent research on reading and its relation to vocabulary, and I provide background discussion of issues in vocabulary teaching: What lexical items do EAP students need to learn? How are these items acquired? What problems do learners face in acquiring new vocabulary? I recommend the use of concordancing activities as a productive means of providing EAP learners with rich exposure to new lexical items in a wide range of contexts. I also describe some learning activities using an online lexical tutor.

Vocabulary Acquisition and Classroom Practice

Reading, especially extensive reading, has long been recognized and recommended as a means of vocabulary acquisition for first language (L1) and second language (L2) learners. At the same time, vocabulary size and depth "are highly, and positively correlated" (Qian 1999, ¶1) and can be used to predict reading comprehension scores. In fact, "for the task of academic reading, the main knowledge type of interest is lexical . . . contributing more to L2 and reading success than other kinds of linguistic knowledge, including syntax" (Cobb and Horst 2001, 318). It may be more appropriate to discuss the relationship between the two as interdependent (Paribakht and Wesche 1997, 1998) and to consider teaching methodologies that integrate vocabulary learning more fully into EAP instruction.

Consideration must also be given to how vocabulary is learned. Although the process of incidental learning is not clear, it is generally viewed as "a by-product, not the target, of the main cognitive activity, reading" (Huckin and Coady 1999, 182). Explicit learning of vocabulary is accounted for by the *depth of processing* hypothesis (Craik and Lockhart, cited in Hulstijn and Laufer 2001a), which suggests that the probability of retaining information in long-term memory is related to the "shallowness or depth with which it is initially processed" (p. 5). Hulstijn and Laufer (2001b) propose vocabulary task design that increases the involvement load, and thus deeper processing, by incorporating *need* (learner motivation to solve a problem), *search* (a learner's attempt to work out the meaning of a new L2 word or to find an L2 word that expresses a concept by checking a dictionary or asking for help), and *evaluation* (choosing a word or meaning after comparing it to other words or meanings). As Hulstijn and Laufer (2001b) have found, tasks with a higher involvement load, for example, those that require students to use new words in compositions, indeed result in better retention.

Nation and Newton (1997) report that learners make greater vocabulary gains when performing communicative activities. This result relates to the characteristics of group communicative tasks:

1. Learners must adjust their level of speech to the needs of their listeners.
2. Communication takes place in meaningful contexts.
3. Communicative activities offer repeated exposure to new vocabulary.
4. Learners must use new vocabulary in meaningful ways.
5. In peer-focused activity, learners have less anxiety about error and so will speak (and therefore use vocabulary) more freely than if a teacher were present.

Communicative activities encourage depth of processing. However, little learning can take place before a learner has acquired a basic vocabulary.

The strategy of using contextual clues to learn new words is, like extensive reading, a time-honored practice, and learners are often trained and advised to do so. However, a number of difficulties may arise. First, many learners do not know enough words in a text to be able to employ contextual clues effectively (Haynes 1993). It is estimated that a learner needs to know 95–98 percent of the words in a text in order to use this strategy effectively (Huckin and Coady 1999). In addition, clues need to be present in the text, and learners need to interpret them correctly (Laufer 1997). As noted earlier, extensive reading is often proposed as a means to provide vocabulary input, but even when English language programs provide extensive reading opportunities, large vocabulary gains do not always result. In one study, students learned an average of only five words while reading a 109-page simplified novel over a period of nine days (Horst, Cobb, and Meara 1998). It is not clear, then, how much exposure to new words is needed for successful learning.

Indeed, Hulstijn (cited in Read 2004) recommends a "complementary" relationship between extensive and intensive vocabulary activities, balancing "quality and frequency of information processing activities" (p. 148). Nor, adds Read, should learners avoid old-fashioned approaches to vocabulary learning, such as memorizing words in lists. However, Coxhead (2000) suggests that words should be introduced in context.

So learners need not only exposure to new language in order to acquire vocabulary incidentally or implicitly, but also deeper processing in order to retain new items in long-term memory. Although the role of reading in vocabulary acquisition is important, extensive reading appears to be an inefficient means of providing input for this process. More focused reading activities and other types of communication activities may well prove to be more effective in achieving the goal of vocabulary learning. Here is where corpora and concordancing software can be of great use.

Corpora and Concordancing in Lexical Teaching

Defined as "naturally occurring examples of language" (Hunston 2002, 2) that are usually stored and accessed electronically, a corpus can be any collection of texts—spoken or written, formal or informal. Examples of written corpora include collections of newspaper and journal articles, lab reports, court proceedings, and literature, while spoken corpora may include transcripts of academic lectures, speeches, movie scripts, and conversations recorded in diverse locations, from coffee shops to professors' offices. Many corpora are widely available on the Web. Examples of these include the following:

- Bank of English (2004)
- British National Corpus (BNC; Oxford University 2005)
- Brown Corpus (Frances and Kucera 1979)
- British Academic Spoken English (BASE) corpus (Nesi and Thompson 2006)
- Cambridge International Corpus (CIC; Cambridge University Press 2006)
- Michigan Corpus of Academic Spoken English (MICASE; University of Michigan 2002)

(For lists of commercial and publicly available corpora for both native and nonnative English speakers, see Flowerdew 1996; Ma 1993; Pravec 2002. A full list of corpora referred to in this chapter appears in the appendix.)

A *concordance* is a list of lines of text from a corpus, in which a particular word is embedded. The first concordances, constructed in the Middle Ages, were based on the Bible, and even now a title search of *concordance* in one university library contains far more references to literary works (e.g., Dante Alighieri's *Divine Comedy*) than to English language teaching. For classroom teaching and research purposes, however, one is likely to turn to one of the many online *concordancers* (tools that create concordances) that are already linked to one or more corpora. Figure 3.1 shows an example, based on the Brown Corpus, of thirty lines (some concordancers extract entire sentences) with the word *make*, using The Compleat Lexical Tutor (Lextutor; Cobb 2006).

A strong argument for using corpora in language teaching is that doing so provides many samples of language in a natural context. As with Figure 3.1, students can be exposed to the word *make* thirty times and draw conclusions about how it is used. Acting as researchers, students are engaged in data-driven learning (DDL; Johns, cited in Robertson 2001). However, if they were to analyze the different uses of the word, they would find that its *col-*

```
 1 the very week of our war against Katanga, we make a $133 million grant to Kwame Nkrumah,
 2 bility for his death. Just as I know I would make a bad soldier even though I cannot sincerely
 3 ts where you can dine, see a movie, shop, or make a bank deposit, the ever-increasing number
 4 ion Survival" which has many facets. Why not make a beginning with a united and disarmed G
 5 not asham'd to Say They want Onely a head to Make a beginning". The final issue of the Engl
 6 ward the shoulders. Arch the back upwards to make a bridge. Be sure the head drops backward
 7 ards, bring his heels together with a click, make a brisk pirouette, skirts flaring, and march
 8 he ruled that the state had been "unable to make a case". Contempt proceedings originally had
 9 said it was stupid butchery to order men to make a charge like that, no matter who gave the o
10 e essence of contract is that one is free to make a choice of what one will or will not do. He
11 ness Act, as amended, authorizes the SBA to make a complete inventory of the productive fac
12 ra-personal responsibility it is possible to make a compromise between the ethical and the pur
13 Finally he reported that Nasser was ready to make a concrete commitment in return for Israeli
14 ility in relation to the world. We shall not make a decisive advance in the ecumenical movem
15 oing this will incur obligations which would make a Democratic victory absolutely fruitless ..
16 acitus was talking about when he said, "They make a desert, and call it peace" ("Solitudinem
17 s foremost marine geologists. He was able to make a detailed inspection of the waves. Their o
18 eel, core, and slice across enough apples to make a dome in the pie tin, and set aside. In a s
19 the most part unproductive, even though they make a fetish of devoting themselves to some c
20 owth have been omitted. It is possible to make a few generalizations about the six giants t
21 this enlarged role in mind, I should like to make a few suggestions: What we in the United St
22 's on maneuvers. In combat, helping your CO make a fool of himself might mean getting your
23 embarrassing silences and have been known to make a fool out of myself just to prevent one.
24 mes is too "unorthodox" and "theoretical" to make a good detective. Why do the police find
25 visitors to Mars should be persons likely to make a good impression, and when he was asked,
26 ect sincerity, but they exhibit a concern to make a good job out of his pious impersonation.
27 vote as Question No. 1 on Nov. 7, would not make a good Mayor out of a bad one. There is n
28 r for official meals. So the President would make a hearty breakfast official by inviting Gove
29 ves can do and how and when to feed them can make a highly competitive business more pro
30 efore his death Papa had agreed with Mama to make a joint will with her in which it would be
```

Figure 3.1. Concordance for the Word *make* in The Compleat Lexical Tutor (Brown Corpus)
Source: Cobb 2006.

locates, the words that "go with" it, vary a great deal. *Collocation* is the tendency for a vocabulary item to co-occur in a sentence with another item, especially in the context of a specific language corpus.

Corpora and concordances are powerful tools that have many applications. One of the most immediate uses is lexicography; using concordancers, lexicographers can determine the most frequent words and their most frequent meanings. Using large corpora, teachers and materials writers can realistically identify what language items should be selected for teaching and learning. In the EAP classroom, corpora provide input for language analysis tasks for researchers and learners alike. Teachers can devise tasks for using corpora, and learners can be trained to manipulate them independently. Learners could, for example, search for concordances that demonstrate a particular grammar rule or that can be compared to their own writing (see Table 3.1; Flowerdew 1996; Gavioli and Aston 2001; Tribble and Jones 1990). Smaller corpora that focus on a particular genre, such as medical reports, can help learners identify the features of that genre (Hunston 2002).

Although concordancing is increasingly being used by teachers and students, it does not seem to have entered the mainstream of vocabulary-building tools to the same extent as other lexical resources such as the Academic Word List (AWL; Coxhead 2000), which has now been incorporated into commercially available materials such as the Academic Word Power series (e.g., Hollinger and Obenda 2004) from Houghton Mifflin. Nonetheless, a range of vocabulary activities can be developed using concordance lines, as shown in Table 3.1. Further examples are given later in this chapter.

The only use of concordance lines in a published textbook that I am aware of is in Thurstun and Candlin's (1997) *Exploring Academic English*. Their approach (Thurstun and Candlin 1998) is worth considering, not least because it can be easily adapted to online concordancing. Focusing on rhetorical purposes associated with academic writing, such as stating the topic, conducting a literature review, and hedging, they used concordance data based on Xue and Nation's (1984) University Word List to create a list of examples of language associated with each purpose. Selecting examples from the Microconcord Corpus of Academic Texts (Scott and Johns 1993), Thurstun and Candlin then devised exercises for writing: asking learners first to look at and think about the meanings of key words in the context of the concordance lines, then to move more deeply into the texts to study the language associated with the key words. Learners are subsequently given opportunities to practice their use of the words and to create compositions using the words they have studied. However, a major advantage of online concordancing, as opposed to viewing concordance lines in a book like Thurstun and Candlin's, is that students may manipulate their own writing and choose from a variety of corpora to study.

Table 3.1. Vocabulary Activities for Concordancing

Learning Purpose	Task
• Raise awareness and/or remediate use of language features associated with particular text genres (e.g., the appropriate modals for hedging) • Extend knowledge of word definitions; polysemy	Gap fill of concordance lines from academic articles
• Develop knowledge of a word's collocates; contrastive analysis (e.g., *bored* and *boring*) • Determine which lexis is associated with particular levels of formality, text types, and writing style	Read and compare paired concordances of selected words or phrases
• Learn special lexis (e.g., abstract nouns)	Analyze concordance lines
• Analyze errors to raise awareness of and remediate problems in collocation, reporting verbs, and so on	Compare student writing with concordanced material
• Expand knowledge of a word's form and how form affects grammatical context	Wild-card searches (e.g., *economic**)

The Compleat Lexical Tutor and EAP Learners

In this section, I introduce in more detail The Compleat Lexical Tutor (Lextutor), developed by Cobb (2006). Although it is not the only Web site devoted to vocabulary learning, it is by far the most comprehensive (for other online concordancers and corpora, see the appendix). What follows is a description of concordancing activities on the Lextutor Web site and some suggestions for task construction. While this chapter's focus is online concordance-based activities in EAP, Lextutor encompasses a great deal more. Learners can access online vocabulary tests, listen to the pronunciation of new vocabulary, and analyze their own writing with a Web Vocabulary Profiler; instructors can use templates for exercise construction, analyze reading material for difficulty level, create video-based cloze activities, and much more. Resources are also available for instructors and learners of French and Spanish. For a quick view of a modest online concordance, users may type a word into the QUICK LOOK-UP box at the top of Lextutor's welcome page (Figure 3.2), select >ENG[LISH]: CONC[ORDANCE] or FR[ENCH]: CONC, and click on the >> button. The resulting concordance uses Princeton University's relatively small WordNet corpus (G. A. Miller et al. 2005).

Lextutor is divided into three sections expressed in the menu columns: Tutorial, Research, and Teachers (see Figure 3.2). I look first at the most important features in the Research column, which is a good starting point for teachers new to concordancing. It should be noted that Cobb frequently updates his Web site, and thus some buttons or features may have moved or changed since this volume went to press.

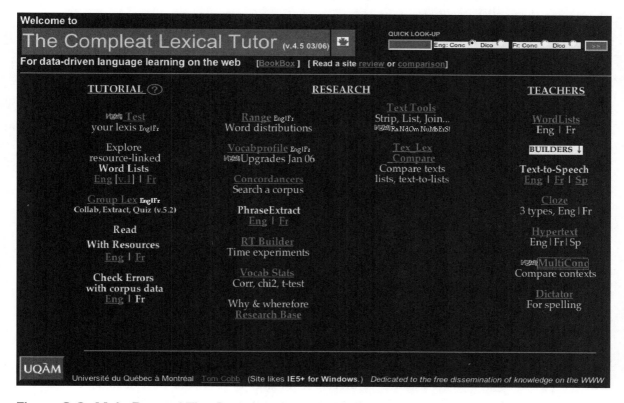

Figure 3.2. Main Page of The Compleat Lexical Tutor
Source: Cobb 2006.

The Research Column

In exploring the Web site, teachers new to concordancing are advised to first read some of the articles in the Research column in *Why & wherefore* >RESEARCH BASE for discussion of how and why frequency lists and concordancing aid language acquisition. In addition, the Research column includes links to other Web sites related to DDL and corpus linguistics.

Also located in the Research column is the >CONCORDANCERS button, which links to three different types of online concordances (corpus-, text-, and story-based) that are useful for correcting errors, studying collocation, and teaching and reinforcing academic vocabulary. *Story concordancers* in Lextutor feature literature that is read aloud and presented in text form with hyperlinks to view concordances of words in the story. However, this chapter considers in detail only the first two types of concordancers as being the most relevant to academic intensive English programs.

One way to begin using Lexutor is to click on the >CONCORDANCERS button and then select a language (English or French) under *Corpus-based concordances* on the Online Concordancer page. The user can then input a word in the *Keyword(s)* "equal to" box, select a corpus from the drop-down menu, and then click on the >GET CONCORDANCE button. The default for English is the Brown Corpus, but other choices are available, depending on the size and focus required, ranging from the University Word List to the BNC Written and Spoken Corpora to the Starr Report (Office of the Independent Council 1998), as well as lists from less formal sources written by teachers and learners of English. Teachers will need to specify which corpus students are to use. See Figure 3.3 for a comparison of outputs from three corpora for the word *language*.

Upon examining the concordance output for the word *make* in Figure 3.1, students can see that its uses are primarily in the infinitive form and that they are nonlexical, often linked to other words that carry the semantic load (e.g., *make a case, make a public statement, make his name, make some sense, make sure*). If users wish to focus on one of those terms, they can return to the Online Concordancer page and select *OPTION 1: With associated word* or *OPTION 2: Collocates table*, organized either alphabetically or by frequency. Users can also set various controls, such as the width of the line, the number of lines desired, and the position of the collocated word in the line (e.g., right-sorted). Based on these concordance lines, one teaching point may come to mind immediately: many learners express recommendations by using the phrase *make sure to* (verb). Since it is possible to concordance fixed phrases, a useful error-correction exercise is to ask students to search for an erroneous example from their own writing (e.g., *seek for help), which may yield no matches—a disconcerting result, but nonetheless useful information for students.

A major source of learners' vocabulary errors is collocation, both lexical and grammatical. The concordancer can be used to raise student awareness by giving focused feedback to help correct errors. The collocation task (at the top of p. 34) focuses on reporting verbs.

Knowledge and use of academic vocabulary can be expanded with contrastive analysis tasks (such as the one on the bottom of p. 34), which help to reinforce for learners the importance of co-occurrence and the inherent "chunkiness" of English. Moreover, the presentation of words in multiple sentences expands learners' knowledge of the word's meanings and appropriate contexts for its use.

Brown Corpus: Concordances for *language* with Associated Words = 10/111

1 om his travel experiences than the limits of **language** allow, he still can charm and astound. To
2 The apostle Paul said the same thing in the **language** and faith of the New Testament: "He that
3 It should have a dramatic form with pleasing **language**, and it should portray incidents which s
4 revolution compete with sensitive surveys of **language** and literature, the common law, parlia
5 erdeveloped country where the diet, culture, **language** and living conditions will be different.
6 an example where the property is absent. The **language** and notation introduced are standard th
7 ty of the external world, and the ideas that **language** and things perceived by consciousness we
8 These narratives of coarse action and crude **language** appeared first in local newspapers, as a r
9 r object of scrutiny, and the effects of the **language** are palpable even if sometimes inevitable
10 : Paragraph Meaning, Word Meaning, Spelling, **Language**, Arithmetic Computation, and Arit

University Word List: Concordances for *language* with Associated Words = 10/63

1 approval seem unable to bring the Classical **language** alive and learn from the resourcefulness
2 roached the problem of making the Classical **language** alive and useful in modern conditions. I
3 ickly resolved. Generally, within a natural **language**, ambiguity is resolved rapidly using recent
4 social stock of knowledge, symbols, common **language** and ideas. But at the same time, these
5 rica with one ethnic group, one culture, one **language** and one religion should be the most deep
6 g of the past, irradiated with the light of **language** and preserved with almost reliquary devotio
7 s. By pressing an extra button you hear one **language** and then another, or, if you want, both si
8 ow the Chinese government. He used the same **language** as that employed by the Chinese gove
9 ore, Hong Kong, or even Japan, the lack of a **language** barrier is India's big advantage. Many o
10 quite, that he has translated it into film **language**. Branagh's version retains a Chorus - Derek

British National Corpus: Concordances for *language* with Associated Words = 10/106

1 us truth led to computer programs (say, for **language** analysis) being regarded as failures if the
2 aking. Visual art has a rich and abundant **language**, and by learning to express and translate it
3 the seats. Regional pride, the growth of **language** and caste- based movements, suspicion of th
4 achieved so that document titles, indexing **language** and classification can be searched interacti
5 es, including the faults and limitations of **language** and notion in some of the operas, are Britte
6 p to Okapi '87 were written in Z80 assembly **language** and operated on a network of Apple IIe
7 capable of rising above the limitations of **language** and other cultural barriers. As Brend Shehu
8 matic presentation of these ideas on logic, **language**, and philosophy. Advertised in 1930 as a j
9 sted in the history of the development of a **language**, and study the speech habits of particular
10 the majority of the Romanians in religion, **language** and traditions – have nothing to expect f

Figure 3.3. Comparison of Output for *language* from Three Corpora
Source: Cobb 2006.

A second type of concordancing offered on the Online Concordancer page in Lextutor allows the input of small corpora of up to fifty thousand words. After selecting *Text-based concordances*, learners can paste or type in their own text(s) and produce a concordance index that can be useful in understanding variation in academic writing. The column to the left of the concordance output lists all the words that are used in the text, with frequencies; thus, students can tell immediately if they are using the same words repeatedly.

Learners can also be trained to use feedback from *type-token ratios*, another type of frequency indicator, in this case determined by dividing the number of different words (types) by the total number of words (tokens). In the Web Vocabulary Profilers area (linked from the >VOCABPROFILE button in the Research column on the main page), learners can compare their type-token ratio to that of an academic text in the corpus. If the same words or sets of words appear repeatedly, the learner must develop more variation in writing and can use the concordance for examples.

The most useful aspect of text-based concordances and vocabulary profiling is the ease with which they allow instructors to set up small parallel concordances. For example, a class set of twenty 400-word compositions saved as text files could be input to compare with one of the academic corpora. Using the frequency data from the profiler and the lines generated by the concordancer, instructors can identify particular problems more accurately than by using intuition; learners can be instructed to compare their work to writing in a corpus of academic essays and study how their language could be used more appropriately.

The Teachers Column

After exploring how the concordancer can identify weaknesses in lexical usage and variation, instructors will need to think about how to give students further exposure to and practice with problematic items. The Teachers column has many tools for this purpose. For example, the Multi-Concordance (accessed through the >MultiConc button) is an intricately designed program offering three different types of practice. Learners can review target language by looking at sets of ten or more concordance lines, use a cloze concordancer (with target words blanked out), and then take a quiz either online or printed out on paper.

An added bonus to the Multi-Concordance tool is easy access to concordances of word forms from the AWL. For example, say a student wrote the following, misusing *economy* for *economic*:

*I think Canada can sustain the economy growth.

Typing *econom'* in the box at the top of the page and pressing the >BUILD button will produce an output of different forms of that stem, as shown in Figure 3.4. The learner can then compare the original use of *economy* with the output and, one hopes, see that the *-y* indicates a noun form. A closer look at the sentence structures in which the different forms of the word are used could also expand a learner's lexical knowledge, in this case that *economic* is the form of *economy* used to modify the noun *growth*.

Hypertext Builders (accessed from the >HYPERTEXT link in the Teachers column) gives any short text a hyperlinked concordance output. This tool is well suited to an academic reading activity in which students work in pairs or groups to read short texts such as article abstracts. They can select any unknown word and, by double-clicking, get its concordance based on the Brown Corpus. (A single click allows students to hear the word pronounced, using a downloadable text-to-speech feature.) Instructors might instead prefer to designate

---

Hits: 020

[001] banks, you do something to the **ECONOMy**," he said. "You take out of circ
[002] e use of the Organization for **ECONOMic** Cooperation and Development (when
[003] itute reforms in military and **ECONOMic** aid policies in the critical area
[004] ped to give greater emphasis to **ECONOMic** aid and to encourage political
[005] Department of Conservation and **ECONOMic** Development, has retired after
[006] c are rapidly expanding their **ECONOMic**, technical and military assistanc
[007] d more than $1,000,000,000 in **ECONOMic** aid alone last year, according to
[008] mium on population instead of **ECONOMic** strength, as in the past, would b
[009] fficer, a department head or an **ECONOMist**, to start. #@# Each member wou
[010] foes that he has not tried to **ECONOMize**. Any tax bill also will revive a
[011] more important than aiding them **ECONOMically**, E. M. Martin, assistant se
[012] istant secretary of state for **ECONOMic** affairs told members of the World
[013] , the assistant secretary said. **ECONOMically**, Martin said, the United St
[014] rtment-building field. Although **ECONOMic** and personal circumstances vary
[015] took top senior individual home **ECONOMics** honors with a demonstration ca
[016] able segment of Dallas business **ECONOMy**. New car sales in Dallas County
[017] r steady momentum to lift the **ECONOMy** to a new historic peak by this aut
[018] s autumn," Beryl W. Sprinkel, **ECONOMist** of Harris Trust + Savings Bank,
[019] that the recent improvement in **ECONOMic** activity was not a "temporary f
[020] l expansion that will carry the **ECONOMy** back to full employment levels full

Figure 3.4. Lextutor's Multi-Concordance Output for *econom'*
Source: Cobb 2006.

related items in a particular discipline for study (e.g., *benefit, compensate, fees*), perhaps from the AWL, so that learners can expand their knowledge of these terms by examining concordance lines. Files generated by the Hypertext Builders can also be linked to the instructor's Web page for further use in review or testing. (Note: I have only been able to use Hypertext Builders on computers running Microsoft Windows, not Macintosh computers.)

Cloze passages are one of the old reliables of language teaching, and the Teachers column has three versions of concordance-linked cloze activities: standard rational or nth-word deletion, gaps from the AWL, and video cloze. Each works with drop-down menus of all the deleted words, so texts need to be fairly short (i.e., fewer than two hundred words). If learners click on one of the restored words, a concordance from the Brown Corpus appears in a new window. Instructors can supply short texts, or learners can exchange their own texts in a "cloze swap" with partners.

Also intriguing, video cloze (accessed through the >CLOZE link) can use short video clips that have text transcripts as a basis for nth-word and rational deletion cloze; although teachers must find the videos, Lextutor provides links to video sources, such as the Public Broadcasting Service and the Australian Broadcasting Corporation, so that instructors (or learners) can develop their own video cloze tasks based on course themes. Exercises can be saved and linked to class Web pages. English Bridge Program students at Simon Fraser University seem to benefit from the multimodal input of the video cloze and the audio version of the basic cloze.

The Tutorial Column

While the Tutorial column is for the most part self-explanatory, it should be mentioned that with *Explore resource-linked Word Lists*, learners can engage in either focused work or ad hoc, unplanned learning. *Explore* offers helpful self-editing and practice tools for learners who are experimenting with language, as it gives concordance and online dictionary options to check meanings and the opportunity to listen to words with the downloadable speech plug-in. Learners can type or paste in text to check a difficult item, such as *due to*, or type in a longer phrase to see if their usage corresponds to that of items in a corpus.

The Group Lexicon (linked through the >GROUP LEX button in the Tutorial column) is a collaborative vocabulary exercise builder that uses concordances for advanced-level quizzes. Learners working individually or in teams select vocabulary and input definitions, examples, and parts of speech from their papers. In some classes, instructors make corrections; in other classes, the students peer-edit. Entries can then be used in a multiple-choice quiz, created by selecting from a drop-down menu listing all the words input by the group. When learners have completed this quiz and wish to try something more challenging, they can click on the red >TOUGHER QUIZ link (Microsoft Windows only) and be reexposed to the same vocabulary, this time using a gapped Multi-Concordance format based on the Brown Corpus. In this way, learners who input the vocabulary will have had to process it, and then will have a second exposure to it in quiz format and a third exposure in the tougher quiz mode. Because the material is online, learners can access the information from outside the classroom or computer lab, and when an ongoing collaborative effort is involved, there is always new vocabulary from others' texts. The collaborative features are an especially interesting aspect of Lextutor.

Challenges and Future Directions

Learners differ; their needs and interests differ. It is unfair to assume that they all enjoy linguistic research. At the same time, EAP students may be highly critical of work that appears to be merely fun, such as games or puzzles like Hangman or a crossword. It is essential to provide a rationale for concordancing tasks, with which they may be unfamiliar. Teachers should also link vocabulary work to reading assignments and/or items on the AWL and encourage students to use their vocabulary in other course assignments in order to give added weight to concordance activities.

Another concern (though some would call it an asset) is that Lextutor does not present a ready-made set of plug-and-play exercises. Instructors need to take the time to become familiar with the activity choices and to guide learners through them. In a concordancing activity on *claim*, for example, I found it helpful to advise students to search for *claimed*, rather than have them be confused with *claim* in its noun form. Instructors can also incorporate detailed worksheets into search tasks, such as the following, based on Thurstun and Candlin's (1997) guided discovery approach.

Worksheet with Guided Discovery Task

Using ALL the corpora, find 10–12 concordances in which *claim* is used as a verb, and paste them here:

Now analyze them by answering these questions:

1. What are the subjects of the sentences, i.e., what nouns are used with this verb?
   People: _____ time(s)
   Inanimate subjects: _____ time(s)
   Other: _____ time(s)
   In your concordance lines, do objects usually follow *claimed*? Yes/No
   What structure usually follows *claimed*?
   Find five examples of how *claimed* is followed by a statement that what the speaker is saying is true.

2. Is a claim always believable? Why or why not? (If you are not sure, check the dictionary.)

3. How can you use *claim* in your Reading Report or IRP writing?

Further control can be accomplished by preselecting the corpora students use. When students see only the University Word List corpus in the *claimed* exercise, fewer distracting lines emerge, and the analysis is simpler because it more closely reflects the academic texts they read. While this manipulation smacks of microcontrol, reading even concordance lines takes time, so this guidance helps learners focus more efficiently on what they need to learn.

Despite the promise of corpora and concordancing for vocabulary acquisition, the path is not completely smooth. Among the objections and concerns voiced, the following seem to relate most closely to EAP learners:

- the issue of authenticity
- the problem of collocation
- the problem of time
- the need for learner training

Authenticity. Not all would agree with the assertion made earlier that the use of corpora gives students opportunities to sample "natural" language in authentic contexts. Mishan (2004) argues that the process of inserting text into a corpus and then extracting lines from it in a concordance may be robbing it of its form and social context. Certainly, strips of sentence parts in a list will never be encountered outside a classroom or computer laboratory. Nor do they bear much resemblance to the research reports or articles commonly used in academic English courses. However, in considering this point, authenticity must be viewed beyond the parameter of language alone. The use of concordances is not for students an end in itself, but a means of gaining access to the material they must master in mainstream courses—an authentic goal for EAP students.

Collocation. Although the study of collocation is a popular use of concordancing, the type of collocations most productively analyzed is limited. Collocations that are idiomatic or invariable, or that are specific to genres (e.g., fixed amount, control group, research question) in research parlance, are most productive for study. (For a further look at genre comparison through the use of concordancing, see VIEW [Davies n.d.] or MICASE [University of Michigan 2002], to name two, in the appendix.)

Time. It is true that concordance lines provide time-saving exposure to large amounts of language in a short time. However, Willis (cited in Hunston 2002) points out that many DDL consciousness-raising tasks take up a great deal of classroom time. Whether they are really worth the effort is especially relevant when such tasks focus on obscure or unusual language. While consciousness-raising is exciting, the value of dedicating class time to analyzing items such as *agog* or *Double Dutch* in the face of the other demands made on EAP learners is questionable. Hence, I find myself on the controlling end of the teacher spectrum, focusing students on specific language patterns in their respective academic disciplines.

Learner training. When first experimenting with concordancing, students are often confused and frustrated not only by concordancing but also by the interfaces and even the terminology used. Learner training activities, both practical and metacognitive, along with clear demonstrations, rationales, and course materials can help students navigate and adapt to learning from concordance tasks with little difficulty. (Examples of such tasks can be found in Sevier 2005.) Most students quickly learn that the payoff is great: a vast reservoir of language resources is at their disposal for writing tasks outside of and beyond their English class.

The increasing use of corpora and concordancing offers learners new and motivating ways to improve their rates of vocabulary acquisition. However, more research is needed on the effectiveness of concordance-based activities in promoting vocabulary acquisition. Widening the range of research in concordancing and encouraging international collaboration among users would benefit instructors as well as learners. Within Lextutor itself, a comparison of the effectiveness of different exercises for different types of vocabulary learning (and learners) would be useful. Beyond this, comparisons of parallel native- and nonnative-speaker corpora and their concordanced output could enable EAP learners to identify frequent sources of lexical and collocation errors and develop ways of overcoming them. Work has begun in this area (see, e.g., Granger 1998; Hinkel 2002), but relatively little has been done in North America, compared to other parts of the world.

Once considered a poor relation of language learning, vocabulary study has come into its own and is now considered an essential aspect of language acquisition. Despite the recognized value of extensive reading as a means of exposing learners to language, focused vocabulary and collocation study is also necessary to assist EAP students in academic literacy practices. Using corpora and concordancing activities online can help solve the problems of time and exposure by giving EAP learners access to the new genre-specific lexis that they need. Concordancing has provided my students with a rich and motivating set of opportunities to investigate academic vocabulary in real contexts and, ultimately, to incorporate it into their own lexicon in both discussion and writing. In so doing, they begin to make stronger connections to the academic community they look forward to joining.

Appendix—Chapter 3
Online Concordancers and Corpora

Advanced Reader's Collocation Searcher (ARCS)	http://www.geocities.com/Athens/Acropolis/7033/
The Bank of English *short sample items only*	http://www.collins.co.uk/books.aspx?group=153
British Academic Spoken English (BASE) Corpus	http://www2.warwick.ac.uk/fac/soc/celte/base/
British National Corpus	http://www.natcorp.ox.ac.uk/
Brown Corpus of Standard American English	http://helmer.aksis.uib.no/icame/brown/bcm.html
Cambridge International Corpus (CIC)	http://www.cambridge.org/elt/corpus/
The Compleat Lexical Tutor (Lextutor)	http://www.lextutor.ca/
Michigan Corpus of Academic Spoken English (MICASE)	http://www.hti.umich.edu/m/micase/

MicroConcord Corpus of Academic Texts	http://langbank.engl.polyu.edu.hk/corpus/microconcord.html
Starr Report	http://icreport.loc.gov/icreport/
University Word List	http://jbauman.com/UWL.html
Variation in English Words and Phrases (VIEW)	http://view.byu.edu/
WordbanksOnline *subscription service*	http://www.collins.co.uk/books.aspx?group=154
WordNet	http://wordnet.princeton.edu/

Chapter 4

Using Online Academic Writing Modules in an IEP Environment

Randi Reppen
Northern Arizona University
Flagstaff, Arizona USA

Camilla Vásquez
University of South Florida
Tampa, Florida USA

Preview

A major challenge for students in intensive English programs (IEPs) is how to make the big leap from small, closely monitored language classes to the more impersonal university or college academic content courses that expect them to be familiar with aspects of extended writing: organization of researched materials, rhetorical devices, various conventions of essay structure, what stands as evidence, and so forth. Students transitioning from secondary school bilingual programs, EFL, or other foreign language classes may encounter similar difficulties in more advanced classes. Reppen and Vásquez describe their IEP's solution: online composition modules that provide autonomous yet guided practice with larger writing issues.

Before you read:

- What are some of the essay structures that students must master to write an academic paper in a content course?

- What computerized tools do you use with your language learners to help them write essays?

- What types of skills do students need in order to organize and synthesize content-area research in English for academic purposes (EAP)?

Academic Writing for Language Learners

Producing writing in and for academic contexts is a complex task that challenges even many native speakers as they begin their college studies. For ESOL students, academic writing presents many additional issues, including organizing a paper for a particular rhetorical goal, meeting the cultural norms of the academic paper in English, presenting an argument, understanding what stands as evidence, working with texts that present conflicting information, dealing with issues related to plagiarism, and using connectors and transitions effectively. To date, most research studies have focused on second language writers and the academic essay, or investigations of particular linguistic features across different types of writing (e.g., Grabe and Kaplan 1996; Hinkel 2002; Hyland 2002; Reid 1993). Other scholarly research has also addressed how best to provide instruction and feedback on ESOL student writing (Ferris and Hedgcock 2005; Leki 1998). These types of research have provided valuable information on challenges faced by second language (L2) learners and their teachers; however, not to be overlooked is less-scholarly attention to issues that arise with L2 writers as they deal with more extended types of academic prose (e.g., the research paper; but see Ferris 1994).

After informally surveying the undergraduate students in our IEP during the past five years, we have found that the vast majority have had no prior experience with writing research papers in either their first language (L1) or English. In order to bridge the gap between what our students learned in their ESOL classes prior to enrolling in our IEP and the specific writing-related skills needed for success in the U.S. university setting, we looked to the use of computer-assisted language learning.

In recent years, the use of computers in ESOL classrooms has become increasingly popular as a means for introducing students to a variety of text types and providing writing practice. Uses include surfing the Web for information and electronic chat, guided instruction and self-contained units, and more recently, language learning Weblogs (blogs; e.g., Blatt 2000; Dieu 2004; T. Nelson 2000). Given the easy access to computers on most university campuses, we determined that developing Web-based modules focused on academic writing issues would be a way to address several needs of university L2 writers. Our modules are not only about the conventions of academic prose (e.g., appropriate use of connectors and transitions), but also about developing the particular skills necessary (e.g., avoiding plagiarism, evaluating sources, dealing with texts that present conflicting information) for students who will soon be writing academic research papers, perhaps for the first time in their academic careers.

This chapter describes the development and use of online writing modules in a university IEP to increase students' control of certain aspects of academic rhetoric and composition. Online modules provide students with autonomous yet guided practice in areas of academic writing that have proven challenging for many IEP students in the past.

Research Related to L2 Writing and Technology Practices

Academic writing demands that writers control many aspects of writing beyond the basic ability to put words together to form simple sentences. Successful writers are able to organize information, incorporate various rhetorical and grammatical devices, and weave information together to create an effective text (Bereiter and Scardamalia 1987). In order to write in this manner, writers need to have a firm control of basic grammar, sentence, paragraph, and essay structures so that they can organize and synthesize information in a coherent manner. They must also use discourse patterns to create a text that is complex, yet reader friendly.

Studies such as Carson's (2001) and Kroll's (1990) investigate types of reading and writing tasks as well as faculty expectations across a range of academic disciplines. These studies show that students are expected to control higher-order skills of academic writing, such as the "knowledge transforming" writing described by Bereiter and Scardamalia (1987, 5). In other words, faculty expect students to produce texts that interpret data, identify connections between theory and practice, and synthesize information that they have read from various sources (Hinkel 2002). Faculty are also concerned with students' abilities to write grammatically, incorporate sources accurately, and format papers according to certain style sheets.

Web-Based Modules for L2 Academic Writing Instruction

Our small IEP (ten to forty students per semester) is designed to prepare L2 students to meet the demands of U.S. university courses, so academic writing plays a crucial role in many of the courses in our curriculum. Full-time course work includes a three-hour-per-week writing class, and writing is integrated across our curriculum. The writing class is also a popular choice for part-time students taking a combination of mainstream academic courses along with one or two courses in the IEP.

We are well aware of the diverse experiences that students bring to the writing classroom in areas such as exposure to academic writing in both their L1 and L2, prior experience with writing extended academic prose, cultural and educational backgrounds, and learning styles and preferences. Our recognition of this diversity provided the impetus for creating a series of versatile stand-alone writing modules that could be incorporated into a writing class or be used by students independently for additional practice with skills covered in class. Because our modules are stand-alone units (i.e., not dependent on a particular curriculum or order of use), teachers and students can use them as needed for additional practice or support, allowing the curriculum to be individualized in order to respond to student needs and backgrounds.

We identified several key areas that were problematic for advanced L2 writing students composing academic papers (e.g., narrowing a topic, paraphrasing, using connectors, incorporating citations). We designed our modules to allow individual learners to work on skills and aspects of academic writing that were challenging for them individually, rather than having an entire class march through the same modules at the same time, thus avoiding the problem of the one-size-fits-all approach to L2 writing pedagogy described by Silva and Brice (2004). We decided it would be easier for students to use materials on our school's reliable Web page, materials created especially for them with a uniform interface, than to have them look for exercises on the Internet where they would encounter a variety of formats or "page not found" messages when an external server was down. We could also tailor our materials specifically to the gaps revealed by investigation of our program's needs. Some materials were adapted from or inspired by a number of other Web sites, for example, The Lupton Library (University of Tennessee at Chattanooga n.d.) and e-Library @ Iowa State University (Iowa State University 2000–2005).

Our approach in developing the academic writing modules has two key aspects. First, our modules are not a set of linked lessons. Rather, each module is a self-contained unit that specifically focuses on aspects of composition that have proven difficult for L2 writers (e.g., using citations, paraphrasing). Second, several modules use corpus-based materials or findings from corpus linguistics (see, e.g., Aston 2001; Granger, Hung, and Petch-Tyson 2002) to shape the content presented in the modules. Information from corpus linguistics offers students the opportunity to reflect on the use of certain linguistic features that are typical of academic writing (e.g., transitions, verb choices; see Sevier, chapter 3 in this volume) and to view examples drawn from authentic language use.

A modular approach might be appropriate to many situations, from middle school classes through graduate university adjunct courses for dissertation writing. The modules we developed for undergraduates follow Alessi and Trollip's (2000) recommendations for effective tutorial design. The modules discussed in this section include four phases of instruction: presentation, guidance, practice, and assessment. The ten modules are divided into two categories: the first two modules focus on technology, and the remaining eight focus on various aspects of academic research and writing. (See this chapter's appendix for a complete list of module titles and Web addresses.)

Technology Modules

The two technology modules, Word Made Easy and NAU Scavenger Hunt, are strong examples of how the Web-based modules allow us to address individual student needs. Most students enter the IEP with some computer literacy. However, although they are able to send e-mail and surf the Web, many lack one or more of the basic skills associated with navigating the Web and with word processing. In these cases, teachers are usually able to identify students' needs and refer students to work on the appropriate modules on their own.

Word Made Easy, the word-processing tutorial, enables students to focus on particular skills associated with various aspects of Microsoft Word (2006), such as saving documents, changing font size, and cutting and pasting. Students can review a skill that they are unsure of, or they can practice new skills. Each section of the module is followed by a short, self-administered quiz so that the students can measure how well they control each skill. The module begins with a list of skills that can be used as an informal self- or teacher-directed assessment. Teachers can ask students to rate their ability/comfort level with the various skills and assign whole-class or individual work in each area. The Web-based module provides a more efficient alternative to using valuable class time for addressing issues that relate to only a few students. The modules can also be incorporated into instruction in writing or integrated skills classes. In addition, the online availability of these resources, including a clear table of contents menu, promotes learner autonomy and encourages students to take active responsibility for their learning.

The Web search module, NAU Scavenger Hunt, begins with an explicit presentation of tips about conducting a focused Web search (e.g., taking notes, using keywords, scanning). Students then embark on a focused search of our university's Web site, collecting various bits of information from different pages. This module is often incorporated into the writing class during the first week of the semester, and it provides teachers with an idea of each student's comfort level with the computer, while acquainting students with information about the university (e.g., library and cafeteria hours of operation) and orienting them to various services available on campus (e.g., health clinic, recreational facilities).

Academic Writing Modules

The remaining eight Web-based modules address topics that include both format issues (e.g., using citations, adhering to a style sheet) and composition issues (e.g., selecting and narrowing a topic, paraphrasing, summarizing, developing paragraphs, using linking adverbials, evaluating online sources; see the appendix for full titles and Web addresses of all modules). Several of these Web modules (e.g., Incorporating Sources, Summarizing, Linking Adverbials) can be completed by students without any interaction from the teacher. However, other modules, such as How to Choose/Narrow a Topic, are designed so that after working independently, students print out their writing and receive feedback from a teacher, group of peers, or writing tutor.

Other tasks central to academic writing that have proven particularly challenging (e.g., summarizing or using quotes) are addressed in more than one module. Teachers are able to direct students to these modules, or students may self-select them for additional work. For example, in the Quoting, Paraphrasing, and Summarizing module, students are presented with tips and strategies to help them with these tasks. Another module, Summarizing, provides a review of what summarizing means, followed by a task that requires students to compare two summaries, one from a textbook and another written by a student. At the end of the module, students are asked to write a summary of what they have learned from the module. This task helps to reinforce the knowledge gained from the information presented in the module, while providing students with the chance to practice writing a summary. The teacher or peers can then provide feedback.

Web Features

The Web medium facilitates the use of fonts and colors to highlight the focus of instruction, and allows for various types of input enhancement (as recommended by Chapelle 2003). For example, the Quoting, Paraphrasing, and Summarizing module shows three texts: the original; an unacceptable paraphrase, in which the writer changed only a few words (presented in a different color); and an acceptable paraphrase. The module then explains in detail the differences between the unacceptable and acceptable paraphrases. A variety of colors immediately focuses students' attention on the relevant areas of the paraphrases. Other modules use colors to identify certain text structures, such as introductions or topic sentences. In addition to helping focus attention on particular relevant aspects, the use of colors and different fonts also appeals to visual learners.

The Incorporating Sources module provides an example of enhanced interactivity made possible by the Web. Students are guided through the different sections of the module, with important concepts highlighted in color and bold font; they then write responses to various prompts and compare their responses to those of "Javier," a virtual student writing a paper on a similar topic. Figure 4.1 shows how the students interact with Javier to work on the paper's introduction. Throughout the self-paced module, the students are asked to compare the information they have written to examples of how Javier responded to the same tasks. This type of reflective instruction has been helpful in developing students' ability to write and self-edit their compositions.

A good example of the use of colors and font enhancement can be seen in the Paragraph Development module. After reading a description of what a paragraph is, students

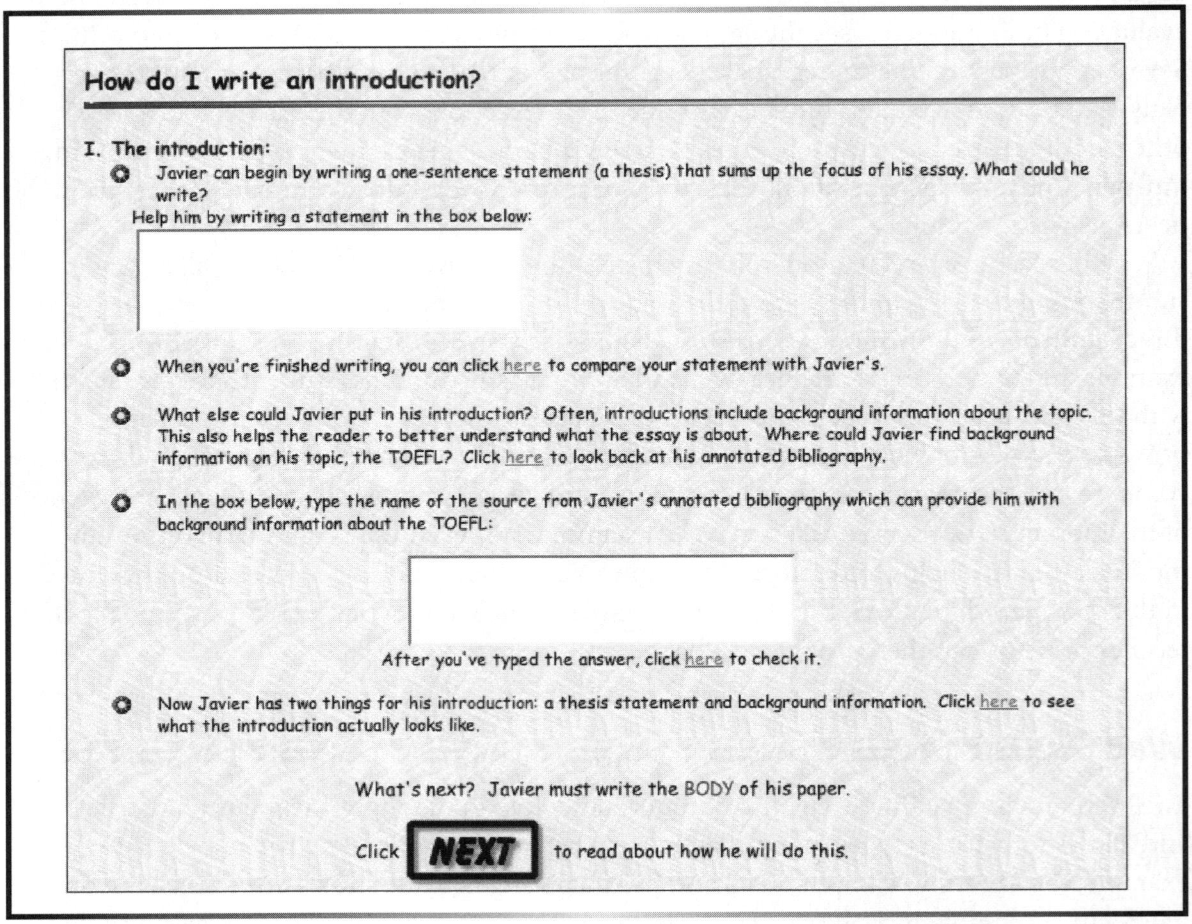

How do I write an introduction?

I. The introduction:

◎ Javier can begin by writing a one-sentence statement (a thesis) that sums up the focus of his essay. What could he write?
Help him by writing a statement in the box below:

◎ When you're finished writing, you can click here to compare your statement with Javier's.

◎ What else could Javier put in his introduction? Often, introductions include background information about the topic. This also helps the reader to better understand what the essay is about. Where could Javier find background information on his topic, the TOEFL? Click here to look back at his annotated bibliography.

◎ In the box below, type the name of the source from Javier's annotated bibliography which can provide him with background information about the TOEFL:

After you've typed the answer, click here to check it.

◎ Now Javier has two things for his introduction: a thesis statement and background information. Click here to see what the introduction actually looks like.

What's next? Javier must write the BODY of his paper.

Click **NEXT** to read about how he will do this.

Figure 4.1. Writing an Introduction with Javier

are guided through the process of writing one. Color fonts and bold type are used to draw students' attention to various parts of the paragraph, such as the topic sentences or transition words.

Taking advantage of the Internet's possibility for interactivity and immediate feedback, we created quizzes using Hot Potatoes (Arneil and Holmes 2005) for various modules. Interactive quizzes are particularly helpful with tasks involving questions of format, where there is little chance for ambiguous answers. For example, a task that students often find challenging is mastering the art of properly citing the sources they use in their papers. Because most of the students in our program are asked to use the format of the American Psychological Association (APA) in their academic course work, we designed the APA Format module to provide practice. In addition to providing examples of in-text citations and references, the module presents three feedback activities in order of increasing difficulty. The activities mirror the tasks that students need to master to use citations successfully in their papers. In the first two activities, students are provided with information or citations and must arrange the reference information properly. In the third task, students are presented with a sample library record and must create a correct citation based on that record. Because the task of creating citations in proper format is one that has little ambiguity, it is an ideal activity to follow with short quizzes that provide immediate feedback (see Figure 4.2). Hot Potatoes allows the designer to input content, design feedback, and generate Web pages for student practice. The quizzes provide immediate feedback on right and wrong answers and collate self-test scores that can then be printed out or sent to the teacher via e-mail.

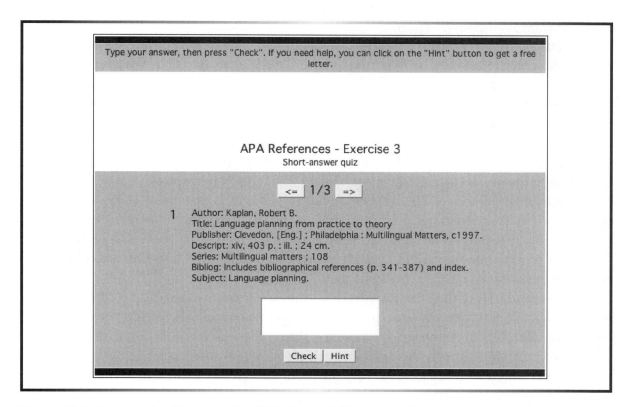

Figure 4.2. Interactive Quiz for the APA Format Module Using Hot Potatoes

Many students now use the Internet as a major source of information for papers and presentations. Evaluating online information is a challenge for all students, but particularly for international students who may come from cultures in which the written word is not questioned. The task of reconciling information from texts that present opposing or contradictory views on the same topic can also be difficult. Sifting through the enormous amount of information presented on the Web only adds to this challenge. To begin to address this problem, we developed the Web Source Evaluation module, which presents a set of questions and criteria designed to help raise awareness about who created a Web site and how that authorship impacts the reliability of the information presented. The quiz at the end of the module asks students to identify and categorize five different sources of information. These questions reinforce students' heightened awareness of Web page authorship. The tasks in the module can be completed individually, in pairs, or in small groups.

For more detailed grammar work, we used corpus-based research to inform instruction on the use of linking adverbials, grammatical items that contribute significantly to discourse cohesion in written academic English. The absence or presence of appropriate cohesive links may influence readers' judgment of how well written a particular text is (Yule 1996, 141). Following recommendations for applying corpus linguistics research to the development of language learning materials (Conrad 1999), we selected two primary areas to target in the Linking Adverbials module: sentence position and semantic category. Specifically, we included activities recommended by Conrad, in which students could "analyze the types of connections that are most often overtly expressed in academic prose (i.e., analyze semantic categories) . . . [and] practice the variable placement of linking adverbials . . . [e.g.,] medial *thus*, *therefore* and *however*" (p. 16).

In our analysis of academic writing, we found that while linking adverbials occur most frequently sentence-initially, certain linking adverbials (e.g., *for example*, *therefore*, *hence*) occur most frequently sentence-medially. Our corpus-based module allows students to learn inductively that linking adverbs may occur in several places in the sentence. The module asks learners to examine two sets of concordances that were prepared using MonoConc Pro 2.2 (2005) and were drawn from a representative corpus of academic writing. Students must then draw conclusions about the frequency of sentence position for each adverbial. (See examples on the next page regarding *thus* and *however* from the corpus.)

Occasionally, novice or ESL writers use linking adverbials that are more typical of spoken registers. Although our module does not treat these register differences per se, our examples (because they come from authentic academic texts) address only those linking adverbials most commonly found in academic writing. Students who tend to use colloquialisms may be asked to compare their writing to the corpus examples.

The second part of the Linking Adverbials module consists of a multiple-choice activity, which asks students to read an excerpt from an academic text and then select the appropriate linking adverbial to connect the discourse. Once students select a response, they receive a detailed explanation of why their answer is either correct or incorrect. Learners are not explicitly presented with rules; rather they are required to read each text closely to decide which linking word or phrase most accurately expresses the semantic relationship in the text. Realizing that this task may prove quite challenging for some learners, we included a linked

Help page, which presents the different semantic categories of linking adverbials, provides a brief explanation of their meanings, and offers a fairly comprehensive list of adverbials in each category (adapted from Biber et al. 1999; for more on the uses of concordancing, see Sevier, chapter 3 in this volume).

Challenges and Future Directions

Any instructional resource has aspects related to either the creation or the use of the resource that pose challenges. This is also true with the online modules. The development of modules is a time-consuming process and typically involves a group of individuals who plan, design, create, edit, and test the content. However, the modules can become reusable learning objects that may find additional applications in the future.

In addition to the initial time commitment, because the modules are not linked to specific classes, teachers may not make the best use of the modules. We introduce our modules as part of our program orientation, but we also need to remind teachers during the semester that the modules are a resource for providing students with additional practice. In spite of the large time commitment and coordination efforts needed to develop, produce, and implement online modules, we feel the benefits for teachers and students outweigh the drawbacks.

The modules presented in this chapter provide a glimpse of some of the many ways the Web can be used to enhance writing instruction in a second language. Modules like ours provide a means for helping students who desire or need additional practice with various skills related to university-level academic composition. Because these modules are delivered online, students can access learning materials and practice academic writing skills at their convenience. This accessibility, in turn, allows instructors the flexibility to address individual student needs by assigning specific modules to students who need extra help with a particular aspect of writing, thus freeing class time to focus on issues relevant for the majority of students in the class.

We plan to continue developing modules that provide additional instruction and practice in areas that have been identified as problematic for L2 writers. We also plan to expand the number of modules that use corpus-based material to inform the structures and activities presented, such as including linguistic patterns found in different disciplines and lexical bundles typical in academic prose and university lectures (as suggested by Biber et al. 1999). In the future, we hope to be able to develop an interface in which students can interact with language corpora to discover patterns of use and to carry out their own searches on particular linguistic structures or features (T. Johns 1994, 1997; see also Sevier, chapter 3 in this volume).

Acknowledgments

We would like to thank Kimberly Becker, Tadayoshi Kaya, Mindy Visser, and Tim Cullen, who were central to the creation of the modules presented in this chapter. We are also grateful for support from a grant from Northern Arizona University's Center for Research, Assessment, and Development of Learning in Electronic Environments.

Appendix—Chapter 4
Web-Based Modules, Online Program Models, and Development Tools

Technology Modules at Northern Arizona University (NAU)	
NAU Scavenger Hunt *linked from the Welcome page*	http://www.nau.edu/english/tesl/scavenger/Scavengerhunt1.html
Word Made Easy *word-processing tutorial*	http://www.nau.edu/english/tesl/wordwebpages/wordpage1.htm
Academic Writing Modules at NAU	
APA Format	http://www.nau.edu/english/tesl/apa/index.htm
Linking Adverbials: A Corpus-Based Interactive Grammar Module for Students	http://www.nau.edu/english/tesl/linkad.swf
How to Choose/Narrow a Topic	http://www.nau.edu/english/tesl/narrowing/choosing-narrowing_topics_home.htm
Incorporating Sources	http://www.nau.edu/english/tesl/incorporate/incorporating_sources_home.htm
Paragraph Development	http://www.nau.edu/english/tesl/paragraph/
Quoting, Paraphrasing, and Summarizing	http://www.nau.edu/english/tesl/quoting/quoting.htm

Summarizing	http://www.nau.edu/english/tesl/summarizing/summarizing_home.htm
Web Source Evaluation	http://www.nau.edu/english/tesl/websources/web_source_evaluation_module_home.htm
Online Models	
e-Library @ Iowa State University	http://www.lib.iastate.edu/
The Lupton Library	http://www.lib.utc.edu/
Tools for Building Modules	
Hot Potatoes *exercise-building software*	http://hotpot.uvic.ca/
MonoConc Pro 2.2 *concordancer*	http://www.athel.com

Chapter 5

Developing a Web-Based Listening Course

In-Seok Kim
Dongduk Women's University
Seoul, South Korea

Preview

The online environment has great appeal for many ESOL teachers, especially as a resource for listening. Web-based listening offers the student control in responding and listening repeatedly. However, exercises are for the most part fairly basic and may not relate directly to the needs of a local curriculum. Kim describes how he developed an online listening comprehension course in English at Korea's Open Cyber University, including multimedia content derived from his own textbook. He explains the relationship between various online and offline elements and suggests that, based on students' positive responses, the Internet is an especially appropriate environment for developing both micro- and macrolistening skills.

Before you read:

- What processes should be planned to teach a listening course entirely online without meeting students face to face (f2f)?
- What kinds of Web-based tools would enable a teacher to encourage commitment to the course, collaboration among peers, and language practice opportunities?

Development of E-Learning

Many people believe that the Internet has fundamentally changed the way foreign languages are taught. Most universities now offer classes that use technology in some form, either as an enhancement to f2f classes for their own on-campus students or for distance learning (Palloff and Pratt 2001). Some universities use this method of language education to reach students who cannot otherwise attend classes, while others adopt it as a way to deliver more effective instruction. In fact, many universities are feeling pressure from students to develop online language courses because students want to have access to learning materials at home. In the Korean educational context, almost all universities offer their students a large number of online language courses in one form or another, thanks to the Internet and communications infrastructure prevalent across all walks of life (Kim 2003). Seventeen cyber universities are fully accredited by the Ministry of Education in Korea and enroll some thirty thousand students. These universities are allowed to offer bachelor's degrees in a variety of disciplines. Among them is Open Cyber University (OCU), one of the earliest virtual universities known to have established a stabilized academic program on a par with that of a brick-and-mortar degree-offering university. I have been teaching a cyber listening course by invitation at OCU since 2001, while also teaching full time at my home institution.

This chapter describes the procedures by which I developed an online listening comprehension course in English that I have taught at OCU for the past three years. The chapter explores the theories underlying online learning and describes how they relate to the processes of developing online multimedia content derived from a course textbook. Finally, it explains the relationship between various online and offline elements in e-learning.

Theoretical Bases for an Online Listening Course

The theoretical underpinnings for an online listening course can be derived from existing, widely accepted second language acquisition (SLA) theories. Among those, *noticing* (Schmidt 1990, 1994a, 1995), *learner autonomy* (Dickinson 1987; White 2003), and *engagement* (Kearsley 2000) are the most relevant to principles of computer-assisted language learning and the pedagogy of listening.

Schmidt's Noticing Theory

Schmidt (1995) defines the term *noticing* as the process of bringing some stimulus into focal attention. For example, noticing comes into play when learners spot the odd spelling of a new vocabulary word or the ungrammaticality of a syntactic structure. The success or failure of learning depends on how noticeable the new words and structures are. Schmidt (1994a) argues that "noticing is the necessary and sufficient condition for the conversion of input to intake for learning" (p. 17; see also Batstone 1996; Thornbury 1997).

An online listening program is one of the best ways to provide materials with a certain degree of noticeability. A case in point is the distinction between the /l/ and /r/ sounds, which typically poses a problem for Japanese and Korean EFL students. In a Web-based listening program, the learner may choose the word *late* for the word *rate* in a sentence. By clicking the answer icon, the learner finds out immediately if the word is incorrect, and what the correct word is. This interactivity maximizes the degree of noticeability for the learner in a matter of seconds. Additionally, the student can receive immediate, completely confidential feedback. In a typical classroom, the teacher's corrections may not be consistent and may cause the student to feel ashamed or embarrassed in front of others. In the privacy of the Web, the learner may focus solely on the content of the correction, and as a result, more effective learning may occur.

Dickinson on Learner Autonomy

Autonomous language learning refers to situations in which learners make decisions about what and when to study, and when and how to be tested (Dickinson 1987). If an instructor tries to work with a large number of students in a confined classroom, little attention can be given to students' individual needs, differences in individual learning strategies, and varying attitudes and feelings toward language learning. Listening skills are particularly difficult to individualize in a large class, where the teacher can give only a few moments of attention to each student. Autonomous learning outside the class may be the solution.

An online listening program allows learners maximum autonomy, and autonomy serves as one of the guiding principles in the creation of multimedia applications (Brett 1999). Originally, multimedia applications were developed for the purpose of self-study, as an adjunct to, or in place of, classroom courses. Although noncomputer media, such as books, audiotapes, and videotapes, can be used in isolation by learners, computer and Internet applications incorporate multimedia elements and user-friendly controls that cannot be found in traditional media. The online listening course that I developed is a stand-alone, multimedia program that does not require students' attendance in class, and most learning activities can be done without the classroom teacher's presence. The Web pages contain model answers, explanations, and Korean translations of target sentences. Behind this approach lies my belief that low-level listening practice calls for rather extensive human labor that can more effectively be performed by giving students the tools to take charge of their own practice and learning. The resultant savings in class time allows for more creative, communicative activities led by the instructor. Autonomy, with good tools, results in more efficient learning.

Kearsley's Engagement Theory for Web-Based Learning

A host of learning theories and models can explain the complex phenomenon that takes place when one is engaged in learning foreign languages; however, *engagement theory*, proposed by Kearsley (2000), seems to have the most direct bearing on Web-based learning. Engagement theory is deeply rooted in constructivism, in which students are given the chance to create their own learning environment. According to Kearsley, Web-based learning has the three major characteristics of constructivism: collaboration, problem solving, and authenticity. *Collaboration* refers to the various types of interactions between the instructor and students or among students themselves. In a Web-based context, these include e-mail exchanges, text and voice chatting, videoconferencing, and discussion forums. *Problem solving* involves group work in completing assignments, projects, or research. Optimal

Web-based learning does not focus on tests or quizzes, but rather on providing a context in which students discover things and experiment with them while working in pairs or small groups. The third characteristic, *authenticity*, is inherently embedded in optimal Web-based learning. Web-based language courses are full of authentic video scenes from all over the world, reporters' live voices, graphics, and animations—all of which can be linked to one Web page—revealing authentic voices and settings that a foreign language instructor could not possibly simulate in a typical classroom.

Course Conversion to the Web

As demand for online language courses grows, instructors may become overwhelmed. Nine out of ten instructors tend to give up developing multimedia (Ko and Rossen 2001). However, teachers can shorten the development process by converting their traditional courses into multimedia content using ready-made Web tools. There are basically two types of course conversions: (1) combine f2f classroom teaching with selected online elements in a blended environment and (2) teach exclusively over the Internet, which involves recasting the entire class into an online mode. The second type requires more of the course developer's dedication and energy and is the mode I chose for the online listening course described in this chapter. After developing the materials, I devoted most of my assigned course time to online chatting, answering students' e-mails, and individual phone conferencing.

Elements involved in course conversion include the following, some of which take place simultaneously:

1. Needs analysis
2. Construction of the syllabus
3. Design of appropriate Web pages to support the course
4. Design of multimedia content
5. Integration of offline and online course elements

Each of these aspects is considered in more detail in the remainder of this chapter.

Needs Analysis

The background for this course is as follows:

Importance of listening to language learning. Listening comprehension skills are the basis on which other language skills can be built. According to Rivers (1987), native speakers spend 40–50 percent of their communication time on listening, 11–16 percent on reading, and 9 percent on writing (for an update, see Oxford 1993). Listening seems to engage people in their daily lives far more than other types of language skills. Rubin (1995) echoes this view: listening is such a critical skill that 50 percent of a person's time is spent on it (p. 7). Rubin also argues that the need to focus on listening has increased.

Student needs. Every year, over one million Korean university students take standardized tests such as the Test of English for International Communication (TOEIC), the Test of English Proficiency (TEPS), and the Test of English as a Foreign Language (TOEFL), and, in general, their listening comprehension scores are considerably lower than their reading scores. Furthermore, Korean students' TOEFL scores ranked 109th among students of 153 countries who have taken the TOEFL Computer-Based Test (CBT) in recent years (J. Lee 2002). Thus, there is a dire need to improve Korean students' listening comprehension skills.

Availability of appropriate materials. I had already developed a listening comprehension textbook with accompanying audio. Thus I had no problems with copyright, and a significant body of content at the appropriate level was readily at hand.

Availability of resources. No matter how good the idea is, multimedia content is almost impossible to develop without funding. A developer might consider the following questions: Is there a computer lab with Internet connection? Do students have Internet access at home?

Additional local factors. Local conditions often indicate that technology offers the optimal solution. I committed myself to developing this online course for several local reasons, which may apply in other regions of the world as well:

1. Many Korean students suffer from listening to meaningless, discrete English phonemes. I wanted to give students the opportunity to listen to sounds contextualized in authentic content.

2. In a land-based course, students are not given enough time to listen to the materials that pose extreme difficulties, and they may not receive enough individualized help because classes are too large. Students' learning could be enhanced by activities such as listening to native speakers, having access to immediate correction after multiple repetitions, and having multiple chances to review the same materials.

3. Explanations and translations into Korean could speed the learning process and could be selected individually by the student, as needed.

4. The online course would benefit students who had to miss the f2f class due to a tight work schedule.

Construction of the Online Syllabus

The online course syllabus for my course, Strategic English Listening Comprehension, consists of three elements: course description, week-by-week syllabus, and contact information (see Kim 2001–2004).

Course description. This three-credit elective for first-year college students runs fifteen weeks. Regardless of their major, students also take several other language courses along with this course. The course combines bottom-up and top-down listening strategies. Assessment involves midterm and final exams delivered online, two quizzes, and two group listening projects. Originally, final exams were given to all students f2f at the same time for security reasons, but since 2003, these have also been delivered online.

Week-by-week syllabus. The syllabus (see Table 5.1) uses the traditional organization of microlevel listening first. Units 1–7 focus on individual phonemes and short sentences; students practice listening to the sounds that pose the most difficulties for Koreans and distinguishing phonemic differences between sounds that are close to each other. Units 8–14 focus on macrolevel listening with paragraphs or dialogues that are semantically more dense and contain syntactically longer and more complex sentences, comparable to TOEIC and

Table 5.1. Syllabus for Strategic English Listening Comprehension

Skills	Week/Unit	Web Page Contents
M **I** **C** **R** **O**	1. Sounds that are difficult for Korean students to distinguish	/l/ vs. /r/ /b/ vs. /v/ /f/ vs. /p/ /i/ vs. /l:/ /ch/ vs. /sh/
	2. Contracted sounds within a word and between words	Modal auxiliary contraction, *who's, what's, going to*; /s, z, t, d/ + *your*; *what are you, what do you*
	3. Accent and intonation	*Object, desert, present, estimate, separate, black board, smoking room* Rising and falling intonation Tag questions
	4. Pronunciation of colloquial expressions	Differences between written and spoken language Idioms and collocation phrases
	5. Sounds that are likely to be misheard	*Below-low, because-cause, remember-member* Minimal pairs: *nodes-nose, braise-braids, rise-rides, speech science-speech signs*
	6. Listening through paraphrasing	*I am afraid that I don't agree with you* *I don't like the idea*
	7. Listening through schema	Speaking of a snake in your culture—scary feeling Marriage ending in divorce—terrible feeling
	Midterm test given online: 40 multiple-choice items	
M **A** **C** **R** **O**	8. Listening with visual aids	Paragraph listening while viewing graphs, tables, statistics, etc.
	9. Listening with visual clues	Paragraph listening while viewing maps, landmarks, etc.
	10. Fill-in practice after listening to the paragraphs	Filling in the blanks based on paragraph listening
	11. Listening with pictures	Choosing the picture that corresponds best to the short sentence heard
	12. Listening with a set of pictures	Sequencing pictures based on information heard in a paragraph
	13. Listening with background pictures	Identifying things misrepresented in the picture after listening to a paragraph
	14. Listening with a set of pictures	Choosing the picture that best represents the conversation heard
	Final test given online: 50 multiple-choice items	

Source: http://www.eflcall.com/.

TOEFL test items. Other teachers might place macrolevel listening first, as recommended by Gilbert (1995).

Instructional Design of Course Web Pages

Web pages allow students to access the course content at their own convenience, wherever they have Internet access. Web page design involves placing functional buttons and planning page layouts so as to facilitate student access (Da 2000). The course developer also needs to possess broad knowledge of how to create multimedia in accordance with the principles of good pedagogy (see Alessi and Trollip 2000; Boettcher and Conrad 1999; W. Lee and Owens 2000). Observation of other instructional Web pages and computer courseware also provides a good basis for understanding design. My online course includes lectures in streaming video, Internet-mounted slide shows, tests, quizzes, homework, and group projects, and emphasizes student-initiated learning. The following description points to how I incorporate the elements of language acquisition theory into the instructional design.

Noticing. Multiple interactions with instructional materials are needed for effective learning (Ellis 1997). In my course, for example, students are asked to listen to target sounds or sentences and choose the picture that represents what they heard (see Figure 5.1). Then

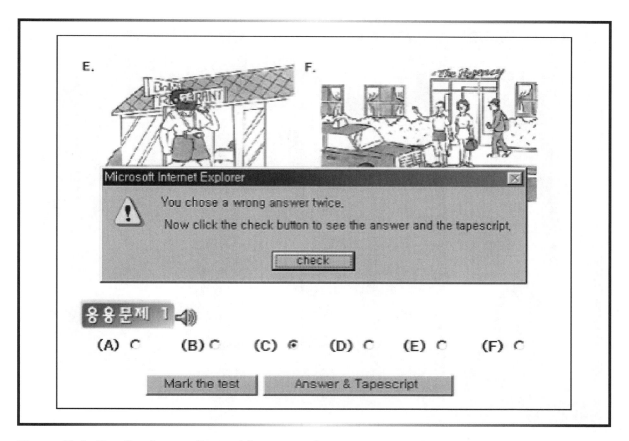

Figure 5.1. Feedback on a Second Incorrect Attempt
Source: http://www.eflcall.com/.

they click an icon to check whether they are correct, and they can see the correct answer as well as read an explanation and a Korean translation, comparing their answers with the model. These interactions maximize the students' ability to notice the difference between what they do and do not know (Schmidt 1994a). If students choose a second incorrect answer, they are asked to view the correct answer and listen to the audio again. Thus, students with a higher level of inaccuracy receive more passes at an item, rather than simply obtaining a score passively.

Autonomous learning. It is important for learners to have an environment in which they can figure out what to do for themselves. Naturally, the instructor's expertise is needed to point students in the right direction and assist them when they run into problems (for more on teacher guidance see Robb, chapter 6 in this volume). At the microlistening level, students first watch an online video lecture about the target sounds, with appropriate media enhancements (see Figure 5.2 for a sample screen). Students then enter the Web page and practice choosing the correct words, checking the answers immediately. They can study transcripts and Korean translations of the sentence examples. If they have questions concerning listening practice items, they can contact the instructor by e-mail, phone, or Internet chat during virtual office hours. The extent of students' listening practice is autonomous: the instructor provides the materials, information, means to practice, and guidance; it is up to the students

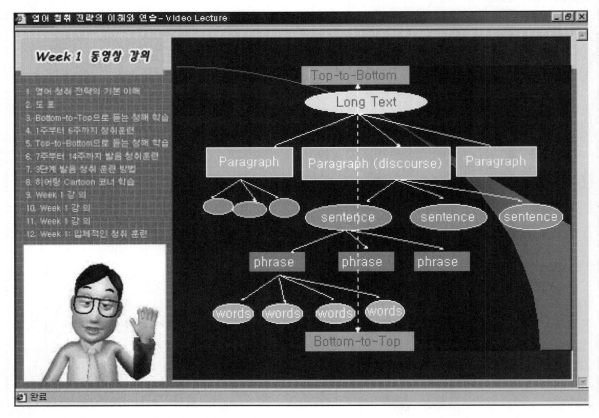

Figure 5.2. Instructor's 3D Avatar
Source: http://www.eflcall.com/.

to practice as much as they feel necessary. I believe that a low-level skill, such as listening practice with discrete sounds, can be cost-effective and instructionally valuable on the Internet since students can practice listening as often as they want and focus specifically on their weakest sounds with the most patient and forgiving of drill masters, the computer.

At the macrolevel, Units 8–15 of the syllabus focus on meaning rather than on discrete sounds, so they use a somewhat different teaching sequence. Students first work offline with the textbook, reading explanations about how to comprehend a paragraph unit and answering comprehension questions concerning these strategies. Students then enter the Web page, watch my streaming video, complete practice items, read the explanations, and check the Korean translations if they wish. Here again, student learning remains autonomous since it takes place through the book and Web pages. The major advantage of this type of learning is that students can repeat the items as many times as they want and focus on working on their weakest items. In an f2f listening comprehension class, students do not usually receive enough time to work on items individually or enough personal time to listen as often as they wish. In the online environment, students can work at their own pace, listening as often as needed to complete the tasks.

Engagement theory. As discussed earlier, Kearsley (2000) proposes three major characteristics of Web-based learning—collaboration, problem solving, and authenticity—all of which I implemented when designing the listening comprehension course. First, the course relies on various types of interaction between students and me or among students, carried out through e-mail exchanges, text and voice chatting, videoconferencing during virtual office hours, and discussion forums. These methods attempt to replace some of the interactivity recommended for the classroom (see Rivers 1987). Second, the course draws on students' engagement in Web learning by assigning two group projects, during which students are asked to relate what they learned from the course to new listening material. For example, students in groups of four or five were asked to watch two streamed ten-minute video segments from a major motion picture (purchased by the university lab center), identify examples of the pronunciation rules (e.g., contractions, blending, deletion) that they were studying in the course, and explain their meanings. Third, I uploaded or hyperlinked authentic materials (e.g., live news reports, dialogues extracted from drama) on the Web pages for optional additional learning. In a land-based classroom, the instructor cannot easily bring such materials to class.

Multimedia Content Development

Multimedia files for Web pages ought ideally to be created by professional graphic/multimedia designers (Da 2000); however, hiring such experts for the course would have been extremely expensive, so with help from a graduate assistant with advanced knowledge of multimedia, I developed the materials. In other situations, teachers may begin with ready-made materials and gradually acquire expertise in media, particularly as digital cameras and videocams become increasingly affordable and easy to use (for more on teacher- and student-made digital video, see Gromik, chapter 9 in this volume). A quick Google Image Search (Google 2006b) turns up copyright-free photos and drawings that may be used to good effect, and several major news services, such as the British Broadcasting Corporation

(BBC) and Voice of America (VOA) News, have transcripts and audiotapes available on their Web sites.

HTML conversion. Simple text materials can be scanned or produced through a word processor and converted into HTML documents using any free Web editor. I converted existing documents from my book (Kim 2002) into HTML files using Namo WebEditor (2005).

Digital images. Creating digital images is one of the easiest parts of preparatory work for a Web program. Images on paper, in books, on slides—even from film negatives—can easily be converted into digital format using a scanner. Once the files are created, they can be modified using an image-editing program such as Adobe Photoshop (2006). If the teacher has access to a digital camera or hand-held device (e.g., PDA, cell phone with camera), images from these devices can be converted to a Web-compatible format such as GIF or JPEG. My course used cartoons in Units 1–5 that contained dialogues in which misunderstandings were caused by mis-hearings. I was lucky enough to have a cartoonist/graphic designer create the cartoons I used. However, classroom teachers may be able to find something comparable in the comics section of newspapers, blank out the speech balloons, and have native speakers record the dialogue, although care for copyrights must be taken. Even stick figures are useful, and a search among one's students may turn up a good sketch artist to help.

Video content. Creating video content might be considered one of the hardest parts of the preparatory process for developing online courses. As of this writing, there are a wide variety of formats (see T. L. Smith and Ransbottom 2000); which one of these a teacher chooses depends on the kinds of computers and bandwidth available to him or her. One thing that any language instructor can do, perhaps with a little assistance from technical staff, is to transfer analog videos to digital video format. Video cameras and computers come with free software for this purpose, but loading the analog movie may require a special converter, available for about $200 at the present time. With a little practice, video files can be created and incorporated into Web pages. Streaming media are recommended because they allow users to view a video clip as the file is being transferred, thus avoiding lengthy waits for downloading. Although video production is becoming easier, it may be best to enlist the help of one's institution if video media are to be made from scratch. Again, one's students may turn out to be helpful in creating video, especially graduate students who are paid or are working on service-learning projects.

Audio lectures. In order to add interest and humor to the video lectures on pronunciation, my graduate assistant learned how to align my recorded audio lectures and presentation software slides with a three-dimensional avatar using the relatively inexpensive Avatar 3D (2003) software. The advantage of an avatar is that one can emphasize certain key points with appropriate hand motions, head movements, winks of the eye, and so forth (see Figure 5.2) while using much less file space than traditional video. Avatars can be made to look like the instructor and have the potential to personalize lectures, mimicking interpersonal actions from the traditional classroom.

Conversion of audio into digital files. There are several ways to create audio for the Web, including converting existing CDs or tapes into digital format. Speech may also be recorded directly on the computer using free sound-editing software, although a professional program gives clearer results. A variety of helpful technical files may be found on the Internet, but changes occur so fast that it would be better to work with only the latest information, perhaps enlisting the institution's technical help. Fortunately, media creation is becoming simpler all the time. Professional actors are not needed for classroom purposes: several native speakers of U.S. English recorded the exercises for each chapter in my textbook, and these recordings were then edited and encoded, with a very professional result, into files that could be used by a plug-in offered by most Web browsers.

Interactive exercises. Professional programmers, or those willing to spend some time learning programming, can use CGI or JavaScript to write interactive Web-based exercises with scoring and feedback. I used JavaScript to convert my textbook pages using a free version and tutorials that were available online. However, most teachers should choose one of the prepackaged authoring programs, such as Hot Potatoes (Arneil and Holmes 2005; for other exercise-authoring programs, see González, chapter 2 in this volume). Since these exercises are the heart of instruction and practice, great care should be taken to make the feedback informative and positive, as well as immediate. Students can receive high-quality instruction if feedback suggests not only what was wrong but why.

Ancillary online resources. In addition to materials that I created, the Web pages for my course are hyperlinked to other resources, including dictionaries, text, and sound files, so when students have a problem with the pronunciation or meaning of a particular word, they can search for help. In addition, links lead to sites related to English pronunciation rules and jokes in English (*Internet TESL Journal* 1998–2005). The latter site is intended to provide additional ways of looking at pronunciation and to relieve stress by injecting an element of humor into the discourse.

As the various pieces of multimedia content are created, care should be taken to build a flowchart, which can also become the basis for an entry menu to the Web site (see Figure 5.3).

Faculty developers should also be aware of the needs of their institutions' course management system (CMS), if they have one, and consult with their system administrators early in the process of development to ensure that they are prepared for a Web-based course and can handle large-scale Web pages with interactive media content.

Integration of Offline Teaching with Online Learning

Offline teaching elements. Using the textbook and CD, students train their ears by listening to English. On the Web pages, they practice listening comprehension at a higher or more intense level. Materials shown on the Web pages do not appear in the text and vice versa. My intent was for students to train their ears extensively in their spare time, possibly listening to the CD on the subway on their way to work, while Web work is corrected online by the software and monitored by both the student and me. By possessing the text and CD or audiotapes, students have resources available for learning long after the course ends.

Student activities in the online environment. A variety of communication tools can be used in online courses, including e-mail, bulletin boards, and online conferencing. Using

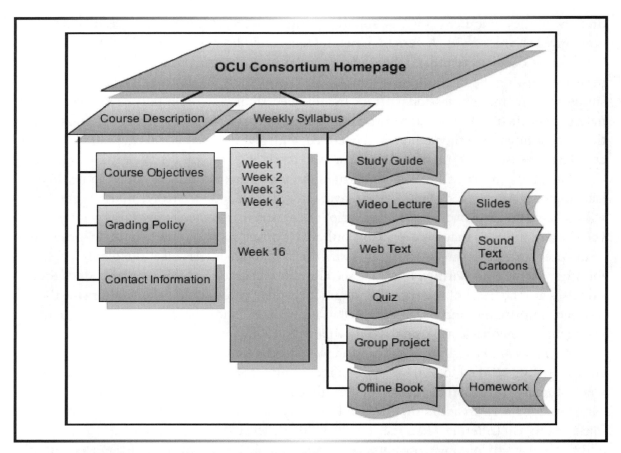

Figure 5.3. Flowchart of Strategic English Listening Comprehension
Source: http://www.eflcall.com/.

these tools leads to the growth of not only each member's knowledge but also the whole community's knowledge base (Adams and Freeman 2000), as students share insights with each other and the instructor responds to their queries. My course utilizes the following communication modes in addition to the weekly virtual lecture:

- *icebreakers*—Students need opportunities to get to know each other and build some sense of community while they take a course online. In this course, students upload brief self-introductions in English or Korean on the Web site's bulletin board. Students welcome this idea, and it often leads to vibrant communications among them. Such social activities make peer-to-peer connections highly motivating.

- *collaborative listening projects*—An end-of-class survey showed that the projects students liked best were the two group projects (involving the movie described earlier). They also liked the idea that male and female students from seventeen participating universities could work together on a single project. (I suspect that interesting exchanges among students outside of course media may have bonded them to the projects to some extent.)

- *e-mail exchanges*—Since most students cannot see me, the instructor, in person, exchanging e-mail is one of the predominant ways that they communicate with peers and with me. I receive approximately ten e-mails daily, asking specific questions about the video lectures and exercises on the Web pages; responses are sent within a day or so. Most are routine questions that can be answered by a graduate assistant; I respond to the queries that call for special attention to instructional points.

- *bulletin board*—I make announcements of general interest on the Web site's bulletin board. Students also exchange opinions about what is being taught in the course, and I answer their general questions using this feature as another instructional opportunity.

- *online synchronous discussions*—Using text, audio, and video chatting in real time, students discuss with their peers what is being taught.

- *virtual office hours*—Because of distance or conflict in work hours, students sometimes have difficulty getting in touch with me in person. I announce virtual office hours at various times on the course bulletin board, during which I take phone calls or engage in instant messaging, Internet chatting, videoconferencing, and so forth. Many students prefer to communicate via synchronous text chat.

Web-based instruction relies heavily on information technologies, which are in turn made possible by digital advances. However, personal contact with students remains a significant part of course structure, whether online or off. The variety of technologies used for communication in the listening course is schematized in Figure 5.4, including push technologies that learners and teachers can use to upload and download material from the target site.

Students' Responses to Online Learning

The number of students enrolled in the online listening course has grown gradually from 230 in the first semester, spring 2000, to over 450 in the fall semester of 2005. When the number of enrollees is more than 200, two full-time graduate assistants are assigned to help. Students generally upload no more than forty questions per week to the bulletin board since most questions can be answered by reading the explanations in the course textbook. Students help each other answer questions on the bulletin board, and when their discussions appear to go nowhere or are headed in the wrong direction, I intervene and settle the debated issue. Students have reported no serious problem with access. If they have an access problem due to slow Internet speed, the graduate assistants set up an individualized file transfer protocol (FTP) site from which students can download large digital files.

Analysis of an informal survey taken during each of the past two semesters reveals students' opinions that this online listening course is better than average in terms of the quality of the language materials and course management (see Table 5.2).

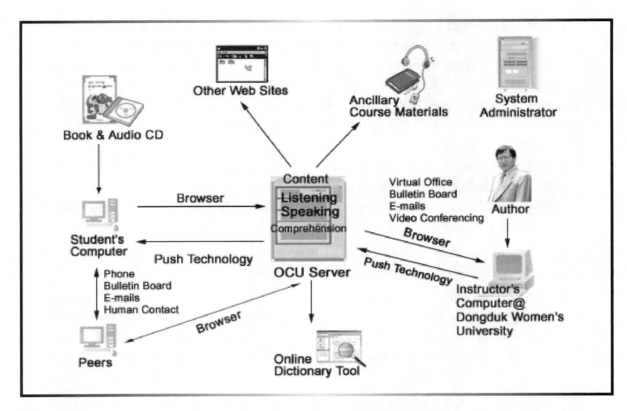

Figure 5.4. Communication Structure for Strategic English Listening Comprehension
Source: Kim 2002.

The survey also revealed the following:

- A majority of students showed a favorable response to the online environment.
- A majority of students indicated that this online course was effective because it had a great deal of good-quality English listening materials, video lectures, and many interesting hyperlinked sites.
- Many students expressed a positive response to my avatar video lectures that summarized what was being taught on the Web and in the course book.
- Many students liked participation in group listening projects because they could establish human relationships among fellow students in the course, an important trait that tends to be lacking in typical Web-based courses (and often in campus-based courses as well).

Challenges and Future Directions

As clearly shown throughout this chapter, the development of a good Web-based course is greatly advanced by well-orchestrated efforts among experts in a number of fields from content to technology. It would be ideal for the language expert to collaborate with a professional multimedia designer and a computer programmer at the onset when developing Web

Table 5.2. Students' Opinions about the Online Course

Question	Yes	So-So	No	No Answer
1. Did this course help you listen better?	68.9%	31.1%		
2. Would you recommend this course to a friend?	88.9%		8.9%	2.2%
3. Do you think that this online course was more effective than the one taught in class?	51.0%	26.9%	13.1%	9.0%
Why?	good listening materials, video lectures, many interesting sites			
4. Which part of this online course did you like the most?	avatar video lecture, group listening projects			

Note: N = 33.

content. However, a teacher with the willingness to learn and experiment may successfully mount such a course with some practice, training, and institutional support, perhaps adding Web materials very gradually over several semesters. In any case, the success of the course cannot be guaranteed unless an instructor is committed to time-consuming preparations and management. Further, constant revision is necessary for the instructor to improve the quality of online instruction by incorporating authentic listening materials that students may encounter in their daily lives.

Other challenges make online instructors feel overwhelmed more often than not. For example, monitoring students from so many different universities is time-consuming. Students from different universities send me e-mails mainly asking questions about the course content and/or reporting problems that occur on the receiving end of Web instruction. Attending to these questions has substantially increased my assistants' and my workloads. Another challenge stems from my adherence to the OCU grading policy, which requires that the maximum number of As through Ds be predetermined on a curve. When the number of scores that fall within a certain grade band exceeds that allowed by the grading policy, it is extremely difficult to readjust the grades in compliance with that policy. Needless to say, many students complain to me about the unfairness of this grading policy.

Four years ago, when I first offered a cyber listening course at OCU, I almost regretted my involvement in it primarily because it took so much time to develop and monitor the course simultaneously. Over a period of several years, however, the course has become well grounded, based on the learning experience through trial and error along with the advancement of Web technology. Now it is fair to say that my experience with teaching a cyber listening course at OCU has shifted from the initial agonizing stage to a stabilized, well-balanced period during which I can easily tend to and maintain the course.

The number of online university courses for language learners is rapidly growing, although it is impossible even to estimate the quickly increasing volume at this point. Students' favorable responses to my online listening course are by no means surprising. Youths growing up in the information age are being weaned on interactions with multimedia and are accustomed to using them to seek knowledge and entertainment (Palloff and Pratt 2001; see Sokolik, chapter 11 in this volume). The integration of digital media into foreign language instruction brings immeasurable power to language learning. Online course work connects learners at a distance and actively engages them through collaboration, group work, and interaction. Teaching foreign languages online constitutes a new powerful paradigm for language instruction. Although it is unlikely that Web-based language instruction will totally replace contact with a human instructor in the university classroom, it seems clear that foreign language instructors who possess broad knowledge and hands-on experience in Web-based instruction will replace those teachers who resist using the powerful, new interactive teaching tools of the twenty-first century.

Appendix—Chapter 5
Web Sites, Internet Tools, and Software

Adobe Photoshop	http://www.adobe.com/products/photoshop/overview.html
Avatar 3D	http://www.interveg.co.kr/index.html?Mode=intProduct&subMode=2&Lang=EN
British Broadcasting Corporation	http://www.bbc.com/
Cyber EFL CALL Academy	http://www.eflcall.com
Google Image Search	http://images.google.com/
Hot Potatoes	http://hotpot.uvic.ca/
Jokes in English for the ESL/EFL Classroom	http://iteslj.org/c/jokes.html
Namo WebEditor	http://www.namo.com/products/webeditor.php
Voice of America	http://www.voanews.com/english/portal.cfm

Chapter 6

Issue: *CALL and the Nonautonomous Learner: Build It, but Will They Come?*

Thomas N. Robb
Kyoto Sangyo University
Kyoto, Japan

Preview

With the advent of the World Wide Web, it has become relatively easy for instructors to create sites, lists of links, and tailor-made exercises and activities to access via the Internet. Given the limitations of the various Web languages, such as HTML and PHP, most of the easy-to-use exercises are of the traditional tutorial-drill type: presentation, question and answer, multiple choice, and fill in the blank. Robb's contention in this chapter is that many of these sites may be quite valuable for language practice, but are probably underutilized due to teachers' overly optimistic assessment of students' willingness to do "outside" work. This chapter examines the phenomenon of student autonomy and concludes with some recommendations about how to encourage access that more closely meets educators' expectations.

Before you read:

- Are you an autonomous learner? If so, how would you demonstrate this?
- How can you tell if a student is an autonomous learner? How do you promote learner autonomy in your classroom(s)?
- Have you ever taught or learned using self-access materials? Were these in paper form or Internet based? What success did you have with these materials?

The Problem with CALL

Over fifteen years ago, I wrote an article for the *JALT Language Teacher* called "Homework: How to Get Them to Do It" (Robb 1990). The basic thesis was that students could not be expected to do homework unless there was some way to hold them responsible for it. Fast forward to 2006—nothing has changed in this respect, but now, thanks to the Internet, teachers are creating not just homework assignments for their students but megabits of supplementary material, which in many cases is simply left to languish with only an occasional student taking advantage of the teacher's well-meaning efforts to offer independent study.

When computers first made their presence felt in the world of ESL, there was no problem with getting students to do computer-based work since the relative scarcity of personal computers meant that most work was done during scheduled class periods in classrooms or labs with the teacher present. Furthermore, apart from the applications that had been installed on local computers for tutorial use, there was little else that students could do with them—no e-mail to check and no Web to surf. In the past decade, however, personal and open lab access to the Internet has become widely available in industrial nations. It has also become extremely easy for teachers to build their own Web sites or create links to other sites and materials using Web publishing tools, such as their school's learning management system or external services such as Yahoo! Groups (2006) and Quia Web (Quia 1998–2006). Sites such as the *Internet TESL Journal* (1995–2006), with thousands of activities and links, are a paradise for eager students capable of studying on their own.

Hubbard and Bradin (2004) discuss the general trend away from tutorial computer-assisted language learning (CALL) activities, such as those found on CDs, to more open, communicative uses of CALL, but they could not take into account the recent explosion of browser-based activities in the past few years. A Google search for "grammar blanks ~correct," to find Web sites with grammar exercises, yielded over sixty thousand pages.

Unfortunately, the experience of many instructors is that most of their students are not autonomous learners who take advantage of such freely available material just because it is there. Nonetheless, the current mind-set of the ESL world places a high priority on learner autonomy to the extent that material is often prepared under the assumption that students will naturally flock to use it.

Learner Autonomy and Self-Directed Learning

The concepts of *learner autonomy* and *self-directed learning* (see Benson 2001) have come to the fore in recent years, and there is no denying that our goal as teachers should be to foster learner independence. We may take the following statement, in an article concerning the application of virtual reality to language learning, as representative of current thinking: "Current concepts in language learning such as learner autonomy also encourage learners to take control of their own learning and to reflect on the learning process, yet many CALL applications show little effort in supporting reflective processes in learners which would allow them to plan, monitor and evaluate their development as language learners" (Schwienhorst 2002, 223). The following two communications from teachers of adults illustrate how these concepts shape their approach to teaching and learning:

To my way of thinking, the teaching/learning process is a two-way tango and both parties are responsible for its success or failure. In my teaching situation, it is important to begin the process of helping students to take some responsibility for their learning. Especially with regards to online learning, I would think students need to be mature and motivated enough to do it on their own. (Deborah Wilson, personal communication, 2003)

I also usually teach adults, at least post high-school, so the attitude I take is that it's their responsibility to do the work I give them, and if they don't, then their failure is their responsibility. If they do the work and they still fail, then it's my failure as well. (Saskia Kameron, personal communication, 2003)

While these assumptions may be true for autonomous, self-directed adult learners, not all students are autonomous learners, not all students can be self-directed, and surely not all students are adults. Therefore, we as teachers cannot assume that the same approach to learning will be useful for all students.

Benson (2001, 48), citing Holec, mentions five tasks of a truly autonomous learner:

1. Determining the objectives
2. Defining the contents and progressions
3. Selecting methods and techniques to be used
4. Monitoring the procedure of acquisition (rhythm, time, place, etc.)
5. Evaluating what has been acquired

Few of the students that I teach—Japanese university students majoring in English—are capable of managing these tasks. Virtually 100 percent of university students in Japan are so-called traditional students. Unlike students in many Western societies, most Japanese students still graduate in four years without taking any time off for a job or other pursuits that might influence their motivation or future goals. Furthermore, the educational culture emphasizes an examination-oriented, teacher-directed approach toward learning. A further exacerbating factor in Japan is the infrequency of class meetings. Classes traditionally meet only once a week for ninety minutes, and the students, particularly freshmen, might be carrying a load of fourteen to sixteen courses, many of which require a certain amount of preparation in addition to class attendance. Facing problems such as these at my university, even a conscientious program to cultivate autonomy through learning awareness activities, learning diaries, and the like has had an effect on only a small proportion of the students.

Teachers need to look at the reality:

- Students in many instructional settings are not self-directed, autonomous learners.
- Students have competing goals—social, work, and study.
- Students may come from cultural backgrounds in which teachers have strict homework requirements.
- Students may be in school simply because it is the thing to do and may have little intrinsic motivation to study.
- Even adults have differing learning styles and may not be self-directed learners.

A more realistic view of learner autonomy is provided by Kerka (1994): "rather than asserting that all adults are self-directed and that self-direction is a hallmark of adulthood, it may be fairer to say that SDL [self-directed learning] is a lifelong phenomenon in which adults differ from other adults and from children in degree: some people are or are not self-directed learners; some people are or are not in different situations" (¶4).

As educators, we cannot completely abdicate our authority and assume that students are, or will be, self-directed. Our approach to teaching should not assume that complete autonomy is the best strategy, even in an ideal world.

Self-Access and Autonomy

Traditionally, student access to CALL materials has been considered a simple dichotomy; there was either *access as a class* or *self-access*. Neither of these is ideal. Access as a class implies the presence of an instructor who most likely sets the learning tasks and the pace of the class. This type of total control runs counter to many of the originally touted advantages of CALL: pacing oneself, repeating material until mastered, and selecting material that meets one's personal goals and learning styles. Furthermore, most structured learning activities, such as those that teachers are likely to put up on the Web (given its present state of development), do not require the presence of an instructor. To perform skill-based exercises, usually focused on discrete grammar points, in a drill-and-kill format in a class setting raises issues of cost and efficiency of staff management. Self-access, on the other hand, is consistent with the concepts of self-pacing and autonomy, but such access is best suited to the so-called, and possibly mythical, autonomous learner—a student who is highly motivated and who can learn independently without the guidance of an instructor.

From observing how students access CALL materials, I consider a four-way distinction of CALL access types to be useful:

1. *True self-access* is perhaps the ideal that many have in mind. Students go to the self-access center of their own free will to study materials that they have determined to be beneficial at their current stage of language mastery.

2. *Recommended self-access* occurs when an instructor or tutor points out to a student that specific self-access materials are available and might be useful for remedial work on an aspect that the rest of the class has perhaps already mastered. The teacher or tutor in this case has diagnosed a need and determined a remedy for the student.

3. *Required self-access* is an access mode that has thus far received little attention and is the focal point of this chapter. Rather than being supplementary, the CALL materials are considered integral to the course, but are best covered by the students independently, outside of class. This approach allows students to spend as much time as needed on the material, in a manner that does not require the instructor's presence. It frees up class time for learning activities that do require a teacher. Since the materials are requirements, students are more likely to complete self-access tasks and activities.

4. *Class access* is simply the logical end of this continuum. The instructor is present in a class that meets in the CALL lab or *smart* (electronically outfitted)

classroom during a regularly scheduled class hour. The instructor can introduce new applications and monitor students' comfort with their use.

The differences among these access modes are summarized in Table 6.1. The differentiating variables are whether guidance is provided, whether use of the materials is required or voluntary, and whether their use is supervised by an instructor present in the computer room or lab.

In my opinion, the class-access mode is used much more than it should be, apparently because of the perceived need for supervision, without which teachers cannot be sure that students are doing the work. Of course, other reasons for the class-access mode exist, such as the possibility that the lab would not be available to students if a time slot were not scheduled (a common case in secondary schools), or the fact that the teacher is using aspects of CALL that require his or her presence. Traditionally, CALL activities have been performed in lab mode with the teacher present. However, since most skill-based activities require little student-teacher interaction, many instructors understandably prefer activities that make the most use of their presence.

The types of CALL activities (skill-based exercises) that I have been concerned with thus far do not appear to be consistent with some contemporary learning theories because such activities are intended to be performed by individuals alone. Even so, skill-based material may be an effective adjunct to communicative classes. Nation (2001) proposes four fundamental modes of study that are required in roughly equal proportions for effective language learning: (1) meaning-focused input, (2) meaning-focused output, (3) deliberate study, and (4) fluency development. Skill-based materials can easily fit in with both the deliberate study mode and the fluency development mode. In fact, such materials can be a useful component in almost any course, but they are best completed in an unsupervised, required self-access mode. Because students do not often use self-access materials as expected, these materials are often ineffective. Guidance and occasional class-access sessions help eliminate ineffectual use of the materials, promote a better understanding of them, and aid in acquisition of the target concepts or forms.

Table 6.1. Variables of Access

	Guided	Required	Supervised
True self-access	no	no	no
Recommended self-access	yes	no	no
Required self-access	yes	yes	no
Class access	yes	yes	yes

The Central Problem with Autonomy

Hwu (2003) observes that "learner autonomy and learner control do not necessarily yield optimal uses of the materials" (p. 8). This is particularly true if the materials do not incorporate a record-keeping (tracking) system and the instructor has made no other provision for accountability. As Hwu asks, "Did making the course materials accessible outside the classroom facilitate students' learning? The answer is *yes* with regards to motivated students and *no* with regards to unmotivated students" (p. 15).

One may well ask, "Why would students not do required work?" After all, they (or someone) have paid good money to enroll in the course. In most Japanese universities, students attend full time and do not have the pressures of work or family responsibilities, so the reasons behind students failing to complete requirements outside of class are complex. Many of my students feel that if the teacher does not check the homework, then it is not worth doing. On an intellectual level, this attitude may seem odd, since outside work is an excellent way for students to practice, consolidate, and extend what they study in class. Assigned work could well be an integral part of the curriculum—material that must be covered—but if it is deemed by the department or instructor to be best mastered in a required self-access mode, it may not seem critical to students. If students' primary concern is not the mastery of the material in a particular course, then other distractions may receive higher priority. Even for students who are truly concerned about their studies, the fact is that they have limited time. How should they invest that time—in ungraded, unobserved, out-of-class assignments, or in additional work for another course that they know will be graded?

One could also ask, "If students do not want to study, why force them to?" Thanasoulas (2002) observes that "learner autonomy does not mean that the teacher becomes redundant, abdicating his/her control over what is transpiring in the language learning process" (¶1). Many adult learners appreciate strict requirements and close supervision and support. When it comes to students who wish that they did not have to study, teachers are responsible for making sure that they do. This position may smack of authoritarianism, but someone has paid the students' tuition, perhaps their parents or the government, and they certainly are not paying for a four-year vacation. Furthermore, the reputations of university programs are at stake. Poor performance will result in poor educational outcomes.

The Tracking Solution

The following message on a technology-related TESL forum highlights one reason that students tend not to do work that is not required. Adato, who was teaching a writing course, faced this dilemma:

> The first semester that I taught the course, I was overwhelmed with the amount of work because I had students sending me too many things to correct. Since then, I have streamlined and made more activities self-correcting by providing the answers online. *I don't think this is the best way for the students because many of them ignore the activities and exercises and only submit the graded assignments.* When I had them submitting everything to me, I gave them points for each activity and because of that, I got a much better response. However, it took far

too much time to correct and respond to each student. (TESLCA-L posting, March 16, 2002; emphasis mine)

In a follow-up e-mail message on March 17, 2002, Adato states, "for the motivated, self-disciplined student who really wants to improve, I feel that independent exercises are valuable and offer a degree of flexibility that can't be provided in a classroom setting." Tracking and acknowledging student work seem essential in CALL. Without a means for the instructor to keep track of who has done what, and with what success, CALL materials cannot be used as an integral part of a course unless presented in class-access mode. Whereas in the early history of CALL, tracking was not technically feasible in any but the most expensive systems, it is now readily available, and with the current diffusion of computers, class access for skill-based CALL is no longer necessary or desirable. However, as Jones (2001) states, "[we need to] recognize that students can only learn from computers with the instruction and supervision of teachers: CALL will not be effective without this essential interaction of teachers and students" (p. 366). One form of interaction can be electronic monitoring of students' CALL work, in other words, tracking or reporting scores in some form so that students understand the significance of their work.

Teachers must be aware of the difference between making CALL materials available and using those materials effectively. Striving to adopt materials and delivery systems that have a record-keeping function or that lend themselves to tracking is one, perhaps essential, way to effectively use such materials. Not only does tracking allow teachers to hold students accountable, it also enables them to see if the software is being used in the intended manner, with full exploitation of its features.

Much of the current crop of commercial software records student activity. For those who use free, Web-accessible activity pages, it would be helpful to have a course management system that minimally tracks when students have clicked on an outside link. Moodle (2005), a popular open-source course management system, has a quiz feature and allows Hot Potatoes (Arneil and Holmes 2005) quizzes to be tracked, including reporting the score as well as errors made. In cases when CALL material does not have a record-keeping feature, teachers can institute the following, albeit a bit more troublesome, policies:

- printouts of completed activities

- announced, in-class quizzes administered using screenshots of the activities; with a strict time limit, only students who have used the material beforehand will be able to perform well

- student-maintained diaries, record sheets, or Weblogs (blogs) of their activities and scores; experience shows, however, that self-reporting only works if teachers check the records frequently for compliance

Challenges and Future Directions

Computers, Internet access, and even software are becoming more affordable, which may entice administrators to encourage their use simply as labor-saving devices. But administrators need to understand that exposure to computer-displayed material does not in itself constitute learning. This is particularly true in Japan, where schools believe that purchasing a tutorial program for the Test of English as a Foreign Language or the Test of English for International Communication is a quick fix for their lack of appropriate preparation courses.

Future prospects for autonomy are not, however, altogether grim. With recent advances in technology, structured CALL activities, more than ever before, can permit students to study those aspects of language that benefit from self-pacing and the lack of peer pressure, and that don't particularly benefit from the presence of a teacher. Removing such activities from the classroom and placing them in required self-access mode allows the instructor to spend more class time on those aspects of learning that do in fact require face-to-face contact. With many students, however, unless there is a way to hold them accountable for their work, self-access will be ineffective. With a little ingenuity, though, I believe that tracking systems can be implemented for most skill-based CALL activities.

If students are aware that their participation is being tracked and calculated as part of their grade, this obvious extrinsic motivation will further their language learning through CALL activities. If teachers build such activities, students will have to come.

Appendix—Chapter 6
Web Sites, Internet Tools, and Software

Hot Potatoes	http://hotpot.uvic.ca/
Internet TESL Journal	http://iteslj.org/
Moodle	http://moodle.org/
Quia Web	http://www.quia.com/web/
Yahoo! Groups	http://groups.yahoo.com/

Section I
Questions and Activities

Questions for Discussion

1. González (chapter 2) demonstrates how language skills can be integrated in an online learning environment (e.g., combining voice chat for speaking and listening, Web pages for reading, blogs for writing and reading, and online video for listening). How could you best integrate language skills into your educational context? Is it necessary or desirable to integrate all skills? Explore your institution's resources, perhaps interviewing technology staff to discover what tools and support may be available to realize your goals.

2. Sevier (chapter 3) and Reppen and Vásquez (chapter 4) advocate the use of concordance programs to demonstrate and practice lexical patterns, such as collocations. What are the advantages of using concordance software for assisting learners with vocabulary and phrasal pattern acquisition? Could you use The Compleat Lexical Tutor (Lextutor; Cobb 2006) with your students? What would be the benefits for you as a teacher, researcher, or materials developer?

3. Language patterns in English for academic purposes and English for specific purposes texts, such as vocabulary and collocation choices, may differ from those in general reading texts such as newspapers. What e-texts could you use with Lextutor (Cobb 2006) for corpus investigation of language patterns in learner task/materials development? Using Lextutor, plan, gather, and explore a small corpus for a specific purpose (e.g., engineering lab reports to investigate graphic-textual interfaces, sample native-English-speaking student essays in a given subject area that display a specific rhetorical pattern). Use your findings to develop a teaching unit for your learners with concordance-supported materials and tasks. Try out the materials you developed, and share your pedagogical findings with other teachers.

4. Reppen and Vásquez (chapter 4) describe a number of writing tasks for university ESL learners. How could their learning modules be adapted for a different learner population (e.g., high school students, EFL learners)? Which would be most useful in your teaching context and why? What should be the role of models or mentors in such a tutorial environment?

5. Kim (chapter 5) bases his online listening course on a textbook he prepared for his students. His material is disseminated widely through an open university. He had technical support from his institution for developing the online course, and support from student assistants in addressing routine issues. Explore how you might obtain support from your institution to develop online courses or materials. What types of support personnel would be necessary for your project? Which skills do you already have, and which will you need to augment through further training or consultant assistance?

6. Robb (chapter 6) poses the problem of what to do when students are not as autonomous or self-guided as we educators would like. How do you support learners in developing autonomous learning strategies? What effect does tracking serve in your program or specific course, and how does tracking affect student participation and motivation in online (or other) activities? If you have used a course management system (CMS), what successes or problems have you had with student participation or motivation?

Activities for Further Study

1. Many educational institutions provide access to an online CMS. CMSs are also available free of charge online. Check out your institution's CMS, or explore a free CMS such as Moodle (2005) or Yahoo! Groups (2006), both cited by González (chapter 2). (Your teacher may wish to assign each group to a different CMS in order to share information.) How would you integrate a CMS into your instructional objectives? What features do you find particularly helpful? Would any hinder the development of a community online? Are there any features you would like to add?

2. Explore the free concordance program Lextutor (Cobb 2006; described by Sevier, chapter 3), which links to corpus texts online. Search several words or phrases, choosing two or more corpora, to find out what you can discover about English vocabulary with a concordancer in different kinds of texts. Suggest specific lessons or units that would involve your learners in doing this kind of search, perhaps referring to specific vocabulary items or grammatical constructions from their own compositions.

3. Explore online one of the writing modules that Reppen and Vásquez developed for their intensive English program (listed in the appendix to chapter 4). Also explore other online activities for writing, such as those offered at Diana Hacker's Web site, A Writer's Reference, to accompany her book (Hacker 2003), or the OWL at Purdue (1995–2006). Are the exercises useful? Why or why not?

Which might be most appropriate for your learners and why? How would you tailor your own lessons to encourage autonomous or supervised use of online writing resources for individuals or groups?

4. Begin a collection of online activity sites of your own using Web software such as Filamentality (2006) or The WebWizard (n.d.). Share your discoveries with classmates or fellow teachers.

5. Explore several Web sites for authentic listening, such as National Public Radio (2006), Voice of America (n.d.), or the British Broadcasting Corporation (2006). Using the authentic texts and digital media at these sites, prepare support materials, such as lesson plans and Web references, for your learners.

6. Explore some of the hundreds of exercises and activities at Randall Davis's (1998–2006) Randall's ESL Cyber Listening Lab or at the *Internet TESL Journal* (1995–2006). Which of these might be useful for your students? Which of these are authentic activities? How would you guide your students in using these exercises?

7. Join Real English Online (Marzio and Hanson-Smith 2006), a support group for students and teachers using video and audio online. Try some of the free video-based exercises created by teachers (see the >Links area of this Yahoo! Group). Many of these lessons have been created with Hot Potatoes (Arneil and Holmes 2005), a free utility program that allows the user to create a wide variety of exercises with multimedia content. (Dreamweaver [2005] allows for the creation of similar materials, and it may be free at your institution.)

8. Download and try out Hot Potatoes (Arneil and Holmes 2005; or Dreamweaver [2005]). Many examples of activities can be found at Michel Barbot's (n.d.) Hot Potatoes Exercises Web page. If you have problems, join the Hot Potatoes Users (2006), a support group for language teachers, and ask for help. Experiment with making online support materials, quizzes, and games for your learners with audio or video files.

9. Explore some of the multimedia activities available online, for example, Groupboard (n.d.) for drawing and chat, Sitepal (Oddcast n.d.) for voice mail, simple exercise generators at Quia Web (Quia 1998–2006) or Module Maker (McKenzie 2000), Interesting Things for ESL Students (C. I. Kelly and Kelly 1997–2006), or video trailers used for ESOL language learning at English Trailers (n.d.). Create one or more lesson plans for using such materials in a blended or wholly online class.

Web Sites in Section I Questions and Activities

British Broadcasting Corporation	http://www.bbc.com/
The Compleat Lexical Tutor (Lextutor)	http://www.lextutor.ca/
Dreamweaver	http://www.macromedia.com/software/ dreamweaver/
English Trailers	http://www.english-trailers.com/
Filamentality	http://www.filamentality.org/wired/fil/
Groupboard	http://www.groupboard.com/
Hot Potatoes	http://hotpot.uvic.ca/
Hot Potatoes Exercises	http://perso.wanadoo.fr/michel.barbot/hotpot/ exercises.htm
Hot Potatoes Users	http://groups.yahoo.com/group/hotpotatoesusers
Interesting Things for ESL Students	http://www.manythings.org/
Internet TESL Journal	http://iteslj.org/
Module Maker	http://questioning.org/module/module.html
Moodle	http://www.moodle.org
National Public Radio	http://www.npr.org
OWL at Purdue	http://owl.english.purdue.edu/owl/ http://owl.english.purdue.edu/handouts/esl/index .html
Quia Web	http://www.quia.com/web
Randall's ESL Cyber Listening Lab	http://www.esl-lab.com/
Real English Online	http://groups.yahoo.com/group/Real_English_Online
Sitepal	http://www.oddcast.com/sitepal/
Voice of America	http://www.voanews.com/english/portal.cfm
The WebWizard	http://www.the-webwizard.co.uk/
A Writer's Reference	http://www.dianahacker.com/writersref/index.html
Yahoo! Groups	http://groups.yahoo.com

Content-Based and Task-Based Learning: Collaborative CALL

This section points out how well the Internet supports the exploration of content-rich sites online and demonstrates the need for ensuring that students work collaboratively. Each chapter in this section proposes interesting technologies as a means to invent new ways of using resources. Kennedy (chapter 7) brings students together in a hands-on environmental project to benefit the whole planet. Susser (chapter 8) focuses a composition course on one of the new industries fostered by the Internet: the content and culture of Web tourism. Gromik (chapter 9) promotes new skills, such as digital video and editing, to meet the needs of a visual age. To bring writing assistance to learners at a distance, Rilling (chapter 10) offers an online writing lab, developed through research in the content genres. Sokolik (chapter 11) discusses the issue of how well teachers are keeping up with their students' rapidly expanding familiarity with the latest technologies. Teachers who grew up with the typewriter are facing students who have iPods plugged into their ears and whose fingers guide the mouse and video game controller with the greatest of ease. While teachers may still be fearful of technology, their students are spending hours every night chatting or playing multipartner games in virtual environments. How will teachers keep up with the information age?

Chapter 7

Making Content Connections Online via the GLOBE Program

Teresa J. Kennedy
University Corporation for Atmospheric Research
Boulder, Colorado USA
University of Idaho, NASA Idaho Space Grant Consortium
Moscow, Idaho USA

Preview

The world is no doubt becoming smaller, at least virtually. Projects connecting schoolchildren around the world can perhaps raise a generation of adults committed to peace and the international protection of the environment. Kennedy describes the GLOBE program, which is active in 109 countries and provides opportunities for integrated language and content instruction. The program weaves interdisciplinary lessons in science, mathematics, social studies, language arts, fine arts, and world cultures into classrooms and across international boundaries through an extensive, interactive Web environment. GLOBE provides learners with opportunities to participate in challenging interdisciplinary projects as they collect environmental data for sophisticated visualization software that will highlight patterns over time and across nations. Ready-made environmental science lessons and simulations with real-world data help learners understand complex phenomena, such as climate change, while developing language and cognitive academic skills and an appreciation of how local effects can have global consequences.

Before you read:

- How have you integrated content into your language teaching/learning? Has it been successful?

- What approaches to language learning are most appropriate for integrating content in elementary or other school contexts?

- What kinds of technology would be most helpful in cross-cultural and cross-national exchanges? Have you used any technologies for such interactions? What results have you had?

Incorporating Language Instruction and Content

Using a second language as the primary vehicle to deliver content instruction has been a common practice in many cultures for thousands of years. Learning a second language for cross-cultural understanding, communicative purposes, or academic advantage implies incorporating a strong language focus into *content-based instruction* (CBI; see Brinton, Snow, and Wesche 2003; Crandall 1992). The process should entail facilitating academic language development through real, hands-on, minds-on learning opportunities that are continuously included throughout and across the daily curriculum.

In CBI, academic subjects become the organizing principle for acquiring the target language; in other words, the content itself influences the selection and sequence of language structures, functions, and vocabulary. Teachers following a CBI approach typically utilize a variety of instructional techniques to present content from multiple subject areas through thematic units (Echevarria, Vogt, and Short 2000). When students are acquiring a new language, it becomes critically important that they have the opportunity to apply new information in an environment that safely encourages discussing, as well as doing, to make abstract concepts concrete. Language learning occurs when students are presented with target-language material in a meaningful, contextualized manner, with the emphasis on acquiring information and knowledge at the same time.

In the United States, teachers representing many academic disciplines have been actively focusing on integration of subjects across the curriculum due to educational reform initiatives, including the No Child Left Behind Act of 2001 (NCLB; U.S. Department of Education 2004a). Recommendations include closely tracking English language learner (ELL) performance, modifying the language utilized on test questions, and encouraging ELL accommodations that have undergone validity testing (Abedi and Dietel 2004). Even more recently, the U.S. Senate designated 2005 as the Year of Language Study. Led by the American Council on the Teaching of Foreign Languages (ACTFL), activities included a strong focus on highlighting the relationship between languages and other subject areas or professional fields.

The renewed emphasis on improving literacy in more than one language empowers teachers to integrate language with academic content. Using CBI, teachers are motivated to assist their students in viewing language as a means to master subject-matter content rather than as the primary focus of their study. Language learning through CBI is deeply contextualized for students, allowing them to focus on meaning while providing a clear purpose for language use. Although teachers are increasingly embedding content in the second language (e.g., using the cognitive academic language learning approach [CALLA; Chamot and O'Malley 1994]), the balance between language and content often varies depending on the academic setting where CBI is used. In immersion and bilingual settings, the success of content-based programs becomes "critically dependent on students' mastery of the academic content to the same degree and level as students in native-language classrooms" (Genesee 1998, 103; see also Swain and Johnson 1997). In ESOL settings, academic content may serve as the medium for language instruction even though greater emphasis is placed on the acquisition of language skills than on the academic or cognitive skills associated with the content (Snow, Met, and Genesee 1989).

Placing significant emphasis on cognitive strength combined with linguistic proficiency is an important tenet of both TESOL's (1997) *ESL Standards for Pre-K–12 Students* and ACTFL's (1996) *Standards for Foreign Language Learning*. Both sets of standards integrate content-based teaching into personal, social, and academic uses of English. ELLs are "expected to learn academic content through the English language and to compete academically with native-English-speaking peers" (TESOL 1997, 9). Thus, incorporating a content-based teaching philosophy is a must in standards-based teaching.

CBI may be expressed in a number of ways. *Interdisciplinary language programs* can provide students with a more integrated view of their own learning, enabling them to see the connection between the various subjects they study. Program models such as theme-based language instruction, language across the curriculum, and English for specific purposes utilize various teaching strategies as students progress toward communicative competence in and across content (Clipperton 1994). *Cooperative learning* is often used with interdisciplinary CBI because it groups students with different linguistic backgrounds and skill levels to work together on a common task with a common goal in a nonthreatening environment, sharing insights, testing hypotheses, and jointly constructing knowledge. Students are assigned roles, such as group facilitator, recorder, reporter, or illustrator. Cooperative learning groups generally utilize a *task-based approach*, which provides appropriate contexts for developing thinking and study skills as well as further developing language and academic concepts. The hands-on, minds-on approach to CBI allows students to learn by carrying out specific tasks or projects, for example, *doing science* (Rosebery, Warren, and Conant 1992) in the target language, not just reading about it.

Implementing interdisciplinary CBI in second language pedagogy presents the challenge of introducing information in such a way that students can understand, remember, and apply it. Teaching methods should utilize a number of strategies: visuals and physical props, logical sequences with beginning-middle-end scenarios (Curtain and Dahlberg 2004), graphic organizers, activity-centered and discovery-based tasks to scaffold new vocabulary, problem solving, communication of information, expression of opinions, and negotiation (Abdullah 1998). Teachers should systematically target language objectives that are integrated with academic objectives to maximize language learning as well as to reinforce knowledge of the disciplines (Genesee 1995), an approach demonstrated in the best immersion and bilingual classrooms.

In the United States, the growing number of K–12 students whose native language is not English—and the desire worldwide to learn English as a foreign language and teach it at increasingly younger ages—suggests an increasing need for academic programs infused with global perspectives and curricula based on thematic, interdisciplinary lessons that apply the principles of CBI. The Global Learning and Observations to Benefit the Environment (GLOBE) program is one such program.

Foundations of the GLOBE Program

The U.S. National Aeronautics and Space Administration (NASA) and National Science Foundation (NSF) are determined to meet science education challenges, such as integrating science and math across the curriculum, and are actively working to promote international programs that provide K–12 educators with enriched science materials, for which students around the world provide the raw data. The international collaboration envisioned by NASA and NSF fostered the development of GLOBE, whose goals include the following:

- Actively include all students regardless of their first language.
- Enhance the academic achievements of the entire student body, especially in the areas of science and math.
- Integrate literacy and numeracy skills with scientific inquiry.
- Provide opportunities and a Web site for K–12 U.S. students to inform and interact with their international peers and the scientific community.
- Give students an authentic means to acquire a second language, and specifically provide ELLs with the opportunity to learn grade-level curriculum.
- Include the entire community in K–12 instruction through Family Science Nights, local science fairs, and informal science community settings.
- Provide the opportunity for family members who speak little or no English to become involved in their child's education.

GLOBE is a hands-on, school- and Internet-based science and education program that unites students, teachers, and scientists around the world in study and research about the dynamics of the Earth's environment (see Figure 7.1).

GLOBE students collect atmospheric, hydrologic, geologic, and biometric data worldwide, each partner school using its own ninety-by-ninety-meter local study site to monitor conditions in its community and make comparisons with other schools around the world. Students report their data via the Internet to the GLOBE network, which can then be accessed by participants at other study sites, scientists at NASA and NSF, and other scientists around the world. These working professionals then pair GLOBE data with information received from satellites to verify, or *ground truth*, the information received from satellite imagery. One benefit of regular and frequent GLOBE data input is that students get to see a satellite image of their own data-collection site, a motivating bonus for hands-on, minds-on learning. Participation in GLOBE data collection improves students' understanding because it involves them in performing real science: calibrating equipment, taking measurements, analyzing data, and participating in research collaborations with students and scientists from around the world. Students engage in activities that are proven best practices in CBI.

GLOBE students have reported data from over fifteen million scientific measurements in the areas of atmosphere and climate, hydrology, soils, land cover, biology, and phenology, and have participated in three international symposia (GLOBE Learning Expeditions) as well as many field campaigns around the world. Data collection and reporting involve the excitement of working with authentic audiences and performing authentic tasks of major significance to the world's environment. Over a million GLOBE students in more than eigh-

Figure 7.1. The GLOBE Program Home Page
Source: http://www.globe.gov/.

teen thousand schools have taken important environmental measurements for use in their own research and that of scientists around the world. Figure 7.2 illustrates a small sample of the types of measurements taken.

Scientists and educators have worked together to develop science education materials (e.g., the protocols in Figure 7.2) as resources for GLOBE teachers. Professional development workshops train teachers to guide their students in taking measurements according to scientific protocols, using the Internet to report and analyze scientific data, and creating partnerships among students at GLOBE schools around the world. Since the program's inception in 1994, over thirty thousand teachers have attended professional development workshops to become certified GLOBE teachers. Participating in the GLOBE program gives teachers the opportunity to put into practice CBI principles that combine technology and creativity, to shape their own content-based lessons, and to share areas of success and questions for improvement within a community of practice (for more detailed descriptions of GLOBE, see T. J. Kennedy and Henderson 2003; T. J. Kennedy and Odell 2000).

An important goal of GLOBE is to provide opportunities for active community involvement that allows leadership opportunities and educational goals to merge, resulting in a true GLOBE Learning Community. A Community might begin as a GLOBE Partner based

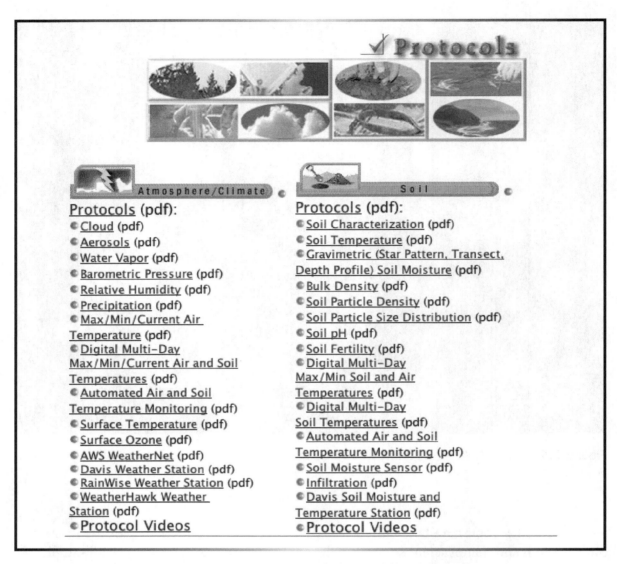

Figure 7.2. Sample Protocols Investigated by GLOBE Partners
Source: http://www.globe.gov/protocols/.

at a university that in turn works with local primary and secondary school teachers and students, and then branches out to include parents, youth clubs, scientists, senior citizens, other colleges and universities, daycare centers, museums, businesses, government agencies, and more. Parents and other community members often work with GLOBE teachers to help students disseminate their research at Family Science Nights as well as to maintain uninterrupted data collection on those days when schools are not open.

Worldwide, the GLOBE program is implemented through a network of partners who facilitate the efforts of the primary and secondary schools in their state or country. GLOBE students initiate their own inquiry-based studies and take part in their scientific projects in several ways:

- developing locally relevant research questions
- taking scientifically valid environmental measurements of the atmosphere, bodies of water, and areas of land at or near their school, following GLOBE protocols (the standard procedures established by scientists, ensuring that all GLOBE data are comparable around the world)
- reporting their data to the GLOBE data archive via the Internet
- creating maps, graphs, and visualizations of data using free software tools available from the interactive GLOBE Web site
- analyzing their data sets and making comparisons to data sets gathered by their peers around the world
- connecting to and utilizing NASA missions and Web-based visualizations
- collaborating with scientists and other GLOBE students around the world on inquiry-based research projects using their local data sets
- communicating with peers around the world through GLOBEMail (Web-based e-mail), videoconferencing, and Web chats
- publishing and disseminating their research at international conferences (GLOBE Learning Expeditions) and on the GLOBE Web site

The GLOBE Program for Language Development

Students must have opportunities to communicate powerfully in the target language if they are going to integrate their language and cognitive development with their growing personal identities. This is a challenge that educators are only beginning to address in immersion and bilingual programs around the world but it is in these programs that there is the most potential for truly preparing citizens who can make highly significant contributions to their own and our global societies. For this to happen, however, immersion educators must explicitly locate their pedagogy and educational vision in the realm of global education and ensure that language policies operating in the school are consistent with this philosophy of global education. (Cummins 1999–2003a, ¶1 under Conclusion)

Matching most of Cummins' suggestions, GLOBE can be an effective tool for working with students who are learning English as a second language or studying foreign languages (see T. J. Kennedy 2005). Authentic materials ready for classroom implementation are available in all six United Nations languages (Arabic, Chinese, English, French, Russian, and Spanish), and at least part of the GLOBE Teacher's Guide (University Corporation for Atmospheric Research [UCAR] n.d.c) is now available in Dutch, German, Greek, Hebrew, Japanese, Portuguese, and Thai, with many other materials becoming available in other languages through GLOBE's international partners. When conducted in English, GLOBE activities can facilitate content-based lessons that incorporate TESOL's (1997) ESL standards and meet ACTFL's (1996) standards for foreign languages by providing students with the opportunity to utilize the language(s) they are studying in content-based language programs. GLOBE activities also meet many U.S. states' requirements for science and math instruction. In addition,

GLOBE provides ELLs with the opportunity to participate in challenging science projects in many languages with little or no extra preparation by the teacher. Studies show that students benefit from using their native language while learning English and suggest that a dual-language approach allows ELLs to maintain their native language, ultimately achieving the valuable goal of becoming bilingual, as well as having greater success in learning English (P. C. Miller and Endo 2004). GLOBE materials actively include all students regardless of their first language and enable ELLs to learn the curriculum at grade level.

The GLOBE Teacher's Guide (UCAR n.d.c), available on the Web and searchable by concept and grade level, provides teachers with more than a thousand pages of sample lessons, unit plans, and pedagogical hints for using GLOBE in the classroom, including foreign language and ESL classrooms for content and literacy instruction (see Figure 7.3). The Teacher's Guide provides language teachers with a content curriculum that can be incorporated into their classrooms, including materials such as cloud and soil charts, instructional slides, and Web pages.

Common areas of interdisciplinary CBI tend to be mathematics, science, technology,

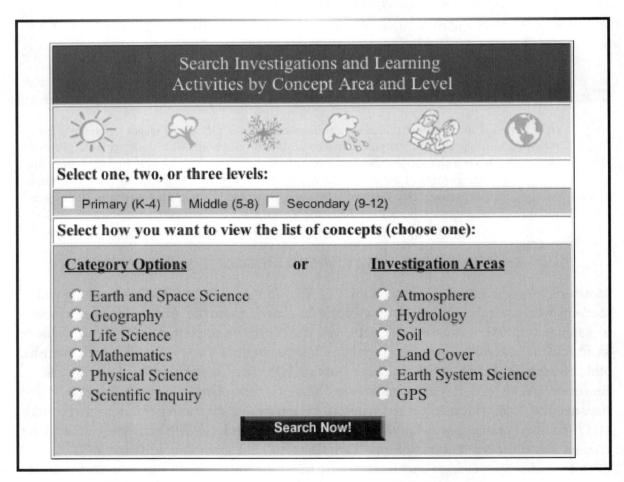

Figure 7.3. Concept Search Page from the GLOBE Teacher's Guide
Source: http://www.globe.gov/tctg/conceptsearch.jsp.

social studies, and art. Two of the most important areas to integrate with language are math and science. Reilly (1988) describes the language of mathematics as having its own special vocabulary, syntax, semantic properties, and discourse features. Instructional activities targeting mathematical concepts should promote second language development through a natural, subconscious process that focuses on communicating the concepts, processes, and applications. These activities should always build on students' real-life experiences and prior knowledge, allowing ample opportunity for social interaction. All lessons that teach new concepts in mathematics must utilize graphics, manipulatives, and other hands-on, concrete materials that clarify and reinforce meaning communicated through language.

Science, on the other hand, generally concentrates on a set of concepts and relationships developed through the process of observation, identification, description, experimental investigation, and theoretical explanation of natural phenomena. Students observe, classify, compare, measure, infer, predict, and find space and time relationships. In science studies, acquisition of new vocabulary can occur through activities such as clustering, using graphic organizers, solving problems in cooperative learning groups, writing journal entries, engaging in discussion circles, and so on (Peregoy and Boyle 2001). The important point to remember is that people learn best by involving themselves in relevant, meaningful experiences.

According to Haley and Austin (2004), "it is important for all language teachers to gain an understanding of how language plays a role in shaping learners' thinking and construction of knowledge, how language is a reflection of our identity, and how language works as a way to develop our relationships with the groups into which we are socialized" (p. 8). Providing students with a variety of opportunities for social interaction (including engaging in open discussion, working with partners and small groups, reporting information orally and in writing, describing experiment results, and listing the steps in a process) actively promotes language development and helps ELLs produce and practice new language and vocabulary. As students conduct science projects and compare their results with those of other GLOBE students around the world, they have authentic opportunities to communicate in the language they are studying. Science, scientific inquiry, and math skills to support such inquiry serve as the locus for oral and literate language to develop. Helping students understand causal effects in the environment around them allows them to incorporate these ideas into their linguistic repertoire (Dobb 2004, 2005). Comparing and collaborating with GLOBE school partners via the program's Web site emphasizes the role that computers can play in cooperative cross-global communications. And ELLs can further develop ideas about scientific phenomena using their expanding second language skills.

GLOBE itself provides the technology to enhance communicative activities. Once a school has joined GLOBE, teachers and their students can communicate with other classrooms by clicking on a country on the world map found on the GLOBE Web site. With each click of the mouse, a more in-depth view of the country appears until finally all the participating GLOBE schools in that country are displayed. By clicking on a particular school, students can make seasonal comparisons, view the school's data (e.g., weather measurements taken by local students, such as temperature, cloud type, and cloud cover), and gain an understanding of climatic differences around the world by asking specific questions of their peers via Web-based GLOBEMail or periodic live Web chats. These interactions provide the perfect venue for authentic language use, consistent with all goal areas of the ACTFL and TESOL standards. Extension activities could include watching a weather report in the target language and later creating weather forecasts that could be videotaped or presented in front of the class.

Another important element of the GLOBE community is involving students in communicative investigations focused on current environmental events. For example, as a follow-up to their GLOBE training in January 2005, teachers and students in Thailand attended a hydrology symposium. An important component of the symposium was inspired by the work of Drs. Mullica Jaroensutasinee and Krisanadej Jaroensutasinee, who initiated the GLOBE Tsunami Study after the destructive event of December 26, 2004. Thai teachers and students are using many different GLOBE program protocols to monitor and assess changes in marine invertebrate species, water and soil quality, and local atmospheric conditions for at least a three-year period. The number of schools participating in this project in Thailand and around the world is expected to grow, eventually involving all regions in discussions about the long-term effects of the disaster (for more information about the Tsunami Project, see UCAR n.d.d).

GLOBE also conducts videoconferences and Web chats in various languages, providing opportunities for spontaneous communication in the target language, helping students develop discussion skills, and furthering collaborative research. One of the many GLOBE events during 2004 was the White Water to Blue Water conference in Miami, Florida, in the United States, which promoted the practice of integrated watershed and marine ecosystem management in support of long-term sustainable development in the Caribbean region. During the event, students representing GLOBE schools in Trinidad and Tobago, Mexico, and Florida participated in two videoconferencing events conducted in both Spanish and English. A follow-up Web chat occurred on Earth Day 2004. In participating schools in the United States, Spanish-speaking students served as translators for the class, taking on leadership roles as they helped their English-speaking peers communicate (see UCAR 2004).

Another innovative Web-based event took place in February 2005, this time allowing students to practice their French and English skills. This French-initiated videoconference brought together students and teachers from the Collège Cantelande in Cestas, France; the School of International Studies in Meadowbrook, Virginia, in the United States; and NASA scientists from various sites. An interesting dynamic took place during the videoconference when a French-speaking foreign exchange student in Virginia served as the English translator for her classmates. As with the Miami conference, bilingual students assumed leadership positions in their classrooms when the discussions and Internet exchanges occurred with other students from their home countries. During the conference, a Web chat for students from Canada, France, and other countries was planned to discuss the launch of the CALIPSO and CloudSat satellites (which were launched from Vandenberg Air Force Base at 3:02 a.m. PDT on April 28, 2006), a collaboration between NASA and the French space agency, Centre National d'Etudes Spatiales, to study airborne particles and clouds (see NASA 2006; Thompson and Rink 2004). Events such as these offer an opportunity for students and teachers to synchronously interact with their peers on an international level (for more information, see Maggi and Geirsch n.d.; NASA 2006).

GLOBE as a Tool for Interdisciplinary Studies

GLOBE provides language teachers with a vehicle for integrating not only science and mathematics, but also a wide range of disciplines in the arts and humanities. As GLOBE students learn more about the world around them by collecting and analyzing environmental data, they develop art skills by working with contour maps, drawing landscape diagrams, and studying soil colors. GLOBE Country Coordinator Anikó Orgoványi (Hungary), a prize-winning artist and advocate of incorporating art into GLOBE, believes that art can help strengthen environmental awareness (UCAR 2005). *The Sound of GLOBE* (KidsGLOBE 1998), a CD featuring music written and performed by GLOBE participants from all over the world, is a wonderful addition to the music classroom. Students learn about photography as they take pictures of their local study sites and describe the pictures in written and conversational settings. GLOBE has developed primary-level storybooks to provide elementary students in the language arts with a connection to many of the science investigation areas targeted by the program. The GLOBE Teacher's Guide (UCAR n.d.c) also provides content information for rich reading activities at the secondary level. Writing descriptive and technical reports about their projects helps students hone composition and science writing skills. GLOBE projects that require independent research on different countries help students gain in-depth cultural understanding and foster global collaboration and cooperation.

GLOBE activities involve virtually all aspects of the curriculum. The multicultural study of geography gives students hands-on experience with understanding latitude, longitude, scale, map elements, and spatial analysis. Students build weather stations in their industrial technology classrooms. Students in agricultural education classrooms actively help scientists and farmers in the field to better track environmental events affecting crop production. GLOBE One, an agricultural field campaign taking place in Black Hawk County, Iowa, in the United States, has been collecting data since spring 2004 from a variety of sources, including participating schools, students on field trips, automated weather stations, volunteers, and specially organized events. The main focus of the campaign transitioned from data collection to data analysis in 2005 in order to answer research questions posed by local students as well as scientists (see UCAR n.d.a). GLOBE also provides authentic, life-centered curricula and opportunities for meeting the special needs found in classrooms where students have a broad range of abilities and learning styles. Opportunities exist for cross-age tutoring, encouraging schoolwide collaboration and respect for all students' backgrounds and perspectives, and fostering enhanced content learning and cooperation. GLOBE activities are also ideal for afterschool clubs and community service-learning projects (for details on service learning, see T. J. Kennedy and Pedras 2004).

GLOBE also recently teamed up with the National Geographic Education Foundation in a five-year, multimedia campaign called My Wonderful World, which is aimed at improving the geographic literacy of young people from eight to seventeen years old by motivating parents and educators to expand geographic learning in school, at home, and in their communities. GLOBE partners, teachers, and former GLOBE students encourage and motivate all members of their communities to become involved in GLOBE student research activities. This includes motivating parents to take an active role in helping their children learn more about the world within and beyond their borders.

GLOBE for Academic Cognitive Skill-Building

Integrated language and content instruction offers a means by which students can continue their academic or cognitive development while acquiring greater language proficiency in a second language. Utilizing an approach that integrates second language instruction with the content of other curricular subjects has been shown to assist classroom teachers in reinforcing designated content areas and to ensure that second language instruction is meaningful to students (Armstrong and Rogers 1997; Curtain and Dahlberg 2004; Krashen 1997). The GLOBE program serves as an excellent means for language teachers to integrate a variety of subjects into their instruction (G. Kelly et al. 2002; T. J. Kennedy and Canney 2001).

GLOBE focuses on *real science* activities for K–12 students in their own local and world environment. Teachers and science educators have found GLOBE to be effective in demystifying science inquiry for both themselves and their students by making science relevant through authentic activities and investigations. It provides an integrated sequence of instructional units and investigations that stress students' use of scientific inquiry to address concepts and topics. Pedagogically, GLOBE helps teachers understand and deal with the following:

- using process, conceptual, content, and inquiry approaches to science, social studies, and language
- teaching the interconnectedness of the earth's systems
- teaching observation and analysis of data and visualizations
- teaching higher-order thinking skills for science applications

GLOBE provides a variety of user-friendly data protocols, lesson plans, and technology applications. It encourages teachers to use its model in developing new materials and teaching strategies appropriate for unique local contexts. In the face of the dreary economic circumstances of most schools, GLOBE offers amazingly rich teaching resources, keeping implementation costs to a minimum while maintaining the scientific integrity and currency of the curriculum.

To summarize, the salient characteristics of GLOBE include the following:

- teacher-friendly lessons tested by classroom teachers
- authentic lesson-by-lesson assessment in line with the standards
- a choice of flexible sequential or thematic instruction
- inquiry opportunities for students
- technology skills development
- little requirement for previous in-depth science knowledge on the part of teachers

Schools that have joined GLOBE over the past ten years report success in fostering students' and teachers' positive attitudes toward science and in increasing the amount of real science that is taught, including the percentage of daily instruction dedicated to science (see Means, Coleman, and Lewis 1998). GLOBE allows teachers to collaborate across disciplines, providing students with a more integrated view of their own learning and enabling them to see the interconnection among the various subjects they study. Students' motivation to learn is piqued when they are inspired to see their studies as meaningful. Because students collect and report on data from their local environments—the schoolyard and community—they can perceive how school relates to life in an immediate, authentic way. Because GLOBE links teachers and students throughout the school and around the world, it fosters alliances among students and increases their environmental awareness and a sense of responsibility for the planet, an understanding of other age groups and cultures, and a sense of a global community. GLOBE allows teachers to put the concepts of authentic learning, student-scientist partnership, scientific inquiry, and standards-based pedagogy into practice on an unprecedented scale. The program encourages all students to behave as scientists and mathematicians while promoting collaboration among all content disciplines in school (for examples of how GLOBE is used in ELL, bilingual, and foreign language classrooms, see T. J. Kennedy 2005).

Challenges and Future Directions

As with any supplemental program, implementing GLOBE in the classroom can be challenging. In many schools, the focus on mathematics, literacy, and NCLB testing requirements (in the United States) has diminished the amount of time available for teaching science at the elementary level. However, NCLB also requires that, beginning in 2007, U.S. states measure students' progress in science at least once a year in each of three grade spans (3–5, 6–9, and 10–12). In implementing GLOBE, teachers may have more opportunities to enhance the usual curriculum by incorporating science experiences (for more information on NCLB and science achievement, see U.S. Department of Education 2004b).

Another challenge for educators is that inquiry-based instruction takes time. Some schools have addressed this issue by using a thematic approach and integrating GLOBE throughout the curriculum. An interdisciplinary approach, working to weave various protocols and learning activities directly into the fabric of the curriculum, offers an excellent solution to time concerns.

Equipment can also be a problem for schools implementing GLOBE. As resources for education become tighter, schools struggle to support any new program. Because this is a worldwide academic issue, GLOBE has worked hard to keep implementation costs to a minimum. Schools are not required to use all the program's protocols, but rather are encouraged to focus on those activities that support what content teachers are already doing. As a result, many schools can implement GLOBE with minimal expenditures, and, in fact, many GLOBE schools receive donations from partners, community members, and local businesses to purchase equipment and supplies. Many protocols can also be performed with little or no equipment, using resources available on the GLOBE Web site, materials readily available in the home, or equipment students build themselves—another bonus for the CBI approach.

GLOBE has a proud tradition of success around the world since its debut in 1994. The next phase in its evolution, referred to as the Next Generation GLOBE, is a closer partnership with NASA and NSF to provide greater access to top scientists around the world in order to expose students, teachers, and communities to the cutting edge of Earth systems science research. To achieve this vision, GLOBE promotes increased student-teacher-scientist collaborations on inquiry-based investigations of the environment. This transition of the program is being accomplished while retaining its essential elements as a worldwide collaborative community of practice that promotes inquiry-based educational activities.

How to Join the GLOBE Program

GLOBE is open to all teachers and students in the United States, and GLOBE materials are freely available to anyone, regardless of partner school status. Internationally, countries must sign bilateral agreements with the U.S. State Department and NASA before taking part in official program activities, which are conducted under the guidance of GLOBE-trained teachers. The first step in becoming a GLOBE teacher in your school is to attend a training workshop in your region. Schedules for workshops and registration forms are available on the GLOBE program home page, as is contact information for partner schools where you may explore options.

GLOBE is an interagency program funded by NASA and NSF, supported by the U.S. State Department, and implemented through a cooperative agreement between NASA; the University Corporation for Atmospheric Research in Boulder, Colorado; and Colorado State University in Fort Collins.

Chapter 8

CALL and Content-Area Teaching

Bernard Susser
Doshisha Women's College
Kyoto, Japan

Preview

An unforeseen consequence of the Internet has been the creation of new industries, such as the global garage sale on eBay, or e-tourism, which allows travelers to book their own flights and vacation packages. Susser's course, Tourism, Culture, and Technology, is content based (students cannot use it to fulfill an English requirement) and gives technology a central role, since so much of the industry is available on the Web. Susser describes how computer-assisted language learning (CALL) pedagogy that is implicit in, for example, the democratization of the classroom and new instructional formats is revising notions of content-based instruction (CBI). Technology makes teachers rethink instructional practices. Susser discusses advanced word-processing functions to analyze reading passages, writing assignments based on CALL and Internet activities, and multimedia presentations. He also considers new technologies with a potential to further enhance CALL-based CBI.

Before you read:

- How do language and content support each other in CBI?
- How can English for specific purposes (ESP) courses support language instruction?
- What kinds of CALL practices might transform traditional notions of content-based learning?

The Need for CBI

> One of the greatest challenges in the ongoing expansion and innovation of content-based instruction is the search for the right balance of language and content teaching. (Snow 2001, 315)

CBI has always been an important part of second language education, but today it is emphasized even more as schools respond to broad social changes. In the United States, the increasing number of nonnative English speakers enrolled in local school systems is one factor; the growing popularity of bilingual education and immersion programs is another. Around the world, EFL programs are adding more content courses as students seek job opportunities in the global market and demand specialized instruction beyond language skills training. In addition, information and communication technologies are forcing people to rethink how they teach and learn all subjects.

This chapter introduces aspects of CBI and CALL theory to suggest how computers and the Internet can be used to teach content and language together. I use a course involving technology, culture, and the new industry of e-tourism to show how a specific content-based language course might be situated in theoretical constructs. I then describe how CALL activities may be changing the way people look at CBI, and suggest future directions for the application of CALL to content learning.

CBI and CALL Theory

Content-based language instruction is defined as "the integration of particular content with language-teaching aims" (Brinton, Snow, and Wesche 2003, 2). The emphasis in CBI is on both content and language, but for many educators the concern is actually language acquisition (see, e.g., Brinton, Snow, and Wesche 2003) or language development. Goodwin (2001) emphasizes the systematic incorporation of grammar into content-based English for academic purposes (EAP) courses, while Peterson (1997) stresses that "content-based language instruction *is* language instruction" (p. 158). Often in response to local demands, some course content is selected based on language teaching considerations (Stryker and Leaver 1997), such as arranging the content in the order of a language acquisition syllabus. For other educators, CBI is very much a contested arena of conflicting approaches with a wide gradation of content and language mixes. Looking at collaborations between content specialists and language teachers, Crandall and Kaufman's (2002) case studies show a range of types in both EFL and ESL. Snow (2001) proffers a good selection of CBI models, from the most content driven to the most language driven (p. 305).

Sustained-content language teaching (SCLT), or sustained CBI, has been proposed as a way to resolve the conflict between language and content. "Teachers who pursue an SCLT approach are not obliged to make tough decisions between either teaching content or teaching language" (Murphy and Stoller 2001, 4) because SCLT focuses on second language learning as well as exploration of a single content area. Pally (1997) emphasizes that sustained content study helps to develop critical thinking skills because it allows students to learn the information that forms the basis for questioning and evaluation, and it familiarizes students with discipline-specific rhetorical conventions.

CALL research extends to the domain of content-based learning. For the purposes of this chapter, Chapelle's (2001) discussion of CALL tasks and Meskill, Mossop, and Bates's (1999) ideas about the features of electronic texts are the most useful. Chapelle looks at CALL tasks from the point of view of language acquisition (pp. 55–57); her criteria for the appropriateness of such tasks (language learning potential, learner fit, meaning focus, authenticity, positive impact, and practicality) serve not only as evaluative standards, but also as guidelines for the use of CALL. (Of course, most of these criteria are not specific to CALL, but apply equally to any language learning task; there are other problems with her argument, summarized by Susser [2002].) Her approach to CALL in content disciplines and her emphasis on tasks in CBI are congruent with the role of CALL tasks proposed by Hanson-Smith (1999): content areas lend themselves to authentic tasks that can replicate real-life skills and promote critical thinking (see also Gromik, chapter 9 in this volume).

A review of elementary and middle school ESL classes that used technologies for learning found instances in which "particular electronic text features appeared to coincide with some of the conditions considered optimal for learning" (Meskill, Mossop, and Bates 1999, 5). These features, which are discussed in more detail in the next section, include anarchy, publicness, instability, malleability, democratization, and anchored referents, most of which apply also to adult ESOL learners using computers and the Internet. *Electronic text* is broadly defined as "any information displayed on a computer, including audio, video, graphics, and the written word" (Meskill and Mossop 2000, 586). These aspects of electronic texts enhance learning in content areas by involving multisensory experience.

Practice Situated in Theory

Tourism, Culture, and Technology is an elective content course that I teach in the tourism major at a large four-year women's university in Kyoto, Japan (total university enrollment is almost six thousand). The course is a two-semester sequence for second-year students and above (ages nineteen to twenty-two), taught for ninety minutes once a week in a networked computer lab. There are no lectures; each class consists of discussing reading assignments and Internet-based projects. I use only standard application programs such as word-processing and Internet browsing software. The focus of the course is threefold: (1) tourism as a cultural phenomenon, (2) the impact of technology on the tourism industry, and (3) language acquisition. I assign readings from standard works in tourism. The content for the cultural aspect of tourism is based on work in the anthropology of tourism. Topics include representations of destinations; tourist-host conflicts; ecotourism, heritage, and identity; and cultural aspects of museum displays. Topics focusing on the impact of technology include the Internet's effects on tourism, Internet aids to travelers, and design and evaluation of destination Web sites. All materials are authentic English texts. The goals of the course are for students to gain some understanding of important issues of culture and technology, to learn how technological advances and the growth of the Internet have changed how the tourism industry operates, and to learn how to be more sensitive to cultural issues in tourism.

To situate this course in CBI theory, I apply the constructs used by Brinton, Snow, and Wesche (2003, 19) to define various models of content-based teaching, and I have added two constructs that I believe are definitive (see Table 8.1).

Six CALL features proposed by Meskill, Mossop, and Bates (1999) demonstrate CALL's emphasis on pedagogy: anarchy, publicness, instability, malleability, democratization, and anchored referents. Several of these are instantiated in my course:

- *Anarchy* suggests that the computer classroom is not teacher centered but is a place where students can "make judgments and negotiate selections" (Meskill, Mossop, and Bates 1999, 7). Two-thirds of class time in my course is devoted to independent or group project work using the Internet. Learners "exercise volition and control over the order and direction of their interaction with electronic texts" (p. 5). Projects range in complexity from simple searches for sites with useful travel-related information, such as maps, currency exchange, weather reports, and world time information, to in-depth research on museum Web sites or online booking systems.

- *Publicness* of electronic texts "facilitates rich discourse on the part of learners and their teachers" (Meskill, Mossop, and Bates 1999, 8). Thanks to the excellent U-shaped layout of our lab, the students' screens are always visible to me. They can turn to partners or gather at tables in small groups to discuss projects with each other, or use computer-mediated communication for project organization and management. I regularly engage students in discussions about what they are looking at or working on, at times individually and at other times with pairs or small groups.

- *Instability* promotes critical thinking (Meskill, Mossop, and Bates 1999, 9). While often frustrating, this aspect of electronic texts forces students to be resourceful and plan ahead. It is also an incentive for students to learn the software functions that are designed to help users cope with instability, such as turning on the

Table 8.1. Constructs Defining Relative Emphasis of the Course

Constructs (Brinton, Snow, and Wesche 2003)	Language-Focused	Content-Focused
Primary purpose: I see this course primarily as a content course, but a disinterested observer might see it as a language course with a specific topic.	• I select the readings carefully to be within *i + 1* of the students' competence. • I correct the organization and surface features of their writing.	• I see the course primarily as a content course. • Others might consider it a language course with a specific topic.

(Continued on p. 101)

Constructs	Language-Focused	Content-Focused
Instructional format: This class is not linked to any other course, so it is an EFL content course.	• Some students are not tourism majors, but take the course primarily because it is offered in English.	• Some students are majoring in tourism studies and have had other courses in the field. • The course is not applicable to the foreign language requirement.
Instructional responsibilities	• I am a language teacher, not a content specialist, and language learning is more than incidental to the course.	
Student population	• The students are all nonnative-English-speaking EFL learners. • Some are tourism majors with previous course work, but others are English majors; both groups hope to work in the travel industry.	
Focus of evaluation	• About 20 percent of evaluation focuses on student language skills.	• About 80 percent of a student's grade is based on content knowledge.
Additional Constructs		
Course credit	• Students cannot use the course to fulfill part of their foreign language requirement. (See Rosenkjar 2002, on the important issue of credit.)	• The course counts as an elective content course.
Teaching methodology: Peterson (1997) points out that "[K–12] subject-area specialists are urging a more student-centered pedagogy that should coincidentally ease the process of collaboration for ESL and content-area teachers" (p. 173).	• I plan a communicative, student-centered course with discussion and hands-on projects with authentic tasks on the Internet. • There is little lecture or top-down teaching.	• I utilize a CBI approach using computer-supported tourism projects and tasks.

automatic backup function in word processing or saving useful URLs in relevant bookmark/favorite folders.

- *Malleability* stimulates thinking "that pertains to changing and shaping both form and content" (Meskill, Mossop, and Bates 1999, 11). Word processing is the ideal tool for teaching writing with a process approach, which shapes compositions through multiple drafts; I have students rewrite their projects to improve both content and English expression. Also, students use information found on the Internet in the production of their own texts, which they modify as they locate additional source materials and integrate these new materials into their projects.

- *Democratization* is "the potential for a leveling of authority" (Meskill, Mossop, and Bates 1999, 12) that computers foster. Through the process of researching their projects on the Internet (including the school library's databases of print materials), students soon become more expert on their chosen topic than I am, especially when they use Japanese-language as well as English-language materials.

- *Anchored referents* in electronic texts provide points "to which talk can be anchored" (Meskill, Mossop, and Bates 1999, 12). This is an additional aspect of the publicness of electronic texts, that is, my discussions with students about their projects are anchored to what is on the screen. The referents "establish a base structure for the teacher's building of instructional scaffolds" (p. 13) for both content and language.

At first glance, the CBI constructs and the CALL features seem to be in different dimensions, the former concerned mainly with content and the latter with pedagogy. However, the practicing teacher soon discovers that the relationship between the two sets of issues is not so simple. For example, the CBI construct of *instructional responsibilities* in theory applies to the instructor's expertise as a teacher of either content or language. But the CALL feature of *democratization* suggests that in a CALL CBI class, the instructor becomes the guide on the side; in other words, a CALL approach forces the rethinking of a CBI principle. A similar change takes place with *instructional format*; the neat CBI categories are challenged, or deconstructed, by the CALL feature of *anarchy*. Using CALL in CBI is not just a matter of holding a standard CBI class in a computer lab; as discussed in the following section, CALL activities require important changes in CBI.

CALL Activities in CBI

Reading instruction through electronic annotation. Word processors provide an excellent example of how technology makes teachers rethink instructional practices. For example, word-processing software functions can be used to represent text structure graphically. Text organization, discourse markers, cataphoric and anaphoric references, and so forth can be made explicit using features such as underlining, bold, italics, borders or boxes, colors, highlighting, footnotes, comments, and graphics such as arrows and callouts. The instructor can prepare assigned readings with these tools, but it is a useful exercise for students to do it themselves. This task is based on research showing that identification of text structure and organization improves comprehension (reviewed in Grabe 1995); it works as a kind of knowledge framework (Mohan 2001; Tang 2001).

The following hypertextual annotation task has been shown to benefit learners (Rouet and Levonen 1996). Copyright-free readings are scanned into text files and distributed to students on disk or by e-mail. Each student is asked to annotate one reading for use by classmates. (This task could be done by teams of students to deal with the ratio of students to readings assigned for the semester.) The annotation consists of the graphic representation of text structure and the addition of footnotes with Japanese translations of difficult or technical vocabulary pasted in from one of the numerous online bilingual dictionaries, a resource valued by students. Word-processing functions are only one way to annotate texts; mind-mapping software is also popular for this use (see Innovation Tools 2002–2006; for a list of electronic resources used in my course, see this chapter's appendix).

Internet-based reading materials. The Internet provides a vast amount of reading material on any content topic; more important, according to Caverly and Peterson (2000), research shows that working through the hypertextual structure of Web documents requires "developmental readers to have strategies for comprehension monitoring and for strategically selecting text" (p. 301). They indicate that "the computer can be an effective tool for readers to reason with text as they make decisions about how to organize information, make inferences, and draw conclusions" (p. 303). The instructor helps students select texts through consultation as they gather material for their projects.

As an introductory task, I ask students to study Google's (2005) Help Center: Search Results Page to understand how search engines work. I then teach a *skimming for details* reading strategy for their first page of hits (using search keywords in the field of tourism) to find relevant items, rather than clicking on each link in turn. This activity combines language skills and content instruction well, since it requires some critical thinking about the types of resources that would make good references.

Critical Web searches. Experts in CBI emphasize computer literacy and research skills, especially teaching students how to evaluate the quality of what they find on the Internet (see Kasper 2000; Stapleton 2003). To develop these skills, I made an online worksheet that takes students through the following stages: reading URLs, understanding advanced search techniques and the variety of search engines, evaluating Internet sites, and citing Internet sources. This worksheet is supported by an online resource guide based on sources such as Schrock's (1995–2006) Critical Evaluation Surveys.

Advanced word-processing functions. At this point, writing papers on a computer can hardly be considered a CALL activity; the benefits of word processing for ESOL writing are too well known to need further discussion here (see Ferris and Hedgcock 1998, 264–289; Pennington 2004). Less well known, perhaps, but certainly helpful, is using the outline function in word-processing software to assist students in organizing their essays and using color coding for correction (see D. F. Campbell 2004; Rilling, chapter 10 in this volume).

Web site evaluation and design. One of the tasks in my course is the detailed evaluation of a tourism destination Web site; students must consider both page design and tourism content aspects. A variation on this task is a short project completed in cooperation with a Web design class taught in another department by a specialist in that field. Students in both classes read Nielsen and Tahir's (2001, 274–279) and Carton's (2002) critiques of previous versions of the popular Web tourism site Travelocity, as well as articles on the basics of page design (Nielsen 1999) and usability (Nielsen 2000). Learners then study the current Travelocity site to consider what changes have been made and why (see Susser and Ariga 2006).

An extension of this project is to have students design their own tourism site, either as a mock-up or using an HTML editor. Having students create Web pages is a widely used CALL activity (see Isbell and Reinhardt 2000; Kitao 2002; Robb 2000; see also several chapters in this volume). Shetzer and Warschauer (2001) show how a course in making Web pages meets the principles and goals of CBI as students merge content with the process and product of Web publishing.

Brochure production. Besides making tourism Web pages, students in my course make brochures or leaflets for tourism destinations using the desktop publishing (DTP) features of their word-processing program or specialized DTP software (see Fowlie 1999; Jewell, chapter 13 in this volume). In fact, one DTP activity described by Butler-Pascoe (1997) is the production of a brochure for tourism. The key point here is whether students have the computer skills needed for this project, and if they do not, whether it is worth taking class time to teach them. This decision depends on an instructor's syllabus and curriculum, but computer-friendly instructors often recommend that honing such skills is in itself a form of constructivist learning, offering ample opportunity to practice language while performing the authentic real-life tasks of brochure design and production.

Speaking skills. Students can practice these skills by giving presentations supported by software such as Microsoft PowerPoint (2006) or the free Impress (included in the Open Office.org Suite [2005]). Schcolnik and Kol (1999) claim that presentations with such software support are more effective than traditional oral presentations because using the software motivates students, helps them to better organize their presentations, and gives them practice writing for a real audience. Further, Hanson-Smith (2000) points out that teaching ESL students to use presentation software "satisfies the creative instinct and allows students to deploy a wide variety of learning strategies" and skills (p. 137). On the other hand, there have been some strong criticisms of presentation software. Parker (2001), for example, argues that PowerPoint shapes people's thinking and limits what they can present and communicate to information that is linear and superficial (see also Tufte 2003). Whether and how one uses presentation software is a matter of individual teacher preference, but its multimedia and hypertextual properties can be quite valuable if used imaginatively.

Authentic communication. Communicating with people outside the classroom is an increasingly popular CALL activity (see Fotos 2004; Nozawa 2002; various chapters in this volume), and it has been used in many different CBI contexts. The students in my tourism course have cooperated with students in the United States who are studying Kyoto. The exchanges are kept simple: the U.S. students send questions about the places they are studying, and the Japanese students respond. The students complete short exchanges by e-mailing each other and using the discussion board function of our course management system (CMS). As with all such projects, much planning and encouragement by the teachers is required to elicit successful, sustained, and consistent communication.

Content-based software. Many CBI courses use subject-specific or content-based software or simulations that were originally created for native speakers. Hanson-Smith (1999) argues that content-based software "creates or shapes relevant tasks to allow learners to practice language skills in an environment safe from misunderstandings and social ridicule" (p. 137); she describes a number of programs that were made for native speakers of English but are suitable for ESL students. Teachers should be aware, however, that many of these programs have been criticized severely for giving students the wrong message about the nature of the environment and the place of human beings in it (Bowers 2000; see also Turkle 1997). Although teachers need to consider the appropriateness of content as well as language, such software may offer good opportunities to apply critical thinking.

Concordancing. The use of concordancing software or online concordancers (e.g., Cobb's Compleat Lexical Tutor [2006]) for studying the specialized vocabulary of disciplines has been widely described in the ESP literature (e.g., Rilling and Pazvant 2002; Weber 2001). Concordancing also supports other aspects of language learning (see Reppen and Vasquez, chapter 4; Sevier, chapter 3; both in this volume), and many concordance tasks could be adapted for CBI. For example, students can download travel brochures from the Internet and run them through a concordancer to see what words collate with *vacation* and other key terms; this helps students write their own brochures more accurately. A more ambitious project is to compare concordance results to a similar search through a different genre, such as articles in travel magazines.

Challenges and Future Directions

The greatest challenge to the CBI instructor is the issue of expertise. There is no simple answer to this problem, but an ESL instructor assigned to teach a content course has several options for developing some expertise: reading in the field, taking courses, subscribing to a journal, joining a professional organization and attending the meetings, and so forth. One particularly valuable resource is a journal devoted to teaching a particular field; in tourism, for example, it is the *Journal of Teaching in Travel & Tourism*. Another resource is World Lecture Hall (University of Texas at Austin 2005), which provides course materials in almost any imaginable field. Such resources make the task of gaining expertise much easier than it used to be.

Another challenge that faces all teachers (and learners) who use technology is making the best use of what technology offers. As Bowers (2000) cautions, software that implies students have the power to change history or rewire nature is educationally unsound. On the other hand, Weigel (2005) warns that educational applications (e.g., CMSs) are unlikely to improve teaching if they accept a traditional classroom model uncritically. In other words, technology is not able to help instructors teach by placing students in a kind of science-fiction *virtual unreality*, nor will it help them if it simply reproduces the existing classroom and traditional learning approaches. The challenge is to find the best pedagogies for the current state of technology.

Even so, as technology advances, many exciting possibilities have opened up for content-based CALL, three of which apply particularly well to CBI: open courseware initiatives, CMSs (also called virtual learning environments), and reusable learning objects (RLOs).

One example of open courseware is MIT OpenCourseWare, a large-scale project that offers "Web-based publication of the educational materials from the MIT faculty's courses . . . [including] open access to the syllabi, lecture notes, course calendars, problem sets and solutions, exams, reading lists, even a selection of video lectures, from 1250 MIT courses" (Massachusetts Institute of Technology 2005, ¶3). While most institutions have not yet gone this far in offering Web-based course material, the trend is likely to accelerate. As a result, teachers will have no trouble finding high-quality course material on the Web to adapt for their own content-oriented or CBI language classes, or to educate themselves in a particular subject area.

The widespread use of CMSs, "Internet-based software that manages student enrollment, tracks student performance, and creates and distributes course content" (Ullman and Rabinowitz 2004, ¶1), opens up two possibilities for ESOL teachers assigned to a content course. First, they can enroll in a distance course in that topic and learn the basics. This was always possible through traditional distance learning, but CMS technology has vastly increased the number and variety of courses available—and their convenience for the working professional. Second, a CMS makes team teaching much easier because the instructors do not have to be at the same institution; linking an on-site language course to a virtual content course becomes a practical possibility.

RLOs are small, self-contained digital resources. They can be aggregated, they are tagged with metadata (so they can be found easily by searching), and they conform to Internet standards so they can be used across platforms and systems (see McGreal 2004; Polsani 2003; Wiley 2002). RLOs include lesson plans, activities, applets, animations, simulations, Web pages, and so forth. They can be found in repositories such as MERLOT (1997–2006; described in McMartin 2004). Strictly speaking, a repository is simply a place to store electronic objects and their tags, but many do much more than that; for example, the peer review function at MERLOT is valuable for deciding if a particular item would be useful for your purposes. RLOs are available for many subject areas and thus promise to be a major resource for CALL in CBI.

This review of the intersection between CBI and CALL has highlighted two key issues: the flexible balance between content and language instruction for CBI, and the effectiveness of teaching practices and tasks with CALL approaches. The combined issues demand attention while planning and conducting courses. Brent (2005) describes two approaches to pedagogy that are especially applicable in the context of CALL and CBI: teaching as a dialogic social performance in which teachers as well as students participate, and teaching as the transfer of knowledge from text to audience. CBI is often limited to the latter approach. Brent warns that "if the group that values teaching as performance has the most influence, we will put more energy into developing flexible courseware that promotes social engagement and interaction. . . . If the group that sees teaching as textual has the most influence, we will develop more elaborate technologies for delivering courses as online texts, emphasising the role of the student as audience rather than as participant" (¶3 under Conclusion).

The example of tourism described in this chapter reveals the extent to which the features of CALL can help language teachers in a content-based course make the CBI classroom more learner centered, constructivist, and communicative.

Appendix—Chapter 8
Web Sites, Internet Tools, and Software
Used in the Course

The Compleat Lexical Tutor (Lextutor)	http://www.lextutor.ca/
Critical Evaluation Surveys	http://school.discovery.com/schrockguide/eval.html
Google Help Center: Search Results Page	http://www.google.com/help/interpret.html
Impress (OpenOffice.org)	http://www.openoffice.org/product/impress.html
Innovation Tools: Mind Mapping Resource Center	http://www.innovationtools.com/resources/mindmapping.asp
MERLOT: Multimedia Educational Resource for Learning and Online Teaching	http://www.merlot.org/
Microsoft PowerPoint	http://office.microsoft.com/powerpoint/
MIT OpenCourseWare	http://ocw.mit.edu/OcwWeb/index.htm
Travelocity	http://www.travelocity.com/
World Lecture Hall	http://web.austin.utexas.edu/wlh/

Chapter 9

Meaningful Tasks with Video in the ESOL Classroom

Nicolas Gromik
Tohoku University
Sendai, Japan

Preview

Audiovisual resources have long been an integral part of the language teacher's repertoire. Since the advent of inexpensive and easy-to-use digital video equipment, film or video creation by students is becoming established as a legitimate approach to enhance language learning. Gromik documents how video production and editing tasks fit in with current second language acquisition (SLA) theory and provide students with important technology skills. The issues discussed here include focus on form, negotiation of meaning, input and output, and the technological preparation needed for teachers. Gromik then describes the task-based activities that he uses in his film course in Japan. He sees video projects as a means to empower students to think critically and become active, autonomous learners and producers of the target language.

Before you read:

- Have you ever produced a home movie? What were the steps involved?
- What kinds of language and metacognitive skills do students develop in filming and editing?
- How can students' creative projects best be evaluated?

Making Movies as Task

Teachers have long used videotape and movies to expose students to the language and culture of the target language. More recently movie trailers available online have offered an appealing new resource that allows teachers to develop exciting lessons promoting various communicative possibilities and targeting students' interests and abilities. However, one perspective on films that has so far received little attention is moviemaking. This approach takes learners away from the screen and positions them behind the lens. Video creation requires some knowledge of the operation of the technology itself, but it also demands that teachers understand how to implement task-based activities in order to facilitate learning outcomes that include both language skills and practical and specific technological skills.

My Communicative Language course is an elective at Tohoku University, an urban university in Japan, and students from various departments (such as nursing or engineering) can enroll without a prerequisite course. These students possess six years of school-based English study plus one year of English preparation in their first year of university. The majority of these students have basic computer skills, but no knowledge of film- or video-editing technique. Filming and editing were perceived as the most preferable project-based approaches to motivate students to utilize their prior knowledge and experience with English as well as to provide an environment conducive to gaining and developing computer skills in a task-based, cognitively challenging setting.

In this chapter I review research on SLA using computer technology in the language classroom and offer guidelines for organizing and managing a film production course using free software, such as Apple's iMovie (2005) or Microsoft's Windows Movie Maker (2004). I make recommendations on how to introduce video production and editing as authentic, task-based learning activities designed to enhance students' technological skills while encouraging language acquisition. I also describe some approaches to evaluating and presenting students' creative products.

Using Video for SLA and Life Skills

The integration of computer-assisted language learning (CALL) into the curriculum has been slow at times, but in the past decade has expanded to a wide variety of activities: attractive drill-and-practice exercises, both online and on CD (see Beatty 2003); aids to language correction (Hada, Ogata, and Yano 2002); computer-assisted explorations of language, for example, with concordancing (Cobb 2006); authentic tasks (Chapelle 2001; Hanson-Smith 1999); and computer-mediated communication between learners via local area networks or the Internet (Warschauer, Shetzer, and Meloni 2000; see also Almeida d'Eça, chapter 12 in this volume). Video has been suggested as a teaching strategy in foreign language classes (Kondo 2002; Ryan 2003); as a tool to assist in training teachers (Coniam 2001; Kamhi-Stein et al. 2002); as a means to investigate second language interactions (Dufon 2002), including both verbal expression and body language (Hoelker, Nimmannit, and Nakamura 1999); as a way to obtain cultural information (Herron et al. 2000); and as a writing stimulus (Gromik 2003). What is most noticeable throughout the body of research on video is the opinion that students, as well as society in general, are becoming increasingly attentive to visual forms of expression and possess finely tuned viewing skills (Herron et al. 2000). Students are increasingly familiar with this technology (Meskill and Ranglova 2000) and realize the benefits of using computers as a tool to learn another language (Warschauer 2000b). Video production and editing can also provide students with a learning experience that is influential for life. Like other aspects of CALL, which Shetzer and Warschauer (2000) see as "essential to success in the age of information" (p. 176), video will no doubt have great importance. Students will someday make video portfolios for self-reflection and evaluation by others, send video messages by podcast or e-mail, and, even more certainly, sift daily through a wealth of visual images that target them for entertainment, education, and marketing.

To meet students' needs in a visual age, teachers need to prepare themselves with both technical information and an understanding of the pedagogical foundations of filming and editing. Fortunately, the tools for becoming video-literate are increasingly easy to master. The steps to prepare for a course in video production—or a short-term workshop to help students create video projects—include the following:

- assembling resources, both hardware and software
- preparing and selecting projects appropriate for curricular goals
- assisting students in the performance of filming and editing
- creating the means to evaluate students' creative work
- finding a forum for students' presentation of their projects

Training students to use the equipment and software, and eventually investigating aspects of the film industry, form the core of each of these steps, which are considered in more detail throughout the rest of the chapter.

Assembling Resources

Hardware

The hardware and software used in the course or project will be governed by the local computer facilities that are available. Nevertheless, consideration should be given to the ratio of computers to students. Two students per computer is conducive to creating language exchanges, while groups of three to five may work together for larger projects if each student is assigned a specific role on the team. At a minimum, the following equipment is required:

- a camcorder or digital video camera
- a compatible computer
- videotapes (if a camcorder is used); a flash drive for the digital camera
- associated batteries and battery charger
- compatible cables to transfer film or digital video to the computer
- a CD or DVD recorder and CDs or DVDs to archive projects

The following are also very useful:

- a tripod (Hand-held cameras produce very jumpy films.)
- extra flash drives for larger projects

- an external microphone (Most cameras have a built-in microphone, but an external one will improve sound quality and range.)
- lights to enhance indoor filming (To avoid the expense of professional light sets, construction lights may be purchased cheaply at a hardware store.)

Software

Windows Movie Maker (2004; see Figure 9.1) and iMovie (2005; see Figure 9.2) are free with new computers (or downloadable with newer operating systems) and are perhaps the most suitable software to use when starting to learn about filming and editing. Both software items are user friendly, and their manufacturers provide tutorials online (see Apple Computer 2006b; Microsoft 2006a). Reviewing a software-specific tutorial assists teachers in introducing these learning aids during the project. The easier the software is to use, the faster students will be able to familiarize themselves with it and take the initiative in investigating it to create more sophisticated products.

Whichever software is selected, it should have certain features. It must allow video to be taken directly from the film or flash drive, retrieved from another device, or imported from other files. Once a digital video camera is connected to the computer on which the software

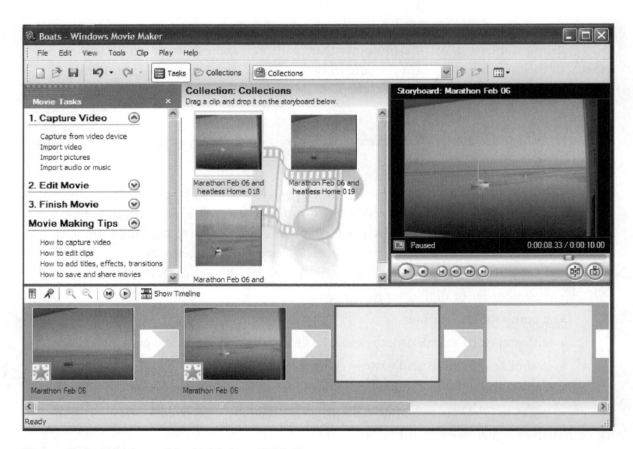

Figure 9.1. Windows Movie Maker (2004)
Source: E. Hanson-Smith. Microsoft product screenshot reproduced with permission from Microsoft.

Learning Languages through Technology

is loaded, the recorded movie should be found and downloaded automatically, or with just a few clicks. Once the film is stored on the computer, it should be easily retrieved for editing. The software must also allow music or voice to be imported and edited to fit in with movie segments. Easy access to slide effects or transitions and title creation should be visible in a point-and-click editing environment. Cutting and pasting should be simple to achieve, with the software allowing such options as deleting a film segment or moving a sequence to another part of the movie. The timeline must be easy to understand and operate (see the timeline under the image in Figure 9.1 and the slidebar in Figure 9.2). Finally, the Help documentation must be easy for language learners to read because that can empower them to work more autonomously.

Preparing

The aim of a film course is to place the equipment and learning strategies in the hands of the learners; doing so takes the focus away from the teacher and encourages students to gain confidence in the technology and their abilities. Through guidance and assistance, the teacher can facilitate students' technical operation. Discussion of film design also creates an

Figure 9.2. Apple iMovie (2005)
Source: E. Hanson-Smith. Macintosh product screenshot reproduced with permission from Apple Computer.

opportunity for teachers to assist students in developing metacognitive learning and thinking strategies.

To realize the goal of giving students responsibility for their own learning, teachers first need to determine what hardware is available at their school and possibly approach the administration about equipment-borrowing protocol. The next step is to develop a plan to manage the classroom and access the resources, especially since students will probably have to share equipment and stagger its use. Establishing a reservation schedule and determining whether the equipment can be taken out of the classroom should also be considered. Because film projects take a little time to develop, teachers need to consider a long-term approach when designing their curriculum and decide whether or not filming will be an in-class activity. Writing a script, planning filming options, filming, and reviewing the first unedited film usually takes students one month, with at least ninety minutes each week devoted to the project. A second month is needed for editing workshops conducted in a computerized or "smart" classroom. Activities that extend student learning should also be taken into account, for example, vocabulary-building activities both before and after the films are created; extensive writing, such as journals or Weblogs (blogs) reflecting on the experience (which may also be part of formative evaluation); and oral presentations to peers, parents, other classes, or a global audience on the Web. These activities may take another month.

Teachers also need to decide how best to organize the class for collaborative learning so as to enhance student interactions and allow for scaffolded approaches to learning with and through the technology. While Sharp (2005) suggests whole-class work in the production of a single film, depending on the magnitude of the project, pair or small-group work is also a viable option.

Selecting Projects Appropriate for Curricular Goals

As Worth and Adair (cited in Dufon 2002) indicate, the less the videographer is taught about the equipment, the more authentic the film becomes. Fortunately, unlike in the days of Worth and Adair, digital video cameras are now fully automated; there is very little to teach aside from zooming. This is not necessarily the case with student film projects, however; the timing of a school term has an effect, and some training with the equipment can facilitate instructional goals. Some types of projects and related levels of technology training are suggested in Table 9.1.

Among many other objectives, a film project aims to stimulate creativity. As students and teachers become more sophisticated in using video, they benefit from reading about film design, but for first attempts, viewing other schools' online productions prepares the students for the task ahead. Apple's (2006a) iLife Educator Award Winners Web page provides links to a wide range of school productions as well as lesson plans and objectives behind the films. In the archives of Nexus (ABC Asia Pacific 2006) and The My Hero Short Film Festival (n.d.), teachers can find ideas for more advanced students. While some of the films are more professional, others are developed by schoolchildren. The content of these links can also be used as discussion resources for generating ideas, evaluating filming and editing strategies, and noticing how film equipment is used.

Table 9.1. Film Project Suggestions

Student Level before the Course	Teaching Strategy	Types of Projects	Further Readings
Beginner/ easy: no prior knowledge of filming or technology	• Self-discovery of equipment and technology • Collaborative investigation of linguistic forms • Class or school presentations	• Select and film props and settings to illustrate a vocabulary item. • Act out/dramatize a familiar story. • Show how to make a particular local food item or craft object. • Take a guided tour of the city by focusing on specific sounds (e.g., picture of a forest, sound of animals).	Gromik 2003; Kamhi-Stein et al. 2002; Katchen, Morris, and Savova 2005; Sharp 2005
Intermediate: knowledge of equipment and software operation	• Self-guided study of software potential and video recording • Exposure to scriptwriting and film genre • School or Web presentations	• Select a genre (e.g., game show, documentary), and film with local color. • Create a mood to illustrate vocabulary using music and images. • Write and dramatize a story.	Sherman 2003
Advanced: extensive knowledge and skills	• In-depth guided study • Character analysis • Film analysis • School or Web publication • Online competitions	• Video activism: alert film consumers to manipulation in editing. • Eco-activism: use video of local urban and rural land uses to portray a problem. • Produce longer documentaries (e.g., on an aspect of culture). • Produce an instructional video for other learners (e.g., how to register for university classes). • Produce a fundraising video for school or local needs.	Harding 2001; Moore 2005

Organizing a Video Project

The aim of my Communicative Language course is to provide students with as much experience as possible with various communicative genres, including giving oral presentations, creating films or videos, and learning about and practicing various computer skills. The film and editing project is an integral part of the course, and final productions are assessed.

Throughout the video project, students have the opportunity to enhance and expand their acquisition of language. In writing a script and structuring a film outline, students rely on their knowledge of the language but also experiment with varied linguistic features to bring meaning to their film sequence (Tschirner 2001). Editing gives students the opportunity to select their best performance, and they learn to stimulate certain reactions in the viewing audience by analyzing and evaluating their linguistic performance (Ryan 2003) or their nonverbal expressions (Hoelker, Nimmannit, and Nakamura 1999). While conceptualizing their films, students begin not only to form a perception of what the end product will look like but also to develop important metacognitive skills. However, some students appear to deduce meaning far more from the written words than the visual effect that their dialogue should exploit. To help students connect the text with the visual, the teacher should allocate a lesson to the design of *storyboards*.

Storyboards display the visual intentions or pictures that make up a scene (see Figure 9.3). The dialogue is written under each picture. Storyboarding is an important feature of scriptwriting because it forces students to plan the relationship among words, actions, and scenes. It answers many planning questions, such as where, when, and how the interaction between the characters will take place. Storyboards that connect image and language help students determine in advance how far from the main subject the camera should be, when a

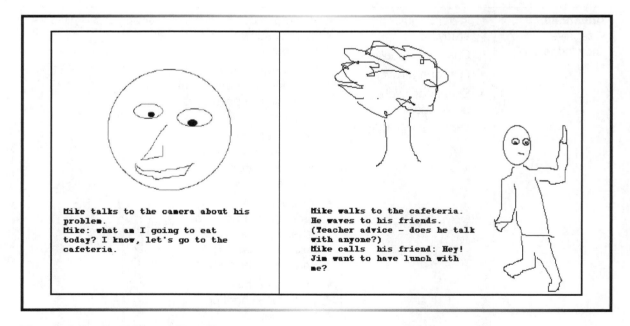

Figure 9.3. Storyboard Panels

close-up is needed, and how to use light effectively. Taking the time to consider these questions makes students more satisfied with their efforts and ensures that they have a good film to start editing. (For an online example of storyboarding, see Shulman 1997–1999.)

Another written element that can greatly assist learners is the *editing log*. This document notes the timing and records the length of scenes so that students can readily find where the sequences are on their film, how long they are, and how to utilize them effectively. Keeping written notes (or a blog) throughout the filming process speeds up the editing and offers further practice in an important academic language skill. As a repertoire of films develops in a school, the teacher can offer the editing logs as examples of how to create and maintain an editing log.

In the process of preparing for their films, students undertake a series of steps that Wenden (2002) explains as forming part of the objectives of self-directed learning: planning, monitoring, and evaluation. *Planning* is defined as the students' decisions about the process through which the task is completed. The learners decide how and when they engage in which type of learning. *Monitoring* refers to the adjustments students make to learn and acquire the target language. Skehan (2003) identifies three stages in the monitoring phase. Learners analyze the intention of the original meaning of their script and decide to refine it to something more comprehensible. Such decisions might reveal the need for more advanced lexical combinations. While refining their work, learners engage in automatic correction of written text, aiming for sentence structure and content accuracy. Finally, they attempt to reach a higher level of fluency (Skehan 2003). *Evaluation* is identified as "the end stage in a learning project whereby a learner determines whether the results achieved are in line with a selected objective and how effectively the selected means of learning contributed to the desired outcome" (Henner-Stanchina and Holec, cited in Wenden 2002, 36). These three elements of learning are also fulfilled in the editing process, which is described in more detail in the next section and summarized in Table 9.2.

Metacognitive knowledge, "what the learner knows about learning" (Wenden 2002, 35), is also crucial to the video project at several points. This form of knowledge helps learners evaluate their work at the creation, performance, and editing stages. While film allows

Table 9.2. Organizing a Film Project by Using Self-Directed Learning

Objective	Filming	Editing
Planning	Storyboard, dialogue, props, location, weather, time, camera	View and select best performance
Monitoring (analyze, refine, become more fluent)	Practice, role play, rewrite, film scene more than once	Explore effects of music, pictures, titles, and transitions
Evaluation	Discuss performance in groups	Discuss editing strategy outcomes in groups

Source: Henner-Stanchina and Holec, cited in Wenden 2002; Skehan 2003; Wenden 2002.

students to view the ongoing production and to think about quality, editing allows them to reflect on what they see, to review their purpose, to recollect how they have achieved it, and to modify the results as needed to make improvements. Reflecting on their work and viewing audience reaction to it thus promote higher learning skills.

Editing

Once all the student films or portions of films are completed, the teacher's next task is to transfer the data from the digital tapes or flash drives to the computer and save them on individual CDs or DVDs so that students, individually or in teams, can work on them. This technical activity usually takes approximately one week to complete, depending on the number of films. During this one-week transition, I provide students with reading comprehension activities (based on MightyCoach.com [Root 2000–2003]) revolving around the concept of film editing, followed by discussion of potential editing strategies. This discussion focuses the students on the editing task and reassures them that it is manageable. In addition to MightyCoach.com, Atomic Learning (2006) provides online video-based tutorials on filming and editing tasks for both iMovie (2005) and Windows Movie Maker (2004).

The editing process can be treated as a workshop in which students interact and communicate to complete their task. It is important for teachers to be familiar with the editing process themselves so that they can assist learners efficiently. Sometimes the technology does not function as rapidly as the students would like, and familiarization allows the teacher to anticipate problems that may arise. Learners working collaboratively have a chance to become experts with part of, if not the entire, editing process. Not only does the collaborative approach bring out students' confidence in their abilities, but it also frees the teacher to work with students who have difficulty with the task at hand. While using the editing software, students engage in authentic communication with the teacher to facilitate problem solving. The conversation is no longer about lexical item definition or grammatical structures; it is about the intended software operation and objectives. The class is no longer guided or directed by a text; it becomes a free arena in which students attempt to explain a problem and understand the solution. By letting the students decide when to seek assistance, the teacher allows them to become active agents involved in their own learning.

Students participating in my film and editing EFL course attend one ninety-minute lesson per week. The technical routine during the editing phase includes the following:

- collecting the software CD from the teacher and turning on the computer (five minutes)
- uploading the film with the editing software (up to five minutes depending on the size of the film)
- seeking resources to add to the film and/or editing with the software (fifty to sixty minutes)
- saving the newly edited film to disk (fifteen to twenty minutes)
- checking that the edited file was carefully saved (two minutes)
- shutting down the computers (two minutes)

Students learn to operate the technology in a responsible and independent manner, and I encourage them to check that they have carefully saved their work. Keeping a copy of the students' original unedited films provides a safety net in case the files are accidentally lost.

When designing the task assignments, teachers should allow ample time for students to make several drafts of the film. Repetition in using the editing software ensures that students review their progress, gain control over the task, and take more creative design risks. In addition, as students engage in reflecting on the outcome of their work, they consolidate their new technology and language skills.

Assessing

To engage students in reflection on their production, the teacher should formulate assessment criteria that provide purpose and offer strategies for project completion. When designing the assessment criteria, the rubric or outline must not offer too much freedom of interpretation, as this might make the task too complex for some students to conceptualize. Furthermore, the overall project must be achievable and clearly designed. The information that students are asked to collect for the project should be something they can research easily, on a topic that is familiar to them and can be completed within the time allocated (Skehan 2003).

Producing a film is a complex task that involves writing, communicating, acting, embracing the technology of filming, and engaging in the creative processes of conceptualization and editing. Therefore, assessment criteria should be balanced among these various tasks. One approach is to offer a general outline of assessment criteria (see Table 9.3); another is to provide students with a rubric from which they can clearly ascertain what skills they need to develop (see Table 9.4). Rubrics can also be designed as checklists to help learners ensure that they have paid attention to all the filming or editing steps. A combination of rubric and outline offers the most flexibility in assessing overall film production. With more advanced learners, it is possible to negotiate the content of the rubric, an additional self-reflective step.

When addressing the issue of performance, teachers should be cautious because performance is a subjective art that is open to interpretation, motivation, emotion, and other such factors. To assess performance is also to expose personal opinion and bias. The rubric guides the students in comprehending the intentions of assessment; however, there should be some discussion of its purpose and value in terms of the overall grade.

The rubric provided in Table 9.4 is not exhaustive; Rubrics for Web Lessons (Pickett and Dodge 2001) provides other suggested formats (for more on rubrics, see Jewell, chapter 13 in this volume). A rubric that is presented to students in advance guides them in appraising their performance at the individual and team levels. It also sets clear goals, including language development objectives; allows for interpretation and negotiation of the task to be completed; focuses on the students' development of technical and problem-solving skills; and may also define new and possibly more challenging tasks while encouraging students to self-direct their learning.

Table 9.3. General Assessment Outline

1. Design, film, and edit a movie about a relevant topic or theme. Save it on a CD or flash drive, and give the final production to your lecturer.
2. Language, content, and concept are interrelated, and your ability to express your ideas in the most effective manner is important.
3. This project also requires display of technological ability, creativity, and, where appropriate, use of researched content.

	Description	Marks	Score
Language	Appropriate information—content		
	Appropriate information—quantity		
	Appropriate and clear pronunciation		
	Correct sentence structure—grammar		
Content	Appropriate for theme/issue/topic		
	Appropriate to language needs and level ($i + 1$)		
	Meaningful and coherent sequencing		
Presentation	Use of design features—colors, sound, pictures, titles, music, transitions, etc.		
	Appropriate time length		
	Ability to use technology		
Concept	Overall production—final edited product		
	Ability to express opinion clearly and to the point		
	Turned in on time		
Total			

Presenting Student Work

To give closure to a video project, students should have the opportunity to present their work to an authentic audience as part of a self-assessment process. Planning, reflecting on, and discussing the presentation are further steps in the language acquisition process.

One approach is to set up the computer lab as a sort of film festival and allow students to walk around the classroom or lab and view productions on individual monitors. With the aid of a checklist or rubric, learners record any techniques or strategies that they might consider using for future projects. Thereafter, discussion can critically review the films while targeting either new collaborative work or improvement of current film projects. Students could then nominate the best productions for their own Academy Awards. For a larger authentic audience, a school festival or parents' night could provide an occasion for displaying productions. Organizing a room, writing appropriate promotional posters (see Jewell, chapter 13 in this volume), and generating short movie trailers for publication on

Table 9.4. Rubric to Assess Student Video Projects

Steps	1 Needs Improvement	2 Satisfactory	3 Accomplished	4 Excellent
Planning: research, script, and story-boarding	Students need help to research and write a script. The storyboard is basic, with limited evidence of planning.	Students need some help to research and write a script. The storyboard follows a logical structure but remains very limited.	Students research and write a clear and purposeful script. The storyboard is carefully designed with some short explanations.	Students research independently and write a clear and purposeful script. The storyboard is drawn carefully, with set design and shot explanations.
Production: technical use of equipment and strategies for conveying meaning	The final production has technical errors. Students do not appear to have any clear acting or composing strategies (e.g., back to the camera, forgotten lines, unclear speech, poor framing).	The final production has some technical errors. Students are familiar with the script but still display lack of acting or visual strategies.	The final production is free of technical errors. Students display familiarity with scripting and acting strategies. They use some visual and audio effects to convey meaning.	The final production is free of technical errors. Students display knowledge of scripting and acting. Students reveal consideration for such audio and video details as music selection and camera placement.
Content: topic of the presentation	The film is confusing and does not follow a logical structure. Factual content may be inaccurate.	The film is confusing, but individual sequences seem logically structured. Factual content is mostly accurate and researched.	The film is coherent. Planning and production render a well-balanced outcome. Factual content is accurate and well researched.	Planning and production render a coherent and original production. Factual content is well researched and used to good effect.

the school Web site provide participants with a greater understanding of the film industry and the various services it requires, thus supporting content-based learning. The films could also be saved as a DVD publication and incorporated into the school's repertoire of learning resources. (Examples of many school video projects are available at Apple Computer 2006a.) Finally, students could submit their productions to online film competitions, for example, The My Hero Short Film Festival (n.d.), the Hometown Video Festival (Alliance for Community Media n.d.), iLife Educator Awards (Apple Computer 2006a), or Video Nation (British Broadcasting Corporation n.d.; only U.K. residents may submit videos for publication).

Another method of presentation to reach an authentic audience is to have students load their projects to Web pages. Although Warschauer, Shetzer, and Meloni (2000) state that the Internet is a great resource for teaching and learning, it still often keeps the learner in the consumer seat. But filming and editing, combined with Web page design, turn consumers into experts about their own culture, ecology, and lives, and creators of a product for a global audience of peers. Using simple HTML editing tools, such as Microsoft's FrontPage (2003), the free Netscape (2003) or Mozilla (2005) Composer feature, or the relatively expensive Dreamweaver (2005), students can, with a little practice and possibly help from an online tutorial (see Atomic Learning 2006; Hanson-Smith n.d.; Stevens 2005b), create Web pages with explanatory text surrounding their embedded video files. Files can be loaded on the school server or saved to a free site, such as Geocities (2006) or Tripod (Lycos 2006). Another approach to creating a suitable means to present student projects is to use presentation software, such as HyperStudio (2005) or Microsoft PowerPoint (2006), either of which allows the importation of media objects. Most presentation software can generate a slide show, a movie, or Web pages as a final product. Displaying students' productions online obviously requires their and/or their parents' permission, and usually the school's as well, depending on the students' age.

Challenges and Future Directions

Filming, editing, and creating individual or group film projects may seem difficult at first, and there are several challenges that teachers must anticipate. For example, although the video-editing software is fairly simple to master, one challenge is ensuring that students have saved their video files appropriately. Most students' instinct is to first click >FILE and then >SAVE PROJECT AS . . . , as they might with a word-processing program. However, this saves their video only as an incomplete project and not as a formatted file, which means that they will most likely lose their work. To overcome the habit of using the >FILE menu, I recommended guiding the students through the correct procedure, which is to use >SAVE PROJECT tool within the movie editing software itself. Teachers need to be very familiar with the software and experiment with it themselves.

Another set of challenges may arise from the local cultural context. For example, the average Japanese student spends a great deal of time studying grammar and vocabulary. Filming and editing, in my context, may be the first project-based learning experience that encourages students to use their knowledge for a meaningful end. Therefore, even though technology now allows Internet users to produce, for example, videoblogs, I think that students who enroll in this type of structured course gain more from producing small-scale semiprofessional documentaries. Once they possess the appropriate skills for creating a film and editing it, they can venture out on their own to other forms of presentation, including streaming webcasts.

Video filming and editing can become an invaluable resource for language development. Collaboration on a complex, authentic task such as a video project stimulates intake and consolidates retention because students share their knowledge of the language and focus on problem solving for authentic purposes. Students develop linguistic, technological, cognitive, and metacognitive skills when they are encouraged to make and edit films. Most important, filming provides students with a medium to express their perceptions of the world.

Acknowledgment

I would like to express my gratitude to Elizabeth Hanson-Smith, whose consistent guidance has been invaluable.

Appendix—Chapter 9
Web Sites and Software for Video and Editing

Tools, Tutorials, and Web Sites for Creating Video Projects	
Atomic Learning	http://www.atomiclearning.com/
Create Home Movies with Windows Movie Maker *tutorial*	http://www.microsoft.com/windowsxp/using/moviemaker/default.mspx
iMovie	http://www.apple.com/ilife/imovie/
iMovie HD Support *tutorial*	http://www.apple.com/support/imovie/
Microsoft PowerPoint	http://office.microsoft.com/powerpoint/
MightyCoach.com	http://www.mightycoach.com/
Rubrics for Web Lessons	http://webquest.sdsu.edu/rubrics/Weblessons.htm
Storyboarding Activity	http://pblmm.k12.ca.us/TechHelp/Storyboarding.html
Windows Movie Maker 2.1 *download*	http://www.microsoft.com/windowsxp/downloads/updates/moviemaker2.mspx
Online Film Competitions	
Hometown Video Festival	http://www.alliancecm.org/index.php?page_id=7
iLife Educator Award Winners	http://www.apple.com/education/ilifeawards/
The My Hero Short Film Festival	http://www.myhero.com/myhero/go/filmfestival/
Video Nation	http://www.bbc.co.uk/videonation/
Web Page Editors and Guides to HTML	
Atomic Learning	http://www.atomiclearning.com/
Dreamweaver	http://www.macromedia.com/software/dreamweaver/
Embedding Media in Your Webpages	http://www.geocities.com/ehansonsmi/embedding_multimedia.html
FrontPage	http://office.microsoft.com/frontpage/
Mozilla Composer (in Mozilla Suite)	http://www.mozilla.org/products/mozilla1.x/
Netscape	http://www.netscape.com/
Vance's e-Zguide "10+ steps to creating simple HTML files"	http://www.homestead.com/prosites-vstevens/files/pi/very_basics/starthere.htm

Chapter 10

An ESL OWL Takes Flight: Social and Curricular Issues in an Online Writing Lab

Sarah Rilling
Kent State University
Kent, Ohio USA

Preview

Springing up around the world, online writing labs (OWLs) in university writing programs and student support centers respond to the need for assistance in second language composition. These labs provide Web-based tutorials and resources to writers at all levels and help students become more autonomous and expert academic writers. As Rilling notes, OWLs can be a very flexible alternative to face-to-face (f2f) writing centers. She discusses the development of and rationale for an advanced language learners' OWL as a dialogic space serving writers across disciplines, and offers tips for teachers and administrators on hatching new OWLs of their own.

Before you read:

- What kinds of tutoring services does your institution offer to English language learners?
- What types of technology could recreate those support services in an online environment?

In Search of OWL Theory

A review of theory and research helped a development team launch Kent State University's (n.d.) ESL OWL. In forming a mission statement, we understood writing to be a recursive process, and we attempted to create a balance among purpose, process, and product (Ferris and Hedgcock 2005). As we engaged with writers in computer-mediated communication (CMC), we explored ways to make the OWL tutorials interactive, not just one-time exchanges. Submissions from students in a range of disciplines expanded our engagement with texts from various academic departments, causing us to adopt an English for specific purposes (ESP) approach.

The following central questions emerged from our engagement with design and implementation of the OWL:

1. *Genre in writing*—How can we best serve writing needs across academic disciplines?

2. *Feedback on ESL writing*—How and why do second language (L2) writing teachers and tutors provide feedback? What should be the focus and process of providing feedback to writers?

3. *Collaborative dialogue online*—If writing is a social practice, how best can tutor and writer interact online to improve the writer's process and products? Is e-mail alone adequate for the purposes of expanded dialogue?

Genre and ESP in Writing Development

Cross-disciplinary tutorials distinguish Kent's ESL OWL from f2f writing centers at the university. The ESL Center serves visa/international students; the Writing Program Center serves mainly students in composition courses, especially basic writing and freshman composition; and the Academic Success Center accommodates the needs of first-generation immigrant undergraduates, low-income students, and students with disabilities. The ESL OWL was devised to assist all of Kent's multilingual writers, both on and off campus, whether they were in composition courses or the academic disciplines. This exceptionally broad clientele demanded an understanding of theory and pedagogical applications in ESP in order to serve students who had a variety of writing goals and composition assignments for sometimes radically different course and degree requirements.

Although L2 teachers are becoming better prepared to teach language for specific purposes, many lack adequate background and the genre awareness necessary to interact with ESP writers in meaningful ways about their specialized fields (Hyland 2000). Writing centers have been slow to incorporate *writing across the curriculum* or *writing in the disciplines* approaches to online tutoring because many of the software support systems they use (e.g., WebCT [2004]) take a traditional, teacher-centered approach (Palmquist 2003). Johns and Swales (2002) question whether writing center tutors have adequate skills to deal with writing needs across disciplines, since tutors are often students in the humanities and may have only limited experience writing in other academic disciplines. Thonus (2002) argues that there are few negative effects on satisfaction when tutor and writer do not share a common discipline, yet we have found tutor training in ESP essential to serving L2 writers across the university.

In the past decade, ESP has focused on a *genre-based approach* to the linguistic and rhetorical forms in various academic specialties (Dudley-Evans and St. John 1998; Feak and Reinhart 2002; Hyland 2000; Swales and Lindermann 2002). *Corpus linguistics* for ESP materials development has also come into favor (see, e.g., Biber, Conrad, and Reppen 1998; Rilling and Pazvant 2002), as has *awareness training* of text conventions in various professional discourse communities (Christie 1999; Flowerdew 2000; Wennerstrom 2003). If ESP writing is reader centered (Boyd 2002), student writers need to be able to identify the reader and provide appropriate discourse for that particular audience, including both graphic and verbal representation systems (Tardy 2005). Combining these various approaches, we felt it would be crucial to offer student writers training in locating and exploiting genre conventions in their own disciplines for specific writing tasks. If the burden of genre knowledge is placed on the student writer, then the tutor, especially when he or she lacks the writer's disciplinary background, is free to encourage writer autonomy in exploring and adapting to the expected written forms. The tutor's role becomes that of assisting writers in "unlocking that door for themselves" and in finding the "architectures" of their disciplinary texts (Swales and Lindermann 2002, 118).

Types of Feedback in L2 Writing

Our collective experience in teaching and tutoring L2 writing prior to, and concurrent with, OWL development matched Kern's (2000) description of the rift between a product-oriented approach (focus on accuracy) and a process-oriented approach (focus on the development of content and ideas). The ideal for our tutorials is to point out students' problems and potentials in writing while considering their purpose and proficiency level.

We know that L2 learners have special needs regarding the feedback they receive (Bloch 2002). They expect help with content, structure, grammar, lexical choices, and sometimes information flow, while their native speaker tutors more generally worry about coherence in writing (Paulus 1999). Thus, tutors in university writing centers often deal more with global concerns of organization and idea development and less with the local concerns of grammar and error correction. Powers and Nelson (1995) indicate that L2 writers ask for assistance from writing tutors with problems of correctness and style at more than twice the frequency of native-English-speaking writers.

The tension created by this social and pedagogical discord between the expectations of writers and those of tutors led us to consider the notion of *indirect coded feedback* (supported by, among others, Chandler 2003; Ferris 2003). However, we also believed that teachers and tutors might be better served in focusing on students' *pursuit of meaning* (Knoblauch and Brannon 2002). If our goal is to provide feedback on students' writing that helps them move to the next phase of their interlanguage (Yates and Kenkel 2002), a narrow focus on student error could give the illusion of a quick fix, one that has limited results for long-term learning and construction of meaning through writing. Error feedback, not correction, allows the tutor to attend to issues of coherence and information as well as structure and usage.

ESP professionals promote learner autonomy in genre acquisition, and writing specialists promote autonomy in L2 writing practices (Ferris 2002). Autonomous writers can self-edit and create a balance in their writing between linguistic complexity and accuracy (Li 2000). Our role as tutors became training students to use independently the strategies that help writers locate error while attending to the development, content, and flow of their text. (For further discussion of the need for guided autonomy, see Robb, chapter 6 in this volume.)

Collaborative Dialogue Online

Breuch and Racine (2000) define writing as social action and social activity, explaining that student writers need an awareness of their anticipated audience's needs and reactions as well as information about how to build cohesive and well-developed arguments. By discussing a text, tutors can demonstrate through their response how an informed, authentic audience might read and interpret the student's textual intentions (Breuch and Racine 2000). By engaging the writer in discussion and promoting and provoking response, tutors can draw on their strengths in knowing how and what to write (Thonus 2003) without appropriating the student's text. However, tutors and clients need to work over time toward negotiating the mismatch between the writers' expectations for error-free text and the tutors' desire for dialogue about text production (Coogan 1999; Hyland 2002; Thonus 2002). Since social interactions between students and tutors may be limited without f2f contact, one of the goals of our OWL was to enhance social interaction between tutor and client.

Thonus (2002) explores the relationship between the tutor and the client and suggests how tutors can draw on shared status in their written response (e.g., native language status, gender, shared subject knowledge). She finds that successful tutorials occurr when

- tutors are academics (either students or faculty),
- tutors are not authoritative,
- tutors acknowledge that they are not always the expert (especially in cross-disciplinary tutorials),
- tutors and clients agree on issues that need attention in further drafting.

Clearly, both social connection between tutor and writer and a consideration of text as social artifact are helpful in composition tutorials. In terms of tutor feedback, Thonus (2002) also notes that with L2 clients, native-speaking tutors spoke more, gave more directives (compared to more mitigated suggestions with first language clients), and focused more on the students' text than on the student as a client, thus diminishing social relations. The OWL offers a space for tutors to provide suggestions and pose questions that involve the writer in reshaping and revising his or her text. We discovered early that our clients respond best, as measured through resubmitted papers and subsequent submissions, when tutors identify themselves personally and engage the clients with questions rather than dictates.

How social interactions would play out online was of primary concern as we developed the OWL. E-mail has frequently been used in L2 learning to exchange information, share ideas, conduct debate, and so forth (see, e.g., Li 2000; Vilmi 1999; Warschauer, Shetzer, and

Meloni 2000). In addition to e-mail, writing tutorials can take place via file exchange, fill-in forms (which might include spaces to post short compositions), or conferencing through real-time text chats (Harris and Pemberton 1995), all with only modest technical support. Electronic files are easy to store, use, and transfer, so online tutorials using these media have the potential to be highly effective and accessible. In comparing online with traditional f2f tutorials, Liu and Sadler (2003) find that students who receive electronic feedback make a larger number of revisions on their texts, but f2f tutorials enable more effective revisions that result in texts being rated higher by instructors, perhaps due to the higher levels of inter-activity in the traditional context. We quickly perceived that extended engagement by both tutor and student is needed in online tutorials, such as by personalizing interactions and providing a structured response. The tutor must also discover the nature of the assignment and the potential audience for the composition—targets that may not be apparent in a single e-mail from the writer—while moving the writer toward the form and content expected in the discipline.

Breuch and Racine (2000) make several suggestions for improving online tutoring. They find that effective, interactive writing tutorials via e-mail take an average of ninety-four minutes of tutor time per response, while f2f tutorials are often conducted much more quickly. However, through the social activity of interacting via e-mail about writers' texts, rather than merely transferring documents back and forth, tutors and clients engage in a dialogue: tutors respond to the clients, not to the documents. To personalize the potentially depersonalizing CMC environment, Breuch and Racine suggest presenting tutor profiles to clients in advance. Even something as simple as using names, both the tutor's and student's, fosters a more natural interpersonal connection. They further propose a three-part struc-tured response to papers received for online tutorials, which we hoped would work well in our ESL OWL:

1. The tutor makes front comments with a personal introduction, uses the stu-dent's name, and provides response specifications (e.g., explaining the type of notes that the tutor has used on the student's text, noting how much of the text the tutor has marked).

2. The tutor makes intertextual comments, directly writing into the student's text as an interruption to focus the client on form-related issues and to ask ques-tions related to lexical choices, organizing structures, content flow, and so forth.

3. The tutor writes endnotes, pointing to needed work and encouraging further submissions to the online writing center. (Adapted from Breuch and Racine 2000)

Both front comments and endnotes provide a personalized element to encourage exchange and do not focus solely on surface features of the text. With the front comments and endnotes, tutors can give instruction on disciplinary writing conventions while offering comments, questions, and suggestions intertextually. In many ways, the tutor becomes guide and cheerleader, serving as a peer reader rather than an evaluative pedagogue. A nondirec-tive approach to tutoring requires active participation from both tutor and writer; the roles of the client-writer and the tutor-reader merge as they examine the developing text together.

OWLs as Virtual Space

The traditional university writing center is often a multifunctional environment where a variety of physical spaces and textual resources are available. The question for online writing centers remains how far to go in replicating the physical writing center, including both human and material resources (Miraglia and Norris 2000). OWLs can mimic physical spaces through high-tech applications such as simulated environments and video chat; yet commonly in OWLs, simple electronic text exchanges, such as e-mail with attachments or Web-based forms with paste-ins, suffice to develop students' writing.

Text-based CMC is often viewed as faceless interaction, providing a measure of anonymity, or even depersonalization (see Andrianson 2001; Wolfe 2000). Even if the only physical presence in CMC is textual, however, a personal voice may still be present. Jordan-Henley and Maid (quoted in Breuch and Racine 2000) state that "although cyberspace can certainly dehumanize a situation . . . it can also focus a situation to the matter at hand—the writing" (p. 248). By mimicking an interpersonal physical space, tutors in the ESL OWL can connect with L2 writers about their texts and provide personalized and personable writing feedback, even at a distance.

A brief review of existing OWLs demonstrated to the Kent development team that there is a range of physical presence in online tutorials. Many OWLs associated with U.S. universities offer Web sites with resources prepared in-house as well as links to online dictionaries and useful external sites (see, e.g., the pioneering Writing Lab at Purdue [OWL at Purdue and Purdue University 1995–2006]). Tutoring can take place through a number of technology applications, including online self-access tutorials (see, e.g., Writing@ CSU [Colorado State University 1993–2006]) and one-on-one tutoring via e-mail or other electronic exchanges with real people, including the potential for voice chat (see examples given by González, chapter 2 in this volume). The following sections deal with how our ESL OWL evolved as both a physical and a virtual space as we tried to put into practice what our research had indicated would be most effective pedagogically.

Developing ESL OWL Tutoring Practices

After experimentation with posting in-house materials to the Web, we initially used our meager resources to focus on developing tutoring practices for CMC-based writing feedback. In subsequent phases of development, we created links to external Web sites keyed to the types of issues that we found our clients needed.

The logistical components of our OWL comprise the following:

- *development team*—The staff consists of seven tutors—one faculty member and graduate teaching assistants on partial assignment, sharing duties in the ESL Center and the Writing Program Center. All staff are at least minimally literate technologically; they are able to use word-processing software effectively and use the Internet for communications and information retrieval.

- *physical computer space*—There is none. Tutors use university computers in labs or personal computers at home.

- *Web site*—Due to technical difficulties, the ESL OWL Web site at first was used only on a limited basis. We have since, however, added resource links to make it more useful.

- *e-mail account*—This is the chief means of interaction between clients and tutors. During initial development, most writers used the e-mail account only. In our second phase, writers are guided to the Web site's links to assist them with language and writing concerns.

- *evaluation team*—A pair of graduate students completing service-learning projects created a database of information for each client-tutor exchange, which includes, when possible, data on the nature of the exchange.

- *mission statement*—This statement enables advertising and delineation of our work. (See Mission Statement of the Kent State University ESL OWL below.)

The mission statement declares that we will not edit compositions for students. We propose to work with writers on improving their composing and revising strategies, including brainstorming, improving organization, and using sources effectively; we did not want to become a line-by-line editing service. Most students contact us directly through our e-mail account since many hear about the OWL through other students or our tutors, who recruit students and talk with faculty in many departments on campus. In addition, students learn of the OWL through our informational brochure, which is updated each semester and distributed around campus.

Creating a Social Space for Dialogue on Writing

We continue to struggle with e-mail exchange as the means to tutoring. Ideally, in the initial e-mail we would receive enough background information to help us contextualize and situate the composition, and to understand the background and needs of the writer. However,

---

Mission Statement of the Kent State University ESL OWL

At the ESL Online Writing Lab (ESL OWL), tutors can consult with Kent State second language writers in almost every discipline and at every level of education, from undergraduate to doctoral students. We are willing to assist you at any stage of the writing process on any writing assignment. We will not edit your work for you, but we can offer suggestions for you to consider. Some things we can help you with are

- brainstorming how you will approach your writing;
- shaping the focus of your writing;
- revising and improving your writing, including organization and clarity;
- using and documenting outside sources effectively;
- strengthening different sections of your writing;
- identifying and correcting your own sentence-level errors.

Source: http://dept.kent.edu/english/eslowl/.

---

students generally submit their writing projects directly to our e-mail address without consulting the specific instructions posted on our Web site. (See Instructions for E-mail Submission of Papers below.) Thus, tutors often do not know what course the piece of writing is for, when it is due, or what the nature of the assignment is. In initial contacts, we found that the tutor must first take the time to establish the context of the writer's submission (e.g., the nature of the class assignment), often while simultaneously planning how to engage the writer in revising. The lack of information has hindered our ability to engage students in treating their writing as a situated act that is addressed to a targeted audience within a defined genre and discipline.

Since student writers sometimes submit a composition only once, each writing tutorial session becomes an isolated teaching event that cannot be expanded as it would be in an extended classroom context. Students might expect a quick fix, and they might be attempting to produce assignments on a tight schedule with little time for engagement or revision. While we would like to work with a student over a period of time and through several assignments, so that the writing can truly show improvement, we have had to adapt our approach to providing feedback in what might be a one-time exchange.

Because students usually come to the OWL expecting primarily error correction, we have found that tutor training and experience is the key to creating dialogue and changing the students' expectations. Powers and Nelson (1995) explain how connections between f2f writing centers and OWLs can be productive: online tutors can better envision and emulate a high level of personal engagement if they have experienced f2f tutorials. All our tutors now work in two writing centers, an f2f center and the OWL, and practices in the f2f tutorials support their work with L2 writers online.

Instructions for E-mail Submission of Papers

Address your e-mail to eslowl@kent.edu from your kent.edu account. Please include

- the name of your course,
- the due date of your assignment,
- a description of your assignment,
- any questions or concerns you have.

Attach your paper to the e-mail OR copy your paper and paste it into the e-mail message. Send it to the OWL. You should hear from one of our tutors within about 24 hours.

Important Note
Since we are not a professional proofreading service, our tutors will usually only look at 900–1200 words (about 4 pages) of your paper in one day. Feel free to submit the whole paper if it is longer than 4 pages, but please specify which pages you would like us to focus on. You may resubmit your paper again on another day for more assistance.

Source: http://dept.kent.edu/english/eslowl/.

Responding Online to Writing

In responding to student writing, tutors first identify themselves to the client and explain how they marked the text. Breuch and Racine (2000) advise using searchable punctuation marks to mark tutor comments (e.g., **word form**); however, since most submissions come as word-processed attachments to e-mail, we decided to color-code our feedback within the text, highlighting responses, questions, and suggestions with various colors to show recurring error patterns. For example, blue can be used to highlight inaccurate grammar or word choice. Yellow can indicate precisely specific and local problems (e.g., subject-verb agreement), and green can bring attention to more global comments and questions.

In an endnote, the tutor summarizes the general strengths and weaknesses perceived in the text and urges the writer to resubmit the composition, ask questions, or use the OWL service again in future papers, thereby providing closure to the exchange. (Coogan [1999] describes the potential for communication problems with an L2 writer when closure is missing.) Our color-coded, routinized system of response through e-mail has been effective, as reported by several users. It encourages writers to articulate the nature of the writing assignment, their goals for the composition, and questions and comments they have about the process of writing and receiving feedback. Through such social engagement, we feel we are successfully moving many of our clients away from the expectation that the OWL tutors are one-shot editors and toward the idea of the tutors as collaborators and supporters of writing development.

Enjoying the ESP Effects

Our efforts to encourage submissions from members of the broader campus community have benefited the university. Previously, the Writing Program Center had served students only in composition courses. But with assistance from our tutors, many of whom had worked in the Writing Program, and active recruiting of clients around campus, composition tutors in the f2f writing center gained increased expertise in working with L2 students as well as students studying in the academic disciplines.

The ESL OWL evaluation team noted that composition submissions came from a broad range of academic disciplines (e.g., education, library science, nursing, political science). They also noted a range of genres, from short, somewhat informal homework assignments to technical reports, theses, and dissertations. When a tutor lacked expert knowledge about the writer's discipline, the tutor deferred to the student as a developing expert in a specialty community. By encouraging autonomy in understanding the features of writing types, styles, and language choices in students' academic disciplines, tutors enabled writers to apply their own developing genre knowledge not only to one particular writing project but also to future compositions. Helping clients become autonomous learners who can consider audience, text, and rhetorical structures independently is one goal of writing instruction and tutoring. Students are very receptive when tutors acknowledge that they, the tutors, are not experts in the subject matter. Instead, tutors ask questions, for example, about word choices or the appropriate use of what might be technical vocabulary. This engages the writers in considering their developing discipline-specific discourse and the expectations of their faculty members or other potential expert readers.

Providing Feedback through CMC

Since many writers who submit to the ESL OWL expect their writing to be edited, tutors provide some feedback about formal aspects of style, grammar, and lexical choice, but in a manner that moves the writer toward self-editing. Depending on the writer's language proficiency, we attempt to use a *triage approach*, focusing on the major and consistent error patterns. This approach is extremely productive with long submissions, such as theses and dissertations. Tutors color-code errors of a certain type on a sample of the word-processed text (e.g., the first three pages of a ten-page essay) and suggest that writers search the rest of the text to self-edit their work. Tutors also point to other issues of organization and composition on a sample of the text (or the whole text, depending on the length of the submission) for students to consider. Clients are always encouraged to resubmit their work for further feedback.

One of the main feedback issues the OWL has dealt with is plagiarism and appropriate citation of texts. We find that some L2 writers copy materials from sources without citation. This strategy of assembling a text may become obvious when one section of an essay is written in the student's voice and another section is a compilation of borrowed bits from a variety of authors. Issues of plagiarism reflect cultural conflict in learning academic writing conventions (Swales and Lindermann 2002; Williams 2002). By raising writers' awareness of the effect that the pastiche has on the reader and by focusing on conventions within the relevant academic discipline, including appropriate practices for citation, we can demonstrate strategies for effectively incorporating source material while recognizing others' intellectual contributions.

A related issue is tutor appropriation of student text. Rather than mandating how to change a text, tutors encourage students to make their own decisions and to consider alternatives for structuring information and arguments. They refer students back to the writing styles and conventions used in their disciplines, their professor's (or another audience's) expectations, and note error patterns with suggestions for lexical or syntactic choices. Students are then equipped to reconsider the purpose of the writing and make informed decisions in redrafting. Students take responsibility for and become expert in their own writing.

Challenges and Future Directions

An important challenge in building an OWL is to enhance and maintain the personal interactions of tutors and clients. To this end, we have three immediate plans for expanding our services in the ESL OWL beyond e-mail exchange:

1. Create a bulletin board on the OWL Web site for students to post their writing for access by tutors and potentially other writers.

2. Implement a MOO (multi-user, object-oriented domain) for providing resource materials and real-time follow-up chat with individuals or groups on their writing projects and processes.

3. Use online concordancing to provide detailed ESP feedback on language forms and usage in various academic disciplines.

Tutors can meet clients in real time in a MOO to further discuss writing when the tutors have already provided feedback through e-mail. (For an excellent tutorial on educational MOOs, see Holmevik and Haynes 2000.) An existing MOO, such as Tapped In (SRI International 1995–2004), could be used for such purposes, and its virtual offices have the look and feel of real faculty offices that could further personalize the tutorial experience. (In contrast, CMSs do not always provide such social space.) Clayton (1998) used a MOO successfully to organize collaborative writing tutorials for groups of advanced ESL writers working on common projects or interlanguage issues (e.g., consideration of audience, creation of organizing frameworks, such as outlines, for essays). In the MOO, groups of writers can be organized by discipline to work with a tutor on genre issues. The tutor arranges meeting times by discipline, and the writers post their texts to the bulletin board so that the group can read them in advance. During the chat, the tutor raises issues for group discussion relating to a specific text or to the genre. By carefully structuring these online discussions, the tutor can build a collaborative environment in which group members help each other understand the conventions of their discipline, as well as convey common information to all group members, and help writers build their own strategies for independent editing and revising.

Another challenge in writing across the disciplines is how best to profit from online or computer-based corpora from specific genres. In the future, OWL tutors will benefit from training on concordancing with corpora from specific academic disciplines in order to provide detailed feedback to students. Using information from the evaluation team regarding past student submissions, we can design and build several small corpora of texts to use in analyzing key features of writing within academic disciplines. For example, if a suitable nursing corpus is not available publicly or through our university, we will collaborate with our colleagues in nursing to select a representative sample of texts (perhaps even student texts), scan them, and create a corpus for use with our concordancer, MonoConc Pro (2000). When providing feedback to a nursing student client, we could then search for lexical items and other patterns that the student appears to be using incorrectly or patterns that the student seems to be avoiding. The concordance output on frequencies of use and samples of patterns can then be shared with the client during a tutorial. Tutors should also be able to assist writers in using online concordancers independently (for more on concordancing, see Sevier, chapter 3 in this volume).

Those who intend to create an OWL should consider the following:

- *Seek collaboration in using existing university resources.* In our OWL, we developed a collaborative synergism with the Writing Program Center. The traditional writing center tutors benefited from developing useful techniques in tutoring L2 learners. Our continued outreach to other disciplines resulted in collaborations, interconnections, and support from faculty and knowledgeable tutors. Support from our colleagues in the university library enabled direct links from online library reference materials and search functions to resources on the OWL Web site.

- *Set priorities.* Resources for development work are often sparse. Our initial resources went into university outreach and protocols for providing feedback to student writers. Further development work is gradually expanding on these practices and the bank of resource materials.

- *Complete evaluation cycles.* Initial evaluation has pointed to academic disciplines and resources that need our future attention, including connections with colleagues, corpus identification, and materials preparation. Analysis of existing data will help us understand patterns, such as planning tutor time to coincide with heavy submission times, evaluating client satisfaction with use of our services (demonstrated through frequency of resubmissions), and understanding and refining interactions between tutors and clients.

- *Plan for tutor training time within the tutors' work assignments.* Allowing time for tutors to become familiar with resources, feedback protocols, and tutoring theory and practices, both online and off, can only strengthen OWL services. In our case, since OWL submissions tend to be low near the beginning of the semester, tutors read and discuss a selection of articles on teaching composition, as well as analyze past tutor-client interactions to see what worked well and what needs improvement. The training process helps initiate tutors prior to actually working with clients as the semester unfolds.

OWLs are exciting electronic spaces for educators to meet and provide support for writers from a variety of backgrounds and with a variety of purposes. OWLs support the educational goals of academic and technological literacy, and they may even shape the academic textual landscape of the future.

Appendix—Chapter 10
Web Sites and Tools for OWLs

Kent State University ESL OWL	http://dept.kent.edu/english/eslowl/
MonoConc Pro	http://www.athel.com/
Tapped In	http://tappedin.org/tappedin/
WebCT	http://www.webct.com/
Writing Lab at Purdue	http://owl.english.purdue.edu/writinglab/
Writing@CSU	http://writing.colostate.edu/

Chapter 11

Issue: *Mismatch or Missed Opportunity? Addressing Student Expectations about Technology*

Maggie Sokolik
University of California
Berkeley, California USA

Preview

Sokolik points out that the apparent acceleration in the pace of technological advances in communication seems matched only by its mirror image: instructors are falling rapidly behind in understanding technology and its potential for education. She presents views collected in surveys of university English language learners in the United States. Students tend to feel that instructors know less about computer technology than their students do. She discusses how the mismatch between student expectations and instructor practice can undermine the teacher's expertise and authority. Should teachers be taking Remedial Multimedia Literacy 101 from their students? Sokolik offers specific suggestions for professionals about how to improve their understanding of language teaching through technology.

Before you read:

- If you are a student, do you feel that you know more about technology than most of your instructors? Give some examples of how you arrived at your conclusion.

- If you are a teacher, do you feel that your students are far ahead of you in technological matters? If so, how can you regain authority?

The Technology Gap

> **Q:** Do you think you know more about the Web than your professors do?
> **A:** Yes, most instructors that I have had have trouble figuring out how to bring down a screen for the overhead. (student respondent)

Second language educators generally accept that pedagogical materials and related teaching techniques are among the factors that affect the motivation and involvement of learners (Clément, Dörnyei, and Noels 1994; Crookes and Schmidt 1991). This belief has been extended specifically to the use of computer and Internet technology in the second or foreign language classroom (Stepp-Greany 2002; Warschauer 1996). Several studies have focused on the use of specific technologies (e.g., chat rooms, e-mail, bulletin boards) within language classrooms and mention their motivating effects, though few have looked at the collection of technologies as one body, how it is used, and how it affects student attitudes toward language learning.

In spite of the acknowledged importance of technology in communication and language education, a major issue faces classroom practitioners: the mismatch between students' use of technology and their perceptions of instructors' knowledge of it. In many cases, this mismatch is becoming increasingly stark, with the patience of many students (and technologically savvy instructors; see Berge 1998) running thin with teachers who, as indicated by the student cited earlier, cannot even operate projection screens, let alone navigate the world of short message service (SMS), instant messaging (IM), moblogs (blogs whose content is posted via mobile/cell phone), or podcasts—all current media of communication for many university students around the world.

What is at the root of this technology gap? Prensky (2001) characterizes the current generation of technology users—those who have grown up with digital technologies—as *digital natives.* He contrasts them with *digital immigrants*, those of a certain generation for whom developing facility with information technology may be more akin to assimilating into a foreign language and culture than to simply learning a practical skill. Prensky's symptoms of being a digital immigrant include "printing out your email (or having your secretary print it out for you . . .); needing to print out a document written on the computer in order to edit it (rather than just editing on the screen); and bringing people physically into your office to see an interesting web site (rather than just sending them the URL). . . . My own favorite example is the 'Did you get my email?' phone call" (p. 2).

Digital natives, on the other hand, have been socialized differently and thus have communication preferences that, at the core, differ from those of the digital immigrants. This contrast has consequences for the classroom, of course. As Prensky (2001) states, "Digital Immigrant instructors, who speak an outdated language (that of the pre-digital age), are struggling to teach a population that speaks an entirely new language" (p. 2). Prensky (2002) goes on to say, "faculty should be attending remedial courses in 'multimedia literacy' taught by the students!" (p. 3).

Of course, Prensky's categories are not as clear-cut as he proposes: everyone can name instructors who behave like digital natives and students who seem like digital immigrants. However, these categories may serve well as a metaphor for the broader generational differ-

138

ence in technology use and understanding, an issue that needs to be examined for its educational implications.

The media of communication are expanding dramatically, potentially increasing the ways that language learners can access not only authentic forms of a language, but also native speakers of that language. Regardless of whether the reader agrees with those who believe that people are in a period of momentous historical change, teachers are faced with unprecedented student use of and easy familiarity with computers in their daily lives, both as sources of communication and entertainment and as everyday tools of the workplace. Several questions arise surrounding the shift to digital technologies:

- What are the implications for language education when instructors understand and use information technology differently than students do?

- What can instructors do to understand and use more effectively the tools of communication that may seem foreign to them, and to identify the pedagogical uses of these technologies?

- How might the instructors' authority in the classroom be affected by students' superior knowledge of information technology, or even by students' perception of their own superior knowledge?

- If instructors do not adapt to these new modes of communication through technology, what opportunities will they miss in teaching English?

The results of a study surveying student attitudes follow, as does an examination of the literature on faculty attitudes toward information technology. This chapter then suggests how the two groups may be brought together.

Externalizing Problems

Several studies examine teachers' use of classroom technology (e.g., Berge 1998; Britt 2000; Meskill et al. 2002). Similarly, others look at how particular technological tools are used or the discourse they elicit (e.g., Almeida d'Eça 2003c; Jepson 2005). Yet students have rarely been asked to discuss at length their experiences with and perceptions of classroom technology or their instructors' use of it.

To gain insight into student attitudes, I conducted a small ($n = 30$) study over the course of three years at a major public research university, asking students to elaborate in writing on their experiences, feelings, and ideas about information technology (IT). Student and faculty access to technology at the university can be classified as average: Internet and computer availability in labs, dorms, and classrooms; a free campus e-mail system; and Web hosting for instructionally related activities. Course management systems (CMSs) such as Blackboard (2005) and WebCT (2004; now merged with Blackboard), as well as a nascent university-developed CMS, are increasingly used in courses, although the specific tools that instructors use within the CMS vary greatly, as details of the study indicate (explained in more depth later). Webcasts are increasingly used in the larger lecture courses, although a few student respondents indicated that they wish webcasting were more widely used. Some courses are experimenting with personal-response systems that allow students to interact electronically during lectures, and with podcasting and RSS (really simple syndication) newsfeeds for course announcements and information, although these are by far the exception.

The purpose of this survey is not to prove a generational difference in attitudes toward technology or to get a sense of the majority of feelings about IT. In fact, given the rapid changes in information and communication technology, along with the increasing access to technology, any such study would quickly become outdated. However, the study gives a quick snapshot of the disparity between student and instructor attitudes toward technology and its potential to undermine classroom relations.

I offer the responses from thirty nonnative-English-speaking undergraduate students. They were all students in a first-semester composition course, although not all were first-semester students. (One was a third-year student; six were second-year students.) They were asked the following six questions and given twenty minutes to answer freely:

1. What kinds of technology have been used in your classes?
2. What aspects of technology use in class do you think you learn from most?
3. What difficulties do you face in using technology for your classes?
4. In general, do you think you know more about the Web than your professors do? (Consider all your instructors.)
5. What other uses of technology do you think would enhance your classes?
6. Other thoughts about classroom technology?

Students were encouraged to include any thoughts they had on the subject, even if they did not relate to a specific question. Since their answers about classroom technology were wide ranging and did not always directly address the questions, the responses are grouped under the varying themes that emerged from their answers. Their responses are compared to instructor experiences as reported in several published studies.

What Difficulties Do You Face in Using Technology for Your Classes?

Students typically reported few, if any, problems. They tended to externalize any problems they had—in other words, they perceived problems as intrinsic to the technology, not to themselves as users or learners. Students cited server problems, lost files, "buggy" programs, lost e-mails, outdated technology, long downloads, and slow connections as the major problems in dealing with technology at the university. Twenty-five percent of the students reported that they had no problems dealing with technology at all, and one student reported, "I have never had any ma[j]or problems with technology that could not be solved."

Only two students discussed problems with the substance or content of the technology—one referring to information overload and the difficulty of searching, the other referring to the speed with which instructors present Microsoft PowerPoint (2006) lectures (although this seems more an instructional problem than a technology problem). Again, however, the causes cited are external: there is too much information, and the professor goes too quickly.

Instructors, however, report in various studies that the problems they face are more intrinsic to their own knowledge and training. For example, in a study of French as a second language instructors, of 112 who do not use technology in their classrooms, 41 percent reported that the cause was inadequate training (Turnbull and Lawrence 2002). In a study with 28 university faculty, Marvin et al. (1999) report that faculty felt that "preparation time for technology greatly exceeds any time saved by technology" (p. 11) and "expressed anxieties regarding the use of technology in the classroom such as time required for training, conversion of current teaching materials to another medium, and the burden of being expected to use the technology properly" (p. 16).

In General, Do You Think You Know More about the Web than Your Professors Do? (Consider All Your Instructors.)

The majority (66 percent) of students surveyed said they knew more about technology and the Web than their instructors did. Responses included statements like "By far" and "In general, yes." However, many of these students were quick to qualify their statements by indicating that their instructors knew more in their own fields and did not spend as much time as students did using the Web for "leisure purposes." Of the students who did not think they knew more than their instructors, one pointed out that she was not "a computer person," but then added that she was not typical among her classmates. Another said she did not devote her "leisure time" to computers. Another stated that she knew "about the same amount, but for different purposes." These comments are representative of those made by students who indicated they knew the same or less about the Web than their instructors did.

These student perceptions reinforce Prensky's (2001) idea that facility with or *nativeness* to technology is associated with leisure time or total involvement with electronic media. Faculty often admit to knowing less than their students in this regard. As Price (2001) reports, "students are arriving at schools everywhere with technology skills that exceed those of their teachers. U.S. elementary principals tell of using students for technical support" (n.p.). This fact is reinforced by a multisite study of 1,144 students done for McGraw-Hill Ryerson, in which statistics show that "students perceive themselves as having a high ability for using the Internet" (Schönwetter and Francis 2002, 23). In the same study, students expressed concern about faculty's "lack of use of existing technology and/or poor management and utilization of technology" (p. 15). The lack of teacher technology skills, of course, has implications for the authority structure of the classroom, an issue I return to later in this chapter.

How Do Students and Teachers Describe Technology?

The students in my survey responded enthusiastically to the use of technology in their classes. In looking at the words used in their answers, very positive attitudes emerge. In fact, aside from the technical difficulties cited earlier, students had nothing negative to say about the use of IT in their courses. The following responses represent their opinions (emphasis mine):

- I think technology makes class **way more interesting** than classes that do not use it.
- Technology in my class **definitely** makes class **more interesting**.
- I think the increasing use of technology in classroom has a **very positive effect** on students.

- I think the use of technology helps students **decrease the stress**.
- I feel that I'm **very lucky** to use technology in learning English.
- Over all, I **love** to apply technology to learn English.
- Technology can help us to learn things in an **easier** way. It makes teaching and learning **more interesting**.
- The website makes the learning material **less boring, and more fun**, because the pretty pictures, text, and design will attract the reader to learn.
- Because formal English class is often boring and dry, but with technology, students tend to have **better participation** in class and thus makes the class to be **more fresh and lively**.
- Technology is **interesting** because we challenge ourselves to learn new things about it, while the speed makes technology **fun and practical** altogether.
- Technology provides both the **attractive** visual and oral materials that catches my attention and **increased my interests** in learning. In addition technology also **increased the efficiency** of the learning process.
- It's more **lively and interesting**.
- I **enjoy** doing in-class assignments . . . in computer labs.
- The use of technology **really improves** the way of **learning.**
- [Turning in essays and papers through the Internet is] **easier and efficient.**

A comparison of these responses to the language of instructors who do not use technology, or who are just beginning to learn how to use it, reveals a very different vocabulary:

- It was a **burden** to me to learn how to use the computer (Meskill et al. 2002, 48).
- Many [faculty] expressed concern that technology often **gets in the way** of the original learning objectives of a course (Marvin et al. 1999, 11).
- Some educators **fear** that an increase in the use of distance learning technologies may decrease the need for teachers (Muilenburg and Berge 2001, 21).
- Many instructors **don't know** about the medium **and don't want to know** (Berge 1998, ¶3 under Cultural Barriers).

The contrast between students' and teachers' attitudes about IT is stunning and, as I explain later, results in many unforeseen and usually unexamined consequences in the language classroom.

How Do Students and Teachers Most Often Use Technology?

Students see a variety of benefits in using information technology as a mode of communication in their courses, while instructors often disregard this use of technology or focus more on its potential to disseminate information. In particular, as the following student responses show, improvements in communication contribute to students' positive attitude toward technology use in an educational environment ("chatting" in these comments refers to text chats):

- Another technology that really impresses me is the use of in-class chatting function. We use it to discuss our reading assignments. I think this is a very revolutionary idea, which can help "shy" students to speak up. Even though some students have difficulties with typing, but I think the chatting feature really provides opportunities for fair discussions. I, for example, gained confidence to speak up in class orally after using the in-class chatting feature. This is probably because I learned how to express my ideas to other people without too much pressure by using the chatting feature.

- Using the Internet for class discussion is the part I like the most because I often don't like to speak in class; I'm just not used to speak in front of a crowd. But, by using the Internet for discussion, it makes me feel more comfortable; I often have more to say on the screen than facing other people, and I learn more during the discussion.

- In class discussion, some people have opinion, but maybe they are too shy, they think their idea would be stupid. They won't say their opinion out, because they think that it's embarrassed for them to say something in front of the class. But technology makes this possible and easier for people who are shy to express their opinion in their group.

- I feel more comfortable sharing my opinions in WebCT chat room rather than in class because I can always revise my "speech" before I published/said it.

- Students can be reluctant to ask question in class but they are not intimidated to ask questions via email.

- The internet is a great way to help increase student communication. It helps students organize and keep in touch with their professors.

- Being able to contact my classmates and instructors through emails, in my opinion, is one of the most convenient ways of communications.

In contrast, faculty are often more concerned with noninteractive content delivery and frequently do not use the interpersonal communication avenues offered to them by technology:

- The professor often says that please don't send him/her email; the best way to ask question is to come to his/her office hours. However, sometimes I could not come to their office hours because I have another . . . class at that time. (survey respondent)

- Most of the technology-based programs we are using are just to retrieve assignments and grades. (survey respondent)

- No PowerPoint through the whole lecture, please! (survey respondent)

- For those faculty who see technology as a barrier to teamwork and interaction, they see technology more as a tool for information dissemination than as a networking tool (Marvin et al. 1999, 20).

- According to Schönwetter and Francis (2002) roughly 85 percent of the student respondents report that their instructors do not use online communication activities such as online chat rooms or discussion lists (p. 18).

For students, the power of technology appears to lie mainly in its ability to facilitate and create flexibility in communications. This use should provide comfort to English language instructors. However, it is equally apparent that many instructors still see the power of technology as lying in its ability to deliver large amounts of information.

Control Issues

The issue of classroom authority is often cited as being at the root of some instructors' reluctance to introduce IT in their classrooms. University students' feelings of superiority in certain aspects of technology use may inhibit educators from structuring courses or curricula in ways that make the instructors appear to be less expert than the students they are teaching. As Marvin et al. (1999) report, "faculty feared a loss of control due to the use of technology in the classroom" (p. 18) and "teachers are afraid of being replaced by the computer" (p. 22).

Students, however, seem able to separate the different functions of technology and instruction, and the roles that technology and instructors play. Several survey respondents address this issue:

- Since the Internet contains so much information, sometimes it is hard for me to find the exactly information I want. Also, credibility is another issue because some web pages are more on personal opinion instead actual facts and I can't really tell. . . . Technology itself does not give opinions or personal thoughts. It is the professors who lead the students to the realm of reasoning and thinking.
- I prefer to have the professor lecture than go through a slide show because that is more distracting, trying to follow what he is saying and what he has posted.
- Having a class that uses the Internet every week has taught me many things, like how to research better and how to detect unreliable information.
- Don't get carried away with the technology, we may have invented the technology, but we're not it.

It is reassuring to find that students believe the proper role of teachers is to guide them through the content and processes, that is, how to reason and think or how to distinguish reliable information, rather than to be experts in technology.

Bringing the Two Worlds Together

The opinions presented in the previous sections, and others found in my survey as well as other researchers' surveys, are summarized in Table 11.1.

Is there a middle ground between the two extremes expressed in Table 11.1? Schönwetter and Francis (2002) report that roughly 85 percent of students surveyed indicate that their instructors need to increase the use of technology in the classroom. However, many instructors look at the burgeoning number of technological tools and products and do not have a

Table 11.1. Summary of Student and Instructor Opinions about Information Technology

Students	Non-IT-Using Faculty
Embrace and experiment with new technology	Find learning new "gadgets" to be a burden and time-consuming
Feel online discussion gives them confidence in class	Fear the loss of human interaction
Use technology for communication and information gathering	Use technology for information dissemination
Feel they need instructors to guide them through information	Feel overwhelmed by technology, or fear they will be replaced by computers
Are enthusiastic about "new" classroom methods and departures from "traditional classrooms"	Fear the loss of the "traditional" classroom structure and authority

clear idea where to start. Many universities offer training, but as Meskill et al. (2002) find, training does not usually include how to use technology in pedagogically appropriate ways: "It becomes clear that training may not be sufficient for the needed conceptual development that leads to the kind of ease and repertoire characteristic of expert users. Indeed, those novice teachers who had received 'state of the art' training in classroom technologies use were far less comfortable in their implementations than the more experienced teacher who had no formal training with computers but a great deal of classroom experience" (p. 54).

As Meskill et al. (2002) conclude, training programs at universities often focus solely on the *how* of a particular piece of educational software, rather than the larger question of *why* to incorporate it into the classroom at all.

In this section, I present goals for classroom teachers to help address student-instructor mismatch in technology use. The overarching principle is for teachers to engage students in the learning process while maintaining an important role as instructor and facilitator. These practices do not advocate learning specific software packages; instead, since the types of software used will change over the years, I refer only to broad classes of software. Further, these goals and strategies focus on the areas of need identified by the students themselves.

Goal: Improve Access and Communication

One vast difference between students' and instructors' use of technology is communication. Typically, departments still insist that faculty hold regular face-to-face office hours, in spite of the fact that they often end up underattended (except at exam time) because students have other commitments during the class day. By contrast, students complain of faculty who do not allow them to send e-mail or who do not answer e-mail in a timely fashion, in spite of the fact that "students who use telecommunications across different geographic locations are more motivated and learn more" (Faigley 1999, 138). At various training workshops I conduct, faculty often express fear that they will be overwhelmed by student e-mail if they allow it. The good news is that most instructors already use e-mail for personal purposes, so it is only a matter of finding strategies to make student e-mail manageable.

An alternative communications tool is instant messaging (IM), which can supplement or even replace actual office hours. I establish IM office hours, which occur at specific times during the week—times when students are more likely to be available, such as evening hours—when they know I will be online to take questions or discuss classroom issues. All that is required is an Internet connection, IM software (which is freely available), and keyboarding skills. A wide variety of IM software supports audio and video communication, so IM office hours can incorporate a voice and a face given sufficient student and instructor access to appropriate technology resources.

Another option is the incorporation of an online class bulletin board (BB) as a central place for students to pose and answer questions. Using a BB (also called a message board or forum) has the advantage of creating an archive of questions and answers, or discussion topics. Several packages of course management software (e.g., Blackboard, Moodle) incorporate BBs into their larger system, and many commercial, free, or open-source BBs are available. Some can be installed on a local server to ensure total privacy and security for students. See Action Plan 1 for this goal.

The choice of software tools for improving communication is less important than establishing a goal for increasing interaction between students and instructors and among students themselves, as well as a plan to achieve this goal.

Action Plan 1: Improve Access and Communication

- Establish a set of guidelines that lay out for students the parameters of e-mail communication for the class.
- Determine what types of e-mail messages are acceptable. Let students know whether you will answer questions about grades, offer study tips, review material, and so forth.
- State the time frame within which you will generally answer.
- Learn how your e-mail filters or rules work so that student e-mail can be filtered into a mailbox or folder of its own. This allows you to separate it from your other e-mail and deal with it according to your guidelines.
- Follow the academic literature on e-mail's best uses in the English language classroom. Books such as *E-Mail for English Teaching* (Warschauer 1995) or *Managing Your E-Mail* (Cavanagh 2003) are good starting points.
- Download and experiment with IM software. Ask your students which IM services they use.
- Ask what course management software your school has a license to, and find out if you can access it. Examine the BB feature and think about how it could be used.
- If course management software is not available to you, ask knowledgeable colleagues about free or open-source BB software that you could use for your class.

Goal: Improve Students' Abilities to Evaluate Materials

As indicated earlier by one of the survey respondents, instructors fill an important need in teaching students to identify and critique sources of information. Learners and instructors are both faced with an enormous amount of resources. Students spend more time online and less time in the library (Schönwetter and Francis 2002), and thus may feel like they are lost in a jungle of information without a compass when searching for online information. Action Plan 2 speaks to this goal.

Goal: Create More Variety in the Classroom

While some instructors fear losing traditional methods of teaching, students are motivated by new approaches. Fortunately, IT allows the possibility of broadening the scope and number of classroom activities, without abandoning tried-and-true practices. As Godwin-Jones (2005) points out, "if the millennial generation is increasingly drawn to the digital third spaces [that is, not the physical 'first space' that is home or the 'second spaces' that are school or work], it behooves us as language educators to do as we have done in the past, use technologies and tools intended for other uses, to create richer opportunities for language learning" (p. 20). Action Plan 3 targets this goal.

Goal: Embrace the New, Don't Fear It

Unfortunately, fear seems to be a prevalent theme throughout the research on instructor attitudes toward incorporating IT pedagogically. Every day, students in ESOL classrooms

---

Action Plan 2: Improve Students' Abilities to Evaluate Materials

- Learn which search engines are currently most popular with students, and conduct sample searches on topics taught in your class. Examine the results, and share them with students.
- Find out which search engines have *sponsored results* (i.e., results based on advertising revenue), and alert students to this feature.
- Discuss issues of authorship and reliability with students.
- Establish or locate a rubric for evaluating Internet information to share with students.
- Teach students the proper way to quote and cite Internet materials.
- Talk to your librarian or resource person about digital collections held at your institution, such as online catalogs, indices, or databases. Learn how to access these and what purpose they might serve in your course.
- If your library offers workshops on how to use the library or online resources, set one up for yourself and/or your students.
- Type "evaluating Internet resources" into a search engine, and investigate several of the results.

Action Plan 3: Create More Variety in the Classroom

- Survey students about the technology they use. Ask them for ideas about how these technologies help them or might help them learn English.
- Organize a faculty meeting or seminar to encourage faculty members to share best practices with each other.
- Create a written inventory of the tasks and techniques you use in your courses. Identify any that might successfully incorporate IT.
- Keep in mind the following guideline from the (U.S.) National Research Council (2002): "To be truly effective, information technology needs to be *embedded* in instruction, not just provided as an additional activity to a standard course or program" (p. 37).

are asked to overcome their own fears in fulfilling the complex task of learning a new language. Instructors can meet them halfway in this task by learning the students' language as well—not just their first language, but the language of technology that they use daily. Again, the incorporation of IT does not mean that an instructor must begin by learning complex software systems. As one student survey respondent says, "one of the uses of technology that I think would enhance the class is to use better technology, and what I mean by 'better' is that it doesn't necessarily have to be some very powerful and expensive technologies but rather ones that most people are familiar with and are most widely used." See Action Plan 4 for this goal.

Challenges and Future Directions

I return to one of the questions I asked at the beginning of this chapter: if instructors do not adapt to these new modes of communication through technology, what opportunities will they miss in teaching English?

Action Plan 4: Embrace the New, Don't Fear It

- Assign students to present or demonstrate some aspect of technology that they use in their everyday lives.
- Attend a conference presentation or workshop on a technology-related topic.
- Adjust your attitude. Monitor yourself for statements like "I'm not a computer person" or "I can't deal with technology."
- Do not delegate technology tasks, such as setting up a VCR or data projector, to your students. Learn to do it yourself, and refuse to be frustrated by your own slowness or failure to do it perfectly. As one survey respondent says, "know how to use your own classroom technology."

Reviewing some of the vocabulary that students use in describing their interactions with IT, I recall the words *fun, interesting, positive, easier, practical, fresh, less boring*, and *attractive*. In other words, students appear to be highly motivated by the technology. Instructors cannot dismiss this motivation as merely attraction to new fads—after all, for most students now entering the university, these are not new technologies. Many of today's eighteen-year-olds have been using the Internet and playing sophisticated computer games for a good portion of their lives. Instructors need to entertain the idea that, as Prensky (2001) claims, "today's students *think and process information fundamentally differently* from their predecessors. These differences go far further and deeper than most educators suspect or realize" (p. 1). Thinking about information and communication differently should have a profound effect on the way teachers conceive of presenting and discussing information in and out of the classroom.

What happens to education when teachers fail to tap their students' motivation and excitement and fail to use today's tools of communication to further the goal of successful language learning? The answer to this question should by now be evident: teachers miss an opportunity to garner intrinsic learner interest by insisting that the "old ways are best" or that this is merely a passing fad. They lose, rather than gain, authority in their own classrooms by appearing ignorant of major social and cultural changes happening around them. Teachers become irrelevant to the English language learning process because they are no longer speaking the same language as their students.

Not surprisingly, students are not alone in expressing concerns about their instructors' lack of technological expertise and experience. More technologically oriented instructors, often new practitioners in the field of ESOL, also express their frustration. Berge (1998) describes the situation as "creating a serious culture gap, and computer-literate faculty must now proselytize their colleagues even as they try to become more familiar with the requirements of the medium. If we don't make more converts, it's going to be even harder to deal with the changing technology: we'll be a minority perennially at odds with the majority, and we'll be too few to share the workload of keeping up with improved technology, adapting curriculum, etc." (¶3 under Cultural Barriers).

As a final note, I present some students' opinions about the future direction they see for educational technology:

- Maybe one day, all homework are submitted online and I don't have to submit messy handwritten assignments anymore (regardless of the fact that I do enjoy imagining my [TAs] trying to decipher my writing with frustration).

- All classes should be webcasted. I'm not saying that for the sake of skipping classes, but I think it would be much easier to go back to something the instructor have said in class if the sessions are recorded.

- Have class notes posted on line before lecture.

- Webcast is a good reviewing tool, also to catch things that you missed in class.

These dreams are all technologically possible today. It is up to the educational infrastructure, as well as individual instructors, to put these dreams into action, and create an educational future that continues to excite and motivate students.

Section II
Questions and Activities

Questions for Discussion

1. Kennedy (chapter 7) describes the GLOBE program for primary and secondary school science education, which is supported by NASA and other government agencies. Can the GLOBE program Web site activities and worksheets be modified to suit your student population? How would you integrate science and math skills with language learning goals for your learners?

2. When is the next GLOBE workshop available in your part of the world? If you already have a GLOBE site at or near your educational institution, how can your learners become involved? What language skills are needed to participate successfully in GLOBE? What preparation will students need in order to undertake activities such as data gathering and database input, especially with small groups working together? How can you foster collaborative interactions in such project work, both face-to-face and online with international partners?

3. Susser (chapter 8) uses a variety of online resources in teaching content-based language in a tourism course in Japan, allowing students to judge and negotiate the process of gathering information through Internet resources. Citing Meskill, Mossop, and Bates (1999, 5), he describes anarchy, publicness, instability, malleability, democratization, and anchored referents as aspects of student-centeredness. How do various aspects of your classroom instruction fit one or more of these ideals? How does or would computer use affect these aspects of your teaching and learning?

4. Gromik (chapter 9) describes video tools that can be used with varying degrees of technological know-how. What video tools do you use in your daily life? How would you envision using these with your learners? How much preparation will your students need, that is, how familiar are your students with video or photo editing already, and how much support will you need to provide to help them produce and edit their own digitized videos? What might drive the content of the videos your learners produce?

5. Rilling (chapter 10) describes using an online writing lab to support second language learners with their academic writing in various disciplines at a university. What practices do you use to support your learners' writing? How have you moved, or would you move, these practices online?

6. How do you use computer-mediated communications (CMC; e.g., e-mail, chat) for your own purposes? How might learners be effectively engaged in CMC for language practice? What language skills can be supported through interactive online discussions? Describe your practices or goals to your peers, and discuss their pedagogical appropriateness. Are there ways you might expand on the use of CMC for language learning?

7. Sokolik (chapter 11) describes learners' frustrations with their instructors' lack of skill in using technology. How can you assess what your learners already know about technology? How can you make use of their knowledge of technology to enhance their language skills? Can your learners assist you in improving your own skills, or can they assist each other? How can you support ongoing technological curiosity and expertise in yourself and your learners? As professionals, what type of support do teachers need, and how can they obtain it?

Activities for Further Study

1. After exploring the teachers' guides at the GLOBE Web site, search for other educational materials online (e.g., learning resources to supplement news magazines). What ideas and materials can you transfer to your own content-based language teaching context?

2. What human resources are available to support a GLOBE project near you? Are there community volunteers or graduate students performing community service who can assist you in the establishment of and follow-through with such a project? For example, a local senior citizens' group or retired faculty from a regional university might have the resources and expertise to undertake a volunteer program with students. Explore online potential local resources, such as the Tutor/Mentor Connection (Cabrini Connections 2000) in Chicago.

3. What content do you teach in your ESOL courses? Identify and explore several useful Web sites with authentic interactive possibilities that are focused on that content area. Are networks of professionals available online to support you in developing content and language in this area? Who? Add these resources to your Filamentality (2006) or WebWizard (n.d.) page, as suggested in Section I, Activity 4.

4. Explore content-based videos and support materials at such sites as the Discovery Channel's educational page, DiscoverySchool.com (2005), or its Global Education Partnership site (2006). How might you use these resources with your learners? Using Hot Potatoes (Arneil and Holmes 2005) software, develop some support materials tailored to your learners.

5. Spend time teaching your learners how to use the electronic search features of your institution's library or the local public library. What useful resources can they access? What search features must you teach in order to help your students limit their searches to relevant resources? Have your learners explore some of the advanced search features of common Web search engines such as Google (2006a), AltaVista (Overture Services 2006), or Ask.com (IAC Search & Media 2006a). (The Google Help Center [2005] has a good Web page to help students interpret search results.) Demonstrate how advanced search strategies can limit the number of hits that the learner will have to sort through, both in the electronic library and on the Internet. Work with learners to evaluate the reliability and relevance of the materials they locate.

6. Join the teachers using online videos for language instruction at the user's group Video & Editing 4 ESOL (Gromik 2006). Ask about ideas for using or creating video with your learners. If possible, participate in a free six-week session on video creation and editing provided by the TESOL CALL Interest Section's Electronic Village Online (announced every December at the CALL IS Web page [2005]).

7. After viewing some of the models suggested by Gromik (chapter 9), have your learners create a video. In the planning stages, ask them to prepare storyboards using a drawing program or the graphics program in, for example, Microsoft PowerPoint (2006). Through the storyboards (as Gromik explains), students must visualize what will happen in each segment of the film and write a short description of it. Have students use and improve the storyboards during the production of the film. Have learners compile a portfolio including the storyboards, their scripts, and a written description of their filming and editing processes. If possible, load the completed videos onto your institution's Web site or to a videoblog (vlog) such as Ourmedia (n.d.). (For examples of what students can accomplish, see ESOL Video Stories [South Birmingham College n.d.] for adult students or iMovie Examples for K–12 [Springfield Public School District 186 n.d.].)

8. Have learners explore specific countries' Web sites to learn more about their own or a partner's home culture; or for science education, they can explore the Web site of a national park or wildlife refuge. They may find useful links through commercial travel sites, such as Expedia (2006) or Travelocity (1996–2006; mentioned by Susser in chapter 8). For younger learners, you may wish to control more closely the content and sites they visit by using a WebQuest format (see QuestGarden [Dodge n.d.] for directions and an interactive template). Have the learners prepare to talk formally or informally about their choices and findings, or have them write about and share their projects with other classes in an online exchange such as the Email Projects Home Page (Gaer 2005).

9. For learners who are highly computer literate, ask groups to complete a show-and-tell of technologies that they use in their daily lives. One group of students could, for example, explain how cell phones can be used to send text messages, photos, or video, while another group could explain some of the abbreviations and acronyms used in text messaging. Alternatively, learners can explore the Web for amazing inventions (such as tools from Fab Central at MIT's Center for Bits and Atoms [2006]), which could be the basis for reports.

10. In less technologically developed areas, learners can be involved in activities that ask them to write or talk about the technologies they use in daily life (e.g., television, movies, video or hand-held games, telephones). Have them predict what kinds of technologies they might use commonly in the future.

Web Sites and Software in Section II Questions and Activities

AltaVista	http://www.altavista.com/
Ask.com	http://www.ask.com/
Discovery Channel Global Education Partnership	http://www.discoveryglobaled.org/
DiscoverySchool.com	http://school.discovery.com/
Electronic Village Online	http://darkwing.uoregon.edu/~call/
Email Projects Home Page	http://www.otan.dni.us/webfarm/emailproject/email.htm
ESOL Video Stories	http://www.sbirmc.ac.uk/all/all_showcase.htm
Expedia	http://www.expedia.com/
Massachusetts Institute of Technology Center for Bits and Atoms	http://fab.cba.mit.edu/
Filamentality	http://www.filamentality.org/wired/fil/
GLOBE Program	http://www.globe.gov/
Google	http://www.google.com/
Google Help Center: Search Results Page	http://www.google.com/help/interpret.html
Hot Potatoes	http://hotpot.uvic.ca/
iMovie Examples	http://www.springfield.k12.il.us/movie/
Microsoft PowerPoint	http://office.microsoft.com/powerpoint/
Ourmedia	http://www.ourmedia.org/

QuestGarden	http://webquest.org/questgarden/author/
TESOL CALL Interest Section Web page	http://darkwing.uoregon.edu/~call/
Travelocity	http://www.travelocity.com/
Tutor/Mentor Connection	http://msg.uc.iupui.edu/TMC/html/index.php
Video & Editing 4 ESOL	http://groups.yahoo.com/group/video_editing4esol/
The WebWizard	http://www.the-webwizard.co.uk/

Section III

Authentic Audience in a Web-Based World

This section describes how technology is used in several different school settings, either through blended (on- and off-campus) or wholly online courses. As learning increasingly takes place outside the walls of a school, teachers must reduce isolation by promoting interconnections among students and between students and their communities, as suggested by Jewell (chapter 13). Trites (chapter 15) explores the significance of interactions between students and teachers as the classroom opens to the world. The technologies spotlighted in this section range from the conventional word-processor (Jewell, chapter 13) and computer-assisted language learning exercises, to Weblogs and Web pages (Almeida d'Eça, chapter 12; Stanley, chapter 14). As elsewhere in this volume, the authors agree that one of the most important uses of technology is to foster social interactivity that is both emotionally rewarding and educationally inspiring. The issue that Trites (chapter 15) raises is not whether courses will go online, but rather, whether online courses will follow what she calls the "nouveau-correspondence model" or instead generate their own new interactive dynamics.

Chapter 12

First Steps in Experimenting with Computers

Teresa Almeida d'Eça
Escola de Santo António
Parede, Portugal

Preview

Authentic audiences of native speakers and other language learners provide a motivating resource for even the youngest students. Almeida d'Eça takes the reader step by step through her explorations with youngsters learning with and through technology in a blended environment. As her knowledge of technology grows, so do her expectations of what her students can accomplish and how much she can attempt with her classes. Her curricular projects for students in fifth through ninth grades demonstrate how individual and class e-mail exchanges, Weblogs (blogs), and voice messaging provide exciting enhancements to the EFL curriculum.

Before you read:

- Have you ever experienced computers with young learners? How?
- When and how should computer technologies be integrated into childhood education?
- How can a teacher find international collaborators for e-mail, voice, or other exchanges?

Entering the World of NetLearning

One of the long-term problems to overcome when teaching a foreign language is motivation. Abstract goals, such as "everyone will need a foreign language when they grow up" or "English is spoken all over the world" may not be successful with youngsters, particularly in competition with immediate gratifications—such as television, video games, or sports—because children do not see immediate effects or gains. The use of information and communications technologies (ICTs) may begin as a result of extrinsic motivation or curiosity about the new technology but, based on my experience, quickly leads to intrinsic motivation: the desire to communicate with others around the world. The possibility of anytime, anywhere contact between peers in distant parts of the world is fascinating. And so is the idea of bringing down the four walls of the classroom and its inherent constraints. ICTs supply a whole new atmosphere—the beginning of some fresh air in education.

While there has been some evidence that computers used unwisely in the early years can be a distraction and hindrance to academic achievement (see MacDonald 2004), many educators believe that computers and the Internet are crucial for success in school and in life. For a teacher new to ICTs, e-mail exchanges can be a good beginning; many publications describe e-mail projects over the Internet (see, e.g., Warschauer, Shetzer, and Meloni 2000). When I first began studying online exchanges, I drew on Serim and Koch's (1996) idea of the Internet as just a tool, but one that can help the teacher create an effective learning environment in undertaking what they call *NetLearning*: "using the Internet in education . . . to transform today's classrooms into global learning environments" (p. 4).

This chapter delineates a gradual progression from e-mail exchanges to full curricular components in *blended* (online and face-to-face) learning environments for young foreign language learners. Teachers attempting to begin using ICTs with young students may find that this type of step-by-step approach allows teachers and students alike to develop experience and confidence as they harness the power of the Internet for language learning.

E-mail Exchanges

Start small. That is the golden rule I learned from Serim and Koch (1996). My first e-mail exchange was carried out between seven of my sixth graders (eleven to twelve years old) in Lisbon, Portugal, and six fifth graders (ten to eleven years old) in Navarre, Florida, in the United States (Almeida d'Eça 1998). Both groups attended public schools. The U.S. class had a couple of gifted students, which I believed would be an added value. In my Portuguese class, I chose a mixed-ability group of students to participate in the exchange: two A students, three B students, and two C students. I expected the better ones to motivate the weaker ones, which they did. I met with the group and explained that it was my first time ever on such a venture, so they were going to be my guinea pigs. In addition, the project had to be extracurricular, during afterschool hours, since I was working with only part of a class. Nonetheless, the students agreed, in part, I believe, because they felt very proud to be invited to join a pioneering project in our school.

A U.S. colleague put me in e-mail contact with my e-partner-to-be, Glenn Rutland (to read more about Glenn's innovative work, see WGBH Educational Foundation 2006b). She immediately felt enthusiastic about embracing a project to create a social and cultural e-mail exchange. I sent her an outline of a possible project, and since I recognized the pedagogical value of negotiating the exchange with the students, as suggested by Serim and Koch (1996), I proposed the plan for the students' approval. I was open to criticism, suggestions for change, or a simple refusal, but the students enthusiastically accepted the project.

As my students were in only their second year of English, Glenn chose a small group of native-English-speaking fifth graders for her side of the exchange so there would be more similarities in the students' grasp of the language. We decided on two sessions a week on my side of the Atlantic: one for students to think about and write a message on paper (they were not required to prepare anything in advance) and the other to type the message into the computer and send it. Glenn's students met only once a week on the project during their normal class time—the benefit of being native speakers and having technology at hand.

Each group was to write about a topic every other week, replying to their peers' messages. There were four items to deal with: personal introductions, descriptions of the school, descriptions of the student population, and descriptions of the surrounding community. At the end of the eleven-week project, students would reflect on similarities and differences between the two contexts and draw conclusions.

On the Portuguese side, we had access to only one multimedia computer with Internet access and e-mail. However, we soon found that our Internet access at school was limited, so students wrote to a word-processor file and copied the messages to a floppy disk for me to send from my computer at home. Despite the technological limitations, my students carried out the exchange enthusiastically. I was amazed and pleasantly surprised to see them commit so much of their afterschool time with such interest and responsibility. For some, this was their first contact with foreign peers, and for a couple of them, it was their first experience with computers and the Internet. To their amazement, they concluded that young people from two distant continents could have common interests and hobbies.

Both Glenn and I committed ourselves wholeheartedly to the project and helped students keep to the plan and deadlines so that the exchange could run smoothly. We both got along very well, a significant factor in this type of project, since it can make the difference between a success and a flop. Not least of all, we became good friends.

Starting with a small group provides a better opportunity to get the feel of things, to learn by doing, to gain experience at an adequate and controllable pace, and to make timely and necessary adjustments without major disturbance or confusion. In addition, if the first project is extracurricular and modest in its goals, it reduces the stress of possible logistical and technological failures now and then.

Curricular Projects by E-mail

After the success of the small-scale project, I felt I should give other students the same type of opportunity. In the second project, Glenn involved an entire sixth-grade class of twenty-five students (eleven to twelve years old), and I attempted a curricular project within the normal school day, though at times students needed some afterschool time.

The subject for exchange again was cultural: family traditions, including traditional family recipes, and cross-generational interviews. (For an example of the kinds of activities that were carried out, see Almeida d'Eça 1999.) Both classes (one in Portugal, the other in Florida) were divided into groups, each one dealing with a specific part of the project. Some students researched typical family recipes; others translated the recipes or interviewed parents and grandparents about family traditions. We gave specific instructions regarding the layout of recipes, and we discussed references to vocabulary and sentence constructions in class. Because it was important to keep to the schedule, a sense of responsibility regarding both the in- and out-of-class tasks was imperative. In addition to the content, my students' desire to do everything right—after all, the project was going to be published on the Internet for anyone to see!—struck me as very special. The following is some practical advice on building such a project.

Practical Advice on Creating a Curricular Exchange Project

Planning

- Jot down all ideas—brainstorm projects.
- Plan a curriculum-based project; it offers more apparent usefulness and involves students more in the learning process.
- Structure objectives, tasks, and expected outcomes very clearly.
- Define ages, grade levels, knowledge level, and number of students involved.
- Set beginning and finishing dates, as well as deadlines for tasks or phases within the project.
- Find a partner you relate to, discuss the project thoroughly, and be open to suggestions.

Execution

- Discuss the outline with your students (if possible, plan the project with them).
- Write a clear and concise call for collaboration.
- Be quick to answer requests for explanations.
- Start by breaking the ice—let students introduce themselves and talk about their hobbies, interests, and so forth, in order to get to know each other and discover things in common.
- Stimulate genuine personal contributions from your students.
- Be flexible about content—the unexpected may be enriching.
- Keep a record or log of everything.

Beyond the Project

- Share the end product with everyone involved and, if possible, with a wider audience—the school, the parents, the community, the Web.
- Send thank-you messages to everyone!

A special, though unrelated event took place during this project: the U.S. students took a field trip to the NASA Space Center. The vivid descriptions of their daily experiences, including the science fiction–like lodgings and the live launch of John Glenn's second mission in space, were very exciting for everyone. This event was not on our agenda, but *flexibility* is a principle to bear in mind at all times in all things related to education, especially in the wide-open world of ICT. Teachers need to be able to take advantage of unique events and incorporate them into the curricular exchange, even if they do not at first seem directly related. Writing and reading about such experiences help motivate students to develop and expand on curricular concepts, express emotions in a foreign language, and apply critical thinking skills.

This second exchange was more demanding of all the human resources involved on the Portuguese side. Classes were exhausting for both teachers and students, with individual groups working simultaneously and students frequently asking for guidance. Afterschool time was needed to keep everything on track. However, despite the workload, there were always rotating volunteers, and no one ever complained. Unlike the first project, this one was assessed as group work. An unexpected reward came a year later when the students and teachers involved saw the project published in *Internet for English Teaching* (Warschauer, Shetzer, and Meloni 2000).

The third and last e-mail exchange was carried out in 2000 between a seventh-grade class (twelve to thirteen years old) in my school and adult students in a private language school in Brazil. It was my way of taking part in the celebrations of the five-hundred-year anniversary of the discovery of Brazil by the Portuguese (see Almeida d'Eça 2000). This time the aim was to compare certain aspects of both cultures sharing the Portuguese language, arrive at similarities and differences, and conclude whether there was indeed a common culture. This exchange had its ups and downs. A more or less floating group of students on the Brazilian side made it difficult to maintain specific pairs of corresponding students over the entire project, and my students were initially uncomfortable with the older range of ages of the Brazilians, though they eventually found the differences to be interesting. The more hands-on experience I gained and the more I probed other e-mail exchanges—such as Kids as Global Scientists (Best and Peek-Brown n.d.) for middle school students; The Official Flat Stanley Project (Hubert n.d.), an international literacy activity for primary and junior students; The Image of the Other (Savli 2006), a European multilanguage school exchange; and the Email Projects Home Page for adults (Gaer 2005)—the more I became convinced that it was a means of communication that could be used for many projects across the curriculum.

Experimenting with New Approaches

After taking my first exclusively online teacher education course, Krauss's (1998–2005) Integrating the Internet into the Classroom, I felt confident in applying a new range of Internet features in my classes. During the course, I prepared three different tailor-made computer-assisted language learning (CALL) activities for my ninth-grade students (fourteen to fifteen years old, fifth-year EFL). Visiting Kenya (Almeida d'Eça 2001b) is a subject sampler created with Filamentality (2006), fill-in-the-blank software on the Internet that guides users through the process of selecting a topic, searching the Web for good links, and turning them into learning activities. New York City (Almeida d'Eça 2001a) is a scenario, a format that poses a question or explores a problem to be solved through Web research. Finally, to celebrate the launch of the euro in Portugal, I created a task-based project, The Euro Is Here to Stay (Almeida d'Eça 2004a), with curriculum-based exercises and quizzes using Quia Web (Quia 1998–2006), education-oriented software.

Shortly after my experience in Krauss's course, I joined an online community of practice called Webheads in Action (WiA; Stevens 2006b; see also Stevens, chapter 19 in this volume), which provides significant online emotional, professional, and technological support for the blended teaching endeavors of its members. Through WiA, I collaborate with colleagues by chatting in voice, text, and video; plan common projects; explore new technology tools; and receive almost instant answers, suggestions, and help. I strongly recommend that teachers who are considering blended teaching join an online group both for training and ongoing peer support (see Rovai and Jordan 2004; Stevens, chapter 19 in this volume).

Let's Blog! Third-Year EFL

Computer-mediated communication can assume many forms beyond e-mail, such as voice mail, electronic lists and bulletin boards, discussion forums, text and voice chat, instant messaging, and blogs, which allow for easily updated commenting. I decided to try blogs with my third-year EFL students after reading Campbell's (2003) "Weblogs for Use with ESL Classes." He considers three ways that blogs can be put to immediate use with ESOL classes: the tutor blog, the student blog, and the class blog. I called my creation a *teacher-student blog*.

The interactivity made possible by inserting comments directly at a specific blog entry attracted me at once because it created a dynamic bi- or multidirectional means of *threaded communication*, a feature lacking in the usual online bulletin board or Web page. At present, in addition to text, comments, and links, blogs can also include audio files (audioblog), photos (photoblog) and slide shows with text, video clips (videoblog), and mobile communications (moblog). Having evolved from online personal journals to multimedia pages about anything and everything, blogs are extremely popular in almost any field (see Stanley, chapter 14 in this volume).

Starting a blog meant that I could have a two-way channel permanently open with my students, convenient to either end of the communication. It provided many benefits. Students could practice English in an authentic way, whenever they felt like it, beyond the four walls of the classroom and outside of school. They could discuss any topic, suggest activities, post clickable links to Web pages, and have an archived record of their progress in English and discoveries on the Internet. Since most of the messages were posted from home in their free time, students could be themselves, free of the constraints of the curriculum and free to write about what interested and pleased them. They would have someone to answer their messages and try to keep the conversation going. They would have a broad audience; anyone could click and send in a comment.

However, because they were young learners, I wanted to safeguard them from exposure to possible undesirable content published instantly at the click of the mouse. So as an initial experiment I decided against using a blog provider. Instead, I used readily available, easy-to-manage Web-editing software to create my own simulated blog called Let's Blog! (Almeida d'Eça 2004b). I used a simple but attractive format, with my own personal touch (see Figure 12.1).

I knew a homemade blog meant more work for me, because I would be responsible for replying to every message (I made a pledge to do that because otherwise there would be no sense in using this new means of communication), updating the blog Web page whenever students posted new comments, and inserting new content and links regularly. For anyone considering creating a blog for the first time, it is worth considering using a blog provider, especially one created specifically for educational settings, such as KidzBlog (2005; it can be run offline on a local computer or published on the Internet through file transfer protocol [FTP]), and setting the features to allow only class members to participate.

I carried out my blog experiment with seventh graders in their third year of EFL. As soon as the Let's Blog! Web page was ready, I talked about it in class, explained my objectives, and gave the students the Web address. Then I waited for the first messages to flow in. As an enticement, I included a simple contest to decipher the welcome message at the top left of the page (see Figure 12.1). The winner would be awarded a prize in class.

To my surprise, the students showed little interest in this project, and the lack of involvement disappointed me. The reason was not lack of access, because those with no computers or Internet access at home could use computers at school. I never found a

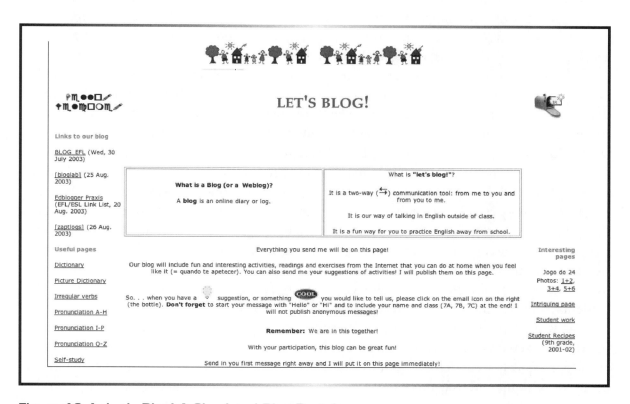

Figure 12.1. Let's Blog! A Simulated Blog Portal
Source: http://64.71.48.37/teresadeca/school/blog7.htm.

satisfactory explanation for the students' inactivity; however, I did not give up. *Persistence* is another attribute needed in online (and offline) teaching. Eventually I found that placing an assignment on the blog with no class explanation forced students to go to the site to find out what to do. During the summer vacation, I received a few additional messages. However, once the face-to-face contact was lost, it was very difficult to maintain students' interest in the project. The experience led me to believe that, for students to get involved in a blog, they needed both an authentic reason to participate and some face-to-face incentive.

Have Fun with English! First-Year EFL

In the 2003–04 school year, I had two fifth-grade classes (ten to eleven years old) studying English for the first time. Would blogging work with beginners? After getting a feel for both groups during the first half of the term, I risked a very elementary blog called Have Fun with English! (Almeida d'Eça 2003b), using the same simulated blog template as Let's Blog! (see Figure 12.1). I explained the idea in class and had students write the Web address in their notebooks. Although only 40 percent of them had Internet access at home, they could use several computers during breaks and lunch hour at school. However, there was no e-mail access for them (an unfortunate but frequent problem in school settings), so I came up with a practical, if not high-tech, solution: I took a screenshot of an e-mail window, pasted it into a text file, and gave photocopies of the page to students who wanted to send me messages. At the following lesson, they would hand in their messages, written in English. I would copy the content to the blog and reply to it. It was the next best thing to real e-mail and solved the problem of lack of technology. *Inventiveness* is important in using technology to avoid lost opportunities that may lead to indefinite postponements and the possible failure of a project. The idea is to keep the spark going at all times.

Naturally, the student messages at this age and grade level were short and simple, and had spelling, linguistic, and structural mistakes. But it was obvious from the start that students practiced what they learned in the classroom, as they used expressions from class and from each other's writings. Some students wanted to go much beyond their actual linguistic level, asking me to translate sentences from Portuguese, but I discouraged that type of writing. I advised them to think of simple sentences in English, based on what they had already learned. I wanted their messages to be authentic personal communications and to reveal exactly what they could do with language at a communicative level, not what I could do for them. I never corrected mistakes before posting a message unless the content was unintelligible or could generate misunderstanding. In my replies, I sometimes modeled subtle corrections (a form of scaffolding) and used simple language, although usually (as recommended by Krashen's Natural Approach) I went a step or two further to demand a little more of the students' comprehension skills (the $i + 1$ model; Krashen 1982).

As with the earlier Let's Blog!, I regularly introduced new content, such as custom-made interactive exercises and various links: Christmas games and activities, Carnival pages, or any other topical or curricular event (for examples, see Almeida d'Eça 2003b). I also created pages for relevant and well-presented student work done in class or at home. The tips on the following page describe how to get blogging started and how to promote student writing and involvement in projects.

Tips to Promote Blogging

- Talk about the blog activity in advance, and explain your objectives to students.
- Set aside a time for composing messages, either in class or in lab periods.
- Grade only when the assignment is a curricular activity done by all students.
- Include good content, lesson assignments, minicontests, and other tidbits to entice students to read and write.

When using Internet software or commercial providers:

- Choose a provider that targets educational uses, such as KidzBlog (2005) or Dekita.org (Ammann, Campbell, and Dieu n.d.a).
- Set the comment features to allow only your class members and invited guests to participate.
- Remind students never to give the password to another person.

Beyond Blogging

Voice Mail

A very pleasant surprise happened a few weeks after the blog experiment began: two Polish boys joined our group. When I was comoderating an online course, a Polish colleague asked if her ten-year-old nephew could participate with my young students. Her seven-year-old son also asked to join the fun when he read the first welcome message from the Portuguese children and understood it. As if this were not excitement enough, both my classes became galvanized when the Polish children sent their first voice mail. My students had no idea what was in store for them when I opened my laptop in class that morning. *Communication* is another concept to keep in mind when planning online lessons. Authentic communication with peers—particularly with the exciting new, and generally free, technologies available—is one of the most motivating aspects of online learning. My students' enthusiasm for the project gradually increased as they created their own voice mails with free HandyBits (2005) software and saw their work shared online—and so did their excitement for computers in the English class when they read and heard messages from peers at a distance.

Structured CALL Lessons

A month later, in an effort to have all students experience learning through technology as well as to build on the wave of student enthusiasm inspired by blogging and voice mail, I progressed to more structured CALL lessons (see, e.g., Almeida d'Eça 2003a). My experiences and conversations with other online teachers had convinced me that using the computer would give my students additional practice in language, as well as motivate them through the novelty of using technology. I had twenty-eight children in each class, but only six computers. Controlling part of the class at the computers while the others were at their desks would have been a difficult task. Luckily, I shared the targeted classes with a colleague during a joint study hour, so I proposed a plan whereby I would take some students to the computers for pair work (two students per computer), while my colleague would supervise the rest of the students in the study hall. *Improvisation* and *collaboration* were at work.

I started with a demonstration lesson to give students an idea of what they would be doing. For some, it was their first contact with a computer and the Internet. Their enthusiasm was such that I immediately decided to offer computerized practice every two weeks instead of every three, as originally planned. Even so, after the first lessons, some students wanted lessons every week, saying that it was fun (no doubt more so than the ordinary study hour) and they were learning.

I planned a different activity for each CALL session, always starting with simple and clear instructions in English. During the first several lessons, I helped with the language (even explaining things in Portuguese when necessary) and guided the students who were new to computers with software navigation, keyboarding, and using the mouse. Then I stepped back as the students went to work. I observed them and took note of what they did, how they worked in pairs, and how they got along. I was always there for guidance, either with the computer or with the lesson content. It was interesting to see the amount of mutual help that went on, but even more interesting to see how motivated, involved, and well behaved the students were in general. I evaluated them on a qualitative basis: how well they understood the task and collaborated with their partner to carry it out, and their level of autonomy, behavior, and ability to complete the task in the allotted time. Now and then, when there were exercises with scores, students would report them, and I would take the quantitative results into consideration, too. There was a great deal of competition in these sessions, with everybody wanting to complete the activities in the shortest possible time and with the best results. (See Tips on Using CALL Software below.)

I created custom-made activities related to the syllabus mainly with Quia Web (Quia 1998–2006) and Hot Potatoes (Arneil and Holmes 2005), both fairly simple authoring appli-

Tips on Using CALL Software

- Remember that the computer facilitates learning; it does not teach. CALL works well for practice and extra input.
- Stay in the computer lab at all times. You need to be there as support for content and technology, even for simple tasks.
- Consider scores and quantitative measures as secondary elements. If CALL is used for practice, students should feel that they can learn from mistakes.
- Evaluate qualitatively. Are students really practicing or just going through the motions?
- View computers and CALL as a means to an end, not a goal in itself. Define your goals first; then find the software you need.
- Use a variety of lessons and software. Students will get bored using the same old stuff.
- Have students share computers if there aren't enough to go around.

cations that allow the teacher to insert content into different types of templates. However, I also used activities that were created by colleagues and freely available on the Internet, such as Kelly and Kelly's (1997–2006) Interesting Things for ESL Students and Zieba-Warcholak's (2002) English Interactive Quizzes.

Talking Avatars

One of the most exciting recent developments for students has been the use of SitePal (Oddcast n.d.) to create talking avatars with their own voices (see Figure 12.2). This variation of voice messaging is even more exciting for young learners because it blends sound with a customized image. Two students created their avatars and first messages in class; that same afternoon, several other students followed their example from home. I immediately wrote a brief tutorial for the remaining students and had the class undertake a tutoring exchange—community language learning—with Aiden Yeh, a colleague in Taiwan, and her ten-year-old son, CJ. They taught my students to say words in Chinese and Tagalog, and my students taught them the same words in Portuguese. The students were glued to their screens. Since the free demo avatars were available for only a short time, students had to respond quickly to messages—another motivational strategy, as it turns out. (I have re-recorded messages and placed screenshots of student avatars on my Web page as examples; see Almeida d'Eça 2003b.)

The CALL activities were motivating because of the novelty of the tools—the computer and the Internet—and the variety involved. These sessions were an escape from the normal classroom, and students received additional English practice time while being exposed to technology and learning to use it. It is important to view technology as just another tool that can motivate students and enhance learning. It is a means, not an end.

The students' enthusiastic end-of-year feedback (June 2004) gave me considerable anecdotal evidence that the lab practice had been helpful. These are just four of the many positive responses (translated from the original Portuguese by me):

> I think these lessons are very important, because in addition to playing games, we are learning at the same time. We write messages in English to other children and we make friends. I

Figure 12.2. Rodrigo's and Pedro's Talking Avatars Created at SitePal
Source: http://www.oddcast.com/sitepal/.

love to hear the voices of the boys and girls in the messages sent to us through the teacher's computer. I love these lessons and if next year you are our teacher, I'd love to have these lessons again. (Diana, fifth grade, class F)

The games helped me understand things better. (Verónica, fifth grade, class F)

The CALL lessons were interesting because I learned to work with the computer and several things in English. (André, fifth grade, class G)

I learned a lot in the CALL lessons. . . . We had three friends: Tommy, Wojtek and Katia. We exchanged ideas with them and it was fun. (Mateus, fifth grade, class G)

Challenges and Future Directions

Teachers face certain challenges, including the following, when they decide to introduce blended lessons into the learning process:

- *their level of expertise*—Is it adequate for the task(s) ahead?
- *their school's computer equipment*—Is it adaptable to the tasks and activities?
- *computer facilities and availability*—Are they adequate for the number of students? Are they easily accessible when necessary?
- *technical support*—Does it exist? Can it respond in a timely fashion?

Teachers may also face psychological challenges. Although my school has had good computing equipment since the mid-1990s, the majority of teachers have not taken advantage of it. The reasons lie beyond the scope of this chapter. Additionally, although I have never had any problems with technical support or official acceptance of my projects, the school has never shown interest in or recognition of the pioneering work that my students and I have carried out since early 1998. Indifference and a lack of understanding are more widespread than is desirable in the twenty-first century, and they present an emotional and psychological challenge that teachers may need to anticipate and overcome to go forward with a technology plan. It is unpleasant to feel isolated, but look at the bright side: when students are the top priority and work with them leads to significant involvement and gratifying learning, what better motivation and inspiration can a teacher have?

Since my first days of using the Internet in the classroom, my school has regularly upgraded its computing equipment. In the past three years it has installed a network with a DSL connection, put one computer in every classroom, and recently installed a wireless connection in part of the school. Although all this improvement may seem quite rosy, it does nothing to solve a significant problem: large classes. I have followed two strategies based on specific circumstances: (1) divide students in two groups and be with one group at a time in the computer lab, generally with two students at each computer; and (2) work with a whole class using my laptop (loaded with all the software), wireless Internet, and a video projector. With the latter strategy, all work is done collaboratively, with students taking notes and deciding on the wording of messages as a group, and one student keying in the text. Voice mail is recorded by one student, sometimes by the whole class, after scripting. With the right technology, one computer can do it all!

Both options work well, but a few students prefer the former because it allows them to have more hands-on involvement and generates a great deal of motivation. With either option, it is essential to plan carefully and double-check everything in the lesson plan, including Web sites, although doing so is not a foolproof guarantee against technical glitches. If you work on school computers, plan well ahead and have any necessary software installed in advance. And always have a plan B; technology can play unexpected last-minute tricks on you.

In addition to large classes, teachers also face students of mixed ability and different cognitive levels; therefore, maintaining motivation, commitment, participation, involvement, and good behavior is another challenge. If these elements have been previously achieved in the traditional classroom, they are easily transferred to the blended classroom, but only when the task level and demands cater to the majority of the group. Thus, I believe that the first and biggest task faced during the implementation phase of technology is to set successive challenges for the students in order to have them all occupied at all times:

- Diversifying the activities and tools helps prevent boredom and routine.

- Having students volunteer for different tasks motivates them to do better work.

- Believing in the less-skilled students and giving them a chance boosts their egos and makes them participate more in the long run.

- Raising curiosity and expectations in advance piques anticipation.

- Having a surprise now and then generates excitement.

- Setting higher standards may encourage the less-skilled students to follow the more-skilled ones.

- Involving students in everything—they are the actors; teachers are the directors orienting and guiding—generates eagerness to learn and enjoyment in doing so.

Because students move from class to class over the years, giving continuity to technology-enhanced projects should be a desirable goal and a priority. Such continuity generates motivation and learning and prepares students for real life. However, this goal is not always realistic or achievable due to specific circumstances: changes in teachers and schools, a shortage of tech-savvy teachers, technophobic teachers. In my case, the fifth graders' blog was continued when they moved to the sixth grade. Although the message flow has been somewhat irregular and maybe a bit slow at times, there have been significant developments. In February 2005, two students on their own initiative sent their first voice messages from home, attached to an e-mail, after having downloaded the free HandyBits (2005) software I had reminded them about in class that morning. In response to their efforts, colleagues taking part in an online teacher training workshop that I was comoderating sent text messages to the students, a few of which had photos and voice mails attached. Several students then replied through the blog. In a related project, I loaded a brief tutorial on HandyBits and an accompanying pictorial narrative of a family holiday, created with the free software Photo Story (2004). The program creates slide effects for the user's photos, similar to those of presentation software. A sound file with narration or background music can also be added. I am now trying to motivate students to use this tool to create simple narrations in English on their own. We have come a long way in a year's time, and the results have exceeded my wildest dreams. As I have become more expert in technology, my students have kept pace.

I believe that online activities are more effective when related to the curriculum, particularly for younger students who need more guidance, control, and supervision. However, diversifying and innovating by incorporating extracurricular elements now and then is a winning recipe. Some teachers believe that CALL and the Internet should be used to do only what is hard or impossible to bring about in a traditional classroom. I believe, however, that these tools should be added even for things that could be done with paper and pen, because the innovation in the process, or the appeal of the tool itself, leads to motivation, involvement, and learning for most students. The more I experiment with these constantly evolving tools, the more pedagogical potential I find in them; the more diverse their features become, the better they cater to different learning styles, and thus the more easily they embrace all students.

As for future directions for my fifth and sixth graders, I will continue a teacher-student blog, but next time I intend to use an online blog provider, most probably mo'time (Tipic 2001–2006). I will also continue to reinforce listening through different online ESOL sites and encourage voice mails from home. I will offer extra speaking practice through exchanges of voice and video mail and simple voice chats with foreign peers early in my students' study, so that they can experience and see for themselves how important and useful it is to learn a foreign language that opens communication doors all over the world. I also intend to use Audacity (2005) to record students' oral practice so that they can detect mistakes and correct themselves after listening. All these activities will be documented in the blog so the students and I will have an ongoing record of their achievements. I have also collected a list of useful tools, resources, and Web pages I have created in a separate index (Almeida d'Eca 2005a).

To sum up, these are the elements I have found most effective in taking one's first steps with CALL:

- Start with small steps and gradually build on your experience.
- Generate and enhance communication in and outside of school.
- Be flexible; do not be afraid to try innovative new technologies.
- Have patience and persistence; things do not always work at first.
- Be inventive and improvise when something does not work.
- Seek peer support and collaboration from online colleagues.

I wholeheartedly advise you to embrace technology in education and gradually try some of these tools. I hope you will find, as I have, that they are so motivating for you and your students that there is no going back.

Appendix—Chapter 12
Web-Based Tools and Student Projects

Tools and Software	
Audacity *desktop recording software*	http://audacity.sourceforge.net/
Dekita.org *blog site devoted to EFL/ESL*	http://www.dekita.org/
Filamentality *software for creating and storing Web pages with users' own links*	http://www.filamentality.org/wired/fil/
HandyBits *voice mail*	http://www.handybits.com/voicemail.htm
Hot Potatoes *six kinds of exercises and activities generated from users' input*	http://hotpot.uvic.ca/
Interesting Things for ESL Students *games, quizzes, activities*	http://www.manythings.org/
KidzBlog *blog software oriented to K–6 students; can be self-contained on a school's Web site*	http://www.haranbanjo.com/kidzblog/
mo'time *blog provider*	http://www.motime.com/
Photo Story *software for creating slide shows, presentations, and albums from users' photos with media enhancements*	http://www.microsoft.com/photostory/
Quia Web *subscription-based software for creating exercises and quizzes*	http://www.quia.com/web/
SitePal *subscription-based software for creating avatars with audio files on users' Web sites; thirty-day free trial*	http://www.oddcast.com/sitepal/
English Interactive Quizzes *teacher-made quiz page*	http://www.wsl.edu.pl/~azetka/

Student Projects	
EFL/ESL Exchange	http://www.dekita.org/exchange/
Email Projects Home Page	http://www.otan.dni.us/webfarm/emailproject/email.htm
The Image of the Other	http://www.europeanschoolsproject.org/image/
Kids as Global Scientists	http://www.letus.org/kidsglobalscientists.htm
The Official Flat Stanley Project	http://www.flatstanley.com
Additional Resource	
First Steps in Experimenting with Computers: Resources	http://64.71.48.37/teresadeca/tellrefs-exp.htm

Chapter 13

Real-World Contexts, Skills, and Service Learning for Secondary School Language Learners

Mary Jewell
University of San Diego/San Diego State University
San Diego, California USA

Preview

Language teachers are excited about the many uses of the Internet and the opportunities it offers for communications around the world. Jewell reminds readers, however, that not all schools or students have immediate access to the Web. Jewell suggests that even a modestly furnished school lab or a single desktop computer in a classroom can offer amazing resources to motivate students and to help them practice language. Familiar applications that the teacher may take for granted, such as a word processor, can be used to produce remarkable, authentic student projects if the approach is task based.

Before you read:

- What computer applications does your school or institution use regularly that might be turned into teaching tools for language and professional skill development? How?

- Have you ever participated in service learning or incorporated it into your instruction? With what success?

- What kinds of projects might your students produce that would benefit the community in which they live?

The Value of Non-Internet CALL

The Internet is king. It rules the world, and the world of computer-assisted language learning (CALL) is no exception. There are hundreds of Web sites devoted to establishing e-mail connections between students in different parts of the world, online writing labs, and even distance education language courses. Students can learn language and culture without ever leaving their computers.

Sadly, though, most non-Internet CALL applications have been left in the digital dust. Little research on stand-alone applications has been conducted since Internet access became widely available, and a brief survey I made of online versus print-based CALL resources makes clear that Web-based chat, discussion groups, and e-mail occupy more space in the curriculum than other technologies. However, many computer applications, such as Microsoft PowerPoint (2006) and the advanced word-processing and template features of such applications as Microsoft Word (2006), the free OpenOffice.org Suite (2005), or AppleWorks (2004) for the Macintosh computer, provide language learners with the opportunity to use English in a variety of authentic contexts. Students improve their language skills through research and by sharing their findings in oral presentations, as well as by preparing and producing planners, budgets, calendars, brochures, and newsletters. These experiences provide valuable real-world contexts and technological skills and enable students to develop confidence in their language abilities. This chapter explores the potential of these programs to enhance language acquisition with high school English language learners.

I have used non-Internet CALL applications with my high-school-aged English language learners for several years and have always been pleased with both the computer and language skill development. Ours is a large, urban high school in a city near San Diego, California, in the United States. Nearly all of the students are from Latin America, and many are studying English for the first time. For some of our students, using a computer is a completely new experience. Students study English in my ESL class and take their content-area classes in Spanish or in specially designed classes for English language learners. Class periods are ninety minutes long, which allows for extended research or project development time. Few students have computers at home, so nearly all of the computer work is completed at school.

Authentic Information and Context

There is general consensus in the language acquisition community that the most effective forms of language instruction in schools are those that focus on communication of real information with authentic value for the learner, rather than solely on grammar or memorization of vocabulary (Cummins 1999–2003b; Cummins and Sayers 1997; Hudelson, Poynor, and Wolfe 2003; Krashen 1983, 1987; Lapp, Flood, and Farnan 1993; Mora 2002). The creation and presentation of informational brochures, posters, and other documents based on word-processing templates provide authenticity and relevance, and thus create an optimal environment for language learning. In developing these kinds of documents, students study and present real-world information within a context that is applicable to their lives and benefits their communities. For example, students creating an informational brochure on high school graduation requirements or the college application process must collect information from multiple authentic texts, work with classmates to decide what is most relevant, and then write their findings in a way that accurately summarizes information and appeals to their audience. Students or the teacher then invite subject-matter experts or community members to view the documents and observe the presentations in order to provide learners with authentic feedback on their products. Service learning supports English for specific purposes and can be employed in many situations. For example, students can create a brochure for a community nonprofit organization, assist job training centers in creating business cards or flyers for their clients, or publicize a school issue. This type of authentic work can provide students with a sense of professional purpose and accomplishment while serving a community need (see Figures 13.1 and 13.2 for examples of student-created brochures).

When creating advanced word-processing documents and computer-supported presentations, the emphasis is on the messages that the language is communicating, not the language itself. Students are concerned mostly with understanding and expressing their thoughts and ideas about the material, not with grammatical correctness. They are motivated to improve their language to better communicate within a given context. When all, or most, of the listening, speaking, reading, and writing activities in the class are focused on the topic of the document under development, language learning takes place in an authentic, useful context (Benrabah 1997; Cummins and Sayers 1997; Mora 2002). Students may still need direct instruction in the form of minilessons for grammar, punctuation, purpose, or format,

Figure 13.1. Student Informational Brochure about School Violence

depending on the tasks involved in creating documents and presentations, but concrete, product-oriented goals are the focus of the project, rather than the language mechanics involved. This integrated, focused approach to project development reinforces key vocabulary and language structures within the authentic, communicative contexts.

Collaboration and Support

Creation of brochures and informational presentations involves the collaboration of students, teachers, and subject-matter experts. For example, students might consult a police officer or psychologist for a project on school violence, or work with a community service organization to create a flyer advertising a new teen center. Collaboration is critical to language development; providing teacher and expert support throughout the project encourages students to increase their skills in language as well as technology. Presentation and desktop publishing activities, when well planned and scaffolded, can provide students with real-world comprehensible input. What they already know about the problem is related to the ongoing vocabulary and new information they encounter as they work through the task together.

Students benefit from working with teachers and experts who can provide input and feedback, but more capable peers, either native speakers or learners at higher levels of English proficiency, can further enhance language learning opportunities. Structuring activities and teams or groupings that include native English speakers as well as English language learners can be difficult to arrange at a secondary school, but it is worth the effort. When brochures or presentations are part of a computer-supported interdisciplinary project that incorporates one or more content areas in addition to English, there are even greater benefits for students. For example, a more advanced English class could work with a newcomer group to research and publicize employment or health care information.

Technology as a Means to an End

Using technology to enhance language learning allows for increased learner autonomy and control, providing for a more student-centered pedagogy. Students are more actively engaged in their learning than in traditional direct-instruction methods, and the teacher's role changes from one of authority to one of facilitator and coach (Cummins and Sayers 1997; Padron and Waxman 1996; Warschauer 1997). Anyone who has ever worked with teenagers understands the importance of their perception of control. By allowing teens to have increased autonomy in technology use and content development for their presentations and desktop publishing, the teacher turns over important aspects of control to the learners.

In addition to the language acquisition benefits of using presentation software and word-processing templates, students also develop useful and marketable computer skills. Technological savvy is a must for success in higher education and the working world (Shetzer and Warschauer 2000). Interdisciplinary authentic projects, such as the development and production of brochures and presentations, can give students the real-world computer experience and language skills they need for success beyond the classroom.

Finally, the motivation factor involved in working on these projects is not to be overlooked. Students nearly always enjoy working on the computer, and will, like anyone else, work hard on something that interests them. Creating professional-looking documents and presentations is fun and challenging for teenagers, and most are willing to attempt to experiment with the assignments, using their creative energies and demonstrating pride in themselves and their efforts when they present the final product. In sum, creating useful documents and presentations can provide the following:

- authentic audience
- authentic content
- comprehensible input
- motivation
- service to a community

The next sections of this chapter offer examples and instructions for creating documents and presentations with readily available software.

Word-Processing Templates

Word-processing software usually provides a variety of templates for creating brochures, posters, spreadsheets, Web pages, resumes, and other documents, as illustrated in Figures 13.1 and 13.2. These templates may already be inside your software or are easily downloadable and can be customized to meet individual student needs. In AppleWorks (2004), go to >File >Show Starting Points, and click on the >Templates tab. In Microsoft Works (2004), the >Templates icon is clearly visible on the front page. Depending on your system configuration, in Microsoft Word (2006) you may need to install the components for the template in advance and make them available on a school network. To install these plug-ins, download the templates you will be using from the Microsoft Office Online Web site (Microsoft 2006b) and save them to a folder on the school file server. Students can then open the original template from your folder, choose >File >Save As . . . , and save their own copies of the template to the local computer hard drive or their personal diskette. For example, *brochure_template* can become *brochure_maria*, *brochure_amir*, and so forth. Ensure that students always work on their own copy of the file so that they do not get confused with multiple versions of the same document, and do not delete the original. (See Creating Templates with Microsoft Word on the following page.)

Even more template options are available at the Microsoft Office Online Web site (Microsoft 2006b), free to Office users. (For templates for Apple computers, follow the links to Microsoft's associated Web page.) Use the directions in the box on p. 181 to locate and download templates from the Internet. In AppleWorks (2004) the >Web tab in the >Templates menu links to further resources on the Internet, including downloadable templates created especially for children's projects.

In my secondary school ESL class, students spend about six weeks each year creating informational brochures and posters about problems common to teenagers. Their topics

---

Creating Templates with Microsoft Word

Word for Windows XP

- From within Word, choose >FILE >NEW.
- In the window that opens on the right of the screen, under Templates, select >ON MY COMPUTER.
- Select the template you wish to use, then click >OK.

Word for Mac

- From within Word, choose >FILE >NEW BLANK DOCUMENT.
- Create the document in the format you want your students to use.
- Choose >SAVE AS . . . and select >DOCUMENT TEMPLATE in the drop-down menu.
- Save a document for each of your students, using their names as the new file names.

You may also use Microsoft Word Forms to create templates.

For other operating systems or software, check the relevant Help files.

Always save a backup copy of the template in a safe place.

---

usually include teen pregnancy, suicide, school violence, drug abuse, and getting into college. Students follow a carefully scaffolded series of steps to complete and then present their original and informative brochures. (See Figures 13.1 and 13.2 for completed examples.)

We begin the informational brochure project by brainstorming issues that are important to the students, and then assign groups based on student interest, for example, teen pregnancy or violence in the school. Students use the Internet, library and community resources (e.g., materials distributed by government agencies), and expert interviews to gather information about the problem under study. They complete text journals and logs (these could be Weblogs at schools that have Internet access), writing about what they are learning and the problems they are having with the project. When students have collected sufficent information, and have several ideas for ways to address the problems, we begin with the layout of the informational brochure.

Before sitting down in front of the computers, students examine several real-world examples of informational brochures and note the important features, such as columns, titles, subtitles, and graphics. We discuss and chart the vocabulary of page layout and design so that we can use it easily throughout the project. I then share with the students the brochure that I created, so they see that a real person can produce a near-professional-quality document. Students then create a basic paper-and-pencil outline or rough draft of their brochures, and finally they begin work on the electronic versions of their documents. I demonstrate the basics of the technology, and the students soon become proficient users. For example, I walk them through cutting and pasting template elements, inserting graphics and bulleted lists, and saving to the correct location. They work together in groups at the com-

Downloading Microsoft Office (2003) Templates from the Web

Office for Windows

- Under the >HELP menu in Word, choose >MICROSOFT OFFICE ONLINE. The Web page will open in a new browser window (you must be connected to the Internet).
- Click >TEMPLATES in the frame on the left.
- Select the template you wish to use. (Brochures and flyers are found in the Marketing section.)
- Ensure your computer system meets the requirements specified, then click >DOWNLOAD NOW. The template will open in a new window.
- Save the template.

Office for Mac

- Under the >HELP menu in Word, choose >VISIT THE MACTOPIA WEB SITE. The Web page will open in your browser (you must be connected to the Internet).
- Select >TEMPLATES from the >INFORMATION, PLEASE . . . column in the center of the page.
- The >TEMPLATES page contains a gallery of selections. You may preview the templates before downloading.
- Select the template you wish to use.
- Click the >DOWNLOAD icon.
- Save the template, being careful to retain the original extension (.pot).

Always save a backup copy of your templates in a safe place.

puters, taking turns "driving" with the mouse. As they learn to use the brochure format, they ask me for help, consult each other, address the charts we have made of the vocabulary, and examine the real-world examples. Invariably, there are setbacks, but most groups produce a high-quality product that incorporates information, new vocabulary, and improved writing skills. Students learn to use correct grammar and punctuation, to write clearly for the audience toward which the presentation is directed, and to incorporate graphic and other design features enabled by the technology. New vocabulary emerges from the issue being presented and is practiced as students discuss their projects. (See the brochure in Figure 13.2.)

The final step in the project is the presentation of the documents. We usually invite community members, other teachers, and parents to a presentation event. I normally schedule the presentations for the class period just prior to lunch time, so any guests can stay and chat with the student-presenters or the school staff. The event takes place in my classroom, which can seat about forty people. Students dress nicely, and I provide juice and cookies for the presenters and guests. The teacher's computer workstation in the classroom is connected to a large television, so computer slide presentations are easily visible. We make copies of the brochures and flyers to distribute to the community members and students at the event. Sharing their brochures with a real audience provides an authentic context for students'

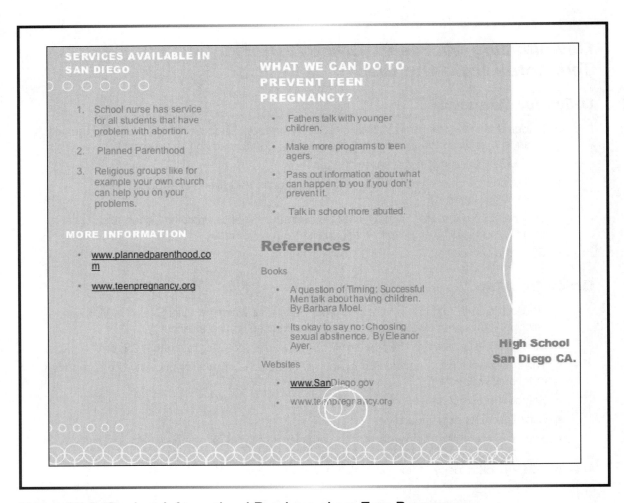

Figure 13.2. Student Informational Brochure about Teen Pregnancy

verbal language skills. Students also reflect on the computer and research skills they learned, and how they would do the project differently next time.

Presentation Software

Many language instructors use Microsoft PowerPoint (2006), AppleWorks (2004) Presentation, or other presentation software such as HyperStudio (2005) or the free OpenOffice.org Suite's (2005) Impress to create presentations for their lectures, yet few secondary school language students have the opportunity to employ this type of easy-to-use presentation tool. Students can use presentation software to present any type of content, such as new vocabulary, the problems they researched in the brochure project, information about themselves, or other topics. A computer-enhanced presentation is ideal for developing students' oral communication skills, especially pronunciation, intonation, and confidence. Pronunciation is one of the most difficult areas of any foreign language to learn (and to teach), yet it is one of the most important (Benrabah 1997). Students must also prepare by writing and organizing their information, thus building their written communication skills as well. When students critique each other's presentations, listening also becomes part of the project, thereby incorporating all of the key skills in language learning, as well as critical thinking.

Students can use any of the many presentation design templates provided in the software, download additional templates online (as in the process for Microsoft Word [2006] templates described earlier), or create their own color and layout schemes. The graphics and the small amount of text in bullet points provide just enough support for students to refer to during their presentations, but not enough for them to rely on completely, so they must learn the information as well as rehearse their presentation of it. Repetition and practice are critical elements of pronunciation improvement and successful oral delivery. Presentation programs also allow for the insertion of audio or video files, which can offer further opportunities for listening/speaking activities, if the school or teacher can provide a microphone. Such programs are easy to use, offering intuitive interfaces for anyone who has used a word processor and many Help files to guide the user through the program.

Tips for Computer Integration in Service Projects

Consider the following points in planning a computer-enhanced service project with students:

Take the time to experiment with the templates your students will be using. There is no better way to learn the pitfalls and shortcuts than to make a brochure, calendar, or presentation yourself. Having a realistic model for students to follow is also extremely helpful. If they know you can do it, they will be more likely to believe that they can do it, too.

Identify resources and places to find help ahead of time, and enlist the aid of librarians and others on campus. Where the Internet is accessible, create folders of useful Web sites on the network or at a designated workstation. Assemble the books or encyclopedias students need, including links to online dictionaries and bilingual dictionaries. Research skills are important, of course, but preselecting some resources helps students make the best use of their research time. Remind them of the people and places on (and off) campus that can provide them with further information or language assistance.

Ensure that students have at least an intermediate level of language proficiency. Before beginning a project, students should be able to converse in at least simple sentences, interact with other learners using language strategies to complete simple tasks, and read and write short documents in English. Otherwise, the frustration at gathering information from text sources may impede students' progress and motivation.

Practice group dynamics beforehand. Model and practice the key skills of listening, questioning, discussing, and providing feedback for group interactions. Provide key phrases and questions students can practice, such as "I'm not sure I understand what you mean. Could you explain it again?" Fishbowl activities, in which one group of students is engaged in a process while the rest of the class observes from outside the circle, work well in this situation.

Encourage students to create brochures, flyers, calendars, or other documents that have an authentic use within and beyond the school community. Students can perform service learning by creating posters and flyers for a nonprofit company or social service in the community, such as a community food bank or a youth sports organization. They can also make paper or digital school-year calendars for home and school use, and duplicate them for distribution to other students and parents.

Build instruction into design elements by having students read, analyze, and discuss model brochures and flyers. Ensure that they have a say in what projects they will undertake.

Create charts and other visuals with key vocabulary and grammar. Students must be able to easily use the specialized vocabulary of the software and project, such as *slide, layout,* and *subtitle.* Displaying charts and other graphics with these key terms allows students to quickly refer to the definitions when working in their groups, completing self-evaluative logs, or preparing presentations. The following terms might be included:

- *format/layout:* the organization of the brochure
- *graphics:* pictures, clip art, or graphs
- *subtitle:* a smaller title that tells the reader what a section is about
- *text:* the words
- *column:* a vertical section of text

Create a group of student experts. Enlist the help of a few motivated students to become the class experts on technology. Teach them the basics of the software application, and encourage them to experiment with and refine their work. Once they become proficient, they can serve as tutors or assistants to other students during class. Becoming a tutor provides additional speaking practice.

Make spell check, online revision, and print preview required tasks several times before printing. Paper and toner cartridges are costly, and printing multiple drafts of the same document is wasteful. Set the printer to print in draft mode until the final copy, and use recycled paper whenever possible. By training students to use software functions such as >PRINT PREVIEW, which allows them to see a formatted document on the monitor before printing, teachers can train a new generation of ecologically informed and efficient computer users.

Take frequent metacognitive breaks. Together in class, discuss and write about how the groups are functioning, the new language structures and vocabulary being used, and the content being learned. Teachers can use these reflective discussions and notes to check for understanding of key vocabulary and concepts, as well as to measure students' writing progress and technological literacy development.

Conference with individual students and groups. Regular conferences with each student and group are critical in order to check understanding; track oral language development; and provide content, language, or technology assistance when necessary. Evaluate the final written work and presentations against a rubric that you share with students prior to the final due date; the rubric should measure the specific standards under study. (See Table 13.1 for a sample rubric.)

Help students organize a presentation event where they can show off their projects. An authentic audience of community and family members and pride of ownership in their work are powerful motivational factors for learners.

Table 13.1. Informational Brochure Evaluation Rubric

Criteria	Full Points (Each item is evaluated on a four-point scale.)
Statement of the problem	A problem affecting young people is clearly stated.
Evidence of research	Sufficient supporting facts and statistics from reputable sources are offered.
Synthesis of information	Facts are fully explained and connected.
Suggested action/solution	Specific actions for solving the problem are suggested, and additional resources are provided.
Language and mechanics	The brochure is free from spelling or grammatical errors and utilizes appropriate register and vocabulary.
Layout/page design	Layout is organized and attractive and includes graphics, subtitles, and white space.
References	A list of resources used in preparing the document is included.

Challenges and Future Directions

Although interesting and rewarding, the types of CALL projects described in this chapter are not without their challenges. Invariably, the file server or printer is not functioning when you most need to access it, or the projection screen is not connected properly. Always have a backup, especially if you have guests at the presentation. You can always have guests gather around one screen. Copy the projects to a CD and to a flash drive, and e-mail them to yourself so that a backup is always available. Allow ample time for project completion, but not too much time, as technology projects tend to expand to fill the time available. Having access to a technology expert who can solve problems and soothe nerves is also valuable. If your school does not have an expert on staff, recruit a community volunteer or capable student. Drawing on more technologically savvy students in class to assist others moves projects forward and provides multiple opportunities for learner-to-learner interactions.

Students, especially of high school age, often take valuable learning time to have fun or socialize while working on tasks such as the development of a brochure. And the administration or other faculty may feel that project-based learning is not entirely serious, especially if one considers the hectic and sometimes noisy task-based learning environment where groups of learners are exchanging ideas while working in teams. Focusing on presentation to an outside audience, such as the guests we invite to view our student informational brochures, can lend a touch of seriousness to the project and eliminate much of the unproductive playing by students and dismissal from colleagues.

More troubling, however, is the danger that a CALL project will become focused on the technology, and not on the language learning involved. Students can become bogged down in formatting or preoccupied with graphics and sounds, losing sight of the more important information and skills they are learning. While good design and effective placement of text and graphics lends a professional air to document design, students should also be made mindful of the language skills they are mastering. Ensuring that students adhere to the rubric criteria can assist in this process. (For templates of rubrics to use with creative projects, see RubiStar [ALTEC 2000–2006].)

Finally, which are the best technologies: new or old? The answer to that question is complex. As the technological world develops, people are continually faced with new arrays of programs and services. However, the newest and most expensive applications are not always the most effective at helping students learn language. Much of technology's effectiveness depends on how we, as professionals, choose to apply the tools with students. We must constantly strive to evaluate any new technology against what we know to be sound pedagogy, and not be tempted to discard older tools simply because they are older. The technology itself will not enhance language learning. It is what we do with it that matters. By mastering the functions of computer-based presentation software and the template features of a word processor for document layout and design, teens can expand their computer literacy skills while processing new information, serving their school or community, and developing a variety of language skills.

Appendix—Chapter 13
Software for Word-Processing and Presentation Projects

Multiplatform Software	
HyperStudio *presentation software*	http://www.hyperstudio.com/
Microsoft Office • Word (in Office) • PowerPoint (in Office)	http://office.microsoft.com/
OpenOffice.org • Writer (in OpenOffice.org) • Impress (in OpenOffice.org)	http://www.openoffice.org/
RubiStar *online rubric creator*	http://rubistar.4teachers.org/index.php
Win/DOS-Specific Software	
Microsoft Works *office suite*	http://www.microsoft.com/works/
Apple-Specific Software	
AppleWorks • Word Processing (in AppleWorks) • Presentation (in AppleWorks)	http://www.apple.com/appleworks

Chapter 14

Redefining the Blog: From Composition Class to Flexible Learning

Graham Stanley
The British Council and ESADE Turismo Sant Ignasi
Universitat Ramon Llull
Barcelona, Spain

Preview

This chapter provides an overview of the way Weblogs (blogs) can be integrated into the teaching of ESOL or, for that matter, any world language. Stanley argues that blogs have far more to offer teachers and learners than their conventional use for free writing to improve reading and composition skills. He suggests how teachers can incorporate blogs into their teaching to help develop relationships between classes in different countries, to build a better sense of community in the classroom, to implement formative assessment, and to encourage greater student autonomy and more reflective learning. The Pew Internet and American Life Project (2005) reports that 27 percent of online adults read blogs and that 48 percent of bloggers are under the age of thirty. The increasingly widespread use of blogs for ESOL indicates that the blogosphere is not just a passing fad, but an authentic virtual space for language learning.

Before you read:

- If you already use paper-based student journals in your classes, how often do you read them? Are they private or public? What type of feedback or response do you provide?

- What might be some advantages of an online journal as opposed to a paper version?

Entering the Blogosphere

> What is a weblog? A weblog is a form and a format: a frequently updated website containing entries arranged in reverse-chronological order. . . . [W]eblogs are organizing businesses, creating and strengthening social ties, filtering the World Wide Web, and providing a platform for ordinary people to publish their views to the world. (Blood 2003, ¶1)

Blood's definition can be applied to the *edublog* (a blog used for educational purposes) and rewritten to reflect how the present community of ESOL edubloggers is currently using blogs as online personal and reflective learning journals and as platforms that give learners a real audience for their writing. Some teachers use blogs as Internet portals for their classes, providing course information and homework, and filtering online resources by level and interest to direct learners to those of value. Other teachers use edublogs to involve their classes in international cross-cultural projects, creating new social ties between students in geographically dispersed locations. Blogs also help increase the sense of community in a class, and they have the potential to be portals and repositories for teaching and learning e-portfolios. They can also be useful to teachers implementing a system of formative assessment with their learners. Finally, blogs are a valuable tool for fostering learner autonomy, as students take more responsibility for their own learning and teachers move from being the provider of knowledge to the facilitator of understanding and new learning.

I have used blogs in my own courses with a wide range of ages, from undergraduate university students, in order to promote autonomous learning and to encourage process writing in English for specific purposes classes, to youngsters studying English at a private EFL academy. Because these students had classes only once a week, we used blogs as a way of extending the classroom environment. Both of these settings were in Europe, where students had relatively easy access to computers in school and at home.

In this chapter, I place blogs in context by examining the theory and research that support the use of this technology in English language teaching. Then I look at current practice, using examples of projects that are in progress or that have already been completed, suggesting how teachers can incorporate blogs into their own teaching and learning situations. I also review the less obvious uses of blogs suggested by the definition of edublog. Finally, I suggest emerging and future trends in the blogosphere, with information about where to get help in using this technology.

Blogs in Context

ESOL edublogs have come a long way since their first use by teachers as a means to keep in touch with friends and family while working away from home. The use of blogs as student online journals, as mentioned by Campbell (n.d.) and Duber (2002), has become a popular function. Many online journals are extensions of traditional student language learning journals (widely documented by, for example, Bailey and Nunan 1996; A. K. Johnson 2002; Peachey n.d.).

The idea of using blogs with ESL classes was taken further by Campbell (2003) in an influential article proposing three types of blogs:

- *tutor blog*—Teachers use this type of blog to post information about the syllabus and homework assignments. Sometimes teachers write about their lives, sharing reflections about local culture or the target culture and language to stimulate online and in-class discussion. Students can respond only by writing comments to the teacher's posts. An example is Campbell's (2006) The New Tanuki (this, and all Web addresses for blogs in this chapter, are listed in the appendix).

- *class blog*—This is a shared discussion space between students and teacher, where resource links may also be quickly accessed. It is an extracurricular space, and as such can be used to encourage students to reflect on themes touched upon in class, as in the Goin' Upstream (2005) blog. Learners have a greater sense of freedom and involvement with this type of blog than with the tutor blog.

- *learner blog*—This is probably the most rewarding type of blog for learners. Each student has an individual blog that becomes his or her personal online space. Learners are encouraged to use the blog to write about what interests them; they can post photos and audio, make comments on other students' blogs, and quickly save links to favorite resources. The online journal mariichigo (2005) is a good example.

As in Campbell's (2006) blog, The New Tanuki, it is common for teachers to combine tutor or class blogs with learner blogs connected by hyperlinks. Such a grouping of interconnected blogs forms a virtual learning environment that has some advantages over more sophisticated courseware management tools because it is flexible for the learner and usually offers a public, open environment that is easy to use.

I also add a related category to Campbell's list:

- *teacher blog*—Teachers use blogs, often for self-reflection and as learning journals, but also for recording Web site links and information. An advantage to using a blog instead of a paper-based teaching journal is that teachers can obtain an online audience of peers to help the reflective process through their comments. One example of a reflective teacher blog is Random Thoughts (McKeand 2006). Another example of a more information-based blog is my own Blog-EFL (G. Stanley 2006).

Apart from being self-reflective tools, journals have enormous potential as a device for research (L. Miller 2004; Richards and Lockhart 1994). Nunan (1992), for example, says that "diaries, logs and journals are important introspective tools in language research" (p. 118), and Suzuki (2004) comments that the emergence of blogs may be changing the problem that McDonough and McDonough (1997) identified: few studies exist of teachers researching their own work in diary form. With increasing numbers of publicly available reflective teacher blogs, research based on what they report will no doubt expand.

Blogs for Writing

Raimes (1983, 4) recommends techniques to get students beyond sentence-level exercises. The blog lends itself well to this purpose and has been promoted as an excellent tool for engaging students in writing, especially as a way of focusing on the writing process rather than the finished product (Barrett 2004; G. Stanley 2004; Ward 2004). Kennedy (2003) mentions that "students will write when they have something to say, when they have an audience, and when they get feedback" (p. 11), and Ward (2004) sums up nicely, stating that the blog "provides a genuine audience, is authentically communicative, process-driven, peer reviewed, provides a dis-inhibiting context and offers a completely new form with unchartered potential" (p. 8). There are over eight million blogs on the Internet, with the number growing exponentially; this is an enormous potential authentic audience for learners.

Blogs work well when teachers (or peers) respond immediately to the content that students produce. Blogs not only encourage teachers to become readers who take more interest in what students say than how they say it, but also offer a wider, more authentic audience for what students write about. The audience can be limited to other members of the class or can include students from other classes, other teachers, the students' family members, or indeed just about anybody in the world with an Internet connection who might be interested in reading what they have to say. (Ganley [2005] discusses many of these uses in her classes at a WorldBridges [n.d.] webcast.) Because learners are writing for a real audience, it is important that they focus on audience and content as well as form. The huge potential audience makes blogging not only highly motivating but also very relevant to a communicative approach to language teaching.

Johns's (1990) landmark essay in the literature of college composition mentions that the writing problems of college students are largely due to their inability to move from "writer-based" to "reader-based" prose, a problem of identifying and understanding audience needs (p. 30). The comment feature of blogs can help writers with this problem, as it solicits immediate feedback. Blogs provide what Vallance (2004) calls "a platform for students to write and obtain quick responses to their text" (p. 51). Comments on blogs help student writers get a better feel for their audience. As Ford (2006) states, "an awareness of audience is one of the underlying principles across the whole curriculum, yet so often students have to make do with an imaginary audience, or one limited to the teacher and any random individuals who might peruse a classroom display. With blogs the audience is real and is, in most cases, large" (¶8).

Blogs for Reading

Apart from writing in their own blogs, students should be encouraged to visit and read the blogs produced by other students in the class or in the wider blogosphere of ESOL. Students are encouraged to write more when their peers comment on their posts, and if they write about subjects of interest to them personally, their blogs can provide meaningful reading practice for other students. Plenty of evidence suggests that this type of meaningful reading is vital in the development of reading skills (Grellet 1981; A. Johnson 2004). Getting students to read peers' blogs can also be a way of generally improving second language reading habits.

Of course, there is no reason the reading of blogs needs to be limited to those written by other ESOL students since it is beneficial for students to read widely. To this extent, James Trotta has established at ESL go net (n.d.) a list of ESOL-friendly content blogs arranged into categories. The owners of these blogs have been approached and have accepted the idea that language learners will post comments on their blogs, thus giving students a chance to engage in discussion with native speakers about a subject of mutual interest.

Blogs for Listening/Speaking

Audioblogs, usually referred to as *podcasts* (iPod + broadcast) are now among the easiest Web tools to use. At podcasting sites, such as Odeo (n.d.) or PodOmatic (2006), students can record their voices and make recorded comments on each other's work using their computer's own sound capability and a microphone. These sites also allow written comments, so teachers may clarify or extend the assignment in writing, and students may obtain writing practice as they critique their own and others' oral productions. For an example of the effective use of student podcasts, see Aiden Yeh's Speech Class podcast (Yeh 2006). *Vlogs* (videoblogs) are also coming into more widespread use, and these offer further listening and speaking practice with the added advantage of multimedia components (for an example of a vlog provider, see Ourmedia [n.d.]; see also Gromik's discussion of video in chapter 9 in this volume).

Teaching Implementations

Apart from practice in various language skills, there are less obvious teaching applications of blogs, suggested by my earlier definition of edublog:

- foster relationships between classes in different countries
- build a sense of community in the classroom
- manage large groups
- aid in constructing learning e-portfolios and other formative assessment in a class of learners

As I discuss these four topics in particular, I also demonstrate how blogs have a role to play as learning devices to promote greater student autonomy.

Collaborating across Cultures

One of the Internet's most powerful features for language learners lies in the possibility of making connections with the target language community and with language learners in other cultural contexts (Lafford and Lafford 1997). The ability to take learners outside the confines of the classroom and into the real world is what makes using computer-mediated communication (CMC) so attractive to teachers. But CMC has other benefits. It provides "an engaging environment for real use of the language" (Lafford and Lafford 1997, 259). When teachers first started looking at the possibilities of using CMC with classes, e-mail attracted the most interest. Setting up e-mail exchanges with classes in other countries became a popular way of exploiting the communicative potential of the Internet (see, e.g., Dudeney 2000; Eastment 1999; Warschauer, Shetzer, and Meloni 2000). Students can write to key pals in the same way that they write paper letters to pen pals, but with a much faster response rate and, hence, greater motivation.

Blogs can also be used in cross-cultural collaborations, especially because they provide an easy way for students to share information that can be referenced again and again. A class blog can be created around specific projects (related, e.g., to the culture and customs of the country of each class; the city or town where the students are based; other varied topics such as TV culture, tourism, local food). A good indication of the potential comes from teacher and active edublogger Ford (2006b): "Christina was in the process of researching her weblog-based project on the Rainforests when she received a message via her weblog's built-in discussion board from someone who was trekking through forests in Costa Rica. He gave her a firsthand account to work with" (¶1). Imagine the motivation to use the kind of language that such an audience can provide. Other examples produced by students are on Ford's (2006a) site, The FordLog.

Even though standard blogs are used to great effect in international exchange projects, another attractive way of blogging that can be motivating for cross-cultural communication projects is the photoblog. Photographs can be added easily to blog sites such as Blogger (1999–2006), or by using free services such as hello software (2004; for computers running Microsoft Windows only). These tools enable easy uploading and free storage of photos in addition to the usual text-only blog. However, there is much to be said for using a special online photo management host, such as Flickr (2006), which serves as a repository for photographs that can then be easily linked to and viewed in any blog. Blogger even produces its own Help files to assist users in the process of linking files from Flickr. Another advantage of Flickr is that it will store the photos and blog privately (available only to friends and family who have a password), a useful feature if you wish to avoid uninvited comments. If you want to focus on the text interactions rather than the photos (Flickr is really a photo managment tool with blogging capabilities), then Buzznet (n.d.) is probably the best free photoblog tool at the moment, and it has recently added video storage capacity. Buzznet also allows settings to make your students' photos accessible only to registered friends or by password.

Using Blogs for Community Building

Online international exchange projects require careful planning and coordination, and they work better if a variety of CMC tools are available, such as text chat or e-mail in addition to blogs (see Almeida d'Eça, chapter 12 in this volume). One of the best ways to organise your project is by looking at examples of successful projects that other people have undertaken, for example, Dieu's (2005) Bee Online class blog. Tracing the development of this blog by looking through the archive, the reader sees that after successfully introducing her Brazilian students to blogging in a class blog, she asked them to set up their own learner blogs (which are linked to the class blog in the Classroll sidebar; see Figure 14.1). Soon afterward, she organized an international link-up to the class blog with students from a school in Italy. The blog became a lively discussion space for both the Brazilian and Italian students as they asked and answered each other's questions about life and culture in their hometowns in English, their shared language of communication. Dieu has been involved in many other blogging projects with students since, and says of the phenomenon, "in blogging, teachers and students become partners beyond the classroom walls" (2004, 27). Another exemplary educational site that Dieu is involved in is EFL/ESL Exchange (Ammann, Campbell, and

Figure 14.1. Barbara Dieu's Class Blog, Bee Online
Source: http://beeonline.blogspot.com.

Dieu n.d.b; initiated in early 2005), whose main purpose is to raise awareness of blogging projects in ESOL, create blog exchanges among classes, and celebrate the individual work of students involved in those projects.

Hamilton (2004) notes that blogs can also improve class dynamics: "When the class-room door closes, the communication pathway is still open" (p. 51). Hamilton mentions that using bulletin boards helps "students to bond with each other and their teacher" (p. 51), and Farmer (2004) provides evidence that using blogs to share information is even better than using bulletin boards or forums. Frequency, however, is crucial to the success of a blogging project. If learner posts are not responded to promptly, students will soon lose interest. Thus, it is good to encourage collaboration and posting between learners, which can be accomplished in many ways:

- Tell students to check the class blog to find out about homework instead of telling them about it in class.

- Post preclass tasks for students on the class blog.

- After school, write something on the class blog about the progress made that day. This instant evaluation can be great for motivation.

- When you respond to individual learner posts, always end with a question, thus encouraging students to reply.

- Encourage students who cannot attend class to send their excuses and apologies to the class blog.

- Use a tutor blog to clarify grammar points, discuss vocabulary, offer links for further research, and so forth. Students then have the option to make a screen print for further study.

- Exploit the fun factor. For example (adapted from Hamilton 2004), ask students to bring something blue to class. Such a task is also a good way of checking to see who has read the blog before coming to class.

In general, anything that exploits the blog's potential as an engaging environment for communication should be explored.

Managing Groups of Blogs

Management is the key to building a successful community of blogs. Imagine keeping track of a group of thirty or more student blogs. Although blogs "break down the rigid idea of the once-a-week class" (T. Black 2003, 11), leading to improved communication and a better, more autonomous language learning environment, the effort to read and respond to dozens of learner blogs requires a considerable investment of time from the teacher. The worst-case scenario is motivated students updating their blogs and checking them every day to see if someone has responded, but to no avail. After a few days students will become disappointed and may well stop blogging. But, you might ask, how can teachers be expected to find the time to visit each of their students' blogs every day to see if anything new has been published? The answer is a piece of software called an *aggregator*, or newsreader.

Aggregators work by noticing when a blog has been updated or changed, and then pointing the new content to one central place. Almost all blogs now have a tiny red icon labeled *RSS* (really simple syndication), *XML*, *Atom*, or *Feed*. There are different types of feeds, but it is not necessary to know the differences among them. Clicking on the button will take you to a Web page showing code. Ignore the code and simply copy and paste the Web address shown at the top of your browser into your aggregator (many educators use Bloglines [IAC Search & Media 2006b], which is free). When new posts are detected, the name of the blog in your aggregator will be put in bold font. With one click, you can read all the new posts in a frame without leaving your own site (see Figure 14.2 for the Bee Online blog as viewed through an aggregator). The process of adding new blog feeds can also be automated by placing a button on your browser toolbar, a process that has simple directions on any aggregator Web site. A click on the browser button at an interesting site sends the RSS information (or its equivalent) to your aggregator. Now that all the blog updates can be seen as a list gathered in one place, and you do not have to visit thirty different sites to see if any have changed, they will be much easier to read and respond to.

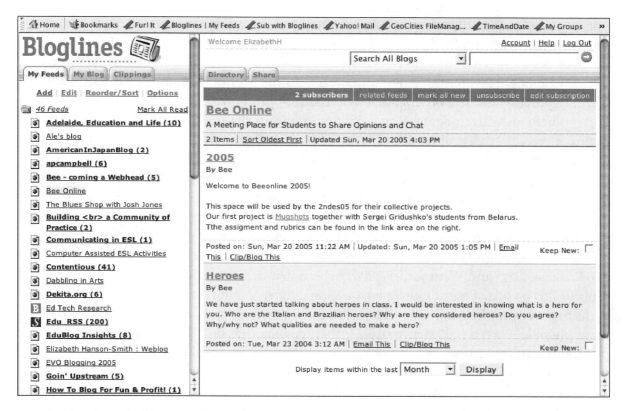

Figure 14.2. Bloglines, a Blog Aggregator

Source: http://www.bloglines.com/.

Note: Blog addresses in bold in the left-hand frame have new content, which can be accessed in the frame on the right. The >SUB WITH BLOGLINES button in the center of the browser menu bar at the top automates blog RSS address capture.

Conducting Formative Assessment with Blogs

Assessment, as defined by Black and Wiliam (1998), includes all activities that teachers and students engage in to obtain information that can be used diagnostically to alter teaching and learning. Assessment is *formative* when this information is used to change the ongoing teaching and learning situation to meet student needs. *Summative* assessment, in contrast, is used to judge if a student has learned something after the study process has been completed, for example, through scored tests or graded compositions.

Formative assessment has been called assessment *for* learning rather than *of* learning. (Assessment Reform Group 1999). Formative assessment is more learner centred because it can be used to diagnose whether students are learning; the teacher uses the result to change the learning situation. The teacher can try reteaching, change an approach, or give more opportunities for students to practice. Formative assessment further alerts students to their strengths or to areas in need of improvement, creating a more autonomous learner in the process.

The adoption of portfolios is often a considerable step toward formative assessment. Barrett (2004) says "the use of portfolios in high stakes assessment of learning is problematic, but the use of portfolios in formative assessment (for instruction) and assessment for learning is powerful" (¶1 under Assessment of Learning). Nunes (2004) mentions that there is a range of definitions of the portfolio: "For some teachers, the portfolio is part of an alternative assessment programme. . . . For other teachers, the portfolio documents the students' learning process, and still others use it as a means of promoting learner reflection" (p. 327). Using portfolios with students, Nunes continues, means the teacher can "become aware of their preferences, styles, dispositions, and learning strategies, thus being able to adopt a more learner-centred practice" (p. 327). Recently, the *e-portfolio* has caught the attention of educators. Lindsay (2002) defines the e-portfolio as "a goal-driven, organised collection of artefacts that demonstrate a growth or expansion of knowledge and skills over time" (p. 3). One advantage of the e-portfolio over the traditional portfolio is the ease of access that it offers to teachers for formative assessment and to students for frequent updating.

A growing number of educators (e.g., Barrett 2004; K. Kennedy 2003; Lindsay 2004, 2005a; Tosh and Werdmuller 2004) believe that there is a place for blogs in student e-portfolios because blogs can help create a low-anxiety environment that encourages students to reflect on their learning. This is just the right situation to make formative assessment possible. Barrett (2004) also stresses that the blog "has potential to make electronic portfolios more engaging" (¶1 under Web logging or "blogging"), especially when it comes to recording student reflections.

Julie Lindsay, a teacher who has used blogs for EFL student portfolios, has perhaps done more than others to promote the idea of using blog-based e-portfolios. She has worked hard to create a community for the development of student digital portfolios at the International School Dhaka in Bangladesh, "using a class weblog for interactive instructional delivery, online discussion and peer evaluation as well as personal weblogs and blogging for journal processing, electronic communication and portfolio publication" (Lindsay 2004, ¶2 under Abstract). Lindsay (2005b) created an excellent set of resources that can help any teachers who would like to start using blog-based digital portfolios with their own classes.

Challenges and Future Directions

As with any technology, teachers should become familiar with blog capabilities before using them with students. The best way for teachers to do this is to start a tutor blog and post to it regularly in order to understand what it means to do so and if it is something they can ask their students to do. It is also wise to start small. When I first discovered blogging, I found it was easy to become a *blogvangelist* and to try to use blogs with all my classes. This is obviously a mistake, as it is difficult if not impossible to respond to all students. It is better to begin with just one class blog, and then mention it in class to encourage students to participate. If this trial is successful, especially if students post to the blog frequently, learner blogs are a good next step. These are more work for teachers, but far more rewarding for students. It is important to remember to use an aggregator (e.g., Bloglines [IAC Search & Media 2006b]) to make it easier to keep track of student output.

Another difficulty is that sometimes, although students are interested at first in blogging and seem to have a great deal to say, the enthusiasm may wane after a few weeks of posting. Teachers can do many things to keep levels of interest (and number of posts) high. It helps greatly if the blog is an integral part of the course, and not a bolted-on extra, because teachers can frequently remind students about the fact that they receive credit for blogging. Other types of blog use may be encouraged by inviting a mystery guest (e.g., another teacher, a friend, a relative) to write to the blog. Teachers can ask students to write questions and try to guess the person's nationality, job, or hobbies based on responses.

Teachers can also try to involve people from outside the classroom (e.g., students in other countries, parents, another class) to write comments. The most demotivating situation for bloggers is trying to write when they think there is no one reading. Teachers need to write comments regularly and encourage others to do so, too, since receiving comments on the blog is the most obvious sign that someone is reading. If students know that their blog has an audience, they will keep writing. One way of getting an audience is to publicise a class blog or project at places such as EFL/ESL Exchange (Ammann, Campbell, and Dieu n.d.b), a venture designed specifically to make student publishing projects known to others.

In closing, I wish to mention several emerging themes in the blogosphere. As mentioned earlier, audioblogging or podcasting is becoming popular, thanks to the affordability of Web space (an important consideration if you wish to provide audio files for students to listen to); high-speed Internet connections; and free, easy-to-use audio tools such as Audacity (2005). There are also free or reasonably priced services, such as Hipcast (2006; formerly Audioblog), which make posting audio files from a telephone directly to a blog very easy. Teachers and students alike can record anything from anecdotes, instructions, and jokes to interviews, advertisements, and poems. Thus, blogs can become a means to practice speaking and listening as well as reading and writing. Of great interest is that podcasts can be located and transferred directly to a portable player for listening whenever and wherever anyone wants, using tools such as Juice (2005) and Apple's (2006c) iTunes. There are now hundreds of ESL-targeted podcasts (English Idioms and Slang [2006] being one of them), and more are sure to follow. Good places to find ESL podcasts for use with students are Englishcaster (2006) or the Podcasting-ELT Yahoo! Group (Diem, Lockman, and Stanley 2006). Because of the ability to comment on the content, almost all podcasts use blogs such as PodOmatic (2006) as their Web home.

Audio, and the use of mobile telephones to carry out what has been called *moblogging* (posting audio to your blog using a mobile/cell phone), could grow in popularity with ESOL teachers and learners, especially while there are interested researchers such as Coghlan (2005) and Duber (2002). Duber's (2004) LetsTalk Web site stresses how much adding audio to blogs can benefit language learners. The mobility of Internet telephony means that students can study, post homework, and join community events, even during long commuting hours on a train or bus.

Videoblogging is also becoming popular, especially as the technology that is available to produce and edit video—and video mobile phone technology—becomes cheaper and easier to use. One stumbling block has been the lack of free space to store video online; however, sites such as Internet Archive (n.d.) and YouTube (2006) seem to have resolved this problem. Videoblogs for language learning will no doubt become more widespread in the near future: "The allure of authentic video materials lies in the fact that students can observe real language in its full context, tapping a wealth of extralinguistic information to support learners in interpreting and comprehending not only the language but the culture as well" (Pusack and Otto 1997, 7). *Tagging* (the labeling of files with key words) at video archives allows users to search for content related to a specific interest or curriculum topic.

The world of the twenty-first century, as blogging commentator Blood (2002) notes, "demands that we broaden our view, not narrow it further. We have in the Weblog an unprecedented tool with which to share ideas and understand other worldviews" (p. 163). Teachers who are interested in investigating contemporary trends and the possibilities that blogging offers should consider joining an online community of practice, such as Evo2005: Using Weblogs in ESL/EFL Classes (2006) or the Blogstreams Salon at Tapped In (SRI International 1995–2004). Teachers in the groups share what they know and seek to learn more about blogging.

Acknowledgments

Many thanks to Barbara "Bee" Dieu in Brazil and Aaron Patrick Campbell in Japan, my two virtual colleagues and online friends, for their encouragement and advice. Much of what I have learned about blogging, especially recently, has been because of, through, or with them. Thanks for the endless enthusiasm, advice, and friendship.

Appendix—Chapter 14
Blogs, Web Sites, and Web Tools for Bloggers

Web Tools, Hosts, and Software for Blogging	
Audacity *recording software*	http://audacity.sourceforge.net/
Blogger *blog host*	http://www.blogger.com/
Bloglines *RSS aggregator and blog host*	http://www.bloglines.com/
Buzznet *photo- and videoblog host*	http://www.buzznet.com/
Dekita.org *edublog host*	http://dekita.org/
Englishcaster *podcast directory*	http://www.englishcaster.com/
ESL go net *edublog directory*	http://www.eslgo.net/
Flickr *photo software and blog host*	http://flickr.com/
hello *photo transfer software*	http://www.hello.com/

Hipcast (formerly Audioblog) _audio- and videoblog host_	http://www.hipcast.com/
Internet Archive: Movie Archive _video host_	http://www.archive.org/details/movies/
iTunes _podcast software and directory_	http://www.apple.com/itunes/
Juice _podcast directory_	http://juicereceiver.sourceforge.net/
LetsTalk _media edublog host_	http://duber.com/LetsTalk/
Odeo _audioblog host_	http://www.odeo.com/
Ourmedia _videoblog host_	http://www.ourmedia.org/
PodOmatic _audioblog host_	http://www.podomatic.com/
Tapped In _educational online community host_	http://tappedin.org/
YouTube _videoblog host_	http://www.youtube.com/
Blogs and Users' Groups	
Aiden Yeh's Speech Class podcast _audioblog_	http://aidenyeh.podomatic.com/
Bee Online _blog_	http://beeonline.blogspot.com/
Blog-EFL _blog_	http://blog-efl.blogspot.com/
Blogstream Salon _users' group_	http://www.tappedin.org/ (login required; go to the Blogstream Salon office)
English Idioms and Slang _blog and podcast_	http://www.englishcaster.com/idioms/
The FordLog _blog_	http://www.weblogs4schools.co.uk/TheFord/
Goin' Upstream _blog_	http://goinupstream.blogspot.com/
mariichigo _blog_	http://www.livejournal.com/users/mariichigo/
The New Tanuki _blog_	http://thenewtanuki.blogspot.com/

EFL/ESL Exchange *online community blog*	http://www.dekita.org/exchange/
Random Thoughts *blog*	http://namckeand.blogspot.com/
Evo2005: Using Weblogs in ESL/EFL Classes *users' group*	http://groups.yahoo.com/group/weblogging/

Chapter 15

Issue: *The Teacher's Critical Role in Effective Online Courses*

Latricia Trites
Murray State University
Murray, Kentucky USA

Preview

As earlier chapters demonstrate, many schools and universities already offer some or all of their curricula online or in blended environments. The great fear of teachers, however, is that online learning will either replace them or create tremendous overloads in their schedule. Trites looks at the different ways that courses have been transferred to the online medium, usually in one of three major modes: nouveau-correspondence, group dynamics, and the interactive online class. She compares these approaches, describing how they are supported by online tools and course management systems such as Blackboard (2005). Her experience indicates that interactive and constructivist components are the most valuable, but that teacher involvement in the learning process is also crucial. She offers tips and suggestions to guide teachers as they develop or redesign their own online courses.

Before you read:

- Have you ever taught or been a learner in an online distance course? What problems did you encounter?

- What level of student interaction and teacher involvement is needed to have a successful distance course? What role can computer technologies play in enabling involvement?

- What tools are required to prevent online distance learning from becoming merely a glorified correspondence course?

Expanding Online

While online courses and programs have become plentiful in the past decade, the quality and merits of each course must be evaluated individually. As technology has allowed educators to reach more prospective students than ever before, the success of a program ultimately hinges on the effectiveness of the instructor to assist learners in the acquisition of knowledge. Unfortunately, little research has been conducted on the effectiveness of online instruction. Some research is observational and anecdotal in nature, exploring the different activities and practices in online education, specifically focusing on experiential—trial and error—evidence (Chang and Huang 2002). Other research compares the effectiveness of online instruction and face-to-face (f2f) instruction (Bennett and Green 2001) or contrasts different modalities of instruction within the online medium (Carr-Chellman and Duchastel 2001; Easton 2003). However, the majority of articles written about online education focus on techniques and strategies to foster effective teaching and learning practices as they fit within broader cognitive and pedagogical learning theories (e.g., Benbunan-Fich, Hiltz, and Harasim 2005; Hall 2002; Huang 2002; Schrum 1998).

Because of the limited research in the field of online education, there are many critics, but most skeptics have yet to fully explore the strengths and weaknesses of the medium as a mode of instruction. Noble, for example (cited in Bianco and Carr-Chellman 2002), argues that the purported need for online education is only created by administrators trying to increase profits for an institution at the cost of educational quality. Others argue that online courses, in a race to tap the distance education market, take the teacher out of the learning process, rendering instruction ineffective (Carr-Chellman and Duchastel 2001). Often, teachers simply translate traditional lecture courses to the online medium, sacrificing the critical interactive component between teachers and students that is present in f2f classes.

I have been teaching online courses since the spring of 2001, when the MA program at Murray State University in Kentucky, in the United States, expanded its ESL Certificate Endorsement component to include online courses. To obtain endorsement, certified teachers are required to take four courses, three of which are offered as part of the full MA in TESOL program, in addition to passing an oral exam and an ESOL content exam. With several refugee resettlement areas as well as other immigrant populations in Kentucky, the state experienced a rapidly increasing need for certified ESL teachers. By expanding our program to include online classes, Murray State, which is located in the remote southwest corner of the state, has been able to reach teachers across the state, nation, and world. While most of the university's online students are pursuing an endorsement, many regularly enrolled students opt for the online section of one of the three required MA courses rather than enrolling in an on-campus section.

Even though most of our MA program is offered on campus, many courses are heavily supported by Web-based media. Syllabi, course materials, and course assignments are posted on Blackboard (2005), a course management system (CMS), so that students may access these materials at any time. Also, students are encouraged to submit assignments to their Blackboard class sites, which allow for ease in archiving and for electronic grading. Many of our courses are taught in a blended (both f2f and online) format. Students are often placed in groups within a class and participate in asynchronous journal discussions or use other communicative features of the CMS to complete group assignments. Current plans include the expansion of many of our courses to the online medium, providing students with greater flexibility and eventually the ability to complete their entire master's degree online.

Theoretical Models

As teachers begin to develop courses for online settings, they "are often adopting a curriculum to fit the technology rather than selecting technology to fit the curriculum" (Bennett and Green 2001, 1). Three broad educational models are generally used in instructional design: *behaviorism*, *cognitivism*, and *constructivism*. The behaviorist model is based on stimulus-response approaches in which students are given repeated drills and exercises to show that they have successfully learned the material that is being taught.

The cognitive model is based on theories from cognitive science, proposing that new knowledge is built upon existing knowledge. Online activities in this model include note taking, peer assessment, and "information seeking through search engines" (Mishra 2002, 495), all building on previously learned classroom skills.

The constructivist model of learning, based on the work of cognitive scientists such as Bruner (1966), Dewey (1933/1998), Piaget (1972), and Vygotsky (1978), is often used in online classes. Many researchers argue that the constructivist model is the most effective for online education (see Stevens, chapter 19 in this volume). Huang (2002) summarizes these historic educational psychologists' definitions of constructivism as a learner's ability to create new knowledge based on the assimilation of that knowledge with the learner's prior knowledge. Instructional practices in this paradigm include the negotiation of goals between instructors and students, learner-centered activities in which peers negotiate meaning together, and assessment measures that are "designed around real-life problems and promote self-evaluation and reflection and maximize learner responsibility" (Mishra 2002, 495). Online instructional activities can include the use of asynchronous discussion forums, synchronous text chats, e-mail, group work, streaming media, and various other social tasks.

Organizational Models

As teachers move from theory to practice in the online distance class, teaching can predominately be formatted in one of three ways: correspondence mode, asynchronous-only mode, or truly interactive mode. The predominant way that online classes have been designed is what I term the *nouveau-correspondence model*. In this model, reflective of behaviorist theories, the teacher posts reading assignments and gives students step-by-step tasks, and students submit assignments for grades to the teacher via e-mail or some kind of digital "drop box" (as it is called in Blackboard [2005]). Student progress is evaluated through objective-based assignments and tests. In this model, teachers simply export their land-based learning materials to the online environment (Carr-Chellman and Duchastel 2001). In fact, online lecturers traditionally place lecture notes online for the students to read. Real-time interaction is missing; knowledge is seen as something to be transferred from teacher to student.

The second most common design of online courses is the *group-dynamics model*. In such courses, the teacher posts reading assignments and possibly lectures online, and gives students a variety of tasks to complete. Students are assigned to post responses to monitored asynchronous discussion boards where other students and the teacher respond to each other's comments. Sometimes these boards or forums are organized as small-group discussions; other times they are organized by topic. Students are also sometimes assigned to work in groups to complete projects. In order to familiarize the students and teachers with each other, students post minibiographies that can include photos. The only synchronous communication occurs when students contact teachers during designated office hours to ask for clarification of course-related information. In this course model, knowledge is seen as something to be discovered by the students from the information that the teacher provides, either directly or through reference to library and Web resources.

While the second model is interactive and possesses constructivist characteristics, in a truly *interactive online class model*, communication among teachers and students is multidimensional, both synchronous and asynchronous. In this third design, the teacher posts reading assignments and gives students typical classroom tasks. Students meet with the teacher for weekly synchronous, teacher-led text chats based on the readings; students also meet in small-group synchronous chats to discuss questions based on the readings and assignments. Sometimes these are guided reading questions provided by the teacher to stimulate conversation; other times students discuss the homework assignments or are asked to lead discussions, taking charge of or adding new materials to the class. In addition to synchronous chat formats, asynchronous discussion forums may also be implemented. Students send assignments to group members for peer review before submitting them to the teacher for a grade. Besides traditional class assignments, the teacher can allow for a "getting to know you" atmosphere at the beginning of the course by holding an initial virtual "happy hour." Teachers hold virtual office hours in synchronous chat so that students can ask questions in real time. Physical office hours can be kept for telephone conversations. Students are assessed through written assignments that reflect their synthesis and evaluation of the course content and through tasks asking them to apply to real-life problems what they have learned and discussed.

Interactive Model

Based on the theoretical models and research, it is evident that interaction is critical to effective online instruction. Bober and Paz Dennen (2001) theorize that "intersubjectivity" (p. 242) develops through interaction, creating deeper learning. They state that intersubjectivity develops through a learner-centered environment that helps foster peer interaction and promotes community building through which students can share their own viewpoints and validate them by understanding the positions of others. Interaction also seems to be critical in overcoming the challenges of online course development that Schrum (1998) identifies: (1) the increased time for course delivery, (2) the need to develop an online community, and (3) the necessity to encourage students to become independent learners.

Promoting Interaction

Jung et al. (2002) indicate four interactions that are critical to successful learning:

1. *Learner-learner*—Learners discuss ideas in asynchronous and synchronous small-group and teacher-led chats, e-mail, and discussion boards.

2. *Learner-content*—Learners are asked to grapple with information, transforming and blending it with their existing knowledge and experiences to construct a new knowledge base (see also Roberts 2002).

3. *Learner-teacher*—Learners feel that teachers are available and invested in students' learning. Rogers (cited in Roberts 2002) states that "the foundation of effective learning is the personal relationship between teacher and learner" (p. 47). Learner-teacher interaction is also highly valued because the teacher is perceived to be the expert and more experienced participant; teacher-student interactions are validated more than peer-peer interactions (see Bober and Paz Dennen 2001).

4. *Learner-computer*—Learners' positive and negative interactions with technology can foster or hinder motivation and learning.

Additionally, Jung et al. (2002) observe three types of interactions: academic, collaborative, and interpersonal—all important in the development of higher learning. They find that social interaction with instructors and collaborative interaction with peers enhance learning and active participation in online courses. Their research shows that social interaction is significantly related to student learning outcomes, while collaborative interaction is significantly related to student course satisfaction. To succeed in online education, students must feel connected with each other as well as to the teacher. The implication is that the correspondence model of online education offers insufficient attention to the interpersonal and collaborative aspects of learning, resulting in poor student outcomes (Collins 2000; Thirunarayanan and Perez-Prado 2002).

Asynchronous vs. Synchronous Interactions

Both synchronous text chats and asynchronous discussion forums are common interactive features of online courses. While some researchers argue that asynchronous discussion forums are sufficiently interactive (Bober and Paz Dennen 2001), others argue that the addition of synchronous chat is critical to the design of an online class (Thomas 2002). Table 15.1 lists the common pros and cons of asynchronous discussion forums and synchronous chats, the most important of which are discussed in this section.

Self-paced, self-directed, asynchronous forums and e-mail provide anytime, anywhere learning. They can promote student reflection and encourage students to build an online identity and become responsible for their own learning. In addition, asynchronicity provides students with time for reflection instead of requiring an immediate response, allowing them to respond at length and in detail to concepts presented in class (Benbunan-Fich, Hiltz, and Harasim 2005; Carr-Chellman and Duchastel 2001). Time for reflection is also a benefit for nonnative speakers of the language of instruction since these students have better

Table 15.1. Characteristics of Asynchronous Discussion Forums and Synchronous Text Chats

Asynchronous Discussion Forums		Synchronous Text Chats	
Pros	*Cons*	*Pros*	*Cons*
• self-directed • flexible schedule • development of student relationships • ability to respond to peer postings • linear display • time for reflection • detailed responses possible	• heavy time commitment • possibility of parallel essays instead of collaborative discussion • lurking • perfunctory responses • selective reading • log-in lags • serial monologues	• democratic environment • immediate feedback • greater teacher presence • greater virtual proximity • development of personal identity • collegiality • reduced feeling of loneliness	• scheduling issues • perhaps too large to manage • dominance of fast typists • ignorance of chat protocols • chaotically overlapping discussion threads • lack of depth

opportunities to formulate their comments and responses to others before posting them and may even make use of dictionaries without feeling self-conscious, as they might in a traditional class.

Students, however, find synchronous text chats more rewarding and less complex than asynchronous discussion forums. They also prefer tasks conducted in synchronous chats because they allow for greater *virtual proximity* (Rice, Hiltz, and Spencer 2005). Wang and Newlin (2001) note that students may find chats a "liberating experience" (p. 3) that removes the feeling of "loneliness" (p. 4) generated by learning at a distance in isolation, even though synchronous communication is limited in the "amount of depth of interaction regarding course materials and procedures" (p. 2). However, Smith, Ferguson, and Caris (2001) remark that synchronous chats, emphasizing the written word, are often broader and deeper than land-based classroom discussions or forum postings. One of the most interesting benefits of the synchronous chat is that as students emerge from anonymity at the beginning of an online course, their identity development removes the worry of online cheating, that is, the fear that anonymity will allow another student to perform the work (Bennett and Green 2001; G. G. Smith, Ferguson, and Caris 2001).

Drawbacks to synchronous text chats and asynchronous forums must also be considered. Hughes and Daykin (2002) criticize asynchronous communication, noting that students are often reluctant to post responses and that forum postings are often found to be perfunctory and lacking in substance. Academically strong students tend to post a response first, and then other students simply agree. With discussion forums, students also may selectively listen to different threads or to messages only from specific classmates, ignoring other posts (Bober and Paz Dennen 2001; Thomas 2002). With log-in lag, students may offer comments so late in the posting period that little interaction is possible. Thomas (2002) argues that asynchronous forums lack the characteristics of actual conversation and that the structure and organization of the messages inhibit discussion, with the result that students are still participating in an isolated mode of communication. In addition, nonnative speakers often feel inadequate about their limited writing competence in the target language or language of instruction (Weasenforth, Biesenbach-Lucas, and Meloni 2002). Pawan et al. (2003) reveal that without explicit directions and teacher presence, students tend to engage in "serial monologues" (p. 119). Additionally, fast typists may dominate the conversation and protocols may be ignored, leading to confusing interlaced threads and disjointed discussions. Questions may be overlooked due to the speed of interaction. In fact, graduate students have commented that they would allow a concern to pass rather than hold up the flow of conversation (Bober and Paz Dennen 2001). However, well-designed courses using appropriate course management tools in combination with planning and grouping by the teacher can reduce or eliminate these concerns.

The combination of synchronous and asynchronous communication appears to be the most beneficial means of contributing to students' online learning in that both methods promote strong collaboration in complementary ways (Ronteltap and Eurelings 2002). Thomas (2002) proposes a *conversational model* of learning that is in line with the constructivist paradigm. This model, which theoretically could be implemented in both synchronous and asynchronous formats, involves "internal and interactive dialogue in students' construction of knowledge" (p. 351). If teachers adopt this conversational model, learners will show increased motivation in learning and will develop deeper levels of understanding, higher-order thinking skills, and divergent thinking: "Through the act of articulating their own emergent understanding . . . [they] are led towards the construction of personal meaning which is not individualistic, but rather a product of the students' interaction" (p. 352). While Thomas's research shows that students engaged in online discussion forums are more active cognitively and use more critical thinking skills than subjects in traditional classrooms do, his results also show that such conversational skills do not develop in asynchronous forum interactions exclusively. He concludes that, for a conversational model of learning, students must engage in normal discussions, which are more closely mimicked in synchronous chats than in asynchronous forums. I argue, however, that these communication forms alone are not enough to provide adequate interpersonal opportunities and that the teacher's presence online is absolutely necessary if students are expected to use higher-order thinking skills.

Implementation of Online Distance Courses

As I stated at the beginning of the chapter, online education still lacks a deep, practical research base. Most research suggests that online education is very effective and that students enrolled in online courses do as well as, if not better than, those in on-campus classes (Bennett and Green 2001; A. Schulman and Sims 1999). Counter-evidence is present but must be examined very thoroughly. One study (Thirunarayanan and Perez-Prado 2002) shows that while there was no significant difference in student performance between the two class environments, the online class did better on a posttest than the on-campus class. A second study conducted by Collins (2000) over a four-semester period shows that students enrolled in a traditional biology course did better than students enrolled in a Web-based version.

However, students in the online classes in both of these studies had little or no interaction, leaving one to wonder whether the results are more typical of a glorified correspondence course than of a truly interactive Web class. These findings raise the question of what level of interaction and teacher involvement is needed to develop successful online classes.

Teacher involvement is critical in promoting deep learning (Bober and Paz Dennen 2001; Roberts 2002; Rosie 2000; Speck 2002; Thomas 2002; Wang and Newlin 2001). Teachers must make strong social connections with students and show that they are invested in student success. Arbaugh and Benbunan-Fich (2005) state that "the extent to which an instructor engages in immediacy behaviors appears to be strongly associated with student outcomes" (p. 128). These *immediacy behaviors* include using personal examples, using humor, providing and inviting feedback, addressing students by name, and asking about personal issues such as students' and their families' health. Evans and Nations (cited in Roberts 2002) note that "collaboration between students and teachers to create educational experiences" (p. 47) is essential for students' development of critical reflection. Thus, in creating our wholly online ESL Certificate Endorsement program at Murray State, we insisted on program elements that would serve to connect students interactively. The decisions we made in designing instructional elements and interactive opportunities can readily be adapted to content and language courses as well.

We made the following programmatic decisions:

1. We must have a strong teacher presence in the course so that students feel that they are not isolated. To accomplish this goal, the teacher must visit the class Web site daily and provide e-mail responses within a twenty-four-hour time frame.

2. Because of the text-based nature of many online courses, we must make our syllabi and course assignments as clear and unambiguous as possible.

3. We must be flexible in our assignments, especially during the first semester of online teaching while we implement a new online version of the course (see also Schramm and Mabbott, chapter 18 in this volume).

4. We must make ourselves approachable to our students. They must feel that they can contact us at anytime for clarification.

We then began developing our endorsement courses using Blackboard (2005; other CMSs operate in basically the same manner, including the free, open-source Moodle [2005]). Classes in our program consist of a foundation course (Linguistics and English Grammars), two theoretical courses (Language and Culture, Applied Linguistics and L2 [second language] Learning), and a theoretical and practical applications class (Methods and Materials in L2 Teaching). Because of the rotation of the courses and because we believed that the Methods and Materials course would be the easiest to implement through online instruction, it was the first to be created.

Designing the Original Course

Since I was scheduled to teach Methods and Materials, I began designing the online course with input from colleagues. Even though the medium of instruction was different, the content of the course needed to be consistent with the material taught on campus. However, some activities, such as student teaching demonstrations, would not be transferable unless I required students to videotape their teaching and submit the video to me either digitally or by regular mail. I decided to substitute observations of ESL classes for the demonstrations on the assumption that teachers returning for endorsement already had or were currently engaged in practical experience. Other activities included reading the same required texts as the on-campus students; conducting classroom observations; posting responses to questions concerning the readings to an asynchronous forum; and participating in small-group, synchronous text chats. Written assignments were the same for both classes, including lesson plans, instructional units, and textbook evaluations. In place of exams, online students were evaluated using a take-home test: they had one week to complete short essay questions that required them to apply what they had learned by analyzing, synthesizing, and evaluating the information covered in the course.

To make the course interactive, I designed two major assignments: weekly discussion board postings and an activity notebook. I informed students that I would begin the discussion forum by posting questions concerning each week's readings; they were required to respond early in the week and return later in the week to respond to other students' postings. After a few weeks of modeling, I required students to post appropriate questions themselves. (See Discussion Forum Instructions below.)

The activity notebook assignment demanded a gradually evolving final project. Since students were already placed in groups for weekly synchronous text chats, I had them work in the same groupings to complete this final project. Students were required to design fifteen lessons or activities that reflected five of the different methodological approaches to language teaching addressed in class. Students had to contact each other and work in groups to decide what lessons they would teach and which methods they would use. They then had to develop and assess the effectiveness of each resulting lesson plan. Finally, the group had to write a two- to three-page statement detailing information about the intended audience, the needs of the audience, and the rationale for the methods and activities chosen. (See Activity Notebook Instructions on the next page.)

Experimenting with Course Implementation

From the initial course design, it is evident that we viewed interaction as a key component to learning, just as in our traditional on-campus classes; however, until I taught our more theoretical class on second language acquisition, we did not realize how important teacher

---

Discussion Forum Instructions

- Each week, read the required readings for the course.
- Initially, I post discussion questions to be addressed in the discussion forum. Later, you are responsible for developing these questions.
- Respond to the questions during the first half of the week; then respond to each other's responses during the second half of the week.

---

presence was in stimulating critical thinking and substantive interactions. Using an approach similar to that for Methods and Materials, I next developed our theoretical course, Applied Linguistics and L2 Learning. After only a few weeks, it became evident that students were experiencing more difficulties in this course than in the previous, more practice-oriented one. On reviewing the archives of the small-group chats and discussions, I found that students frequently made comments indicating that they had not understood the readings for the week and, therefore, were unable to answer the discussion questions effectively. As a result, I developed short summaries of the readings so that students could understand the major issues. However, based on further continuous evaluation, it became evident that the course was not progressing well and that something had to be done to ensure student comprehension of the theoretical concepts. I worried that I would fall into the trap of providing only lecture notes and reading keys online, that is, information, but not interaction that promoted critical reflection.

After much thought and consultation with colleagues, I restructured the course. Instead of posting to a discussion board, students were required to meet synchronously online with me once a week for a one-hour, teacher-led discussion using the chat feature in Blackboard. I scheduled three different chat times; students were required to attend one chat and read the archives of the other two. Within the chats, to ensure that students reflected on the readings,

I posed critical questions or had group leaders offer questions or provide topics for group discussion.

Within a short time, I began to see a marked improvement in student understanding and progress in the course. Fortuitously, I taught both an online and an on-campus version of this course at the same time and was able to monitor the progress of both sets of students. I noted that students in the online course eventually participated more fully in the class discussions (in their case, chats), came to class more prepared, and asked more in-depth questions.

Developing the Online Curriculum

Because of the success of these courses, all of our online courses have been designed to include both teacher-led and small-group synchronous text chats. Asynchronous discussion boards have been minimized. Anecdotal feedback from students reveals that they feel more connected to class members, to the teacher, and to the content because of the synchronous discussions. For theoretical material, such as second language acquisition theory, students comment that the interaction with the teacher is essential for comprehension. Working alongside class members and building a community of learners in their groups also helps them not feel isolated as they sit alone at their computer screens. From an instructor's standpoint, I find that engaged students come to class more prepared for learning. When compared to on-campus students, interactively engaged students online seem to ask questions that are more challenging and make better connections between materials and between courses.

Challenges and Future Directions

One of the greatest challenges to designing an effective online class is the commitment of time required of both the teacher and the student. Responding to multiple e-mails and developing and responding to discussion forums takes much more time than answering student questions in a traditional class. Also, because students do not have f2f access to their teachers, their tolerance of ambiguity when it comes to course expectations is rather limited. Extremely detailed instructions for every assignment must be written, which adds to the teacher's workload.

Other challenges to successful online courses include the management of students during synchronous text chats. As noted earlier, sometimes fast typists dominate the chat. Students who arrive late may apologize, greet others, and disrupt productive discussion. Fortunately, a feature in Blackboard (2005; and other CMSs) allows the teacher to send a private message to the offending students, reminding them of the chat protocol while at the same time not embarrassing the students in front of the rest of the class. Protocols must be spelled out before chat sessions begin.

Students often use technology as an excuse for late assignments, and unstable Internet connections can create valid problems. However, teachers cannot allow students to use ignorance of the technology and the platform as an excuse for failure to participate actively in the course. While teachers need to be flexible, students must be informed at the onset of the class that they will be expected to be competent in the medium. Since the primary responsibility of the teacher is the curricular learning objectives, students must realize that the teacher may not be able to answer technology questions and that they must take responsibility for their own technical problems by contacting the technical support in place at the institution offering the course.

Several of the publications mentioned in this chapter give a comprehensive list of characteristics for the development of a successful online course. The following are some basic suggestions:

- Do not directly translate a traditional lecture course into a Web course (Pyle and Dziuban 2001). Instead, combine pedagogical activities that draw on academic, collaborative, and interpersonal learning modes, which can build literacy, oracy, and critical thinking.

- Give students the "big picture" in order to enhance motivation (Bober and Paz Dennen 2001; Hall 2002).

- Lay out every aspect of the course in detail to avoid misunderstandings (G. G. Smith, Ferguson, and Caris 2001).

- Do not allow technology to be an excuse for not completing assignments or being absent from chats. Devote time at the beginning of the course to making sure that the technology functions for everyone.

- Make chats authentic and direct (Roberts 2002). To foster collaboration, cooperation, and interaction, vary who presents questions and issues to discuss in class. Have students become experts on course readings and share what they know interactively online.

- Be personal with the students (Zielinski 2000). Just because text chats and e-forums are "faceless" does not mean that participants have to remain anonymous. (For adding voiced and faced communications online, see González's discussion of voice and video chat in chapter 2 and Almeida d'Eça's discussion of avatars in chapter 12, both in this volume.)

- Redefine class time, making clear that class does not happen at one specific time but is often distributed throughout the entire week (Easton 2003).

The following is a more comprehensive list of tips to ensure a high level of student involvement:

- Start each teacher-led chat with social interactions. Welcome students to the course individually, if possible. Address student questions about class procedures, assignments, and exams; then progress to the actual course content.

- Have students take turns being the discussion leader for a chat, but model appropriate questions first. This activity places the responsibility for learning squarely on the students.

- Give students prompt feedback on their work.

- Allow students to critique each other's work, which is one way to promote interaction among them. By reading others' work, students can see the strengths and weaknesses in their own work. Students also learn to examine the purpose of assigned tasks and to see the learning goals of the course.

- Provide students with guidelines for e-mail content and responses. Students should understand that responding to many individual e-mails is time-consuming and that bulletin boards or announcement boards should be checked daily for the teacher's responses to general class queries and directions for upcoming assignments. Otherwise, students will simply resort to e-mailing the instructor rather than exploring the course site for answers (Hughes and Daykin 2002).

- Hold virtual office hours on the telephone, in chat, or through videoconferencing. Inform students about these hours and make sure they know that only during these hours can they expect an immediate response to a course procedural question.

- Develop clear protocols for chat structure concerning both attendance and content. Offer more than one chat per week, but require students to attend one and read the archives of the others. Use both teacher-led and small-group chats. Tell students that questions related to information found on the course site, such as the date of the next test, should be saved for virtual office hours.

- Keep groups for project work and discussions small. Groups of three or four are ideal. If groups are larger, students do not feel as obliged to participate. If groups consist only of pairs, serious problems can ensue if a student drops the course.

While developing online classes, I came to understand that "technology does not produce instructional outcomes; it is merely one variable among many that contribute to effective learning experiences" (Head, Lockee, and Oliver 2002, 261). However, as Carr-Chellman and Duchastel (2001) remind, "online education is a specific medium in its own right and thus it will have its own design considerations for effective instruction" (p. 149). Perhaps the "most important factor for successful distance learning is a caring, concerned teacher who is confident, experienced, at ease with the equipment, uses media creatively, and maintains a high level of interacting with the students" (Sherry, cited in Hitch and Hirsch 2001, 15). While developing courses for online delivery is time-consuming, the rewards of engaged students producing quality work and interacting at a higher level of reasoning make the time commitment worthwhile.

Section III
Questions and Activities

Questions for Discussion

1. Almeida d'Eça (chapter 12) shows how information and communication technologies can be used to improve language skills through class exchanges. What kinds of cooperative educational exchanges can you envision with an online teaching partner? What type of support would you need to realize such an exchange? How can you avoid some of the initial problems Almeida d'Eça had in her collaboration? Discuss the strategies that would help create a sense of community and commitment during the online learning experience.

2. Jewell (chapter 13) involves her learners in producing brochures that will be of use to the community, thereby weaving computer literacy and volunteerism into language instruction. Community service benefits all partners—volunteers, agencies, and clients—at every age. Service may involve sending your learners outdoors in multilingual groups to clean up a park or to a classroom to offer assistance with ESL and bilingual learners. What kinds of service learning can you involve your students in to support your institution or community? What role could technology play?

3. Stanley (chapter 14) presents distinctions among the tutor blog, the class blog, and the learner blog. Which of these do you use with your learners, or which would you like to implement? What do you see as its most important potential? What roles do audio and video play when added to text-based blogs? How do audiovisual technologies change the dynamic of tutor, class, and learner blogs? How can you promote oral and literacy skills through the blogging process in a blended or distance learning environment? How might blogging be used for formative or summative assessment?

4. Trites (chapter 15) works to fit available technological tools to the pedagogical demands of her distance learning courses. Think about existing practices in a language or ESOL course that you are familiar with. How can these best be transformed into online activities and tasks? What new practices might be involved? What are the advantages of a blended classroom environment, and what are those of the distance learning virtual classroom? What modifications and adjustments are needed for each? What roles do students, language, and interaction play in the online curriculum? How does online learning change the dynamic of your class, your teaching style, and your time management?

5. A variety of computer-mediated communications and course management tools can be used to establish and maintain connections with learners on the Web. Which tools have you used? Which might you like to explore for use in your course(s)? How can interaction be built into language instruction online? How would you balance the use of synchronous and asynchronous communications, that is, which medium can be used effectively for which purposes? What role do older technologies, such as the telephone, play?

Activities for Further Study

1. Explore creating an exchange with an international teaching partner. (You might explore possibilities with a sister institution or city abroad, or seek out one of the educational exchanges mentioned in this volume.) Involve your learners in projects across classrooms and national boundaries to foster the exchange of knowledge and content-based interactions. What theme or content will form the focus of your joint project? What products will be shared (e.g., synchronous and asynchronous interactions, student-created Web sites with useful links, group reports on shared blogs, Web-based presentations)? What are the specific duties of the participants at each site (instructors as well as learners)? What contingency plans will you need to make? What level of teacher and learner control, oversight, and accountability will be built into the project? How will you report the results of your collaborative experiences?

2. Explore some of the PBS teacher support materials, such as NOVA Teachers (WGBH Educational Foundation 2006a) for NOVA television programs or PBS TeacherSource for K–12 (Public Broadcasting Service 1995–2006). How can you use one or more of these resources with your learners? What materials are already available online, and which will you need to modify? How?

3. Visit several community organizations that might appeal to students at the level you teach. What kinds of brochures or pamphlets do they already have? Use some of these as samples in class when teaching brochure design. Have students evaluate how desktop publishing software might improve the brochures. Apply desktop and Internet publishing to service learning projects for the community or your class or school (e.g., a nonprofit agency informational brochure, an online newsletter). Could your students mentor agency volunteers in the uses of technology?

4. Explore some of the blogs that Stanley lists (in the appendix to chapter 14). How can you create and make the best use of blogs with your learners? Use blogging with your class. Provide feedback and promote interaction among students. Use an aggregator to manage your students' blogs. Report your

experience to a colleague or classmate, or present your ideas at a conference or in-service session.

5. Try several of the blogging tools that Stanley presents (chapter 14), such as Blogger (1999–2006) or Flickr (2006). Then have your learners create a blog and upload pictures of family or illustrations for literature, history, science, or whatever content they are currently reading. (For younger students or others, you may wish to follow some of the safeguards suggested by Almeida d'Eça in chapter 12, instead of using a commercial public blog.) Have students write about their illustrations, and be sure to have them share and comment on each other's work through their blogs.

6. Trites (chapter 15) advocates the strong presence of a teacher in online distance courses as being a key to successful pedagogy. Plan and present to your colleagues several online activities in which the teacher has a strong presence in shaping students' critical thinking. What types of activities lend themselves to teacher presence in this way, and which may be best left to students on their own? (You may wish to refer also to Robb, chapter 6, on the value of tracking student work.)

7. Think of language learning tasks in which student expertise can be pooled to benefit the class. Design online versions of these projects or tasks to promote learner autonomy while providing adequate teacher and peer scaffolding. Try one or more such projects with your students. List teacher and learner responsibilities and tasks. Share these with the learners, and provide an opportunity for negotiation. Hold all participants accountable for contributing to the project.

Web Sites in Section III Questions and Activities

Blogger	http://www.blogger.com/
Flickr	http://www.flickr.com/
NOVA Teachers	http://www.pbs.org/wgbh/nova/teachers/
PBS TeacherSource	http://www.pbs.org/teachersource/

Section IV

Constructivism in Professional Development

This last section is not as theoretical as it might sound at first. Authors in this section offer practical advice for structuring meaningful educational situations that can be applied in subject matter and language courses, not just in teacher education. Constructivism has been mentioned in other parts of this book, and Stevens (chapter 19) suggests that it is the approach that online learning demands. Important aspects of constructivist learning, particularly as enhanced by technology, include reflection on one's own educational processes (Dahlman and Tahtinen, chapter 16), collaboration with others in the completion of tasks and projects (Gommlich and Minick, chapter 17), and social interactions that create and sustain communities of practice (Stevens, chapter 19). The significance of technology in opening up educational possibilities to distance learners, a theme encountered in several chapters in other sections, is emphasized by Schramm and Mabbott's (chapter 18) discussion of a fully online degree program in teacher education. Stevens (chapter 19) considers the issue of how teachers, particularly after graduation, can keep up with the rapidly changing world of technology. He points out the need for teachers to join or create a community of practice for continuous peer mentoring and experimentation with the collaborative practices supported and enhanced by new technologies.

Chapter 16

Virtual Basegroup: E-Mentoring in a Reflective Electronic Support Network

Anne Dahlman and Sarah Tahtinen
University of Minnesota
Minneapolis, Minnesota USA

Preview

Teachers beginning their careers face time-consuming tasks of enormous complexity. Dahlman and Tahtinen present a process for creating an electronic support *basegroup* to help novice language teachers survive once they leave the comforting surroundings of their training institution. Modeled after weekly face-to-face (f2f) reflection sessions that all student teachers attend during their preservice experience, e-mentoring groups help bridge the gap between theory and practice that new teachers experience most acutely in their first years in the field. Dialogue journaling, an e-forum, and a Web site for resources are some of the main elements of a network to support reflective teaching practices.

Before you read:

- What kind of teacher support did you receive during your teacher education?
- What kinds of issues do new teachers face in their first years of teaching? What were your experiences?
- What would be the advantages of and difficulties with electronic support for practice teaching or for new teachers entering the profession?

The Need for Postgraduation Support

During the first few years of their career, teachers are often consumed with keeping their head above water: struggling to learn a new curriculum; developing lesson plans and materials; dealing with behavioral issues; tracking down supplies; and responding to the various needs of students, parents, colleagues, and administrators (Moskowitz and Stephens 1997). Lacking the seniority of veteran educators, many new teachers are also placed in the most difficult assignments: remedial classes, multiple preparations, and classes of students with the most diverse and challenging needs (DePaul 2000; Halford 1999). Unfortunately, 20–30 percent of new teachers leave the field within the first three years of teaching, and over 9 percent leave during the first year alone (DePaul 2000). Most disappointing is that after five years, roughly 50 percent of beginning teachers have left the teaching profession (Anderson 2000). Support systems are clearly needed to help reduce the high turnover of new teachers. Torres-Guzman and Goodwin (1995) suggest that beginning language teachers fare best when they are assigned mentors who teach the same grade level, content area, and language of instruction. However, in many cases, there are few if any opportunities for teachers to find this kind of support, often when it is needed the most.

In addition to the practical demands imposed on new teachers, novice instructors often struggle with seeing the connections between what they have learned in their teacher education programs and what they experience when teaching independently in the classroom. Teachers may feel reluctant to use theoretical knowledge acquired through lectures, research reports, and books, relying instead on knowledge they have acquired through direct teaching and learning experiences (Drever and Cope 1999; L. M. Nelson 1999) and their own belief systems, which are deeply rooted and thus difficult to change (see Golombek 1998).

This chapter presents a critical reflection on the experiences of a collectively created support network and proposes ways of maximizing the benefits of this kind of reflective network for novice language teachers. The network described here included two second-language teacher educator–mentors and three novice language teachers in the Twin Cities area in Minnesota, a large metropolitan region in the Midwestern United States. The participating novice teachers were K–12 language teachers in U.S. public schools, teaching either ESL or a world language such as Spanish or French. All teachers held a master's degree in education from the University of Minnesota. They had also completed a postgraduate initial licensure program in second languages and cultures education, specializing in K–12 ESL and/or a foreign language. Each participant was asked to assist with designing and participating in the support network, an electronic mentoring model that aimed to take into consideration the following needs:

- providing emotional support for novice teachers, especially at a distance
- creating tasks and functions that assist novice teachers in seeing theory-practice connections
- providing continued learning opportunities

The participating novice teachers had all belonged to the same preservice teacher cohort the year before this experience, so they all knew each other. Participants had contributed to reflective sessions during their student teaching, and they had identified these basegroups as one of the most useful components of their teacher education program. The postdegree online support network attempted to simulate the functions and format of the f2f reflective training sessions. The virtual support network took place using electronic media that enabled novice teachers to connect with each other anytime, anywhere. Even though all the participants had stayed in the Twin Cities area after their preservice year, they reported that their work kept them so busy that they simply did not have the time to get together with their cohort members in person. The virtual support network was intended to be as personable and intimate as possible in order to provide authentic emotional, social, and technical support. The tasks involved e-mail journaling, an e-forum, Web sites, and electronic lists.

To maximize the success of the network and the participants' learning opportunities, we explored what research could tell us about the kinds of knowledge teachers perceive to be useful. We also looked for descriptions of other experiences in setting up an electronic support network. Our research made quite clear that when it comes to useful knowledge, teachers typically prefer practical experiences to theoretical readings (Drever and Cope 1999; L. M. Nelson 1999). For example, Golombek (1998) discovered that second language (L2) teachers' own experiences as learners and teachers strongly informed their instructional decision making. Freeman and Johnson (1998) also found that "much of what teachers know about teaching comes from their memories as students, as language learners, and as students of language teaching" (p. 401; see also Freeman and Johnson 2005; Tarone and Allwright 2005). Educational theory is not perceived as useful or applicable because teacher education programs often do little to bridge theoretical and practical knowledge, thus leaving teacher trainees (even when they find theory important) on their own in applying what they have learned (R. G. Smith and Coldron 2000; Stigler and Hiebert 1999).

Teachers' many daily tasks leave little time for reading about current best practices (Reiman and Thies-Sprinthall 1998). A number of affective factors also contribute to teachers' reluctance to apply theory. For example, they might be antipathetic to research because they perceive researchers as removed from the classroom, or they may not be able to understand highly technical research articles that leave them frustrated. In addition, many teachers are disappointed by the lack of specific improvements accomplished through research (see Borg 2003). Teacher education programs may fail to sufficiently take into consideration the existing knowledge-base of student teachers, namely their "prior experiences, personal values, and beliefs" (Freeman and Johnson 1998, 401) about teaching and learning and how these inform instructional decisions. In other words, pre- or in-service teachers are not "empty vessels" (Freeman and Johnson 1998, 401) to be filled with theoretical knowledge and methodologies. Teachers must be encouraged to view the new information and articulate it in relation to what else they know about teaching and learning in order to make informed decisions.

Given these findings and perceptions, one of the main objectives of our electronic support network was to find ways to bridge the theory-practice *teaching gap*, as Stigler and Hiebert (1999) call it. The reflective exchanges between the facilitators and the novice teachers served as an optimal platform for making meaningful connections between theory and practice in the classroom. Our exchanges took into account beliefs and personal values of the novice teachers concerning theoretical knowledge, and we treated their view of reality respectfully.

Reviewing the literature in the area of e-mentoring informed us of models and programs to support teachers through online networks. Mentoring new teachers through formalized support programs has been widely acknowledged as an important aspect of teacher development; however, the concept of virtual teacher mentoring through online technologies is relatively new. Technological advances in computer-mediated communication (CMC), such as electronic lists, e-mail, chat groups, and Web conferencing, now offer possibilities for enhancing the mentoring process (Bierema and Merriam 2002), especially for people with limited access to mentors in their field, or those who are disadvantaged by distance (O'Neill, Wagner, and Gomez 1996; see also Stevens, chapter 19 in this volume). These mentoring programs extend beyond the traditional boundaries of professional education to enhance development and provide support for new teachers (Klecka, Clift, and Thomas 2002).

Bierema and Merriam (2002) define e-mentoring as a reciprocal process, "a computer mediated, mutually beneficial relationship between a mentor and a protégé which provides learning, advising, encouraging, promoting, and modeling, that is often boundary-less, egalitarian and qualitatively different than traditional face-to-face mentoring" (p. 214). They highlight the importance of relationships within the mentoring environment and demonstrate that time is necessary to foster relationships. Commitment and clear expectations for participation, including frequent and consistent interaction, are also essential. O'Neill (2001) compares relationships between online and more traditional mentoring in using telementoring, also known as online mentoring or e-mentoring, as a means to support a middle school science curriculum. In many studies, the definition and importance of structure in programs had an effect on their success. Single and Muller (2001) focus on the key elements in a structural model of online mentoring by defining the advantages of e-mentoring as increased opportunities and flexible participation times and places. In their model, the three essential areas of e-mentoring are planning, structure, and assessment. While e-mentoring offers exceptional opportunities for creating connections between people at a distance from each other, it takes careful planning and implementation to create an online mentoring relationship that is able to fulfill the functions of f2f relationships.

Several Web sites are dedicated to teachers interested in a mentoring relationship, and many programs have begun to offer mentoring by creating virtual communities for communication. For example, Teaching.com (ABCXYZ 2006) offers free forums that enable teachers to mentor each other via e-mail. Another program created specifically to support beginning teachers, primarily in rural areas, is the Novice Teacher Support Project (University of Illinois 2005), sponsored by the Partnership for Professional Development, a collaboration among various universities, schools districts, and teachers' associations in Illinois, in the United States. Welcoming Interns and Novices with Guidance and Support (WINGS; University of Texas at Austin n.d.) is a telementoring Web site whose primary purpose is to support novice teachers who have graduated from, or are currently enrolled in, teacher education programs. Graduate students can receive individual support or join online communities to mentor them during their course work and into their beginning years of teaching.

The literature on virtual mentoring reflects the need for further research and dissemination of information on how to tap into existing support networks. Using the tools of CMC to create mentoring relationships between beginning and experienced language teachers provides promising potential. We have observed, however, that while many online programs emphasize the importance of relationships between the network participants, little effort is actually devoted to facilitating those relationships. Most of the networks include a large number of participants who do not know each other, and the focus seems to be on the technical components of teaching. Little understanding and consideration are given to treating teachers as holistic beings with underlying beliefs and assumptions within specific teaching contexts that present vastly different challenges. In the following section, we describe our experiences with creating an individualized, reflective online network for novice L2 teachers, recent graduates from a K–12 ESL initial licensure program. Unlike many other programs, our network attempts to pay careful attention to the affective variables of its participants: their feelings, perceptions, and beliefs regarding teaching and learning, and the kind of support they believe would be useful to them.

Mentoring Novice Teachers

Simulating the Basegroup Online

The support network described here was designed for a group of first-year ESL and foreign language teachers who had all belonged to the same cohort of about twenty-five preservice student teachers the year before. Due to the cohort format of our licensure program, students commonly form close relationships with one another, and a close-knit community of novice language teachers emerges from their interactions. The support network was modeled after one of the best-liked components of the preservice experience, the basegroups: weekly sessions led by university supervisors who are doctoral candidates in the area of second languages and cultures. Basegroups are designed to offer preservice teachers a medium for reflection, an integral part of teacher development (see, e.g., Farrell 1998; Kullman 1998; L. Schulman 1986; C. Stanley 1998; Thiel 1999). Preservice teachers engage in reflection through a variety of activities, including discussions of videotaped lessons, the proffering of emotional support and guidance, generation of ideas for instruction, assistance in problem solving, rehearsals, exploration of instructional resources, and the sharing of knowledge about teaching. The basegroups were typically quite small in size, consisting of only five to eight members, which resulted in intimate gatherings characterized by trust; genuine care; concern for one another; and deep understanding of the strengths, weaknesses, and needs of each member.

The idea for a similar reflective electronic support network emerged from our discussions with the preservice teachers, who often expressed how valuable the f2f basegroups had been and how the support they had received in these groups had played a central role in their professional development. We hoped that the electronic network could simulate the f2f mode and thus continue to serve similar functions after the semester's end by providing support, facilitating theory-practice connections, and offering continued learning opportunities. The remainder of this section outlines the tasks and functions we felt were of value in creating a supportive online environment.

Tasks and Functions in the Virtual Basegroup

At an initial f2f planning meeting, the teacher educators and novice teachers brainstormed and agreed on the network's activities: dialogue journaling, an e-forum, and a Web site with personalized links for further support and development. (Our Web site, Virtual Basegroup, has since been taken down; similar Web sites may be seen at comparable programs such as WINGS [University of Texas at Austin n.d.] and the Novice Teacher Support Project [University of Illinois 2005], listed in this chapter's appendix.)

E-mail dialogue journals. We implemented dialogue journaling to give the novice teachers an opportunity to share their experiences in their classrooms, reflect on challenges, ask for guidance, present ideas, brainstorm solutions, and generally seek emotional support. The participants could decide whether to send their e-mails to one or both of the teacher mentors or to the whole group. The participants were to check in at least once a week to let everyone know how things were going, but they were encouraged to contact the network members more often if need arose.

E-forum bulletin board. We set up an e-forum, an online bulletin board, to provide the participants with a way to get together as a group to reflect, show and receive support, brainstorm ideas, solve problems, and educate one another. The e-forum functioned as a means for the participants to learn more about one another's teaching contexts; the issues, commonalities, and differences among them; and each teacher's questions and concerns. In addition, questions raised on the e-forum provided opportunities for teacher mentors to assist novice teachers in applying theoretical knowledge to their teaching practice; the mentors helped them draw connections between classroom practices and research findings and theory. The e-forum was a communication medium that closely resembled the basegroups; teachers came together to share their experiences with other teachers whom they knew well and genuinely cared about.

Web site. We created a Web site (no longer online) as an additional way to connect theory and practice. The site offered a collection of readings, online resources, tips, and materials related to the questions and concerns brought up by the novice teachers. Novice teachers requested more information on topics such as how to collaborate effectively in K–12/ESL inclusion settings (where nonnative speakers are mainstreamed with their age-group cohort), how to create responsive classrooms that directly address motivational and affective issues, and how to integrate language and content in L2 instruction. These issues arose from the novice teachers' current teaching contexts.

The three types of tasks and media designed for the project are summarized in Table 16.1, together with their rationale and the f2f basegroup activities they replaced.

Given the overwhelming success of the f2f basegroups that participants attended during preservice, and the fact that teachers and teacher mentors alike were highly motivated to participate in the electronic version, we were surprised that the reflective online support network did not seem to work the way it was intended. The main problem was that the novice teachers only rarely participated. It was clear that this was not due to a lack of interest or need. The participants' explanations for their failure to participate are summarized in Table 16.2, which delineates, despite the participants' strong interests in the electronic network,

Table 16.1. Tasks and Functions of the Electronic Reflective Network

Tasks/Activities	Function—How It Fulfills Novice Teachers' Needs	Simulated Basegroup Activity
E-mail dialogue journaling—once a week, or more often if need arises		
Triads: novice teacher, experienced teacher, and university supervisor • Novice teacher initiates questions. • Topics and themes emerge from classroom practice. • Spontaneous e-mails elicit support, advice, or reflection, as need arises.	• Sharing information and experiences • Focusing reflection on teaching • Dialoguing on issues • Problem solving • Encouraging one-on-one support from university supervisor, experienced teachers, and peers • Brainstorming for ideas • Accessing both practical and theoretical knowledge • Making research useful	• Structured pre- and postobservation reflection sessions • Supervisor commentary on lesson plans • f2f reflection sessions
E-forum—once a week		
Electronic discussions and virtual exchanges • Novice teachers initiate discussions, comments, observations, and so forth. • Experienced teachers and supervisors offer prompts, questions, observations, and so forth. • Novice teachers respond to postings.	• Reflecting • Providing group support • Sharing information and experiences • Providing peer support • Providing experienced teacher or university supervisor support • Accessing both practical and theoretical knowledge • Problem solving • Making research useful	• f2f reflection sessions with peers and university supervisor
Web site—available on a continuous basis; teachers determine the frequency for accessing the resource sites		
• Coordinate various functions from a central location. • Provide links to e-forum. • Provide links to resources and Web sites related to topics of interest.	• Accessing useful information—both theoretical and practical • Reflecting	• Resources, ideas, advice, tips, and suggestions provided by basegroup leaders (university supervisors)

that a wide array of external circumstances posed substantial challenges to the network and impeded its functioning.

In the following section, we reflect further on challenges to e-mentoring and on possible solutions described by the participants and facilitators.

Table 16.2. Comparison of Face-to-Face Reflection Sessions and the Online Support Network

Face-to-Face Basegroups	Online Support Network
Mandated meetings • Weekly meetings were held, and attendance was mandatory for partial course credit.	*Participation not mandatory* • Novice teachers were encouraged to participate weekly at times that were convenient to their individual schedules.
Allotted time • Program load included three hours each week for basegroups.	*Additional load* • Beginning teachers were asked to spend time each week beyond their teaching duties.
Sharing of emotions easy • Physical presence made it easier to share emotions. • Novice teachers were able to share f2f in extemporaneous ways. They could share examples from their work, ask questions, and get immediate feedback. They could sense who needed more encouragement and less critique.	*Sharing of emotions difficult* • It was harder to address emotional needs online. • While the discussion could include similar topics, the benefits of f2f discussion did not occur. Teachers found it difficult to fully describe emotional aspects without expending large amounts of energy in recording their thoughts.
Instructor-initiated topics • Topics came from the course syllabus and included issues generally relevant to beginning teachers, second language pedagogy, and questions generated by student-teachers. Readings and assignments were similar. • Teaching placements were unique, but all student teachers were experiencing similar expectations and evaluations in their placements. • Participants had extensive time to get to know their peers' contexts through shared videotaped lessons and extended contact time in the program.	*Participant-initiated topics and questions* • Discussion topics were mainly determined by the novice teachers based on their experiences and challenges in the classroom. • Teachers in various situations from large urban schools to smaller suburban districts worked with dissimilar curricular guidelines and insufficient background knowledge of others' contexts.
No technology • Technology was not utilized for the f2f basegroup sessions.	*Issues with technology* • Some teachers found it easy to log on and participate while others had technical problems. Time and accessibility played a role in participation rates.

Challenges and Future Directions

Lack of external pressure or support. Even though participants agreed on how often they thought they would like to and could participate in the network, participation was entirely voluntary; there was no financial incentive for devoting time to participation, and no penalties or tangible costs for not participating regularly. Clair and Adger (1999) identify a lack of external support for professional development as one of the key challenges for providing teachers with successful, meaningful, and long-term professional development opportunities. To overcome this challenge, we consider it crucial that teachers receive financial compensation or other incentives, such as release time, for participating in a network such as ours. Financial and moral support should come from all levels of administration, from the local school context—school administration and teacher colleagues—all the way up to the district and even state level.

Integration and significance. Another important factor in establishing a successful mentoring experience is to assure that the activities associated with it are fully integrated into the teachers' daily structure (i.e., the tasks and duties necessary for a teacher to complete his or her work). This kind of integration helps the participants receive external and tangible credit for the work and effort they invest in the network. Such credit could be in the form of having the experience count toward tenure or as professional development, for which teachers receive clock hours, pay-step increases, and/or university credit. The main point is to make it count, as we heard repeatedly from our participants.

Time issues. Research has identified lack of time as a major challenge in participating in support networks (e.g., Clair and Adger 1999). Even though the activities in the electronic network were designed to take up as little time as possible, the participants nevertheless had difficulty finding the time to post questions and comments on the e-forum and submit their e-mail journal entries. Issues related to Internet access (e.g., slow dial-up, the need to find an Internet café) can also create time problems.

One way to address time issues is to find ways for teachers to share their experiences quickly and without laborious effort. Teachers should have a variety of channels for different reporting needs and purposes, that is, there should be a way to quickly share any pressing emotions without having to catch up with others' responses or think about the technological system set up for the network. Sharing should be done through a medium that teachers naturally use every day, such as an e-mail list. Newer and easier-to-use technology, such as a Weblog (blog) or audioblog accessible by telephone (see Stanley, chapter 14 in this volume), can also serve the purpose.

Alternatively, teachers can be paired up with a peer, in which case they report only to that person, who would be familiar with the school context and issues the partner is facing. This pairing would enable teachers to send quick and spontaneous reflections because no information regarding the school context would have to be submitted with the entry. It could enable teachers to engage in more in-depth reflection and dialogue with other participants in real time, using a resource such as voice chat (see González, chapter 2 in this volume).

Difficulty with sharing emotions. Although we made great efforts to create a communication medium that was intimate, personable, and reflective of genuine concerns and interests among members, the electronic network did not sufficiently succeed in meeting the participants' emotional needs. We believe that electronic communication devices, whether e-mail, an e-forum, or another online mechanism, unavoidably create a distance between the people participating in these interactions. This distance can be in the form of a time lag and/or the lack of physical or emotional proximity between individuals, obstacles that are especially difficult to overcome during a short-term session such as a single semester. Much communication in daily life takes place through nonverbal means that enable a person to read subtle social cues, interpret signals sent by other group members, and respond to them according to their needs. It is difficult to achieve this kind of social subtlety through text-based CMC. In addition, sharing emotions through writing, as opposed to f2f communication, involves different cognitive functions. In written communication, reflection is more structured and delayed; the process of writing one's ideas serves as an additional round of reflection and thus fulfills a different need than the more extemporaneous desire to share one's emotions in a less filtered fashion in real time.

CMC tools such as synchronous text and voice chat, which allow for instantaneous communication and feedback, and videoconferencing may minimize the distance between participants. It would also be advantageous to complement the electronic channels of communication with more conventional types of support, such as phone conversations and occasional f2f get-togethers with other participants, if possible. These would be viable options for the teachers who participate in our network because they all teach in the Twin Cities area. We feel that this f2f interaction would be critical in fostering opportunities for emotional support in particular. By reinforcing collaborative professional relationships, teachers have multiple opportunities for professional growth through a variety of channels and modes.

Participant-initiated discussions. Participants were given the opportunity to ask questions and post discussion topics that pertained to their individual needs. These topics were then addressed by others in the group, including the teacher mentors. Based on this input from the participants, the mentors posted additional links to informative Web sites and related articles. While this spontaneity helped make discussions relevant to each individual, it may have contributed to the lack of coherence within the group because teachers were dealing with a wide variety of issues in specific teaching contexts (see also K. E. Johnson 1996).

A further drawback was the tone of the participants' postings. When they shared their frustrations, they often focused only on negative aspects of the experience (e.g., mainstream teachers' unwillingness and reluctance to collaborate) rather than on solutions. It would have been more productive for the novice teachers to focus not only on their beliefs but also on those of their colleagues in the local setting, and on how to facilitate better understanding of each other's views. We also felt occasionally that giving novice teachers the freedom to focus on issues that they felt needed to be addressed resulted in the discussion of symptoms rather than underlying causes.

To address these challenges in the future, we will pose questions arising from our knowledge of participating schools and districts. Mentors must bring in the contextual factors and view novices' issues consistently against the broader school environment, while allowing participants from a variety of teaching contexts to vicariously experience educational realities throughout Minnesota. Another way to provide the participants with more information about each teacher's context and situation would be to have them share video-taped lessons online, which would enable peers to see and experience firsthand the students and the classroom under discussion. We could also assign teachers to write a case study or a plan for action research based on their teaching context and their most pressing issues, all of which can be shared through the support network's central Web site.

Problems posed by technology. While there seem to be clear advantages to using technology, it can present issues of access and ability. Cuckle and Clark (2002), in their study of 216 teacher mentors, show a wide range of availability and access to technology as well as widely varying views on how to integrate technology into teaching. Inequitable access and the time needed to learn how to use CMC may inhibit the use of technology, especially when involving a network of peers in the field. In our case, all group members were knowledgeable about computer technology. They had taken a course in technology during their preservice year and reportedly used computers on a daily basis. Nevertheless, the participants experienced challenges with the CMC tools. Some issues related to technology included limited access to computers, lack of knowledge of specific computer facilities, and low comfort level with and preconceived ideas about using technology. While all the participants eventually learned how to log on to the support network and contribute to the discussions, they often felt that the use of technology complicated the reflection process and distracted their attention from the teaching issues. We learned that teacher reality can be so unbelievably hectic that having to remember any, no matter how little, additional information feels like an overwhelming task.

Given the realities of daily teaching, when planning and preparing for a support network, it is essential that facilitators pay careful attention to even the most minute and seemingly simplistic details. They should set up an easily accessible tutorial online. In the beginning, they should check and double-check to be sure that everyone knows what to do and feels comfortable doing it. Facilitators should urge participants to submit questions so that answers can be posted online as Frequently Asked Questions that can benefit everyone. When people are under a great deal of stress, as teachers often are, they have very low tolerance for systems that do not work in a smooth and predictable way, so facilitators should expect to spend extra hours during the first weeks of e-mentoring to ensure that the technology works efficiently for every participant.

As we continue to create our e-mentoring network, we intend to focus on teachers' emotional needs while seeking professional development support through their schools and districts. While a support network must provide advice and tips related to classroom practice, it must also offer mental and emotional support. Teachers view their realities through an affective lens. If we do not address teachers' emotional needs at the same time as we address their need for factual knowledge, our response will most likely not reach the audience. By addressing their emotional needs first, we remove the affective filter that inhibits teachers from making connections to the more factual knowledge.

Based on our experiences in setting up and maintaining the electronic support network, we believe that computers can facilitate this kind of emotional support through such functions as text and voice chat and videoconferencing, which are developing at a fast rate and can enable increasingly impediment-free f2f and other real-time interactions online. We also think that it makes sense to supplement electronic media with more traditional means of communication, such as site visits, if participants feel that their emotional needs are not being properly met. A carefully blended environment, with appropriate administrative recognition and support, would go a long way toward remedying the plight of the novice teacher, especially in a state like Minnesota, where teachers can be great distances from one another and in widely varying teaching contexts.

Appendix—Chapter 16
Web Sites and Communities for
Teacher Mentoring Online

Teaching.com	http://www.teaching.com/
Novice Teacher Support Project	http://ntsp.ed.uiuc.edu/
WINGS	http://www.edb.utexas.edu/ties/wings.html

Chapter 17

Reinvention of an Online Teacher Education Course: From Cooperation to Collaboration

Klaus Gommlich and Theresa Minick
Kent State University
Kent, Ohio USA

Preview

Many universities are realizing that they must move quickly to take advantage of the new online teaching and learning environment offered by the Internet. They fear, however, that courses and curricula may not be of the same high quality online. Gommlich and Minick created a master's-level teacher education course incorporating ESL methods, multimedia, and U.S. culture in an online learning environment. Teacher educators and novice teachers transformed their traditional roles in the process of developing content, postmethod pedagogical goals, and forms of collaboration. This chapter reveals how the course developed toward constructivist activities, especially how both teaching and learning intersected in collaborative practices. Their course, which offers group tasks infused with new technologies, can be replicated in many different content areas.

Before you read:

- The authors refer to information-centered versus inquiry-oriented pedagogy. What would be some of the features of each?
- How would the teacher's and learner's roles differ in each model?
- What kinds of technology could each type of pedagogy employ?

Teacher Education and Postmethod Pedagogy

In the context of a rapid development of linguistic, sociolinguistic, cognitive, and sociocultural models of second language acquisition in the past fifteen years, a holistic interpretation of foreign and second language pedagogy, including more complex approaches using computer-assisted language learning (CALL), increasingly reflect the constructivist process of learning embedded in real social situations that embody a variety of exchanges, activities, and interactions. Not surprisingly, researchers and practitioners are strengthening their cooperation to better inform practices, knowing well that the times of *one approach for all* in foreign or second language teaching and learning have long passed. Following the basic principles of particularity, practicality, and possibility in a postmethod pedagogy (Kumaravadivelu 1994, 2001), foreign language teaching concentrates on autonomous learners and teachers who—in their particular way and from their own perspectives—are capable of self-determining and self-directing their approaches to learning and teaching. However, an essential issue in this process remains the problem of how to instill the concepts of a postmethod pedagogy in both the learner and the teacher.

ESOL teachers know very well that some (if not the majority of) learners still expect to be loaded down with theoretical knowledge, and they regard techniques to practice skills as "add-ons." The need to build and rely on learning strategies as guarantors for continued learning is a vague or even unfamiliar notion to many learners. Likewise, González (2003) shows that foreign/second language teachers retain relatively traditional expectations when they are trained or retrained. Even though many foreign language teachers intuitively investigate and revisit teaching approaches, they may still lack systematic skills to turn experience into theory and enrich their views and reflections. In this context of change, Kumaravadivelu (2001) demands that the training of teachers, as well as their continuing education, be fundamentally adjusted from an "information-oriented system into an inquiry-oriented one" (p. 553). This transformation necessitates changing teacher educators' attitudes toward the novice teachers' learning processes, as well as altering the teacher educators' roles and responsibilities in the process.

Inquiry-oriented systems of education and further education can be sustained by offering many opportunities for teacher educators and novice teachers to engage in tasks (i.e., social activities) that lead to

- furthering general problem-solving abilities, thus building strategies;
- incorporating learners into various learning situations;
- understanding the process of content-relevant solutions to problems;
- appreciating and assessing achievements;
- most important, developing the ability to practice continuous learning.

Creating that potential repertoire of activities is of paramount importance for successful formation of long-term learning habits in novice teachers. Such activities include situations in which the social function of language is conditioned by various cultural frames as well as pedagogical tasks such as course planning, lesson implementation, and assessment.

Task-based and project-based language teaching (Beglar and Hunt 2003; H. D. Brown

2001; Skehan 1998; Stoller 2003; Warschauer 2000a) have long been accepted as communicative approaches, and have been used primarily to integrate the learner into activities beyond dyadic verbal exchanges. Applied to the multimedia context, an inquiry-oriented system of pre- and in-service teacher education not only focuses on the ability to create, implement, and assess tasks for the language learner, but also applies task-based approaches to the teacher education itself. Consequently, such an approach includes creating pedagogical projects, such as needs analyses, flexible or reusable teaching materials, and assessment models for skills-oriented and task-based language learning.

In this chapter, we describe how we practice an inquiry-oriented approach to teacher education through the genesis of an online course on U.S. culture. We will discuss two separate courses: (1) a graduate-level, one-semester course for novice teachers who, in turn, develop (2) an online course for ESOL learners. We elaborate on the learning processes of the teacher educators and novice teachers as developers of the online course, and we reflect on the function of cooperation and collaboration. By describing a two-year period, we demonstrate how our work fundamentally changed our ways of teaching and learning, especially how both teaching and learning by teacher educators and novice teachers intersected and overlapped, becoming almost inseparable. Finally, we offer the opinions and assessments of novice teachers to substantiate our findings.

American Culture Online

Integrating CALL in teacher education and continuing education became an indispensable requirement during the 1990s. Following the rapid development of new instructional technologies, content and approaches to courses preparing teachers for CALL have changed continuously. According to Hubbard (2003), "a language teacher being trained today should either have one or more full courses in CALL or be engaged in a professional training program where CALL issues permeate the whole curriculum" (¶2 under Introduction).

At Kent State University in Ohio, in the United States, we changed our orientation from information-centered to inquiry-oriented pedagogy in the training of students in a master's program. Empowering future teachers of ESOL to use new media and technologies in their classrooms has been the main driving force in creating an online course on U.S. culture for ESOL learners. Two forms of development were institutionalized: (1) a graduate course, Computers in L2 [second language] Teaching, to introduce the main concepts of CALL and build basic technological skills through mini projects, followed by (2) a workshop integrating online materials into a coherent language and culture learning course, which over two years developed into a teacher education course called Multimedia, Online Instruction and Second Language Acquisition (MOISLA). The novice teachers of diverse cultural backgrounds who enrolled in MOISLA all had graduate student status, were in at least their second or third semester of a two-year master's program, were trained in issues of task-based teaching, and had previously completed Computers in L2 Teaching.

The content and result of MOISLA was American Culture Online (2004), a Web-based content-oriented ESOL course for learners at the high-intermediate/low-advanced proficiency levels. The main content of American Culture Online familiarizes ESOL learners with a number of cultural institutions, behaviors, and expectations typically experienced by newly admitted international students at U.S. institutions of higher education. Topics include preparing for the journey to the United States; arriving at a destination; arranging one's student life; and learning about the host country and its institutions, people, cities, and so forth. All topics are arranged along a Road Trip (see the Course Map, Figure 17.1), which provides the environment for information, comparison, confrontation, and problem solving.

All units are designed to address the real needs and interests of international students who are new to the United States while incorporating a task-based pedagogy. For example, a unit called Home Sweet Home includes such subunits as Arriving in the US, Living On-Campus, Furnishing an Apartment, Shopping, and Saving Money. Living On-Campus opens with a presentation on major Kent State dormitories, including impressions of students who live in them. Students have to select a dorm where they want to live and fill out the Residence Services Application Form. Choosing a dorm is a task that comprises several activities, such as reading about various dormitories (including, e.g., their location, food plan options, types of rooms, facilities), chatting online with students who currently live in these dorms, and e-mailing partners in the course. After performing these activities and deciding where to live, students fill out the forms and e-mail them to their teachers. Then students can move

Figure 17.1. Menu for the American Culture Online Course Web Site (2004; available by course registration only)

on to learn dorm lingo, read a particular dorm's manual, practice requesting various room services, or request room cancellations. To be approved for room cancellation, students have to compose a persuasive letter in which they must use convincing arguments to explain their situation. The task is successfully completed if students manage to get their room cancellation request approved.

American Culture Online provides opportunities for learning through text, video, sound files, and Web references, as well as synchronous and asynchronous communications media such as chat rooms, e-mail, and discussion boards. All students are matched with key pals—other students in the course—whom they contact to exchange opinions, receive feedback, and share knowledge in order to learn from each other.

Phases of Course Development

Since its inception, the entire project of creating American Culture Online in MOISLA has been a work in progress, mainly due to continuous improvement of the technological tools available to the developers, a more refined understanding of realistic pedagogical principles in the online teaching context, and an improved understanding of how to enable the novice teachers as developers to achieve their goals pedagogically and technologically. Because students change from semester to semester, there has also been a continuous redefinition of workshop goals, procedures, and the teacher educators' and developers' roles in the online course development process. Pedagogically, the current version of the online course is the result of three consecutive phases differentiated by content and pedagogical goals as well as quality of collaboration among team members.

Phase I: Teacher-Directed Learning

Phase I was characterized by a clear separation between teacher educators' and novice teachers' responsibilities, and during this phase the course followed a very traditional construct in which the teacher educators created the aims and goals of the course and organized a syllabus to distribute the workload throughout fifteen weeks of class. It should be noted that the three teacher educators were a collaborative team with individual areas of expertise: (1) theory and methodology, (2) application and implementation, and (3) technology tools. The teacher educators determined the assignments, dates, and deadlines, including the dates by which students should learn how to use specific technology tools and how to integrate technology with second language acquisition theories (see Objectives for Phase I on the next page).

The majority of expected outcomes were predetermined. Before the new semester even began, the teacher educators had selected the technology tools and critical articles for reading and discussion. They defined the projects that novice teachers would create to demonstrate their understanding and knowledge of the tools and pedagogy, and they predetermined their own roles as well as the roles of the novice teachers. Very little change would occur in those roles during the semester.

Phase I produced over a dozen individualized projects threaded together by the common theme of U.S. culture and by the integration of specific technologies, but it did not

Objectives for Phase I

Teacher educators should

- provide novice teachers with the pedagogical and technical skills necessary to create multimedia materials for online distributed learning using task-based instruction.

Novice teachers should

- examine pedagogical issues related to online courses and task-based instruction;
- design multimedia lessons following the methodology of task-based instruction;
- create and edit graphics, sound files, and videos;
- use various vehicles for delivering multimedia materials.

By the end of the course, novice teachers should be able to

- manage three online editing tools,
- create pedagogically sound lessons based on the principles of task-based instruction,
- create multimedia projects appropriate for dissemination on the Web for distributed learning and/or distance learning courses,
- design and create task-based multimedia projects with accompanying lesson and assessment plans, and digitized video.

represent a shared vision of design and curricular goals. The rigidity of our approach interfered with the novice teachers' willingness and desire to freely unfold their creativity and deepen their involvement.

Phase II: Task-Based Team Development

A major shift in paradigm occurred in Phase II, when we transformed our *knowledge to practice* approach into an action plan of *knowledge in practice*. Phase II was characterized by cooperative and collaborative forms of interaction between teacher educators and novice teachers as they took a team approach to project development. Although the aims of the course were similar to those of the workshops taught in Phase I, the task-based approach in Phase II changed the dynamics of the teaching and learning environment and how we achieved those aims and goals. Teacher educators and novice teachers modeled for each other the methodology that we advocated, and in that process, the level of cooperation and collaboration among all participants increased. Educators as well as novices were learning to teach and learn together. We all experienced the multiple roles that we wanted our language students to experience. Changing from a prescribed to a task-based approach for the workshop was immediately reflected in students' assessments of their own learning, as demonstrated in this excerpt from a reflective essay:

> Working in this class showed me what it means to work on a task because contributing to this online course was a task in itself. We had to develop our own ways of accomplishing our

goals. Also, we had to manage our own time and set our own schedule. At the beginning, it was a bit confusing, because we expected more help from the instructor. With time, it became clearer. I think that experiencing all this "from within" added to my development as a teacher. (Student A)

Some of the changes in MOISLA that gradually resulted from a task-based methodology helped the teacher educators and novice teachers

- create and design the online course together (an outcome with real-world use of learning and knowledge);

- develop technology skills to complete the task (as opposed to skills for skills' sake);

- become involved in problem solving;

- seek feedback and advice from peers as well as from a community of experts;

- present their work to a committee of outside reviewers, consisting of former students who had completed the course and the director of the ESL Center (an intensive English program);

- discuss the committee recommendations and modify projects accordingly.

In addition, as novice teachers and teacher educators began to take on multiple roles, the novices more actively contributed in decision-making processes. They decided whether they wanted to work on their projects individually or as members of a team. They organized the presentation to the external committee and responded to the committee's feedback and suggestions. The most difficult challenge was to define, design, and create the online learning environment, which required multiple negotiations in order to reach a consensus. Novice teachers elaborated on the process of building collaborative work groups in their own words:

I experienced the challenges of group cooperation in terms of differences in culture, personalities, and beliefs. At times it was hard for me to give up individual control to the group. I realized how strongly my beliefs were about different parts of the task. However, I am grateful to have worked with others with diverse perspectives. I feel that our project is richer, stronger and more sensitive to learner's needs because of it. (Student B)

Working together helped me understand better what it means working as a team, what it means to listen to others, to get your own ideas across, and to compromise. In cooperative learning, you have to take into account personal traits of the people you work with, their background knowledge, their culture, etc. (Student A)

Phase III: Collaboration, Cooperation, and Continuity

The gradual transition from Phase II to Phase III was brought about by several facilitating factors:

- a more in-depth understanding of task-based instruction by novice teachers and teacher educators

- a better understanding of the role of collaboration and cooperation

- a collective interpretation of both the history and the future of the multimedia course, which was articulated through various documents and artifacts that were integrated into the course portfolio, thus establishing continuity from one generation of students and teachers to the next

Collaboration and cooperation in Phase III existed on multiple levels, requiring all parties involved in the project to adopt multiple roles: individual course members, members of work groups of varying size, and reviewers and evaluators in a community of experts.

Novice teachers began the course with their own questions and goals and ended it with questions for the next generation of participants:

- How do we evaluate what has been previously created?
- How can we continue to contribute to the American Culture Online course?
- What tasks should we (re)design?
- How should we (re)evaluate the lessons?
- What do I (we) need to learn in order to accomplish my (our) goals?
- What is our timeline?
- How can multimedia enhance the Internet-based learning experience and reinforce language use?
- What technology skills do I (we) already have? What skills do I (we) need to develop?

Throughout the course, these questions led to a more complex set of inquiries related to design, terminology, tutorials, copyright issues, and instruments, as summarized in Table 17.1.

In Phase III, whenever the course participants could not provide specialized knowledge to solve problems, a community of experts was sought. In addition to outside reviewers and experts, ongoing self-assessment and peer feedback provided information to the group, who then used that knowledge to determine their next steps. The voices of the novice teachers reflect knowledge-seeking strategies:

> In order to communicate with experts outside of classroom walls, we consulted with the staff at Student Multimedia for technical support with video editing. I also consulted my siblings who had previous training with Sound Forge and [Adobe] Photoshop. These consultations are important as they are coming from a different perspective and can give more technical explanations. (Student B)

> I had a chance to show the online culture course to an instructor in the ESL program who I might be helping to use the online materials for intermediate learners. I found it interesting that some of the lessons she liked the most were designed by non-native speaker graduate students, and this prompted me to think that sometimes as a native speaker, I may not even be aware of my own culture and how to present it to other people, because I may take for granted things that non-native speakers readily notice as distinctive about American culture. Because of this, it would probably be useful for me to consult with non-native speakers when designing a course on culture, because they may have more of a sense of what international students want or need to know about America. (Student E)

Among the important contributions of the students in Phase III was the selection of critical articles on instructional design theories, computer-mediated communication,

Table 17.1. Trainee Inquiries

Design	• At what levels of the project should there be cohesive design elements? • What aesthetic control does a team have in the development of their specific task-based lesson? • Which technologies support the design of specific tasks?
Terminology	• What terms do we need to define for the students in the American Culture Online course? • What words can be used consistently throughout the project? For example, should *final project* be used as the culminating activity for each task or for the completion of the entire course?
Tutorials	• What resources do the learners need in order to meet with success through online delivery of the content? • Do the learners need specific technological skills to accomplish the online tasks?
Copyright Issues	• Who are our resource people? • What release forms do we need to create for permissions from people in photos and videos?
Evaluation	• How can we evaluate multimedia use? • What instruments do we need to research or create? • How can we measure competencies (technology/content)? • How can we gather information about background knowledge and interests? • What survey or observational tools do we need to develop to measure the success of the online course?

discourse functions, syntactic complexity in synchronous and asynchronous communication, learning communities, and video in virtual communities. Everyone participated in the construction and dissemination of knowledge by reading the research and sharing findings with the class. As one participant notes,

> sometimes, we researched a certain area of knowledge, and then shared what each of us found. It proved to be very useful and time-saving. Besides, each person would have a certain "angle" to the problem, and it made the whole process so much more interesting and valuable. (Student A)

Other changes during Phase III related to removing the constraints of a traditional syllabus. In Phase I, the technology was taught in steps at preassigned dates. By Phase III, the novice teachers themselves determined when it was appropriate to learn, for example, how to edit video, edit images, and record and edit sounds based on the needs of the teams, their progress, and the consensus of the group. Formative assessment focused on the processes of group project development, so that dates could be made flexible without lowering the quality of final products, which were evaluated both formatively (during the course of a task or project) and summatively (at the end of the term), thus creating an understanding that even a so-called final product requires further development. Therefore, several novice teachers felt encouraged to continue working with the multimedia project after the course ended.

In Phase II, the novice teachers decided to create various documents and instruments to be archived for the next generation of novices enrolled in the course. In Phase III, the novice teachers went one step further by taking an active role in the course content and design for the following semester. Their suggestions and ideas were thoughtful and revealed the level of their engagement in the course. The impact of the evaluative process was more profound due to the development of joint ownership of work and knowledge about how everything linked together. For example, novices

- recognized the need for more in-depth evaluation and articulated their suggestions;
- reviewed the role of the external committee and when their participation would be most beneficial;
- determined what documents should be archived for future generations of designers and organized them into a portfolio;
- created and adopted a rubric for evaluating each task-based lesson, among other ideas and suggestions for assessment;
- recognized gaps in the design and content of American Culture Online and sought ways to address them;
- recognized gaps in their own individual or team or group knowledge base and sought ways to improve their understanding;
- recognized gaps in a syllabus constrained by tradition and sought ways to make the course more dynamic, with the flexibility to evolve and meet new challenges. (See the students' class philosophy in this chapter's appendix.)

Challenges and Future Directions

Throughout the different phases of the project, teacher educators and novice teachers were faced with a variety of challenges, such as the cultural diversity of the class and everyone's multiple perspectives, different degrees of familiarity with technology, the availability of technology, the sustaining of interest over an extended time, and interaction with outside experts. Also, for the first time, teacher educators and novice teachers were learning together in a task-based environment and needed to develop the necessary skills to work together in a variety of configurations (teacher educator to teacher educator, novice teacher to teacher educator, novice teacher to novice teacher). The course development process enabled us to challenge our beliefs and examine our teaching and learning strategies. Phase III demonstrates that the contextualization of learning provides collaborative experiences and more opportunities for observation and reflection. We focused less on assessing the skills acquired and more on the application of knowledge and skills, as called for in task-based instruction.

The result of this approach is very promising. First, it demonstrates that teacher training goes beyond simulating real-world situations. Novice teachers investigate pedagogical issues related to online courses, distance learning, and distributed learning; they investigate task-based instruction and select topics for inclusion in the online course based on learners' actual needs, requests, and demands; and they design and manage the vehicle for delivering the online course materials (in this case, the course management system WebCT [2004]). At the same time, they learn to use the tools needed to design their own multimedia projects and experience how to learn from each other. They come to understand that cooperation and collaboration are preconditions for preparing highly successful individuals in graduate education today. Novice teacher commentary summarizes these findings:

> I think I have changed as a teacher. I have become especially aware of what it's like to be a student of a task-based curriculum, and I have discovered aspects that I particularly like, as well as one I find frustrating. Perhaps what I mean is that, I have learned what works for me, what kind of input I need, when I need it, and when I just need to be left alone to work on the task at hand. While testing the tasks, I really started to think that a lot of the CALL instruction—as it is now—might be more beneficial if it were part of a wider curriculum. (Student C)

> Working together with my two project partners has turned out to be most beneficial, not only in terms of sharing workload, but also as regards the range of ideas that flew into the final project as well as the work process itself. Arranging responsibilities for the different parts of the work load and sections within the production process was one example for the collaborative nature of collaborative learning. (Student D)

> Overall, I think I have changed most as a language teacher through learning how to really look at overall goals and design of a course. . . . I have learned to be more cognizant of the fact that not all lessons will be useful for all goals, and that meeting actual learner needs is one of the keys to language teaching success. Specifically with technology, I have learned that it can be useful for teaching language, but that it is very time-consuming to design. However, I feel that I can now be confident to use technology as a research tool for myself and students, for communication . . . as an information resource, as a presentation tool, and finally as a language learning lesson itself. (Student E)

In short, by concentrating on the construction of meaning through hands-on projects involving collaboration and cooperation, we believe we meet the current challenges of a postmethod approach to teacher education. Teachers leaving a course such as the one described in this chapter are capable of steering their own professional development in foreseeable and unforeseeable social contexts in the future.

Acknowledgments

We would like to express our thanks and appreciation to the following novice teachers involved in the project since 2002: Brita Banitz, Tatyana Bystrova, Anja Graube, Jessy Hendrickx, Amber Hoyt, David Kadas, Katsumi Kawamata, Dragica Kosanovic, Karen Kreutel, Diane Lamb, Rebekah Lee, Robin Manning, Kasey McCullough, Justin Nicholes, Thelma Peres, Mathew Porter, Lyudmila Portnova, Susanne Rizzo, Amanda Robinson, Jeff Ross, Sara Ryan, Leona Salewsky, Philip Stokes, Martha Sutter, Lauren Vogel, Kamaria Wolf, Na Wu, Kim Yoder, Liying Zhao, and Katrin Zimmermann.

Appendix—Chapter 17
Philosophy of Fall 2004 Multimedia Class

Our Class Philosophy

Our class philosophy was to create a collaborative and cooperative working environment, to build on previous groups' contributions, and to move the American Culture Online project forward by refining extant materials and incorporating new elements. Part of the way we created a collaborative and cooperative working environment was to develop the tasks in teams. Although one of us chose to work solo, we all participated in each other's projects in both formal and informal ways.

One aspect of the collaborative and cooperative process was to compile the "6+6" evaluation of the American Culture Online course at the very beginning of the semester. Based on our evaluation, we were able to come up with some guidelines for our own work. For example, we decided to maintain the road trip structure of the course and to extend the simple design features (e.g., the white background, the impact font, the blue lettering) from the initial level to all levels of the task. Another aspect of design features we specifically wanted to incorporate was to keep each Web page short with simple navigation tools. Furthermore, we decided to provide students with more points of entry into the online experience, principally through the features of a sensory introduction to each location and the use of persona or storylines for each task.

With respect to the tasks themselves, we resolved to create tasks that required shorter, specific time limits to accomplish—ideally, 20 to 50 minutes. We also realized that for many of the tasks, quizzes had been a significant (or only) form of feedback. Therefore, we resolved to pay close attention to varying the ways students obtain feedback during and upon completion of the tasks. Also important to our class philosophy was a commitment to brainstorm "big," emphasizing creativity, breadth, and depth in our ideas. Once we had developed some exciting ideas, we carefully narrowed our focus so that we were able to divide tasks into manageable chunks.

By the end of the semester, we recognized a significant need in the American Culture Online course design, which we were able to articulate only after some discussion. Whereas the students have a roadmap by which to navigate the course, there is no similar guide for the instructor. We realized that it would be useful if not necessary for there to be some classification of the tasks themselves that would enable an instructor to structure the course based on his or her pedagogical goals. For example, it might be helpful to know which tasks focused on which skills. If we had had more time, we would have compiled such a "pedagogical roadmap."

On the whole, we have found the collaborative and cooperative environment to have been a satisfying one in which to work. The course has offered us exciting learning opportunities. We wish the best to the next generation of American Culture Online creators!

Chapter 18

Implementing an Online ESL Teacher Education Program

Andreas Schramm and Ann Mabbott
Hamline University
St. Paul, Minnesota USA

Preview

Demand for online learning is growing rapidly, yet the planning and execution of an online program may seem daunting, and faculty who are not familiar with Internet-based learning often remain skeptical about the possibility of developing high-quality online courses. Schramm and Mabbott describe what is needed to expand an existing on-campus ESL teacher accreditation program to outlying rural areas by developing a distributed-learning program online. Based on an ethnographic study of classroom communications, they decided on four primary initiatives: (1) re-creation of campus-based courses on the Web, (2) online academic and instructional support systems, (3) hardware and software to deliver learning content and facilitate interaction online, and (4) student recruitment and assistance.

Before you read:

- What differences in teaching and learning do you anticipate between a Web course and a traditional course? Are there interactions that may be accomplished better through the Internet?

- What are traditional course components that you would not want to miss? Which ones might you improve?

- How can teacher educators provide quality professional development in ESL for teachers who work in remote areas?

The Need for ESL Teacher Education

The number of English language learners (ELLs) in the United States has been growing at a steady rate. Between 1989–90 and 2003–04, the number of students with limited English proficiency in the K–12 public school system more than doubled in the United States, from 2,030,451 students to 4,999,481 (Padolsky 2005). This growth rate challenges public schools to find teaching professionals with expertise in language acquisition to facilitate appropriate education for these students. The federal government's No Child Left Behind Act of 2001 (U.S. Department of Education 2004a) further pressures schools to hire only highly qualified teachers by threatening sanctions against schools that hire unlicensed instructors.

Although most states have at least one teacher education program at the tertiary level that specializes in working with ELLs (Kindler n.d.), professional teachers who want to get additional certification in ESL often do not live close enough to such institutions for their participation to be practical. Thus, the challenge for existing ESL teacher education programs is to determine how to reach all those who need their services. One solution, also used by the special education field for similar reasons (S. B. Smith, Smith, and Boone 2000), is to develop an accessible, distributed distance learning ESL teacher program that is equal in quality to programs that are provided in person on campus. Such a solution may be appropriate in EFL contexts also.

In this chapter, we describe how an existing on-campus ESL teacher accreditation program can expand its services to outlying areas by developing an online program that allows all teachers in the state and beyond to access ESL teacher education. We demonstrate theory and strategies for converting traditional campus classes to the Internet environment, using as the backdrop the experiences of Hamline University in St. Paul, Minnesota, in the United States. After briefly describing the content of the program, we discuss the initiatives needed to recreate our high-quality, on-campus program in a distributed format. In particular, we address the pedagogical underpinnings used to convert our courses to the Web, areas of academic and instructional support that differ online, software systems to deliver content and facilitate learning, the challenges we faced in advertising and attracting students to our online courses, and the issues of program quality revealed in a study of on-campus and online modes of delivery.

Hamline University's Graduate Online ESL Teacher Program

Regarding its ELL population, Minnesota is fairly typical of the United States as a whole. The state had an ELL growth rate of 172.9 percent between 1994 and 2004 (National Clearinghouse for English Language Acquisition 2005). Minnesota has several ESL teacher education programs, but most are located in the Twin Cities area of St. Paul and Minneapolis and are not accessible to many teachers in the rural areas, which have seen some of the greatest growth. This situation is similar to that of many countries, which may have urban education centers but a great need for teachers in less accessible, rural areas. With this need in mind, Hamline University's Center for Second Language Teaching and Learning decided to develop an online program that would duplicate the accredited, on-campus program as closely as possible but make it accessible to teachers who live outside the metropolitan area. Most of the teachers who participate in our courses, both on campus and online, are already working in ESL or bilingual positions in schools but are not yet certified in ESL by Minnesota. Others are preservice teachers who need to take additional education courses that are required of all teachers, regardless of content area. Leaving their jobs to attend courses in the city would present a serious hardship, both for them and for their schools.

The online program has been in operation since 1997 and serves graduate students almost exclusively. Although our intention was to serve teachers in rural Minnesota, we have found that teachers in other states and countries have also chosen to join our program. We also serve local teachers with childcare and scheduling problems that were solved by the distributed online course work. This chapter deals solely with the ESL-specific content courses.

ESL educator licensing in Minnesota is prescribed by the Board of Teaching. Hamline University has incorporated the licensing guidelines into a series of ESL pedagogy courses that teachers take in addition to general education courses. Courses balance theory and practice and endeavor to make the content applicable to K–12 classrooms. After the publication of the *TESOL/NCATE Standards for the Accreditation of Initial Programs in P–12 ESL Teacher Education* (TESOL 2003), we reviewed our course work to ensure inclusion of those standards. We strive to maintain a student-centered, constructivist style of education for all classes and programs (Duffy and Kirkley 2004b; Mezirow 2000), whether they meet on campus or online. A list of Hamline's ESL licensure courses is given in Table 18.1. All but the

Table 18.1. Courses in Hamline University's ESL Licensure Program

Course	Credits (1 credit = 12–15 student contact hours)
Linguistics for Language Teachers	4
Basics of Modern English (grammar)	4
History of English	1
Second Language Acquisition	3
Testing and Evaluation (assessment)	2
Language and Society (sociolinguistics)	4
Development of Literacy Skills	3
ESL Methods (not online)	4
Practicum (student-teaching supervised by practicing licensed teachers as well as an instructor in the graduate program; not online)	1–6 (depending on previous teaching experience)
Total	**26–31 credits/hours**

last two are currently offered online. Please note that this table includes only ESL-specific courses; it does not include the general education courses required of all teacher candidates.

The courses that are not available online, ESL Methods and the Practicum, are provided to students in person either by Hamline faculty who live in or travel to rural locations, or during summer school when some students are able to come to the Twin Cities campus. The online courses are not independent studies. Each class has an involved professor and group of students and is as interactive as the available software, Blackboard (2005), allows. Each course has start and end dates, and since the courses are conducted throughout a semester, the students have to keep up with the course work on a weekly basis.

The decision to recreate the existing on-campus program in an online format was pragmatic. The Minnesota Board of Teaching closely controls teacher licensing program quality, and it obligated our university to provide distance learners with the same program that it approved for us to deliver to on-campus students. At the same time, we felt that using a program that had proven effective over time would most likely lead to success in exploiting an online environment for teacher education at a distance.

Course Transfer to the Web

The re-creation of traditional courses on the Internet, or the creation of online courses from scratch, requires a planned and deliberate approach within a theoretical framework. This section is devoted to a short description of one such framework. We complement the description by brief comments on how theory can be, and has been, put into practice.

The relationship between online and face-to-face (f2f) courses has received much attention in the literature (e.g., Duffy and Kirkely 2004a; Warschauer 1999). As one might expect, there are some major differences between f2f and online courses: access, language medium, amount of interaction, learner control, and interactivity, to name but a few (Herring 1996; Warschauer, Shetzer, and Meloni 2000). Yet there are also clear parallels between traditional and online courses. In both cases, participants need to be motivated to learn; the setting is designed for learning; and learners communicate through language, visuals, and other channels and codes (Herring 1996). We have chosen to focus on similarities between the two educational settings, which is not to say that the differences are less important. We have found that for many developers of online courses, differences seem to dwarf similarities; once the similarities become apparent, however, the major shifts required to accomplish teaching and learning in an online format become easier to envision.

In moving our courses to the Web, we made a conscious effort to apply our teaching philosophy to our entirely Web-based courses. In our traditional program, we espouse a student-centered, constructivist philosophy of education (Duffy and Kirkley 2004b; Mezirow 2000). Thus, interactivity is central to our teaching. What follows is a short description of how an interactive, student-centered, constructivist classroom experience can be recreated on the Web. (For a more detailed study of the ethnographic strategies employed in course development, see Schramm 2005.)

Communication is central to teaching and learning, and courses can be viewed as communicative events. To identify the communicative characteristics of a teaching situation, an ethnographic analysis of its components can be conducted (Bauman and Sherzer 1975; Hymes 1964). Such an analysis considers all aspects that are relevant to a particular communication and identifies their form and content. In this case we looked at the following components: setting, participants, events, forms, and topics. The resultant components and their characteristics can then be reproduced in a Web-based setting, thus providing a communicative template. This template applies equally to f2f and Web-based courses unless obvious differences, such as physical setting or written versus spoken language, are concerned.

In designing our Web courses, we first conducted an ethnographic analysis of each traditional on-campus course in order to recreate the most significant components of their communication in their Web-based counterparts. Table 18.2 lists the results of our analysis. The most important characteristics are examined in more detail in the following sections.

Participants and Events

Although in communication all components are connected, for the purpose of the ethnographic analysis they were separated. The first two analytical components are discussed jointly here. Probably the most important characteristic within the participant course component is *public communication*, which is very common during instruction. It is labeled "public" because all participants can potentially interact with one another and benefit from these interactions. It includes such public participant-event combinations as the *lecture* in a classroom, the classroom as a place for *whole-class plenary meetings,* and the classroom as a place for *small-group meetings.* These three types of events had to be implemented appropriately on the Web. The lecture is characterized by the instructor's public, one-way delivery of information while he or she holds the floor. To recreate this communicative component, the lecture content can be written up statically as a Web page or more dynamically through linked pages carefully designed to be accessed by all students; thus, the online course allows for public, instructor-focused, one-way content delivery.

Table 18.2. Ethnographic Components and Characteristics of a Course Setting

Participants	Events	Web Equivalents
Public Communication		
• Student-instructor • Student-student	• Lectures • Whole-class plenary meetings • Small-group meetings • Informal exchanges	• Web pages/Web slide show • Class bulletin board • Group bulletin board or chat room • Student bulletin board or chat room without instructor
Private Communication		
• Student-instructor • Student-student	• Side conversations during class breaks • Office hours • Study-group meetings	• E-mail • Private bulletin board or chat room

The next most important public participant-event combination in courses is whole-class plenary meetings. In such meetings, all course members might interact with one another and the instructor, which in contrast to lectures makes them nonstatic, interactive, and multidirectional. They can be reproduced on the Web using an electronic bulletin board, a tool that allows dynamic, equal access to the "floor." Students and instructors may interact publicly by posting and responding to messages. Each message constitutes a turn in the whole-class dialogue. Bulletin boards can further be used for public communications as a forum for announcements of upcoming events and assignments.

Small-group meetings to conduct exercises are also a public participant-event combination in traditional courses. Again, there is equal access to the floor by group members and by the instructors when they are present. This event can also be recreated on the Web by using bulletin boards that are limited to a specific group. Bulletin boards allow asynchronous discussions (which according to our experience provide the highest quality of discussion) or chat rooms for synchronous discussions. Group members post public messages and replies that constitute turns in the group discussion. Just as in traditional courses, the instructor can "visit" groups and take turns as well, or archive and analyze interactions and thereby provide feedback to the group.

Finally, public classroom events also include *informal exchanges* when students chat with each other before and after class and during breaks. Informal student-to-student interactions can be implemented on the Web using the bulletin board or chat room as well. For this purpose, students are given forums that are not accessed by the instructor.

Ethnographic analysis also identifies two private participant-event combinations between students and the instructor that typically take place during a course: those that take place (1) *off to the side* during class breaks or (2) during *office hours*. E-mail was used to reproduce these communicative components online. E-mail provides an individualized channel for private point-to-point exchanges between student and instructor. Furthermore, we have found that e-mail is more accessible and flexible than talking to an instructor in a traditional setting; students appreciate the promptness of instructor replies, which necessitates that the instructor check and reply to student queries frequently. Each e-mail message represents a turn in the instructor-student dialogue.

Groups of students in traditional courses also often meet to work on research projects, study for tests, or explore readings. Such *study-group meetings* take place in settings away from the classroom, and for this reason, these interactions can also be viewed as private. As in the other group settings described in the previous paragraphs, electronic bulletin board discussions or chat rooms can accommodate such private group meetings. However, unlike the public discussion groups, which are created automatically and require participation, such forums are set up based on requests from students, and access is limited to group members.

Forms and Topics of Communication

Among the communicative concerns we investigated were (1) topics discussed in courses; (2) nonverbal, visual elements employed for communicating course content; and (3) study resources, such as the course reader or library materials, that students access for additional course content. Forms of the language, such as informality and humor, are not considered here, as we felt this aspect of communication is universal, peripheral to developing our Web courses, and well documented elsewhere (e.g., Kötter 2002).

We decided to keep the topics of our campus-based courses intact as much as possible when reproducing them on the Web. As an example, we retained speech sounds, a topic in a linguistics course, and used audiocassettes, sound files on CD, or downloadable files to send to students. It is thus relatively easy to transfer the audio components of a lesson to distributed learning and retain the similarity to their counterparts in a traditional course. To help students study another topic (how to assess language proficiency) in the Testing and Evaluation course, we provide the same videotaped student speech samples as in the campus-based course and create an online forum that allows students to discuss how to conduct such an assessment. The instructor reads the postings in the student forum and can guide the discussion as needed.

For somewhat more abstract concepts, such as the topic of sound systems in a linguistics course, it is very helpful to use concrete objects. On campus, we demonstrate these concepts with a set of toys composed of multicolor struts and connectors that snap together, or with an organic chemistry model set. Online, digital photos of the toys are presented to the students, and the movements of the physical demonstration are described verbally with captions on a Web page. Such visual aids are not ideal but help certain students who struggle with grasping abstract concepts. Since visualization is one of the strengths of the Web, we also recommend other options such as animation or screen capture files.

We are in the initial stages of videotaping best practices in real ESL classrooms as a supplement to both our online and on-campus classes. We have identified ESL teaching techniques—such as cooperative learning, coteaching between ESL and mainstream teachers, and the language experience approach—and hope to find good examples of each in classrooms in our local area so that we can create CDs or DVDs to be viewed by our university students when they take online or f2f classes. To finance this endeavor, we are seeking funding from the federal government in conjunction with our local public television station.

Online Staff Support Systems

It is tempting to assume that online courses can be supported in the same or a similar way as traditional courses, but this section outlines several support areas that differ in an online course. We give concrete examples from our courses to show one way to implement systems for academic and instructional support, as well as the costs inherent in converting traditional courses into an online format.

Within the area of academic support, we found that professors have to spend more time teaching online than they would for an on-campus class. For example, in online discussions, every student is required to participate; *lurking* (just listening to or reading exchanges) is not an option. Thus, more instructor time goes into discussions. Similarly, every assignment, quiz, or exam must be handled electronically (e.g., downloaded, saved, opened, sometimes printed) before it can be graded; such individual handling takes extra time. Instructor time may increase 25–33 percent compared to the same course taught in a traditional campus setting. Some course management systems (CMSs; see the next section) can be set up to quiz students online, but this applies mainly to fact-based, summative evaluation; authentication of student work remains problematic.

Program assistant or secretarial time commitment also increases. Online courses typically require electronic preparation and mailing of materials (e.g., videos, audiocassettes, course orientation materials) that are traditionally hand-delivered or picked up by students. Although such tasks can initially be handled internally by program staff, it seems prudent and cost-effective to outsource much of this work to an online bookstore. In addition, someone must handle, and sometimes answer immediately, students' technical questions about hardware and software. We ended up splitting program assistant personnel into high- and low-tech assignments because of the differences in background required for each. We found that we needed an additional 40 percent full-time equivalent (FTE) position to accommodate both efforts.

If the library has not already caught up with new electronic materials, an institution also needs to allow for an increase in library staff, that is, a technically trained librarian to assist in distributed learning. Students in online courses may not be able to physically visit the library on campus. Services to accommodate their needs include online or phone reference desk work as well as ordering and delivering materials online. It is reasonable to expect over 40 percent FTE for a librarian to meet these needs, and a part-time student worker may also need to be hired. Furthermore, special software for the preparation and electronic delivery of library research materials will have to be obtained to keep resources equivalent in scope and quality to the traditional setting. As most university libraries come into the digital age, these costs and concerns will lessen.

Online courses also require additional involvement by the instructional technology staff, who address issues surrounding the conversion of class activities and materials to online formats, as well as the identification and use of instructional software supported by the institution. Issues regarding the hardware on which instructional software runs also arise regularly. The administrator in charge of technology services must provide input for capacity and cost planning for both software and hardware. In concrete terms, an online program may need to employ a 50 percent FTE instructional technologist. Hardware personnel support will be needed for approximately one hour per week per semester, and the administrator in charge of technology services may contribute about half an hour during the same period. The institution must include these personnel items in budgeting for course conversion and ongoing maintenance.

Instructional support is needed to redesign courses or help instructors with the course design, planning, and coordination once courses are converted and implemented. These functions can be provided by either an instructional technologist or an instructor with the necessary technological skills and knowledge. The advantage in the latter case is having someone who knows both appropriate pedagogy and the program of study. In our case, the design, support, and coordination of colleagues replicating five courses online took 33 percent FTE of a technologically savvy instructor over the course of one semester during development work.

Course Delivery Systems

In lieu of classrooms, online courses require CMSs to deliver an experience to distributed learners that is equivalent to what students encounter on campus. The main objectives of a course are to deliver content to learners, allow students to interact with the material, and facilitate their learning of that content. Two models are available to deliver content and the interaction with that content: using off-the-shelf software components via a server at the institution, or using the courseware of an off-site company on its server. The former model is rather expensive because the institution has to provide all the expertise and support for the various software products needed to deliver online course content locally. Among other things, a new server and operating software may have to be purchased and dedicated services put in place just for course delivery. Thus, leasing an off-site CMS, such as WebCT (2004) or Blackboard (2005), may be more prudent. A number of free or relatively inexpensive server and CMS products are also available, such as Moodle (2005) or Angel (2005). However, based on our experience, we advise creating a campus-wide support system for the CMS product to ensure course and service quality.

Since the goal is to provide the same level of support to both distance and on-campus students, the system must deliver handouts, visual materials, and course texts online. This can be achieved by using either the CMS or a specialized electronic reserve system, such as Docutek ERes (2005). Both allow faculty to post any course-related materials to a secure, password-protected Web page. Faculty can post any information they want to distribute to all students in the course, including documents in any format, spreadsheets, audio and video files, and links to other Web sites.

Resources for cross-disciplinary student research in education, sociology, psychology, linguistics, and language acquisition are essential to successful online learning. For students in distributed learning courses, timely access to documents can be provided in two ways: full-text databases and electronic document delivery. Typically, today's libraries subscribe to several electronic databases that are available to on-campus and online students alike. Among the most important library subscriptions are FirstSearch (Online Computer Library Center 2005), Wilson Education Abstracts Full Text (Ovid Technologies 2006), Educational Resources Information Center (ERIC; Cambridge Scientific Abstracts 2006a), PsycINFO (Cambridge Scientific Abstracts 2006b), Sociological Abstracts (Cambridge Scientific Abstracts 2006c), and InfoTrac (Thomson Learning n.d.). These databases are updated frequently.

The university library also needs to provide students with more traditional, non-Web sources of information. For articles that are not available in full-text databases, specialized delivery systems of copyrighted articles are needed. For this purpose, libraries can use electronic document delivery, with software such as EDDplus and DocuFax, both modules of Docutek ERes (2005). With this type of software, students are able to send an electronic request to the library, which digitizes the article for retrieval on the Web. Consequently, providing this type of service requires a librarian with the appropriate training to coordinate and supervise the research component of a program to ensure adequate resource access. With online courses, a whole new model of research service becomes necessary, and development of that model requires an initial investment in additional staff resources as well as CMS access and support.

Student Recruitment and Retention

Having a high-quality, accessible, online teacher education program in place does not automatically draw students, even when there is a great need for qualified teachers. Traditional means for recruiting students, such as catalogs, do not suffice because students are not accustomed to seeking online institutions or distance learning options for their education. In addition, prospective students often have financial constraints that could keep them from participating in an online program. In rural areas, teacher salaries are comparatively low, and positions are frequently part-time only. But supplemental grants, such as those supported by the federal Title III act in the United States, may increase accessibility to courses by reducing the cost of tuition. Students in the program may pay a small fee, such as one hundred dollars per course, and the rest of the tuition is paid for by the federal grant. A well-informed local recruiting agent can help school districts apply for such grants for their students.

In addition to announcing courses through the traditional university course bulletin, we reach potential students by advertising on the Internet, through educational cooperative service units located throughout the state or region, and on the database of the Minnesota Department of Education. Another option is to send tailored mailings to rural schools. Yet none of these methods has been as successful as sending a local recruiter who travels to schools and contacts prospective students in person.

Online Program Quality

Online programs need to be examined rigorously for quality as reflected in student performance and satisfaction. Assessment of student performance may be accomplished through traditional measures, such as grades on assignments. Student satisfaction with the courses can be determined by retention rates and course evaluations. In addition, explicit comparison of online and on-campus learning environments is needed to ensure uniformity in meeting standards.

We started the process of examining program quality by conducting a pilot study comparing the on-campus and online versions of two courses: Linguistics for Language Teachers, a foundation course, and Testing and Evaluation of ESL Students, a more applied course. Our research question was the following: is it possible to maintain the same instructional and course design quality in such courses when they are moved from the traditional on-campus setting to an online format?

Results of the study show no significant differences between the two modes in terms of grades or retention rates. Only one of the fully anchored rating scale statements from the course evaluations resulted in a higher rating for the on-campus environment: *Instructor had good rapport with class participants*. None of the other fourteen statements on the course evaluation showed a significant difference for Testing and Evaluation of ESL Students, while the online Linguistics for Language Teachers class was rated as superior to the on-campus version by students on two of the statements: *Handouts were appropriate and informative* and *Instructor demonstrated competency in his/her area*. The open-ended questions that followed the rated statements showed that students in both online classes were quite satisfied with the interactions they had with one another, confirming that we achieved success in making them feel like part of an academic learning community. (For a complete description of this study, see Mabbott and Schramm 2004.)

Challenges and Future Directions

As a result of our study, we have drawn several conclusions about online learning for ESL teacher candidates. Like other studies (Shea et al. 2004; S. B. Smith, Smith, and Boone 2000), our research found that students can learn as much in an online class as they do on campus. Another conclusion is that professors should make a conscientious effort to help online students feel welcome in class and to establish a rapport with them. Although students did not rate online classes poorly in this respect, it is the one area in which the online courses did not do as well as the on-campus classes. Although instructors were actually quite "present" in their online classes through monitoring student discussions, the perception by some students was that they were left alone more than they liked. Professors need to find a way to make their presence more transparent, perhaps by simply responding more often to student comments. The third conclusion is that students who choose online learning are quite happy about other aspects of it, including interactivity with their peers. We see these results as quite positive, and they give us good reason to continue building interactions and connections within the online courses to ensure personal engagement and intellectual challenge.

Enrollment in online classes has been high, so our challenge is not to convince students of the viability of online options, but rather to convince our skeptical colleagues that online learning can be high quality. Naturally, professors are people who enjoy interacting with their students, and some doubt that one could have the same supportive academic experience online as one has in the physical classroom. In addition, language teacher education and teaching languages have traditionally been hands-on, in-person communicative endeavors. However, skeptics may want to put their reservations about virtual education on hold and consider the following: online programs can empower students who have nowhere else to go for their education, and can serve them well. Such programs can therefore improve the quality of the education available for language minority students or language students in general, especially those in more rural areas.

Another challenge is to see whether we can facilitate a completely online program. So far, most of our program is online, but we still require that students attend an on-campus ESL Methods class and do student teaching in a physically supervised setting. This in-person contact reassures us that our students are actually effective teachers. We know, however, that even the minimal on-campus requirement is prohibitive for some student teachers. If we are able to use technology to assist us, we actually may be able to develop a fully online program. We plan to continue to upgrade our technology use and improve our online courses as new technological resources become available. We hope to soon have videos of best practices in ESL instruction that can be streamed as video or played on a computer CD or DVD drive and viewed during online instruction. If we are able to obtain high-quality classroom models in a video format, we may be able to move the ESL Methods course online. We are also exploring the possibility of using video cameras or Webcams so that university supervisors can visit ESL teachers in their classes and coach their instruction virtually, and teachers can review their own performance in the classroom. As we, and students, become more tech savvy, our educational programs can only improve.

Our efforts thus far have been professionally satisfying. Because of the flexibility in course options, hundreds of teachers who would not otherwise have had the chance have been licensed in ESL. These professionally prepared teachers are much better able to advocate for the social and academic needs of their students than they were in the past. Before they were licensed, many of these teachers were well intentioned, but they did not know, for example, about schools' legal requirements to educate ELLs, or how to assess language proficiency and determine who should be in an ESL class and who should not. They did not understand language systems and second language acquisition processes adequately enough to become highly skilled language teachers. If they were already experienced teachers, they may have developed appropriate teaching skills for ELLs, but these teachers were not able to defend their skills or programs to their colleagues and administrators with sound, research-based evidence. Providing an ESL teacher education program online means that all ELLs, not just those who live near universities with ESL teacher education programs, can have access to high-quality teacher education.

Chapter 19

Issue: *Tools for Online Teacher Communities of Practice*

Vance Stevens
Petroleum Institute
Abu Dhabi, United Arab Emirates

Preview

Stevens is the founder of Webheads in Action, a teachers' community of practice (CoP) existing almost entirely online, which explores technology collaboratively through the extensive use of computer-mediated communication (CMC) tools. In this chapter, Stevens documents the birth and development of this community. He explores how teachers learn to use CMC tools in a constructivist setting, such as that offered by the Webheads. Teachers' hands-on professional development, in turn, informs their interactions and approaches to language pedagogy with their own students. Stevens describes several Webhead classrooms and argues that if teachers pursue ongoing professional development in the context of CoPs, they will work within a constructivist paradigm, where scaffolding occurs in a shared zone of proximal development.

Before you read:

- What professional interactions have you engaged in while developing your pedagogical skills? Were any of these online?
- How do the ways in which teachers learn throughout their schooling affect how they teach their students? What are some examples?
- What constructivist techniques do you feel are appropriate for your students, either online or face to face?

Writing for Webheads: Growth of an Online Community

Language teachers have often shown themselves to be on the leading edge of computer-based technologies because of their involvement in communication. The Internet is an excellent means of putting people in touch with one another, and this characteristic has been exploited by language teaching professionals. The tools with the most potential for learner interaction can also be used by teachers to learn about these tools and how to use them with students. In fact, to use CMC tools successfully with students, teachers must gain experience with these tools themselves. One significant solution to the problem of incorporating rapidly developing CMC and other technologies into ongoing teacher training has been the formation of CoPs online, where teachers share and learn how to use techniques that benefit their students in online or blended settings.

Wenger is perhaps the best-known proponent of the concept of *communities of practice* (1998). He defines CoPs as simply "groups of people who share a passion for something that they know how to do and who interact regularly to learn how to do it better" (2002, 1). Wenger (1998, n.d.) distinguishes CoPs from other communities (e.g., a neighborhood) because they share three crucial elements:

1. A common domain of interest (a specialty, sometimes recognized as such only within the CoP)

2. Cohesion and interaction within the community (as opposed to simply shared membership in an organization)

3. A practice or expertise (as opposed to a common passive interest, for example, in books or movies)

I came to realize the importance of online community in language learning during the 1990s, when I began teaching a writing course at Winet's (n.d.) project, StudyCom English for Internet, for students from around the world. StudyCom matched volunteer teachers with volunteer students in free online courses. However, I soon saw that sending composition assignments via e-mail did not engage the students beyond the initial correspondence. When one of my students made a Web page for our course, I was so impressed that I took it upon myself to learn the Web-authoring language HTML. This was an awakening for me, a realization that what was missing in the fleet of e-mail messages passing in the night was an anchor. This student had demonstrated the importance of having such an anchor—a portal that would focus the course on its objectives and expand its purview infinitely through hyperlinks to other relevant documents on the Internet.

Another significant leap came in the late 1990s, when Winet introduced what he called *3D classes* in English and encouraged his teachers to explore virtual chat rooms in The Palace (2001–2006), a free online space where participants were represented by avatars (characters that could be created from personal photos or graphics). The illusion of three-dimensionality was created by endowing each Palace (a graphical chat space unique to a given server) with objects such as doors and windows hyperlinked to other graphical spaces, so visitors had the impression of moving from room to room. My writing classes used a Palace chat room called the Virtual Schoolhouse. The interface gave visitors great leeway in expressing themselves not only in text but also with emoticons (small images that represent feelings) and tools that allowed them to control the environment in imaginative ways. For example, visitors could share graphical objects by dropping them, virtually, and letting others capture them. (Other multi-user, object-oriented domains [MOOs], such as schMOOze University [n.d.], are similar in concept.) My students, now known as *Webheads*, liked the graphical Palace environment and saw it as an enjoyable way of improving their language skills.

Members of this early Writing for Webheads (WfW) group (see Stevens 2006c) tended to range in age mainly from secondary school students to young working professionals, although we had a septuagenarian grandfather in the group (a former minister of culture from Argentina) as well as a young schoolboy from Saudi Arabia. The students shared a desire to improve their English, often for career enhancement; an attraction to the Internet; self-motivation as volunteer learners; and sufficient English ability to cope with unfiltered interaction with native speakers. They also tended to be empathetic with each other and appreciative of the opportunity to learn on the Internet. A small subset of the group consisted of nonnative-English-speaking language teachers practicing in their respective countries. These teachers, as well as the native-English-speaking teachers in the group, benefited from having the opportunity to try online techniques with genuine students, and all parties appeared to have sufficient self-interest in the arrangement to develop and sustain it over a period of several years. (The teachers in our WfW group would eventually become the Webheads in Action.)

In addition to e-mail and the MOO for chat, I found the following tools to be beneficial to sustaining the emerging community:

- ICQ (2006), Internet chat software, introduced a revolutionary means of seeing when friends are online, and we used this tool as a *back channel* to get in touch with each other, help each other download and install needed software, and meet in whatever other chat tool we were experimenting with that week.

- I used my new HTML skills to help students and teachers get to know one another by posting their writings on the Internet. (In the current Internet world, this can be readily accomplished through Weblogs [blogs].)

- I requested that students send me photos, and I eventually mounted a gallery of portraits with links to individual student Web pages. These efforts served to create a far better sense of community than simple e-mail exchanges.

- Eventually students and teachers started e-mailing audio files to each other, using Pure Voice and Real Audio (now called RealPlayer [2005]). The voices added another dimension to what we were learning about one another, and audio had pedagogical value as well. One student uploaded recordings of her reading aloud and asked for feedback on pronunciation. We often heard from students that aural training was something they felt was lacking in an online environment, so they were happy when they had a means of practicing with other group members, some of whom were native speakers.

- A *Eureka!* moment came when we first tried an early version of HearMe (no longer available), a synchronous, audio-enabled chat service that worked as a plug-in through our Internet browsers. The makers of HearMe sent us code that we simply copied into our own Web pages. By visiting these pages, we could speak to each other.

WfW participants could now find each other in ICQ, drop by The Palace for text chat, and then speak to one another in HearMe. We were well on our way to becoming a group who, despite having never met personally, knew a great deal about one another: what we looked like, what we sounded like, and through our writing, how we perceived the world and one another. We had, in short, become a CoP, despite being divided by great physical distances.

Community Building 101: Webheads in Action

By the early 2000s, WfW had branched out from simply meeting online regularly to participating in online events. For example, the WfW teachers gave a presentation at the April 2000 Teaching in the Community Colleges online conference, and we invited our students to participate. We realized that having students meet and interact with language teachers exposed the students to authentic language, and their confidence and motivation grew when they found that they could communicate successfully in a live presentation (see Coghlan and Stevens 2000).

Our use of voice chat at that time was innovative and, combined with our foray into online conferencing, gave us the opportunity to invite newcomers to our online gatherings. We began to submit proposals for online events at land-based conferences, and when they were accepted, we posted to electronic lists frequented by language teachers to announce our live online voice events. In this way, we engaged live conference audiences on land in impromptu interactions with remotely participating WfW members. We were pleased to find not only that these events worked, but also that we could count on members within the group to make and keep appointments online. Another important aspect in online community development was having confidence that reputations could be staked on unseen colleagues who were responsible enough to one another to keep their promises.

Our use of voice technology had a different kind of impact on WfW, one that changed the character of our community. Voice chatting, and its potential to reach learners and peers online, brought attention to our work and enabled us to become more involved with teachers who wanted to learn about CMC and how to use it with their students. Unfortunately, the increasing involvement of teaching professionals ultimately had a dilatory effect on student participation. Students who popped by our regular Sunday synchronous chats found that their voices were being drowned out by native-speaker banter, and the discussion on the mailing list was tending toward teacher talk.

As a result of this divergence in purpose and audience, I took advantage of an opportunity at the end of 2001 to deliver an online workshop (Stevens 2006a) in the second annual TESOL CALL Interest Section–sponsored Electronic Village Online (EVO; for a description of this volunteer effort, see Hanson-Smith and Bauer-Ramazani 2004). The workshop was meant to show teachers how an online community could be formed by involving the participants in an actual community formation experience, and then relating this experience to the context of language learning. Many teachers in WfW joined the workshop, which came to be known as Webheads in Action (WiA) to distinguish it from WfW. (See the group site at Stevens 2006b). Although many of the teachers tried to keep a foot in both communities, it soon became clear that the most stimulating contributors were focusing on WiA. Consequently, WiA has flourished and expanded, and as of this writing four years later, it continues to generate many e-mails each day and produce frequent collaborations among members (Figure 19.1 shows the portal page [Stevens 2006b]). While the student WfW group still exists at around four hundred members (about the same number as WiA) and continues to enjoy sporadic interaction, the dynamic of the group has diminished, and its members hardly know each other as well as in the early days.

Figure 19.1. Webheads Portal Page with Community Member Images
Source: http://www.vancestevens.com/papers/evonline2002/webheads.htm.

Webheads Workshop Outcomes

The content of the EVO WiA workshop was both skills (instruction in the use of the free text, voice, and video synchronous and asynchronous CMC tools in learning environments) and pedagogy (a discussion of how these tools could be used to help bind a group of diverse online participants into a cohesive community). By using these tools, WiA members met online as a CoP and got to know each other while sharing experiences and expertise. There is no doubt that the participants enthusiastically embraced the global community that emerged, as shown by evidence left throughout our Web archives (see, e.g., Almeida d'Eça 2005b; Stevens 2006b).

In addition to the split from WfW, there were two particularly important outcomes of the EVO WiA session. First, many of the group members applied to their teaching what they had learned from participation in this online community. WiA members regularly document their teaching experiences with online CMC tools, and several have specifically documented changes in their teaching by comparing their work before their encounter with WiA to more recent work influenced by the CoP (e.g., al-Othman 2001–2004; D. González 2003a; Yeh 2003a).

Second, unlike other EVO sessions that met during this eight-week period, the Webheads did not disband. Throughout the year, we continued to meet at our regular Sunday chat at Tapped In (SRI International 1995–2004). Group members continued to participate in special online events as well as face-to-face (f2f) and online conferences, and even launched their own traditions, such as an annual HalloWebhead party at the end of each October. WiA attracted new members, in particular those who became interested in the group through their research into CoPs (e.g., C. M. Johnson 2003; Steele 2002) and those who participated in what have since become annual EVO sessions, Becoming a Webhead (see D. González and Almeida d'Eça 2006) and its many sequels run by "graduates" of the original group, to inculcate in others the Webhead model of community formation. Through interaction with new members, the community-of-practice paradigm has been embraced as a model for the learning that takes place through a loose yet strengthening association (Lave and Wenger 1991).

Since the 2002 EVO WiA workshop, the CoP model has been replicated with consistent success in the formation of similar communities, for example, Real English Online for teachers and students who use video (Marzio and Hanson-Smith 2006), and the bloggers of Dekita.org's (Ammann, Campbell, and Dieu n.d.a) EFL/ESL Exchange (Ammann, Campbell, and Dieu n.d.b), who meet in weekly chats, present at online conferences together, and publish a communal blog and interlinked blogs with the work of students from around the world. As Brown and Gray (1995) say about CoPs, "what holds them together is a common sense of purpose and a real need to know what each other knows" (¶3 under Communities of Practice Emerge). The Communities of Practice group, com-prac (J. Smith 2006), is one of many CoPs that have come together out of an interest in CoPs themselves; these are often excellent sources of material on the topic.

An examination of long-term CoPs suggests that the following components are integral to their formation and maintenance in a distributed online environment:

- *engaged coordination*—To retain vitality, CoPs need intensive nurturing by a committed and skilled coordinator (or coordinators). The coordinator ensures that all the other components are managed, and that members of the group feel personally welcome, appreciated, and involved.

- *pictures*—Posting community member pictures on the Internet is a trademark of our CoPs and helps members get to know one another.

- *voices*—Voice over Internet Protocols (VoIPs) are common CMC tools these days, and voice recordings can be stored at community portals and made available through Web sites and blogs. Some members of our community feel that voice is more powerful than photo images in forming impressions and leading to bonding, but certainly, in tandem, these two help CoP members get to know and relate to one another.

- *community Web pages*—Webheads develop Web pages where member details, such as place of residence, workplace, professional and even sometimes personal links and vignettes are recorded, again for the purpose of helping others in the CoP form impressions of personality and professional background.

- *asynchronous interaction*—WiA members utilize free electronic lists and community portals, such as Yahoo! Groups (2006), and set up wikis (Web pages that can be edited collaboratively online), blogs, Moodle sites, discussion boards, and so on to establish asynchronous contact among members.

- *synchronous interaction*—Webheads establish regular weekly online meeting times using freely accessible Web portals, and we encourage use of instant messaging in our groups.

- *archives*—Members post transcripts of conversations with each other on the Internet; archive collaborative presentations, publications, and other accomplishments; compile syllabi developed during collaborative online sessions; and link these to pictures and biographical details to enable the community to recognize and get to know the contributors and the classes they teach.

- *informality*—We recognize that we are essentially human, and we front the phatic (social and emotive) elements of our interpersonal relationships. This style of interaction has resulted in collaborations of the highest professional quality.

- *tolerance*—A member once remarked that among our strengths is downplay of any personal agenda among members. Acceptance of boundary members (sometimes called *lurkers*) is also a Webhead characteristic; members are welcome to make contributions whenever they feel comfortable doing so.

The Importance of Chat in Community Cohesion

What is usually called *chat* is discouraged in many language learning settings because of its association with telegraphic discourse and paucity of content. Some see chat as a frivolous waste of time—anathema to learning and a panacea for lonely hearts. Many regard it as potentially dangerous because people can misrepresent interactions or reveal too much of their identity and expose themselves to abuse. Tudini (2003), for example, notes a problem with "interlocutors seeking virtual sex" (p. 154; see also Privacy Rights Clearinghouse 2005; Rao 2003). However, the telephone is also susceptible to these pitfalls: people can waste time on the phone or use their mobiles to arrange trysts. Yet the telephone is perceived as a remarkable tool that facilitates communication and helps people accomplish tasks that would be impossible or difficult if left to other means of communication. Nonetheless, the telephone suffers severe limitations as a pedagogical tool. It is expensive over long distances and impractical for use by more than two people without special equipment or venues. If only people could pick up the phone and call anyone (or a group of people) anywhere in the world at any time for as little as they spend on their Internet connection. Chat tools allow people to do this and more, in combinations of text, voice, and video image.

For teachers to gain more realistic perspectives on the benefits of chat with students, they must use it themselves in their own professional development. The activity most pertinent to this outcome is teachers joining a chat to find out from each other how to use CMC tools and best apply them in teaching. Setting conditions whereby teachers are able to interact in CoPs exposes them to synchronous communication in safe and healthy environments and helps them realize that such environments can be created for their own students as well. (See examples in Almeida d'Eça 2003c, chapter 12 in this volume; D. González 2003b; Trites, chapter 15 in this volume.) For commonly used software or Internet tools to be used effectively in professional learning environments, they must be freely available to all concerned, that is, both low cost and cross-platform, in order to encourage participation from all group members. Because of our activities as innovators and pedagogically cutting-edge users of CMC, Webheads have been fortunate over the past few years to have been granted free use of various voice-enabled presentation tools whose costs are born by the host services, such as LearningTimes (2006), Alado (n.d.), and WorldBridges (n.d.). See CMC Tools Used by WiA on the next page.

Community Building 201: Constructivism in Blended Communities

Reflection on WiA suggests that teachers must experience participation in a CoP to understand the range of CMC tools available to them, to gain some expertise in orchestrating their use, and to practice the pedagogical principles appropriate to them. A CoP provides a *zone of proximal development* (Vygotsky 1978) and *scaffolding* in training techniques to offer an authentic and rewarding experience for teachers, who learn at their own pace with the support of other language teaching professionals. After such experiences, members can put expertise back into the community, extending the scaffolding to others. An online CoP is unique in that it necessitates communication through the tools that are being learned.

Techniques for scaffolding in CoPs introduce teachers firsthand to learning through constructivist models. Much has been written about constructivism in learning (for a comprehensive list of Web resources on the topic, see Ryder 2006). Hsiao (n.d.) provides a succinct definition:

Constructivist approach to learning emphasizes authentic, challenging projects that include students, teachers and experts in the learning community. Its goal is to create learning communities that are more closely related to the collaborative practice of the real world. In an authentic environment, learners assume the responsibilities of their own learning, they have to develop metacognitive abilities to monitor and direct their own learning and performance. When people work collaboratively in an authentic activity, they bring their own framework and perspectives to the activity. They can see a problem from different perspectives, and are able to negotiate and generate meanings and solution through shared understanding. The constructivist paradigm has led us to understand how learning can be facilitated through certain types of engaging, constructive activities. (II.2)

"Engaging, constructive activities" are precisely those that Webheads encourage (for examples of activities, see Stevens 2004; for a continuously updated index of WiA work, see Almeida d'Eça 2005b). One of the interesting results of WiA has been the conscious transfer of community-building strategies from the online experience, where overt strategies are required, to f2f or blended environments, which might not seem at first blush to require such strategies.

In constructivist thought, learning is considered a social phenomenon, and the presence of a community (others within one's zone of proximal development as well as experts leading the way) is a strong influence on learning. Teachers have long sought to make use of the notion that learning is aided by the social interaction that results from putting students into small groups and having them provide feedback to one another. However, I now find that the community-building techniques that I apply to my online classes, by which students get to know each other through their Web presence, work equally well in my f2f classes when they are blended with online experiences. The feeling of community within the class develops when student work is made available online for scrutiny by an audience of appreciative peers. The students work to project the right presence, and others in the class come to appreciate the personality quirks that show through (especially when students are encouraged to illustrate their work with digital art).

The following are techniques for community building that are mirrored in WiA and that I use in my blended but largely f2f language classes:

- Have students create Web presences through blogging and/or creating Web sites.

- Create community Web pages where member introductions and links to personal and professional Web sites, voice mail, and blogs can be accessed.

- Post these community member pages, with pictures, on the Internet.

- Encourage interchange between the local student community and others around the world.

Blogging gives a voice on the Internet to students who do not have direct knowledge of HTML, and it can be an important element in building community online (A. P. Campbell 2003; Galloway n.d.; see also Stanley, chapter 14 in this volume). The advantage of blogs is that students can get themselves online instantly (see Stevens 2005a). They do not have to bother with creating Web pages or deal with any of the normal aspects of Web hosting and file transfer. Furthermore, students can personalize their blogs with photos and links to other Web spaces. I think of blogging as a message in a bottle because it also grants students access to an audience of readers and interactants beyond their immediate school confines. Many Webheads are doing significant work with blogging (e.g., Dieu n.d.; G. Stanley 2005, chapter 14 in this volume; Suzuki 2004).

Other Webheads have found unique ways to utilize the Webheads community in their f2f or, more usually, blended language teaching situations. González (2003b), for example, notes parallels between lessons learned in a community of peers and their applications in the classroom with regard to chat, which she considers "an unexploited tool for language learning and teacher development" (¶1 under Conclusion). González used her experience with Webheads to create a blended, chat-suppported, video-enhanced English course for architecture students in Spain and Venezuela (González, chapter 2 in this volume; D. González and St. Louis 2002).

Al-Othman (2003–2004) applied some Webhead-inspired insights to her teaching when she announced that her Kuwait University end-of-term student presentations would be delivered live online through the Webheads' Alado (n.d.) voice chat room. She invited community members to participate by listening and then helping to evaluate the presentations. Yeh (2003a) also applies CMC techniques to her blended classes in Taiwan; she has created a graphically appealing set of Web pages documenting her students' work with other Webhead community members. One example of her ongoing work is her online sessions with Webhead songwriter Michael Coghlan. Yeh's students listened to recordings of Coghlan's songs and then met the composer online to discuss the lyrics with him (Yeh 2003b, 2004a). Yeh also has her students record and critique each other's speeches in an audioblog (or *podcast*) on the Internet (Yeh 2006). An example of her work with total physical response features a charming online video of her students talking their way through a Tai Chi demonstration (Yeh 2004b).

Challenges and Future Directions

Despite evidence of the benefits cited in this volume, teachers typically are not taking advantage of available technologies to put their students in optimally communicative, interactive, constructivist, student-centered learning environments. There are many reasons for this situation. Foremost may be that these technologies are emerging and evolving faster than teachers are able to keep up with them. Teachers are typically overworked with their day-to-day tasks, and it is the exceptional teacher indeed who takes the time necessary to stay current with technology. Many teachers are simply not interested in the technology for its own sake, and only consider using it in situations where it can marginally enhance what they have always done with students. This is a laudable first step, but the most appropriate applications of technology in education require both skill and art. Technology as a tool most resembles a paintbrush—using the brush to refresh a surface the way sailors apply paint to ships involves a much lower level of skill and familiarity than manipulating it like an artist. Producing truly stimulating material requires finesse in applying technology so that students will not only benefit from the immediate implementation but also be able to manipulate the tools themselves in an imaginative manner in pursuit of their lifelong learning objectives. Therefore, the most successful uses of technology in education tend to be innovative, and for innovation to occur, it is necessary to have both an interest in technology for its own sake and a means of efficiently pursuing that interest and applying it to one's particular situation.

Innovation and application are far from impossible goals. This chapter supports the assertion that if teachers pursue professional development in the context of a CoP, they can achieve these goals by working within constructivist learning environments, where scaffolding occurs among those in a shared zone of proximal development. To apply community-building techniques to online or blended teaching practices, teachers need to experience participation in a CoP in which these techniques are used for their own learning. Then teachers are in a position to apply these principles to their own classrooms with confidence. To begin the process of becoming Internet-literate, teachers are urged to join online courses such as the EVO or the Principles and Practices of Online Teaching Certificate sponsored by TESOL, and to join a CoP such as Webheads in Action, or for newcomers to technology, its spin-off group, Learning with Computers (Baya 2005–2006). This invaluable experience will lead to a lifetime of satisfactory teaching and learning in the global network. (To join any of the communities discussed in this chapter, visit the site addresses listed in the appendix.)

Online Communities for Teachers and Students	
Australian Flexible Learning Framework	http://www.flexiblelearning.net.au/
Communities of Practice *com-prac home page*	http://groups.yahoo.com/group/com-prac/
EFL/ESL Exchange	http://www.dekita.org/exchange/
Global Educators' Network	http://vu.cs.sfu.ca/GEN/welcome/welcome.html
Learning with Computers	http://groups.yahoo.com/group/learningwithcomputers/
LearningTimes *community home pages*	http://www.learningtimes.net/
Merlot: Multimedia Educational Resource for Learning and Online Teaching	http://www.merlot.org/
MiddleWeb: Exploring Middle School Reform: Some Teacher Mentoring Resources	http://www.middleweb.com/mentoring.html
Novice Teacher Support Project	http://ntsp.ed.uiuc.edu/
OpenSource for Educators	http://www.opensource.idv.tw/moodle/
The Palace	http://www.thepalace.com/
Teacher Support Network	http://www.teachersupport.info/
Teaching.com	http://www.teaching.com/
Real English Online	http://groups.yahoo.com/group/Real_English_Online/
schMOOze University	http://schmooze.hunter.cuny.edu/
StudyCom English for Internet	http://www.study.com/
EVOnline2002—Webheads Community Event *WiA home page*	http://groups.yahoo.com/group/evonline2002_webheads/
Webheads in Action: Communities of Practice Online *WiA portal page*	http://www.vancestevens.com/papers/evonline2002/webheads.htm
Worldbridges	http://worldbridges.net/
Writing for Webheads: An Experiment in World Friendship through Online Language Learning *WfW portal page*	http://www.homestead.com/prosites-vstevens/files/efi/webheads.htm

Tools for Community Building	
Alado Webcasts *voice chat platform*	http://www.alado.net/
Dekita.org *blog host*	http://www.dekita.org/
Elluminate *voice and video chat platform*	http://www.elluminate.com/
ICQ *instant message and chat software*	http://www.icq.com/
iVisit *instant message software*	http://www.ivisit.com/
LearningTimes.org *online community host*	http://www.learningtimes.org/
Moodle *CMS software*	http://www.moodle.org/
NetMeeting 3 *chat software*	http://www.microsoft.com/windows/netmeeting/
Nicenet *chat host*	http://www.nicenet.net/
The Palace *chat host*	http://www.thepalace.com/
Paltalk.com *chat software*	http://www.paltalk.com/
Pure Voice *voice mail*	http://www.pure-voice.net/
RealPlayer *media player*	http://www.real.com/
Talking Communities *voice chat host*	http://talkingcommunities.com/
Tapped In *online community host*	http://www.tappedin.org/
Windows Live (formerly MSN) Messenger *instant message and chat software*	http://get.live.com/messenger/overview/
Yahoo! Groups *online community host*	http://groups.yahoo.com/
Yahoo! Messenger *instant message and chat software*	http://messenger.yahoo.com/

Section IV
Questions and Activities

Questions for Discussion

1. Dahlman and Tahtinen (chapter 16) provide support to in-service teachers new to the field who live great distances from one another. What types of assistance did (or do) you find helpful as a new teacher? Are these forms of assistance supported by online networks, or could they be? Does your institution or educational system have a mentoring process? How might it be supported through an online network? If your institution already has online mentoring, how does it compare to or contrast with that described by Dahlman and Tahtinen?

2. Gommlich and Minick (chapter 17) use in-house collaborative networks consisting of teacher trainees, teacher trainers, and technologists in the development of online curricula for language learners. Which specialists at your institution or within your network of professionals could you enlist to help support the development of online courses and curriculum? What are the advantages of such networks? Which technologies support such collaborative inquiries?

3. Schramm and Mabbott (chapter 18) argue that online classes can be developed from traditional classes, and in Minnesota online courses are required to be equal to their land-based equivalent. Can you transform classes that you have taught face to face into online classes? What technologies would you use? What modifications would you need to make to transform your courses or materials into a high-quality online environment? How similar are the two types of courses in practice? How does technology enable pedagogical practices? (You might want to make a list of counterpart pedagogical practices in each environment to use as a basis for discussion.)

4. Stevens (chapter 19) describes the Webheads as collaborative professionals in a community of practice (CoP) who support each other online with the use of computer and technology enhancements to instruction. Why should professionals participate in CoPs? How do CoPs foster lifelong learning? What pedagogical and technological tips would you seek from a CoP? What areas of expertise can you offer?

Activities for Further Study

1. Support networks, or communities of practice (see Stevens, chapter 19), for beginning and experienced teachers have an increasing presence on the Internet. Explore sites such as the Webheads in Action portal page (Stevens 2006b); the Teacher Support Network (n.d.) in England, Scotland, Wales, and Northern Ireland; some of the resources linked from MiddleWeb's (2002) page, Some Teacher Mentoring Resources (for middle school teachers); Teaching.com (ABCXYZ 2006); or the Novice Teacher Support Project (University of Illinois 2005; the latter two mentioned in chapters 16 and 19). Experiment with becoming involved as a mentor or mentee. What are the benefits to each of the participants? How could you get colleagues or peers at your institution involved in support networks?

2. Join the free six-week Electronic Village Online session Becoming a Webhead (sponsored by TESOL's CALL Interest Section) in January–February to see how a community of practice forms. If you are between sessions, join the Learning with Computers group (Baya 2005–2006). If you are interested in video online, join the Video & Editing 4 ESOL group (Gromik 2006). Be sure to respect the rules of netiquette, such as introducing yourself to the group in your initial post, observing or lurking for a time to see how the group operates, and including references when making a contribution.

3. Schramm and Mabbott (chapter 18) use an ethnographic approach to analyze their courses for transformation into an online course setting. Using the table they provide, analyze the following aspects of a course you teach: setting, participants, classroom events, forms, and topics. How does such analysis help you to better envision your course in an online format? What language learning needs of students become apparent in performing such an ethnographic investigation?

4. A fair amount of support from experts who specialize in library and technology services was required to convert the teacher education program presented by Schramm and Mabbott (chapter 18) into distance education courses. Create a plan for gaining such support at your institution. Consider the following: With whom would you network? What sources of funding might be available? What incentives are there for moving courses or course components online? What kinds of access do learners have or need for success?

5. With colleagues or other students, explore one or more of the Internet-based communication environments freely available online, as suggested by Stevens (chapter 19), such as Tapped In (SRI International 1995–2004) or Learning-Times (n.d.). Which of these would work well for your learners as a communications tool or in the development of a community of practice? Design a lesson plan for your ESOL students using an Internet communication tool.

Web Sites in Section IV Questions and Activities

Becoming a Webhead *Electronic Village Online session*	http://darkwing.uoregon.edu/~call/ (click the link for the Announcement page)
Learning with Computers	http://groups.yahoo.com/group/ learningwithcomputers/
LearningTimes.org	http://www.learningtimes.org/
MiddleWeb: Exploring Middle School Reform: Some Teacher Mentoring Resources	http://www.middleweb.com/mentoring.html
Novice Teacher Support Project	http://ntsp.ed.uiuc.edu/
Tapped In	http://www.tappedin.org/
Teacher Support Network	http://www.teachersupport.info/
Teaching.com	http://www.teaching.com/
Video & Editing 4 ESOL	http://groups.yahoo.com/group/video_editing4esol/
Webheads in Action *portal page*	http://www.vancestevens.com/papers/evonline2002/ webheads.htm

References

ABC Asia Pacific. 2006. Nexus: Previously on English Bites. http://abcasiapacific.com/englishbites/archives.htm.

ABCXYZ. 2006. Teaching.com. http://www.teaching.com.

Abdullah, M. H. 1998. Problem-based learning in language instruction: A constructivist model. ERIC Digest. ERIC Document Reproduction Service No. ED423550. http://www.ericdigests.org/1999-2/problem.htm.

Abedi, J., and R. Dietel. 2004. Challenges in the No Child Left Behind Act for English-language learners. *Phi Delta Kappan* 85:782–85.

Adams, E., and C. Freeman. 2000. Commuting the "distance" of distance learning: The Pepperdine story. In *Distance learning technologies: Issues, trends and opportunities*, ed. L. Lau, 157–65. Hershey, PA: Idea Group.

Adobe Photoshop CS2. Software. 2006. San Jose, CA: Adobe Systems. http://www.adobe.com/products/photoshop/overview.html.

Alado webcasts. n.d. http://www.alado.net/.

Alessi, S. M., and S. R. Trollip. 2000. *Multimedia for learning: Methods and development.* Boston: Allyn & Bacon.

Alliance for Community Media. n.d. Hometown video festival. http://www.alliancecm.org/index.php?page_id=7.

Almeida d'Eça, T. 1998. Parede, Portugal and Navarre, Florida: An email cultural exchange. http://64.71.48.37/teresadeca/school/culturalexchange.htm.

_____. 1999. The spirit of Christmas. http://64.71.48.37/teresadeca/school/spiritofxmas.htm.

_____. 2000. Portugal and Brazil: A 500-year-old common culture? http://64.71.48.37/teresadeca/school/portugal-brasil.htm.

_____. 2001a. New York City. http://64.71.48.37/teresadeca/school/new-york-scenario.htm.

_____. 2001b. Visiting Kenya. http://web.archive.org/web/20021221183755/http://www.kn.pacbell
.com/wired/fil/pages/samtravellite.html.

_____. 2003a. CALL lessons 2003–2004. http://64.71.48.37/teresadeca/school/call-lessons03-04.htm.

_____. 2003b. Have fun with English! http://64.71.48.37/teresadeca/school/fun-with-english5.htm.

_____. 2003c. The use of chat in EFL/ESL. *TESL-EJ* 7(1). http://writing.berkeley.edu/TESL-EJ/ej25/
int.html.

_____. 2004a. The euro is here to stay. http://64.71.48.37/teresadeca/papers/tesol2004/if04-euro.htm.

_____. 2004b. Let's blog! A teacher-student blog for 7th grade students (third year of EFL).
http://64.71.48.37/teresadeca/school/blog7.htm.

_____. 2005a. First steps in experimenting with computers: Resources. http://64.71.48.37/teresadeca/
tellrefs-exp.htm.

_____. 2005b. Index of "Webheads in Action" Web pages and related sites. http://www.malhatlantica
.pt/teresadeca/webheads/wia-index.htm.

al-Othman, B. 2001–2004. How participation in a CoP informs and influences personal teaching?
Presentation at the 37th Annual TESOL Convention and Exhibit, Baltimore, Maryland. http://
www.geocities.com/esl_efl_ku/.

_____. 2003–2004. First live webcast project by Kuwaiti students. http://alothman-b.tripod.com/
wia_162finalproj.htm.

ALTEC, University of Kansas. 2000–2006. RubiStar. http://rubistar.4teachers.org/index.php.

American Council on the Teaching of Foreign Languages (ACTFL). 1996. *Standards for foreign
language learning: Preparing for the 21st century*. Yonkers, NY: ACTFL.

American culture online. 2004. Kent State University. http://dept.kent.edu/esl/. Available with course
registration only.

Ammann, R., A. Campbell, and B. Dieu. n.d.a. Dekita. http://www.dekita.org/.

_____. n.d.b. EFL/ESL exchange. http://www.dekita.org/exchange.

Anderson, T. 2000, Spring. New teacher-mentor project: Moving teachers into the second millennium. *Schoolwide Northwest* 4–5. Portland, OR: Northwest Regional Educational Laboratory.

Andrianson, L. 2001. Gender and computer-mediated communication: Group processes in problem
solving. *Computers in Human Behavior* 17:71–94.

Angel LMS. Software. 2005. Indianapolis, IN: Angel Learning. http://www.cyberlearninglabs
.com/Products/.

Apple Computer. 2006a. iLife educator award winners. http://www.apple.com/education/ilifeawards/.

_____. 2006b. iMovie HD support. http://www.apple.com/support/imovie/.

_____. 2006c. iTunes. http://www.apple.com/itunes/.

AppleWorks Version 6.2.9. Software. 2004. Cupertino, CA: Apple Computer. http://www.apple
.com/appleworks/.

Arbaugh, J. B., and R. Benbunan-Fich. 2005. Contextual factors that influence ALN effectiveness.
In *Learning together online: Research on asynchronous learning networks*, ed. S. R. Hiltz and
R. Goldman, 123–44. Mahwah, NJ: Lawrence Erlbaum.

Armstrong, P. W., and J. D. Rogers. 1997. Basic skills revisited: The effects of foreign language instruction on reading, math, and language arts. *Learning Languages* 2 (3): 20–31.

Arneil S., and M. Holmes. 2005. Hot Potatoes Version 6. Software. Victoria, BC, Canada: Half-Baked Software. http://hotpot.uvic.ca/.

Assessment Reform Group. 1999. *Assessment for learning: Beyond the black box.* Cambridge: Cambridge University School of Education. http://k1.ioe.ac.uk/tlrp/arg/publications.html.

Aston, G., ed. 2001. *Learning with corpora.* Houston, TX: Athelstan.

Atomic Learning. 2006. Atomic learning: Click. See. Hear. Learn. http://www.atomiclearning.com/.

Audacity Version 1.2.4. Software. 2005. http://audacity.sourceforge.net/.

Avatar 3D. Software. 2003. Seoul: InterVEG. http://www.interveg.co.kr/index.html?Mode= intProduct&subMode=2&Lang=EN.

Bailey, K. M., and D. Nunan. 1996. *Voices from the language classroom.* Cambridge: Cambridge University Press.

The bank of English. 2004. http://www.collins.co.uk/books.aspx?group=153.

Barbot, M. n.d. Hot Potatoes exercises. http://perso.wanadoo.fr/michel.barbot/hotpot/exercises.htm.

Barrett, H. C. 2004. Electronic portfolios as digital stories of deep learning: Emerging digital tools to support reflection in learner-centered portfolios. http://electronicportfolios.org/digistory/ epstory.html.

Batstone, R. 1996. Key concepts in ELT: Noticing. *ELT Journal* 50:273.

Bauman, R., and J. Sherzer. 1975. The ethnography of speaking. *Annual Review of Anthropology* 4:95–119.

Baya, G. 2005–2006. Learning with computers. http://groups.yahoo.com/group/ learningwithcomputers/.

Beatty, K. 2003. *Teaching and researching computer-assisted language learning.* Harlow, England: Pearson Education.

Beglar, D., and A. Hunt. 2003. Implementing task-based teaching. In *Methodology in language teaching: An anthology of current practice*, ed. J. C. Richards and W. A. Renandya, 96–106. Cambridge: Cambridge University Press.

Belz, J. 2004. Learner corpus analysis and the development of foreign language proficiency. *System* 32:577–91.

Benbunan-Fich, R., S. R. Hiltz, and L. Harasim. 2005. The online interaction learning model: An integrated theoretical framework for learning networks. In *Learning together online: Research on asynchronous learning networks*, ed. S. R. Hiltz and R. Goldman, 19–38. Mahwah, NJ: Lawrence Erlbaum.

Bennett, G., and F. Green. 2001. Student learning in the online environment: No significant differences? *Quest* 53 (1): 1–13.

Benrabah, M. 1997. Word-stress—A source of unintelligibility in English. *International Review of Applied Linguistics* 35:157–65.

Benson, P. 2001. *Teaching and researching autonomy in language learning.* Harlow, England: Longman.

Bereiter, C., and M. Scardamalia. 1987. *The psychology of written composition.* Mahwah, NJ: Lawrence Erlbaum.

Berge, Z. 1998. Barriers to online teaching in post-secondary institutions: Can policy changes fix it? *Online Journal of Distance Learning Administration* 1 (2). http://www.westga.edu/~distance/Berge12.html.

Best, S., and D. Peek-Brown. n.d. Kids as global scientists. Center for Learning Technologies in Urban Schools (LeTUS). http://www.letus.org/kidsglobalscientists.htm.

Bianco, M. B., and A. Carr-Chellman. 2002. Exploring qualitative methodologies in online learning environments. *Quarterly Review of Distance Education* 3 (1): 251–60.

Biber, D., S. Conrad, and R. Reppen. 1998. *Corpus linguistics: Investigating language structure and use.* Cambridge: Cambridge University Press.

Biber, D., S. Johansson, G. Leech, S. Conrad, and E. Finnegan. 1999. *Longman grammar of spoken and written English.* London: Pearson.

Bierema, L. L., and S. B. Merriam. 2002. E-mentoring: Using computer mediated communication to enhance the mentoring process. *Innovative Higher Education* 26:211–27.

Black, P., and D. Wiliam. 1998. Assessment and classroom learning. *Assessment in Education* 5:7–74.

Black, T. 2003. Get learners learning outside your lesson! *IATEFL Issues* 171:11–12.

Blackboard Academic Suite Release 7.0. Software. 2005. Washington, DC: Blackboard. http://www.blackboard.com/.

Blatt, I. 2000. Internet writing and language learning. In *Writing across languages*, ed. G. Brauer, 89–98. Stamford, CT: Ablex.

Bloch, J. 2002. Student/teacher interaction via email: The social context of Internet discourse. *Journal of Second Language Writing* 11:117–34.

Blogger. Software. 1999–2006. Mountain View, CA: Google. http://www.blogger.com/.

Blood, R. 2002. *The Weblog handbook.* Cambridge, MA: Perseus.

_____. 2003. BlogTalk—A European conference on Weblogs: Web-based publishing, communication and collaboration tools for professional and private use. http://2003.blogtalk.net/.

Bober, M., and V. Paz Dennen. 2001. Intersubjectivity: Facilitating knowledge construction in online environments. *Education Media International* 38:241–50.

Boettcher, J., and R. Conrad. 1999. *Faculty guide for moving teaching and learning to the Web.* Mission Viejo, CA: League for Innovation in the Community College.

Bogatz, H. 1997. Advanced reader's collocation searcher (ARCS). http://www.geocities.com/Athens/Acropolis/7033/.

Borg, S. 2003. Teachers' involvement in TESOL research. *TESOL Matters* 13 (2): 1–8.

Bowers, C. A. 2000. *Let them eat data: How computers affect education, cultural diversity, and the prospects of ecological sustainability.* Athens: University of Georgia Press.

Boyd, F. 2002. An ESP program for students of business. In *English for specific purposes*, ed. T. Orr, 51–56. Alexandria, VA: TESOL.

Brent, D. 2005. Teaching as performance in the electronic classroom. *First Monday* 10 (4). http://firstmonday.org/issues/issue10_4/brent/index.html.

Brett, P. 1999. The design, implementation and evaluation of a multimedia application for second language listening comprehension. PhD diss., University of Wolverhamton.

Breuch, L., and S. Racine. 2000. Developing sound tutor training for online writing centers: Creating productive peer reviewers. *Computers and Composition* 17:245–63.

Brinton, D. M., M. A. Snow, and M. B. Wesche. 2003. *Content-based second language instruction*, Michigan Classic ed. Ann Arbor: University of Michigan Press.

British Broadcasting Corporation. 2006. http://www.bbc.com/.

_____. n.d. Video nation. http://www.bbc.co.uk/videonation/.

Britt, J. 2000. Student teacher perceptions of technology integration during internship. Athens State University. http://www.athens.edu/pt3/3.html.

Brown, H. D. 2001. *Teaching by principles: An interactive approach to language pedagogy.* White Plains, NY: Addison-Wesley Longman.

Brown, J. S., and E. S. Gray. 1995. The people are the company: How to build your company around your people. *Fast Company* 1(1): 78. http://www.fastcompany.com/online/01/people.html.

Bruner, J. 1966. *Toward a theory of instruction.* Cambridge, MA: Harvard University Press.

Butler-Pascoe, M. E. 1997. Visit our city. In *New ways of using computers in language teaching*, ed. T. Boswood, 47–48. Alexandria, VA: TESOL.

Buzznet. n.d. http://www.buzznet.com/.

Cabrini Connections. 2000. Tutor/mentor connection. http://msg.uc.iupui.edu/TMC/html/index .php.

Cambridge Scientific Abstracts. 2006a. ERIC. http://www.csa.com/factsheets/eric-set-c.php.

_____. 2006b. PsycINFO. http://www.csa.com/factsheets/psycinfo-set-c.php.

_____. 2006c. Sociological Abstracts. http://www.csa.com/factsheets/socioabs-set-c.php.

Cambridge University Press. 2006. Cambridge international corpus. http://www.cambridge .org/elt/corpus/.

Campbell, A. P. 2003. Weblogs for use with ESL classes. *The Internet TESL Journal* 9 (2). http://iteslj .org/Techniques/Campbell-Weblogs.html.

_____. 2006. The new tanuki. http://thenewtanuki.blogspot.com/.

_____. n.d. Learner attitudes towards a tutor-run Weblog in the EFL university classroom. http:// www8.ocn.ne.jp/%7Eapc33/newtanuki.htm.

Campbell, D. F. 2004. Delivering an online translation course. *ReCALL* 16:114–23.

Carr-Chellman, A., and P. Duchastel. 2001. The ideal online course. *Library Trends* 50 (1): 145–58.

Carson, J. 2001. A task analysis of reading and writing in academic contexts. In *Linking literacies: Perspectives on L2 reading-writing connections*, ed. D. Belcher and A. Hirvala, 48–83. Ann Arbor: University of Michigan Press.

Carton, L. 2002, February 26. Travelocity.com's homepage: Lessons to be learnt. http://evolt .org/node/21795.

Cavanagh, C. 2003. *Managing your e-mail: Thinking outside the inbox.* Hoboken, NJ: John Wiley & Sons.

Caverly, D. C., and C. L. Peterson. 2000. Technology and college reading. In *Handbook of college reading and study strategy research*, ed. D. C. Caverly and R. F. Flippo, 291–320. Mahwah, NJ: Lawrence Erlbaum.

Chamot, A. U., and J. M. O'Malley. 1994. *Learning strategies in second language acquisition.* Cambridge: Cambridge University Press.

Chandler, J. 2003. The efficacy of various kinds of error feedback for improvement in the accuracy and fluency of L2 student writing. *Journal of Second Language Writing* 12:267–96.

Chang, T., and J. Huang. 2002. A pilot study of role-interplay in a Web-based learning environment. *Education Media International* 39:75–85.

Chapelle, C. A. 2001. *Computer applications in second language acquisition: Foundations for teaching, testing, and research.* Cambridge: Cambridge University Press.

_____. 2003. *English language learning and technology.* Amsterdam: John Benjamins.

_____. 2004. Technology and second language learning: Expanding methods and agendas. *System* 32:593–601.

Chen, J., S. Belkada, and T. Okamoto. 2004. How a Web-based course facilitates acquisition of English for academic purposes. *Language Learning & Technology* 8 (2): 33–49.

Christie, F. 1999. Genre theory and ESL teaching: A systemic functional perspective. *TESOL Quarterly* 33:759–63.

Clair, N., and C. T. Adger. 1999. Professional development for teachers in culturally diverse schools. *CAL Digest.* Washington, DC: Center for Applied Linguistics.

Clayton, T. 1998. Learning to write collaboratively. In *Teaching in action*, ed. J. C. Richards, 232–34. Alexandria, VA: TESOL.

Clément, R., Z. Dörnyei, and K. Noels. 1994. Motivation, self-confidence and group cohesion in the foreign language classroom. *Language Learning* 44:417–48.

Clipperton, R. 1994. Explicit vocabulary instruction in French immersion. *Canadian Modern Language Review* 50:736–49.

Coady, J. 1997. L2 acquisition through extensive reading. In *Second language vocabulary acquisition: a rationale for pedagogy*, ed. J. Coady and T. Huckin, 225–37. New York: Cambridge University Press.

Cobb, T. 2006. The Compleat Lexical Tutor Version 4.5. Software. http://www.lextutor.ca/.

Cobb, T., and M. Horst. 2001. Reading academic English: Carrying learners across the lexical threshold. In *Research perspectives in English for academic purposes*, ed. J. Flowerdew and M. Peacock, 315–29. Cambridge: Cambridge University Press.

Coghlan, M. 2005. Voices from the edge. Presentation at the 2005 TESOL CALL Interest Section Electronic Village Online. http://users.chariot.net.au/~michaelc/blog/edge_voices.htm.

Coghlan, M., and V. Stevens. 2000. An online learning community—The students' perspective. Paper presented at the Fifth Annual Teaching in the Community Colleges Online Conference. http://www.chariot.net.au/~michaelc/TCC2000.htm.

Collins, M. 2000. Comparing Web, correspondence and lecture versions of a second-year non-major biology course. *British Journal of Educational Technology* 31:21–27.

Colorado State University. 1993–2006. Welcome to Writing@CSU. http://writing.colostate.edu/.

Commonwealth of Australia. 2006. Australian flexible learning framework. http://www.flexible learning.net.au/flx/go/.

Coniam, D. 2001. The use of audio or video comprehension as an assessment instrument in the certification of English language teachers: A case study. *System* 29:1–14.

Conrad, S. 1999. The importance of corpus-based research for language teachers. *System* 27:1–18.

Coogan, D. 1999. *Electronic writing centers: Computing the field of composition.* Stamford, CT: Ablex.

Coxhead, A. 2000. A new academic word list. *TESOL Quarterly* 34:213–38.

Crandall, J. 1992. Content-centered learning in the United States. *Annual Review of Applied Linguistics* 13:111–26.

Crandall, J., and D. Kaufman, eds. 2002. *Content-based instruction in higher education settings.* Alexandria, VA: TESOL.

Crookes, G., and R. Schmidt. 1991. Motivation: Reopening the research agenda, *Language Learning* 41:469–512.

Cuckle, P., and S. Clarke. 2002. Mentoring student-teachers in schools: Views, practices and access to ICT. *Journal of Computer Assisted Learning* 18:330–40.

Cummins, J. 1999–2003a. Immersion education for the millennium: What we have learned from 30 years of research on second language immersion. I teach I learn.com. http://www.iteach ilearn.com/cummins/immersion2000.html.

———. 1999–2003b. Putting language proficiency in its place: Responding to critiques of the conversational/academic language distinction. I teach I learn.com. http://www.iteachilearn .com/cummins/converacademlangdisti.html.

Cummins, J., and D. Sayers. 1997. *Brave new schools.* New York: St. Martin's Press.

Curtain, H., and C. A. Dahlberg. 2004. *Languages and children—Making the match: New languages for young learners, grades K–8*, 3rd ed. Boston: Allyn & Bacon.

Curtis, D. 2003, December 16. The Maine event. *Edutopia.* http://www.glef.org/php/article .php?id=Art_1119&key=137.

Da, J. 2000. Web-based interactive CALL courseware development: A primer. Middle Tennessee State University. http://lingua.mtsu.edu/call/interactive/.

Davies, M. n.d. Variation in English words and phrases (VIEW). Brigham Young University. http:// view.byu.edu/.

Davis, R. 1998–2006. Randall's ESL cyber listening lab. http://www.esl-lab.com/.

De Pew, E., and S. K. Miller. 2005. Studying L2 writers' digital writing: An argument for post-critical methods. *Computers and Composition* 22:259–78.

DePaul, A. 2000. *Survival guide for new teachers: How new teachers can work effectively with veteran teachers, parents, principals, and teacher educators.* Washington, DC: U.S. Department of Education.

Dewey, J. 1916/1966. *Democracy and education.* New York: Free Press.

———. 1933/1998. *How we think*, rev. ed. Boston: Houghton Mifflin.

Dickinson, L. 1987. *Self-instruction in language learning.* New York: Cambridge University Press.

Diem, R., S. Lockman, and G. Stanley. 2006. Podcasting-ELT. http://groups.yahoo.com/group/ podcasting_elt/.

Dieu, B. 2004. Blogs for language learning. *Essential Teacher* 1 (4): 26–30.

———. 2005. Bee online. http://beeonline.blogspot.com/.

———. n.d. Blogging and presence online. http://members.tripod.com/the_english_dept/blog04/.

Discovery Channel Global Education Partnership. 2006. Global education partnership. http://www .discoveryglobaled.org/.

Discovery Education. 2005. Discoveryschool.com: Teaching tools. http://school.discovery.com/teachingtools/teachingtools.html.

diSessa, A. A. 2000. *Changing minds: Computers, learning, and literacy*. Cambridge, MA: Massachusetts Institute of Technology.

Dobb, F. 2004. *Essential elements of effective science instruction for English learners*, 2nd ed. Los Angeles: California Science Project. http://csmp.ucop.edu/downloads/csp/essential_elements_2.pdf.

_____. 2005. Inquiry-based instruction for English language learners: Ten essential elements. In *Integrating inquiry across the curriculum*, ed. R. H. Audet and L. K. Jordan, 201–26. Thousand Oaks, CA: Corwin Press.

Docutek ERes. Software. 2005. Burlingame, CA: Docutek. http://www.docutek.com/.

Dodge, B. n.d. QuestGarden 1.0. http://webquest.org/questgarden/author/.

Dreamweaver 8. Software. 2005. San Francisco, CA: Macromedia. http://www.macromedia.com/software/dreamweaver/.

Drever, E., and P. Cope. 1999. Students' use of theory in an initial teacher education programme. *Journal of Education for Teaching* 25:97–109.

Duber, J. 2002. Mad blogs and Englishmen. *TESL-EJ* 6 (2). http://www-writing.berkeley.edu/tesl-ej/ej22/int.html.

_____. 2004. LetsTalk: home page. duber dot com. http://duber.com/LetsTalk/.

Dudeney, G. 2000. *The Internet and the language classroom*. Cambridge: Cambridge University Press.

Dudley-Evans, T., and M. J. St. John. 1998. *Developments in English for specific purposes: A multidisciplinary approach*. Cambridge: Cambridge University Press.

Duffy, T. M., and J. R. Kirkley. 2004a. *Learner-centered theory and practice in distance education: Cases from higher education*. Mahwah, NJ: Lawrence Erlbaum.

_____. 2004b. Learning theory and pedagogy applied in distance learning: The case of Cardean University. In *Learner-centered theory and practice in distance education: Cases from higher education*, ed. T. M. Duffy and J. R. Kirkely, 3–13. Mahwah, NJ: Lawrence Erlbaum.

Dufon, M. A. 2002. Video recording in ethnographic SLA research: Some issues of validity in data collection. *Language Learning & Technology* 6 (1): 40–59.

Eastment, D. 1999. *The Internet and ELT*. Oxford: Summertown Publishing and the British Council.

Easton, S. 2003. Clarifying the instructor's role in online distance learning. *Communication Education* 52:87–105.

Echevarria, J., M. Vogt, and D. Short. 2000. *Making content comprehensible for English language learners: The SIOP model*. Boston: Allyn & Bacon.

Egbert, J. 2005. *CALL essentials: Principles and practice in CALL classrooms*. Alexandria, VA: TESOL.

Egbert, J., C.-C. Chao, and E. Hanson-Smith. 1999. Computer-enhanced language learning environments: An overview. In *CALL environments: Research, practice, and critical issues*, ed. J. Egbert and E. Hanson-Smith, 1–13. Alexandria, VA: TESOL.

Egbert, J., and E. Hanson-Smith. 1999. *CALL environments: Research, practice, and critical issues*. Alexandria, VA: TESOL.

Ellis, R. 1997. *SLA research and language teaching*. Oxford: Oxford University Press.

Elluminate. 2001–2006. http://www.elluminate.com/.

English idioms and slang. 2006. http://www.englishcaster.com/idioms/.

English trailers. n.d. http://www.english-trailers.com/.

Englishcaster. 2006. http://www.englishcaster.com/.

ESL go net. n.d. http://www.eslgo.net/.

Evo2005: Using Weblogs in ESL/EFL classes. 2006. http://groups.yahoo.com/group/weblogging/.

Expedia. 2006. http://www.expedia.com/.

Faigley, L. 1999. Beyond imagination: The Internet and global digital literacy. In *Passions, pedagogies, and 21st century technologies*, ed. G. E. Hawisher and C. L. Selfe, 129–39. Logan: Utah State University Press.

Fairclough, N. 1999. *Critical discourse analysis.* London: Longman.

Farmer, J. 2004. Communication dynamics: Discussion boards, Weblogs and the development of communities of inquiry in online learning environments. incorporated subversion. http://incsub.org/blog/index.php?p=3.

Farrell, T. 1998. Reflective teaching: The principles and practices. *English Teaching Forum* 36 (4): 10–17.

Feak, C., and S. Reinhart. 2002. An ESP program for students of law. In *English for specific purposes*, ed. T. Orr, 7–23. Alexandria, VA: TESOL.

Ferris, D. 1994. Rhetorical strategies in student persuasive writing: Differences between native and non-native speakers. *Research in the Teaching of English* 28 (1): 45–65.

_____. 2002. *Treatment of error in second language student writing.* Ann Arbor: University of Michigan Press.

_____. 2003. *Response to student writing: Implications for second language students.* Mahwah, NJ: Lawrence Erlbaum.

Ferris, D., and J. S. Hedgcock. 1998. *Teaching ESL composition: Purpose, process, and practice.* Mahwah, NJ: Lawrence Erlbaum.

_____. 2005. *Teaching ESL composition: Purpose, process, and practice.* 2nd ed. Mahwah, NJ: Lawrence Erlbaum.

Filamentality. Software. 2006. San Ramon, CA: SBC Knowledge Ventures. http://www.filamentality.org/wired/fil/.

Flickr Beta Version. Software. 2006. Sunnyvale, CA: Yahoo! http://flickr.com/.

Flowerdew, J. 1996. Concordancing in language learning. In *The power of CALL*, ed. M. Pennington, 97–113. Houston, TX: Athelstan.

_____. 2000. Using a genre-based framework to teach organizational structure in academic writing. *ELT Journal* 54:369–78.

Ford, P. 2006a. The FordLog. http://www.weblogs4schools.co.uk/TheFord/.

_____. 2006b. Weblogging in schools. The FordLog. http://www.weblogs4schools.co.uk/TheFord/WhyWeblogs.

Fotos, S. 2004. Writing as talking: E-mail exchange for promoting proficiency and motivation in the foreign language classroom. In *New perspectives on CALL for second language classrooms*, ed. S. Fotos and C. Browne, 109–29. Mahwah, NJ: Lawrence Erlbaum.

Fowlie, J. 1999. Doing the news in the EFL classroom: A practical project. *IATEFL ESP SIG Newsletter* 14. http://www.unav.es/espSig/fowlie14.htm.

Francis, W. N., and H. Kucera. 1979. Brown corpus of standard American English. Brown University. http://helmer.aksis.uib.no/icame/brown/bcm.html.

Freeman, D., and K. E. Johnson. 1998. Reconceptualizing the knowledge-base of language teacher education. *TESOL Quarterly* 32:397–417.

_____. 2005. Toward linking teacher knowledge and student learning. In *Second language teacher education: International perspectives*, ed. D. J. Tedick, 73–96. Mahwah, NJ: Lawrence Erlbaum.

FrontPage 2003. Software. 2003. Redmond, WA: Microsoft. http://office.microsoft.com/frontpage.

Gaer, S. 2005. Email projects home page. Outreach and Technical Assistance Network. http://www.otan.dni.us/webfarm/emailproject/email.htm.

Galloway, I. n.d. Blogging in TESL. Presentation at the 39th Annual TESOL Convention and Exhibit, San Antonio, Texas. http://www.sfu.ca/~igallowa/blogging.

Ganley, B. 2005, November 6. EdTechTalk#24. Worldbridges. http://worldbridges.com/livewire/2005/11/06/edtechtalk24-november-6-2005/.

Gass, S. 1997. *Input, interaction and the second language learner.* Mahwah, NJ: Lawrence Erlbaum.

Gavioli, L., and G. Aston. 2001. Enriching reality: Language corpora in language pedagogy. *ELT Journal* 55:238–46.

Genesee, F. 1995. Integrating language and content: Lessons from immersion. ERIC Digest. ERIC Document Reproduction Service No. ED390284. http://www.ericdigests.org/1996-3/immersion.htm.

_____. 1998. Content-based language instruction. In *Critical issues in early second language learning*, ed. M. Met, 103–5. Reading, MA: Scott Foresman-Addison-Wesley.

Geocities. Software. 2006. Sunnyvale, CA: Yahoo! http://geocities.yahoo.com/.

Gilbert, J. 1995. Pronunciation practices as an aid to listening comprehension. In *A guide for the teaching of second language listening*, ed. D. Mendelsohn and J. Rubin, 151–65. San Diego, CA: Dominie Press.

Glennan, T. K., Jr., and A. Melmed. 1996. *Fostering the use of educational technology: Elements of a national strategy.* Santa Monica, CA: RAND. [MR-682-OSTP/ED]

Global educators' network. n.d. http://vu.cs.sfu.ca/GEN/welcome/welcome.html.

Godwin-Jones, R. 2005. Messaging, gaming, peer-to-peer sharing: Language learning strategies and tools for the millennial generation. *Language Learning & Technology* 9 (1): 17–22. http://llt.msu.edu/vol9num1/emerging/default.html.

Goin' upstream. 2005. http://goinupstream.blogspot.com/.

Golombek, P. R. 1998. A study of language teachers' personal practical knowledge. *TESOL Quarterly* 32:447–64.

González, A. 2003. Who is educating EFL teachers: A qualitative study of in-service in Colombia. *Íkala, Revista de Lenguaje y Cultura* 8 (14): 153–72.

González, D. 2003a. My journey with webheads. http://dafnegon.tripod.com/myjourneywithwebheads/.

_____. 2003b. Teaching and learning through chat: A taxonomy of educational chat for EFL/ESL. *Teaching English with Technology* 3 (4). http://www.iatefl.org.pl/call/j_review15.htm.

_____. 2004a. Bringing colleagues into Web-based learning and teaching. *Essential Teacher* 1 (4): 22–25.

_____. 2004b. Colaboración en línea: Un curso de inglés para arquitectura. *Temas de Educación* 10:57–71. La Serena, Chile: Departamento de Educación, Universidad de La Serena.

_____. 2004c. Dilemas de la evaluación del aprendizaje del Inglés con propósitos específicos a través de soportes electrónicos: Estudio de un caso. PhD diss. Universidad de Valencia, Spain.

_____. 2005. Blended learning offers the best of both worlds. *Essential Teacher* 2 (4): 42–45.

González, D., and T. Almeida d'Eça. 2006. Becoming a Webhead 2006 (BaW-2006). http://groups.yahoo.com/group/baw-06/.

González, D., and R. St. Louis. 2002. Content-based English for specific purposes course design: The case of English for architecture. In *Content-based instruction in higher education settings*, ed. D. Kaufman and J. Crandall, 93–106. Alexandria, VA: TESOL.

Goodwin, J. M. 2001. EAP support for matriculated university students. In *Understanding the courses we teach: Local perspectives on English language teaching*, ed. J. Murphy and P. Byrd, 259–80. Ann Arbor: University of Michigan Press.

Google. 2005. Google help center: Search results page. http://www.google.com/help/interpret.html.

_____. 2006a. Google. http://www.google.com/.

_____. 2006b. Google image search. http://images.google.com/.

Grabe, W. 1995. Discourse analysis and reading instruction. *The Journal of TESOL France* 2 (2). Reprinted in T. Miller, ed. 2000. *Functional approaches to written text: Classroom applications*. Washington, DC: United States Information Agency. http://exchanges.state.gov/education/engteaching/pubs/BR/functionalsec1.htm.

Grabe, W., and R. Kaplan. 1996. *Theory and practice of writing*. New York: Longman.

Granger, S., ed. 1998. *Learner English on computer*. Austin, TX: Addison-Wesley Longman.

Granger, S., J. Hung, and S. Petch-Tyson, eds. 2002. *Computer learner corpora, second language acquisition and foreign language teaching*. Amsterdam: John Benjamins.

Grellet, F. 1981. *Developing reading skills*. Cambridge: Cambridge University Press.

Gromik, N. 2003. Stimulating creativity in a Japanese school—using the Internet. *The ETJ Journal* 4 (2): 16–17.

_____. 2006. Video & editing 4 ESOL. http://groups.yahoo.com/group/video_editing4esol/.

Groupboard. Software. n.d. Calgary, AL, Canada: Group Technologies. http://www.groupboard.com/.

Gruber, S. 2000. Technology and tenure: Creating oppositional discourse in an offline and online world. *Computers and Composition* 17:41–55.

Hacker, D. 2003. *A writer's reference*, 5th ed. Boston: Bedford/St. Martin's.

Hada, Y., H. Ogata, and Y. Yano. 2002. Video-based language learning environment using an online video-editing system. *Computer-Assisted Language Learning* 15 (4): 387–407.

Haley, M. H., and T. Y. Austin. 2004. *Content-based second language teaching and learning: An interactive approach*. Upper Saddle River, NJ: Pearson Education.

Halford, J. M. 1999. Policies to support new teachers. *Educational Leadership* 56 (8): 85.

Hall, R. 2002. Aligning learning, teaching and assessment using the Web: An evaluation of pedagogic approaches. *British Journal of Educational Technology* 33:149–58.

Hamilton, M. 2004. Communication pathways. *Modern English Teacher* 13 (2): 51–55.

Handley, Z., and M.-J. Hamel. 2005. Establishing a methodology for benchmarking speech synthesis for computer-assisted language learning (CALL). *Language Learning & Technology* 9 (3): 99–119. http://llt.msu.edu/vol9num3/handley/default.html.

HandyBits Voice Mail Version 5.5. Software. 2005. Oslo, Norway: Teknum Systems. http://www.handybits.com/voicemail.htm.

Hanson-Smith, E. 1999. Classroom practice: Content-area tasks in CALL environments. In *CALL environments: Research, practice, and critical issues*, ed. J. Egbert and E. Hanson-Smith, 137–58. Alexandria, VA: TESOL.

_____. 2000. Hands-on teacher training: Presentation software. In *Technology-enhanced learning environments*, ed. E. Hanson-Smith, 137–48. Alexandria, VA: TESOL.

_____. n.d. Embedding media in your Webpages. http://www.geocities.com/ehansonsmi/embedding_multimedia.html.

Hanson-Smith, E., and C. Bauer-Ramazani. 2004. Professional development: The electronic village online of the TESOL CALL Interest Section. *TESL-EJ* 8 (2). http://www-writing.berkeley.edu/TESL-EJ/ej30/int.html.

Harding, T. 2001. *The video activist handbook*. London: Pluto Press.

Harris, M., and M. Pemberton. 1995. Online writing labs (OWLs): A taxonomy of options and issues. *Computers and Composition* 12:145–59.

Haynes, M. 1993. Patterns and perils of guessing in second language reading. In *Second language reading and vocabulary learning*, ed. T. Huckin, M. Haynes, and M. Coady, 24–45. Norwood, NJ: Ablex.

Head, J. T., B. Lockee, and K. Oliver. 2002. Method, media, and mode: Clarifying the discussion of distance education effectiveness. *Quarterly Review of Distance Education* 3:261–68.

hello. Software. 2004. Mountain View, CA: Google. http://www.hello.com/.

Herring, S., ed. 1996. *Computer-mediated communication: Linguistic, social and cross-cultural perspectives*. Amsterdam: John Benjamins.

Herron, C., S. Dubreil, S. P. Cole, and C. Corrie. 2000. Using instructional video to teach culture to beginning foreign language students. *CALICO* 17 (3): 395–427.

Hinkel, E. 2002. *Second language writers' text: Linguistic and rhetorical features*. Mahwah, NJ: Lawrence Erlbaum.

Hipcast. 2006. http://www.hipcast.com/.

Hitch, L., and D. Hirsch. 2001. Model training. *Journal of Academic Librarianship* 27:15–19.

Hoelker, J., S. Nimmannit, and I. Nakamura. 1999. Exploration through video. *Proceedings of the Second Pan Asian Conference: Teaching English: Asian contexts and cultures,* ed. KOTESOL, 145–57. Seoul: Korea Teachers of English to Speakers of Other Languages. http://www.kotesol.org/publications/proceedings/1999/abs_145hoelker.shtml.

Hollinger, L., and D. Obenda. 2004. *Academic word power 1*. Boston: Houghton Mifflin.

Holmevik, J., and C. Haynes. 2000. *MOOniversity: A student's guide to online learning environments*. Boston: Allyn & Bacon.

Horst, M., T. Cobb, and P. Meara. 1998. Beyond *A clockwork orange*: Acquiring second language vocabulary through reading. *Reading in a Foreign Language* 11 (2): 207–23.

Hot Potatoes Users. 2006. http://groups.yahoo.com/group/hotpotatoesusers/.

Hsiao, J. W. D. L. n.d. CSCL theories. http://www.edb.utexas.edu/csclstudent/Dhsiao/theories.html.

Huang, H. 2002. Towards constructivism for adult learners in online learning environments. *British Journal of Educational Technology* 33:27–37.

Hubbard, P. 2003. An invitation to CALL: Foundations of computer-assisted language learning. Stanford University Linguistics Department. http://www.stanford.edu/~efs/callcourse/.

Hubbard, P., and C. Bradin. 2004. Another look at tutorial CALL. *ReCALL* 16:448–61.

Hubert, D. n.d. The official Flat Stanley project. The Education Network of Ontario. http://www.flatstanley.com/.

Huckin, T., and M. Coady. 1999. Incidental vocabulary acquisition in a second language: A review. *Studies in Second Language Acquisition* 21:181–93.

Hudelson, S., L. Poynor, and P. Wolfe. 2003. Teaching bilingual and ESL children and adolescents. In *Handbook of research on teaching the English language arts*, ed. J. Flood, D. Lapp, J. Squire, and J. Jensen, 421–34. Mahwah, NJ: Lawrence Erlbaum.

Hughes, M., and N. Daykin. 2002. Towards constructivism: Investigating students' perceptions and learning as a result of using an online environment. *Innovations in Education and Teaching International* 39:217–24.

Hulstijn, J., and B. Laufer. 2001a. Incidental vocabulary acquisition in a second language: The construct of task-induced involvement. *Applied Linguistics* 22:1–26.

———. 2001b. Some empirical evidence for the involvement load hypothesis in vocabulary acquisition. *Language Learning* 51:539–58.

Hunston, S. 2002. *Corpora in applied linguistics*. Cambridge: Cambridge University Press.

Hwu, F. 2003. Learners' behaviors in computer-based input activities elicited through tracking technologies. *Computer-Assisted Language Learning* 16:5–29.

Hyland, K. 2000. *Disciplinary discourses: Social interactions in academic writing*. Essex, England: Longman.

———. 2002. *Teaching and researching writing*. New York: Longman.

Hymes, D. 1964. Introduction: Toward ethnographies of communication. *American Anthropologist* 66 (6): 12–25.

HyperStudio Version 4.5. Software. 2005. Elgin, IL: Sunburst Technology. http://www.hyperstudio.com/.

IAC Search & Media. 2006a. Ask.com. http://www.ask.com/.

———. 2006b. Bloglines. http://www.bloglines.com/.

ICQ Version 5.1. Software. 2006. Tel Aviv, Israel: ICQ. http://www.icq.com/.

iMovie HD Version 5.0.2. Software. 2005. Cupertino, CA: Apple Computer. http://www.apple.com/ilife/imovie/.

Innovation Tools. 2002–2006. Mind mapping resource center. http://www.innovationtools.com/resources/mindmapping.asp.

Internet Archive. n.d. Internet archive: Movie archive. http://www.archive.org/details/movies.

Internet TESL Journal. 1995–2006. http://iteslj.org/.

———. 1998–2005. Jokes in English for the ESL/EFL classroom. http://iteslj.org/c/jokes.html.

Iowa State University. 2000–2005. E-library @ Iowa State University. http://www.lib.iastate.edu/.

Isbell, K., and J. Reinhardt. 2000. Web integration: A model for task-based learning. In *Technology-enhanced learning environments*, ed. E. Hanson-Smith, 45–55. Alexandria, VA: TESOL.

iVisit Version 3. 2006. Santa Monica, CA: iVisit. http://www.ivisit.com/.

Jepson, K. 2005. Conversations—and negotiated interaction—in text and voice chat rooms. *Language Learning & Technology* 9 (3): 79–98. http://llt.msu.edu/vol9num3/jepson/.

Johns, A. 1990. L1 composition theories: Implications for developing theories of L2 composition. In *Second language writing: Research insights for the classroom*, ed. B. Kroll, 24–36. Cambridge: Cambridge University Press.

Johns, A., and J. Swales. 2002. Literacy and disciplinary practices: Opening and closing perspectives. *Journal of English for Academic Purposes* 1:13–28.

Johns, T. 1994. From printout to handout: Grammar and vocabulary teaching in the context of data-driven learning. In *Perspectives on pedagogical grammar*, ed. T. Odlin, 293–313. Cambridge: Cambridge University Press.

_____. 1997. Contexts: The background, development and trailing of a concordance-based CALL program. In *Teaching and language corpora*, ed. A. Wichmann, S. Fligelstone, T. McEnery, and G. Knowles, 100–115. London: Longman.

Johnson, A. 2004. Creating a writing class utilizing class and student blogs. *The Internet TESL Journal* 10 (8). http://iteslj.org/Techniques/Johnson-Blogs/.

Johnson, A. K. 2002. Journal writing for an audience. *Modern English Teacher* 11 (2): 46–50.

Johnson, C. M. 2003. Establishing an online community of practice for instructors of English as a foreign language. PhD diss., Nova Southeastern University. http://www.scis.nova.edu/~johnschr/.

Johnson, D. W., R. T. Johnson, and E. Holubec. 1988. *Circles of learning*. Edina, MN: Interaction.

Johnson, K. E. 1996. The vision versus the reality: The tensions of the TESOL practicum. In *Teacher learning in language teaching*, ed. D. Freeman and J. C. Richards, 30–49. Cambridge: Cambridge University Press.

Jones, J. F. 2001. CALL and the responsibilities of teachers and administrators. *ELT Journal* 55:360–67.

Juice. 2005. http://juicereceiver.sourceforge.net/.

Jung, I., S. Choi, C. Lim, and J. Leem. 2002. Effects of different types of interaction on learning achievement, satisfaction and participation in Web-based instruction. *Innovations in Education and Teaching International* 39:153–62.

Jung, U. O. H. 2005. An international bibliography of computer-assisted language learning: Sixth installment. *System* 33:135–85.

Kagan, S. 1994. *Cooperative learning*. San Juan Capistrano, CA: Author.

Kamhi-Stein, L. D., N. Besdikian, E. Gillis, S. Lee, B. Lemes, M. Michelson, and D. Tamaki. 2002. A project-based approach to interactive Web site design. *TESOL Journal* 11 (3): 9–15.

Kasper, L. F. 2000. Sustained content study and the Internet: Developing functional and academic literacies. In *Sustained content teaching in academic ESL/EFL: A practical approach*, ed. M. Pally, 54–73. Boston: Houghton Mifflin.

Katchen, J., B. Morris, and L. Savova. 2005. Do-it-yourself video role models. *Essential Teacher* 2 (1): 40–43.

Kearsley, G. 2000. *Online education: Learning and teaching in Cyberspace.* Stamford, CT: Wadsworth Thomson Learning.

Kelly, C. I., and L. E. Kelly. 1997–2006. Interesting things for ESL students. http://www.manythings .org/.

Kelly, G., T. J. Kennedy, M. Eberhardt, and L. K. Austin. 2002. Learning Spanish while practicing mathematics concepts and skills: A winning combination. *Teaching Children Mathematics* 9:141–47.

Kennedy, K. 2003, February 15. Writing with Web logs. *Technology & Learning.* http://www .techlearning.com/db_area/archives/TL/2003/02/blogs.html.

Kennedy, T. J. 2005. GLOBE joins forces with the American Council on the Teaching of Foreign Languages to promote content-based language study around the world. http://www.globe .gov/fsl/html/templ.cgi?actfl_2005&lang=en&nav=1.

Kennedy, T. J., and G. Canney. 2001. Collaboration across language, age, and geographic borders. In *Collaboration for diverse learners: Viewpoints and practices,* ed. K. Risko and K. Bromley, 310–29. Newark, DE: International Reading Association.

Kennedy, T. J., and S. Henderson. 2003. The GLOBE program: Bringing together students, teachers and scientists to increase scientific understanding of the earth through research. *Children, Youth and Environments* 13 (2). http://www.colorado.edu/journals/cye/13_2/FieldReports/GLOBE/ GLOBEProgram.htm.

Kennedy, T. J., and M. R. L. Odell. 2000. GLOBE: An international technology-based interdisciplinary program. In *Case method research and application: Creative interactive teaching, case method and other techniques,* vol. 9, ed. H. E. Klein, 215–18. Boston: World Association for Case Method Research and Application.

Kennedy, T. J., and M. J. Pedras. 2004. Service-learning: The missing link to language study, preservice education and building community. In *JUNTOS: Community partnerships in Spanish and Portuguese,* ed. J. Hellebrandt, J. Arries, L. Varona, and C. Klein, 172–79. Boston: Heinle & Heinle.

Kent State University. n.d. Kent State University's ESL OWL (online writing lab). http://dept.kent .edu/english/eslowl/.

Kerka, S. 1994. Myths and realities: Self-directed learning. ERIC Document Reproduction Service No. ED365818. http://web.archive.org/web/20001018222234/http://www.sit.edu/lcc/sd_learn .html.

Kern, R. 2000. *Literacy and language teaching.* Oxford: Oxford University Press.

KidsGLOBE. 1998. *The sound of GLOBE.* CD. http://www.globe.gov/fsl/html/templ.cgi ?nlfall1998_page8&lang=en&nav=1.

KidzBlog Version 1.3. Software. 2005. San Diego, CA: HaranBanjo. http://www.haranbanjo .com/kidzblog/.

Kim, I.-S. 2001–2004. Professor Inseok Kim's cyber EFL CALL academy. Futech Research Institute of English Language Education and Technology. http://www.eflcall.com/.

_____. 2002. *Strategic English listening comprehension* (English and Korean Bilingual Version). Seoul: Pakmungak.

_____. 2003. *Multimedia-assisted language learning: Promises and challenges.* Seoul: Bookorea.

Kindler, A. n.d. Language and education links: Bilingual education and ESL teacher education programs in the U.S. National Clearinghouse for English Language Acquisition. http://www.ncela.gwu.edu/resfor/preteachers/teachered/index.htm.

Kitao, K. 2002. Teaching cultural awareness through writing: Student Webpage projects. In *The changing face of CALL: A Japanese perspective,* ed. P. Lewis, 203–15. Lisse, The Netherlands: Swets & Zeitlinger.

Klecka, C. L., R. T. Clift, and A. S. Thomas. 2002. Proceed with caution: Introducing electronic conferencing in teacher education. *Critical Issues in Teacher Education* 9:28–36.

Ko, S., and S. Rossen. 2001. *Teaching online: A practical guide.* Boston: Houghton Mifflin.

Kollias, V., N. Mamalougos, X. Vamvakoussi, M. Lakkala, and S. Vosniadou. 2005. Teachers' attitudes to and beliefs about Web-based collaborative learning in the context of an international implementation. *Computers & Education* 45:295–315.

Kondo, I. 2002. Video and learner enthusiasm: Stimulating personal interest as the first step towards autonomy. In *Proceedings of the JALT CUE and TEVAL mini-conferences, Japan,* ed. A. S. Mackenzie and T. Newfield, 83–86. Tokyo: Japan Association for Language Teaching.

Kötter, M. 2002. *Tandem learning on the Internet.* Frankfurt: Peter Lang.

Knoblauch, C. H., and L. Brannon. 2002. Responding to texts: Facilitating revision in the writing workshop. In *Dialogue on writing: Rethinking ESL, basic writing, and first-year composition,* ed. G. DeLuca, L. Fox, M. Johnson, and M. Kogen, 251–69. Mahwah, NJ: Lawrence Erlbaum.

Krashen, S. D. 1982. *Principles and practices in second language acquisition.* Oxford: Pergamon Press.

_____. 1983. *The natural approach: Language acquisition in the classroom.* Hayward, CA: Alemany Press.

_____. 1987. *Principles and practice in second language acquisition.* New York: Prentice Hall.

_____. 1994. *The power of reading.* Englewood, CO: Libraries Unlimited.

_____. 1997. *Foreign language education the easy way.* Culver City, CA: Language Education Associates.

Krauss, M. 1998–2005. Integrating the Internet into the classroom. Lewis and Clark College. http://www.lclark.edu/~krauss/usia/home.html.

Kroll, B., ed. 1990. *Second language writing.* Cambridge: Cambridge University Press.

Kullman, J. 1998. Mentoring and the development of reflective practice: Concepts and context. *System* 26:471–48.

Kumaravadivelu, B. 1994. The postmethod condition: Emerging strategies for second/foreign language teaching. *TESOL Quarterly* 28:27–48.

_____. 2001. Toward a postmethod pedagogy. *TESOL Quarterly* 35:537–60.

Lafford, P. A., and B. A. Lafford. 1997. Learning language and culture with Internet technologies. In *Technology-enhanced language learning,* ed. M. D. Bush and R. M. Terry, 215–62. Lincolnwood, IL: National Textbook Company.

Landauer, T. K., and S. T. Dumais. 1997. A solution to Plato's problem: The latent semantic analysis theory of acquisition, induction, and representation of knowledge. http://lsa.colorado.edu/papers/plato/plato.annote.html.

Lapp, D., J. Flood, and N. Farnan. 1993. Literacy learning for all. In *The power of two languages*, ed. J. Tinajero and A. F. Ada, 294–303. New York: Macmillan-McGraw-Hill.

Laufer, B. 1997. The lexical plight in second language reading. In *Second language vocabulary acquisition: A rationale for pedagogy*, ed. J. Coady and T. Huckin, 20–34. New York: Cambridge University Press.

Lave, J., and E. Wenger. 1991. *Situated learning: Legitimate peripheral participation.* Cambridge: Cambridge University Press.

Lawrence, S. 2002, November 17. Online or invisible? http://citeseer.ist.psu.edu/online-nature01/. Edited print version also available: 2001. Free online availability substantially increases a paper's impact. *Nature* 411 (6837): 521.

LearningTimes. 2006. http://www.learningtimes.net/.

_____. n.d. http://www.learningtimes.org/.

Lee, J. 2002. A report of the TOEFL score comparison among 153 nations. *Dong-ah Daily Newspapers* (Seoul). July 30.

Lee, W., and D. L. Owens. 2000. Multimedia-based instructional design. In *Instructional and cognitive impacts of Web-based instruction*, ed. B. Abbey, 102–17. Hershey, PA: Idea Group.

Leki, I. 1998. *Academic writing: Exploring processes and strategies.* Cambridge: Cambridge University Press.

LeLoup, J., and R. Ponterio. 2000. Cooperative learning activities for the foreign language classroom. *Language Learning & Technology* 3 (2): 3–5.

Levy, M., and C. Kennedy. 2004. A task-cycling pedagogy using stimulated reflection and audio-conferencing in foreign language learning. *Language Learning & Technology* 8 (2): 50–68. http://llt.msu.edu/vol8num2/levy/default.html.

Li, Y. 2000. Linguistic characteristics of ESL writing in task-based email activities. *System* 28:229–45.

Lindsay, J. 2002, December 12. Digital teaching portfolios. Presentation at the Professional Educators Association of Kuwait conference. http://www.lindsayonline.net/Reaching_Out/Teacher_links/digport_pdf.pdf.

_____. 2004. Fostering an online learning community for the development of student digital portfolios. Paper presented at the 19th International Baccalaureate Asia Pacific Regional Conference, Mumbai. http://www.lindsayonline.net/Reaching_Out/Teacher_links/stportfolio.htm.

_____. 2005a. Digital teaching portfolio. http://www.lindsayonline.net/.

_____. 2005b. Weblogs and student portfolio projects: Why and how to implement them. Presentation at the 2005 TESOL CALL Interest Section Electronic Village Online. http://www.lindsayonline.net/Reaching_Out/Teacher_links/Weblogs.doc.

Liu, J., and R. W. Sadler. 2003. The effect and affect of peer review in electronic versus traditional modes on L2 writing. *Journal of English for Academic Purposes* 2:193–227.

Lycos. 2006. Tripod. http://www.tripod.lycos.com/.

Ma, B. K. C. 1993. Small-corpora concordancing in ESL teaching and learning. *Hong Kong Papers in Linguistics and Language Teaching* 16:11–30.

Mabbott, A., and A. Schramm. 2004. Course quality in online English-as-a-second-language teacher education. In *Creating teacher community: Selected papers from the Third International Confer-*

ence on Language Teacher Education, ed. M. Bigelow and C. Walker, 281–99. Minneapolis, MN: Center for Advanced Research on Language Acquisition.

MacDonald, G. J. 2004. Contrarian finding: Computers are a drag on learning. *Christian Science Monitor*. December 6. http://search.csmonitor.com/2004/1206/p11s01-legn.html.

Maggi, B. H., and C. Geirsch. n.d. CALIPSO and CloudSat Education and Public Outreach programs partner with GLOBE and NASA CONNECT. http://www.globe.gov/fsl/html/templ .cgi?calipso&lang=en&nav=1.

Makers Pages. Software. n.d. Mellon Tri-College Language Project. http://lang.swarthmore.edu/ makers/.

mariichigo. 2005. http://mariichigo.livejournal.com/.

Marvin, S., K. K. Franklin, J. S. Chesser, R. Edleston, P. Edwards-Schafer, C. Oberste, I. J. Routen, and T. Satkowski-Harper. 1999. Faculty attitudes about the use of technology in the college classroom. Paper presented at the 28th Annual Meeting of the Mid-South Educational Research Association, Point Clear, AL.

Marzio, M., and E. Hanson-Smith. 2006. Real English online. http://groups.yahoo.com/group/ Real_English_Online.

The Marzio School and Real English. 2006. Real English. http://www.real-english.com/.

Massachusetts Institute of Technology. 2005. MIT OpenCourseWare: Our story. http://ocw.mit .edu/OcwWeb/Global/AboutOCW/our-story.htm.

Massachusetts Institute of Technology, Center for Bits and Atoms. 2006. Welcome to fab central. http://fab.cba.mit.edu/.

McDonough, J., and S. McDonough. 1997. *Research methods for English language teachers*. London: Arnold.

McGreal, R. 2004. Learning objects: A practical definition. *International Journal of Instructional Technology and Distance Learning* 1 (9): 21–32.

McKeand, N. 2006. Random thoughts. http://namckeand.blogspot.com/.

McKenzie, J. 2000. Module maker. http://questioning.org/module/module.html.

McMartin, F. 2004. MERLOT: A model for user involvement in digital library design and implementation. *Journal of Digital Information* 5 (3): Article No. 293. http://jodi.ecs.soton.ac.uk/ Articles/v05/i03/McMartin/.

Means, B., E. Coleman, and A. Lewis. 1998. *GLOBE year 3 evaluation: Implementation and progress*. Menlo Park, CA: SRI International.

MERLOT: Multimedia Educational Resource for Learning and Online Teaching. 1997–2006. http:// www.merlot.org/.

Meskill, C. 1999. Conclusion: 20 minutes into the future. In *CALL environments: Research, practice, and critical issues*, ed. J. Egbert and E. Hanson-Smith, 459–69. Alexandria, VA: TESOL.

Meskill, C., and J. Mossop. 2000. Electronic texts in ESOL classrooms. *TESOL Quarterly* 34:585–92.

Meskill, C., J. Mossop, and R. Bates. 1999. Electronic texts and learners of English as a second language. http://cela.albany.edu/publication/brochure/etext.pdf.

Meskill, C., J. Mossop, S. DiAngelo, and R. K. Pasquale. 2002. Expert and novice teachers talking technology: Precepts, concepts, and misconcepts. *Language Learning & Technology* 6 (3): 46–57. http://llt.msu.edu/vol6num3/meskill/.

Meskill, C., and K. Ranglova. 2000. Sociocollaborative language learning in Bulgaria. In *Network-based language teaching: Concepts and practice*, ed. M. Warschauer and R. Kern, 20–40. Cambridge: Cambridge University Press.

Mezirow, J. 2000. Learning to think like an adult: Core concepts of transformation theory. In *Learning as transformation*, ed. J. Mezirow, 3–33. San Francisco: Jossey-Bass.

Microsoft. 2006a. Create home movies with Windows Movie Maker. http://www.microsoft.com/windowsxp/using/moviemaker/default.mspx.

———. 2006b. Microsoft Office online. http://office.microsoft.com.

Microsoft Office 2003. Software. 2005. Redmond, WA: Microsoft. http://office.microsoft.com/.

Microsoft PowerPoint 2003. Software. 2006. Redmond, WA: Microsoft. http://office.microsoft.com/powerpoint.

Microsoft Word 2003. Software. 2006. Redmond, WA: Microsoft. http://office.microsoft.com/word.

Microsoft Works Version 8. Software. 2004. Redmond, WA: Microsoft. http://www.microsoft.com/products/works/default.mspx.

MiddleWeb. 2002. MiddleWeb: Exploring middle school reform: Some teacher mentoring resources. http://www.middleweb.com/mentoring.html.

Miller, G. A. et al. 2005. WordNet Version 2.1. Cognitive Science Laboratory, Princeton University. http://wordnet.princeton.edu/.

Miller, L. 2004. Teachers as researchers. *Modern English Teacher* 13 (4): 39–41.

Miller, P. C., and H. Endo. 2004. Understanding and meeting the needs of ESL students. *Phi Delta Kappan* 85:786–91.

Miraglia, E., and J. Norris. 2000. Cyberspace and sofas: Dialogic spaces and the making of an online writing lab. In *Taking flight with OWLs: Examining electronic writing center work*, ed. J. A. Inman and D. N. Sewell, 85–103. Mahwah, NJ: Lawrence Erlbaum.

Mishan, F. 2004. Authenticating corpora for language learning: A problem and its resolution. *ELT Journal* 58:219–27.

Mishra, S. 2002. A design framework for online learning environments. *British Journal of Educational Technology* 33:493–96.

Mohan, B. 2001. The second language as a medium of learning. In *English as a second language in the mainstream: Teaching, learning, and identity*, ed. B. Mohan, C. Leung, and C. Davison, 107–26. Harlow, England: Longman.

MonoConc Pro Version 2.0. Software. 2000. Houston, TX: Athelstan. http://www.athel.com/.

MonoConc Pro Version 2.2. Software. 2005. Houston, TX: Athelstan. http://www.athel.com/.

Moodle Version 1.5.3. Software. 2005. East Perth, Australia: Moodle. http://moodle.org/.

Moore, M. 2005. Bowling for Columbine: Teacher's guide. http://www.bowlingforcolumbine.com/library/teachers/index.php.

Mora, J. K. 2002, July 26. A road map for effective biliteracy instruction: A knowledge base and teaching strategies. San Diego State University. http://coe.sdsu.edu/people/jmora/Mora Modules/BiliteracyRoadMap.htm.

Moskowitz, J., and M. Stephens, eds. 1997. *From students of teaching to teachers of students: Teacher induction around the Pacific Rim*. Washington, DC: U.S. Department of Education.

Mozilla Suite Version 1.7.12 (Macintosh). Software. 2005. Mountain View, CA: Mozilla Foundation. http://www.mozilla.org/products/mozilla1.x/.

Muilenburg, L., and Z. L. Berge. 2001. Barriers to distance education: A factor-analytic study. *American Journal of Distance Education* 15 (2): 7–22.

Murphy, J. M., and F. L. Stoller. 2001. Sustained-content language teaching: An emerging definition. *TESOL Journal* 10 (2–3): 3–5.

The My Hero Short Film Festival. n.d. http://www.myhero.com/myhero/go/filmfestival.

Namo WebEditor 2006. Software. 2005. Seoul: Namo Interactive. http://www.namo.com/products/webeditor.php.

Nation, P. 2001. How good is your vocabulary program? *ESL Magazine.* http://www.eslmag.com/modules.php?name=News&file=article&sid=24.

Nation, P., and J. Newton. 1997. Teaching vocabulary. In *Second language vocabulary acquisition: A rationale for pedagogy*, ed. J. Coady and T. Huckin, 238–54. New York: Cambridge University Press.

National Aeronautics and Space Administration (NASA). 2006. CALIPSO: Cloud-Aerosol Lidar and Infrared Pathfinder Satellite Observations. http://www-calipso.larc.nasa.gov/.

National Clearinghouse for English Language Acquisition. 2005. Minnesota data and demographics. http://www.ncela.gwu.edu/policy/states/minnesota/03_demo.htm.

National Public Radio. 2006. http://www.npr.org/.

National Research Council. 2002. *Enhancing undergraduate learning with information technology: A workshop summary,* ed. M. Hilton. Center for Education, Division of Behavioral and Social Sciences and Education. Washington, DC: National Academy Press.

Nelson, L. M. 1999, July. Theory to practice: Utilization of instructional systems design, constructivist pedagogy, and distance learning. Paper presented at the Annual Summer Institute and Conference of Nova Southeastern University, Ft. Lauderdale, FL.

Nelson, T. 2000. Using computers to teach writing in the FL classroom. In *Writing across languages*, ed. G. Brauer, 99–115. Stamford, CT: Ablex.

Nesi, H., and P. Thompson. 2006. The British academic spoken English (BASE) corpus. University of Warwick and University of Reading. http://www2.warwick.ac.uk/fac/soc/celte/base/.

NetMeeting 3. Software. 2000. Redmond, WA: Microsoft. http://www.microsoft.com/windows/netmeeting.

Netscape Version 7.1 (Macintosh). Software. 2003. Mountain View, CA: Netscape. http://www.netscape.net/.

Nicenet. 2003. http://www.nicenet.net/.

Nielsen, J. 1999. *Designing Web usability: The practice of simplicity.* Indianapolis, IN: New Riders.

_____. 2000. *Designing Web usability.* Indianapolis, IN: New Riders.

Nielsen, J., and M. Tahir. 2001. *Homepage usability: 50 Websites deconstructed.* Indianapolis, IN: New Riders.

Nozawa, K. 2002. Keypal exchanges for writing fluency and intercultural understanding. In *The changing face of CALL: A Japanese perspective*, ed. P. Lewis, 187–201. Lisse, The Netherlands: Swets & Zeitlinger.

Nunan, D. 1992. *Research methods in language learning.* Cambridge: Cambridge University Press.

_____. 2001. Aspects of task-based syllabus design. Karen's linguistics issues: Free resources for teachers and students of English. http://www3.telus.net/linguisticsissues/syllabusdesign.html.

Nunes, A. 2004. Portfolios in the EFL classroom: Disclosing an informed practice. *ELT Journal* 58:327–35.

Oddcast. n.d. SitePal. http://www.oddcast.com/sitepal/.

Odeo. n.d. http://www.odeo.com/.

Office of the Independent Council. 1998. Referral to the United States House of Representatives pursuant to Title 28, United States Code, § 595(c) [The Starr Report]. http://icreport.loc.gov/icreport/.

OLPC (One Laptop per Child). 2006, February. Frequently asked questions. http://laptop.org/faq.en_US.html.

O'Neill, D. K. 2001. Knowing when you've brought them in: Scientific genre knowledge and communities of practice. *Journal of the Learning Sciences* 10:223–64.

O'Neill, D. K., R. Wagner, and L. M. Gomez. 1996. Online mentors: Experimenting in science class. *Educational Leadership* 54 (3): 3–42.

Online Computer Library Center. 2005. FirstSearch. http://www.oclc.org/firstsearch/.

OpenOffice.org Suite Version 2.0. Software. 2005. Santa Clara, CA: Sun Microsystems. http://www.openoffice.org/.

Opensource for educators. n.d. http://www.opensource.idv.tw/moodle/.

Orr, T. 1995. Studying the professions we serve. *ESP News* 4 (2): 11.

Ourmedia. n.d. http://www.ourmedia.org/.

Overture Services. 2006. AltaVista. http://www.altavista.com.

Ovid Technologies. 2006. Wilson education abstracts full text. http://www.ovid.com/site/catalog/DataBase/176.jsp?top=2&mid=3&bottom=7&subsection=10.

OWL at Purdue and Purdue University. 1995–2006. The writing lab at Purdue. http://owl.english.purdue.edu/writinglab/.

Oxford, R. 1993. Research update on teaching L2 listening. *System* 21:205–11.

Oxford University. 2005. British national corpus. http://www.natcorp.ox.ac.uk/.

Oxford University Press. 2000–2006. Passport online. http://www.oup-passportonline.jp/.

Padolsky, D. 2005. NCELA FAQ No. 8. National Clearinghouse for English Language Acquisition. http://www.ncela.gwu.edu/expert/faq/08leps.htm.

Padron, Y., and H. T. Waxman. 1996. Improving the teaching and learning of English language learners through instructional technology. *International Journal of Instructional Media* 23 (4): 341–54.

The palace. 2001–2006. http://www.thepalace.com/.

Palloff, R. M., and K. Pratt. 2001. *Lessons from the cyberspace classroom: The realities of online teaching.* San Francisco: Jossey-Bass.

Pally, M. 1997. Critical thinking in ESL: An argument for sustained content. *Journal of Second Language Writing* 6:293–311.

Palmquist, M. 2003. A brief history of computer support for writing centers and writing-across-the-curriculum programs. *Computers and Composition* 20:395–413.

Paltalk Version 8. Software. 2006. New York: Paltalk. http://www.paltalk.com/.

Paribakht, T. S., and M. Wesche. 1997. Vocabulary enhancement activities and reading for meaning. In *Second language vocabulary acquisition: A rationale for pedagogy*, ed. J. Coady and T. Huckin, 174–200. New York: Cambridge University Press.

———. 1998. Reading and "incidental" vocabulary acquisition. *Studies in Second Language Acquisition* 21:196–224.

Parker, I. 2001, May 28. Absolute PowerPoint: Can a software package edit our thoughts. *The New Yorker*. http://www.physics.ohio-state.edu/~wilkins/group/powerpt.html.

Paulus, T. M. 1999. The effect of peer and teacher feedback on student writing. *Journal of Second Language Writing* 8:265–89.

Pawan, F., T. M. Paulus, S. Yalcin, and C. F. Chang. 2003. Online learning: Patterns of engagement and interaction among in-service teachers. *Language Learning & Technology* 7 (3): 119–40. http://llt.msu.edu/vol7num3/pawan/.

Payne, J. S., and P. J. Whitney. 2002. Developing L2 oral proficiency through synchronous CMC: Output, working memory, and interlanguage development. *CALICO Journal* 20 (1): 7–32. http://php.scripts.psu.edu/faculty/j/s/jsp17/articles/calico2002/.

Peachey, N. n.d. Learner diaries. Teaching English. BBC/British Council. http://www.teachingenglish.org.uk/think/write/diary.shtml.

Pelletieri, J. 2000. Negotiation in cyberspace: The role of chatting in the development of grammatical competence. In *Network-based language teaching: Concepts and practice*, M. Warschauer and R. Kern, ed., 59–86. Cambridge: Cambridge University Press.

Pennington, M. C. 2004. Electronic media in second language writing: An overview of tools and research findings. In *New perspectives on CALL for second language classrooms*, ed. S. Fotos and C. Browne, 69–92. Mahwah, NJ: Lawrence Erlbaum.

Peregoy, S. F., and O. F. Boyle. 2001. *Reading, writing, and learning in ESL: A resource book for K–12 teachers*. 3rd ed. New York: Longman.

Peterson, P. W. 1997. Knowledge, skills, and attitudes in teacher preparation for content-based instruction. In *The content-based classroom: Perspectives on integrating language and content*, ed. M. A. Snow and D. M. Brinton, 158–74. White Plains, NY: Longman.

Petrushin, V. A. 2001. Using speech analysis techniques for language learning. In *Proceedings of the IEEE International Conference on Advanced Learning Technologies*, ed. J. R. Hartley, T. Okamoto, Kinshuk, and J. P. Klus, 129–30. http://csdl2.computer.org/comp/proceedings/icalt/2001/1013/00/10130129.pdf.

Pew Internet and American Life Project. 2005. Pew/Internet: Pew Internet and American life project. http://www.pewinternet.org/reports.asp.

Photo Story 3. Software. 2004. Redmond, WA: Microsoft. http://www.microsoft.com/photostory.

Piaget, J. 1965. *The language and thought of the child*. New York: World Publishing.

———. 1972. *The psychology of the child*. New York: Basic Books.

Pica, T. 1994. Research on negotiation: What does it reveal about second-language learning conditions, processes, and outcomes? *Language Learning* 44:493–527.

Pickett, N., and B. Dodge. 2001. Rubrics for Web lessons. San Diego State University. http://webquest .sdsu.edu/rubrics/Weblessons.htm.

PodOmatic. 2006. http://www.podomatic.com/.

Polsani, P. R. 2003, February 19. Use and abuse of reusable learning objects. *Journal of Digital Information* 3 (4): Article 164. http://jodi.ecs.soton.ac.uk/Articles/v03/i04/Polsani/.

Powers, J. K., and J. V. Nelson. 1995. Second language writers and the writing center: A national survey of writing center conferencing at graduate institutions. *Journal of Second Language Writing* 4:113–38.

Pravec, N. A. 2002. Survey of learner corpora. *ICAME Journal* 26:81–114. http://nora.hd.uib.no/ icame/ij26/pravec.pdf.

Prensky, M. 2001. Digital natives, digital immigrants. *On the Horizon* 9 (5). http://www.marcprensky .com/writing/Prensky%20-%20Digital%20Natives,%20Digital%20Immigrants%20-%20Part1 .pdf.

_____. 2002. Evolving instruction? Seven challenges. *On the Horizon* 10 (2). http://www.marc prensky.com/writing/Prensky%20-%20Evolving%20Instruction%20-%20OTH%2010-2.pdf.

Price, B. J. 2001. I was just thinking—When students know more than teachers. *International Education Daily*. June 24. http://members.iteachnet.com/~webzine/article.php?story=20010624 21453526. [Available from the author.]

Privacy Rights Clearinghouse. 2005. Children's privacy and safety on the Internet: A resource guide for parents. http://www.privacyrights.org/fs/fs21-children.htm.

Public Broadcasting Service. 1995–2006. PBS TeacherSource. http://www.pbs.org/teachersource/.

Pusack, J. P., and S. K. Otto. 1997. Taking control of multimedia. In *Technology-enhanced language learning*, ed. M. D. Bush and R. M. Terry, 1–47. Lincolnwood, IL: National Textbook Company.

Pyle, R., and C. Dziuban. 2001. Technology: Servant or master of the online teacher? *Library Trends* 50:130–44.

Qian, D. 1999. Assessing the roles of depth and breadth of vocabulary knowledge in reading comprehension. *Canadian Modern Language Review* 56 (2). http://www.utpjournals.com/product/ cmlr/562/562-Qian.html.

Quia. 1998–2006. Quia Web. http://www.quia.com/web/.

Raimes, A. 1983. *Techniques in teaching writing*. Oxford: Oxford University Press.

Rao, V. S. 2003. MSN to shut down chat rooms. Rediff.com. http://www.rediff.com/netguide/2003/ sep/24msn.htm.

Read, J. 2004. Research in teaching vocabulary. *Annual Review of Applied Linguistics* 24:146–61.

RealPlayer 10. Software. 2005. Seattle, WA: RealNetworks. http://www.real.com.

Reid, J. 1993. *Teaching ESL writing*. Englewood Cliffs, NJ: Regents Prentice Hall.

Reilly, T. 1988. ESL through content area instruction. ERIC Digest. ERIC Document Reproduction Service No. ED296572. http://www.ericdigests.org/pre-929/esl.htm.

Reiman, A. J., and L. Thies-Sprinthall. 1998. *Mentoring and supervision for teacher development*. New York: Longman.

Rice, R. E., S. R. Hiltz, and D. Spencer. 2005. Media mixes and learning networks. In *Learning together online: Research on asynchronous learning networks*, ed. S. R. Hiltz and R. Goldman, 215–38. Mahwah, NJ: Lawrence Erlbaum.

Richards, J. C., and C. Lockhart. 1994. *Reflective teaching in second language classrooms.* Cambridge: Cambridge University Press.

Rilling, S., and Ö. Pazvant. 2002. Computer concordancing for ESP materials. *TESOL Journal* 11 (3): 43–44.

Rivers, W. M., ed. 1987. *Interactive language teaching.* Cambridge: Cambridge University Press.

Robb, T. 1990. Homework: How to get them to do it. *The Language Teacher* 13 (8): 15–16.

———. 2000. Teaching writing with Web projects: Famous personages in Japan. In *Technology-enhanced learning environments,* ed. E. Hanson-Smith, 125–34. Alexandria, VA: TESOL.

Roberts, B. 2002. Interaction, reflection and learning at a distance. *Open Learning* 17:39–55.

Robertson, D. 2001. Classroom concordancing. University of Stirling Institute of Education. http://www.celt.stir.ac.uk/resources/ML24/ddlearning.pdf.

Ronteltap, F., and A. Eurelings. 2002. Activity and interaction of students in an electronic learning environment for problem-based learning. *Distance Education* 23:11–22.

Root, T. 2000–2003. Mightycoach.com: Online video training. http://www.mightycoach.com/.

Rosebery, A. S., B. Warren, and F. R. Conant. 1992. *Appropriating scientific discourse: Findings from language minority classrooms.* Santa Cruz, CA: National Center for Research on Cultural Diversity and Second Language Learning.

Rosenkjar, P. 2002. Adjunct courses in the great books: The key that unlocked Locke for Japanese EFL undergraduates and opened the door to academia for EFL. In *Content-based instruction in higher education settings,* ed. J. Crandall and D. Kaufman, 13–27. Alexandria, VA: TESOL.

Rosie, A. 2000. Online pedagogies and the promotion of "deep learning." *Information Services & Use* 20:109–16.

Rouet, J.-F., and J. J. Levonen. 1996. Studying and learning with hypertext: Empirical studies and their implications. In *Hypertext and cognition,* ed. J.-F. Rouet, J. J. Levonen, A. Dillon, and R. J. Spiro, 9–23. Mahwah, NJ: Lawrence Erlbaum.

Rovai, A., and H. Jordan. 2004. Blended learning and sense of community: A comparative analysis with traditional and fully online graduate courses. *International Review of Research in Open and Distance Learning* 5 (2). http://www.irrodl.org/index.php/irrodl/article/view/192/274.

Rubin, J. 1995. An overview to a guide for the teaching of second language listening. In *A guide for the teaching of second language listening,* ed. D. J. Mendelsohn and J. Rubin, 1–12. San Diego, CA: Domini Press.

Ryan, S. 2003. Practical digital video in the language classroom. *C@lling Japan* 11 (1): 12–16.

Ryder, M. 2006. Constructivism. University of Colorado at Denver. http://carbon.cudenver.edu/~mryder/itc_data/constructivism.html.

Savli, V. 2006. The image of the other. European Schools Project Association. http://www.europeanschoolsproject.org/image/.

Schcolnik, M., and S. Kol. 1999. Using presentation software to enhance language learning. *Internet TESL Journal* 5 (3). http://iteslj.org/Techniques/Schcolnik-PresSoft.html.

Schmidt, R. 1990. The role of consciousness in second language learning. *Applied Linguistics* 11:129–58.

———. 1994a. Deconstructing consciousness in search of useful definitions for applied linguistics. *AILA Review* 11:11–26.

_____. 1994b. Implicit learning and the cognitive unconscious: Of artificial grammars and SLA. In *Implicit and explicit learning of languages*, ed. N. Ellis, 165–209. London: Academic Press.

_____. 1995. *Attention and awareness in foreign language learning.* Honolulu: University of Hawaii Press.

schMOOze University. n.d. http://schmooze.hunter.cuny.edu/.

Schönwetter, D., and H. Francis. 2002. *Student perceptions of learning success with technology: Pilot study report 2002.* http://www.mcgrawhill.ca/highereducation/images/allstudents.pdf.

Schramm, A. 2005. Making online students connect: Ethnographic strategies for developing online learning experiences. In *Distance education and languages: Evolution and change*, ed. B. Holmberg, M. Shelley, and C. White, 230–41. Clevedon, England: Multilingual Matters.

Schrock, K. 1995–2006. Teacher helpers: Critical evaluation information. http://school.discovery.com/schrockguide/eval.html.

Schrum, L. 1998. On-line education: A study of emerging pedagogy. *New Directions for Adult and Continuing Education* 78:53–61.

Schulman, A., and R. Sims. 1999. Learning in an online format versus an in-class format: An experimental study. *T.H.E. Journal* 26 (June): 54–56.

Schulman, L. 1986. Paradigms and research programs in the study of teaching. In *Handbook of research on teaching*, ed. M. Wittrock, 3–36. New York: Macmillan.

Schwienhorst, K. 2002. The state of VR: A meta-analysis of virtual reality tools in second language acquisition. *Computer-Assisted Language Learning* 15:221–39.

Scott, M., and T. Johns. 1993. Microconcord corpus of academic texts. Oxford University Press. http://langbank.engl.polyu.edu.hk/corpus/microconcord.html.

Serim, F., and M. Koch. 1996. *NetLearning: Why teachers use the Internet.* Sebastopol, CA: Songline Studios and O'Reilly.

Sevier, M. 2005. Vocabulary teaching activities. Simon Fraser University. http://www.sfu.ca/~msevier/.

Sharp, S. K. 2005. A blueprint for successful video projects. *Essential Teacher* 2 (1): 36–38.

Shea, P., E. Fredericksen, A. Pickett, and W. Pelz. 2004. Faculty development, student satisfaction, and reported learning in the SUNY Learning Network University. In *Learner-centered theory and practice in distance education: Cases from higher education*, ed. T. M. Duffy and J. R. Kirkely, 343–78. Mahwah, NJ: Lawrence Erlbaum.

Sherman, J. 2003. *Using authentic video in the language classroom.* Cambridge: Cambridge University Press.

Shetzer, H., and M. Warschauer. 2000. An electronic literacy approach to network-based language teaching. In *Network-based language teaching: Concepts and practice*, ed. M. Warschauer and R. Kern, 171–85. Cambridge: Cambridge University Press.

_____. 2001. English through Web page creation. In *Understanding the courses we teach: Local perspectives on English language teaching*, ed. J. Murphy and P. Byrd, 429–45. Ann Arbor: University of Michigan Press.

Shulman, A. 1997–1999. Storyboarding activity. San Mateo County Office of Education. http://pblmm.k12.ca.us/TechHelp/Storyboarding.html.

Siemens, G. 2004. Connectivism: A learning theory for the digital age. http://www.elearnspace
.org/Articles/connectivism.htm.

Silva, T., and C. Brice. 2004. Research in teaching writing. *Annual Review of Applied Linguistics*
24:70–106.

Single, P. B., and C. B. Muller. 2001. When email and mentoring unite: The implementation of a
nationwide electronic mentoring program. In *Implementing successful coaching and mentoring
programs*, ed. L. Stromei, 107–22. Cambridge, MA: American Society for Training &
Development.

Skehan, P. 1998. Task-based instruction. In *Annual review of applied linguistics*, ed. W. Grabe, 268–86.
New York: Cambridge University Press.

———. 2003. Focus on form, tasks, and technology. *Computer-Assisted Language Learning*
16:391–411.

Slavin, R. E. 1995. Research on cooperative learning and achievement: What we know, what we need
to know. *Contemporary Educational Psychology*, 21:43–69.

Smith, B., and G. J. Gorsuch. 2004. Synchronous computer mediated communication captured by
usability lab technologies: New interpretations. *System* 32:553–75.

Smith, G. G., D. Ferguson, and M. Caris. 2001. Teaching college courses online vs. face-to-face.
T.H.E. Journal 28 (April): 18–24.

Smith, J. 2006. Communities of practice. http://groups.yahoo.com/group/com-prac/.

Smith, R. G., and J. Coldron. 2000, April. How does research affect pre-service students' perceptions
of their practice? Paper presented at the annual meeting of the American Educational Research
Association, New Orleans, LA.

Smith, S. B., S. J. Smith, and R. Boone. 2000. Increasing access to teacher preparation: The effectiveness of traditional instructional methods in an online learning environment. *Journal of Special
Education Technology* 15 (2): 37–46.

Smith, T. L., and S. Ransbottom. 2000. Digital video in education. In *Distance learning technologies:
Issues, trends and opportunities*, ed. L. Lau, 132–33. Hershey, PA: Idea Group.

Snow, M. A. 2001. Content-based and immersion models for second and foreign language teaching.
In *Teaching English as a second or foreign language*, 3rd ed., ed. M. Celce-Murcia, 303–18.
Boston: Heinle & Heinle.

Snow, M. A., M. Met, and F. Genesee. 1989. A conceptual framework for the integration of language
and content in second/foreign language education. *TESOL Quarterly* 23:201–17.

South Birmingham College. n.d. ESOL video stories. http://www.sbirmc.ac.uk/all/all_showcase.htm.

Speck, B. 2002. Learning-teaching-assessment paradigms and the on-line classroom. *New Directions
for Teaching and Learning* 91:5–18.

Springfield Public School District 186. n.d. iMovie examples. http://www.springfield.k12.il.us/movie/.

SRI International. 1995–2004. Tapped in. http://tappedin.org/tappedin/.

Stanley, C. 1998. A framework for teacher reflectivity. *TESOL Quarterly* 32:584–91.

Stanley, G. 2004. Introducing your students to blogs. *IATEFL Issues* 178:9.

———. 2005. Blogging for ELT. BBC World Service and British Council. http://www.teachingenglish
.org.uk/think/resources/blogging.shtml.

_____. 2006. Blog-EFL. http://blog-efl.blogspot.com.

Stapleton, P. 2003. Assessing the quality and bias of Web-based sources: Implications for academic writing. *Journal of English for Academic Purposes* 2:229–45.

Steele, J. H. 2002. Herding cats: A descriptive case study of a virtual language learning community. PhD diss., Indiana University of Pennsylvania. http://netdial.caribe.net/~jhsteele/catstoc.html.

Stepp-Greany, J. 2002. Student perceptions on language learning in a technological environment: Implications for the new millennium. *Language Learning & Technology* 6 (1): 165–80. http://llt .msu.edu/vol6num1/STEPPGREANY/default.html.

Stevens, V. 2004. The skill of communication: Technology brought to bear on the art of language learning. *TESL-EJ* 7 (4). http://cwp60.berkeley.edu:16080/TESL-EJ/ej28/int.html.

_____. 2005a, April. Blogging in online communities of practice: Impact on language learning and teacher professional development. Presentation at the Qatar Teachers English Network Conference, Doha. http://prosites-vstevens.homestead.com/files/efi/papers/qten2005/ vancestevens2005qten.htm.

_____. 2005b. Vance's e-zguide "10+ steps to creating simple HTML files." http://www.homestead .com/prosites-vstevens/files/pi/very_basics/starthere.htm.

_____. 2006a. EVOnline 2002—Webheads community event. http://groups.yahoo.com/group/ evonline2002_webheads.

_____. 2006b. Webheads in action: Communities of practice online. http://www.vancestevens .com/papers/evonline2002/webheads.htm.

_____. 2006c. Writing for webheads: An experiment in world friendship through online language learning. http://www.homestead.com/prosites-vstevens/files/efi/webheads.htm.

Stigler, J. W., and J. Hiebert. 1999. *The teaching gap.* New York: Free Press.

Stoller, F. L. 2003. Project work: A means to promote language and content. In *Methodology in language teaching: An anthology of current practice*, ed. J. C. Richards and W. A. Renandya, 107–19. Cambridge: Cambridge University Press.

Strategic Studies. 1999–2002. LessonPro. http://www.lessonpro.net/.

Stryker, S. B., and B. L. Leaver. 1997. Content-based instruction: Some lessons and implications. In *Content-based instruction in foreign language education: Models and methods*, ed. S. B. Stryker and B. L. Leaver, 285–312. Washington, DC: Georgetown University Press.

Susser, B. 2002. Effectiveness and evaluation in CAI. *LET Kansai Shibu Kenkyu Shuroku* 9:1–12.

Susser, B., and T. Ariga. 2006. Teaching e-commerce Web page evaluation and design: A pilot study using tourism destination sites. *Computers and Education* 47 (4): 399–413.

Suzuki, R. 2004. Diaries as introspective research tools: From Ashton-Warner to blogs. *TESL-EJ* 8 (1). http://www-writing.berkeley.edu/TESL-EJ/ej29/int.html.

Swain, M. 1985. Communicative competence: Some roles of comprehensible input and comprehensible output in its development. In *Input in second language acquisition*, ed. S. M. Gass and C. G. Madden, 235–53. Rowley, MA: Newbury House.

Swain, M., and R. K. Johnson. 1997. Immersion education: A category within bilingual education. In *Immersion education: International perspectives*, ed. R. K. Johnson and M. Swain, 1–16. New York: Cambridge University Press.

Swales, J. M., and S. Lindermann. 2002. Teaching the literature review to international graduate students. In *Genre in the classroom: Multiple perspectives*, ed. A. Johns, 105–19. Mahwah, NJ: Lawrence Erlbaum.

Talking Communities. n.d. http://talkingcommunities.com.

Tang, G. 2001. Knowledge framework and classroom action. In *English as a second language in the mainstream: Teaching, learning, and identity*, ed. B. Mohan, C. Leung, and C. Davison, 127–37. Harlow, England: Longman.

Tardy, C. 2005. Expressions of disciplinarity and individuality in a multimodal genre. *Computers and Composition* 22:319–36.

Tarone, E., and D. Allwright. 2005. Second language teacher learning and student second language learning: Shaping the knowledge base. In *Second language teacher education: International perspectives*, ed. D. J. Tedick, 5–24. Mahwah, NJ: Lawrence Erlbaum.

Teacher support network. n.d. http://www.teachersupport.info/.

TESOL. 1997. *ESL standards for pre-K–12 students*. Alexandria, VA: TESOL.

———. 2003. *TESOL/NCATE standards for the accreditation of initial programs in P–12 ESL teacher education*. Alexandria, VA: TESOL. http://www.tesol.org/s_tesol/bin.asp?CID=219&DID=2135&DOC=FILE.PDF.

TESOL CALL-IS. 2005. Electronic village online 2006. http://darkwing.uoregon.edu/~call/.

Thanasoulas, D. 2002, December. What is learner autonomy and how can it be fostered? Karen's linguistics issues. http://www3.telus.net/linguisticsissues/learnerautonomy.html.

Thatcher, B. 2005. Situating L2 writing in global communication technologies. *Computers and Composition* 22:279–95.

Thiel, T. 1999. Reflections on critical incidents. *Prospect* 14 (1): 44–45.

Thirunarayanan, M., and A. Perez-Prado. 2002. Comparing Web-based and classroom-based learning: A quantitative study. *Journal of Research on Technology in Education* 34:131–37.

Thomas, M. J. W. 2002. Learning within incoherent structures: The space of online discussion forums. *Journal of Computer Assisted Learning* 18:351–66.

Thompson, E. H., and C. Rink. 2004, March 29. NASA and France pick up rhythm for CALIPSO launch. http://asd-www.larc.nasa.gov/new_AtSC/its_calipso_info.html.

Thomson Learning. n.d. InfoTrac college edition. http://infotrac.thomsonlearning.com/.

Thonus, T. 2002. Tutor and student assessments of academic writing tutorials: What is "success"? *Assessing Writing* 8:110–34.

———. 2003. Serving generation 1.5 learners in the university writing center. *TESOL Journal* 12 (1): 17–24.

Thornbury, S. 1997. Reformulation and reconstruction: Tasks that promote noticing. *ELT Journal* 51:326–34.

Thurstun, J., and C. Candlin. 1997. *Exploring academic English: A workbook for student essay writing*. Sydney: National Centre for English Language Teaching and Research (NCELTR).

———. 1998. Concordancing and the teaching of the vocabulary of academic English. *English for Specific Purposes* 17:267–80.

Tipic. 2001–2006. mo'time. http://www.motime.com/.

Torres-Guzman, M. E., and A. L. Goodwin. 1995. *Mentoring bilingual teachers.* Washington, DC: National Clearinghouse for Bilingual Education. http://www.ncela.gwu.edu/pubs/focus/focus12.htm.

Tosh, D., and B. Werdmuller. 2004. eportfolios and Weblogs: One vision for eportfolio development. ERADC: ePortfolio research and development community. http://www.eradc.org/papers/ePortfolio_Weblog.pdf.

Travelocity.com. 1996–2006. http://www.travelocity.com/.

Tribble, C., and G. Jones. 1990. *Concordances in the classroom.* London: Longman. Repr., Houston, TX: Athelstan, 1997.

Tschirner, E. 2001. Language acquisition in the classroom: The role of digital video. *Computer-Assisted Language Learning* 14:305–19.

Tudini, V. 2003. Using native speakers in chat. *Language Learning & Technology* 7 (3): 141–59. http://llt.msu.edu/vol7num3/tudini/default.html.

Tufte, E. R. 2003. *The cognitive style of PowerPoint.* Cheshire, CT: Graphics Press.

Turkle, S. 1997. Seeing through computers: Education in a culture of simulation. *The American Prospect* 8 (31). http://www.prospect.org/print/V8/31/turkle-s.html.

Turnbull, M., and G. Lawrence. 2002. *FSL teachers and technology: Findings from a national survey.* Canadian Association of Second Language Teachers. http://www.caslt.org/research/computers2.htm.

Ullman, C., and M. Rabinowitz. 2004. Course management systems and the reinvention of instruction. *T.H.E. Journal* 32 (October). http://www.thejournal.com/articles/17014.

University Corporation for Admospheric Research (UCAR). 2004, May 14. GLOBE Earth Day Web chats a success! http://www.globe.gov/fsl/GB/Display.pl?page=gb14MAY2004_032536&lang=en&nav=1.

_____. 2005, February 4. The art of GLOBE. http://www.globe.gov/fsl/STARS/ART/Display.opl?star=globe_art&lang=en&nav=1.

_____. n.d.a. GLOBE one. http://www.globe.gov/fsl/globeone/.

_____. n.d.b. The GLOBE program. http://www.globe.gov/.

_____. n.d.c. GLOBE teacher's guide. http://gandalf.globe.ucar.edu/tctg/globetg.jsp?rg=n&lang=en.

_____. n.d.d. GLOBE Thailand hosts marine hydrology symposium. http://www.globe.gov/fsl/html/templ.cgi?thailand_hydro&lang=en&nav=1.

University of Illinois. 2005. Novice teacher support project. http://ntsp.ed.uiuc.edu/.

University of Michigan. 2002. Michigan corpus of academic spoken English. http://www.hti.umich.edu/m/micase/.

University of Tennessee at Chattanooga. n.d. The Lupton Library. http://www.lib.utc.edu/.

University of Texas at Austin. 2005. World lecture hall. http://web.austin.utexas.edu/wlh/.

_____. n.d. WINGS. http://www.edb.utexas.edu/ties/wings.html.

University of Texas at Austin, College of Education. n.d. Laptop initiative for future educators. http://www.utexas.edu/education/laptop.html.

U.S. Department of Education. 2004a. The Elementary and Secondary Education Act (The No Child Left Behind Act of 2001). http://www.ed.gov/policy/elsec/leg/esea02/index.html.

_____. 2004b. The facts about . . . science achievement. http://www.ed.gov/nclb/methods/science/science.html.

Vallance, M. 2004. Blogging: Using Weblogs to encourage English language learners to write. *Modern English Teacher* 13 (2): 51–54.

Veermans, M., and D. Cesareni. 2005. The nature of the discourse in Web-based collaborative learning environments: Case studies from four different countries. *Computers & Education* 45:316–36.

Vilmi, R. 1999. Language learning over distance. In *CALL environments: Research, practice, and critical issues*, ed. J. Egbert and E. Hanson-Smith, 427–41. Alexandria, VA: TESOL.

Voice of America. n.d. VOA news. http://VOAnews.com/.

Vygotsky, L. S. 1978. *Mind in society: The development of higher psychological processes.* Cambridge, MA: Harvard University Press.

Wang, A., and M. Newlin. 2001. Online lectures: Benefits for the virtual classroom. *T.H.E. Journal* 29 (August). http://www.thejournal.com/articles/15513.

Ward, J. M. 2004. Blog assisted language learning (BALL): Push button publishing for the pupils. *TEFL Web Journal* 3 (1): 1–16. http://www.teflweb-j.org/v3n1/blog_ward.pdf.

Warschauer, M. 1995. *E-mail for English teaching.* Alexandria, VA: TESOL.

_____. 1996. Motivational aspects of using computers for writing and communication. In *Telecollaboration in foreign language learning: Proceedings of the Hawai'i symposium*, ed. M. Warschauer, 29–46. Honolulu: University of Hawaii, Second Language Teaching and Curriculum Center.

_____. 1997. Computer mediated collaborative learning: Theory and practice. *Modern Language Journal* 81:470–81.

_____. 1999. *Electronic literacies: Language, culture, and power in online education.* Mahwah, NJ: Lawrence Erlbaum.

_____. 2000a. The changing global economy and the future of English teaching. *TESOL Quarterly* 34:511–35.

_____. 2000b. On-line learning in second language classrooms: An ethnographic study. In *Network-based language teaching: Concepts and practice*, ed. M. Warschauer and R. Kern, 41–58. Cambridge: Cambridge University Press.

Warschauer, M., D. Grant, G. Del Real, and M. Rousseau. 2004. Promoting academic literacy with technology: Successful laptop programs in K–12 schools. *System* 32:525–37.

Warschauer, M., H. Shetzer, and C. Meloni. 2000. *Internet for English teaching.* Alexandria, VA: TESOL.

Waxman, H., M.-F. Lin, and G. F. Michko. 2003. A meta-analysis of the effectiveness of teaching and learning with technology on student outcomes. North Central Regional Educational Laboratory and Learning Point Associates. http://www.ncrel.org/tech/effects2/index.html.

Weasenforth, D., S. Biesenbach-Lucas, and C. Meloni. 2002. Realizing constructivist objectives through collaborative technologies: Threaded discussions. *Language Learning & Technology* 6 (3): 58–86. http://llt.msu.edu/vol6num3/weasenforth/.

WebCT Campus Edition Version 4.1. Software. 2004. Lynnfield, MA: WebCT. http://www.webct.com/.

Weber, J.-J. 2001. A concordance- and genre-informed approach to ESL essay writing. *English Language Teaching Journal* 55:14–20.

The WebWizard. Software. n.d. The WebWizard. http://www.the-webwizard.co.uk/.

Weigel, V. 2005. From course management to curricular capabilities: A capabilities approach for the next-generation CMS. In *Course management systems for learning: Beyond accidental pedagogy*, ed. P. McGee, C. Carmean, and A. Jafari, 190–205. Hershey, PA: Information Science Publishing.

Wenden, A. L. 2002. Learner development in language learning. *Applied Linguistics* 23:32–55.

Wenger, E. 1998. Communities of practice: Learning as a social system. Community Intelligence Labs. http://www.co-i-l.com/coil/knowledge-garden/cop/lss.shtml.

_____. 2002. Cultivating communities of practice: A quick start-up guide. http://www.ewenger.com/theory/start-up_guide_PDF.pdf.

_____. n.d. Communities of practice: A brief introduction. http://www.ewenger.com/theory/index.htm.

Wennerstrom, A. 2003. *Discourse analysis in the language classroom: Genres in writing.* Ann Arbor: University of Michigan Press.

WGBH Educational Foundation. 2006a. NOVA teachers. http://www.pbs.org/wgbh/nova/teachers/.

_____. 2006b. NOVA teachers: Featured teacher Glenn Rutland. http://www.pbs.org/wgbh/nova/teachers/featured/2004f_rutland.html.

White, C. 2003. *Language learning in distance education.* Cambridge: Cambridge University Press.

Wiley, II, D. A. 2002. Connecting learning objects to instructional design theory: A definition, a metaphor, and a taxonomy. In *The instructional use of learning objects*, ed. D. A. Wiley, II, 1–35. Bloomington, IN: Agency for Instructional Technology. http://www.reusability.org/read/chapters/wiley.doc.

Williams, J. 2002. Undergraduate second language writers in the writing center. *Journal of Basic Writing* 21 (2): 73–91.

Willis, J. 1996. A flexible network for task-based learning. In *Challenge and change in language teaching*, ed. J. Willis and D. Willis, 52–62. Oxford: Heinemann.

Windows Live Messenger Version 8. Software. 2006. Redmond, WA: Microsoft. http://get.live.com/messenger/overview.

Windows Movie Maker Version 2.1. Software. 2004. Redmond, WA: Microsoft. http://www.microsoft.com/moviemaker/.

Winet, D. n.d. StudyCom English for Internet. http://www.study.com/.

Wolfe, J. L. 2000. Gender, ethnicity, and classroom discourse: Communication patterns of Hispanic and white students in networked classrooms. *Written Communication* 17:491–519.

WordbanksOnline. 2004b. http://www.collins.co.uk/books.aspx?group=154.

Worldbridges. n.d. http://worldbridges.net/.

Xue, G., and I. S. P. Nation. 1984. A university word list. *Language Learning and Communication* 3:215–29.

Yahoo! 2006. Yahoo! groups. http://groups.yahoo.com/.

Yahoo! Messenger. Software. 2005. Sunnyvale, CA: Yahoo! http://messenger.yahoo.com/.

Yates, R., and J. Kenkel. 2002. Responding to sentence level errors in writing. *Journal of Second Language Writing* 11:29–47.

Yeh, A. 2003a. CMC and webheads: Hand in hand in education without borders. Presentation at the 37th Annual TESOL Convention and Exhibit, Baltimore, MD. http://www.geocities.com/aidenyeh/tesol/CMCandWebheads.htm.

_____. 2003b. NKFUST's listening and conversation class with Michael Coghlan. http://www.geocities.com/aidenyeh/michaelc/fear_of_being_too_good_audio/index.htm.

_____. 2004a. Happy online: Online event with Michael Coghlan. http://dcyeh.com/sy0304/2ndsem/groupa_projects/happy/.

_____. 2004b. Let's get physical! TPR and other kinaesthetically based language learning activities. http://dcyeh.com/sy0304/2ndsem/groupa_projects/tpr/students_pres/.

_____. 2006. Aiden Yeh's speech class podcast. http://aidenyeh.podomatic.com/.

YouTube. 2006. http://www.youtube.com/.

Yule, G. 1996. *The study of language.* Cambridge: Cambridge University Press.

Zieba-Warcholak, A. 2002. English interactive quizzes. College of Foreign Languages in Czestochowa. http://www.wsl.edu.pl/~azetka/.

Zielinski, D. 2000. Can you keep learners online? *Training* 37:64–71.

Contributors

Teresa Almeida d'Eça has thirty years of experience teaching Grades 5–11 in Portugal. She is the author of several works on e-mail exchanges and NetLearning, including *NetAprendizagem: A Internet na Educação*. She is a long-time Webhead and regularly offers sessions for TESOL's Electronic Village Online.

Anne Dahlman is a doctoral candidate in the Second Languages and Cultures Education Program at the University of Minnesota, in the United States, where she teaches in the K–12 ESL and foreign language initial licensure program. Her research interests include computer-assisted language learning (CALL) and second language teacher education, especially teacher cognition and learning.

Klaus Gommlich is an associate professor and director of the ESL Center at Kent State University, in Ohio, in the United States, where he teaches in the MA TESL program. His research interests are cognitive issues in second language acquisition, methodology of TESL/TEFL, functional linguistics, and translation studies.

Dafne González is a full professor of ESP and technology-related courses at Universidad Simón Bolívar, in Caracas, Venezuela, where she also coordinates the Graduate Programs in Education. She holds a master's degree in applied linguistics and a doctorate in education. A member of the TESOL Electronic Village Online coordination committee and a moderator of online courses for TESOL, she also serves on the Advisory Board of *ESL MiniConference Online* magazine.

Nicolas Gromik is a CALL/EFL lecturer in Japan. His research interests are developing computer and lifelong learning skills. He has been a moderator of TESOL's CALL Interest Section Electronic Village Online sessions in video and editing for the past two years and serves on the coordination team.

Elizabeth Hanson-Smith is professor emeritus at California State University, Sacramento, in the United States, where she cofounded and directed the graduate TESOL program. She has authored several works on technology-mediated language learning, and volunteers on the TESOL CALL Interest Section's Electronic Village Online coordination team. Her software design credits include Oxford Picture Dictionary Interactive, Live Action English Interactive, and Constructing the Paragraph.

Mary Jewell is an ESL teacher in San Diego, California, in the United States, and a doctoral candidate at a joint program of the University of San Diego and San Diego State University. She has published several articles on CALL and its uses in secondary schools, including "Electronic Discussion Forums and English Learners," *CATESOL Journal* 15 (1): 57–64.

Teresa J. Kennedy is an affiliate associate professor of bilingual/foreign language education at the University of Idaho, in the United States, and the director of international/U.S. partnerships and outreach for the GLOBE Program at the University Corporation for Atmospheric Research in Boulder, Colorado. For fifteen years, she taught in K–12 content-based foreign language, bilingual, and ESL programs, and for nine years she has taught ESL, bilingual, and foreign language methodology courses as well as general education pedagogy and technology courses at the university level. She has also taught science education courses and workshops around the world. Her Web site is http://www.teresakennedy.com/.

In-Seok Kim is a professor of ESL and applied linguistics in the Department of English Language at Dongduk Women's University in Seoul, South Korea. He earned a master's degree in TEFL at Southern Illinois University and received a doctorate in applied linguistics at Teachers College, Columbia University. He did postdoctoral work at Massachusetts Institute of Technology and Harvard University and taught at Brown University. His major research interests are second language acquisition, multimedia-assisted language learning/teaching, and design and development of multimedia English content. He is a chairman of the national English Curriculum Committee for the Korean Ministry of Education and Human Resources.

Ann Mabbott is director of the Center for Second Language Teaching and Learning at Hamline University, in Minnesota, in the United States. Her interests include K–12 teacher education in ESL, second language literacy, ESL program models, and online teacher education. She has a doctorate in second languages and cultures education.

Theresa Minick is coordinator of basic language studies in the Department of Modern and Classical Language Studies at Kent State University, in Ohio, in the United States. She teaches the technology and multimedia courses for pre- and in-service teachers across languages. Her research interests are related to CALL, computer-mediated communication, task-based methodology, and second language acquisition.

Randi Reppen is an associate professor in the TESL/Applied Linguistics Program at Northern Arizona University, in the United States, where she is also the director of the Program in Intensive English. Her scholarly works include two coauthored books and publications in scholarly journals, including *TESOL Journal, TESOL Quarterly, Journal of Applied Linguistics*, and *Studies in Second Language Acquisition*.

Sarah Rilling is an associate professor at Kent State University, in Ohio, in the United States, where she teaches graduate and undergraduate courses in applied linguistics. Since the early 1980s, she has taught languages using computers with software, MOOs, and other computer-mediated communications. Her research interests include corpus-based approaches to analyzing language in specific contexts and discipline-based writing and the nonnative speaker. She regularly uses computers in teaching and research.

Thomas N. Robb is a professor in the Faculty of Foreign Languages at Kyoto Sangyo University, in Japan. He received his doctorate in linguistics from the University of Hawaii. He served as president of Japan Association for Language Teaching and on the TESOL board of directors as well as two terms as chair of TESOL's CALL Interest Section. He has created a number of Web sites for students and teachers, including the SL-List project and Passport Online (Oxford University Press 2000–2006). His current passion is Moodle, an open-source course management system.

Andreas Schramm is associate professor at the Center for Second Language Teaching and Learning at Hamline University, in Minnesota, in the United States. He teaches linguistics, history of the English language, and research methodology. His research interests include effective methods for teaching linguistics, research methodology, online teaching, sociolinguistics, psycholinguistics, and pragmatics.

Marti Sevier has taught in the English Bridge Program at Simon Fraser University in Vancouver, British Columbia, Canada, since 2000. She has also taught and trained teachers in China, Singapore, Japan, and the United States. Her professional interests include using technology in the teaching and learning of vocabulary and cross-cultural education.

Maggie Sokolik is the director of the Technical Communications Program of the College of Engineering at the University of California, Berkeley, in the United States. She is the former director of the Berkeley Summer ESL Workshop. She is editor of *TESL-EJ*, an international scholarly journal focusing on English language teaching and learning. She is the author of several textbooks.

Graham Stanley teaches at the Universitat Ramon Llull and at the British Council in Barcelona, Spain. He recently completed his master's degree in ELT and educational technology at the University of Manchester and was co-moderator of the TESOL Electronic Village Online 2005 session Using Weblogs in ESOL.

Vance Stevens is a computing lecturer at the Petroleum Institute in Abu Dhabi, United Arab Emirates. With ESL and CALL experience dating back to the 1970s, he has conducted research, produced many publications and CALL software, and served on various editorial boards and committees of professional organizations, including TESOL's CALL Interest Section. He develops communities of practice for students and teachers based on the Webheads model he conceived.

Bernard Susser teaches in the Information and Media Department of Doshisha Women's College in Kyoto, Japan. He has published extensively on the writing process, computers and writing, CALL, and cross-cultural communication in journals such as *CALICO Journal, Computers and Composition, JALT Journal, Journal of Second Language Writing*, and *ReCALL*.

Sarah Tahtinen has been teaching and coordinating K–12 ESL and bilingual-bicultural programs for over sixteen years. Currently, she is completing her doctoral studies in the Second Languages and Cultures Education Program at the University of Minnesota, in the United States. Her research interests include CALL, second language learner support systems, and grounded theory as a research methodology.

Latricia Trites is an associate professor at Murray State University in Murray, Kentucky, in the United States, serving as professor in the MA TESOL Program. She has designed and taught several online courses in the teacher certification program that reaches many students worldwide. Besides online instruction, her interests include reading instruction and assessment.

Camilla Vásquez received a doctorate in applied linguistics from Northern Arizona University, where she also served as coordinator for the university's Program in Intensive English. She is currently assistant professor of linguistics in the Department of World Languages at the University of South Florida, in the United States.

Index

Page numbers followed by an italic *f* or *t* indicate material in figures or tables, respectively.

Autonomous learning, 3, 69–76
    central problem with, 74
    challenges and future directions in, 75–76
    definition of, 55
    as goal, 70–71
    in Japanese settings, 71, 76
    in online listening course, 55, 60–61
    in online writing labs, 128, 133
    realistic view of, 71–72
    self-access and, 72–73
    student willingness to do work and, 69, 70, 74
    tasks of learner in, 71
    teacher control in, 74
    in teacher education, 234
    technology and, 178–179
    tracking solution in, 74–75
Avatar(s), talking, 169–170, 169f
Avatar 3D, 62, 68
Awareness training, genre, 127

B

Back channel, for communities of practice, 259
Bank of English, 28, 39
Basegroup for e-mentoring, 221–232
    challenges and future directions in, 229–232
    comparison with face-to-face sessions, 228t
    e-forum bulletin board in, 226, 227t
    e-mail dialogue journals in, 226, 227t
    emotional support and sharing in, 222, 229–230
    integration and significance in, 229
    lack of external pressure or support in, 229
    participant-initiated discussions in, 230–231
    problems posed by technology in, 231
    simulation of face-to-face mode in, 224–225
    tasks and functions in, 226–228, 227t
    time issues in, 229
    Web site in, 226, 227t
Becoming a Webhead, 262, 273
Bee Online blog, 192, 193f, 194, 199
Beginner's paradox, in vocabulary acquisition, 25, 26
Behaviorism, 203
Bible, concordance from, 28
Bilingual settings, content-based instruction in, 84
Blackboard, 139, 146, 202, 208, 210, 253
Black Hawk County, Iowa, 93
Blended communities, constructivism in, 264–267
Blended course
    challenges and future directions for, 22–23,
        170–172
    communication centers for, 16
    conversion to, 56
    designing of, 16–17

first steps and progression in, 159–174
    student comments on, 23
    Web page for, 16–17
Blended practices, 3
Blog(s), 12, 16, 187–200
    aggregator for, 194, 195f, 196
    audio, 164, 191, 197
    authentic reason for participating in, 166
    challenges and future directions for, 196–197
    class, 189
    class dynamics with, 193
    for collaborating across cultures, 191–192
    collaboration between learners with, 193
    in communities of practice, 266
    for community building, 192–193
    context for, 188–189
    definition of, 188
    entering the blogosphere, 188
    for e-portfolios, 196
    ESOL-friendly content, 190–191
    for formative assessment, 195–196
    homemade versus provider use, 164–165, 167
    learner, 189
    for listening/speaking, 191
    managing groups of, 194
    mobile/cell phone, 164, 197
    for reading, 190–191
    real (authentic) audience for, 190, 197
    sustaining enthusiasm for, 196–197
    teacher, 189
    teacher-student, 164–166, 172
    teacher use of, 188
    teaching applications of, 191–196
    tips for promoting, 167
    tutor, 189
    types of, 188–189
    video, 164, 191, 197–198
    for writing, 189–190
Blog-EFL, 199
Blogger, 192, 198, 217
Bloglines, 194, 195f, 196, 198
Blogstreams Salon at Tapped In, 198, 199
Blogvangelist, 196
BNC (British National Corpus), 28, 39
BNC Written and Spoken Corpora to the Starr
    Report, 32
British Academic Spoken English (BASE), 28, 39
British Broadcasting Corporation (BBC), 61–62,
    68, 80
British National Corpus (BNC), 28, 39
Brochure(s), 175–186
    authentic information and context in, 176–178
    authentic use of, 183

Brochure(s) *(continued)*
    collaboration and support in, 178
    computer integration for, tips in, 183–184
    conferencing on and assessment of, 184, 185*t*
    group dynamics with, 183
    level of language proficiency for, 183
    presentation of, 104, 181–182, 184
    as real-world task, 175–186, 182*f*
    resources and places for, 183
    student experts on, 184
    word processing for, 177, 177*f*, 178*f*, 179–182
Brown Corpus, 28, 29*f*, 32, 35, 39
Bulletin board, 146
    in e-mentoring, 226, 227*t*
    in online listening course, 63–65
    in online writing labs, 134–135
Buzznet, 192, 198

C

CALL. *See* Computer-assisted language learning
CALL Environments: Research, Practice, and Critical
        Issues (Egbert and Hanson-Smith), 3
Cambridge International Corpus (CIC), 28, 39
CBI. *See* Content-based instruction
Cell phones, 1–2
Centre National d'Etudes Spatiales, 92–93
Chat
    in communities of practice, 258–260, 263–264,
        266–267
    in-class functions, 143
    potential for abuse, 263–264
    synchronous interaction in, 205–207
    text
        in communities of practice, 258–260
        consulting hours via, 22
        in-class uses of, 143
        management of students during, 211
        for online course (distance learning),
            203–204, 210–211
        synchronous interaction in, 205–207
    video, 20
        in GLOBE program, 92–93
    voice, 11, 15–24
        activities, 11, 17–21
        application in online learning, 15
        audio and text log in, 15
        authentic audience in, 21
        characteristics of, 15
        collaboration in, 17–21
        in communities of practice, 260, 263–264,
            266–267
        consulting hours via, 22

    expert jigsaw reading in, 18–20
    in GLOBE program, 91–93
    image descriptions and drawings in, 17
    interaction in, 20
    international experts participating in, 20, 23
    jigsaw reading in, 18
    negotiation of meaning in, 20
    online presentations in, 20–21, 21*f*
    planning of online learning via, 16–17
    research on, 4
    typical environment for, 11
    whiteboard use in, 15, 16*f*, 17
Chatlogs, 15
Class(es). *See specific types and programs*
Class access, 72, 73*t*
    versus self-access, 72–73
Class blog, 189
Cloze activities
    concordance-linked, 36
    nth-word, 36
    rational deletion, 36
    video, 36
Cloze concordancer, 34–36
Cloze swap, 36
CMS. *See* Course management system
Coghlan, Michael, 267
Cognition, in language learning, 13
Cognitive skill-building, GLOBE program for, 94–95
Cognitivism, 203
Collaboration
    in blogs, 193
    in CALL lessons, 168
    cultural, blogs for, 191–192
    definition of, 55
    in GLOBE program, 86, 93, 95
    in Lextutor, 36–37
    in online listening course, 55, 61, 64
    in online teacher education course, 233–244
    in online writing labs, 126, 128–129, 135
    in real-world tasks, 178
    in synchronous communication, 11–24
    in video tasks, 114, 118, 122
Collaborative activities
    expert jigsaw group, 18–20
    image descriptions and drawings, 17
    jigsaw reading, 18
    online presentations, 20–21, 21*f*
    in video chat, 20
    in voice chat, 17–21
Collaborative interaction, 205
Collège Cantelande (Cestas, France), 92–93
Collocation, 28–29, 32, 38
    definition of, 29

Control, teacher
    learner autonomy and, 74
    student *versus* instructor use of technology and,
        144
Conversational model, 207
Conversational skill, research on, 4
Conversion of course to Web
    combination of face-to-face with online
        elements, 56
    elements in, 56
    exclusion online teaching, 56
    listening course, 56–65
    needs analysis for, 56–57
Cooperative learning, 13–14
    in content-based instruction, 85
    definition of, 14
    mixed-ability students in, 14
    in teacher education, 239–243
CoP. *See* Communities of practice
Corpus (pl. corpora), 28–40
    in academic writing, 44, 48, 49*f,* 50
    applications of, 29
    argument for using, 28
    authenticity of, 38
    available on Web, 28
    challenges and future directions for, 37–39
    The Compleat Lexical Tutor, 31–37
    consciousness-raising with, 38
    definition of, 25, 28
    in EAP classroom, 29
    formal *versus* informal, 28
    guided discovery approach to, 37
    learning training for use, 38–39
    in lexicography, 29
    online, 39–40
    in online writing labs, 135
    output for *language,* comparison of, 32, 33*f*
    preselection for student use, 38
    smaller, genre-focused, 30
    spoken *versus* written, 28
    time use for, 38
    for vocabulary acquisition, 28–31
Corpus-based concordances, 32
Corpus linguistics, 127
Correspondence mode, 203–204
Course management system (CMS), 139
    Blackboard, 139, 146, 202, 208, 210, 253
    for content-based instruction, 104, 105–106
    financial options in, 253
    for online listening course, 63
    for tracking student work, 75
    WebCT, 136, 139, 143, 243, 253
Creative language, 3

Critical Evaluation Surveys, 107
Critical thinking skills, in content-based instruction,
    98–99
Critical Web searches, 103
Crossword puzzles, 20, 37
Cultural collaboration, blogs for, 191–192
Culture gap, 149
Current events, in GLOBE program, 92
Curricular e-mail exchange, 161–163
Curriculum
    language across, 85
    writing across, 126
Cyber EFL CALL Academy, 68

D

DDL (data-driven learning), 26
Dekita.org, 173, 198, 262, 269
Deliberate study, 73
Democratization
    in CALL, 102
    definition of, 102
Depth of processing hypothesis, 27–28
Desktop publishing, 104, 178
Dickinson's learner autonomy, 55
Dictionary, student creation of, 20
Digital files, conversion of audio files to, 62–63
Digital images, for online listening course, 62
Digital immigrants, 138–139
Digital natives, 138–139
Disciplines, writing in, 126
Discovery Channel Global Education Partnership,
    154
DiscoverySchool.com, 154
DiscoverySchool.com: Teaching Tools, 16–17, 24
Discussion forums, 205–207, 209
Discussion via text chat, 143
Distance learning, 3, 54. *See also specific courses*
    challenges and future directions in, 211–212
    designing original course, 208–209
    experimenting with course implementation,
        209–211
    implementation of courses, 207–208
    interaction in, 204–207
    teacher's critical role in, 201–213
DocuFax, 253
Document delivery, electronic, 253–254
Docutek ERes, 253
Doing science, 85
Drawings, whiteboard for, 15, 16*f,* 17
Dreamweaver, 80, 122, 123
Drop box, 203

online education course for teachers of, 233–244

technology opportunities in, 149

video tasks in, 109–123

English for specific purposes (ESP)

challenges in teaching, 12

collaborative use of synchronous communication in, 11–24

content-based instruction in, 85

content on Web for, 12–13

genre-based approach in, 127

online writing labs in, 126

English Idioms and Slang (blog and podcast), 199

English Interactive Quizzes, 169, 173

English language learner (ELL)

GLOBE program for, 89–90

need for teachers of, 246

rate of growth, 246

secondary school, real-world tasks and service learning for, 175–186

testing requirements and accommodations for, 84

English Trailers, 80

Environmental education, GLOBE program for, 83–96

E-portfolios, 196

blogs for, 196

definition of, 196

versus traditional, 196

ESL. *See* English as a second language

ESL Certificate Endorsement, 202–203, 208

ESL go net, 190, 198

ESL Standards for Pre-K-12 Students, 85

ESOL. *See* English for speakers of other languages

ESOL Video Stories, 154

ESP. *See* English for specific purposes

Essays. *See* Academic writing

Ethnographic study, for online ESL teacher education program, 245, 249–255, 249*t*

The Euro Is Here to Stay, 164

Evaluation, in self-directed learning, 117, 117*t*

Evo2005: Using Weblogs in ESL/EFL Classes, 198, 200

EVOnline2002–Webheads Community Event, 268

Expedia, 154

Expertise

in blended lessons, 170

in content-based instruction, 105

Expert jigsaw group, 18–20

Explicit learning, of vocabulary, 27

Explore resource-linked Word Lists (Lextutor), 36

Exploring Academic English (Thurstun and Candlin), 30

Exposure problems, in vocabulary acquisition, 25–40

Exposure to computer material, *versus* learning, 75–76

Extended writing. *See also* Academic writing

aspects of, 41

Eye gaze recording, research on, 4

F

Face-to-face (f2f) classes

blended with online classes, 3, 56

conversion of, 56

online courses *versus,* 202

online ESL teacher course *versus,* 248–249

technological enhancement of, 54

Family Science Nights, 88

Feed (blog icon), 194

Feedback

in academic writing, 42

in academic writing module, 47

indirect coded, 127

in listening course, 55

in online learning, 12

in online listening course, 59–60, 59*f,* 63

in online writing labs, 126, 127–128, 133, 134

in optimal language learning environment, 3

f2f. *See* Face-to-face classes

Filamentality, 16–17, 24, 80, 154, 163–164, 173

Film competitions, 114, 120–122, 123

Film festivals, 114, 120–122, 123

Film production course, 109–123. *See also* Video tasks

FirstSearch, 253

First steps, 159–174

First Steps in Experimenting with Computers: Resources, 174

Flat Stanley Project, 163, 174

Flexibility, 50, 163

Flickr, 192, 198, 217

Florida, GLOBE program in, 92

Flowchart, for online listening course, 63, 64*f*

Fluency development, 73

The FordLog, 192, 199

Formative assessment

blogs for, 195–196

definition of, 195

France, GLOBE program in, 92–93

Free templates, 16–17

FrontPage, 122, 123

Immersion settings, content-based instruction in, 84
Immigrants, digital, 138–139
iMovie, 110, 112–113, 113*f*, 118, 123, 154
iMovie HD Support, 123
Impress (presentation software), 104, 107, 182
Improvisation, in CALL lessons, 168
Incidental learning, of vocabulary, 27
Incorporating Sources module, 46, 50
Indirect coded feedback, 127
Informal exchanges, as course component, 250
Informality, in communities of practice, 263
Information and communication technologies
          (ICT), first steps and progression in,
          159–174
Information-gap activities
     expert jigsaw groups, 18–20
     jigsaw reading, 18
Information-oriented system, *versus* inquiry-
          oriented, 234–235
Information technology (IT)
     student *versus* teacher use and opinions,
          139–144
     transnational online degree program in, 1
InfoTrac, 253
Innovation Tools: Mind Mapping Resource Center,
          107
Inquiry-oriented system, in teacher education,
          234–235
Instability in CALL, 100–102
Instant messaging (IM), 146, 265
Instructional format, in content-based instruction,
          102
Instructional responsibilities, in content-based
          instruction, 102
Instructor-based learning, *versus* computer-assisted,
          6
Integrating the Internet into the Classroom, 163
Intensive English programs (IEPs), online academic
          writing modules in, 41–51
Interaction
     academic, 205
     in academic writing module, 46–47, 46*f*, 47*f*
     asynchronous *versus* synchronous, 205–206
     collaborative, 205
     in collaborative synchronous communication,
          11
     in communities of practice, 263
     in GLOBE program, 91–92
     interpersonal, 205
     learner-computer, 205
     learner-content, 205
     learner-learner, 205
     learner-teacher, 205

     in listening course, 55, 63
     in online course (distance learning), 204–207
     in online writing labs, 126, 128–129, 131–134
     in optimal language learning environment, 3
     in personal-response systems, 139–140
     promotion of, 205
     social, 7
     in teacher-to-student blog, 164–166
     in voice chat activities, 20
Interconnection promotion, 6–7
Interdisciplinary language programs, 85, 90–91
Interdisciplinary studies
     content-based, 83, 85, 90–91, 93–94
     GLOBE program for, 93–94
Interesting Things for ESL Students, 80, 169, 173
International School Dhaka (Bangladesh), 196
Internet. *See specific applications and techniques*
Internet Archive, 197
Internet Archive: Movie Archive, 199
Internet for English Teaching, 163
Internet TESL Journal, 63, 70, 76
Interpersonal interaction, 205
Intersubjectivity, 204
Inventiveness, 166
Iowa, GLOBE program in, 93
Iowa State University, 44, 51
iPods, 1
Isolation reduction, 6–7
iTunes, 197, 199
iVisit, 265, 269

J

JALT Language Teacher, 70
Japan, learner autonomy in, 71, 76
Jaroensutasinee, Krisanadej, 92
Jaroensutasinee, Mullica, 92
Jigsaw group, expert, 18–20
Jigsaw reading, 18
Jokes in English for the ESL/EFL Classroom, 68
Journal of Teaching in Travel & Tourism, 105
Journals, online. *See* Blog(s)
Juice (podcast), 197, 199

K

Kearsley's engagement theory, 55–56, 61
Kent State University
     ESL OWL of, 125–136
     online teacher education course of, 235–244
Keystroke recording, research on, 4
Kids as Global Scientists, 163, 174
KidzBlog, 165, 173

instructional design of Web pages for, 59–61
integration of offline teaching with online learning, 63–65
interactive exercises for, 55, 63
learner autonomy and, 55, 60–61
local factors and, 57
multimedia content development for, 61–63
needs analysis for, 56–57
noticing and, 54–55, 59–60
offline teaching elements in, 63
problem solving in, 55–56, 61
sites, tools, and software for, 68
student activities in, 63–65
student responses to, 65–66, 67t
students' need for, 56–57
synchronous discussions in, 65
theoretical bases for, 54–56
video content for, 62
virtual office hours in, 65
week-by-week syllabus for, 57–59
The Lupton Library, 44, 51
Lurkers/lurking, 251, 263

M

Maine, laptop initiative of, 1–2
Makers Pages, 24
Malleability in CALL, 102
mariichigo blog, 189, 199
Marzio, Mike, 20
Matching words, 20
Math, language learning in, 90–91
Meaning
  creation of, 7
  negotiation of, 3, 12
    in task-based approach, 13
    in voice chat activities, 20
  pursuit of, 127
Meaning-focused input, 73
Meaning-focused output, 73
Memorization of words, 27
Mentoring, electronic, 221–232
  challenges and future directions in, 229–232
  commitment and clear expectations in, 224
  comparison with face-to-face sessions, 228t
  e-forum bulletin board in, 226, 227t
  electronic, definition of, 224
  e-mail dialogue journals in, 226, 227t
  emotional support and sharing in, 222, 229–230
  importance of relationships in, 224
  integration and significance in, 229
  lack of external pressure or support in, 229
  need for postgraduation support, 222–225

participant-initiated discussions in, 230–231
problems posed by technology in, 231
simulation of face-to-face mode in, 224–225
tasks and functions in, 226–228, 227t
time issues in, 229
virtual basegroup for, 221–232
Web site in, 226, 227t
Web site resources for, 224, 232
MERLOT: Multimedia Educational Resource for Learning and Online Teaching, 106, 107, 268
Meskill, Carla, 1
Message board. *See* Bulletin board
Message forums, asynchronous communication via, 12
Metacognitive knowledge, 117–118
Mexico, GLOBE program in, 92
Michigan Corpus of Academic Spoken English (MICASE), 39
MicroConcord Corpus of Academic Texts, 30, 40
Microsoft FrontPage, 122, 123
Microsoft Office, 186
Microsoft Office Online, 179, 181
Microsoft PowerPoint, 21, 24, 104, 107, 122, 123, 154, 182, 186
Microsoft Windows Movie Maker, 110, 112–113, 112f, 118, 123
Microsoft Word, 44–45, 176, 179, 180
Microsoft Works, 186
MiddleWeb: Exploring Middle School Reform: Some Teacher Mentoring Resources, 268, 273
MightyCoach.com, 118, 123
Mindfulness, in learning process, 3
Minnesota
  electronic mentoring model in, 222–232
  ELL population in, 246
  online ESL teacher education program in, 245–256
Mismatch in technology use, student-teacher, 137–149
MIT OpenCourseWare, 106, 107
MIT Technology Center for Bits and Atoms, 154
Mixed-ability students
  challenge of involving, 171
  in cooperative learning, 14
Moblog, 164, 197
Module(s), online
  academic writing, 41–51
    accessibility and convenience of, 49–50
    approach in developing, 44
    assessment in, 44
    challenges and future directions in, 49–50

Peer-focused activity, for vocabulary acquisition, 27
Persistence, 166
Personal digital assistants (PDAs), 1–2
Personal-response systems, 139–140
Photoblog, 164, 192
Photographs
    in communities of practice, 259, 261*f*, 263
    whiteboard for, 15, 16*f*
PhotoStory, 171–172, 173
Plagiarism, in online writing labs, 134
Planning, in self-directed learning, 117, 117*t*
Podcasting, 139–140, 191, 197
Podcasting-ELT Yahoo! Group, 197
PodOmatic, 191, 197, 199
Portfolios, 195–196
Portugal, online learning and instruction in, 159–174
Posters, as real-world task, 179–182
Postmethod pedagogy, 234–235
PowerPoint, 21, 24, 104, 107, 122, 123, 154, 182, 186
Presentation(s), online, 20–21, 21*f*
Presentation software, 182–183, 186
Principles and Practices of Online Teaching Certificate, 267
Print-based CALL, 176
Privacy, student, 16
Problem solving
    definition of, 55–56
    in online listening course, 55–56, 61
Professional development
    communities of practice in, 257–269
    online ESL program, 245–256
        challenges and future directions in, 255–256
        communicative characteristics of, 248–249
        course delivery systems in, 253–254
        course included in, 247–248, 247*t*
        course transfer to Web, 248–254
        ethnographic study for, 245, 249–255, 249*t*
        versus face-to-face courses, 248–249
        forms and topics of communication in, 250–251
        participants and events in, 249–250, 249*t*
        quality assessment of, 254–255
        research services for, 253–254
        staff support systems for, 251–252
        student recruitment and retention in, 254
        study resources in, 250–251
    and postmethod pedagogy, 234–235
    reinvented online course, 233–244
        American Culture Online developed for ESOL in, 235–244, 236*f*
        challenges and future directions in, 242–243
        class philosophy for, 244

collaboration, cooperation, and continuity in, 239–242
        information-oriented *versus* inquiry-oriented, 234–235
        task-based team development in, 238–239
        teacher-directed learning in, 237–238
        trainee inquiries in, 240, 241*t*
    virtual basegroup for e-mentoring, 221–232
Pronunciation, in student presentation, 182–183
Proximal development, zone of, 264, 267
Proximity, virtual, 206
Psychological challenges, for teachers, 170
PsycINFO, 253
Public communication, as course component, 249–250
Publicness in CALL, 100
Purdue University, 80, 130, 136
Pure Voice, 259, 269
Pursuit of meaning, 127

Q

QuestGarden, 155
Quia Web, 20, 24, 70, 76, 80, 168–169, 173
Quizzes, in academic writing module, 47, 47*f*
Quoting, Paraphrasing, and Summarizing module, 45, 50

R

Randall's ESL Cyber Listening Lab, 80
Random Thoughts (blog), 200
Rational deletion cloze, 36
Reader-based *versus* writer-based prose, 190
Reading
    blogs for, 190–191
    in GLOBE program, 93
    instruction through electronic annotation, 102–103
    Internet-based materials for, 103
    skimming for details strategy in, 103
    vocabulary acquisition through, 25, 26
Reading comprehension, in film or video editing, 118
Real English Online, 20, 24, 80, 262, 268
RealPlayer (Real Audio), 259, 269
Real science, in GLOBE program, 94–95
Real-world contexts and skills, 175–186
    authentic information and context for, 176–178
    authentic use in, 183
    challenges and future directions in, 185–186
    collaboration and support in, 178
    computer integration in, tips for, 183–184

conferencing on and assessment of, 184, 185*t*

group dynamics for, 183

level of language proficiency for, 183

presentation event for, 184

resources and places for, 183

student experts in, 184

student motivation in, 179

technology as means to end in, 178–179

Recommended self-access, 72, 73*t*

Record-keeping, in learner autonomy, 74–75

Reflective network, for e-mentoring, 221–232

Required self-access, 72, 73*t*

Research

on academic writing, 42–43

changed focus of, 5

new methodologies in, 5

online journal resources, 4–5

services for online courses, 253–254

on technology in language learning, 4–6

Research column (Lextutor), 32–34

Research papers. *See* Academic writing

Reusable learning objects (RLOs), 105–106

RSS (really simple syndication), 139–140, 194

RubiStar, 186

Rubrics for Web Lessons, 119, 123

Rutland, Glenn, 160–161

S

Scaffolding, 166

in communities of practice, 264, 267

Schmidt's noticing theory, 54–55

schMOOze University, 268

School of International Studies (Meadowbrook, Virginia), 92–93

Science education

doing science in, 85

GLOBE program for, 83–96

positive attitudes toward, 95

real science in, 94–95

Search engines, 103

Secondary school language learners, real-world tasks and service learning for, 175–186

Second language acquisition (SLA), video tasks for, 109, 110–111, 122

Self-access

versus access as class, 72–73

and autonomy, 72–73

recommended, 72

required, 72

true, 72

Self-directed learning, 70–72

evaluation in, 117, 117*t*

in film or video project, 117, 117*t*

monitoring in, 117, 117*t*

planning in, 117, 117*t*

in teacher education, 234

Self-pacing, 72–73

Serial monologues, 207

Service learning, 175–186

authentic information and context in, 176–178

authentic use of, 183–184

computer integration in, tips for, 183–184

group dynamics in, 183

level of language proficiency for, 183

presentation event for, 184

resources and places for, 183

student experts in, 184

Simon Fraser University, vocabulary acquisition program in, 26

Sitepal, 80, 173

Skill-based activities, 73

Skimming for details, 103

SLA. *See* Second language acquisition

Small-group meetings, as course component, 249–250

Smart classroom, 72–73, 114

Social interaction, 7

Social phenomenon, language learning as, 12, 13

Sociolinguistic competencies, 13

Sociological Abstracts, 253

Software. *See also specific titles and applications*

CALL, tips on using, 168

content-based, 104–105

in optimal language learning environment, 4

for video tasks, 112–113, 112*f*, 113*f*, 123

Solar-powered laptop, 2

The Sound of GLOBE, 93

South Africa, e-learning in, 1

South Korea

listening comprehension scores in, 56–57

Web-based listening course in, 53–68

Speaking skills, in content-based instruction, 104

Staff support systems, for online courses, 251–252

Standards for Foreign Language Learning, 85

Starr Report, 32, 40

Stevens, Vance, 257

Storyboarding Activity, 123

Storyboards, 116–117, 116*f*

Story concordancers, 32

Strategic competencies, 13

Strategic English Listening Comprehension, 53–68. *See also* Listening course, Web-based

Stress/anxiety level, 3

Student approval of new technology, 3